THE MEANING OF THE
DEAD SEA SCROLLS

W9-ADA-323

THE MEANING OF THE
DEAD SEA
SCROLLS

Their Significance for Understanding
the Bible, Judaism, Jesus, and Christianity

JAMES VANDERKAM
AND
PETER FLINT

HarperSanFrancisco
A Division of HarperCollinsPublishers

THE MEANING OF THE DEAD SEA SCROLLS: *Their Significance for Understanding the Bible, Judaism, Jesus, and Christianity.* Copyright © 2002 by James VanderKam and Peter Flint. All rights reserved. Printed in the United States of America. No part of this book may be used or reproduced in any manner whatsoever without written permission except in the case of brief quotations embodied in critical articles and reviews. For information address HarperCollins Publishers, Inc., 10 East 53rd Street, New York, NY 10022.

HarperCollins books may be purchased for educational, business, or sales promotional use. For information please write: Special Markets Department, HarperCollins Publishers, Inc., 10 East 53rd Street, New York, NY 10022.

HarperCollins Web site: http://www.harpercollins.com
HarperCollins®, ♣®, and HarperSanFrancisco™ are
trademarks of HarperCollins Publishers, Inc.

FIRST HARPERCOLLINS PAPERBACK EDITION PUBLISHED IN 2004

Library of Congress Cataloging-in-Publication Data
VanderKam, James C.
  The meaning of the Dead Sea scrolls : their significance for understanding the Bible, Judaism, Jesus, and Christianity / James C. VanderKam.—1st ed.
    p. cm.
  Includes bibliographical references and indexes.
  ISBN 0-06-068465-8 (pbk.)
    1. Dead Sea scrolls—History and criticism. 2. Bible. O.T.—Criticism, interpretation, etc.
3. Qumran community. 4. Dead Sea scrolls—Relation to the New Testament. I. Flint, Peter W. II. Title.
BM487 .V27 2002
296.1′55—dc21   20022069730

  05 06 07 08 RRD(H) 10 9 8 7 6 5 4 3 2

To Mary
To Amanda

Contents

Foreword

SOON AFTER THEIR DISCOVERY IN 1947, THE DEAD SEA SCROLLS took the world by storm, and ever since scholars and general readers alike have studied them, read them, or at least talked about them. The first scrolls were published in 1950 in what we now consider primitive editions, but at least they were released; the delay in the publication process occurred only at a later stage. Together with these text editions we have been blessed, usually, by a veritable flood of studies on the Qumran community and individual scrolls. These studies elucidated the content of the scrolls and placed them in the context of the Jewish society and multifaceted literatures of the late Second Temple period. Diverse explanations of these scrolls abounded and theories multiplied, to the joy of researchers of antiquity and those involved in the history of research. However, the more scholars wrote, the greater the confusion grew among readers, and correspondingly the more a need was felt to pull the threads together. At that point, in the 1950s, the first introductions to the Dead Sea Scrolls started to appear; some of them were very impressive and remain so even today, especially those appearing in revised editions.

But as the task of an introduction is to provide a full picture of an area of research, and as this area has expanded many times over due to the recent flood of publications, especially over the last decade, the writing of a new introduction became desirable. Such an introductory volume covering the full range of data presented to the public up to 2002 is represented by this book by Professors James C. VanderKam and Peter W. Flint.

At this point, all the Qumran scrolls have been published in scholarly editions together with translations and extensive technical notes and elucidations of their content. A comprehensive concordance is scheduled to appear in the fall of 2002, and a one-volume edition of all the nonbiblical Dead Sea Scrolls is to follow shortly thereafter.

Early descriptions of the Qumran scrolls mentioned 600 manuscripts, a number that has grown in our imagination to 700, 800, 900, and now 931, according to my calculations of August 2002 based on the data included in the introductory volume to the *Discoveries in the Judaean Desert* series (vol. 39, Oxford: Clarendon Press, 2002). In ten cases these manuscripts contain different texts on their recto and verso. Early calculations were based on mere estimates, while recent ones followed inventory lists. However, any attempt to count these manuscripts is fraught with difficulties due to the fragmentary status of the corpus. As a result of these problems, the totals for the manuscripts are only approximate and the figure 931 has to be taken with a grain of salt. This number refers to texts of different length. Some are long or even very long, such as the large Isaiah scroll from cave 1 and the long copy of the Temple Scroll from Cave 11. Others comprise one-sheet compositions, such as *4QTestimonia* and personal notes such as the Aramaic so-called *4QList of False Prophets* and the Hebrew *4QList of Netinim,* which were written on mere scraps of leather. The number of Qumran manuscripts is not identical to that of the compositions found in the caves, since many compositions are represented by multiple copies. If these multiple copies are deducted from the overall number of manuscripts, we are left with 445 items, including 175 unidentified fragments. Because of the many difficulties relating to the evaluation, we presume that the Qumran caves housed multiple copies of up to 350 independent compositions.

The Qumran library, quite sizable by ancient standards, was initially housed in the community buildings at Khirbet Qumran and later in the adjacent caves, which served as living and work quarters as well as storage areas. The compositions compose a heterogeneous corpus penned in Hebrew, Aramaic, and Greek consisting of various literary genres including not only the sectarian literature of the Qumran community, but also writings composed elsewhere in ancient Israel, including the much older biblical writings. Because of the diverse nature of the Qumran corpus, one cannot speak of a single discipline devoted to Qumran research, for such a discipline would, of necessity, have to include many subdisciplines; in addition to a thorough grasp of the different literary genres found at Qumran, a knowledge of the history of the Jewish people in the Second Temple period, the history of the Hebrew and Aramaic languages, archeology, the history of ideas, and the background of Christianity would all be necessary. The study of the Qumran documents thus involves various disciplines, all of which are covered by this volume.

This introduction by VanderKam and Flint analyzes these 350 Qumran compositions, and often their multiple copies, and describes the societies and cultures within which they were composed. The biblical evidence has been presented in much greater detail than in other introductions, and many novel insights have also been provided. This updated introduction is a very useful and informative tool for Qumran research.

Emanuel Tov
Editor-in-Chief
Dead Sea Scrolls Publication Project
Hebrew University, Jerusalem
August 2002

Preface

THE ADVENT OF THE THIRD MILLENNIUM HAS BROUGHT NEW CHALLENGES in the study of the Dead Sea Scrolls. The official publication of the scrolls—mostly in the series "Discoveries in the Judaean Desert" (see Appendix IV)—is nearing completion, and virtually all the documents are available in English translation. At the same time, comprehensive studies have been written on only certain texts or groups of texts, and a limited number of books dealing with themes such as worship or theology or purity in the scrolls as a whole have been published. In addition, the full impact of recent technological advances such as radiocarbon dating, DNA analysis, imaging by direct digital acquisition, and the Internet is just beginning to be realized.

Several introductions to the Dead Sea Scrolls, many of them offering a wealth of information and valuable insights, were published toward the end of the twentieth century. But now the need for a new introduction to the scrolls—one that takes into account all these texts as a library and incorporates the latest scholarly discussions and technological advances—has become increasingly apparent. And so *The Meaning of the Dead Sea Scrolls* was born in 2000, when we set out to write a new, comprehensive, and up-to-date introduction. Special care has been taken to situate the scrolls and the Qumran community in their Jewish context and to explore their relevance for studying Jesus and the writings of the New Testament. Since the intended audience is the interested public, the information in this book has been made as accessible as possible: technical terms have been explained, and very few Hebrew, Aramaic, or Greek words have been used. We are nevertheless confident that students and scholars, too, will find a wealth of information in these pages.

The entire manuscript has been read and corrected by both authors, but in most cases we were each responsible for certain chapters. James VanderKam composed Chapters 1–3, 9–13, 16, and 18 and a section of Chapter 15. Peter Flint wrote Chapters 4–8, 14–15, and 17 and a small section of Chapter 16, and prepared Appendixes I–IV. Some differences in style may thus be evident, although through the use of formatting, boxes, and tables the book presents itself as a unified whole.

Acknowledgments

With few exceptions, all Scripture quotations in *The Meaning of the Dead Sea Scrolls* are from the *New Revised Standard Version,* copyright 1989 by the Division of Christian Education of the National Council of the Churches of Christ in the United States of America. Almost all quotations from the Dead Sea Scrolls are from two translations issued by the same publisher (Harper San Francisco) which serve as companions to this volume: for the biblical scrolls, *The Dead Sea Scrolls Bible* by Martin Abegg, Jr., Peter Flint, and Eugene Ulrich (1999); and for the nonbiblical scrolls, *The Dead Sea Scrolls: A New Translation* by Michael Wise, Martin Abegg, Jr., and Edward Cook (1996).

The Meaning of the Dead Sea Scrolls would not have been possible without the help and expertise of many people. We wish to extend our gratitude, first, to scholars and colleagues who offered constructive feedback, especially Monica Brady, who read James VanderKam's chapters and suggested many improvements, and Emanuel Tov, Eugene Ulrich, Shemaryahu Talmon, Roy Brown, and Ernest Muro, who read portions of Peter Flint's material and proposed helpful changes. Second, to several colleagues and graduate students who checked sections of the manuscript or provided several photographs used in this book: Catherine Murphy, Angela Kim, Ralph Korner, and Stephen Marler.

Third, to the organizations and individuals who provided permission for and, in several cases, assistance with copyrighted pictures. In alphabetical order these are the Albatross Archive, the Estate of John Allegro, the Ancient Bible Manuscript Center (especially Arik Greenberg), Gregory Bearman, Brill Academic Publishers, the British Library, Crossroad Publishing Company, the Israel Antiquities Authority, the Israel Museum (Shrine of the Book), Ernest Muro, OakTree Software (Roy Brown), John Trever, and West Semitic Research (Bruce Zuckerman and Marilyn Lundberg).

Finally, we thank the team at Harper San Francisco for their vision, patience, and hard work in bringing this book to publication. We especially thank John Loudon, Executive Editor, for his acceptance and oversight of the project; Terri Leonard, Senior Managing Editor, for her patience and expert work; and Kris Ashley, Editorial Assistant, for answering many questions and supplying us with much needed information.

PART ONE

Discoveries, Dating, Archeology, and New Methods

1

The Discovery of the Dead Sea Scrolls

THE STORY OF THE DISCOVERY of the first Dead Sea Scrolls has become a part of Western lore. Who has not heard about the Bedouin shepherd who threw a rock into a cave, heard a crash, went in to explore, and found the scrolls? The story in that form may be accurate, but it turns out to be something of a simplification. As a matter of fact, much remains unknown about the exact circumstances under which those scrolls were discovered. The story of the discovery at first deals with just one cave; the other ten were located at later times.

The First Cave

What are our sources of information about the episode? The Bedouin shepherds (more than one) who are the heroes have told their story, and that story has been retold and examined by the scholars who first had access to and worked on the scrolls. But different stories are attributed to the discoverers, who did not give a very precise indication of when the incident occurred. Also, a significant amount of time elapsed between the discovery and the first reports about it, and the cave in which the texts were found was not located by scholars until perhaps two years after the first scrolls were removed from it.

The best, most complete source of information about the initial discovery is chapter 12 (supplemented by other parts) in John C. Trever's *The Untold Story of Qumran*. Trever was the first American scholar to come into contact with the scrolls, and he took it upon himself to investigate as carefully as possible the circumstances under which they were found. His conclusions are based on interviews with the Bedouin and evidence from others.[1] The following summarizes the account given by the Bedouin as related by Trever; it is supplemented in places with other early evidence.

THE BEDOUIN TELL THEIR STORY

The discovery of the first scrolls and the long process of bringing them to scholarly and public attention took place at a time of great turmoil and violence in the Middle East. Tensions between Arabs and Jews were high during the British Mandate, and they grew higher and the mayhem increased as the United Nations debated the partition of Palestine. In 1946 or 1947, toward the end of the British Mandate in Palestine, which ended with the partition of the land in May 1948, three men from the Taʿamireh tribe of Bedouin—Khalil Musa, a younger cousin, Jumʿa Muhammad Khalil, and a still younger cousin (fifteen years of age), Muhammad Ahmed el-Hamed, nicknamed edh-Dhib (the Wolf)—were tending their flocks of sheep and goats in the region of Ain Feshkha on the northwestern side of the Dead Sea. The tribe customarily moved about in that region between the Jordan River and Bethlehem and had done so for centuries. They had even proved to be a source of archeological discoveries from time to time. Jumʿa, we are told, liked to explore caves in the hope of finding gold, and so, when the opportunity presented itself, he would check the nearby cliffs for caves. The key events happened at some point in the winter of 1946–47; Trever reports that "the Bedouin think it was November or December 1946."[2] He describes what happened in this way:

> Jumʿa, it was, who happened upon two holes in the side of a rock projection above the plateau where the flocks were grazing. The lower of the two holes was barely large enough "for a cat to enter," as Jumʿa described it in several interviews; the one which was somewhat above eye level was large enough for a slender man to enter. Jumʿa threw a rock through the smaller opening and was startled by the strange sound he heard; apparently the rock shattered an earthenware jar within. Thinking there might be a cache of gold within, he summoned the two other herdsmen to show them the curious holes. In the gathering darkness of evening it was too late to attempt an entrance; the next day had to be devoted to watering their flocks at ʿAin Feshkha, so they agreed to explore the cave two days later.[3]

The youngest of the three, Muhammad Ahmed el-Hamed, returned to the cave openings a few days later while his relatives slept in the early morning; there he climbed into the cave through the larger opening. Returning to Trever's narrative:

> As his eyes became accustomed to the dim light, he saw about ten tall jars lining the walls of the cave, according to his own description. Several of them had covers. Some of the jars had small handles which apparently were used in tying down the covers to seal the contents. In addition, the Bedouins claim that there was a pile of rocks which had fallen from the ceiling, and much broken pottery on the floor of the cave. All but two of the jars proved to be empty. One was filled with reddish earth; from the other one, a jar with a cover, Muhammed pulled two bundles wrapped in cloth which he described as "greenish" in appearance. A third, the largest, was a roll of leather without any wrapping. From his description and hand motions during our interview, as well as from other evidence, it seems quite probable that the larger scroll was the now-famed Isaiah Scroll (1QIsaᵃ) and the two smaller ones, the Habakkuk Commentary (1QpHab) and the Manual of Discipline (1QS). Only these three manuscripts were taken by edh-Dhib from the cave that morning.[4]

According to Trever, the fact that the older cousins were angry with edh-Dhib for entering the cave without them and perhaps hiding treasure he may have found (he did show them the three bundles) accounts for his absence from later events. At any rate, a few days later Jumʿa brought the scrolls to a Taʿamireh site southeast of Bethlehem, where the scrolls were reportedly left for weeks in a bag hanging on a tent pole. During this time, as they were shown to others, at least some of them suffered some damage: the cover broke off the Isaiah scroll, and the *Manual of Discipline*[5] was split in two.

SELLING THE MANUSCRIPTS

The chronology becomes a little more certain after this. In March 1947, the two older cousins brought the manuscripts to a Bethlehem carpenter and antiquities dealer named Ibrahim 'Ijha, who, after being advised they might have been stolen from a synagogue, returned them to Jum'a after several weeks (Trever calculates this was April 5, 1947) and declared them devoid of archeological worth. Jum'a next brought them to another Bethlehem antiquities dealer, Khalil Eskander Shahin (known as Kando), who was a cobbler by trade. The arrangement made was that Kando would put up a guarantee of five Jordanian pounds (a Jordanian pound was worth about $4 at the time) while George Isha'ya Shamoun, a member of the Syrian Orthodox Church whom Jum'a had met in Bethlehem, kept the scrolls. The Bedouin were to receive two-thirds of any amount that Isha'ya and Kando would be able to gain from selling them. The fact that Isha'ya was from the Syrian Orthodox Church leads us into the next stage in the story about the scrolls.

Metropolitan Athanasius Yeshue Samuel

It was during Holy Week (April 7–13, 1947) that Isha'ya contacted St. Mark's Syrian Orthodox Monastery in the Old City of Jerusalem in the hope of finding out what the manuscripts might be. He apparently thought the texts on them might be in the Syriac language. The monastery was so named because tradition held it to be the site where the house of Mark's mother stood, the place where Jesus' disciples were assembled when Peter came to them after his release from prison (Acts 12:12–17). The head of the monastery was Metropolitan (Archbishop) Athanasius Yeshue Samuel (1907–1995), who was to become a very important figure in identifying the scrolls and bringing them to the attention of scholars. The Metropolitan agreed to look at a scroll, and Isha'ya and Kando brought part of the *Manual of Discipline* to the monastery. After examining the piece and hearing the report about how the scrolls were found, he suspected that they might be old and indicated an interest in buying them. That sale was not to be concluded, however, for several months.

Before the sale took place Isha'ya was brought to the cave twice, once by both of the two older Bedouin and once by Khalil Musa alone. Four other scrolls were removed from the cave on the second of these visits, and one of them, apparently the one to be named the *Genesis Apocryphon,* was left with Kando. The other three[6] of this more recent lot of four manuscripts Khalil Musa and Jum'a kept. In June 1947 they sold the three to Faidi Salahi, also an antiquities dealer, for seven Jordanian pounds (about $28). He also purchased two of the jars from the cave.

The original three scrolls (the large Isaiah scroll, the *Commentary on Habakkuk,* and the *Manual of Discipline*), with the fourth one now in Kando's possession (the *Genesis Apocryphon*), were sold to Metropolitan Samuel on July 19, 1947. There is a familiar story about how the two Bedouin and Isha'ya, who were coming to deliver the manuscripts, were turned away from the monastery by a monk who knew nothing of their arrangements with Samuel. The mistake was rectified, however, and Kando, on behalf of the Metropolitan, then paid the Bedouin sixteen Jordanian pounds (about $64), since he had sold the four manuscripts to the cleric for twenty-four pounds. Isha'ya, at the Metropolitan's request, brought a priest of St. Mark's to the cave, thus verifying the story about the discovery told by the Bedouin.

While Mar[7] Samuel suspected the scrolls were very old, several individuals to whom he showed them (none of whom was an expert in such matters) doubted their antiquity. In late July Father J. van der Ploeg, an Old Testament scholar at the University of Nijmegen (the Netherlands) who was staying in Jerusalem at the École Biblique, was shown the scrolls, and was the first to recognize that one of them was a copy of Isaiah. Yet he was not at all convinced of the scroll's antiquity and wanted to see the jar in which it was found. No one ever showed it to him and thus he had no convincing reason to accept the cleric's claim that the scrolls were two thousand years old.

Eleazar Sukenik

Mar Samuel continued to seek the advice of others about the age of the scrolls and even brought them with him on a trip to Lebanon and Syria. Despite his efforts, he had no success in confirming his hunch about the parchments. As his quest continued with regard to the four scrolls in his possession, the fate of the other three—the ones purchased by Faidi Salahi—soon took an interesting twist. An Armenian antiquities dealer in Jerusalem named Nasri Ohan contacted Eleazar Lipa Sukenik (1889–1953), professor of archeology at the Hebrew University of Jerusalem. They met on November 25, 1947,[8] in Zone B of partitioned Jerusalem (a neutral place), at the Jaffa Gate.

> There, through the barbed-wire barricade, the eminent archeologist saw a ragged fragment of leather inscribed in strange Hebrew characters. The dealer told him of its discovery by Bedouins who were seeking to sell many such pieces to their mutual friend, Faidi Salahi. . . . When Sukenik noted a resemblance between the script on the fragment and that which he had often seen scratched on first-century ossuaries, his initial skepticism soon gave way to excited curiosity. He therefore offered to buy the fragments for the Hebrew University and urged the Armenian dealer to get more samples of them from the Bethlehem dealer.[9]

In his diary entry for November 25, 1947, Sukenik wrote: "To-day I met X [antiquity dealer]. A Hebrew book has been discovered in a jar. He showed me a fragment written on parchment. *Genizah?!*"[10] Later that week the dealer, who mentioned the Bedouin story about their discovery in a cave near the Dead Sea, showed Sukenik more fragments at his shop. This made Sukenik resolve to go on a dangerous trip to Bethlehem to see Faidi Salahi, with whom he had dealt in antiquities before. On November 29, 1947, the dealer and Sukenik took the bus to Bethlehem. Salahi told the story of the discovery and showed them his two jars and the scrolls and fragments in his possession. At Sukenik's request, Salahi allowed him to take two scrolls to Jerusalem so that he could make a decision whether to purchase them. He promised to decide within two days.

In a well-known and striking coincidence, as Sukenik was back in Jerusalem taking his first look at the scrolls (the *Thanksgiving Hymns* and the *War Scroll*, also called the *War Rule*),[11] he heard over the radio the news that the UN General Assembly, meeting at Lake Success on Long Island, had voted to partition Palestine and thus to form a Jewish and an Arab state. In a diary entry for December 1, 1947, Sukenik wrote: "I read a little more in the 'parchments.' I'm afraid of going too far in thinking about them. It may be that this is one of the greatest finds ever made in Palestine, a find we never so much as hoped for."[12] When in December Sukenik mentioned the scrolls to a librarian at the university—who happened to have been one of the persons to whom Mar Samuel had earlier shown his scrolls—he informed Sukenik about the ones the Syrians had in their hands. So, by December 1947, Sukenik was aware of all the scrolls found, although the nature of the ones held by the Metropolitan was not clear to him.

At the request of Metropolitan Samuel, Anton Kiraz, a member of the Syrian Orthodox Church and a prosperous businessman, contacted Sukenik about the scrolls held at St. Mark's.[13] A meeting between Kiraz and Sukenik took place on February 4, 1948, at the YMCA. When the archeologist saw the script of the three texts shown to him, he recognized similarities with the ones he had bought from Salahi. He offered to buy the scrolls and asked that he be allowed to show them to the president of the university, Judah L. Magnes, and other interested individuals. He was permitted to borrow the three scrolls (apparently against Mar Samuel's wishes), and copied several chapters of the larger Isaiah scroll while he had it in his possession. At a meeting on February 6 Sukenik offered Kiraz a fairly large amount of money for the scrolls—500 Jordanian pounds and another 500 if Kiraz could convince the Metropolitan to sell. The Jewish Agency had promised to provide the money needed for the purchase. The sums mentioned tipped off Kiraz and the Metropolitan that they had valuable property, and they began to ponder how much they should ask for them.

JOHN TREVER, WILLIAM BROWNLEE, AND MILLAR BURROWS

Rather than meeting again with Sukenik, Kiraz decided to seek expert opinion at the American School of Oriental Research (ASOR) in Jerusalem. Sukenik was forced to wait (although he and President Magnes tried by telephone to convince the Syrians to sell) while Mar Samuel and Kiraz worked out what they would do with the manuscripts. As Sukenik tells it, "Towards the end of February, I received a letter from him [Kiraz] saying that his co-religionists had decided to postpone selling the manuscripts until relations with the outside world were restored and they could ascertain their proper value. He assured me, however, that as soon as this was done the Hebrew University would have the option of first refusal of the manuscripts."[14] As a matter of fact, on February 18, 1948, Father Butrus Sowmy of St. Mark's had placed a telephone call to ASOR. The person who took the call was John Trever, one of only two scholars present there at the time. It happened that the director of the school, Millar Burrows, of Yale University, was on a trip to Baghdad and had appointed Trever acting director in his absence. Also at the school was William Brownlee, who, like Trever, was a recent Ph.D. and recipient of an annual ASOR fellowship. Ironically, all three had been at the Dead Sea near where the cave was on October 25, 1947, but their purpose then was pleasure and they had no idea they were so close to a place that would soon change their lives. Trever reports that the priest said over the phone that he was the librarian at the monastery and "had been organizing their collection of rare books to prepare a catalogue of them. Among the books he had found some scrolls in ancient Hebrew, which had been in the Monastery for about forty years, but he could find no information about them. He was inquiring, therefore, if our School could supply him with some data for the catalogue."[15] Trever asked him to bring the manuscripts to the school, and Sowmy agreed that he would do so the next day. Trever assumed the manuscripts were recent ones and did not think much about them.

Father Sowmy brought the four manuscripts to the school on February 19, 1948, and showed them to Trever, who happened to have a set of slides illustrating the history of the biblical text. He compared the script of one of Father Sowmy's manuscripts with the writing on several texts shown on the slides and found similarities between the manuscript letters and those on the Nash Papyrus, which dated to the second century BCE. He copied out some lines of one of the manuscripts, but told his visitors that it would take some time to do the careful analysis required to date the script. Trever tells the story that, as he examined the scrolls, Father Sowmy's brother, Ibrahim, who was a customs official at the Allenby Bridge and who had accompanied his brother to the American school, related some of his thoughts:

> Ibrahim remarked that while working at the Allenby Bridge he had studied about the history of Jericho and the Dead Sea area. From his studies he had learned about the Essenes who lived in that region during the time of Jesus. As a result he had become very interested in the Essenes. He suggested to the Syrians at the Monastery that these documents might have belonged to that ancient sect of Jews and been deposited by them in the cave during a period of persecution, perhaps when the Romans attacked Jerusalem in A.D. 70. Since the scrolls had been "wrapped like mummies" originally, he added, they must be very ancient, for mummification had long since become a lost art.[16]

It is intriguing that Ibrahim had come to the conclusion, before knowing what the scrolls were, that they were connected with Essenes and predated the destruction of Jerusalem—views that were to become a near consensus among scholars. Trever, after the Syrians left, was able to identify the passage he had copied as coming from Isaiah. He informed Brownlee about the manuscripts and was understandably eager to see them again. Yet the fact that the parchments were now back in the Old City made access to them difficult under the trying circumstances for travel in Jerusalem at that time.

With considerable difficulty Trever was able to visit the monastery and meet with Father Sowmy and the Metropolitan on February 20, 1948. He told them that he was willing to photograph the manuscripts so that scholars could perform the necessary studies preparatory to determining a date for them. After some debate, they agreed to bring the scrolls to the school the next day. Trever was also allowed to examine the manuscript of Isaiah again. He was further convinced of its authenticity by the presence of scribal corrections in different hands and by repairs to the manuscript itself—procedures that he believed no forger would apply to a manuscript.

It is fortunate that Trever, one of the first scholars to see the scrolls, was also a photographer; the pictures he shot under difficult conditions and with whatever materials were available in war-torn Jerusalem have left the field forever in his debt. Metropolitan Samuel and Father Sowmy brought the manuscripts to the school the next day, where Trever had all the necessary equipment in place in the basement. He was concerned about the work because electricity could be cut off at any time in those days. The procedure took most of the day (February 21, 1948), but Trever and Brownlee, with Sowmy's assistance, succeeded in photographing the entire scroll of Isaiah and the *Commentary on Habakkuk*. At the end of the session and just before the Syrians had to leave, Trever says that he was "determined to take a few color shots. The special camera and plates had been carefully prepared for the purpose that morning, so the shift could be made quickly. Then it was that I made two exposures of Columns 32 and 33, with the rest of the scroll rolled on either side—a picture which has been published probably more often than any other one related to the scrolls."[17]

The Syrians agreed to leave the unphotographed scrolls at the school so that they, too, could be repaired and photographed. Trever later photographed what had appeared to be two manuscripts, but proved to be two parts of the same one (the *Manual of Discipline* [*Rule of the Community*]). Trever and Brownlee returned the manuscripts on February 24, when Trever urged the Syrians to move the scrolls to a safer place and to have experts in America attempt to open the one that could not be unrolled (the *Genesis Apocryphon*).

On February 25, 1948, Trever wrote to William Foxwell Albright, a scholar at Johns Hopkins University and the leading paleographer in the world, to inform him about the manuscripts and to say that, if Albright's dating of the Nash Papyrus to the second century BCE was accurate, the Isaiah scroll, whose script was similar to that of the papyrus, was the oldest biblical manuscript yet found. Meanwhile, Trever continued to work on his photographs as he and Brownlee studied the texts. Brownlee was the first to identify one of them as a commentary on Habakkuk, and was later to publish several important studies of the manuscript. When the director of the school, Millar Burrows, returned, the three studied the manuscript photographs intently. It was not until March 5 that the Syrians divulged to Trever that the manuscripts had not been kept in their library for forty years as first claimed; they admitted they had purchased them the previous year from Bedouin living near Bethlehem and that one of their monks had actually visited the cave where the scrolls had been found. They also indicated their desire to take Trever to the cave.

The complications involved in every move can hardly be overstated. Not only was there the constant danger and difficulty of travel from one part of Jerusalem to another, but the Syrians did not want to work with the Jordanian Department of Antiquities, although the American School was obligated to do so for any archeological work. Trever had already mentioned the scrolls to the director of antiquities, R. W. Hamilton, who encouraged him to visit the cave with the Syrians. They, however, now declined to guide him there out of concern for safety. The Metropolitan also informed Trever that he would soon be leaving Jerusalem to visit Syrian communities in the United States.

On March 15 Trever was cheered by the arrival of a letter from Albright which included the following words:

> My heartiest congratulations on the greatest MS discovery of modern times! There is no doubt whatever in my mind that the script is more archaic than that of the Nash Papyrus, standing very close to that of the third-century Egyptian papyri and ostraca in Aramaic. Of course, in the present state of our definite knowledge about Hebrew paleography it would be safe only to date it in the Maccabean period, i.e., not later than the accession of Herod the Great. I should prefer a date around 100 B.C.[18]

Albright added that he doubted the scroll would supply very significant corrections to the traditional Hebrew text of Isaiah, but thought it would "revolutionize our conception of the development of Hebrew orthography. And who knows what treasures may be concealed in the remaining rolls!" Albright's dating of the Isaiah scroll has withstood the test of time, his assessment of the text-critical value of the Isaiah scroll has largely been confirmed, and his hint about other treasures has proved to be prophetic.

After Trever tried unsuccessfully to find a route to the area of the cave that would avoid danger zones, the Americans decided that the time had come to let the Syrians know how important the manuscripts were. On March 17, 1948, Trever and Burrows prepared a statement meant to be a press release, and the next day they showed it to Metropolitan Samuel, who was pleased with it. The statement was then sent for release to the ASOR office in New Haven, Connecticut, although it was not issued until April 11. It was only after the press release was written that the Metropolitan told Trever about the interest of some Jews in the manuscripts, including President Magnes of the Hebrew University. Trever says the Syrians had alluded to this on March 5, when he assumed that Sukenik was one of the individuals involved. On this latter occasion Mar Samuel disclosed that Sukenik had seen the scrolls and wanted to buy them, while Trever informed him that he had let the director of antiquities know about the scrolls. But on March 25 the Metropolitan, after giving Trever another fragment of the *Habakkuk Commentary* that he happened to find in a book he had opened that morning (!), informed Trever that Father Sowmy had left earlier in the day for Lebanon and had taken the four scrolls with him. A controversy was later to erupt about this, because Trever wrote soon afterward about his happiness that the scrolls had been removed from the country—an act that was illegal. As he writes in his book: "It was a great relief to know that at last the scrolls were out of strife-ridden Jerusalem. By what route or means of transportation Sowmy had departed, I was not informed. That the manuscripts would be placed in a bank vault in Beirut was all the specific information revealed to me. The fact that removing antiquities from the country without an export license was technically illegal was foreign to my thoughts. I rejoiced to know that the scrolls were safe."[19] Soon after this the three scholars of the American School had to leave the country because of the mounting violence. Before departing, Trever and the Syrians agreed on a number of points that would go into a contract giving ASOR the right to publish the scrolls of which the Metropolitan claimed ownership. Through most of February and all of March, of course, Sukenik was left waiting for more word about these scrolls.

The office of ASOR issued the press release on April 11, and it appeared in print on April 12. *The Times* of London for that date carried the following announcement:

> Yale University announced yesterday the discovery in Palestine of the earliest known manuscript of the Book of Isaiah. It was found in the Syrian monastery of St. Mark in Jerusalem, where it had been preserved in a scroll of parchment dating to about the first century BC. Recently it was identified by scholars of the American School of Oriental Research at Jerusalem.
>
> There were also examined at the school three other ancient Hebrew scrolls. One was part of a commentary on the Book of Habakkuk; another seemed to be a manual of discipline of some comparatively little-known sect or monastic order, possibly the Essenes. The third scroll has not been identified.

The release says much about the four texts and already uses the name "a manual of discipline," which Burrows (reminded of a Methodist "discipline") had given to one of the scrolls. It is also interesting that already at this time a connection with Essenes is mentioned and that the American scholars, all of whom were Protestants, used the term "monastic order" for the group responsible for the texts. Yet what is most surprising about the statement is how the impression is left that the Isaiah scroll was discovered at St. Mark's. Although by the time the release was written the Syrians had told the Americans about the cave, the press release fails to mention it. Burrows wrote later about the release:

> Unfortunately a mistake had somehow been introduced into the version given to the press. I had written, "The scrolls were acquired by the Syrian Orthodox Monastery of St. Mark." As released to the press in America the statement said that the scrolls had been

"preserved for many centuries in the library of the Syrian Orthodox Monastery of St. Mark in Jerusalem."[20] Who inserted this I do not know. Professor Sukenik, on reading the published account, issued a statement to set the matter right, pointing out that the scrolls had been found in a cave near the Dead Sea within the previous year. From this statement, which I read in the *Rome Daily American* of April 28, 1948, when our ship stopped at Genoa, I first learned that the discovery included manuscripts other than those bought by Archbishop Samuel.[21]

With Sukenik's press release announcing the existence of the three scrolls he had purchased, it became public knowledge that seven manuscripts from the same cave were involved.

By this time apparently other texts had also turned up. In early September 1948, Mar Samuel showed the new director of the American School, Ovid Sellers of McCormick Theological Seminary in Chicago, some additional scroll fragments he had acquired. After he was appointed Apostolic Delegate to North America, the cleric brought the four manuscripts and these new pieces with him to the United States; he showed the new fragments to Trever in early February 1949. They had been removed from the cave by one of the men of St. Mark's whom Mar Samuel had sent there in the fall of 1948. Included were fragments from two copies of the book of Daniel. We will meet the Metropolitan again later in our story.

Locating and Excavating the Cave

By the end of 1948, nearly two years after the initial discovery, no scholar had yet located the manuscript cave. This is understandable when one remembers the dangers of travel in the area while the American trio were still in Jerusalem (they left in April). The British Mandate in Palestine ended on May 15, 1948, and war broke out immediately. Peace was not restored until November 1948, and in January 1949 restrictions on travel were removed so that it became possible to visit the area of the cave. Sellers tried to get the Syrians to keep their promise to help in reaching the cave, but Father Bulos, who was then in charge of St. Mark's, demanded more money than Sellers could pay for the service. At this time Joseph Saad of the Palestine Archaeological Museum was also involved in the delicate efforts to learn about the location of the cave.

The person who was in large part responsible for rediscovery of the cave was a Belgian observer serving on the United Nations staff, Captain Philippe Lippens, who was staying in Jerusalem and became interested in finding the cave. He went around to the various institutions that had had something to do with the scrolls and gathered what information he could, from people and publications, about the location of the cave. Trever reports:

> On January 24, 1949, he succeeded in obtaining an interview with Major General Lash, the British Commander of the 3rd Brigade of the Arab Legion at Ramallah. General Lash called Brigadier Ashton, his archeological advisor, who in turn contacted G. L. Harding, Chief Inspector of Antiquities, in Amman, Jordan [the area in question was now in Jordanian territory]. Harding confirmed the importance of the cave project. Thus, General Lash dispatched Brigadier Ashton with two Bedouins and Captain Akkash el-Zebn to search the area mentioned in my article.[22]

Captain Akkash el-Zebn was the one who actually spotted the cave on January 28, 1949, only four days after Lippens had spoken with General Lash (see Figure 1.1). He saw that

Figure 1.1
Cave 1 at Qumran
Muhammad ed-Dhib crawled through the upper opening to find the first scrolls. The larger opening was made later.
Photograph courtesy of Catherine Murphy

the earth in front of a cave was disturbed and thought it might be the result of excavating work. This proved to be correct, and Harding was then summoned. Despite some initial skepticism, he soon confirmed that the cave was the one in which the manuscripts had been found. What evidence suggested that this was the scrolls cave, when there were many other caves in the area? Pieces of the same sorts of scroll jars as those sold to Sukenik were found, as were fragments that had broken away from the scrolls we have been describing. An example is the *War Scroll*, one of Sukenik's three texts; several pieces of it were spotted in the cave by the excavators.[23]

From February 15 to March 5, 1949, a collaborative excavation of the cave was conducted under the auspices of the Jordan Department of Antiquities, the École Biblique, and the Palestine Archaeological Museum. The leaders were Harding and Roland de Vaux, the director of the École Biblique. Something of the conditions under which they worked emerges from the thanks Harding later recorded to the Arab Legion "for their always willing co-operation and assistance: it is entirely due to the wonderful security which they maintain that archaeological work is possible even in the most remote parts of the country."[24]

The cave is some 8 meters long, 4 meters high, and its width varies from less than 1 meter to about 2 meters. The Bedouin and the Syrians had removed the complete or largely intact manuscripts and the bigger pieces from the cave, but the official excavators found about 600 fragments as well as "numerous scraps of cloth, fragments of wood, olive- and date-stones, palm fibre, leather phylactery cases, and a mass of broken pottery."[25] It turns out that the visitors to the cave who preceded the archeologists had enlarged the lower entrance. It is worthwhile to quote Harding's brief summary of the work of excavation and the finds:

> The dump of the illegal excavations was first examined and produced large quantities of sherds and cloth and a few pieces of inscribed leather, including the first piece we had seen in the Phoenician [= paleo-Hebrew] script. The filling of the cave consisted of very fine powdery grey dust mixed with stones fallen from the sides and roof; there was about 50 cm. depth of this type of fill before undisturbed soil was reached. In view of the earlier clearance no stratification could be observed, but several large clumps of coagulated animal droppings made it clear that the cave had been used as a shelter by small wild animals for a considerable period of time.
>
> The only tools it was possible to use in the clearance of the cave were penknives, brushes, tweezers, and fingers, for the fragments are brittle and easily damaged, and

sieving was not possible because of the presence of the stones in the fill. Several hundred fragments of inscribed leather and a few fragments of papyrus were recovered, varying in size from pieces bearing one letter, or even half a letter, to a piece containing several lines of text in a column. After the two intact jars acquired by the Hebrew University were removed the remainder were apparently broken up, for we found nothing but sherds. Very few other objects were found . . . apart from the linen; one scroll, or part of a scroll, was found still in its linen wrapper, stuck together to the neck of a jar. . . . Having been exposed to dampness for some time it was corroded to a solid black mass, and it was impossible to separate even a small portion of it.

Inscribed fragments were mounted between glass each day as they were found, and photographed on the spot for safe record. Infra-red photographs taken in the studio of the Palestine Archaeological Museum later have revealed texts on pieces which to the naked eye present merely a blank black surface.[26]

His reference to photographing the finds is especially important; photos of the scrolls and fragments have not only preserved a record of what was found but have often proved to be the best way to read the texts they bear. Harding also mentions finding three phylactery cases and a wooden comb.

De Vaux reported on the large amount of pottery (twelve baskets full were taken from the cave), which included the remains of many (at least fifty) jars and covers, some bowls, a pot, a pitcher, and four lamps. In his initial publications on the subject, dating from 1949, de Vaux insisted that almost all of the pottery was from the second century BCE, but later, on the basis of more information, he dated it to the first century CE.[27] In his first report he also bemoaned the disaster left behind by those who had visited the cave after the Bedouin first entered it.[28] According to Mrs. G. M. Crowfoot, who wrote up the results of tests on the linens, they were cleaned "of thick dark brown dust mixed with rat and mouse droppings" and subjected to technical analysis.[29] She estimated that there were pieces from forty, perhaps well over fifty, cloths and divided them into three groups: those with decoration of blue lines, plain cloths (some having fringes), and jar covers.[30] Their uses seemed to be limited to two: as scroll wrappers and as jar covers. Although admitting the difficulty in dating the linens and the lack of parallels to some features in them, she concluded that the dating suggested by a carbon-14 test on a linen piece from the cave (more on this later) and by coins found at Khirbet Qumran (near the end of the first century CE) was consistent with all the evidence pertinent to the linens.[31]

With hindsight, it is intriguing to read a footnote de Vaux attached to his second report about the cave. He reported that the site of ancient habitation nearest to the cave was Khirbet ["the ruin of"] Qumran, about one kilometer to the south: "We took the opportunity during our stay at the cave to examine the site anew. We will soon publish the results of this survey; it suffices to say here that no archeological clue places this human installation in relation with the cave where the manuscripts were hidden."[32] The statement is correct for that time: there was no archeological indication then connecting the cave and the site, after he and Harding had made only a surface examination and excavated just two tombs.[33] De Vaux was soon to change his mind when he excavated the site itself (see Chapter 3).

Once the cave had been found and it was clear that the Bedouin and Syrians had taken most of the written pieces out, it became important to learn whether any other texts they might have removed were now in other hands. Joseph Saad, under instructions from and with the support of Harding, went to considerable lengths to learn the identity of the

Bethlehem antiquities dealer who had sold the scrolls. No informed person had been willing to divulge this information. Dealing in antiquities, which various individuals mentioned in this chapter had done, was illegal, but compromises at times seem unavoidable to ensure that valuable antiquities are properly preserved and so that they can be acquired by the authorities if necessary. Saad became acquainted with Kando and worked out arrangements to purchase for 1,000 Jordanian pounds the additional manuscript fragments he had obtained.

Subsequent Fate of the Cave 1 Manuscripts

Before turning to subsequent discoveries, we should trace what happened to these famous manuscripts, the first of the Dead Sea Scrolls. Publication proceeded rapidly. Sukenik issued two Hebrew fascicles of a work he entitled *Hidden Scrolls from the Genizah Found in the Judean Desert*.[34] The first of these appeared already in 1948. It contained an introduction to the scrolls; parts of the *War Scroll,* the *Thanksgiving Hymns,* and the fragmentary Isaiah scroll; and several photographic plates of the manuscripts. The second (1949), which appeared after the cave had been found that year, offered more of the same, but also some treatment of the *Rule of the Community,* a copy of Leviticus, the longer Isaiah scroll, and the *Commentary on Habakkuk,* with a number of photographic plates. Sukenik died in 1953, but the Hebrew University appointed a committee to publish the material he had left behind. The posthumous volume completed the publication of his three texts, with more photographs, the introductions for the two earlier fascicles, and excerpts from Sukenik's diary.[35]

The American scholars, too, published the texts they had photographed with admirable promptness. The first publication in 1950 presented an introduction followed by photographs of the entire larger Isaiah scroll and the *Commentary on Habakkuk* with transcriptions of the text on the facing page.[36] The *Manual of Discipline* (the *Rule of the Community*) appeared the next year, again with photographic plates and facing transcriptions.[37]

Metropolitan Samuel, who had come to the United States in 1949, attempted to sell the manuscripts in his possession. The story about this is complicated, but his scrolls were displayed several times (including at the Library of Congress in October 1949). No buyer stepped forth, perhaps dissuaded by rumors about a high asking price or by continuing questions about who was the legal owner of these antiquities.[38]

To make a long story short, Mar Samuel placed an advertisement in the *Wall Street Journal* of June 1, 1954. It read: "'The Four Dead Sea Scrolls' Biblical Manuscripts dating back to at least 200 BC are for sale. This would be an ideal gift to an educational or religious institution by an individual or group. Box F 206, The Wall Street Journal" (p. 14). The ad, which ran for several days, was brought to the attention of Yigael Yadin, Sukenik's son, who was in the United States at the time. Working through intermediaries in order to keep his interest a secret, he arranged to have the authenticity of the scrolls verified and then purchased (July 1, 1954). The individual who made the purchase possible—the final price was $250,000—was the philanthropist D. S. Gottesman. Each of the four scrolls was flown in a separate plane to Israel, where, at a press conference on February 13, 1955, the prime minister of Israel announced what had happened.

This meant that the state of Israel now possessed all seven of the first scrolls discovered. The state decided at that time to set up the Shrine of the Book Foundation, a project that Gottesman agreed to fund as well. Eventually the Shrine of the Book was built at the

Israel Museum in Jerusalem, with the inauguration taking place on April 20, 1965. There the seven manuscripts are housed, along with some other texts owned by Israel.[39]

The Other Caves

The scrolls cave that engendered so much publicity and excitement turned out not to be the only one containing written remains. In February 1952, Bedouin explorers found another cave, this time containing only fragments of manuscripts and no complete scrolls. The discovery occurred while Harding, de Vaux, and others were excavating caves farther south in the Wadi Murabbaʿat where material, including documentary texts, dating from the second Jewish revolt against Rome (132–35 CE) had been located by Bedouin in October 1951. The second scrolls cave is just a short distance south of the first, also in the cliffs on the northwest shore of the Dead Sea. In this case, Kando soon offered for sale the fragmentary manuscripts taken from the cave; with the agreement of the Jordanian Department of Antiquities, they were purchased by the Palestine Archaeological Museum and the École Biblique.

After learning about the discovery of the cave, Harding called together William Reed, director of ASOR, Father Dominique Barthélemy of the École Biblique, and Joseph Saad, and they quickly located the cave. An expedition was led by Reed and de Vaux, who were assisted by three others from the École Biblique, three Arab leaders, and twenty-four Bedouin. The group, divided into seven teams, explored the cave and the surrounding region from March 10 to March 29, 1952. De Vaux wrote that the purpose of the caves expedition was not only to verify that the fragments came from this cave, but also and especially to determine the area inhabited by the group who had left the manuscripts. He commented on how thoroughly the Bedouin had cleared the cave of its contents: of the written material, they had left behind only two small fragments, which the archeologists found and studied.[40] It is noteworthy that the debris left behind by the Bedouin also contained fragments of cylindrical jars, as the first cave did.

This cave expedition surveyed all the caves in an 8-kilometer stretch from Hadjar el-Asba in the north to a kilometer south of Ain Feshkha. Khirbet Qumran lies at approximately the midpoint in this stretch of land. De Vaux wrote about the work: "An exploration was made of the holes, caves, and crevices with which the cliffs are everywhere honeycombed. Of the soundings taken 230 proved barren, but 40 of these cavities contained pottery and other objects. These remains range in date from the Chalcolithic to the Arab period, but 26 of the sites explored yielded pottery which was identical with that of the first cave of Khirbet Qumran."[41] Most of the caves with objects in them were to the north of or adjacent to Khirbet Qumran; only a few were farther to the south. Also, two partially paved roads were detected, one connecting Qumran with the west and another leading south from it to Ain Feshkha. De Vaux admitted that the survey was not exhaustive. The heat became oppressive, the workers fell ill or quit, and so the project came to an end.[42] Its nonexhaustive character soon became evident when other text-bearing caves were found in the area.

In the course of the caves expedition, on March 14, the archeologists did find a third cave with inscribed fragments. This was the first time that an official group was able to spot such a cave before the Bedouin did. Cave 3 is located about a half kilometer to the north of Cave 1 and contained bits and pieces of what their editor Maurice Baillet later identified as fourteen manuscripts; the fifteenth text taken from Cave 3 is the famous *Copper Scroll*, a list of treasure sites inscribed on copper. Again, many cylindrical jars were found in the cave.[43]

In August 1952, Bedouin explorers, who were obviously carrying out their own major survey, made a most significant discovery. In July and August they had already found the sites known as Khirbet Mird and Naḥal Ḥever, where important manuscripts had survived. Then also in August they came upon what is now known as Qumran Cave 4 (see Figure 1.2), the cave with the largest number of written remains in the area. De Vaux was to write later that, in conducting the cave survey in March 1952, "we restricted our research to the rock cliffs and did not examine the marl terrace stretching in front of them. The reason was that the nature of the terrain is such as to exclude in this marl terrace the presence of any natural caves suitable for human use. All that we noticed were cavities eroded by water which were archaeologically barren. In this we erred."[44]

It turns out that, according to the story they told,[45] the Bedouin were alerted to the presence of a cave near Khirbet Qumran by an older member of their tribe. One night, as some of the Taʿamireh were discussing their discoveries in the vicinity of the cave, he remembered that when he was young he had chased a partridge in the area of Khirbet Qumran. The partridge went into a hole that turned out to be the opening of a cave, which the Bedouin entered and where he found pottery and other objects. With the information supplied by the older man, younger Bedouin soon found the cave and the mass of fragments preserved in it.

They tried to sell about 15,000 of these in Jerusalem and gave false information about where the cave was in order to protect their treasure and profit. On September 20, 1952, Harding was contacted by de Vaux, who said that Bedouin had offered him a huge quantity of fragments and that he had purchased some of them for 1,300 pounds. Harding went

Figure 1.2

A view of Cave 4 (to the rear, with an opening on the side) and the adjacent Cave 5.

Courtesy of James VanderKam

to the area of Qumran (this much was at least clear about the cave's location) and caught the Bedouin at their work; they had apparently been removing material from the cave for three days before they were stopped. They made off with their valuable discoveries, meaning that what they had taken would have to be purchased from them (no small matter when thin budgets were already strained by the amounts that had been spent to acquire other manuscripts and fragments). An official excavation of the cave was conducted September 22–29, 1952, and fragments from many more manuscripts were recovered. As de Vaux was later to write:

> The Bedouin had already removed more than half the fill of the cave and had worked so carefully that only a few small fragments were found in their debris. But the archeologists themselves explored the lower levels of the cave and a small underground room that the Bedouin had not reached, and they discovered the original entrance. They gathered almost a thousand fragments, belonging to one hundred different manuscripts which are almost all represented among the fragments bought from the Bedouin. This certifies the origin of the lot sold by them. On the other hand this scattering of the parts of the same manuscripts indicates an ancient upheaval.[46]

Eventually scholars were to identify the remains of almost 600 manuscripts in Cave 4.

This cave is located only a short distance from the building ruins at Qumran. It is an artificial cave hollowed out in the marl overlooking the Wadi Qumran. Although called Cave 4, it is actually an "oval chamber opening on to two smaller chambers which had been partially eroded away."[47] De Vaux commented that there was relatively little pottery found in it, although pieces from several jars and other objects were present. Texts were found in both chambers of the cave (called 4Qa and b), but they were mixed by the Bedouin, with the result that texts are identified simply as coming from Cave 4. However, almost all of the texts and pottery came from what de Vaux called the first room of Cave 4, 4Qa.

The sheer number of fragments emerging from Cave 4 changed the way in which the Qumran discoveries were handled. Prior to this find, it was expensive but feasible to purchase all of the material and prepare it for swift publication. The Jordanian authorities had established a going rate of one pound per square centimeter of inscribed surface, and as the fragments poured in, the rate went down to half of that. With the arrival of the Cave 4 fragments, the financially strapped Jordanian government nevertheless made 15,000 pounds available for purchase. When more money was soon needed but was not forthcoming from the treasury, the government, at Harding's suggestion, invited foreign institutions to purchase fragments with the stipulation that, after the work preparatory to editing them was finished, they would be given an equivalent number in quantity and quality to the ones they had purchased.[48] As things turned out, several institutions responded: McGill University (Montreal), the Vatican Library, the University of Manchester, the University of Heidelberg, McCormick Theological Seminary (Chicago), All Souls Church in New York, and Oxford University. In the end, the government reversed its decision and ordered that the texts remain in Jordan, but the institutions were reimbursed. In this way the perhaps 15,000 fragments from Cave 4 were, for the most part, kept in the country and not scattered over the world. John Allegro, one of the team of scholars appointed to work on the scrolls from Cave 4 and a scholar who wrote sensitively about the Bedouin and Jordanian side of things, has commented about the situation:

The Ta'amireh jealously guarded their secrets now, and their cave hunting had become a thoroughgoing business, directed by the leaders of the tribe, and engaged in by all the able-bodied members. Nobody in the world knows that desolate area like these people, and it is certain that if it had not been for them the Dead Sea Scrolls would still have remained undiscovered. If the prices are high, the work is tedious and back-breaking in the extreme, and certainly no member of the expedition who scaled the cliffs and combed the hundreds of caves, sifting the dust between their finger-tips for days on end, in a stifling atmosphere which is just indescribable, would begrudge the Ta'amireh a penny of their gains.[49]

The fact that Cave 4 was so close to the ruins raised the question of a relation between Khirbet Qumran and the scrolls with a new urgency. If it had been plausible to wonder about a connection between the scrolls and the building ruins when only Caves 1–3 were known, it became more difficult to deny a connection with the discovery of Cave 4. One would almost have to pass through the structures to reach the cave.

While excavating Cave 4, the archeologists located Cave 5 some 25 meters farther north. It held fragmentary remains of what have been arranged by editor J. T. Milik into twenty-five units.[50] Although the yield from this cave was nothing like what Cave 4 had to offer, its location so close to the buildings again suggested a connection. Cave 5 was excavated September 25–28, 1952. The Bedouin, early in September, had found another manuscript cave in the cliffs directly west of Khirbet Qumran. Cave 6 held remains of thirty-one scrolls, a large number of which were papyrus rather than leather.[51]

After the excitement of 1952, no new manuscript caves were discovered until 1955, when during an official excavation lasting from February 2 until April 6, archeologists found four more caves during a survey of the entire side of the marl terrace near Khirbet Qumran. All four had been artificially carved out. This brought to six the number of caves immediately adjacent to the buildings. Caves 7–10 yielded few texts: Cave 7 had nineteen, Cave 8 had five, Cave 9 had one, and Cave 10 had only an ostracon. These caves had collapsed and suffered erosion. Though Cave 8 yielded very few texts, it did contain about one hundred leather thongs and leather tabs with eyelets in them—items used for fastening scrolls. It is possible, therefore, that this cave was where such items were made as part of a scroll-producing process; or perhaps their presence means only that Cave 8 was where they were hidden.[52]

The final discovery of a cave housing manuscripts came in 1956, this time by the Bedouin. In January a group of them cleared out the blocked entrance of the cave and found some rather well preserved manuscripts in it. Other than Cave 3, this is the northernmost of the caves. In Cave 11 were the remains of some thirty-one texts, including a long and interesting Psalms scroll and the *Temple Scroll.*[53]

Select Bibliography

Some major accounts of the Qumran discoveries have been mentioned in the backnotes. A brief but detailed chronological survey appears in

Pfann, S. "History of the Judean Desert Discoveries." *Companion Volume to the Dead Sea Scrolls Microfiche Edition.* 2d rev. ed. Edited by E. Tov with S. Pfann. Leiden: Brill, 1995. Pp. 97–108.

See also:

Fields, W. "Discovery and Purchase." In L. H. Schiffman and J. C. VanderKam, eds. *Encyclopedia of the Dead Sea Scrolls*. 2 vols. New York and Oxford: Oxford University Press, 2000. 1:208–12.

Short biographies of some of the principal characters may also be found under their names in the *Encyclopedia of the Dead Sea Scrolls:*

de Vaux, Roland. 1:202–4.
Milik, Józef T. 1:552–54.
Samuel, Athanasius Yeshue. 2:818–19.
Sukenik, Eleazar L. 2:902–3.

A number of the first scholars to work with the scrolls have left reports about the events:

Allegro, J. *The Dead Sea Scrolls*. Harmondsworth, UK: Penguin, 1956. Chaps. 1–2.
Burrows, M. *The Dead Sea Scrolls*. New York: Viking, 1955. Part One. Appeared well before the final cave discovery and went through many printings.
——. *More Light on the Dead Sea Scrolls*. New York: Viking, 1958. An updated version of the earlier book.
Cross, F. M. *The Ancient Library of Qumran*. 3d ed. Minneapolis: Fortress, 1995. Chap. 1. An updated edition of a work that first appeared in 1958.
Milik, J. T. *Ten Years of Discovery in the Wilderness of Judaea*. Studies in Biblical Theology 26. London: SCM, 1959. Chap. 1. First appeared in French in 1957.
Samuel, A. Y. *Treasure of Qumran: My Story of the Dead Sea Scrolls.* Philadelphia: Westminster, 1966.
Sukenik, E., ed. *The Dead Sea Scrolls of the Hebrew University.* Jerusalem: Magnes Press, 1955 [Hebrew].
Trever, J. *The Untold Story of Qumran*. Westwood, NJ: Revell, 1965.
Vaux, R. de, *Archaeology and the Dead Sea Scrolls*. The Schweich Lectures, 1959. Rev. ed. London: Oxford University Press, 1973.

CHAPTER *2*

Dating the Dead Sea Scrolls

PLACING THE DEAD SEA SCROLLS in their proper historical context is a crucial step in interpreting them. When were these scrolls copied and what means are at our disposal for determining their dates? To grasp the nature of the problem, it is helpful to place ourselves in the situation in which the first individuals to see the scrolls found themselves. When Mar Samuel, Eleazar Sukenik, John Trever, William Brownlee, and others had their first looks at the scrolls, they did not know how old they were, and all resorted to whatever means they had for assessing their antiquity. Mar Samuel suspected they were very old and showed them to people who, he hoped, might be able to confirm this; the other three had paleographical experience (see below) and turned to the evidence available for such analysis. The general time frame for the scrolls was settled fairly early on to the satisfaction of most researchers, but some dissenting voices continued to be heard over the next decade or so, including some who maintained that the scrolls were actually medieval in date. Why have the experts found that to be unlikely?

Several scientific methods for situating the scrolls have been adopted by the scholars who have done the fundamental work. In this chapter we survey the three main ones: archeology, paleography (the study of ancient handwriting styles and changes in them), and carbon-14 dating techniques.[1] Each method in itself can lead to fairly specific results and indeed has done so; yet if all three (though they analyze different entities) lead to the same conclusion, reliability is considerably increased. Because the history of archeological work at Khirbet Qumran is the subject of Chapter 3, it receives shorter treatment here; the other two methods for dating scrolls are explored in greater depth.

Archeology

In its literal meaning, *archeology* is the study of ancient things, early times. As the word has come to be used, it is the science devoted to finding and interpreting the material remains of a place. This has become a highly specialized discipline with its own theories and schools about how one should go about recovering the past from the mute remains left in and on the soil. We should remember that the first scrolls were found in 1947 and that excavations in the area of Qumran did not commence until 1949. De Vaux's digs at the site itself began in 1951 and continued through 1956. He used methods that were in vogue at the time and was able to compare the items found during his five campaigns with the pottery and other artifacts then available from excavations at different places. We should keep in mind that the archeological work at Qumran dealt with the nonwritten remains, not specifically with the scrolls. Most have concluded, though, that the scrolls and the physical remains were related, being the possessions of the same group.

What does an archeologist do? Once a site has been selected and officially approved for excavation and the funding has been secured, a team of specialists (usually) and volunteers go about a careful clearing of the site, beginning of course with the top layer and moving downward to earlier levels. That is, an archeological site presents in reverse order the history of its past. An important aspect of the work is distinguishing layers of use or occupation. As one works downward it may be that one can see levels clearly separated by evidence of destruction such as layers of ash. It was the practice in antiquity to rebuild cities on the same spot where they had been destroyed because these were often better (obviously not perfectly) situated for defense, water supply, communication, and the like. As a result, the sites were built up progressively to form *tells,* or mounds, that are clearly visible. Where layers can be distinguished in the earth, the upper must be later than the lower, but that fact in itself does not supply enough information for dating the levels precisely; it yields only a time relative to the other layers. A key element in archeological dating is recovery of items such as pottery and coins from a layer. The pottery styles and composition may then be compared with finds from other sites (which may or may not be dated), while coins often divulge dates within specific chronological systems (e.g., the reigns of kings).

It is crucial to keep an adequate record of the situation in which everything was found and what it looked like when it was unearthed. A photographic record is essential, and field notes complement the visual report. The process is rather slow work, especially if the site in question is a large one. In the case of larger areas, archeologists often choose to make soundings in certain spots rather than uncovering the entire site.

One of the characteristics of modern excavations is association of many kinds of specialists in the work. Paleobotanists, anthropologists, and others help analyze the sundry sorts of materials found. Another characteristic is the attempt to find out everything about a site from the excavation. That is, rather than concentrating simply on finding something that will make the news or be appealing in a museum, modern excavators try to extract as much information as possible about the way of life pursued by the populace at a site, the types of living quarters and public spaces, the local diet, the agricultural areas around a site, the roads, and so forth. As a result, modern excavations tend to be expensive and time-consuming; with so much data to report, the final publications of sites are often badly delayed.

A problem faced by archeologists and by anyone doing careful research is achieving as much objectivity as possible—not letting one's assumptions or hopes influence the reporting of results. This issue is one that has frequently arisen in excavating and explaining the data from places mentioned in the Bible. Depending on one's theological stance, confirming or debunking biblical accounts has been prominent on the agenda. As we shall see, Qumran archeology has not escaped the charge of bias.

For details of the archeological excavations at Qumran, see Chapter 3. The principal excavator, Roland de Vaux, concluded after five seasons of work that the site had been inhabited in the Israelite period (eighth–seventh centuries BCE); it was then abandoned for

Table 2.1	The Strata of the Qumran Site According to Roland de Vaux
Period	**Dates and Other Details**
Israelite Phase	Eighth–seventh centuries BCE
Phase Ia	Began during the reign of John Hyrcanus (134–104 BCE), possibly a little earlier
Phase Ib	Began possibly during the reign of John Hyrcanus, but no later than the reign of Alexander Jannaeus (103–76 BCE), and continued until 31 BCE
Phase II	After a gap in occupation, a new phase began between 4 and 1 BCE and continued until 68 CE
Phase III	Roman soldiers occupied the site briefly after its destruction in 68 CE

a number of centuries before being built up and reinhabited by the people of the scrolls, beginning in the latter part of the second century BCE and continuing until 68 CE, with a short gap in occupation from 31 BCE to about the turn of the era. This occupation by the scrolls community he divided into two main phases (I and II) and subdivided the first into two parts (Ia and Ib).[2] The evidence, he believed, suggested that the buildings served as the center for a sectarian group whose members may have lived in caves or temporary shelters in the area. For a sketch of de Vaux's conclusions about strata, see Table 2.1.

As we will see in the next chapter, modifications suggested by archeologists working since de Vaux's exacavations and reports have altered this outline principally by eliminating phase Ia and by reducing the gap in occupation from nearly three decades to just a year or two. Evidence from coins and pottery has been crucial in establishing the dates for these phases. It remains to be seen whether there is sufficient evidence that the Qumran site was occupied in the last quarter or so of the second century BCE. Y. Meshorer has argued that the coin finds do attest such an occupation, that de Vaux's gap in occupation from 31 to 4 BCE must be modified, and that the site was probably inhabited until 73 CE, not 68 CE as de Vaux maintained. These points do little to change the general picture as far as the rough dating of the ruins goes.[3]

Paleography

As we have seen, the first scholars to determine a rough date for the scrolls drew their conclusions on the basis of paleographical analysis.

METHOD

Paleography is the science that investigates the styles of ancient handwriting, that is, the ways in which scribes formed letters, and the evolutionary changes in those styles over time as a means for establishing a *relative* chronology of texts. It is especially convenient, of course, if an ancient text mentions when it was written; then its date can be transposed into the chronology with which we are familiar—if the dating system used is understood and if the text is not a forgery. Happily, there are some Hebrew and Aramaic texts with date formulas, and they provide anchors, known points, on the paleographical time line. But very often ancient texts have no explicit or even implicit indication of time and thus must be aligned historically using other evidence. E. Sukenik believed the scrolls in his possession came from the late Second Temple period (516/515 BCE –70 CE) because their scripts reminded him of the writing styles on ossuaries from that time, while J. Trever compared the script of the large Isaiah scroll with that of the Nash Papyrus and other texts that had been found and studied. From that time to the present, scholars have continued to use and refine their paleographical analyses of the Qumran texts. There are disagreements about how precise Hebrew and Aramaic paleography can be in setting dates (within 25 years? within 100 years?), but there is little dispute about the general historical parameters within which the Qumran scrolls belong.

Prior to the discovery of the Dead Sea Scrolls there were few examples of texts from the area of ancient Israel, much less dated ones. Some inscriptions and other documents had been found and were of help in evaluating the scroll scripts, but the scrolls themselves have now become the major source of information about Jewish scribal hands in the Greco-Roman period, and discoveries of other near-contemporary texts have added to the paleographer's store of information. The fact that not a single one of the scrolls discloses when it was written means that all of them must be assigned a relative date; we do not know the month, day, or year in which any of the nearly 900 texts from Qumran was composed or copied. We do now have one partially dated ostracon found at the site; it mentions the second year of something, perhaps of the first Jewish revolt against Rome (hence 67 CE).

Paleography is a very helpful tool for *approximate* dating of texts, and at times it is virtually the only method available. One advantage enjoyed by the experts in this field is that they are often working with the productions of professional scribes. Few people in antiquity could write, and the few who did most of the writing were trained in the standard, accepted ways of forming letters. Not all writers were professional scribes, but many were, so that there was little of the massive variety in writing styles that we see today when so many more people are literate. Moreover, it probably means that changes in scripts took some time to develop; the scribal art favored conservatism over innovation.

Before looking more closely at the way in which the work is done, we should keep in mind some limitations that beset paleographical analysis. If a manuscript lacks an internal date and other indications of its time (such as references to historical characters and events), paleographers can establish when the text was likely to have been written only relative to fixed chronological points. They cannot assign it an absolute date like April 21, 63 BCE, or even 63 BCE. Being able to show that a certain scribal hand embodies later developments than the characteristics of a particular dated text is, of course, very helpful, but just how much later than that text would it be? Five years? Ten? Twenty? How can we tell? It may not be possible to specify a date within a very narrow a range unless there are many fixed points provided by other dated texts from the region. Usually we do not know how rapidly changes took place in letter formation or whether we are dealing with a conservative or more innovative scribe. Did developments occur at the same time in all scribal centers? Then, too, there are different styles of handwriting—from the most formal to cursives; all of these may have had different rates and times of significant change.

EARLY HISTORY

It will be useful to give a brief overview of the history of paleography for texts from the time and area in which we are interested. Although paleographical research long antedated it, one of the first studies based on a somewhat more adequate textual basis was W. F. Albright's study of the Nash Papyrus.[4] In this essay he tried to date the papyrus, a fragmentary manuscript containing the Ten Commandments and the Shema' ("Hear, O Israel") from Deut. 6:4. Albright was able to compare the script of this short text with writing samples from several documents and inscriptions and date it relative to them. He also sketched a typology for the development of the Aramaic script (the one we think of as Hebrew) used in the late Persian Empire and the early Jewish formal handwriting that evolved from it. Albright placed the Nash Papyrus in the second half of the second century BCE, that is, between 150 and 100 BCE.

In the early days of scrolls research, several paleographers applied their skills to the scribal hands on the manuscripts. Sukenik and Trever have already been mentioned. Others include S. A. Birnbaum, who wrote a number of articles in which he attempted to date individual manuscripts. He also composed other studies in which he commented paleographically on the scrolls in general, and he published a short monograph on the subject in 1952.[5] Birnbaum devoted the entire work to a refutation of those (mostly nonpaleographers) who opposed his and others' earlier paleographical conclusions. His book *The Hebrew Scripts*[6] is a major work that incorporates the evidence from Qumran as part of a project aiming to cover Hebrew scripts from all periods. Another expert who examined the scrolls paleographically was N. Avigad.[7] Both Birnbaum and Avigad agreed that the scrolls were to be assigned to the last two centuries BCE and the first century CE, although Avigad was aware of 4QSamuel[b], which he put in the third century BCE.

F. M. CROSS

Although these writers made important contributions, when one thinks of paleography of the Qumran texts, the first name that springs to mind is F. M. Cross. His article "The Development of the Jewish Scripts"[8] has been the standard reference work for the scripts of the scrolls and other Jewish texts from the last centuries of the Second Temple. He has more recently updated his work, but has not changed the fundamental outline of the development he set forth in 1961.[9] There are, however, many more dated texts available now than when "The Development of the Jewish Scripts" was published and thus more evidence on which to base firmer conclusions.

In the 1961 essay, after providing an overview of the ancient texts available for comparison (not only from Qumran, but also from Wadi Murabba'at, funerary inscriptions, etc.), Cross wrote: "In the present state of palaeographical study, therefore, we are enabled to draw a typological line of development of several script types, each appearing in scores if not hundreds of documents, inscribed on a variety of materials, the evolution pegged by a series of absolute datings at intervals throughout the Herodian Age [30 BCE–70 CE] and the subsequent era between the two Jewish Revolts against Rome [70–132 CE]."[10] His extensive work with the full corpus from Qumran led him to distinguish three periods for the scripts found in the Dead Sea Scrolls:

1. The *Archaic or Proto-Jewish Period* (ca. 250–150 BCE): Because there are few samples, the dating is less exact and is "largely based on typological sequence."[11]

2. The *Hasmonean Period* (150–30 BCE): "The upper limit of this period, the lower limit of the Archaic period, is marked by the emergence from the slowly evolving Archaic book hand of a characteristic and rapidly developing style, which may be associated naturally with the decline (or suppression) of Greek, the resurgence of Aramaic and especially Hebrew as the official languages of Judaea in the era of Maccabaean nation-

alism."[12] He considered this period "the heyday of sectarian composition"[13] because the major sectarian texts seem to have been composed during it.

3. The *Herodian Period* (30 BCE–70 CE): This age is marked off by some firmly dated texts at the end (e.g., from Masada, which was destroyed in 73 CE) and at the beginning (e.g., an ostracon from Qumran dating from before the end of de Vaux's period Ib, i.e., before 31 BCE). As for the accuracy of paleographical dating, Cross wrote: "Indeed it is not too much to say that, thanks to the rapid evolution of the script in this era, the palaeographer can often fix a characteristic book hand within fifty years in terms of absolute dates, or even to a generation in terms of relative (typological) relationships."[14]

During these three periods different kinds of scripts are attested. Cross distinguished four: *formal, semiformal, cursive,* and *semicursive* (see Figure 2.1).

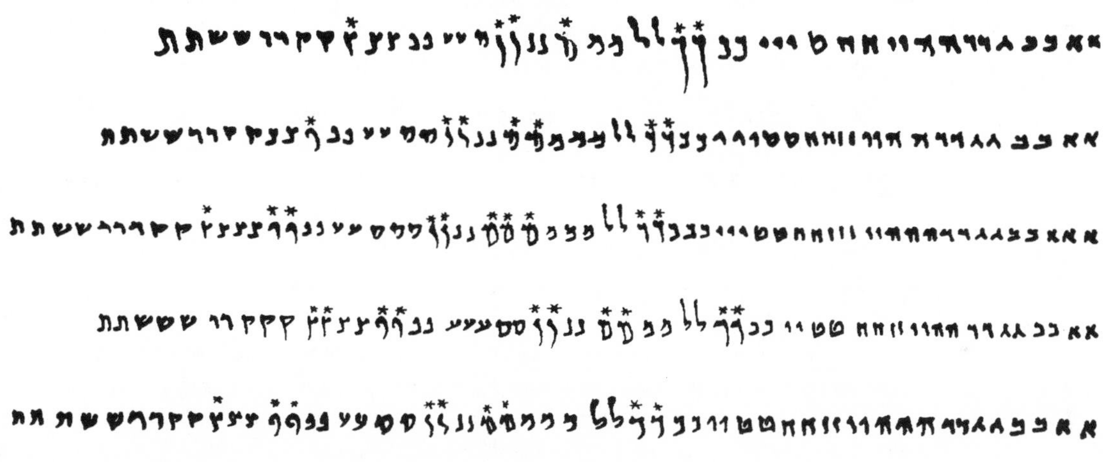

PLATE 10: The Evolution of the Formal Hand in the Hasmonaean and Herodian Periods

Line 1. A script transitional between the Archaic (Proto-Jewish) and Hasmonaean periods (ca. 175–150 BCE). From a manuscript of Deuteronomy from Qumrân (4QDeut^a). Published by Sidnie White in *Qumran Cave 4.IX* (DJD 14) 7–8 + Plate 1.

Line 2. A typical Hasmonaean script (ca. 125–100 BCE). From a manuscript of Deuteronomy (4QDeut^c) published by Sidnie White in *Qumran Cave 4.IX* (DJD 14) 15–34 + Plates 3–9. Compare the hand of the great Isaiah scroll (IQIsa^a) of about the same date.

Line 3. A Late Hasmonaean or Early Herodian hand (ca. 50–25 BCE). From a manuscript of Samuel (4QSam^a). Cf. F. M. Cross, "A New Biblical Fragment Related to the Original Hebrew Underlying the Septuagint," *BASOR* 132 (1953) 15–26.

Line 4. A typical Early Herodian formal script (ca. 30–1 BCE). From a manuscript of the Order of the War (1QM[1Q33]).

Line 5. An Early Herodian "Round" semiformal hand (ca. 30 BCE–20 CE). From a manuscript of Numbers (4QNum^b) published by Nathan Jastram, in *Qumran Cave 4.VII* (DJD 12) 205–67 + Plates 38–49.

Figure 2.1 A Chart of Early Jewish Scripts

From Frank Moore Cross, "Palaeography and the Dea Sea Scrolls," in P. Flint and J. VanderKam, eds., *The Dea Sea Scrolls: A Comprehensive Assessment* (2 vols.; Leiden: Brill, 1998), 1: plate 10.

To these scripts we should add the so-called *paleo-Hebrew* script—an archaic form of writing rarely used at Qumran. In the cases in which a scribe employed this, it was pressed into service for copies mostly of pentateuchal books and Job and in some other manuscripts for writing divine names. Not all of these scripts are as well attested or their sequence as securely established. (For more on the paleo-Hebrew scrolls, see "The Scrolls and the Text of the Hebrew Bible/Old Testament" in Chapter 6.)

The stuff of a paleographical publication is a set of script charts in which samples of each letter of the alphabet are given for a specific text. These are then compared in minute detail, page after painful page, with the data in charts for other texts. The results rarely make for exciting reading, but the comparative exertions are essential and the charts prove to be handy references.

An example will illustrate the data with which the paleographer works, although we should remember that paleographical decisions are not made on the basis of one letter alone. So, for instance, a trait in the earlier periods distinguished by Cross is that letters tend to be of uneven sizes, whereas in the Herodian period they have achieved a more uniform size. To choose a single sample for illustration, we may use the letter *taw* (ת in printed form), the last one in the Hebrew alphabet, which appears in rather different forms, depending on time and script style. In the formal tradition we can see these changes:

> *Taw* in the Archaic period is a very large letter, extending well below the (theoretical) base-line. The left leg is long and doubly curved. By mid-Hasmonaean times, however, *taw* has shrunken, following the general trend towards uniformity of letter-size. The left leg no longer ends in a curved flourish, but in an angular base. By Herodian times, the right leg has lengthened to roughly the same length as the left one.[15]

Using paleographical information, Cross dated the earliest manuscripts from Qumran to the period 250–200 BCE and the latest to not long before 70 CE. For him only three manuscripts showed evidence of being copied in the third century BCE: 4QSamuel[b] (no later than 250), 4QJeremiah[a] (a little before 200), and 4QExodus[f] (275–225). These and other early copies he thought had been brought to Qumran sometime after they were prepared; that is, they were not actually copied at the site. Cross himself established dates for a series of Qumran texts, and, on the basis of his work, the editors of the many other Qumran texts have almost always included in the official publication a study of the scripts in order to help date their texts.

The conclusions reached by the editors and Cross have been tabulated by Brian Webster.[16] Naturally, there are many uncertainties in such a list, but these are the numbers by the overlapping periods that have been identified by the various editors:

Period	Number of Manuscripts
Archaic (250–150 BCE)	21 manuscripts
Archaic to Hasmonean (200–150)	20 manuscripts
Hasmonean (150–ca. 50)	224 manuscripts
Transition to Herodian (ca. 75–1 BCE)	5 manuscripts
Herodian (50 or 30 BCE–68 CE)	418 manuscripts and two ostraca

In this list the numbers for the earliest phases may be somewhat inflated because of the inclusion of fragments in cryptic scripts that have been identified by their editor as coming from many different manuscripts, although at first they were regarded as coming from only two (4Q249–4Q250). But the raw numbers do show that, as we might have expected, almost all of the manuscripts from the Qumran caves were copied in the Hasmonean and Herodian periods.

Carbon-14 Methods of Dating

While archeologists have worked with the material remains and paleographers with the scripts of the manuscripts, another method approaches the problem by attempting to date the material on which the texts were written. Except for the *Copper Scroll,* the Qumran texts were copied on parchment, a treated form of animal hide, or on papyrus. Both types of writing materials are therefore organic substances. In a happy coincidence scientists had developed carbon-14 analysis as a method for dating organic objects at about the time the first artifacts from the Qumran area became available for study.

METHOD

Carbon-14 atoms are absorbed by plants, and the plants are eaten by animals, so that the level of carbon-14 in the two is similar to its level in the atmosphere. When an organism dies, it ceases taking on new carbon atoms. In fact it begins losing carbon-14 atoms at a measurable rate, becoming carbon-12. Calculating the ratio of carbon-14 atoms to carbon-12 atoms allows one to determine how long the organism has been losing carbon-14. The results are then compared with a calibration chart to measure the length of time before the present that the loss of carbon-14 atoms has been taking place. The calibration charts are based on the averages of carbon-14 counts in tree rings. The information supplied by carbon-14 analysis is, therefore, the number of years between the death of the plant or animal and the present, not necessarily the date of a text. We do not know how long a period elapsed between the death of an animal, say, and when its hide was prepared and then used as a writing surface, but it is reasonable to assume that the gap was not a large one.

HISTORY

At a very early time the carbon-14 method was applied to the problem of dating the scrolls. F. W. Libby, of the Institute for Nuclear Studies and the Department of Chemistry at the University of Chicago, was the person responsible for the scientific discovery, and G. Lankester Harding, Director of the Jordanian Antiquities Authority, sent four ounces of linen from one of the Cave 1 scroll wrappers to him in 1950. He sent the material through J. L. Kelso, who was returning to the United States after a year as director of the American School of Oriental Research, and C. Kraeling actually delivered the cloth to Libby on November 14, 1950. Libby then conducted a test on the piece, which revealed that it had a radiocarbon age of 1917 years BP (*Before the Present,* the present being 1950), plus or minus 200 years. He therefore concluded a date for the linen between 167 BCE and 233 CE.[17]

The result was a very helpful but limited piece of information. It established a general framework for the date of the linen, and by implication also for the scroll in which the linen was wrapped. Questions about the connection between scroll and linen could arise because the two came into scholarly hands separate from each other, but the linen almost certainly came from the lone Qumran cave identified at that time. At least the radiocarbon date of the linen scroll wrapper virtually ruled out other periods, whether earlier than 167 BCE or later than 233 CE, for the scroll wrapper in question. As O. R. Sellers of McCormick Theological Seminary, the scholar who had suggested the carbon-14 test, put it: "So epigraphy, archaeology, and nuclear physics now combine to support the genuineness and antiquity of the material found in the cave."[18]

Since Libby's maiden experiments, there have been a number of refinements in the method, and these have required some modifications of his results. His "measurement, however, was made before the necessity for calibration was known. (Libby's margin of error arose entirely from the counting of the radioactivity.) By modern calibration, Libby's measurement gives us 68% confidence that the date of the Cave 1 linen was somewhere between 160 BCE and 390 CE."[19] So, although the range now seems a little larger than originally thought (550 rather than 400 years), the same point remains valid: earlier and later dates are implausible.

In 1950 only a linen wrapper, not a scroll, was subjected to carbon-14 testing because the method at that time required destroying a relatively large amount of material in order to conduct a valid test. Some 2–5 grams were needed to get 1 gram of carbon, which would entail losing too much of the valuable writing material to test a scroll fragment.

A decade later F. E. Zeuner published an essay about two tests on a piece of a roof beam made of date-palm wood and found in locus 86 at Khirbet Qumran (from de Vaux's period II, i.e., the first century CE). The tests were conducted in 1956 and the report appeared in 1960.[20] The same results were reached with both tests: the wood had a carbon-14 age of BP 1940 ± 80 (10 CE ± 80 = 70 BCE–90 CE). "If the wood had been used immediately after cutting, this measurement would reflect a date of building activity at Qumran (some time before the date of the fire which had charred the wood). After allowing a factor for the age of the tree [Zeuner estimated 15–85 years[21]], calibration of these measurements gives us 68% confidence that the cutting of the wood used to make that roof-beam occurred somewhere between 40 BCE and 110 CE."[22]

ACCELERATOR MASS SPECTROMETRY TESTING

In more recent times refinements in radiocarbon-dating methods have made it feasible to subject scrolls and scroll fragments to testing. Once the accelerator mass spectrometry (AMS) technique had been developed, a much smaller amount of material was required for a valid test (about 20–40 milligrams). So, in 1991 and 1994–95 sets of scrolls were subjected to such analysis, and the results have been very interesting for several reasons.

In 1991, Robert Eisenman and Philip Davies, two scrolls scholars, requested that AMS testing be done on the scrolls, and this was done at the instigation of Amir Drori, Director of the Israel Antiquities Authority. Samples from fourteen manuscripts found at six sites (four had internal dates, the others did not) were taken and tested at the Institut für Mittelenergiephysik in Zurich.[23] Then in 1994–95 another twenty-two samples of scrolls were tested at the NSF Accelerator Mass Spectrometry Facility at the University of Arizona in Tucson. These, too, were from several sites and three of the texts had internal dates.[24] For the texts with internal dates (none of which, of course, is from Qumran), these are the results as calculated by G. Doudna in 1998 (1-σ means that there is a 68% level of confidence that the correct year falls within the limits proposed; the letters T and Z in parentheses indicate where the test was done, Tucson or Zurich):[25]

Text	Internal Date	AMS Dates (1-σ, 1997 Calibration)
WDSP 2	352/351 BCE	399–357 or 287–234 BCE (T)
5/6Hev 19	128 CE	131–240 CE (Z)
5/6Hev 21	130 CE	132–324 CE (T)
XHev/Se 11	130/131 CE	32–129 CE (Z)
Mur 30	134/135 CE	77–132 CE (Z)
XHev/Se 8a	134/135 CE	237–340 CE (T)
Mird	744 CE	676–775 CE (Z)

The dates in the internal-date column and the ranges in the AMS column correspond fairly closely, with the internal dates usually falling at or near one end of the AMS range. The notable exception is the second from the last item, for which there is at least a one-hundred-year discrepancy between the internal date and the earliest date in the AMS range. The 2-σ range for this text is 140–390 CE, that is, there is a 95 percent level of confidence that the actual date of the papyrus falls within that range. In other words, it too would then fit the pattern of the others in that the internal date would be near one of the extremes of the AMS date.

Bearing this information in mind, we may turn to the results obtained by the two laboratories for texts lacking internal dates (see Table 2.2 on the following page).

The Tucson laboratory also tested a piece of linen with a leather thong from Cave 4 (165–144 or 117–2 BCE) and a piece of linen from Cave 2 at Murabba'at (1285–1310 or 1355–1386 CE).

Several thoughts arise from perusing the list. Of the twenty texts certainly from Qumran (note that the large Isaiah scroll was tested twice; the provenance of 4Q342, 344–45 is disputed), the latest AMS date in any range is 237 CE (4Q258 in the first of two samples; 81 CE is the upper limit in the second), or, if the second sample of 4Q258 is more accurate, then 82 CE (4Q266) is the highest. Presumably 237 CE is the very latest one could go for any of the texts studied, and the fact that a second test of the same manuscript yielded such different results suggests this may be far too high. The very earliest date in any range is 385 BCE (4Q542, somewhat lower in a second range). This may be regarded as the very earliest one could go in dating any manuscript tested.

We may divide the results for the manuscripts found at Qumran into two categories: those for which the paleographical and AMS ranges overlap or almost do; and those for which the two ranges do not overlap. In the overlapping or nearly overlapping category are twelve examples, only two of which belong in the "nearly overlapping" basket (1QpHab [two-year discrepancy] and 4Q208 [eight-year discrepancy]). For 4Q208, it may be added that Cross did not think, as the editor J. T. Milik did, that the manuscript was from the third century or around 200 BCE. He always dated it later. The other ten have sizable overlaps (included here is the second sample for 4Q258).

For the manuscripts lacking such overlaps (seven, including the first sample for 4Q258), 4Q365, fragment 3 misses an overlap by 72 years, 4Q213 by 55, 4Q266 by 54, 4Q521 by 36, and 4Q267 by 21 years. The first sample of 4Q258 misses by 134 years. In all

Table 2.2	*Paleographic and AMS Dates Compared*	
Text	**Paleographic Dates**	**AMS Dates (1-σ 1997)**
4Q542 (Qahat)	125–100 BCE	385–349 or 317–208 BCE (Z)
4Q365 frg. 3	40–10 BCE	339–327 or 202–112 BCE (Z)
1QIsa[a]	125–100 BCE	201–93 BCE (Z)
4Q213 (Levi)	50–25 BCE	197–105 BCE (Z)
4Q53 (Sam[c])	150–30 BCE	196–47 BCE (Z)
Mas 11 (paraJosh)	ca. 30 BCE–30 CE	166–49 BCE (Z)
Mas 1n	175–125 BCE	38 BCE–78 CE (Z)
11Q19 (T[a])	ca. 30 BCE–30 CE	53 BCE–21 CE (Z)
1QapGen	ca. 30 BCE–30 CE	47 BCE–48 CE (Z)
1QH[a]	30–1 BCE	37 BCE–68 CE (Z)
4Q266 (D[a])	100–50 BCE	4–82 CE (T)
1QpHab	1–50 CE	88–2 BCE (T)
1QS	100–50 BCE	164–144 or 116 BCE–50 CE (T)
4Q258 (S[d])	30–1 BCE	133–237 CE (T), first sample
4Q258 (S[d])	30–1 BCE	36 BCE–81 CE (T), second sample
4Q171 (pPs[a])	1–70 CE (?)	29–81 CE (T)
4Q521	125–75 BCE	39 BCE–66 CE (T)
4Q267 (D[b])	30–1 BCE	168–51 BCE (T)
4Q249 (cryptA)	190–150 BCE	196–47 BCE (T)
4Q317 (cryptA)	?	166–48 BCE (T)
4Q208 (Enastr[a])	225–175 BCE	167–53 BCE (T)
4Q22 (paleoEx[m])	100–25 BCE	164–144 or 116 BCE–48 CE (T)
4Q22 (repair patch)		51 BCE–47 CE (T)
4Q342	ca. 1–30 CE	25–127 CE (T)
4Q344	after 70 CE (?)	68–131 CE (T)
4Q345	60–10 BCE	361–168 or 141–125 BCE (T)
1QIsa[a]	125–100 BCE	341–325 or 202–114 CE (T)

instances (other than the first sample for 4Q258) the paleographical and AMS numbers fall within the range for Qumran and the scrolls suggested by other evidence—the last two centuries BCE and the first century CE.

Although this is the case, there are two sets of results that attract special attention. First, the AMS numbers for 4Q542 (385–349 or 317–208 BCE) are not only outside the normal range for Qumran texts, but they are also distant from the proposed paleographical dates (125–100 BCE). Of course, the paleographical conclusion is open to debate, but is there any reason for questioning the AMS date? Apparently there is. Doudna, who chides Qumran scholars for assuming the AMS date is incorrect and the paleographical one certain, calls the AMS result an "outlier (i.e., a measurement that differs from that of other similar items without known cause)."[26] He refers to 4QLevi[a] (4Q213), which is written in a hand similar to that of 4Q542 but whose AMS dates were 197–105 BCE (1-σ) and 344–324 or 205–53 BCE (2-σ); one would have expected the two to have similar ranges. Doudna writes:

> There is a ready mechanism which may account for the anomaly. That there was contamination from an older source on both samples from 4QTQahat [= 4Q542] before cleaning is a fact. If this contamination was successfully removed by the chemical pretreatment procedure, the radiocarbon date reported by Zurich may be an accurate date. But if some of this contamination was not removed despite the pretreatment procedures of the Zurich laboratory, then the radiocarbon date reported for 4QTQahat is older than the true date of this text. Present data suggests that this latter option is in fact the case.[27]

A second question arises with 4Q258, a copy of the *Rule of the Community*. In the list in Table 2.2, results from two samples taken from different parts of the manuscript are given. A second sample was analyzed because the result on the first was so unexpected (1-σ 133–237 CE, 2-σ 129–318 CE). Tests on the second sample yielded a 1-σ range of 36 BCE–81 CE (2-σ 50 BCE–130 CE), which falls within the expected limits. Although retesting in this instance simply because the results were surprising (really surprising!) may seem a dubious procedure, the second test involved "extensive additional cleaning in acetone in an effort to knock out any possible contamination."[28] The variation in results between the two tests is beyond acceptable limits for AMS dating. "The practically certain explanation for the two results on 4QS^d [= 4Q258] is that some modern contamination was present that was not completely removed in the pretreatment on the first sample; and that this contamination or more of it was removed in the second attempt, or else it was not present to begin with in the second sample."[29] As Doudna adds, however, one wonders what the results would be if manuscripts that yielded expected results were retested.

Doudna's references to modern contaminants should be explained. In addition to whatever foreign substances may have adhered to the manuscripts when in use and during the centuries they lay in the caves, we know that modern individuals have added their own. Not only were the manuscript fragments handled by those who found, showed, and sold them, but the international team of scholars who sorted, cleaned, and studied them treated the parchments and papyri with oils to make them easier to read. Doudna has collected statements from Cross, Allegro, and Strugnell (all three of whom were members of this team) in which they mention the practice. Strugnell, for example, wrote: "Next came some cleaning of the darker patches with oil, to bring out the writing—something chemically harmless, I am told, but some of us used it too generously in the early days; infrared film could probably have given us the same results without permanently darkening the surface."[30] The seemingly harmless procedure of applying a substance like castor oil, which contains modern carbon, could, of course, affect radiocarbon results. The scholars working on the scrolls in the 1950s could hardly have been aware of this, but it happened nevertheless.

The only manuscript included in both the Zurich and the Tucson tests was the large Isaiah scroll. The Zurich lab reported (with modifications for the 1997 calibration) a 1-σ range of 201–93 BCE, while Tucson found a 1-σ range of 341–325 or 202–114 BCE. The Zurich numbers and the second set from Tucson correspond. At the 2-σ level, Zurich found 351–296 or 230–48 BCE, and Tucson reported 351–295 or 230–53 BCE. Again the sets of numbers from the two laboratories coincide almost exactly.

The AMS batteries of tests, then, leave us with important results for dating of the manuscripts. They supply evidence from an independent line of investigation that gives strong reason for thinking that most of the Qumran manuscripts belong to the last two centuries BCE and the first century CE. The radiocarbon analyses also show a high percentage of correspondence with the paleographical dates of manuscripts defended by the editors, although this is not always so. Questions may be raised about the precision of both methods, but when these sorts of results are obtained from a series of tests, they have greater weight than any one sample.

One further note may conclude this section. As indicated above, there is some debate about whether 4Q342, 344–45 come from Qumran Cave 4 or some other place. Because they were originally thought to have come from Cave 4, they received the designations listed; however, A. Yardeni has argued that these and several other manuscripts do not come from Qumran. In support of her conclusion, she includes the AMS results for 4Q342 and 344. Her case is not very strong for 4Q342 (paleography: ca. 1–30, "early first century CE";[31] AMS 1-σ 25–127 CE, 2-σ 43 BCE–214 CE), but it is weightier for 4Q344 (paleography: after 70 CE[?], it "would not seem to predate the end of the Herodian period";[32] AMS 1-σ 68–131 CE, 2-σ 24–226 CE). Even in this case, while it would at the earliest belong at the very end of the de Vaux's period II at Qumran, it is possible that 4Q344 came from it, judging from the AMS ranges. As for the paleographical date, as Yardeni admits, there are problems: "The script is a tiny cursive, and most of the letters are difficult to identify."[33] There would be no difficulties on either paleographical or AMS grounds in dating 4Q345 to the last centuries BCE.

In conclusion, we may represent the evidence from these three methods for dating materials from Qumran in centuries as follows:

Archeology	second century BCE–first century CE
Paleography	third century BCE–first century CE
Accelerator Mass Spectrometry (AMS)	fourth century BCE–third century CE (or fourth century BCE–first century CE)

However the earliest and latest extremes of these date ranges are interpreted, there is indeed a large measure of overlap between them. It would be highly unlikely, therefore, that the scrolls and the buildings at the site belong to any other periods than these, given our current information and interpretation of it.

Select Bibliography

Archeology

Vaux, R. de. *Archaeology and the Dead Sea Scrolls.* The Schweich Lectures, 1959. Rev. ed. London: Oxford University Press, 1973.

Paleography

Cross, F. M. "The Development of the Jewish Scripts." In G. E. Wright, ed. *The Bible and the Ancient Near East: Essays in Honor of William Foxwell Albright.* New York: Doubleday, Anchor Books, 1961. Pp. 133–202.

——. "Palaeography and the Dead Sea Scrolls." In P. W. Flint and J. C. VanderKam, eds. *The Dead Sea Scrolls After Fifty Years: A Comprehensive Assessment.* 2 vols. Leiden: Brill, 1998–99. 1:379–402.

——. "Paleography." L. H. Schiffman and J. C. VanderKam, eds. *Encyclopedia of the Dead Sea Scrolls.* 2 vols. New York and Oxford: Oxford University Press, 2000. 2:629–34.

Carbon-14 Testing: The 1991 Tests

Bonani, G., M. Broshi, I. Carmi, S. Ivy, J. Strugnell, and W. Wölfli. "Radiocarbon Dating of the Dead Sea Scrolls." *'Atiqot* 20 (1991): 27–32.

Ivy, S., W. Wölfli, M. Broshi, I. Carmi, and J. Strugnell. "Radiocarbon Dating of Fourteen Dead Sea Scrolls." *Radiocarbon* 34 (1992): 843–49.

Carbon-14 Testing: The 1994–95 Tests

Jull, A., D. Donahue, M. Broshi, and E. Tov. "Radiocarbon Dating of Scrolls and Linen Fragments from the Judean Desert." *Radiocarbon* 37 (1995): 11–19.

——. "Radiocarbon Dating of Scrolls and Linen Fragments from the Judean Desert." *'Atiqot* 28 (1996): 85–91.

Carbon-14 Testing: A Later Assessment

Doudna, G. "Dating the Scrolls on the Basis of Radiocarbon Analysis." In P. W. Flint and J. C. VanderKam, eds. *The Dead Sea Scrolls After Fifty Years: A Comprehensive Assessment.* 2 vols. Leiden: Brill, 1998–99. 1:430–71.

CHAPTER 3

Archeology of the Qumran Site

ALTHOUGH THE FIRST ARCHEOLOGICAL EXPLORATION pertinent to our area was the excavation of Qumran Cave 1 from February 15 to March 5, 1949 (see the description in Chapter 1), the ruins at Khirbet Qumran were later subjected to five seasons of archeological work (1951–56). In the last two decades there have been a few other studies of the area, but none on the scale of the digs in the 1950s. It should be recalled that during the work on Cave 1, Roland de Vaux mentioned visiting the ruins about one kilometer to the south, but at the time located no archeological evidence connecting the cave with the ruins. Systematic excavations of the ruins supplied the missing evidence and formed the basis for de Vaux's well-known theory about an Essene community living in the area of Qumran from about 130 BCE to 31 BCE and then again from about 4 BCE to 68 CE. (see Figure 3.1).

Early Reports

The seasons of excavations in the 1950s were not the first recorded visits to the site of Qumran. For centuries ruins were visible above the ground and attracted the attention of people who passed through this remote area. One could see piles of stones, a cistern or reservoir, an aqueduct, and a cemetery with many graves. A number of the earlier visitors to the site recorded their observations.

Upon hearing the way in which natives of the area pronounced the name Qumran (as Gumran), *Félicien de Saulcy* (1850–51) declared with no hesitation that it was the site of the notorious biblical city Gomorrah of Sodom and Gomorrah fame.[1]

Among other items, *Guillaume Rey* (1858) described a large wall that separated the dry land from the marsh and ran south from the Wadi Qumran. He took note of the graves, which, his guides informed him, were non-Muslim.[2]

C. Clermont-Ganneau (1873) surveyed the ruin and excavated a tomb (he included drawings of it), but considered the site unimportant. Clermont-Ganneau's description of the cemetery and one opened tomb (done on November 29, 1873) retains its interest and should be quoted:

Figure 3.1
Parts of the ruins
of Qumran, looking
toward the mountains
west of the site.
Courtesy of D. Tal,
M. Haramti, Albatross

The ruins are insignificant in themselves, consisting of some dilapidated walls of low stones and a small *birkeh* [cistern] with steps leading to it. The ground is strewn with numerous fragments of pottery of all descriptions. If ever there existed there a town properly so-called, it must have been a very small one. . . . The most interesting feature of Kumrân is the tombs, which, to the number of a thousand or so, cover the main plateau and the adjacent mounds.

Judging merely by their outward appearance, you would take them to be ordinary Arab tombs, composed of a small oblong tumulus, with its sides straight and its ends rounded off, surrounded by a row of unhewn stones, with one of larger size standing upright at either end. They are clearly distinguished, however, from the modern Mussulman graves by their orientation, the longer axis in every case pointing *north* and *south,* and not east and west. This very unusual circumstance had already been noticed by the Mussulman guides of M. Rey, who made the same remark as our men, that these were tombs of *Kuffar,* that is to say unbelievers, non-Mussulmans.

I made up my mind to have one of them opened. Our two men from Selwan set to work before our eyes. . . . After going down about a metre, our workmen came upon a layer of bricks of unbaked clay, measuring 15¾ inches by 8 inches by 4¾ inches, and resting on a sort of ledge formed in the soil itself. On removing these bricks we found in the grave proper that they covered the half decayed bones of the body that had been buried there. We managed to secure a fragment of a jaw with some teeth still adhering to it, which will perhaps enable us to arrive at some conclusions of an anthropological nature.

There was nothing else whatever to afford any indications. The head was towards the south, the feet towards the north. The accompanying sketches give an exact notion of the dimensions and arrangement of the tomb that I opened up, as also of the general appearance of this puzzling cemetery. The main plateau, which contains the greater number of the tombs, is crossed from east to west by a sort of path, separating these tombs, which are arranged with considerable regularity into two unequal groups.

It is hard to form an opinion as to the origin of these graves, chiefly on account of their unusual orientation. They may very well have belonged to some pagan Arab tribe of the period which the Mussulmen call Jâhilîyeh, that is to say before the time of Mahomet. Indeed, if they had been Christian tombs, they would probably have exhibited some characteristic mark or emblem of a religious nature, for the use of unbaked bricks to cover and protect the bodies, the considerable depth of the cavities, the regularity that pervades the arrangement, and so on, show that these graves were constructed with a certain amount of care and with evident respect for their intended occupants.[3]

E. W. G. Masterman (1902–13?) was commissioned by the Palestine Exploration Fund to measure the level of the Dead Sea in the area of Ain Feshkha. While doing so, he visited Qumran and left a description of the tombs and the aqueduct.[4]

According to *F. M. Abel* (1909), the tombs at Qumran belonged to a Muslim sect.[5]

Gustav Dalman (1914) determined that the ruins were left from a Roman fort.[6]

Martin Noth (1938) was the first to offer the widely accepted suggestion that Qumran was the City of Salt mentioned in Josh. 15:62. In Josh. 15:61–62 there is a list of six towns in the wilderness: Beth-arabah, Middin, Secacah, Nibshan, the City of Salt, and En-gedi. As he wrote in his commentary on Joshua, published in 1938: "The name [City of Salt] . . . points to a place on the Dead Sea, where Khirbet Qumran on the northwestern coast of the sea could be an ancient site."[7] After the first excavations by de Vaux produced no evidence of an Israelite settlement at Qumran, Noth withdrew his identification with the City of Salt.[8] However, when it was announced that they were Israelite ruins, he returned to his original identification.[9]

D. C. Baramki (December 30, 1940) "demarcated the site for the British Mandate government and noted the ruined buildings, reservoir, boundary wall and more than 700 graves. He noted that the graves, 'although crude and resemble Bedu graves are not correctly orientated for Moslem graves.'"[10]

S. Husseini (April 25, 1946) "surveyed Kh. Qumran and the area southward until Ein Feshkha. He noted the ruins, the plastered reservoir, the 'square corner towers,' the cemetery, the aqueduct, and what he called 'the extensive garden walls' lying between Kh. Qumran and Ein Feshkha. Concerning the pottery he concluded: 'Byzantine and Arab including one Iron Age fragment'. . . ."[11]

So, the site had been visited a number of times and some descriptions of it were available before 1947; however, no one had subjected the ruins to a thorough examination.

The de Vaux–Harding Excavations

1951

As we saw in Chapter 1, de Vaux and Harding, while excavating the first cave in 1949, visited Khirbet Qumran, but their quick surface examination and opening of two tombs yielded no archeological evidence linking the site and the cave. De Vaux wrote later, however, that he and Harding were not satisfied with this negative argument and decided to excavate the site. Their first campaign, under the auspices of the Jordanian Department of Antiquities, the École Biblique, and the Palestine Archaeological Museum, lasted from Nov. 24 to Dec. 12, 1951. De Vaux and Harding led the excavation, and were assisted by about fifteen workers.[12]

The excavators concentrated on the main building (loci 1–4) and on some tombs (see Figure 3.2). Coins in the rooms extended in date from near the beginning of the first century CE to the second year of the first Jewish revolt against Rome (67–68 CE). As most were found under the soil of rooms 1, 2, and 4, de Vaux concluded that the building was occupied at the beginning of the common era and was probably abandoned during the revolt.[13] The pottery was not only consistent with this dating, but also included an intact jar just like the ones taken from the scrolls cave.[14] Nine tombs in different parts of the cemetery

---

PROFILE
Roland de Vaux

Roland Étienne Guérin de Vaux was born on December 17, 1903, and died on September 10, 1971. A Dominican priest, he came to the École Biblique et Archéologique in Jerusalem in 1933 after pursuing biblical and oriental studies and taking ecclesiastical vows, and was to remain with the school until his death. At the École he studied for two years and then became a professor in 1935, teaching biblical history, archeology, Akkadian, and exegesis. De Vaux served as director of the École from 1945 to 1965.

After World War II the government invited the school to study the archeology of the part of Palestine occupied by Jordan, and de Vaux accepted the offer. As Benedict Viviano, a scholar later associated with the École, has written: "He had been trained as a historian but trained himself to be an archaeologist, helped by his friendship with Vincent, W. F. Albright, K. Kenyon, B. Mazar, and many others. [De Vaux] learned archaeology by doing it."[1] His archeological experience before the discovery of Cave 1 at Qumran consisted of work on a Byzantine mosaic church floor at Ma'in in Jordan (1937), an Arab caravanserai at Abu Gosh (1944), a Byzantine shrine to John the Baptist at el-Ma'mudiyeh near Hebron (1945–46), and the beginnings of his long-term work at Tell el-Far'ah in Samaria (nine seasons from 1946 to 1960). Later he participated in Kenyon's excavations in Jerusalem (1961–63).

De Vaux's official position at the École and the role of the school in the early days of scrolls discoveries led to his involvement in Qumran archeology. He was also to be appointed as the editor-in-chief for the publications of the scrolls in the series *Discoveries in the Judaean Desert*.

---

1. "Vaux, R. É. G. de," *Dictionary of Biblical Interpretation* (Nashville: Abingdon, 1999), 2:606.

Figure 3.2

A Grid of the site and
buildings at Qumran

From R. de Vaux. *Archae-
ology and the Dead Sea
Scrolls* (The Schweich
Lectures 1959; revised
edition in an English
translation; London: Oxford
University Press, 1973,
plate xxxix)

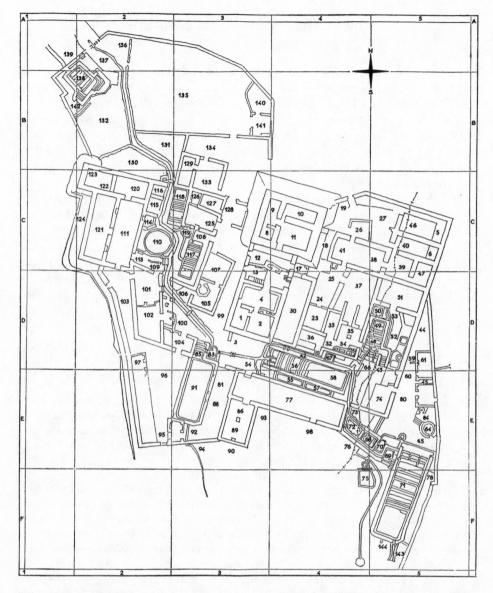

were opened and pieces of bones were sent to H. V. Vallois, director of the Musée de
l'Homme in Paris, for analysis.

Discovery of a jar like the scrolls jars in the caves established a link between the caves
and the ruins. Although the principal phase of occupation was from about 1 to 70 CE, there
was evidence in places for an earlier period of occupation. The cemetery was more difficult
to date, but it seemed certain that bodies were buried there during the time the principal
building was occupied. Moreover, the date of the building and the way in which it was constructed precluded identifying it as a Roman fort (as Dalman had proposed). The building
was not a private dwelling, just as the cemetery was not one for a single family; both served
a community. As de Vaux put it:

PROFILE
Lankester Harding

Gerald Lankester Harding (1901–79) first went to Jordan in 1932 and by 1936 had been named Chief Curator (later Director) of Antiquities. In 1948, after the partition of Palestine, Qumran came under his jurisdiction. He first learned of the scroll discoveries in late 1948 by reading about them in the April issue of the *Bulletin of the American School of Oriental Research* (it had just arrived). Although he was English, Harding acquired a splendid command of Arabic. Religiously an agnostic, he was the central authority figure for scroll-related matters in the government from 1948 on.

Harding was forced to resign his position in the summer of 1956 when, during a time of enthusiasm for pan-Arab nationalism, Western officials lost their jobs. He published his own account about Qumran as chapter 11 in his book *The Antiquities of Jordan* (London: Lutterworth Press, 1959). In 1966 Harding served for a short time as an advisor to the Jordanian Department of Antiquities.

> The khirbeh and the cemetery are only the central meeting place for the living and for repose for the dead of a community which lived spread out over the area but in possession of an organization of which the large building was the seat, a strict discipline to which the arrangement of the cemetery attests, with peculiar funerary rites.[15]

In light of the new evidence de Vaux retracted some of his early conclusions, such as the pre-Roman date of the manuscript jars. Noting that some had already suggested the scrolls were linked with Essenes, he adduced (as others had) the evidence from Pliny the Elder regarding an Essene settlement on the shores of the Dead Sea in a place corresponding exactly with Pliny's description.[16]

1953

The first season of excavation was soon followed by a second, which lasted from February 9 to April 24, 1953. By this time Caves 2–6 had been discovered and the caves expedition had taken place. The campaign was conducted under the banner of the same three institutions as the first excavation at the ruins. The leaders were again Harding and de Vaux, assisted by J. Milik and others; this time more than fifty workers (most from the Ta'amireh tribe) and two Arab leaders from the Palestine Archaeological Museum assisted.[17] Their work focused on the remaining parts of the main building and the tower (loci 5–53). De Vaux brought in equipment used in his excavation at Tell el-Far'ah to help in moving the many rocks and large amount of debris covering the ruins. Several more of the tombs were opened (nos. 12–19).

De Vaux's preliminary report (he stressed its preliminary character) centered on the main building, in the architecture of which he distinguished three levels. The *first level* involved a building of 30 by 37 meters, with the northwest corner occupied by a tower with substantial walls (1.2 to 1.5 meters thick); the lower of the two stories in the tower had no outside access. Evidence in the walls and cisterns in this area of the ruins, especially a fault line running through the eastern side, suggested that the first level came to an end because of an earthquake.[18] The pottery of this level dated it to the end of the Hellenistic period (just before 63 BCE).

After the earthquake the building was restored. In this *second level* the base of the tower was reinforced on the northern and western sides (the sides facing outward). A number of other structural changes took place, and the occupants did not repair the damaged cisterns. De Vaux thought that the changes effected in this level responded to a need for isolation and security, while retaining the general arrangement of the structure.[19] Its pottery placed this level in the early Roman period. In the course of describing level two, de Vaux wrote about the debris from the upper story of locus 30 (the largest room in the building):

> It contained fragments of a mudbrick structure covered with carefully smoothed plaster in curious forms. These mysterious pieces were put together with paste and cloth and brought to Jerusalem. After they had been patiently assembled, they allowed one to reconstruct a narrow table, about five meters in length and .5 in height, along with pieces of one or two other, shorter tables. These tables were associated with low seats running along the walls. Also, a low platform (still in plaster) was reconstructed; it was surrounded by an edge, divided into two by a projection and with two hollowed-out compartments. Is all of this the furniture of a dining room? It is possible, yet the position of the storey and the distance from the kitchens in loci 38–41 are surprising. But included with the debris were two inkwells [in a footnote he mentions a third, found in locus 31], one bronze and the other earthenware, which belong to a type known from the Roman period through discoveries in Egypt and Italy. One of them still contained dried ink. Is it not reasonable to regard these tables and the inkwells as the furniture of a *scriptorium?* The low platform with the compartments would have been used for purifications connected with the copying of sacred texts.[20]

His reading of the evidence from the second floor of locus 30 was to arouse controversy in the years that followed.

Although the evidence suggested to de Vaux that the same group occupied the structures in this second phase, he did wonder whether the restoration of the site occurred immediately after the earthquake or was separated from it by a period of abandonment. It was clear that level two ended through military action, as shown by iron arrowheads in loci 4, 19, and 45 and by a layer of a powdery black substance which implied that the roofs, made of reeds, had burned.

Level three, which contained the remains of numerous changes and signs of a considerable reduction in the area used, led de Vaux to conclude that the purpose of the site had changed. It no longer met the general needs of an organized community but served as a residence for a modest number of people who baked their bread in just one oven near the tower. Its pottery showed that it was slightly later than level two. This was the last phase in the history of the site; after this, only passersby stopped there.

The pottery, when compared with that in the caves, showed that the caves were used at the time of levels one and two at the site, with most of the material corresponding with the pottery of level two.[21] In a section regarding additional objects found in the ruins, de Vaux mentioned, among others, some written material. As he put it: "In these ruins open to the sky discovery of written documents on leather or papyrus would have been extraordinary luck, but certain inscriptions were preserved on pottery."[22] He then listed a name found on a jar, a pitcher with several Greek letters, a seal with the Greek name Josipos, a half dozen ostraca with letters or words in Hebrew characters, and a large piece of pottery with the Hebrew alphabet on it. The poorly formed script suggested that this was a writing exercise of a novice scribe.

Coins have played an important role in dating archeological sites because they regularly have year numbers stamped on them. Many were found in the ruins at Qumran. De Vaux listed 179 coins, with the earliest dating from 136 BCE. Almost all came from the levels he had isolated at the site, but thirteen dated from the second Jewish revolt (132–35 CE), three from the Byzantine period, and two from the Arab periods (these last three groups were found on the surface). The coins from the second revolt, de Vaux thought, did not suggest another period of occupation, but an isolated episode; presumably the few later ones were left by visitors.

The combined evidence of the architecture, pottery, and coins led de Vaux to offer a tentative history of the building: "It now appears that the building was constructed in the reign of John Hyrcanus [134–104 BCE]; it is in any case certain that it was occupied under Alexander Jannaeus [103–76 BCE]; one could not otherwise explain the large number of coins from these two reigns [14 and 38, respectively]. Period 1 [level one] lasted at least to the last of the Hasmoneans, Antigonus Mattathias [d. 37 BCE]."[23] Here de Vaux, building on his earlier conclusion that an earthquake ended period I, cited Josephus's report (*Antiquities* 15.121–47; *War* 1.370–80) that a terrible earthquake had struck Judah in 31 BCE (30,000 people died). The absence of coins of King Herod (37–4 BCE) indicated that the buildings at Qumran remained unoccupied for a time after the earthquake. In the reign of his son and successor Archelaus (4 BCE–6 CE), the debris was cleaned from the destroyed site and the buildings repaired and reoccupied by the same group that had earlier used it.[24] Since the last coins of level two are from the second year of the first Jewish revolt (67–68 CE) and those of level three were struck in the same year, we can conclude that the site was leveled in that year. Josephus reported that in June of 68 CE Vespasian came to the Jordan Valley, to Jericho; while there, he went to the Dead Sea to verify rumors about its waters (he had some men whose hands were tied tossed into the sea; they floated). Vespasian left a garrison at Jericho and in 69 CE his son Titus led the Tenth Legion from Jericho to Jerusalem (*War* 4.450, 477, 486; 5.42, 64). For de Vaux, this information left no room for doubt: "the building of Qumran was destroyed in June 68 by the soldiers of the Tenth Legion."[25] Roman soldiers then occupied the site and may have remained there until near the end of the century when the coin evidence ceases (level three). Qumran was used briefly during the second revolt and then finally abandoned for good.

So, by 1953 (the date when he signed his article) de Vaux had arrived at the following sketch for the history of the Qumran site:[26]

Period I: Construction in the reign of John Hyrcanus (134–104 BCE)
　　abandonment of the site (31 BCE and after)
Period II: Restoration under Herod Archelaus (4 BCE–6 CE)
　　destruction in June 68 CE
Period III: Military occupation from 68 to the end of the first century
　　abandonment
　　brief occupation during the second revolt (132–35)
　　definitive abandonment

1954, 1955, AND 1956

The third campaign to the site continued from February 13 to April 14, 1954. It was sponsored by the same three institutions and was led by Harding and de Vaux, who were joined by some fifty workers, many of whom were veterans from the previous dig. They cleaned out the main building and cleared objects found to the south of it (loci 54–99), especially four cisterns, the large meeting hall and its annex, and the potter's workshop, but no work was done on the cemetery. The fourth season, with the same institutions and leaders and many of the same workers involved, ran from February 2 to April 6, 1955. During it, the focus was on the western side of the site (loci 100–144), with its smaller building, court-yard, and parts of the water system. The team discovered Caves 7–10 and also spotted a small cemetery a little north of the ruins (they excavated two tombs in it). Campaign five, with fewer workers, was shorter than the previous ones, lasting only from February 18 to March 28, 1956. The time was devoted to making tests and soundings to fine-tune the distinction between the periods and to establish a more definitive plan of the site. Work was also done in the large cemetery, where eighteen tombs were excavated. They found a secondary cemetery to the south and opened four tombs in it. The fifth season of work involved moving beyond the immediate area of Khirbet Qumran to examine some structures found between Qumran and Ain Feshkha. Among these were remains of an Israelite building, a long wall, and a small isolated structure. Near Ain Feshkha they found a large building contemporary with the ruins of Qumran. The group also cleared Cave 11, which the Bedouin had discovered just before this season of work began.

Because de Vaux gave the results of the three campaigns in one article, we can summarize the findings from all of them together.[27] He believed the conclusions about the principal phases of occupation reached in his previous publication were confirmed by the results of campaigns three through five but that the more recent work added nuance and greatly enriched the evidence for them.

De Vaux indicated there was now evidence for an earlier occupation than his first phase or level—an Israelite phase. This could be dated by the pottery associated with it to the eighth–seventh centuries BCE. It was possible to trace the wall that surrounded the installation and to determine that the deep round cistern (locus 110) was part of the structure, as was the wall running from the southeast corner of the buildings southward to the Wadi Qumran. Discoveries included a jar handle with the Hebrew inscription meaning "of the king" and an ostracon on which was writing in paleo-Hebrew. De Vaux associated the site with 2 Chron. 26:10, which says that King Uzziah of Judah (who reigned from perhaps 783 to 742 BCE) "built towers in the wilderness and hewed out many cisterns. . . ."

Besides the Israelite phase, de Vaux now divided his level I into Ia (an early, small-scale reuse of the site) and Ib, when the buildings were developed to their full extent.[28] In light of later discussions, we should note what de Vaux wrote about phase Ia:

> It is difficult to to determine exactly the date of these first constructions. One can certainly associate with them only some pieces and pots found in the deep levels of loci 32, 36, and 30 in the south. This pottery is not distinguished from that of period Ib, and no coins specify its date. Period Ib probably began in the reign of Alexander Jannaeus (103–76 BCE); it is possible but not certain that period Ia began during the reign of John Hyrcanus (134–104 BCE) because it seems that it lasted only a short time and that the development of the community very soon required an extension of the buildings which then acquired their definitive plan.[29]

Period Ib received more detailed treatment. He assigned to this period the aqueduct, which brought the winter rain waters from the Wadi Qumran. The water channel entered the installation on the northwest side and made its way indirectly toward the southeastern end of the site, filling various basins as it went and ending in the large cistern at locus 71.

De Vaux considered the water system the most striking characteristic of Khirbet Qumran, one that was carefully constructed to provide for the daily needs of a relatively populous group that had chosen to live in the desert, a group that had (so its writings indicated) substantial purity requirements.[30] All of the large cisterns were equipped with steps, with the upper part divided by a low partition—a feature suggesting that these were pools used as ritual baths. He noted that similar pools had been found in Jerusalem and finally concluded that they were probably simple cisterns, with the steps allowing one to draw water from them. De Vaux did single out two cisterns (in locus 68, on the southeast, and in locus 138, near the northwest entrance), which were certainly baths (whether ritual or secular he did not say).

Belonging to this period was the largest room in the complex, locus 77, which measured 22 by 4.5 meters and must have been, he thought, the community's meeting room. Means for cleaning the floor of this room were present (sloping floor, channel for draining water), suggesting that it also served as a refectory. Additional evidence was furnished by the adjacent room (loci 86, 89) in which more than 1,000 vessels, mostly made at the site, were discovered. These included jars, dishes, jugs, plates, bowls, and beakers. This was, he thought, the crockery, which offered all that would be required for meals in the large room.

The end of period Ib was marked by an earthquake, which damaged the buildings. More evidence of damage from it was uncovered in the later digs at the site, so that a fault line could be seen all along the east side, while areas farther to the west were also affected. The pottery in loci 86 and 89 (off the large room) suggested that the site was occupied when the quake struck; the large amount of material that had to be cleaned from the area before it was later reoccupied pointed toward the same conclusion. At this time de Vaux hypothesized that the earthquake had started a fire, the clearest indication of which was a layer of ash in the open areas next to the buildings. The earthquake and fire were followed by a time of abandonment of the site. The coins provided the clearest proof, but the excavations yielded further evidence. It appeared that the water system was not repaired immediately. Sediment built up and caused an overflow, so that sediment is found in areas around the large basin (locus 130 from the basin in 132). The sediment above the layer of ash in locus 130 and in the northwest area of the secondary building reaches a depth of 75 centimeters; it grows thinner as one moves eastward. He thought this and the subsequent rebuilding could be explained by positing only a short time of abandonment and that the numismatic evidence suggested no more than thirty years.

After discussing the evidence for periods II and III (no new evidence caused him to change his views about them), de Vaux dealt with several other subjects in the remainder of his long article. One was the animal-bone deposits found at Khirbet Qumran.[31] In open spaces between the buildings and around them were found animal bones deposited between large pieces of jars or pots, at times placed in intact pots with lids on them, in one instance covered only by a large plate. There were usually other fragments of pottery found with them, and the deposits were barely covered with dirt. Some even seem to have been placed on the ground. These deposits were found in sundry places, apparently in almost all the noncovered spaces at Qumran. The largest number turned up in locus 130 (northwest side of the site). F. E. Zeuner of the London Institute of Archaeology, who was participating in the excavation at Jericho, examined the bones from thirty-nine of these deposits. De Vaux summarized the preliminary report from the professor. No deposit contained the complete skeleton of an animal; the bones, without flesh on them, were not connected. Twenty-six deposits held the bones of a single animal, nine the bones of two animals, three the bones of three animals, and one the bones of four animals. Bones from five adult sheep, five adult goats, twenty-one sheep or goats, fifteen lambs or kids, six calves, four cows or oxen, and one large unidentified animal (possibly an abnormal cow) were found. The bones were certainly the remains of meals. Judging from the level in which they were found, the pottery associated with them, and at times by the coins located in the immediate vicinity, the largest number of the deposits uncovered belonged to period I, but some came from period II. He thought the care with which the bones were set aside after the meat on them had been cooked and eaten showed a religious intent. As it was known from the literature that some of the community's meals were sacred, it is understandable that what remained from them would have been treated with respect. However, no biblical legislation clarified the bone deposits.

Pottery again came in for treatment, and de Vaux devoted a few pages to the coins.[32] In the last three campaigns, 415 coins (not including the silver ones) were found; of those that could be identified he gave a list by the period in which they belonged. In period I (he could not distinguish between Ia and Ib) there were 63, with the earliest one coming from the reign of John Hyrcanus (134–104 BCE), and the latest 4 from that of Herod the Great (37–4 BCE). Most (48) came from the time of Alexander Jannaeus (103–76 BCE). Period II offered 160 coins. The first 5 were from the reign of Archelaus (4 BCE–6 CE) and the latest 2 from the third year of the first Jewish revolt (68–69 CE). From period III there were just 4 coins, and 6 came from later times. These data were consistent with finds in the earlier excavations, showing again that the site must have been occupied during Jannaeus's reign. The coins from Herod the Great suggested some occupation during his time, but the low number is not in harmony with the length of his reign. So the earthquake of 31 BCE had struck an occupied structure and was followed by an abandonment until the end of Herod's kingship. The reoccupation took place during Archelaus's reign and continued to the first revolt. There were 62 coins from the second year of the revolt, but only 5 from the third year; this again comports precisely with the conclusion that Qumran was taken by the Romans in June of 68 CE.

As for the silver coins, near the door in locus 120 (northwest side) the excavators found two pots buried between the soil of periods Ib and II. The pottery type is strange to Qumran. They were filled with silver coins, one containing 223 and the other 185. Against the north wall of the same locus and level a third vase with more than 150 coins was buried, this time in a pottery type attested at Qumran. M. H. Seyrig, director of the French Institute of Archeology in Beirut, examined the coins. He reported that the contents of the three containers were identical. With some exceptions the coins were from Tyre and most were tetradrachmas. A few coins went back to the last Seleucid kings, but the largest number belonged to the independent coinage of the city, which began in 126 BCE. The latest coins dated from the equivalent of the year 9/8 BCE (after which there was a gap in Tyrian minting of coins for a few years, resuming in large numbers only in 1 BCE or 1 CE). So the coins were hidden at some point between 9/8 BCE and the first year of the common era. Such evidence was helpful to de Vaux in calculating the time of abandonment between levels I and II.

In previous excavations a number of tombs in the Qumran cemetery had been opened. No more were excavated in the campaigns of 1954 and 1955, but in 1955 a small secondary cemetery north of the ruins was discovered.[33] It contained a dozen tombs that were grouped and some others that were scattered around. The two that were opened proved similar to those in the main cemetery. One contained a woman of thirty to thirty-five years, the other a man of more than fifty years. The bones were examined by G. Kurth of Göttingen, who also studied those from the tombs excavated in the large cemetery. In the latter all eighteen contained skeletons of males. As for the tombs on a small hill, where they were less regularly arranged and some were oriented east-west, four had skeletons of women (all in east-west tombs), one a child (east-west), and one a skeleton of undetermined sex (north-south). In a secondary cemetery to the south of Khirbet Qumran another thirty tombs were found, with different orientations. The four that were opened contained a female skeleton (east-west), and skeletons of three infants (one north-west, the other two east-west, one less clearly aligned; see Figure 3.3).

With only 43 of about 1,200 tombs in the various cemeteries excavated, de Vaux was hesitant to draw too many conclusions. The burial places in question are three: the large cemetery with its tombs aligned north-south and its extension on the low hills to the east with tombs less carefully arranged and often differently oriented; and the two secondary cemeteries on the north and south. All of these, despite their differences, were of the same type and appeared to be connected with the principal occupation of Qumran in periods I and II. In the well-ordered part of the large cemetery there were only tombs of males, with the single certain exception of tomb 7, which falls outside the ordered arrangement and is of a peculiar type. In the extension of this cemetery to the east there were four women and one infant; in the cemetery on the north the sexes are mixed, while in the one on the south there were four children and a woman. In the graves of the males no objects were found with the body; three of the five women's tombs had some poor ornaments. Tombs 17 and 19 (dug in 1953) and 32 and 36 (opened in 1956) had the remains of wood coffins, perhaps suggesting the bodies were brought there from elsewhere. In three other cases

Figure 3.3
A view of part of the Qumran cemetery.
Courtesy of Monica Brady

(11, 24, 37) the skeletons were disjointed, possibly indicating cases of reburial, whether from another site or as burials of victims of the earthquake by those who cleaned out and reoccupied the site.

The 1956 archeological campaign, the fifth one at the site of Khirbet Qumran, completed de Vaux's work there. He also conducted a full-scale excavation at Ain Feshkha from January 25 to March 21, 1958.[34] By that time he had distinguished phases of occupation at Ain Feshkha contemporaneous wth periods Ib and II at Qumran. Similarities in architecture and pottery, when combined with their proximity and shared dates, suggested to de Vaux that Qumran and Ain Feshkha were used by the same group. A long wall might have connected the two sites. Ain Feshkha was an agricultural and industrial outpost of the community at Qumran.

De Vaux's fullest statement about the archeology of Khirbet Qumran and the surrounding areas was to come in his Schweich Lectures delivered in December 1959, the year following the excavation at Ain Feshkha. De Vaux gave the lectures in English. As Kathleen Kenyon wrote later: "He lectured in English with enormous verve and fluency, with occasional engaging mispronunciations at which he would laugh as well as anyone. They were the only Schweich Lectures that I can remember which were crowded at the first lecture and more crowded by the end."[35] The British Academy agreed to publish the French text of the lectures that de Vaux had prepared. That French version, *L'Archéologie et les Manuscrits de la Mer Morte,* appeared in 1961. De Vaux himself then prepared a revision of the text into which he was able to place a considerable amount of new information; he completed the revision shortly before his death on September 10, 1971. The revised text was translated into English and published as *Archaeology and the Dead Sea Scrolls* in 1973. In the book de Vaux supplied much of the same information as that found in his preliminary reports, but was able to supplement it (e.g., with a fuller account of the coins) and deal with it in light of the sundry reactions to his principal hypotheses. He retained his understanding of the stratigraphy at Khirbet Qumran as evidencing an Israelite period followed by the Essene periods Ia, Ib, and II and by the brief Roman occupation of period III.

Later Work

After the de Vaux–Harding expeditions to Qumran the site received little archeological attention. De Vaux made some final verifications there in connection with the expedition to Ain Feshkha in 1958. From December 1959 to April 1960 John Allegro was permitted by the Jordanian authorities to work at Qumran as part of his unsuccessful attempt to locate the treasures mentioned in the *Copper Scroll* of Cave 3. De Vaux charged that there were no serious archeological controls to what Allegro's group did at Qumran and that they destroyed the sites in which they dug.[36]

Conservation work was done at Qumran by the Jordanian Department of Antiquities and financed by the United States Agency for International Development from 1965 to 1967. The work received the approval of de Vaux, who thought that it did nothing to modify the conclusions reached in his expeditions to the site. [37] R. W. Dajani, technical assistant to the Jordanian Department of Antiquities, reported the chance discovery of an intact jar dating from the first century BCE or CE. Some stone "mugs" were also found in the cistern in locus 110.[38] The Six-Day War of 1967 led to an Israeli takeover of the area, and restoration work continued under the control of the Israel Department of Antiquities.

On April 9, 1966, journalist S. H. Steckoll, with the approval of the Jordanian Department of Antiquities, opened a tomb at Qumran (he labeled it G.2). Then in December 1966 and March 1967 he excavated eight other tombs in the main cemetery (G.3–10).[39] One of the skeletons exhumed (in G.2) was subjected to proper study by physical anthropologists—the only skeleton to receive such attention until recently.[40] Steckoll later penned a note in which he cited Tom Zavislock, an architect with experience in restoring buildings damaged by earthquakes, who attributed the destruction that de Vaux had credited to an earthquake to either faulty construction or repair of the cisterns in loci 48–50, which cracked when subjected to the weight of water upon reuse.[41]

De Vaux's study of the site was not the only one, although he did have the advantage of having led all of the campaigns (with Harding). One participant in the excavations from 1954 on, E. M. Laperrousaz, published his own interpretation of the finds from Qumran and Ain Feshkha in a book,[42] which followed a number of articles by him on the subject. Laperrousaz argued that period Ia began in 104/103 BCE and soon developed into period Ib, which came to a violent end due to a Hasmonean attack between 67 and 63 BCE. The site was then abandoned for a time and was not reoccupied until about 20 BCE, that is, during the reign of Herod. This period, which he called IIa, ended when Judea became a procuratorial province in 6 CE. It was separated from period IIb by another time of abandonment; the subsequent phase IIb ended in 68 CE. His lower chronology for the beginning of the sectarian occupation of Qumran arose at least in part from his disagreement with de Vaux about what the numismatic evidence implied. As we will see, although little of Laperrousaz's overall theory has carried the day, his lower date for Ia has been defended by several archeologists.

Little work was done with the archeological remains of Qumran between the end of the de Vaux–Harding digs until the mid-1980s. Since then quite a number of studies have appeared, in part supporting de Vaux's conclusions, in part revising or refining them.

In 1984–85, J. Patrich of the University of Haifa led a resurvey of the area covered during the caves expedition of 1952, and his team excavated five caves during four seasons (1986, 1988, 1989, 1991; included were Caves 3 and 11).[43] An effort was made to find the remains of huts or tents, since de Vaux had thought most members of the Qumran group had lived in such dwellings. Patrich thought that, even though they are humble habitations, tents and huts should leave traces. Also, if the members lived in this way, there should be evidence of paths connecting the dwellings with the main center. "Such a network, required especially if the members had to return to their dwelling places at dusk, after the evening meal, is absent in the entire area outside Khirbet Qumran."[44] There is also no indication that the aqueduct was extended to any dwellings elsewhere. "All these considerations lead, in our opinion, to the inescapable conclusion that all members of the community lived inside Khirbet Qumran. This conclusion was confirmed by the excavations as well."[45] Patrich reported that caves in the marl terrace could have been used for living quarters and also thinks that his cave FQ37, about one kilometer south of Qumran, could have served the same purpose; so he concluded that his survey had confirmed de Vaux's view that the caves in the cliffs did not serve as dwellings for the members of the Qumran group. Patrich differed from de Vaux in thinking that the membership of Qumran lived mostly on the upper story at Qumran itself. He estimated that the size of the group, therefore, could have been no larger than 50–70, not the 150–200 postulated by others.[46]

M. Broshi, then curator of the Shrine of the Book in Jerusalem, wrote a summary article that appeared in 1992.[47] He, too, raised the issue of how the evidence of coins was to be used (they indicate a date after which, not necessarily a date during the time of the monarch whose name they bear) and concluded that

> the archeological findings do not provide evidence as to whether the site was settled in the middle or at the end of the second century B.C.E. The same applies to the end of stratum Ia. It is obvious that this stratum extended over a short period only, but the evidence to the exact date it ended is lacking.[48]

He reviewed the suggestions for the end of period Ib and found de Vaux's to be the most likely, with the earthquake of 31 BCE and the fire being simultaneous. Broshi did not, however, accept the thesis of a considerable time gap between periods I and II. The relatively low number of coins from Herod did not entail this; moreover, a sizable amount of sediment can build up in a short time. He also accepted the argument that some of the commentaries relate to the great famine that struck during Herod's reign (25–24 BCE); the fragments in question claim that the group did not suffer while everyone else did. "In short, even if there had been a gap between strata Ib and II, it would seem that it could not have lasted for more than a few years, and by 26 BCE the site was most probably settled and the land cultivated. Thus, stratum II lasted for a period longer than assumed by de Vaux, and at least 94 years (26 BCE–68 CE) should be ascribed to it."[49] We may add that Broshi counters Patrich's claims about where members of the Qumran group may have lived:

> Although evidence of habitations was found in about 40 caves it is quite possible that some of the members of the community lived in temporary structures such as tents and huts, traces of which are rarely found.[50]

This last point has continued to be debated in light of later findings (see below).

While the chronology of the different levels at Khirbet Qumran was being questioned by these writers, a different kind of proposal came from Robert Donceel and Pauline Donceel-Voûte. The article in which they articulated their theory served also as an announcement about a new project to publish the final results of the Qumran excavations.[51] The initiative had come in 1986 from Jean-Luc Vesco, then director of the École Biblique, and Jean-Baptiste Humbert, an archeologist also from the École, and it coincided with the centenary of the school. The intent was to publish several short fascicles to make the Qumran finds available as soon as possible (see below for the only volume that has appeared—hardly a short fascicle). In the essay the authors include two noteworthy hypotheses. First, the Qumran industries may have been part of the wider trade networks in the area, including work with balsam and bitumen; the implication is that Qumran would not have been an isolated monastic settlement, but one incorporated into the broader economy of the region. Second, the writers, struck by the fine ware at Qumran, explained the furniture from the second story of locus 30 (understood by de Vaux as copying tables) as that of a *triclinium*. The room had a podium running along the wall on three sides; on this were couches. The triclinium, a dining room with three couches, is a feature found in many archeological sites in the eastern Mediterranean region. The Donceels thought the inkwells in the locus had no relation to the furniture. As we have seen, de Vaux himself had considered calling this room a dining room, but finally decided in favor of naming it a scriptorium. This idea of Qumran as a country villa has elicited a number of responses—almost all negative.

A similar proposal was put forward by Yizhar Hirschfeld of the Hebrew University. As he saw the situation, Qumran was a "fortified manor house, a sort of castle in which the lord or his representative lived and from which he oversaw the adjacent lands." He came to this conclusion from a comparison of the Qumran ruins with several sites he had excavated.[52]

In the winter of 1995–96, Broshi and H. Eshel (the latter from Bar Ilan University) conducted a six-week season of excavation in an area located just north of Khirbet Qumran, especially some collapsed caves in the marl terrace. Two caves, C and F, were investigated. Broshi and Eshel were drawn to the area by a network of trails. They estimated that there were twenty to forty artificial caves north of the Wadi Qumran and believed they had evidence these were inhabited. This would be consistent with the suggestion that about 150–200 people resided at Qumran in periods Ib and II. Some other remains (pottery, coins, iron nails from shoes, a peg) implied that tents had been erected in the area north of the buildings. Stones appear to have been placed in circles but any traces of tents have eroded away. They found the main path that led from the buildings to Caves 1–3 and 11, along which they spotted sixty iron nails from sandals. Their survey of various areas north of the buildings produced pottery that had parallels in the finds within the buildings.[53]

Our archeological survey closes with considerations of important contributions by two other archeologists. J.-B. Humbert, a scholar from the École Biblique and an archeologist who is involved in the process of making de Vaux's excavation materials available (see above), has proposed a rereading of the archeological remains at Khirbet Qumran.[54] For him, the occupation of the site in the Hellenistic period began with a Hasmonean villa or residence, a structure that served an agricultural purpose in support of nearby Hyrcania. In this way one could account for the presence of Hasmonean coins at Qumran. The structure existed during de Vaux's period Ia and was destroyed in either 57 (by the Roman Gabinius) or in 31 BCE (by Herod). Essenes then took over the site and modified it in stages to serve as a cultic center for their settlements in the area. On Humbert's view, only ten to fifteen "guardians" lived at Qumran permanently (i.e., in the buildings). Other people who worked in the industries at the site came from outside. He, with others, rejects the idea that one can infer the population at Qumran from the number of tombs in the cemeteries (de Vaux himself had indicated that some of the graves contained bones transported there from elsewhere).

At Qumran, Essenes set up a cultic center on the north side of the complex, the side facing Jerusalem. Included was a court for sacrifices and an altar. Later this cultic area was abandoned and another was erected on the south side. The large room (locus 77) was a hall for offerings and included an altar or tables for offerings. At this time the aqueduct was constructed. Sometime later even this cultic area may have been abandoned, but the site itself was destroyed in 68 CE. Summarizing Humbert's proposals, then:

1. The site was first a Hasmonean villa that was destroyed in 57 or 31 BCE.

2. Essenes took over the site after 31 BCE.

3. They transformed it into a cultic center complete with a sacrificial system.

4. There was no break in occupation during the Essene phase, but the site was modified.

Jodi Magness from Tufts University (and now the University of North Carolina at Chapel Hill) has reacted both to de Vaux's theories and to those proposed by others and has offered a revised chronology of the site that is now widely accepted. First we will summarize her reactions to the villa theory and Humbert's sacred space proposal and then give the details of her revised chronology.

Magness (with others) has shown in some detail that the villa (or country manor) theory is unlikely.[55] Although Qumran does have some fine ware, the complex does not look like contemporary villas in the region, whether in layout, architecture, interior decoration, or ceramics. Regarding Humbert's proposals, Magness has offered several serious criticisms. First, the more than 1,000 pieces of pottery in loci 86 and 89 that de Vaux understood as pieces for dining and Humbert as vessels for sacrifice would have to be dated to Humbert's pre-Essene phase, that is, when Qumran was supposedly a secular, farming installation, not a cultic center. Second, Humbert has given some unwarranted help to his villa phase by reconstructing, without supporting evidence, a triclinium at the site. Also, his interpretation of locus 77 as an offering hall complete with altar does not comport with comparative data; rather, de Vaux's interpretation of this as an assembly hall or dining room agrees with evidence from elsewhere. Against Humbert and others she maintains that Qumran is not located in a strategic place: "Qumran differs significantly from contemporary palatial and villa sites in Judaea and Idumea, and is also anomolous in terms of settlement patterns around the Dead Sea in the Hasmonean and Herodian periods. De Vaux's interpretation of the site as a sectarian settlement still makes the most sense."[56]

Although she has supported de Vaux's views about the nature of the site, Magness has advocated important modifications in his chronology. For one, she has argued that there is no period Ia at Qumran. It will be recalled that de Vaux found little evidence for this, and it was marked by no coins or distinctive pottery. She acknowledges that more precision about the phases of occupation will be available only when all of the material from Qumran is published, but thinks that period Ia did not exist and that de Vaux's numismatic argument for placing the beginning of Ib no later than the reign of Alexander Jannaeus is unconvincing (as others have also argued). "This means that the settlement at Qumran was apparently established much later than de Vaux thought, probably some time in the first half of the first century BCE. However, the presence of *miqva'ot* [ritual baths], the pantry containing over one thousand dishes, and the possible evidence for the custom of depositing animal bones outside the buildings in pre–31 BCE contexts indicate that the settlement was sectarian from the beginning of its establishment."[57]

Another point at which Magness has revised de Vaux's chronology is the period of abandonment that he had posited for the site (ca. 31–4 BCE) after an earthquake and fire. She notes that several scholars (e.g., Broshi) have wondered why the same group would abandon the site for three decades only to resettle it. The archeological evidence, especially coins, could solve the problem. In particular she cites the 561 Tyrian silver coins found between levels Ib and II. De Vaux associated these with period II and, as the latest of them came from 9/8 BCE, he thought the site was reinhabited after this date. Magness thinks it is more reasonable to assign them to period Ib. She also reassigns to period Ib some of the pottery that de Vaux attributed to the early part of period II:

> No period of abandonment followed the earthquake of 31 BCE. Instead, the inhabitants continued to occupy the site, repairing some of the damaged buildings and leaving others filled with collapse. In 9/8 BCE or some time thereafter, the settlement suffered a violent and apparently deliberate destruction by fire, causing the community to leave. This period of abandonment lasted from one winter season to several years, during which time the water system fell into disrepair and the site was flooded. Sometime early in the

reign of Herod Archelaus [4 BCE–6 CE], the same population returned to the site, cleared it, and reoccupied it.[58]

So, at this point de Vaux's understanding of the site as a sectarian center seems to have withstood the test of time, although not all accept it. There is some agreement among archeologists that he dated the beginning of the sectarian occupation too early and that there is no evidence the site was occupied until the early first century BCE. There is also no longer sufficient reason to posit a gap in occupation of thirty years between periods I and II. The two seem to have followed in rapid succession, separated by a destructive fire in 9/8 or a little later. Period II followed very soon on period I (early in Archelaus's reign) and lasted until Romans destroyed the site in 68 CE. On this last point, Yaakov Meshorer has questioned de Vaux's conclusions from coins for establishing 68 CE as the destruction date of the site. Although coins from years two and three of the Jewish revolt are present but none from years four and five, this does not entail that the site was destroyed in the third year. Coins of years four and five are rarer than than those from the previous years of the revolt. He suggests that the site was destroyed at the same time as Masada—in 73 CE.[59] The adjustment is small and quite uncertain, but possible.

Population Estimates and the Cemeteries

Several scholars have used archeological data to estimate the population of Qumran. De Vaux, basing his conclusions on the length of time the community was there, the number of tombs, and the average lifetime of the residents (inferred from study of the skeletons), thought that "even at the period of its greatest prosperity the group would not have numbered many more than 200 members. It was an organized group, as is shown by the complex plan of the buildings and water supply, the number of places of common use, and the uniform arrangement of the main cemetery."[60] De Vaux added another factor to the equation: some of the tombs contained evidence that may indicate bodies were transferred there from elsewhere, that is, that not all of the tombs in the cemeteries may have held the remains of members of the Qumran group.[61] Laperrousaz posited a shorter duration for the Essene community at Qumran (121–125 years) and, using the number 1,200 for the tombs while assuming a mortality rate at Qumran of 7 percent (which was the rate in Israel in 1970), arrived at an average membership of 1,428. He then considered various other factors (water supply, per capita use, etc.) and concluded that in period Ib there would have been about 300–350 people at Qumran and in period II about 350–400.[62]

Broshi has rejected such calculations, but arrived at the same numbers as de Vaux through a different means—the seating capacity of the meeting hall (locus 77):

> The dimensions of this hall were 22 × 4.5 m., viz covering an area of 99 sq.m. The members of the community dined here while sitting on the ground (most probably in rows parallel to the longitudinal walls). It can be estimated that four to five rows (each 0.7 m. deep) could be placed in such a hall and each row could seat 30 men (each place 0.7 m. wide). Thus the hall could accommodate 120 to 150 men. We believe this to have been the maximum number of members of this community. To this number should be added a further three age groups [for those in the stages of becoming members] constituting about 10% to 15% of the community, i.e., 12 to 20 men. In all, the community could not have been bigger than 150 to 200 members.[63]

These estimates have been countered by much lower ones. Patrich, who, it should be recalled, found no evidence the members lived in tents or huts in the area, posits a group no larger than a few dozen. They would have lived in the complex on the second floor, as the first floor areas were reserved for other purposes (workshops, etc.). Not even all of the second story would have been available for living quarters (e.g., locus 30), with the result that "hardly enough room remains to house more than a few dozen inhabitants in the entire complex, unless dwelling halls or dormitories existed, hardly the case at Qumran."[64] Similarly Humbert, who thought that only a group of guardians constituted the permanent population at Qumran, put their number at 10–15 and also thought they lived in the complex.[65]

The question cannot be answered definitively because there are too few pertinent data and too many variables, but the low totals of Patrich and Humbert seem unlikely for the Qumran complex. Whether there were huts and tents for residence around Qumran is a debated point. Also, while the cemetery did give reason to think that some burials were secondary, of people not from the site, the number of these is small among the fifty or so tombs that have been excavated (five coffins and two other burials). Hence, the large majority of the tombs may indeed be those of Qumran residents, and if so, the number of inhabitants would have to have been considerably higher than Patrich and Humbert allow.

The population estimates lead naturally to a consideration of the three cemeteries at Qumran. The large cemetery, which begins about 50 meters from the edge of the buildings, has approximately 1,100 tombs. The following discoveries were made during de Vaux's excavations:

> In the *main cemetery* 37 tombs were opened; where the sex of the interred person could be determined, in the regularly arranged area they contained the skeletons of males with one exception (perhaps), while in the eastern extension there were skeletons of perhaps one male, four females, and one child. Two of the female burials contained beads and earrings.
>
> In the *north cemetery* two tombs (9, 10) out of the twelve were opened; they contained the skeleton of one male and one female.
>
> In the *south cemetery* four tombs (1–4) of a total of thirty were excavated; they contained skeletons of one woman and three children.

Steckoll excavated one tomb in the main part of the cemetery (it contained a male skeleton) and eight others (five men, two women, a baby girl). De Vaux clearly thought little of Steckoll's efforts, writing: "The authorities of the Israeli occupation have forbidden this Sherlock Holmes of archaeology to continue his researches at Qumran."[66]

These data have played a major role in the debate about whether the community at Qumran was a male celibate society. We will examine the evidence for that claim later. Most of the tombs opened (and they are only a small fraction of the total) contained skeletons of males, but the presence of a number of females and children naturally raises questions about the nature of the community. It could be argued that their small number and the fact that the tombs containing them are different in character point to some other explanation. For example, they could be the remains of relatives of members or could be the skeletons of travelers. Nevertheless, they pose a problem for anyone who thinks the Qumran community was all male.

A new perspective on the question was opened by Joseph Zias.[67] He notes that the presence of beads, a finger ring, and earrings in the first southern tomb and tomb 32 of the main cemetery (eastern extension) made him skeptical that these were Essene burials, especially as beads are never found in Second Temple Jewish burials. Citing five Bedouin burial practices (east-west orientation, grave goods, shallowness of depth, field-stone coverings, marking stones for the head and feet), Zias infers that tombs 32–36 (eastern extension of the main cemetery) and apparently also those in the southern cemetery (oriented east-west) are Muslim burials, not Jewish ones. Skeletons of women and children, normally the least likely to be preserved intact, were the best preserved at Qumran—another reason to doubt they were burials from Second Temple times. "When one has the opportunity to see the skeletal material firsthand, along with the burial data and grave goods, and to compare it to the poorly preserved and fragmented material from the main cemetery, it is difficult to avoid the obvious fact that these anomalous burials are simply Bedouin burials from recent periods (post–1450 CE) and thus chronologically intrusive."[68] Dental evidence suggests the same: the males in the main cemetery had come from other areas to the desert, whereas the women were desert dwellers whose teeth show greater attrition due to an abrasive diet and the presence of sand in their food. He thinks the skeletons excavated by Steckoll were Bedouin as well.

In an important inference from his study of the evidence, Zias writes:

> The absence here of extended family tombs comprising several generations, as seen in other nearby Jewish sites such as Ein Gedi and Jericho, along with the absence of females and children, strengthens in my opinion the belief that we are dealing here in fact with a celibate community of males. Anthropologically, the only deviation from the Jewish burial norm seen here is the strict orientation of the graves along a north-south axis, which might reflect their opposition towards the priestly class in Jerusalem whom they disdained.[69]

If Zias is correct, then the relevant evidence for a group living at Qumran would come only from the well-organized, so-called main cemetery, since the burials in the other cemeteries and the extension are not ancient.

At least one other cemetery shows the characteristics of the main one at Qumran. At Ein el-Ghuweir, located 15 kilometers south of Qumran, P. Bar Adon excavated nineteen tombs in which he found skeletons of thirteen males, six females, and one child.[70] The cemetery, some 800 meters from a building, is contemporaneous with that of Qumran. Whether this means that a related community inhabited the site is not certain. The excavator thought it was another Essene settlement, but de Vaux was skeptical,[71] and Broshi, after neutron activation analysis of the pottery, has concluded that the ceramics from the two sites were not produced in the same place.[72] B. Zissu has shown that one of the types of tombs at Beit Safafa in southern Jerusalem resembles the Qumran method of burial and wonders whether these were the tombs of Essenes living in Jerusalem.[73]

As noted above, a project is under way to make all of de Vaux's material and notes available. By 2001 only one of the planned volumes in the series Fouilles de Khirbet Qumran et de Aïn Feshkha had appeared: J.-B. Humbert and A. Chambon, *Album de photographies, Répertoire du fonds photographique, Synthèse des notes de chantier du Père Roland de Vaux OP* (Fribourg: Éditions Universitaires: Göttingen; Vandenhoeck & Ruprecht, 1994). Another five volumes are to follow.

Select Bibliography

Broshi, M. "The Archeology of Qumran—A Reconsideration." In *The Dead Sea Scrolls: Forty Years of Research*. Edited by D. Dimant and U. Rappaport. Studies in the Texts of the Desert of Judah 10. Leiden: Brill; Jerusalem: Magnes and Yad Izhak Ben-Zvi, 1992. Pp. 103–15.

Donceel, R., and P. Donceel-Voûte. "The Archaeology of Khirbet Qumran." In *Methods of Investigation of the Dead Sea Scrolls and the Khirbet Qumran Site*. Edited by M. Wise, N. Golb, J. Collins, and D. Pardee. Annals of the New York Academy of Sciences 722. New York: The New York Academy of Sciences, 1994. Pp. 1–38.

Humbert, J.-B. "L'espace sacré à Qumrân: Propositions pour l'archéologie." *Revue Biblique* 101–2 (1994): 161–214.

Humbert, J.-B., and A. Chambon. *Album de photographies, Répertoire du fonds photographique, Synthèse des notes de chantier du Père Roland de Vaux OP*. Fribourg: Éditions Universitaires; Göttingen: Vandenhoeck & Ruprecht, 1994.

Magness, J. "The Chronology of the Settlement at Qumran in the Herodian Period." *Dead Sea Discoveries* 2 (1995): 58–65.

——. "Qumran Archaeology: Past Perspectives and Future Prospects." In P. W. Flint and J. C. VanderKam, eds. *The Dead Sea Scrolls After Fifty Years: A Comprehensive Assessment*. 2 vols. Leiden: Brill, 1998–99. 1:47–77.

——. *The Archeology of Qumran and the Dead Sea Scrolls*. Studies on the Dead Sea Scrolls and Related Literature. Grand Rapids, MI: Eerdmans, 2002.

Vaux, R. de. *Archaeology and the Dead Sea Scrolls*. The Schweich Lectures, 1959. Rev. ed. London: Oxford University Press, 1973.

Zias, J. "The Cemeteries of Qumran and Celibacy: Confusion Laid to Rest?" *Dead Sea Discoveries* 7 (2000): 220–53.

CHAPTER 4

Technology and the Dead Sea Scrolls

SOON AFTER THE DEAD SEA SCROLLS WERE DISCOVERED, scholars turned to scientists and to new technologies for help in dating, imaging, and reconstructing these most precious of ancient manuscripts. This chapter covers seven topics: (1) dating the scrolls with recourse to radiocarbon analysis; (2) the contribution of DNA analysis; (3) assembling and reconstructing the scrolls; (4) preserving and restoring the scrolls; (5) imaging the scrolls by photography; (6) imaging by direct digital acquisition; and (7) the role of computers, databases, and the Internet. We have tried to present the material in a clear but informed manner, with some of the more technical details contained in separate boxes.

Dating the Scrolls on the Basis of Radiocarbon Analysis

The role of radiocarbon (notably carbon-14) analysis has proved vital for dating the Dead Sea Scrolls and for confirming or correcting datings that were arrived at by other means (especially paleography). Since this topic has already been covered earlier in the book, we will not deal with it in the present chapter. For extensive discussion on the carbon-14 method, the history of this technology, and accelerator mass spectrometry (AMS) testing on the scrolls, see Chapter 2 ("Carbon-14 Methods of Dating").

DNA Analysis and the Dead Sea Scrolls

Because the leather parchments that comprise the vast majority of the Dead Sea Scrolls were produced from animal skins, some or many contain molecules of DNA (deoxyribonucleic acid, the molecular basis for heredity). Since the mid-1990s, several experts have been using DNA techniques to analyze fragments of the scrolls, because advances in molecular biology have made it possible to recover DNA from ancient sources.[1] The molecular analysis of *ancient DNA* (aDNA) from several scrolls enables the researcher to establish a genetic fingerprint or signature that is unique for each manuscript. One prospect for the third millennium is that the precision of DNA analysis will allow scholars to identify the species, population, and even the individual animal from which each parchment was

> **TECHNICAL DETAILS**
> ## DNA, Ancient DNA, and PCR (the Polymerase Chain Reaction)
>
> Immediately after death, the rapid degradation of biomolecules begins, a process that usually continues unabated until these molecules return to a native state. DNA, which occurs in large quantities in living tissue, degrades rapidly after death, and in most cases only small amounts of short DNA molecules can be recovered from dead tissue. This normally prevents recovery and analysis of DNA sequences from ancient tissue.
>
> However, the recognition by scientists of PCR (the *polymerase chain reaction*, an in vitro technique for rapidly synthesizing large quantities of a given DNA segment) in 1985 increased the possibility of isolating DNA sequences in extracts in which the majority of the molecules are degraded. Theoretically, a single intact copy of a DNA sequence is sufficient for PCR, which makes this an ideal tool for aDNA studies. PCR products can be sequenced directly from a sample or after cloning, which makes DNA-sequence comparisons a most useful tool for studying kinship relationships between individuals and larger populations.
>
> The amplification of *mitochondrial DNA* (mtDNA) from ancient bones and teeth dated from 750 to 5,450 years BCE has been achieved by several investigators, and aDNA has been used in the sex identification of skeletal remains. PCR has been successfully applied in the analysis of ancient mtDNA from a variety of soft-tissue remains, including a 7,000-year-old human brain and the preserved skins of over thirty kangaroo rats. Numerous reports document the successful extraction and amplification of aDNA from museum skins and field-collected specimens. Some of these skins have been subjected to the same conditions that exist in the Dead Sea Scrolls, and the extraction procedures for such specimens are not very different from those used in previous studies of aDNA.
>
> (Adapted from Parry, et al., "New Technological Advances," 498–99)

produced. Such information should prove valuable in answering specific questions concerning the origin and production of individual scrolls.

DEVELOPMENTS SINCE THE 1980s

The ability to recover biomolecules, especially DNA, from ancient remains provides the opportunity to study the genetic material of past organisms and to identify the histories of individuals and populations. Unfortunately, the DNA that has been recovered from archeological specimens is so degraded that the usual techniques associated with DNA fingerprinting cannot be used. Far more promising, however, is the prospect of determining the origin and identity of biological materials such as preserved skins or parchments. This requires some changes in the traditional procedures that involve the polymerase chain reaction (PCR), short segments of unique DNA from the mitochondria, and nuclear DNA.

As early as 1984, reports on the retrieval of ancient DNA sequences from an extinct animal appeared, followed by the cloning of DNA from the skin of an ancient Egyptian mummy that had been dated at 2,400 BCE. Although these and many subsequent studies employing aDNA analysis have produced positive results, difficulties and methodological problems do arise. The main problem is that PCR technology is extremely sensitive and can be easily affected by contamination from extraneous DNA material. One source of such contamination is people working in the field. Fortunately, in Dead Sea Scrolls research contamination by contemporary human DNA does not pose a serious problem, since it is easy to differentiate from animal DNA obtained from the manuscripts. Another source of contamination is micro-organisms such as bacteria, so sterile conditions and strict controls are necessary in the laboratory. A second problem that scientists face is the presence of inhibitors of unknown origin in aDNA extracts, which pose the danger of interfering with the PCR reaction.

THE VALUE OF DNA RESEARCH
FOR EVALUATING THE DEAD SEA SCROLLS

The aDNA obtained from fragments of the scrolls has provided answers to several questions. What follows applies only to manuscripts made of animal skins; DNA research is not relevant to papyrus or copper (from which some manuscripts were made).

(1) *Assembling scrolls in the Rockefeller and Israel Museums.* Many hundreds of fragments remain unidentified, but a good number of these belong together. Obtaining DNA signatures unique to each scroll will enable scholars to sort out the physical relationships between a large number of fragments. This information will prove useful in sorting out the huge number of tiny pieces that cannot be confidently grouped on the basis of shape, style of handwriting, or contents.

(2) *Making new reconstructions and assessing earlier ones.* Since individual animals can be identified by their unique genetic signature, it is possible to identify the origin of separate parchment fragments based on their genetic information. With recourse to aDNA analysis, pieces belonging to the same skin or to closely related ones can be grouped together. This process should assist scholars in new reconstructions of scrolls and in confirming or dismissing previous reconstructions.

(3) *Parchment used for patches.* The use of aDNA analysis offers important information on patches used to repair scrolls, especially about where a manuscript was when it was patched. If the leather used for the patch is from the same herd as the original manuscript, the scroll may have remained in one place for some time. However, if the patch belongs to a herd from a different region, the original scroll may have been transported or the herd may have been very mobile.

(4) *Scrolls made from more than one animal.* Because of their size, some manuscripts are composed of parchments produced from a number of different animals (e.g., the Great Isaiah Scroll, the *Rule of the Community,* and the *Temple Scroll*). The largest of these is the *Temple Scroll* (at 26 feet, or 8 meters), which is written on nineteen separate sheets of parchment. It appears that between two and four sheets of leather parchment were derived from the same animal. Analysis of different sections of these scrolls will allow us to determine to what extent the parchments in a single manuscript are related, and whether they are derived from the same animal or closely related ones.

(5) *The species of animals used for production.* Most of the scrolls were written on the skins of goats or sheep, but other skins were also used. On the basis of microscopic examination of the distribution of hair follicles that remain in the fragments, the scholar W. Ryder has determined that of four sample groups of scrolls, one group is derived from calf, one from a fine-wooled sheep, one from a medium-wooled sheep, and one from a hairy animal that was either a sheep or a goat.[2]

Biblical sources and at least one manuscript from the Judean Desert (the *Temple Scroll*) suggest that in ancient Judaism strict requirements were imposed to ensure the purity of animal skins. In particular, special requirements were placed on the origin and preparation of skins brought into the temple or the Temple city:

> Nor are you to consecrate a skin from another city for use in My city; for the skins are only as pure as the flesh from which they come. If you have sacrificed the animal in My temple, the skin is pure for use in My temple; but if you have slaughtered the animal in another city, it is pure only for use in other cities. (11QT^a 47.14–17).[3]

Some of the parchments found at Qumran may have been prepared with less strict requirements for cleanliness and purity. It appears that certain skins were from species of animals that were clean, but not necessarily ritually pure or used for sacrifice in the Temple. These may include animal species such as gazelle, ibex, or deer.

(6)*Assessing the scope of the collection.* Does the collection found at Qumran represent a library from one location or from a wider region? Some Old Testament texts emphasize the importance of separating flocks and herds; for example, in Gen. 13:5–9 Abram and Lot separate their herds to different locations, and in Gen. 30:40 Jacob separates his herds from those belonging to Laban. The first text reads:

> Now Lot, who went with Abram, also had flocks and herds and tents, so that the land could not support both of them living together; for their possessions were so great that they could not live together, and there was strife between the herders of Abram's livestock and the herders of Lot's livestock. At that time the Canaanites and the Perizzites lived in the land. Then Abram said to Lot, "Let there be no strife between you and me, and between your herders and my herders; for we are kindred. Is not the whole land before you? Separate yourself from me. If you take the left hand, then I will go to the right; or if you take the right hand, then I will go to the left."

In early Judaism it was apparently vital that animals used for the production of skins in Jerusalem, the Temple city, be derived from flocks and herds that were "known to their ancestors" (Josephus *Antiquities* 12.146). This suggests that flocks and herds were carefully observed and were guarded against contamination through crossbreeding. Analysis of aDNA that has been extracted from goat bones excavated at Qumran and other archeological sites in Israel may well reveal fixed gene patterns that can be compared with gene patterns found in the scrolls. Such an aDNA analysis can determine if the selected scrolls were produced locally at Qumran or if they were collected from different locations. This procedure could be tested by comparing the genetic fingerprints from manuscripts containing works known to have been composed at Qumran (e.g., the *Rule of the Community*) with manuscripts that were most likely brought to Qumran from other locations in Palestine (e.g., the Great Isaiah Scroll).

A SCIENTIFIC REPORT

In 1998 the American scholar Scott Woodward reported that his team had begun to extract aDNA from small portions of the Dead Sea Scrolls, to amplify biologically active DNA using PCR, to obtain DNA sequences, and to identify unique genetic signatures of the fragments.[4] These early results are most promising, since they show that the procedures involved are workable and should prove useful for reestablishing the physical relationships of many scroll fragments. Such identifications may also help clarify the translation and interpretation of specific texts.

The aDNA was extracted from eleven small pieces of parchment. The sequence of six of these fragments is most closely related to wild and domestic goats, but is significantly different from the human sequence—which shows that the parchment material was not contaminated by modern human DNA. The sequences of two more fragments suggest that they were derived from a gazelle, ibex, or similar kind of animal. Woodward and his team also examined six fragments from five different sheets of the *Temple Scroll* and concluded that all were derived from goats.

DNA has also been isolated and amplified from the archeological bones of ibex and goats that were found at Masada. The ability to recover such genetic information from ancient animal remains, Woodward points out, will enable scholars to compare Dead Sea Scroll fragments with the animals from which they were derived. Such a comparison should eventually allow identifications of the parchment sources by geographical location.

Although this research is relatively new, by the late 1990s it had already been shown that aDNA can be recovered from the leather parchment on which most Dead Sea Scrolls were written. Moreover, it has proved possible to recover sequences from this material and to compare these with other sequences. Early results indicate that two ancient scroll fragments do not derive from domestic or wild goats, but most likely a wild species of gazelle or ibex. Seven other scroll fragments, six of them from the *Temple Scroll,* are derived from goats. According to their 1998 report, Woodward and his team had not yet identified any parchment made from a species of sheep.

Assembling and Reconstructing the Dead Sea Scrolls

Assembling and reconstructing manuscripts involves a fundamental issue in scrolls study: the establishment of the text.[5] Since the 1960s, a method for reconstructing scrolls has been developed by the German scholar Hartmut Stegemann and his students. There are two steps in this process. First, scholars attempt as far as possible to assemble the many fragments from Qumran and other sites in the Judean Desert. The second step is to reconstruct scrolls out of these fragments, which involves special methods and techniques that present several challenges and difficulties.

ASSEMBLING THE QUMRAN SCROLLS

The process of assembling manuscripts from Qumran was largely completed over a period of thirteen years: between 1947, when the first scrolls were discovered, and 1960. The labor-intensive task of sorting the thousands of fragments and assembling them into different manuscripts was carried out by the original team of editors under editor-in-chief Roland de Vaux. Since having photographs of assembled manuscripts is fundamental to scrolls research, the enormous contribution of these early scholars in the saga of these ancient texts must be acknowledged.

Although it was usually known from which cave individual pieces came, scholars had to decide which manuscript each piece belonged to. The chaotic mix of fragments was partly caused by the Bedouin and even by archaeologists, but it was also due to the length of time the scrolls lay in the caves. The majority were not deposited in jars, but were stored in a virtually unprotected state. Most of the damage was due to the wind blowing through some caves (especially Caves 2 and 4), to small animals such as rats, and disturbances by earlier looters or explorers (see Figure 4.1).

Figure 4.1

A rat nest containing fragments of scrolls, found at Murabbaʿât, south of Qumran

Photograph from DJD 2.2, plate II, courtesy of the Israel Antiquities Authority

Working in the scrollery of the Palestine Archaeological Museum, de Vaux and his team grouped together fragments using various criteria, which were gradually refined. These include the general appearance and color of the leather; the thickness and preparation of the skin; the dimensions of the manuscript; the columns, margins, and rulings; the ink; the handwriting; the degree of carefulness of the scribe; and the type of spelling. The task of assembling scrolls is rendered more complicated by many factors; for example, differences in thickness and color of skins used in the same manuscript, and the fact that two or more scribes sometimes worked on the same scroll (e.g., the Great Isaiah Scroll [1QIsa[a]] and the *Hodayot* [1QH[a]]).

RECONSTRUCTING MANUSCRIPTS

Material reconstructions can be done with both leather and papyrus scrolls, and serve to provide more insight into the text, structure, content, and genre of the composition than is possible in its fragmentary state. Because they are so fragmentary, several Qumran compositions were previously unstudied by scholars, but with physical reconstruction the appearance and comprehension of several scrolls has been advanced (e.g., 4Q174, known as the *Midrash on Eschatology*[a] or *Florilegium*).

This method is especially important for (1) manuscripts that represent a formerly unknown work and have no overlapping parallel text (e.g., *11QMelchizedek* [11Q13]); (2) cases where several copies of a work exist (e.g., the *Rule of the Community* [1QS, 4QS, 5QS]); and (3) even some biblical manuscripts (e.g., 4QKings and 4QDeut[n]).

Although J. T. Milik undertook a material reconstruction of 1Q22 and 1QSb as far back as 1955,[6] the actual method of material reconstruction of scrolls from scattered fragments was developed by Hartmut Stegemann in his 1963 reconstruction of the *Hodayot* (1QH[a]) and described in his English-language article of 1990.[7] This methodology has also been applied extensively by his student Annette Steudel (1994)[8] and other scholars.

Fundamental to this method of reconstructing manuscripts is the fact that, as scrolls, they were originally rolled up when the process of decay began. The basic principle is to identify corresponding shapes of fragments and corresponding points of damage. Fragments or points of damage within a fragment that appear similar to each other must come from successive layers of the original scroll. The distance between corresponding damage patterns equals the circumference of the original scroll at the point where they were originally situated; thus the smaller the distance between corresponding traces of damage, the closer to the end of the scroll we are. Scrolls were usually stored rolled up with the beginning of the text on the outside. In such cases distances decrease progressively from the beginning of the text (the right side of the scroll) toward the end (the left side).

A few scrolls were rolled up in the "wrong" direction, with the beginning of the text inside instead of outside. In these cases the smaller distances between corresponding points of damage are found at the beginning of the scroll and grow progressively larger the farther one moves toward the end of the text (examples include 1Q22, 1QM, 1QH[a], and 4Q174). The precise amount of increase or decrease from one layer to the next will vary, since it is dependent on the thickness of the leather and on how tightly the scroll was wrapped.

THE RECONSTRUCTION PROCESS

The reconstruction process often enables scholars to calculate the original length of a scroll of which only fragments remain, but only if the middle or the outer part is preserved. Such material reconstructions are frequently helpful for determining just how much of an original text has been preserved. Since these reconstructions have been made using photocopies, they must be checked against the original manuscripts in the museum. Direct joins, for example, can only be confirmed by comparison with the original fragments. The same holds true for the number of hairs per square centimeter of leather, which varies on different parts of an animal's skin. Since fragments that contain a similar number of hairs per square centimeter may come from the same part of the skin, they can be placed close to one another in the reconstruction.

How can a material reconstruction of a scroll be confirmed or proved incorrect? Three criteria are (1) the width of the columns; (2) the division of the sheets (i.e., the number of columns per sheet); and (3) the original

---

TECHNICAL DETAILS
Reconstructing a Dead Sea Scroll

The reconstruction process involves several steps taken by the researcher: (1) ascertaining whether direct joins between fragments exist; (2) identifying definite connections of fragments on the basis of biblical quotations; and (3) comparing the pieces of a scroll and checking whether corresponding points of damage exist in order to identify patterns of damage.

The third step requires two sets of photocopies of the fragments in a scroll; the tracing of the various fragment shapes; and the marking of features such as column dividers, sewing seams, and top and bottom margins. In front of a strong light one of the photocopies is shifted around over the second until corresponding traces of decay are found. For the pieces to be actually part of the same sheet, the distances between lines drawn with ink or a sharp instrument on different fragments must correspond with each other. (An alternative is to use one set of photocopies and one set of transparencies, in which case no additional extra light is needed.) This process demands a great deal of patience, and the accuracy of a proposed arrangement can only be determined after the entire scroll has been reconstructed.

(Adapted from A. Steudel, "Assembling and Reconstructing Manuscripts," 526–27)

diameter of the manuscript. (The reconstruction is called into question if the diameter of the scroll is larger than its height.) The most important factor, however, is whether the text that results from the reconstruction actually works.

RECONSTRUCTING THE TEXT ITSELF

Although unusual or conflicting textual evidence often leads to a redoing of the reconstruction, material reconstructions can be valid even when they yield unexpected results. One interesting example is given by the German scholar Annette Steudel, who placed text quoting from Ps. 6:1–4 (Heb. 6:2–5) after text quoting Ps. 17:1–2 in her reconstruction of *4QMidrash on Eschatology*[b] (4Q177).[9] By quoting verses of Psalm 6 *after* Psalm 17, however, the placement goes counter to the sequence of Psalms in this "thematical midrash," which in general follows the traditional order of the biblical Psalter. Concluding that a different placement in the original scroll is virtually impossible, Steudel examined the contents of 4Q177 more closely, which produced an interesting explanation for the order of quotations. In this document all other quotations from the Psalter are cited without a quotation formula, but Psalm 6 is introduced by *as David said*, which shows that this quotation is subordinate. In other words, while the other Psalms quotations serve to guide the structure of 4Q177, this is not the case for Ps. 6:1–4, which is, instead, an additional biblical quote that has been inserted. This example illustrates how material reconstructions can force scholars to investigate a text more thoroughly and even to avoid errors in interpretation. It also confirms the importance of a careful reading of the text itself, both for confirming aspects of the reconstruction and for providing a solid basis for interpreting the composition.

Other scrolls for which material reconstructions have been done include the *4QHodayot* manuscripts, the *4QMMT* material, the Cave 4 copies of the *Damascus Document, 4QSongs of the Sage* (4Q510–11), and *4QSapiential Work A*. Early results have proved significant. Reconstructions by Eileen Schuller and Hartmut Stegemann, for example, show that certain of the *Hodayot* manuscripts from Cave 4 "do not contain the large compilation of hymns found in 1QH[a], but smaller units of material."[10]

Additional reconstructions that have been proposed or are already under way include *4QTanhumim* (4Q176) and *4QMessianic Apocalypse* (4Q521), which will help assess the character of these two works. Another is *4QBeatitudes* (4Q525), where the reconstruction will determine whether the beatitudes in this fascinating scroll come near the beginning of the composition, as occurs for the Beatitudes in Matthew's Gospel (5:1–12), or whether they come later.

Preserving and Restoring the Dead Sea Scrolls

Preserving and restoring the manuscripts and artifacts found in caves in the Judean Desert has proved a formidable task.[11] In this section, we discuss the efforts made and progress achieved from the time that scrolls were brought to the museums to the present.

EARLY RESTORATION WORK
AT THE PALESTINE ARCHAEOLOGICAL MUSEUM

The vast majority of the scrolls were written on animal skins, some were penned on papyrus, and one (the *Copper Scroll*) was inscribed on copper. The earliest manuscripts from Qumran date from about 250 BCE and the latest to 68 CE, when the community came to an end. It is not surprising that during the more than three centuries that elapsed, different methods of treating hides were adopted, many additives were used (e.g., oil, alums, and other minerals), and tanning was done with vegetables in varying concentrations. These processes produced leather that differed in thickness and color, ranging from pale yellow to dark brown.

Damage and Deterioration

Unfortunately, the scrolls have suffered much damage over the years, which has affected their color and appearance. This deterioration began long before their discovery in modern times. Although a few manuscripts were found wrapped in linen cloths in jars, many were stored in niches in cave walls, and many others lay buried in dust on cave floors. Due to the elements, rats, insects, and molds, as well as the activities of early human intruders, the great majority of these ancient manuscripts are badly damaged and some have almost completely disintegrated.

Further damage occurred when most of the scrolls were brought to the Palestine Archaeological Museum in the Jordanian part of Jerusalem, where (in early 1953) an international team of scholars began processing and preparing them for publication. This team had the unenviable task of sorting and assembling thousands of fragments in a large room named the *scrollery*, which contained about twenty tables. On these rested pieces of manuscripts placed between glass sheets, for a total of more than 1,000 plates (see Figure 4.2).

Early photographs indicate a lack of preservation techniques and environmental control. It should be stated, however, that this was certainly not deliberate on the part of the museum authorities or the scholars, who worked under difficult conditions and with what

Figure 4.2

Sorting fragments of the Dead Sea Scrolls: The early editors at work in the Palestine Archaeological Museum

Photograph courtesy of the Estate of John M. Allegro

today would be considered primitive resources. Scrolls were moistened and flattened between two sheets of glass, and then sorted by document or text. In the course of sorting, cellulose tape ("Sellotape," which was newly invented at the time) was used as backing material and to connect fragments. This tape was affixed to the leather (often in more than one layer)—and occasionally onto the text itself! Sometimes fragments were encapsulated between two layers of tape, and in many cases the adhesive penetrated the leather and soaked right through. Consequently, several fragments are completely transparent or appear black and greasy.

Most pieces were placed between sheets of ordinary window glass, where they lay loose and would sometimes slip out. The glass plates were often piled atop one another, causing added pressure on the fragments themselves, thereby accelerating penetration of the greasy, sticky mass into the manuscripts. In many cases the glass was also dusty, dirty, or even cracked.

Early Attempts to Remedy the Situation

One of the original team of editors, John Allegro, was so disturbed by the deteriorating condition of the Dead Sea Scrolls that he wrote a letter to the editor of the *Observer* on December 11, 1966:

> On a recent visit to the museum, I saw for myself just how perilous is the situation. Fragile fragments, which have been out of their desert habitat now for more than 14 years, are lying still between the glass plates where we left them many years ago, mostly unsecured, and in some cases, as I was horrified to see, subjected to intolerable pressure by the plates lying on top of one another in a large cabinet.

The damage being caused by the cellulose tape was especially troubling, as was pointed out in 1962 by Sir Francis Frank, of the British Museum, in an unpublished letter to Father Roland de Vaux: "The fragments must first be freed of the cellulose acetate tape which was used to hold them together."[12] Another problem was that the edges of some pieces bore a black sticky substance, which was apparently caused by the sustained effects of water on leather. A third difficulty was that many fragments had become stuck to the glass, which could not be lifted without damaging the leather.

In 1962, H. Plenderleith, Keeper of the Research Laboratory at the British Museum, wrote a report on the state of the scrolls,[13] in which he recommended several urgent preservation measures. These included sterilization of the leather to eliminate fungi and bacteria, flattening the fragments, and moisturizing them with an evaporation of water mixed with glycerin (up to 90 percent RH [relative humidity]). His earlier set of technical notes (which were written in 1955) describe how Plenderleith attempted to separate and analyze fragments contained in three boxes that had been sent to London:

> The method eventually adopted was to expose the scroll fragments at 100% relative humidity for a few minutes and then to transfer them to a refrigerator for a like period. The degree of freezing was sufficient to congeal the surfaces of the black material [i.e., the ultimate decomposition product of the animal membrane] while leaving the membrane sufficiently limp.

The procedure of restoring Dead Sea Scrolls was described by Valerie Foulkes, of the British Museum, in her report of 1963.[14] This included the removal of patches from the fragments, moistening and flattening the leather, and then fastening them with thin strips of silk, using gum arabic, or with gold beater's skin, using PVA (polyvinyl acetate) glue. Foulkes also employed British Leather Dressing, a special dressing for softening leather that had been developed at the British Museum. Because this dressing produced a glittering film on the leather surface, she thinned it with benzene, deeming it too dangerous to remove the adhesive tape from papyri and damaged parchment fragments. The adhesive tape was removed with a scalpel and a solvent named trichloroethylene. The fragments were then joined, using gummed silk strips or gold beater's skin and PVA adhesive. Foulkes also removed, with British Leather Dressing, water-soluble salt crystals that were found on the surface of the leather.

In spite of the temporary improvements carried out in the 1960s, the scrolls have continued to deteriorate at an alarming rate. For example, the leather treated with British Leather Dressing has become badly darkened and appears greasy and glossy, and in many cases the text is almost illegible against this dark background.

Half of the parchments and some papyri were sent to the Israel Museum Laboratory for restoration in the 1970s and 1980s. During this time much of the adhesive tape was removed with scalpels, and greasy adhesive spots were eliminated using wads of cotton dampened with trichloroethylene. Many fragments were then backed with white lens-tissue paper (sometimes in several layers) with the help of Perspex glue in a solution of acetone or toluene and polyvinyl acetate. Several glass plates were replaced by acid cardboard of the kind that was available in Israel at the time, and the fragments were treated with a chemical named thymol.

RESTORATION WORK BY THE ISRAEL ANTIQUITIES AUTHORITY

Despite the best efforts of all those involved, the methods of treating scrolls that were used in the 1950s, 1960s, and 1970s proved unsuitable or of temporary effect. The most pressing problem still confronting the conservators was the adhesive tape, which had to be removed without delay.

Progress Made Since 1991

A laboratory for the conservation of the scrolls was established in 1991 by the Israel Antiquities Authority on the premises of the Rockefeller Museum in East Jerusalem. Realizing that removal of the adhesive tape and stains would take many years, the conservators decided as an emergency measure to remove the fragments from the acid boards and glass plates and place them between acid-free cardboard. The fragments were attached to lens tissue with hinges of Japanese paper in the order shown on the original photographs that had been taken in the 1950s (see page 67). In cases where the tape covered the fragment, which would prevent the use of hinges, the piece was placed in a pocket of Japanese paper that was then attached to the sheet of lens tissue. The sheet itself was then enclosed in acid-free boards.

With respect to a method of joining manuscripts that could replace the adhesive tape, the conservators decided to exclude parchment glue and adhesives based on organic solvents due to the difficulty of reversing their effects, and to use instead water-based adhesives such as methylcellulose (MC). Best results were obtained with MC glue in its cold jelly condition, or Clucel G that had been dissolved in ethanol (5 percent).

The Method of Restoration

In seeking the most effective methods, the conservators studied numerous papers, especially the reports of the British conservators who had worked on the scrolls in the 1960s. Many experiments were also conducted, using different adhesives and backing materials. Modern parchment and gold beater's skin were excluded because of their different constitutions in comparison with ancient leather. Eventually, in consultation with specialists in the field of restoration, including members of the International Committee at the Getty Conservation Institute, they developed a method that is most appropriate for conserving the Dead Sea Scrolls.

Additional challenges and problems have been tackled by the conservators. (1) The few patches that were used to reinforce certain scrolls have to be removed very carefully, often with a surgical scalpel. (2) To accommodate editors who usually require a direct view of

---

AN INSIDER'S VIEW
The Method of Restoring Dead Sea Scrolls

Before beginning work on the leather, the conservator checks each fragment under a microscope. Delaminated areas of leather are then reinforced by MC glue in its cold jelly state, and the fragment is pressed under a small weight. Damaged areas are temporarily fastened with Japanese paper and MC glue, and—with the help of a heated surgical scalpel or a scalpel and hot air gun—the adhesive tape is removed piece by piece. The surface previously covered by the adhesive tape often remains coated with a thick layer of greasy and sticky glue, which must also be removed. This procedure is carried out under a protective hood for safety reasons.

The fragment involved is placed on a flexible and transparent sheet (Mylar film), and a strip of filter paper is folded, dampened with a solvent, and placed in a small glass, which is then turned upside down on the spot containing the unwanted glue. After one or two minutes, the softened sticky mass is removed using a small eraser and tiny tweezers. This procedure is repeated until the surface of the fragment is no longer sticky.

At this stage the dark spots may be removed and the greasy glue that has penetrated the leather may be extracted. A mineral powder called Fuller's Earth is strewn on the dark spot, and one or two drops of solvent are placed in the center. The fragment is then covered by another film of Mylar and a heavy piece of glass. Once the powder is completely dried, it is removed from the surface of the leather, mostly by using a fine brush, and the remaining traces are removed by using a tiny eraser under a microscope.

The conservators reinforce weak or torn areas with Japanese paper that has been prepared in advance on glass with glue dissolved in distilled water. In most cases, it is sufficient to dab the deficient area several times with a damp cotton wad over the layer of Japanese paper placed on the fragment, and to dry it under pressure. Such reinforcing treatments are extremely delicate and time-consuming and sometimes have to be repeated.

The conservators at the Israel Antiquities Authority have achieved very good results in uncovering texts that had been completely obscured by stains, using an earth poultice together with solvents. In this process, no loss of natural oils from the skins was reported.

(Adapted from E. Boyd-Alkalay and E. Libman, "Preserving the Dead Sea Scrolls and Qumran Artifacts," 540–42)

both sides of the fragments, the conservators often place these between two pieces of stabil-tex™ stretched on cardboard frames and sewn around with stabil-tex™ thread. The fragments can then be presented to the reader enclosed in a frame made of two clear Perspex plates, and the frames can be turned over without damaging the fragments. (3) Scrolls made from papyrus present a special case. Removing the adhesive tape itself from such a fibrous and delicate material without causing damage is most difficult. Since many of these fragments contain writing on both sides, tape has often been glued on the script, which complicates the process of removal; the most effective method so far is the "hot-air method" (using a heated surgical scalpel or a scalpel and a hot-air gun). In order to reinforce and unite the papyrus fragments, tiny strips of Japanese paper are glued to them. In addition, cotton wads are dampened with a solvent and used to remove any adhesive residues from the papyrus surface. The conservators have also developed a new method for mounting papyrus fragments. A laced pattern of Japanese paper is cut according to the shape of the fragment, and this is carefully fixed in stages, using tiny hinges, on to both sides of the fragment. Then the edges of the cutout are glued to the cardboard frame, and this entire "sandwich" is placed between two sheets of polycarbonate. The tissue pattern serves two functions: reinforcing the papyrus and stretching it.

FUTURE PROSPECTS

Beginning in 1992, several conservators and scientists from the Getty Conservation Institute in the United States, often working with the Israel Antiquities Authority, have investigated the precise nature of damage to the Dead Sea Scrolls. Aspects include physical changes that have occurred, the effect of climate in the caves, the minerals found in the scrolls, and the causes of physical, chemical, and biological deterioration. Studies have also been conducted inside caves where scrolls were found; one of these shows that relative humidity conditions fluctuate not only with changes in seasonal temperatures, but also with changes in daytime and night-time temperatures.

Samples of leather, ink, salt crystals, and mold fungi have also been examined. Early results show that the inks used on the scrolls are carbon-based, and that the mold fungi are fortunately in an inactive state. Moreover, the overall bad state of the leather is largely attributable to the great quantity of salt crystals that has been deposited on the scrolls; this has caused delamination, a process whereby salt first dissolves, then crystallizes, and finally tears the surface of the leather.

Imaging the Scrolls by Photography

PHOTOGRAPHING THE DEAD SEA SCROLLS

Since the discovery of the scrolls, photographers have played an important role in choosing the most effective methods to help decipher specific manuscripts.[15] Because of the deterioration and darkening of many scrolls, techniques such as infrared photography produce images that are often clearer than the manuscripts themselves with regard to readability. In many cases writing that can no longer be seen on the original scrolls is legible on the photographic plates.

The larger scrolls found in Cave 1 at Qumran presented relatively few challenges, since they could be photographed with standard color or black-and-white film, with special consideration needed only for lighting. This is in stark contrast to material from several other caves, in which a multitude of fragments were found scattered across the floor and had been severely damaged by weathering, darkening, shrinking, and cracking. Because darkened leather fragments can be lightened and carbon ink can be darkened with the use of infrared film, manuscripts that were previously illegible became very readable on infrared photographs. The infrared process was refined over the years, up through the photography of scrolls from Cave 11 at Qumran in the early 1960s, but backlighting was not used until much later. The older photographic negatives were made of glass, but most negatives were of celluloid-based film.

Although many individuals have photographed portions of the scrolls over the years, only a few professional photographers have been commissioned to do so with a view to providing a thorough and permanent record of these priceless documents.

PROFILE
Pioneer Photographers of the Dead Sea Scrolls (1948–67)

John C. Trever: The first photographer of the scrolls was John Trever, who was resident at the American School of Oriental Research (now called the W. F. Albright Institute) in Jerusalem when the three best preserved scrolls (all from Cave 1) were brought there. Trever has provided several accounts of his work, with one final volume scheduled for publication in late 2002.[1] He photographed these scrolls using standard black-and-white film and later repeated the process in color; both sets of plates were published on facing pages in 1972.[2]

The Biberkrauts: In contrast, the first scrolls acquired by the Hebrew University were darker and more damaged, and thus very difficult to read. James and Helena Bieberkraut unrolled, cleaned, and photographed almost all the scrolls (one exception is the *Temple Scroll*) that had been acquired by Eliazar Sukenik and his son Yigael Yadin. Not surprisingly, the best results were obtained using infrared film. The photography was mostly done on large-format film, measuring 5 by 7 inches (13 by 18 cm).[3] The Bieberkrauts' plates included manuscripts from Qumran, and others that had been found by Yadin at Masada and Haḥal Ḥever.

Najib Albina: Prior to the Six-Day War in 1967, scrolls from most of the Qumran caves and several minor sites in the Judean Desert of Jordan—for example, Wadi Murabbaʿât, Khirbet Mird, and Wadi ed-Daliyeh—were photographed by Najib Albina of the Palestine Archaeological Museum. Albina used large-format film and mostly broadband infrared photography for all manuscripts on animal skin, which enabled scholars to distinguish the ink from the darkened skin tones of the background, and to see the texture of the skin, which is very helpful for reconstructing fragmentary manuscripts.

---

1. J. C. Trever, *The Dead Sea Scrolls: A Personal Account* (Grand Rapids, MI: Eerdmans, 1977); *The Untold Story of Qumran* (Westwood, NJ: Revell, 1965); and *The Dead Sea Scrolls in Perspective* (North Richland Hills, TX: Bibal, 2002).

2. F. M. Cross, D. N. Freedman and J. A. Sanders, eds., *Scrolls from Qumrân Cave I: The Great Isaiah Scroll, The Order of the Community, The Pesher to Habakkuk from Photographs by John C. Trever* (Jerusalem: ASOR–Albright Institute of Archaeological Research–Shrine of the Book, 1972).

3. See Magen Broshi, "The Negatives Archive of the Shrine of the Book," in E. Tov, with S. J. Pfann, eds., *Companion Volume to the Dead Sea Scrolls on Microfiche,* 2d ed. (Leiden: Brill and IDC, 1995), 135–36.

Cave 4 at Qumran, with thousands of fragments recovered from the floor, presented a special challenge. As these pieces were cleaned, photographed, and sorted, individual manuscripts were reconstructed as fragments were placed together. When the various scrolls were assigned to individual editors, further improvements were made in assembling each one. These stages in the assembling of the fragments were photographed by Najib Albina at regular intervals, with between three and five negatives produced for each of nearly 600 manuscripts over the seven-year period of May 1953 to June 1960. No less than five series of photographs in the PAM (Palestine Archaeological Museum) collection are devoted to the Cave 4 scrolls:

PAM Number	Date Photographed	Description of Cave 4 Plates
PAM 40.575–41.139	May 1953 to June 1954	The original plates of unsorted scroll fragments
PAM 41.140–41.762	June 1954 to July 1955	The plates after general sorting
PAM 41.763–41.995	July 1955 to March 1956	Plates composed by editors, mostly in horizontal format
PAM 41.996–42.941	April 1956 to April 1959	Plates composed by editors, in horizontal format
PAM 42.966–43.701	May 1959 to June 1960	The final composition, in vertical format

For Cave 11, which had been discovered in 1956 by the Bedouin, Albina produced one full set of early photographs for the six manuscripts that were better preserved: 11QpaleoLev[a], 11QPs[a], 11QtgJob, 11QapocrPs, the *Songs of the Sabbath Sacrifice* (11QShirShabb), and the *New Jerusalem Text* (11QNJ). The other, more fragmentary, scrolls were left unsorted and photographed in groups on mixed plates:

PAM Number	Cave 11 Scrolls
PAM 42.171–175	11QpaleoLev[a]
PAM 43.772–795	11QPs[a]
PAM 43.796–824	11QtgJob
PAM 43.981–988	11QapocrPs
PAM 43.989–992	11QShirShabb
PAM 43.994–44.002	11QNJ
PAM 42.175–180; 43.794; 44.002–012; 44.114–117	More fragmentary scrolls

David Shinhav and Ruth Yakutiel: The final manuscript from Cave 11 is the *Temple Scroll* (11QT[a]), which was obtained by Yigael Yadin from the antiquities dealer Kando during the 1967 war. At last this, the largest of all the Dead Sea Scrolls, could be photographed and studied. The *Temple Scroll* proved most difficult to photograph, since the ink was written not on the usual hair side, but on the flesh side, which caused many letters to lift from the surface and adhere to the back of the skin. This manuscript was opened and photographed by David Shinhav and Ruth Yakutiel of the Israel Museum, who made plates of both the front and back sides of the manuscript in standard black-and-white and infrared formats.[16]

In 1967, Israel also won control of the Palestine Archaeological Museum, soon to be called the Rockefeller Museum, where most of the Dead Sea Scrolls are housed. The Israel Department of Antiquities (now the Israel Antiquities Authority) later authorized new photographs of certain manuscripts kept at both the Shrine of the Book and the Rockefeller Museum on 35 mm format black-and-white film.

Tsila Sagiv: The photographs of the Wadi ed-Daliyah manuscripts taken by Tsila Sagiv may be noted, since both front-lighting and backlighting were used, which made visible the lines of the papyrus on both the front and back of each scroll. Later, during the 1990s, a new set of narrow-band infrared photographs of many scrolls from Caves 4 and 11 were taken by Sagiv. These images have a distinct advantage over the earlier ones produced by Albina: the skin tones are almost completely muted, which makes the distinction between the ink and the background far clearer.

Robert Schlosser: Between 1984 and 1986, the American photographer Robert Schlosser made a set of diapositive photographs (i.e., positive transparencies; see next page) from the original negatives in the PAM collection on behalf of the Dead Sea Scrolls Preservation Council. Sets of the Schlosser images are stored in at least three locations: the Ancient Biblical Manuscript Center in Claremont, California; the Huntington Library in San Marino, California; and Duke University in Durham, North Carolina.

Bruce and Kenneth Zuckerman: In the 1980s and 1990s, photographs of selected manuscripts from the Shrine of the Book, the Rockefeller Museum, and the Amman Archaeological Museum in Jordan were taken by Bruce and Kenneth Zuckerman of West Semitic Research in Palos Verdes, California. The brothers made use of new and experimental techniques, including various types of lighting (notably backlighting). The result was improved images in color (or "color-balanced") formats, infrared formats, and standard black-and-white formats. The Zuckermans also experimented with digital photography and computer enhancement of digital images.

THE ORIGINAL NEGATIVES AND REPRODUCTIONS

The original negatives taken in 1948 by John Trever of certain manuscripts from Cave 1 are both technologically and historically important. These include the Great Isaiah Scroll (1QIsa[a]), the *Rule of the Community* (1QS), and the *Habakkuk Pesher* (1QpHab). All are now stored at the Ancient Biblical Manuscript Center, in Claremont, California. A second major collection of original negatives, now housed at the Shrine of the Book in Jerusalem, was produced from the scrolls kept there. The third collection was produced at the Palestine Archaeological Museum (now the Rockefeller Museum), and is housed by the Israel Antiquities Authority in Jerusalem. Taken mainly of fragments from Caves 2 to 11, this collection is by far the most extensive of the three.

A number of the original negatives have suffered various forms of damage, including scratched, cracked, or broken glass-plate negatives (using Ilford and Kodak film). However, the main source of damaged negatives was the use of film produced by the Dupont Corporation. Fortunately, this type of deterioration applies only to negatives in the PAM collection; the negatives at the Shrine of the Book remain in a relatively excellent state of preservation.

TECHNICAL DETAILS
Deterioration of Negatives in the PAM Collection

The negatives stored in the PAM archives were made from Dupont Non-Color Sensitized "Cronar" Commercial-S Sheet Film (not infrared). This film is susceptible to particular forms of damage: (1) *bluing*, which is caused by the original development process and results in a blue tint on the negatives; and (2) *separation* between the three components of the negative, the gelatin anti-hyaline surface, the celluloid base, and the emulsion surface. Separation between the celluloid base and the gelatin surface takes place for two reasons: *reticulation*, or blistering, due to shrinkage of the celluloid negative base; and *separation due to crystallization*, which is the most damaging form of deterioration.

Photographic reproductions were made from the original negatives in three forms: prints on photographic paper, diapositives (positive transparencies), and microfiches (negative transparencies). When the original PAM negatives were produced, *prints* were also made, so that a complete set of contact prints could be stored in an album at the Palestine Archaeological Museum. These photographs are of fine quality and were made on good photographic paper. In other cases, however, reproductions from both the PAM and the Shrine of the Book negatives were limited to sets of full-sized prints. These were produced for the use of each editor in his or her work and for inclusion in the official publications of the Dead Sea Scrolls.

An early set of *diapositives* was made from the original negatives of the PAM collection after 1967 at the request of Yigael Yadin. This collection, which is not complete, is currently housed at the Shrine of the Book. A later set of high-contrast diapositives was made between 1984 and 1986 from the original negatives in the PAM collection by Robert Schlosser on behalf of the Dead Sea Scrolls Preservation Council. In 1993, under the editorship of Emanuel Tov and Stephen Pfann, the Dutch photographer P. Moerkerk produced a set of *microfiches* directly from the original negatives. These images were made from the entire collection of original negatives stored at the Shrine of the Book, the Israel Antiquities Authority, and the Hebrew University of Jerusalem. The exposures were made directly from negative to negative on fine-grain Fuji II High Resolution microfiche film, with the result that information stored only in the layered emulsion has been preserved on each microfiche. The master fiches are in the possession of publishers E. J. Brill and IDC, in the Netherlands.

PUBLICATION OF THE IMAGES

Images of the Dead Sea Scrolls found in published volumes require additional steps beyond the source being used for the reproduction in printed form or on microform transparencies. Publications of these images include the following:

Discoveries in the Judaean Desert: The official edition of the Dead Sea Scrolls includes plates of scrolls that were acquired by the Palestine Archaeological Museum. Almost without exception, the plates that appear in each volume are made from full-sized prints of the PAM negatives. Since 1995, the prints have been digitized and refined by means of a photo-rendering program, which increases the definition of ink in the written text and of the fragment edges.

The Facsimile Edition of the Dead Sea Scrolls: This two-volume collection of plates was reproduced by the Biblical Archaeology Society from a set of reproductions of the PAM negatives in a smaller format.[17] Because the editors tried to limit their selection to scrolls that were still unpublished and to eliminate most prints that had been made from defective negatives, not all the PAM negatives were reproduced in the *Facsimile Edition.* The text found on most pieces is quite readable, but the edges of many fragments are lost along with traces of ink.

The Dead Sea Scrolls on Microfiche: This facsimile edition is the published version of the master fiches, discussed above, that are housed in the Netherlands.

The Huntington Library Microfilm: In 1991 the director of the library, William Moffett, gave permission for this set—which is based on its own collection of Schlosser's second-generation negatives—to be reproduced for the use of scholars. The microfilms that were produced are of generally poor quality and often overexposed.

ULTRAVIOLET AND INFRARED PHOTOGRAPHY

Since the vast majority of the original negatives of the Dead Sea Scrolls remain in very good condition, the use of advanced techniques for acquiring new images is necessary for only a few documents, most of them small fragments. In these cases, more sophisticated methods are required to make damaged fragments readable.

The technology for ultraviolet imaging is easier than that for infrared; hence its routine use from an early date. As early as 1910, photography with ultraviolet light was being used on ancient documents. When a suitable ultraviolet source known as Wood's Lamp was invented in the 1920s, this method of reading manuscripts became common. Although the use of infrared lagged behind that of ultraviolet (the film was developed only later), infrared photography has been used since the discovery of the first scrolls.

Infrared film is sensitive in both the red- and blue-light spectrums, and is usually used with a filter to exclue the blue. It is not clear which filters were employed by Najib Albina for the PAM photographs, but the use of filters by Kenneth and Bruce Zuckerman in the 1980s stimulated interest in

> ### TECHNICAL DETAILS
> ### Visible, Ultraviolet, and Infrared Light
>
> The wavelength of light is measured in *nanometers* (nm). Visible light is in the ~400–720 nm range, with ultraviolet light (UV) below 400 nm, and infrared light (IR) above 720 nm. The *blue light* referred to in this chapter is between 400 and 480 nm. The camera range used by the Zuckermans was in the *near IR* range, or up to 1,000 nm.

> ### TECHNICAL DETAILS
> ### Using Filters in Infrared Photography
>
> The Zuckermans obtained the best results by using filters of the "cut-on" variety. These are filters that let in light only at a specified fixed wavelength and block out the visible and blue part of the light spectrum. As a result, this film records only reflected infrared. The specific filters chosen by the Zuckermans were Kodak 88A, 87, and 87C, which cut on at bandwidths of 740 nm, 750 nm, and 810 nm, respectively. Since infrared film is sensitive only up to about 900 nm, the photography carried out was over a bandwidth of ~90–160 nm.

applying infrared photography to faded or darkened ancient manuscripts. In a number of photographic field trips to the Berlin Museum in 1991 and to Jerusalem in 1992, the Zuckermans observed that the use of certain filters for infrared photography yielded much better results.

Imaging the Scrolls by Direct Digital Acquisition

IMAGING THE DEAD SEA SCROLLS

The digitizing (i.e., scanning) of major photographic collections and archives has come of age in the third millennium.[18] Many libraries have moved or are moving toward digitization of both written texts and photographic collections into databases that can be interrogated by search engines. Images with a higher resolution (which are measured in dots per square inch, or *dpi*) are sharper and less grainy, but occupy a larger amount of disk space on the computer. For example, a 600 dpi image means that each inch of the negative is digitized at 600 discrete spots, with each dot corresponding to a pixel. A scan of 600 dpi produces a computer file that is not too large and is adequate for most purposes. Although much higher resolutions are possible, these are mostly impractical and costly; for example, scans of 3,000 dpi in *Adobe Photoshop* can yield files of 40–50 megabytes each! It has been suggested that the size and cost of images becomes too high somewhere between 1,200 and 2,000 dpi.[19]

It is preferable to acquire digital images directly from an original manuscript, which has several advantages: (1) The images can be examined immediately, which is of great

---

TECHNICAL DETAILS
What Is Digital Imaging?

A digital image is composed of thousands of picture elements known as *pixels*. The intensity or blackness of each pixel (the *pixel depth*) can range from nil (black) to a maximum value (white), which is determined by the camera acquiring the image. Although the human eye cannot discern much of the gray scale, a computer can do so, and information on pixel depth may prove most important.

Most commercial cameras are 8 bits, providing a gray scale of 255 (i.e., $2^8-1 = 255$ shades or intensities of gray); other cameras range from 10 bits ($2^{10}-1 =1,023$) to 16 bits (65,535). Although this scale is far beyond what the human eye can distinguish, the computer has the information and greater pixel depth for providing better detail and dynamic range in both imaging and digitizing. Image quality is to some extent a function of pixel depth.

Another issue that directly affects the legibility of texts and the quality of images is *spatial resolution*. Two questions must be asked: (1) How big is the detector (and thus the image field of view)? (2) What is the spatial resolution of the image (i.e., how much of the document's area is represented by each pixel in the image—a micron, 100 microns, or a millimeter)? When an image is acquired digitally from the original manuscript, spatial resolution is set by the size of the sensor (e.g., 1,024 by 1,024 pixels) and by the magnification of the camera lens.

(Adapted from Bearman, Pfann, and Spiro, "Imaging the Scrolls," 492–93)

benefit to the editor working with the imaging technician; for example, he or she can straightaway select areas for close-up imaging or other special attention. (2) Because the image is being observed directly, the camera can easily be focused. For infrared photography, in contrast, the photographer cannot see the images until they have been developed. (3) Images that are digitally acquired are ready for digital image-processing techniques, without the cost and delay of scanning them. (4) Electronic imaging often works farther in the infrared spectrum than film, the result being images with better contrast.

DIGITAL IMAGING AND RESULTS ACHIEVED

The American scientist Gregory Bearman became involved with imaging Dead Sea Scrolls as a result of his work in electronic imaging and imaging spectroscopy. Bearman, a physicist at the Jet Propulsion Laboratory in California, which conducts research for the National Aeronautic and Space Administration (NASA), realized that NASA technology could be used for commercial or academic applications of imaging and spectroscopy. With the belief that the study of manuscripts might benefit from such technology, he approached the Ancient Biblical Manuscript Center in California. The result was a fruitful collaboration between the Manuscript Center, the Jet Propulsion Laboratory, and the Zuckermans, with a view to applying these new technologies to the Dead Sea Scrolls.

In 1993 this team reported excellent, real-time images of part of the severely damaged *Genesis Apocryphon,* using a new tunable filter that could be set to any wavelength in the infrared spectrum with a very narrow bandpass. Following this breakthrough, in 1994 a team from the Manuscript Center, which included Bearman and the Zuckermans, was invited to image the entire *Genesis Apocryphon* at the Shrine of the Book in Jerusalem. The images that resulted revealed a considerable amount of new text and were used by several scholars for their preliminary edition of the *Genesis Apocryphon.*

In 1997 the Ancient Biblical Manuscript Center sponsored a second imaging field expedition, this time in collaboration with the Israel Antiquities Authority, the Israel Museum, the Shrine of the Book, and the Dead Sea Scrolls editorial team. The results were impressive: new electronic infrared images of approximately 900 fragments that had been selected by editors of the scrolls and other scholars.

The contrast between the ink of the text and the leather background determines how much writing can be read on a scroll. The contrast of any image is determined by the amount of light from the source of illumination that the ink and parchment reflect onto the sensor, which may be film or the sensor of an electronic camera. The greater the difference between the signals of the leather parchment and the ink at the sensor, the greater the contrast—and hence the greater the amount of text that can be read.

As can be seen by the large contrast between the reflection of ink and leather in the first graph of Figure 4.3, fragments with dark ink on light leather are quite easy to read with the unaided eye. The small amount of contrast in the second graph of the figure, however, shows that fragments with darkened leather are virtually impossible to read or (in some cases) have no text that can be detected at all.

There are three important digital collections of images of early photographs of the Dead Sea Scrolls from the Palestine Archaeological Museum and the Shrine of the Book: (1) at Oxford University Press, with pictures taken at 300 dpi; (2) at the Foundation for Ancient Research and Mormon Studies in Provo, Utah, with pictures at 200 dpi; and

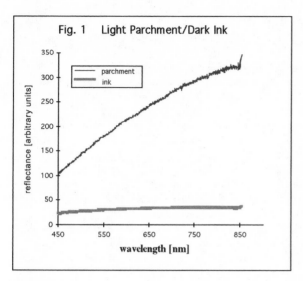

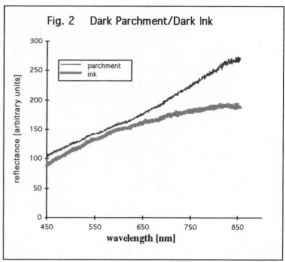

Figure 4.3

The contrast between ink and parchment in direct digital acquisition

From Gregory Bearman, Stephen J. Pfann, and Sheila I. Spiro, "Imaging the Scrolls: Photographic and Direct Digital Acquisition," 1:489. Used with permission.

(3) at the Ancient Biblical Manuscript Center, with pictures at 1,200 dpi (such images with a higher resolution are sharper and less grainy, but occupy a much larger amount of disk space).

Computers and the Dead Sea Scrolls

In view of constant changes in computer technology and software development, some of the following comments on computers and the scrolls may well be outdated after a year or two. In this section we briefly survey the Dead Sea Scrolls publication project, describe *The Dead Sea Scrolls Electronic Reference Library,* profile the *Accordance* Program, and conclude with some pointers to relevant Web sites.

PRODUCING CAMERA-READY COPY
FOR *DISCOVERIES IN THE JUDAEAN DESERT*

Virtually all of the Dead Sea Scrolls have been published by Oxford University Press in the series *Discoveries in the Judaean Desert* (DJD; see Appendix IV). Individual volumes are prepared by the assigned editors, who submit them to one of two main centers: (1) the Hebrew University in Jerusalem, where the Dead Sea Scrolls Publication Project has been led and organized by the editor-in-chief, Emanuel Tov; and (2) the University of Notre Dame in Indiana, where Eugene Ulrich and James VanderKam have overseen the production of many volumes. At one of these locations (the Hebrew University in most cases), the manuscript, including the mounted plates, is finalized for delivery to the Press in camera-ready form.

TECHNICAL DETAILS
Preparing Volumes in the DJD Series

The *Discoveries in the Judean Desert* (DJD) volumes are prepared on the Macintosh plat-form, using the MicroSoft Word computer program. In earlier days, manuscripts were produced in Word 4, but in the early 1990s Word 5.1 became the norm. The basic font is M-Imprint, which is supplied by Oxford University Press. For ancient scripts and diacriti-cal marks, the main fonts are SuperHebrew, SuperGreek, Samaritan and Lachish (for paleo-Hebrew), Estrangela (for Syriac), and Roman (for diacriticals), all of these by cour-tesy of Linguist's Software in Edmonds, Washington.

Some readers may find these details surprising, since Word 5.1 seems antiquated when compared to Word 2001, and fonts such as SuperHebrew and SuperGreek have been superseded by the more modern LaserHebrew II and LaserGreek II. It has also been observed that characters in the SuperHebrew font have a tendency to cramp together, whereas in LaserHebrew II and its predecessor Hebraica the characters are better spaced.

Sound logic, however, has motivated the editors' ongoing caution and conservatism on this issue. First, many of the individual editors, who are from several countries, have little expertise in or access to the more advanced programs. This is by no means a criticism of the editorial team, since only a minority of scholars are also computer experts. Even the earlier change from Word 4 to Word 5.1 presented challenges to several editors, many of whom had to switch from Word Perfect, DOS, or Windows for the sake of the DJD project. Second, and most important, it is vitally necessary to avoid the alterations, even minute ones, that often accompany updated programs or fonts. For example, the Hebrew charac-ters in LaserHebrew II are sharper and better-spaced than those in SuperHebrew—but the keystrokes for some letters are different. For editors who have worked over several years on a volume, with dozens or scores of pages of Hebrew and critical markings already entered on the computer, a universal change from the older font to the newer one can wreak havoc. Similar dangers may hold true for any changeover to Word 2001.

By the late 1980s, as the editorial team expanded, it became clear that the editors would need to use a common computer program, fonts, and style if consistency was to be main-tained. As early as 1988, the basic computer platform, fonts, and style sheet that would be used by all future editors had been developed by the chief editor of the Cave 4 biblical scrolls, Eugene Ulrich, and his team. Although the style sheet would be further refined by both the Jerusalem and Notre Dame teams, the computer platform and fonts remain essentially the same.

With the DJD publication project virtually completed in 2002, the editors felt it was not worth the risk to update software applications and fonts, choosing instead to maintain continuity with the tried and tested program and platform. There is much wisdom in the words of one senior American editor, who—when challenged to upgrade the program and fonts for the DJD project—replied, "If it ain't broke, don't fix it!"

THE DEAD SEA SCROLLS ELECTRONIC REFERENCE LIBRARY

Bibliographical Details: *Volume 1*, edited by Timothy H. Lim in consultation with Philip S. Alexander (Oxford: Oxford University Press; Leiden: Brill, 1997), approximately $2,495.

Volume 2, prepared by Noel B. Reynolds, Donald W. Parry, E. Jan Wilson, and Terrence L. Szink, of the Foundation for Ancient Research and Mormon Studies and the Center for the Preservation of Ancient Religious Texts at Brigham Young University, Utah (Leiden: Brill, 1999), approximately $275.

Following earlier collections of images in microfiche form (especially the *Microfiche Edition* described above), two reference libraries of the Dead Sea Scrolls are now available in electronic format. Due to the efforts of Brill Academic Publishers, Oxford University Press, the Foundation for Ancient Research and Mormon Studies, and many scholars, these two collections offer ready access by scholars to virtually all the Dead Sea Scrolls on a desktop computer.

Features of Volume 1

The first volume comprises 3 CD-ROMs, an installation disk and two image disks. Each scroll fragment has been allocated a card that gives information on where it is housed, where it was published, and related scholarly publications. Fragments are indexed by their various plate numbers, whether PAM (Palestine Archaeological Museum), SHR (Shrine of the Book), or IAA (Israel Antiquities Authority). They are also indexed by cave number, title, microfiche location, or location in the *Facsimile Edition* (described earlier), and searches can be performed on the data found on the cards. Also listed on these cards are related fragments, with the PAM number given for each. An additional feature that many scholars will welcome is that the cards can be searched by biblical passages. In sum, the various types of data contained on each card make it easy to look up fragments and work with other collections such as the earlier *Microfiche Edition*.

The core of this volume of the *Electronic Library* is the approximately 2,700 photographs containing images of the Dead Sea Scrolls. The quality of these images is very good (at 300 dpi); although the resolution could be higher, this would take up far more electronic space and entail a collection much larger than three CD-ROMs. The zoom-in capability allows users to examine fragments more closely, with little diminishment of quality—a feature that is one of the major benefits of a computer photograph. The program allows the user to zoom in and magnify an image from 1 to 300 percent. In this respect the resolution of screen settings and monitor makes a considerable difference: the higher the resolution, the sharper the image when it is magnified. Users can also copy and paste photographs into a word-processing program or into a paint program.

Other tools include the ability to rotate the images 90 degrees and to adjust brightness and contrast. One very useful tool is the ability to make an annotated bookmark for any fragment. The program also has a built-in simple word processor called the Memo Pad, which automatically supplies the reference when anything is copied from one of the cards.

With its hefty price tag, Volume 1 is designed primarily for institutions, libraries, and professional Dead Sea Scrolls scholars.

TECHNICAL DETAILS
System Requirements for Volumes 1 and 2

The minimum configuration for both volumes is an IBM 486 at 66 mhz, 16MB of RAM, 6MB of free hard drive space, Windows 3.1, a 4× CD-ROM player, and a 256 color monitor at 800 × 600 pixels. Not surprisingly, a faster processor and more RAM are recommended, especially when the user is working with a word processor program at the same time.

Optimal performance will be obtained with a Pentium 166 or higher, 32 MB of RAM, 30MB free hard drive space, Windows 98 or higher, a 32× CD-ROM player, and a 17-inch or larger SVGA display set to 1024 × 768 pixels. For the majority of users, the most important element is the size of the monitor and the screen resolution: the larger the monitor and the higher the resolution setting, the better the quality of the photographs.

Features of Volume 2

The second volume of the *Electronic Library* will prove most welcome for scholars and others who desire access to the Dead Sea Scrolls in electronic form, but find the cost of Volume 1 beyond their reach. It features about 800 digitized images of the scrolls, which were selected from the collection housed at the Ancient Biblical Manuscript Center. Also included are Hebrew transcriptions, a database of the nonbiblical texts, the English translation by Florentino García Martínez (*The Dead Sea Scrolls Translated,* 2d ed. [Leiden: Brill; Grand Rapids, MI: Eerdmans, 1996]), and word lists with root forms in Hebrew and Aramaic. Finally, this collection also includes the Septuagint, the Vulgate, and the King James Version of the Old Testament.

Scrolls are classified by language and cave, with a separate window listing the contents for each cave. The title of each manuscript is also provided, together with the volume of the official DJD (Discoveries in the Judaean Desert) edition in which it has appeared, as well as its editor. There follows a list of fragments for the scroll in question, together with its PAM numbers and a Hebrew or Aramaic transcription. Photographic images are displayed when a camera icon is clicked; a most useful feature is the option of viewing both image and transcription side by side. The program allots more monitor space to the photographs than does Volume 1, which means most of the screen contains the image rather than parts of the software program. This is a significant improvement and wastes less space; however, the useful bookmark feature found in the earlier volume has not been included.

A search feature is also available, featuring a search engine known as WordCruncher, which allows the user to search for words or letters, to conduct complex searches, and to construct concordances. It should be noted, however, that searches are limited in their capabilities, since the database features no grammatical tags. There is a lexical assistant that displays various forms of words, but this is based on the Westminster Hebrew Bible text and is not exhaustive; according to the developers, future editions will improve the lexical assistant. The great strength of the search function is its ability to search for words or letters while defining the range, for example, on the same line or within twenty words. One frustration is the fact that Hebrew text cannot be exported into a word processor. This may well be for copyright reasons; it appears that the programmers have deliberately designed any sequence of letters in the text to be reversed when copied.

Volumes 1 and 2 Compared

The two volumes of the *Electronic Library* differ in several ways. First, although the first volume was developed for scholars who make extensive use of the photographs, the second is designed to assist scholars in conducting research on the texts themselves. Second, Volume 2 comprises only one CD-ROM, as opposed to the three in Volume 1, the main reason being that it does not contain as many photographs. Third, the second volume lacks the biblical texts. The 1999 edition contains the important nonbiblical manuscripts and subsequent releases are scheduled to include all the nonbiblical material. In sum, Volume 2 is a markedly different library in comparison with Volume 1.

THE ACCORDANCE PROGRAM

Bibliographical Details: *Accordance 5.3, Accordance Scholars CD–3,* which includes the following modules: (1) *Qumran Sectarian Manuscripts in Hebrew/Aramaic,* with Qumran text and Grammatical Tags, by Martin G. Abegg, Jr., approximately $80. (2) *Qumran Sectarian Manuscripts in English,* based upon *The Dead Sea Scrolls: A New English Translation,* by Michael Wise, Martin Abegg, Jr., and Edward Cook (San Francisco: HarperSanFrancisco, 1996), approximately $30. (3) *An Index of Qumran Manuscripts,* edited by Stephen W. Marler, in consultation with Martin G. Abegg, Jr., approximately $30. Available from OakTree Software, Inc. *(www.oaksoft.com),* 498 Palm Springs Drive, Suite 100, Altamonte Springs, FL 32701.

Accordance is one of the leading Bible software programs, combining ease of use with powerful search features, and original language texts that are not available for other software programs. For students of the Dead Sea Scrolls, this is the program of choice because of one central feature: grammatically tagged texts of these ancient manuscripts. Besides displaying the text of a given scroll, by means of tagging *Accordance* provides precise grammatical information for each word such as gender, number, aspect, stem, and lexical form. This capability allows for a high degree of accuracy and searches for grammatical patterns. A nontagged text, in contrast, is far more limited in search capability.

Accordance currently has three modules for Qumran research, all three of which are designed to work together, but each can also be used separately:

(1) *The Qumran Sectarian Manuscripts in Hebrew/Aramaic* features Hebrew and Aramaic nonbiblical documents that are grammatically tagged, which enables advanced grammatical searches to be conducted in the original languages. Searches can be for a single word, phrases, or grammatically based patterns. The search ranges can also be custom defined. For example, one could find all the verbs occurring in the *pi'el* in the *Rule of the Community* (1QS), and the relationship between words can be graphically laid out using the *Construct Window.*

The parsing information is available in the *Instant Details Window* by pointing the cursor over the Hebrew/Aramaic word. Although the primary texts are unpointed, this parsing information provides the lexical form and access to biblical Hebrew dictionaries, allowing for more detailed research of the word. Other features include the ability to create a concordance of the Hebrew/Aramaic words, ranging from the entire corpus to a single manuscript or even a few lines. The ability to add customized notes to specific lines is very useful for research. The *Notes Feature* also allows for hyperlinking to other Qumran texts (see Figure 4.4). The texts can be copied into word processors and used for research papers, articles, or study notes.

This module allows those who have a basic understanding of Hebrew to conduct research in the Qumran texts, which benefits both their understanding of the scrolls and their ability to use these documents for research in allied areas such as biblical, New Testament, and Jewish studies.

(2) The *Qumran Sectarian Manuscripts in English* features the translation of the nonbiblical scrolls by Wise, Abegg, and Cook (see above) and can be displayed independently of, or in parallel with, the Hebrew/Aramaic module. Although not grammatically tagged like the first one, this module is most useful for conducting research based upon the English text. For example, one can search for "Melchizedek" and survey all the occurrences

TECHNICAL DETAILS
System Requirements for *Accordance*

The minimum system requirements are the Macintosh Operating System 7.1, 12 megabytes of available RAM, and 10 megabytes of free hard drive space. Version 5 can also run native to Operating System X. Although there is no version for the PC, there are apparently several unofficial emulators that can run Macintosh system 7.1 on an IBM PC, which should make it possible for *Accordance* to be used on the PC platform.

Figure 4.4

Parallel Hebrew and English texts of 4Q286 (*4QBlessings*ᵃ), with customized notes by the user, in *Accordance 5.3.*

Courtesy of OakTree Software

of this word in the nonbiblical scrolls. The concordance and notes features discussed above are also available with this module.

(3) The *Index of Qumran Manuscripts* lists all of the Qumran scrolls by cave and provides a brief description of their contents, approximate date, language, and paleographic and bibliographic information. This module can also be used in conjunction with the Qumran texts to identify titles of specific scrolls. For example, if the first module containing the primary texts has 4Q175 as the title of a document, one simply selects this title and clicks on the *Qumran Index* to find out the name of the text (in this case, the *Testimonia*). The *Qumran Index* can also be used alone to gather different types of information about specific documents, such as: (a) If one looks up any manuscript by its title (e.g., 4Q364), *Accordance* will provide a description of the document (in this case, the *Reworked Pentateuch*). (b) If one wishes to survey the Aramaic manuscripts found at Qumran, simply type "Aramaic" in the language field to produce a list of all the relevant scrolls. (c) One can also see if a specific biblical passage is found at Qumran, including quotations in nonbiblical manuscripts.

THE DEAD SEA SCROLLS ON THE INTERNET (WORLD WIDE WEB)

Providing information on the scrolls and the Internet is a difficult enterprise. There are hundreds of sites on the Web that are relevant for studying the writings and archeology of

Qumran and other sites in the Judean Desert, and more are being regularly added. Furthermore, the Internet addresses of a great many sites are subject to change; in some cases the user is rerouted to the new address, but this is by no means always the case. With new sites being added and many address changes taking place every few months, any book that includes such information becomes rather dated soon after it is published. Since the first edition of most books—including *The Meaning of the Dead Sea Scrolls*—remains in print for a few years, any updates and new information can only be included in the next edition.

In this section we describe a few sites of relevance to Dead Sea Scrolls study and list the addresses of a few more. If any of these sites cannot be accessed on the Web because its address has been changed, users may be rerouted to the new address. If not, users should search for the site under "Dead Sea Scrolls" or under "Qumran" on a search engine. One engine of choice for academics is Google *(http://www.google.com)*, which is lightning fast and effective. Another advantage of such searches is that they will yield many more sites than the ones listed below.

The Orion Center for the Study of the Dead Sea Scrolls and Associated Literature

The most important and comprehensive Web site devoted to the Dead Sea Scrolls is administered by the Orion Center, which was established in 1995 as part of the Institute for Jewish Studies at the Hebrew University of Jerusalem.

This Web site *(http://orion.mscc.huji.ac.il)* provides many resources for the study of the scrolls, as well as information about the center's activities and programs. One aim of the center is to encourage research on these ancient documents, especially with a view toward situating the new information gained from the scrolls in the context of Jewish history and religion in the Second Temple period. This integration affects areas such as Old Testament studies, Jewish literature and thought of the Second Temple period, New Testament studies, early Christianity, and early rabbinic Judaism.

The site includes a treasure trove of resources for the study of the Dead Sea Scrolls, including books and on-line resources; a comprehensive bibliography (which can be searched); a Beginner's Guide to the scrolls; a Cave Tour; an index to the official editions of the scrolls ("Discoveries in the Judaean Desert"); details of books relevant to scrolls study from publisher E. J. Brill; a Conference Bulletin Board; relevant news articles; and links to other Web sites.

Other Web Sites

Additional Web sites are listed below, but readers are reminded that addresses of many sites are subject to change and new sites are continually being added. The listing of these Web pages in *The Meaning of the Dead Sea Scrolls* is for information only, and does not imply an endorsement of the opinions found on these sites by the authors or by HarperSanFrancisco Publishers. Many of these addresses, and others besides, are listed on the Orion Web site.

DEAD SEA SCROLLS: GENERAL TOPICS

Biblical Archaeology Review (excavations at biblical sites, topics in biblical archaeology)
 http://www.bib-arch.org

Center for the Study of Early Christianity (an educational institution and research center in Jerusalem; includes a Qumran curriculum and articles on the scrolls by Stephen J. Pfann)
http://www.csec.ac.uk/dss/main.htm

Congress ("The Dead Sea Scrolls: Fifty Years After Their Discovery," Jerusalem, July 20–25, 1997)
http://www.hum.huji.ac.il/ies/deadsea50.htm

Dead Sea Scrolls (Encyclopedia.com)
http://www.encyclopedia.com/html/d/deads1eas1.asp

Dead Sea Scrolls (an introduction to the scrolls, a map of the Dead Sea, and much other information)
http://sunsite.unc.edu/expo/deadsea.scrolls.exhibit/intro.html

Dead Sea Scrolls Project (Norman Golb and Michael Wise)
http://www-oi.uchicago.edu/OI/PROJ/SCR/Scrolls.html

Essenes, The, and the Essene Way of Life (New Age Web site)
http://www.essene.com/

Israel Antiquities Authority (information about the Authority's activities and policies)
http://www.israntique.org.il/

Israel Mosaic (summary of the history of Qumran and description of the Qumran sect)
http://mosaic.lk.net/g-qumran.html

Israel Supreme Court Decision (on the Qimron vs. Shanks copyright case, translated by Dr. Michael Birnhack of Haifa University)
http://lawatch.haifa.ac.il/heb/month/dead_sea.htm

Khirbet Qumran Database (developed by Dr. Ferdinand Rohrhirsch; only available in German)
http://www.chirbet-qumran.de/

Library of Congress (exhibition of the Dead Sea Scrolls at the Library of Congress in 1993)
http://www.ibiblio.org/expo/deadsea.scrolls.exhibit/intro.html

North American Baptist College, Edmonton, Canada (Tyler Williams's course site)
http://www.nabcebs.ab.ca/OT-net/DSS/introductions.html

Oriental Institute Museum, University of Chicago (a Dead Sea Scrolls fragment)
http://www-oi.uchicago.edu/OI/MUS/HIGH/OIM_A30303.html

Rutgers University, Department of Religion, Dead Sea Scrolls page (time line of discovery, resources)
http://religion.rutgers.edu/iho/dss.html

Schoyen Collection (Qumran manuscripts, a jar, and an inkwell)
http://www.nb.no/baser/schoyen/5/5.9/

Shrine of the Book, Israel Museum, Jerusalem (includes a frequently-asked-questions page)
http://www.imj.org.il/eng/shrine/

Taylor-Schechter Genizah Research Unit, Cambridge University Library (manuscripts from the Cairo Genizah)
http://www.lib.cam.ac.uk/Taylor-Schechter

University of Arizona, Department of Physics (on radiocarbon and paleographic dates)
http://www.physics.arizona.edu/physics/public/dead-sea.html

Uppsala University Qumran Seminar
http://www.afro.uu.se/qumran/

SCHOLARLY AND PERSONAL HOME PAGES

Bajot, David (photographs, maps, links)
  http://www.brandx.net/dbajot/deadsea/

Bar-Ilan, Meir (includes photographs of Qumran, the Copper Scroll, and two academic papers)
  http://faculty.biu.ac.il/~barilm/qumran.html

Binder, Donald (photographs, links, partial translations from some scrolls)
  http://www.smu.edu/~dbinder/qumran.html

Flint, Peter (books and electronic resources on the Dead Sea Scrolls and biblical studies)
  http://www.deadseascrolls.org or *http://www.deadseascrolls.ca*

Gunneweg, Jan (archeology and archeometry, with information on the jars found at Qumran)
  http://pluto.mscc.huji.ac.il/~msjan/archaeom.html

Hoselton, Mitchell (large selection of links)
  http://www.flash.net/~hoselton/deadsea/deadsea.htm
  (time line for discoveries, 1946–1955)
  http://www.flash.net/~hoselton/deadsea/timelinm.htm

Kilmann, Jack (includes a downloadable Dead Sea Scrolls scribal font)
  http://www.historian.net/DSSfont.htm

Kraft, Robert (computing in the humanities, course material on scrolls, Septuagint sites)
  http://ccat.sas.upenn.edu/rs/rak/kraft.html

Marler, Stephen (electronic and other resources for scrolls research)
  http://www.steve.marler.com/

Moeller, Fred (includes the Isaiah scrolls)
  http://www.ao.net/~fmoeller/qumdir.htm

Muro, Ernest (on the Greek fragments of Enoch from Qumran Cave 7)
  http://www.breadofangels.com/7qenoch/

Pfann, Stephen (on an English edition of Roland de Vaux's notes)
  http://www.csec.ac.uk/devaux.html

Rohrhirsch, Ferdinand (on the German edition of Roland de Vaux's notes)
  http://home.t-online.de/home/ferdinand.rohrhirsch/

Seland, Torrey (resource pages for biblical studies)
  http://www.torreys.org/bible

Tabor, James (much useful information on the Dead Sea Scrolls)
  http://www.uncc.edu/jdtabor/dss.html
  (results of his four-year investigation of the skeletons found at Masada)
  http://www.uncc.edu/jdtabor/masada.html

Select Bibliography

For this chapter we are especially dependent on several advanced articles in

Flint, P. W., and J. C. VanderKam, eds. *The Dead Sea Scrolls After Fifty Years: A Comprehensive Assessment.* 2 vols. Leiden: Brill, 1998–99:

  Boyd-Akalay, Esther, and Elena Libman, "Preserving the Dead Sea Scrolls and Qumran Artefacts." 1:535–44.

Bearman, Gregory, Stephen J. Pfann, and Sheila I. Spiro. "Imaging the Scrolls: Photographic and Direct Digital Acquisition." 1: 472–95.

Parry, Donald W., David V. Arnold, David G. Long, and Scott R. Woodward. "New Technological Advances: DNA, Electronic Databases, Imaging Radar." 1:496–515 + plate 15.

Steudel, Annette. "Assembling and Reconstructing Manuscripts" 1:516–34.

Also helpful are some articles from

Schiffman, L. H., and J. C. VanderKam, eds. *The Encyclopedia of the Dead Sea Scrolls.* 2 vols. New York and Oxford: Oxford University Press, 2000:

Steudel, Annette. "Scroll Reconstruction." 2:842–84.

Zuckerman, Bruce and Kenneth. "Photography and Computer Imaging" 2:669–75.

PART TWO

The Dead Sea Scrolls and Scripture

CHAPTER **5**

The Hebrew Bible/Old Testament Before the Scrolls

THIS CHAPTER EXPLORES THE TEXTS OF THE OLD TESTAMENT that were available to us before the discovery of the Dead Sea Scrolls. There are three main texts: the Masoretic Text (written in Hebrew and Aramaic), the Samaritan Pentateuch (in Hebrew), and the Septuagint (in Greek). Other, later texts include the Latin, Syriac, and Aramaic Bibles.

The Masoretic Text

EARLY MANUSCRIPTS

Almost all modern English translations of the Old Testament are based on a single manuscript—the Leningrad, or St. Petersburg, Codex (Figure 5.1). Copied in 1008 or 1009 CE, this is our earliest complete example of the traditional Hebrew Bible, or Masoretic Text. The Leningrad Codex is used by most biblical scholars in its published edition, *Biblia Hebraica Stuttgartensia (BHS)*[1] and the earlier edition, *Biblia Hebraica*, edited by Rudoph Kittel *(BHK)*.[2] In the mid-1990s, an international team of scholars began preparing a new edition of the Leningrad Codex, to be known as *Biblia Hebraica Quinta (BHQ)*, at the initiative of the United Bible Societies and sponsored by the German Bible Society. *BHQ* is scheduled to appear for publication in several parts during the first decade of the third millennium.

Another, separate edition of the Leningrad Codex is *Biblia Hebraica Leningradensia (BHL),* which was prepared by Aron Dotan and published in Israel in 1973.[3] A fully revised edition with notes and appendixes in English appeared in 2001.[4] This is the most accurate edition of the Leningrad Codex currently available in the early years of the third millennium.

An important Masoretic manuscript is the Aleppo Codex, which forms the basis of the Hebrew University Bible Project (HUBP), currently under way at the Hebrew University in Jerusalem. This manuscript was copied in about 925 CE, about a century before the Leningrad Codex. A substantial portion, however, has been lost, which means that for some books the Hebrew University project must rely on other manuscripts. Of all modern Hebrew Bible editions, the HUBP includes the most comprehensive collection of variant

Figure 5.1

Carpet page of the
Leningrad Codex

Photograph by Bruce and Kenneth
Zuckerman, West Semitic Research,
in collaboration with the Ancient
Bible Manuscript Center. Courtesy
of the Russian National Library
(Saltykov-Shchedrin)

readings; the first volume to be published was Isaiah (1995), followed by Jeremiah (1997).[5] As of late 2002, the book of Ezekiel was in the final stages of preparation.

DEFINITION, ORIGINS, AND GROWTH OF THE MASORETIC TEXT

But what precisely is the Masoretic Text (MT)? The term is quite complicated since it covers many manuscripts rather than a single one; for instance, both the Leningrad Codex and the Aleppo Codex are representatives of this text. *Masoretic Group* or *Masoretic Family* would thus be a more accurate name. In its broader sense, the *Masoretic Text* refers to any text of the Hebrew Bible that was produced by a group of scholars called the Masoretes (see below) or to any copy of such a text. In the narrower sense, which is more commonly used, the Masoretic Text denotes the standard text of the Hebrew Bible that was finalized by the Masoretes of Tiberias (thus in the "Tiberian Tradition").

The *Masoretes* were a group of scholars from the eighth century onward who maintained traditions for copying the biblical text (the Masoretic Text) for liturgical or scholarly use. Earlier scholars who had maintained these traditions and were concerned to establish and preserve the correct form of the biblical text were known as *scribes*. The Hebrew Scriptures were originally written and copied in consonantal form only; an example of this early unvocalized text (without vowels and other signs) is given in Figure 5.2.

Since all ancient biblical texts consisted only of Hebrew consonants without vowels, many words could be read in more than one way, leading to different readings of the same

תהלים

אשרי האיש אשר לא הלך בעצת רשעים 1:1

ובדרך חטאים לא עמד ובמושב לצים לא ישב

כי אם בתורת יהוה חפצו ובתורתו יהגה יומם ולילה 2

והיה כעץ שתול על פלגי מים 3

אשר פריו יתן בעתו ועלהו לא יבול

וכל אשר יעשה יצליח

לא כן הרשעים 4

כי אם כמץ אשר תדפנו רוח

על כן לא יקמו רשעים במשפט וחטאים בעדת צדיקים 5

כי יודע יהוה דרך צדיקים ודרך רשעים תאבד 6

למה רגשו גוים ולאמים יהגו ריק 2:1

יתיצבו מלכי ארץ ורוזנים נוסדו יחד 2

על יהוה ועל משיחו

ננתקה את מוסרותימו ונשליכה ממנו עבתימו 3

יושב בשמים ישחק אדני ילעג למו 4

אז ידבר אלימו באפו ובחרונו יבהלמו 5

ואני נסכתי מלכי על ציון הר קדשי 6

אספרה אל חק יהוה 7

אמר אלי בני אתה אני היום ילדתיך

Figure 5.2
The unvocalized Hebrew Text (Psalm 1:1–2:7) The chapter and verse numbers are not part of the original text.

verse. Compare the letters *dg* in English, which could be *dig, dog,* or *dug,* depending on which vowel is used. In order to standardize the biblical text, the Masoretes added vowel signs and other components. The effect was to fix the meaning of each group of consonants (e.g., only *dig,* not *dog* or *dug*); see the passage from *Biblia Hebraica Stuttgartensia* in Figure 5.3 and the photograph from the Leningrad Codex in Figure 5.4.

SHAPE OF THE MASORETIC TEXT

Masoretic manuscripts contain the same overall shape for the Hebrew Bible, the threefold arrangement that was developed by the rabbis: the Torah, the Prophets, and the Writings (see Chapter 7). The specific order of books sometimes varies between manuscripts for the following groups: (1) Chronicles; (2) Psalms, Job, and Proverbs; and (3) the Five Scrolls (Song of Songs, Ruth, Lamentations, Ecclesiastes, and Esther). For example, the most widely used printed edition of the Hebrew Bible (*BHS,* like *BHK* before it) places Chronicles at the end of the Writings—even though the Leningrad Codex, the Aleppo Codex, and many other early manuscripts place Chronicles as the first book in that division. Other

The Origins and Growth of the Masoretic Text

The *first stage* originated among Babylonian Jews, the Pharisees, or Temple circles, and ended with the destruction of the Temple in 70 CE (or perhaps with the end of the second Jewish revolt in 135 CE). Documents include many of the Hebrew texts from Qumran (ca. 250 BCE–68 CE) and Masada (before 74 CE) and ancient translations, including one called *kaige–Theodotion* (in Greek, mid–first century BCE). The term *Proto-Masoretic* is commonly used for the precursors of the Masoretic Text in this period, but is really too general since it applies to the following period as well.

The *second stage* extends from the destruction of the Temple until the eighth century CE and is characterized by more and more textual consistency as rabbinic scholars sought to standardize the text of the Hebrew Bible. The main witnesses for the earlier part of this period are several biblical scrolls from the Judean Desert and several translations into other languages. The scrolls were found at Murabbaʿat (parts of the Torah, Isaiah, and the Minor Prophets) and at Naḥal Ḥever–Naḥal Ṣeʾelim (Genesis, Numbers, Deuteronomy, Psalms) and were all written before 135 CE. The term *Proto-Masoretic* is also used for the precursors of the Masoretic Text in this period.

The *third stage* extends from the eighth century until the end of the Middle Ages and is characterized by almost complete textual uniformity. During this period, the Masoretes set out to produce a standard text of the Hebrew Bible that in their eyes was true to the Scriptures revealed by God in ancient times. This standardized text has three main components: letters, vowel signs, and accents. (Accents are signs marked on words of the biblical text relating them to the music to which they are chanted in the liturgy.) Most manuscripts include, at least to some extent, a fourth component: the marginal notes of the Masorah (see Figures 5.3 and 5.4).

differences in order are also to be found; in the following list, the Koren Bible (produced in Jerusalem in 1962) represents the traditional order of books found in modern printed editions. The third column lists yet another arrangement found in some manuscripts of the Babylonian Talmud.

Koren Bible (1962)	Leningrad Codex (1008/9)	*Baba Bathra* 14b and MSS
Psalms	Chronicles	Ruth
Proverbs	Psalms	Psalms
Job	Job	Job
Song of Songs	Proverbs	Proverbs
Ruth	Ruth	Ecclesiastes
Lamentations	Song of Songs	Song of Songs
Ecclesiastes	Ecclesiastes	Lamentations
Esther	Lamentations	Daniel
Daniel	Esther	Esther
Ezra-Nehemiah	Daniel	Ezra-Nehemiah
Chronicles	Ezra-Nehemiah	Chronicles

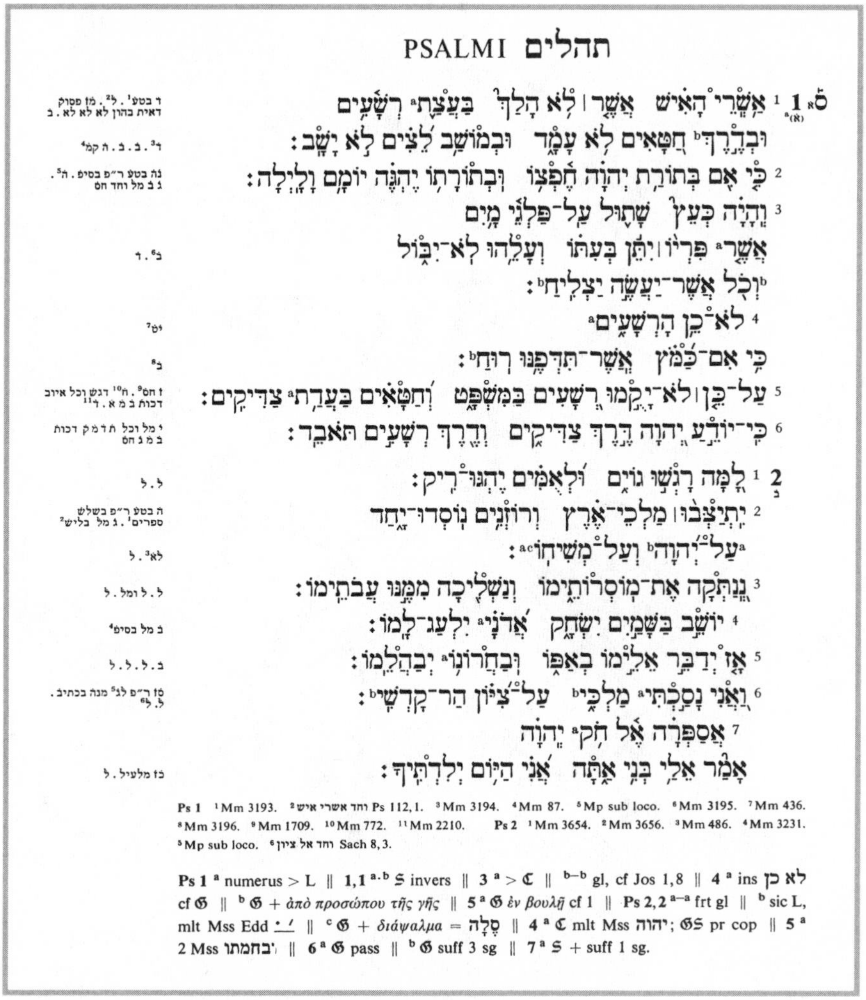

PSALMI תהלים

[Figure reproduction of Biblia Hebraica Stuttgartensia, Psalm 1:1–2:7, with Masoretic text, marginal notes (Masora parva), Masora magna references, and critical apparatus]

Ps 1 ¹Mm 3193. וחד אשרי איש ²Mm Ps 112,1. ³Mm 3194. ⁴Mm 87. ⁵Mp sub loco. ⁶Mm 3195. ⁷Mm 436. ⁸Mm 3196. ⁹Mm 1709. ¹⁰Mm 772. ¹¹Mm 2210. **Ps 2** ¹Mm 3654. ²Mm 3656. ³Mm 486. ⁴Mm 3231. ⁵Mp sub loco. וחד אל ציון Sach 8,3.

Ps 1 ¹ numerus > L ‖ **1,1** ᵃˑᵇ 𝔖 invers ‖ 3 ᵃ > 𝔗 ‖ ᵇ⁻ᵇ gl, cf Jos 1,8 ‖ 4 ᵃ ins לא כן cf 𝔊 ‖ ᵇ 𝔊 + ἀπὸ προσώπου τῆς γῆς ‖ 5 ᵃ 𝔊 ἐν βουλῇ cf 1 ‖ ᵇ sic L, mlt Mss Edd ־ׅ ‖ ᶜ 𝔊 + διάψαλμα = סֶלָה ‖ 4 ᵃ 𝔗 mlt Mss יהוה; 𝔊𝔖 pr cop ‖ 5 ᵃ 2 Mss ובחמתו ‖ 6 ᵃ 𝔊 pass ‖ ᵇ 𝔊 suff 3 sg ‖ 7 ᵃ 𝔖 + suff 1 sg.

Figure 5.3
A sample from *Biblia Hebraica Stuttgartensia* (Psalm 1:1–2:7) The last group of notes below is known as the *Apparatus.*
From K. Elliger et al., eds., *Biblia Hebraica Stuttgartensia* (Stuttgart: Deutsche Bibelgesellschaft. 1966/1977), 1087

The Samaritan Pentateuch

DEFINING AND INTRODUCING THE SAMARITAN PENTATEUCH

The Samaritan Pentateuch (SP) is not a translation, but the Samaritan version of the first five books of the Hebrew Bible. For Samaritan Jews, who still exist as a group in Israel today (especially in Nablus and at Ḥolon), the Samaritan Pentateuch constitutes the entire canon of the Bible. This Pentateuch is an important source for the history and origins of the Samaritan community and a valuable textual witness to one early form of the first part of the Hebrew Bible.

The Samaritan Pentateuch was rediscovered by European scholars only in the seventeenth century, when Pietro della Valle sent a complete copy, now called Codex B, to Europe in 1616. Almost twenty years later, in the Paris Polyglot of 1645, J. Morinus published its

Figure 5.4

Page from the Leningrad Codex
(Exod. 15:14b–16:3a)

Photograph by Bruce and Kenneth Zuckerman,
West Semitic Research, in collaboration with the
Ancient Bible Manuscript Center. Courtesy of the
Russian National Library (Saltykov-Shchedrin)

text, which was corrected by B. Walton in his London Polyglot of 1657. A scholar named E. Castellus appended a sixth volume to the London Polyglot, which included some 6,000 variant readings between the Masoretic Text and Samaritan Pentateuch, 1,900 of which agree with the Septuagint. Because of its ancient form and frequent agreements with the Septuagint and the Latin Vulgate, this text found much support among Roman Catholics, for whom the Greek and Latin Old Testaments were very authoritative.

In 1815, the noted German scholar W. Gesenius published a classic study on the Samaritan Pentateuch,[6] proposing that the Samaritan sect and its text began when Alexander the Great allowed the Samaritans to build their temple on Mt. Gerizim (which remains to this day the holy mountain of the Samaritans). Gesenius believed that Samaritan priests introduced sectarian readings into the Hebrew text they had received, and he attributed the many agreements between the Samaritan Pentateuch and the Septuagint to similar Hebrew manuscripts used by the Samaritans in Palestine and by Jews in Alexandria who had translated the Septuagint. Gesenius referred to this common source as the *Alexandrino-Samaritanus* text, which was of little value for establishing the best or most ancient form of Scripture since it was a "vulgar" text that had been simplified, popularized, corrected, and expanded. This was in contrast to the Judean text (i.e., the precursor to the Masoretic Text), which was produced by the Jews of Jerusalem, who tried to preserve the ancient Hebrew text unchanged. Gesenius's negative view of the Samaritan Pentateuch was followed by most scholars for the next century.

In 1915, however, Paul Kahle offered a much more positive view of the Samaritan Pentateuch by proposing that it was very old, that the Septuagint was derived from several old translations and was standardized by the Church, and that the Masoretic Text was in fact a late creation from older sources. For Kahle, the Samaritan Pentateuch preserved many genuine old readings and an ancient form of the Pentateuch. He also identified an early "pre-Samaritan text" because of agreements between the Samaritan Pentateuch and the books of *Jubilees, 1 Enoch,* and the *Assumption of Moses,* as well as the Septuagint and parts of the New Testament. Kahle's more favorable view of the Samaritan Pentateuch has been adopted by many modern scholars, even though most still view the Masoretic Text as a better text.

MANUSCRIPTS AND EDITIONS OF THE SAMARITAN PENTATEUCH

The text of the Samaritan Pentateuch is preserved in three kinds of sources: manuscripts, translations, and Samaritan literature. Although the manuscripts are all medieval, the other sources indirectly bear witness to the Samaritan text during the first millennium of the common era and interpret obscure passages in the Samaritan Pentateuch.

There are several manuscripts of the Samaritan Pentateuch, such as:

Codex Add. 1846	1100 CE	University Library, Cambridge
Codex B	1345/46 CE	Purchased by P. della Valle
Manuscript E	1219 CE	Book of Exodus
Abishaʿ Scroll	12th–13th century	Text revered by modern Samaritans

For the Samaritan religion, the sacred text is the Abishaʿ Scroll, which introduces itself as written by "Abishaʿ, son of Phineas, son of Eleazar, son of Aaron . . . in the thirteenth year after the Israelites ruled the land of Canaan in its borders round about." As many as nine scribes copied this manuscript.

The Samaritans translated their Torah into Greek, Aramaic, and Arabic, but as of 2002 there was no English translation. The main editions of the Samaritan Pentateuch are (1) A. F. von Gall, *Der hebräische Pentateuch der Samaritaner* (Giessen, 1914–18 [reprint, Berlin, 1966]), an edition that attempts to reconstruct the original form of the Samaritan Pentateuch by selecting readings from various manuscripts, but tends to follow Codex B. It is generally accurate, but contains several errors, is too reliant on the Masoretic Text, and lacks important sources such as the Abishaʿ Scroll; (2) A. and R. Sadaqa, *Jewish and Samaritan Versions of the Pentateuch—With Particular Stress on the Differences Between Both Texts* (Tel Aviv and Jerusalem: Ruben Mass, 1961–65); the basis for this edition is the Abishaʿ Scroll; (3) L. F. Giron Blanc, *Pentateuco Hebreo-Samaritano: Genesis* (Madrid, 1976); (4) A. Tal, *The Samaritan Pentateuch, Edited According to MS 6 (C) of the Shekhem Synagogue,* Texts and Studies in the Hebrew Language and Related Subjects 8 (Tel Aviv, 1994).

CHARACTER OF THE SAMARITAN PENTATEUCH

Readings of the Samaritan Pentateuch that differ from the traditional Masoretic Text may be classified in eight groups: (1) scribal errors; (2) differences in grammar; (3) replacement of old Hebrew forms with later ones; (4) removal of grammatical difficulties and

Figure 5.5

A page from the Samaritan
Pentateuch (Deut. 4:32–40)
Manuscript Cott. Claud BVII
(dated 1362–63 CE)

Reproduced by permission of the
British Library

replacement of rare constructions with more frequent ones; (5) insertion of additions and
interpolations from parallel passages; (6) corrections to remove historical difficulties and
objectionable passages; (7) interpretation and clarification of the text by small changes;
and (8) adaptation to Samaritan theology and ideology.

One example of group 6 is found in Gen. 50:23, where the Samaritan Pentateuch
changes *upon the knees of Joseph* (MT) to *in the days of Joseph,* since it seemed improper for
Joseph's grandchildren to be born upon his knees. Another is in Deut. 25:11, where *his private parts* (MT) is changed to *his flesh,* since it seemed obscene for a woman to grab a
man's private parts during a fight.

The variant readings in group 8 contain specifically Samaritan features, including the
defense of God's honor and the honor of Moses and other ancient heroes; legal differences

Box 5.1	*Variants in Deuteronomy*	
Samaritan Pentateuch	*Masoretic Text (NRSV)*
12:14: But only at **the place that the LORD has chosen** in one of your tribes—there you shall offer your burnt offerings and there you shall do everything I command you.	**12:14:** But only at **the place that the LORD will choose** in one of your tribes—there you shall offer your burnt offerings and there you shall do everything I command you.
27: 4: So when you have crossed over the Jordan, you shall set up these stones, about which I am commanding you today, **on Mount Gerizim,** and you shall cover them with plaster.	**27: 4:** So when you have crossed over the Jordan, you shall set up these stones, about which I am commanding you today, **on Mount Ebal,** and you shall cover them with plaster.

from the Masoretic Text; and specifying Mt. Gerizim rather than Jerusalem as the center for worshiping Yahweh. One example of these characteristic Samaritan features is the addition of a lengthy Tenth Commandment that specifically mentions Mt. Gerizim; Samaritans view the First Commandment in the Masoretic Bible as an introduction to the Ten Commandments. Two additional examples are the implied reference to Shechem as the site that God has already chosen (rather than Jerusalem, which he will choose) in Deut. 12:14; and to Mt. Gerizim (rather than Mt. Ebal) as the place where the Israelites were commanded to erect the first altar after crossing the Jordan river in Deut. 27:4 (see Box 5.1).

THE SAMARITAN PENTATEUCH, THE DEAD SEA SCROLLS, AND OTHER TEXTS

The discovery of the Dead Sea Scrolls has enabled scholars to appreciate the antiquity of the Samaritan Pentateuch and its value for reaching a better understanding of the biblical text. As we shall see in Chapter 6, many Qumran biblical scrolls may be classified as *Palestinian* or *Pre-Samaritan* (one ancient form of the biblical text), since they preserve a text similar to the Samaritan Pentateuch. Examples of this textual form include 4QpaleoExod^m, 4QExod-Lev^f, and 4QNum^b. The pre-Samaritan form of the biblical text dates to the second century BCE or earlier, but does not include the "sectarian readings" that were later inserted into the Samaritan Pentateuch to support the distinctive views of the Samaritan community.

The Samaritan Pentateuch is also of value to Septuagint studies, since it agrees with the Greek Bible in about 1,900 readings (according to E. Castellus). Furthermore, several passages in the New Testament reflect a text that is similar to the Samaritan Pentateuch. One example is in Acts 7:4, where Stephen states that Abraham went to Canaan *after* the death of Terah; this seems to agree with the Samaritan Pentateuch's statement that Terah died at the age of 145 years. In contrast, the Masoretic Text states that Terah died at the age of 205 (Gen. 11:32)—sixty years after Abraham had left. Another example is in Heb. 9:3, which agrees with the Samaritan Pentateuch in locating the golden altar of incense behind the veil of the Holy of Holies, whereas the Masoretic Text and Septuagint locate it in the holy place.

The Septuagint or Greek Bible

DEFINITION AND ORIGINS OF THE SEPTUAGINT

The *Septuagint* encompasses Greek translations of the Hebrew Bible, the additions to some books (e.g., Daniel), entire books now included among the Apocrypha (e.g., 1 Maccabees), and other books that are not among the Apocrypha of the Roman Catholic Church, but are recognized by other churches (e.g., the *Prayer of Manasseh* and *Psalm 151*).

Some scholars understand the Septuagint as referring only to the Pentateuch, while others include the entire collection of Jewish-Greek Scriptures, using the term *Old Greek* (OG) for books that were translated from the Hebrew. Other scholars, recognizing that our surviving Greek manuscripts contain corruptions and errors, use terms such as *Original Septuagint* or *Proto-Septuagint* to describe the text as it was originally translated. Many scholars prefer using a critical text (i.e., a text constructed after careful evaluation of all the available manuscripts) as nearest to the original translation. Others, however, regard the construction of critical texts as subjective and artificial and prefer to use a few well-known Septuagint manuscripts as representative of the Greek translation. Whatever view is adopted, it seems clear that the Septuagint was made in several stages, beginning with the Pentateuch in the third century BCE (probably in Egypt) and ending in the first century BCE or even the first century CE.

The word itself comes from the Latin *septuaginta,* meaning *seventy* (hence the Roman abbreviation LXX), and derives from a fascinating story. According to the *Letter of Aristeas,* which was written probably sometime between 150 and 100 BCE, the Egyptian king Ptolemy II (285–247) ordered his librarian, Demetrius of Phalerum, to collect all the books in the world for his library at Alexandria in Egypt. Since Demetrius believed that this collection should include a copy of the Jewish Law translated into Greek, he arranged for a letter to be sent to the high priest Eleazar in Jerusalem. As a result, seventy-two Jewish elders were sent to Alexandria to translate the Pentateuch. The stated author of the letter is Aristeas, a Jew from Alexandria, who presumably took part in this project. The translation was made by six elders from each of the twelve tribes, for a total of seventy-two. Following the arrival of these scholars in Alexandria, drafts of the translation were made, and the final version was completed in exactly seventy-two days:

> Three days later Demetrius took the men and passing along the sea-wall, seven stadia long, to the island, crossed the bridge and made for the northern districts of Pharos. There he assembled them in a house, which had been built upon the sea-shore, of great beauty and in a secluded situation, and invited them to carry out the work of translation, since everything that they needed for the purpose was placed at their disposal. So they set to work comparing their several results and making them agree, and whatever they agreed upon was suitably copied out under the direction of Demetrius.
>
> And the session lasted until the ninth hour; after this they were set free to minister to their physical needs. Everything they wanted was furnished for them on a lavish scale. In addition to this Dorotheus made the same preparations for them daily as were made for the king himself—for thus he had been commanded by the king. In the early morning they appeared daily at the Court, and after saluting the king went back to their own place. And as is the custom of all the Jews, they washed their hands in the sea and prayed to God and then devoted themselves to reading and translating the particular passage upon which they were engaged, and I put the question to them, Why it was that they washed

their hands before they prayed? And they explained that it was a token that they had done no evil (for every form of activity is wrought by means of the hands) since in their noble and holy way they regard everything as a symbol of righteousness and truth.

As I have already said, they met together daily in the place which was delightful for its quiet and its brightness and applied themselves to their task. And it so chanced that the work of translation was completed in seventy-two days, just as if this had been arranged of set purpose.[7]

After the translation was read to the Jewish community, the leaders pronounced a curse on anyone who might seek to change it in any way, since this was the authorized Greek translation of God's Law. Eventually the translators returned home with a guard of honor, a letter, and gifts for the high priest Eleazar.

Although this story is mostly fictitious (with the title *Septuaginta,* or *Seventy,* rounding off the number seventy-two), it is significant for understanding the origins of the Greek Bible: (1) The term *Septuagint* originally applied only to the five books of the Pentateuch. (2) It is clear that many Greek-speaking Jews, notably in Alexandria, needed a translation of the Scriptures since they spoke little or no Hebrew. (3) At least some Jews viewed the Septuagint as authoritative Scripture. (4) The *Letter of Aristeas* is a propaganda document that supports the authoritative and inspired status of the Septuagint.

EARLY MANUSCRIPTS

Copies of the Septuagint may be grouped under six headings:

(1) *The Dead Sea Scrolls:* Several scrolls were written in Greek and date from the second century BCE to the early first century CE. Most of these manuscripts are biblical (or, rather, scriptural) and from the Pentateuch: Exodus (pap7QLXXExod), Leviticus (4QLXXLev^a and pap4QLXXLev^b), Numbers (4QLXXNum), and Deuteronomy (4QLXXDeut). An important Greek scroll of the Minor Prophets is 8ḤevXII gr, which was found farther down the west coast of the Dead Sea in Cave 8 at Naḥal Ḥever. Another work discovered at Qumran and included in the Septuagint is the Letter of Jeremiah (pap7QEpJer gr). (For further information on these scrolls, see Chapter 6, "Observations on the Biblical Scrolls," and Chapter 8, "The Letter of Jeremiah.")

(2) *Papyri* (plural of *papyrus*): These preserve some of the earliest copies of the Greek Bible, but most are very fragmentary. One of these papyri was discovered in Cave 4 at Qumran (pap4QLXXLev^b) and two more in Cave 7 (pap7QLXXExod and pap7QEpJer gr). Other important examples, which were found elsewhere, include Chester Beatty Papyri IV and V, containing substantial portions of Genesis 8–46 and dating from the fourth and third centuries CE, respectively. Another is Chester Beatty VI, which contains much of Numbers and Deuteronomy and was copied in the second or early third century CE.

(3) *Uncials:* In contrast to very early Hebrew ones, several early Greek manuscripts preserve much or all of the Old Testament. These include a few uncials (i.e., manuscripts written in capital letters). Since they were preserved and handed down by church leaders, these manuscripts contain both the Old and New Testaments. The three most important uncials are Codex Sinaiticus, Codex Alexandrinus, and Codex Vaticanus.

Codex Sinaiticus (abbreviated S or א [the Hebrew letter *'alep*]) was copied in the fourth century CE and brought to Europe from St. Catherine's Monastery in the Sinai Desert. Most of the manuscript is housed at the British Museum in London, and a smaller portion at Leipzig, Germany. Sinaiticus originally contained the entire Greek Bible, but of the Old

Figure 5.6

Page from the printed edition of the LXX Psalter used by scholars (Ps. 1:1–2:1)

From A. Rahlfs, ed., *Septuaginta. Vetus Testamentium Graecum, Auctoritate Academiae Scientiarum Göttingensis editum. Vol. X: Psalmi cum odis.* 3d edition (Göttingen: Vandenhoeck & Ruprecht, 1979), 81

ΨΑΛΜΟΙ

1   **Α΄**

1 ΜΑΚΑΡΙΟΣ ἀνήρ, ὃς οὐκ ἐπορεύθη ἐν βουλῇ ἀσεβῶν
καὶ ἐν ὁδῷ ἁμαρτωλῶν οὐκ ἔστη
καὶ ἐπὶ καθέδραν λοιμῶν οὐκ ἐκάθισεν,

2 ἀλλ' ἢ ἐν τῷ νόμῳ κυρίου τὸ θέλημα αὐτοῦ,
καὶ ἐν τῷ νόμῳ αὐτοῦ μελετήσει ἡμέρας καὶ νυκτός.

3 καὶ ἔσται ὡς τὸ ξύλον τὸ πεφυτευμένον παρὰ τὰς διεξόδους τῶν ὑδάτων,
ὃ τὸν καρπὸν αὐτοῦ δώσει ἐν καιρῷ αὐτοῦ
καὶ τὸ φύλλον αὐτοῦ οὐκ ἀπορρυήσεται·
καὶ πάντα, ὅσα ἂν ποιῇ, κατευοδωθήσεται.

4 οὐχ οὕτως οἱ ἀσεβεῖς, οὐχ οὕτως,
ἀλλ' ἢ ὡς ὁ χνοῦς, ὃν ἐκριπτεῖ ὁ ἄνεμος ἀπὸ προσώπου τῆς γῆς.

5 διὰ τοῦτο οὐκ ἀναστήσονται ἀσεβεῖς ἐν κρίσει
οὐδὲ ἁμαρτωλοὶ ἐν βουλῇ δικαίων·

6 ὅτι γινώσκει κύριος ὁδὸν δικαίων,
καὶ ὁδὸς ἀσεβῶν ἀπολεῖται.

2   **Β΄**

1 Ἵνα τί ἐφρύαξαν ἔθνη
καὶ λαοὶ ἐμελέτησαν κενά;

Inscriptio ψαλμοι B, ψαλτηριον A', ψαλτηριον τω δδ αβ αλληλοια (graecis literis scriptum) Rˢ, *psalmus dauid* LaR(ˢ), legi non potest in He (ψαλ...), nulla adest in S' Sa LaG Ga; reliqui an inscriptionem habeant et quam habeant, nescio

1

1 επι καθεδραν B' Ld He(uid.)] επι -δρα Rˢ Ld(sil)' A': cf. 2 12 5 12 7 9 9 11. 15 etc. et Johannessohn Präp. p. 323 | 1² > LaG | λοιμων *pestium* uel *pestilentiarum* uel *pestilentium* Tert.P (cf. Lag. Probe), *pestilentiarum* Aug. IV 336 A. 1695 C] *pestilentiae* La(etiamAug et Tert.P) Ga

3 ποιη] ποιηση A

4 ουχ ουτως 2° et απο προσωπου της γης] ÷ Ga (cf. Field), > O teste Hi ed. Mo-

rin (S.-St. 2, p. 120) | ως ο B' Rˢ A' = 𝔐] ωσει L' | εκριπτει : sic (cf. 83 11 παραρριπτεισθαι) uel εκριπτει, cf. Thack. p. 244

5 ασεβεις Rˢ Laᵃ A' = 𝔐] pr. οι B' : ex 4 | αμαρτωλοι] pr. οι A

2

init. B'BoP UulgAug L' A' = 𝔐] pr. ωδη τω δαυειδ Sa, pr. ψαλμος τω δαυιδ Rˢ = *psalmus dauid* LaR Ga, pr. ⟨in finem psa⟩lmus ⟨ipsi dauid⟩ LaG, pr. ανεπιγραφος He, pr. προφητεια περι χριστου uel sim. BoP

1¹. ² duo stichi Sa LaG(uid.) Ga, unus rel. | εφρυαξαν *fremuerunt* La Ga] *tumultuatae sunt* Tert.(quinquies) et Cyp.(bis): cf. proleg. § 5 11

Testament only a portion remains. The New Testament is complete, and at the end appear the *Epistle of Barnabas* and the *Shepherd of Hermas.*

Codex Alexandrinus (abbreviated A) is dated to the fifth century and resides at the British Museum. This manuscript originally contained the entire Greek Bible, including the *Psalms of Solomon* (but with a title that separates it from the other books) and (in the New Testament part) the two *Epistles of Clement of Rome.* For the Old Testament part, which comprises three volumes, only a few passages are missing due to damage (the largest being 1 Kingdoms 12:18–14:9 and Pss. 49:19–79:10).

Codex Vaticanus (abbreviated B) was copied in the fourth century and has been housed at the Vatican Library in Rome since before 1481. It originally contained the entire Greek Bible, but the beginning has been lost (up to Gen. 46:28), as well as Psalms 106–138, and Heb. 9:14 through Revelation.

(4) *Minuscules* or *Cursives:* Hundreds of manuscripts written in the cursive script found in printed editions bear witness to all or parts of the Septuagint. These manuscripts were all copied in medieval times.

(5) *Printed Editions:* Critical editions of several Septuagint books have been published by the Göttingen Septuginta-Unternehmen in Germany, and as of 2002 several more were still in preparation. A complete edition of the Septuagint, available in two volumes or in a single compact one, was edited by A. Rahlfs in 1935.[8]

(6) *English Translations:* Unfortunately, very few translations of the Septuagint are available in English. The most widely used is Sir Lancelot Brenton's *The Septuagint Version: Greek and English,* which was originally published in 1851 and has been reprinted several times.[9] The first English translation, one that is far more difficult to obtain, was made in 1808 by Charles Thomson, one of America's founding fathers.[10]

SHAPE AND CONTENTS OF THE SEPTUAGINT

The contents of the Septuagint, as well as its order of books, differ markedly from those in the Hebrew Bible. This is illustrated by the books found in Codex Sinaiticus, Codex Vaticanus, and Codex Alexandrinus. See Table 5.1 overleaf (some books are missing from Codex Sinaiticus, which is damaged).

In addition to the books found in the Hebrew Bible, the Septuagint contains books and additions that are classified by many scholars as Apocrypha: Tobit, Judith, 1 and 2 Maccabees, the Wisdom of Solomon, Sirach (or Ecclesiasticus), Baruch, the Letter of Jeremiah, as well as the Additions to Esther (in eight sections) and to Daniel (in three sections: the Prayer of Azariah and Song of the Three Young Men; Susanna; and Bel and the Dragon). Many Septuagint manuscripts contain additional writings that are usually included among the Pseudepigrapha, although they are accepted as Scripture by some Orthodox churches: the *Prayer of Manasseh, Psalm 151,* the *Psalms of Solomon, 1 Esdras, 3 Maccabees,* and *4 Maccabees* (for further details, see Chapter 8).

Most manuscripts of the Greek Old Testament and early church lists[11] show that the sequence of books from Genesis through 1–2 Chronicles was fairly consistent. These suggest that the Pentateuch was not regarded as a separate group, but rather as history in the same sense as the books that followed. In many cases, Ruth followed Judges and preceded the four books of Kingdoms (i.e., 1–2 Samuel and 1–2 Kings), which were immediately followed by the revisionist history found in 1 and 2 Paraleipomena (1 and 2 Chronicles). The books of Tobit, Judith, and 1–4 Maccabees are found in nearly all Septuagint manuscripts, extending the period being covered into the Hellenistic-Roman period. We may also note that Daniel is grouped with the prophets, often after Ezekiel.

The order of books in the latter part of the Septuagint, however, is by no means clear, since the manuscripts differ. Codex Vaticanus, for example, ends with Ezekiel and Daniel, while Codex Alexandrinus ends with Sirach and the Psalms of Solomon. Since the arrangements of the books beyond 2 Chronicles likely remained fluid well into the Christian era, the final shape of the Septuagint cannot be established with certainty. The Hebrew Bible used by Jews ends with Ezra–Nehemiah and Chronicles, and thus

Table 5.1	Contents of the Septuagint According to Three Manuscripts	
Codex Sinaiticus	**Codex Vaticanus**	**Codex Alexandrinus**
Genesis	Genesis	Genesis
[Exodus]	Exodus	Exodus
[Leviticus]	Leviticus	Leviticus
Numbers	Numbers	Numbers
[Deuteronomy]	Deuteronomy	Deuteronomy
[Joshua]	Joshua	Joshua
[Judges]	Judges	Judges
[Ruth]	Ruth	Ruth
[1–2 Kingdoms]	1–2 Kingdoms	1–2 Kingdoms
[3–4 Kingdoms]	3–4 Kingdoms	3–4 Kingdoms
1 [+2] Paraleipomena	1–2 Paraleipomena	1–2 Paraleipomena
[1 Esdras = Ezra]	1 Esdras (Ezra)	Hosea
2 Esdras (Nehemiah)	2 Esdras (Nehemiah)	Amos
Esther	Psalms	Micah
Tobit	Proverbs	Joel
Judith	Ecclesiastes	Obadiah
1–4 Maccabees	Song of Songs	Jonah
Isaiah	Job	Nahum
Jeremiah	Wisdom of Solomon	Habakkuk
Lamentations	Sirach	Zephaniah
[Esther]	Esther	Haggai

culminates with a clear theological message: the return to the land of Israel after the Exile, in fulfillment of God's covenant promises to Abraham and later Israelite leaders. In contrast, the Old Testament of Christian Bibles ends with the book of Malachi: not with a return, but with prophecies of judgment and the promise of the messianic age (for further details, see Chapter 7).

THE SEPTUAGINT AND THE SCROLLS

The Septuagint plays a significant role in our understanding and evaluation of the Dead Sea Scrolls. In addition to the Septuagint manuscripts found at Qumran and Naḥal Ḥever, several scrolls contain a Hebrew textual form that is similar to that of the Septuagint. As we shall see in Chapter 6, these manuscripts may be regarded as "close to the presumed Hebrew source of the Septuagint." For example, 4QJer[b] and 4QJer[d] contain a Hebrew text

(continued)

Codex Sinaiticus	Codex Vaticanus	Codex Alexandrinus
[Judith]	Judith	Zechariah
[Tobit]	Tobit	Malachi
[Hosea]	Hosea	Isaiah
[Amos]	Amos	Jeremiah
[Micah]	Micah	Baruch
Joel	Joel	Lamentations
Obadiah	Obadiah	Letter of Jeremiah
Jonah	Jonah	Ezekiel
Nahum	Nahum	Daniel
Habakkuk	Habakkuk	Esther
Zephaniah	Zephaniah	Tobit
Haggai	Haggai	Judith
Zechariah	Zechariah	1 Esdras (Ezra)
Malachi	Malachi	2 Esdras (Nehemiah)
Psalms	Isaiah	1–4 Maccabees
Proverbs	Jeremiah	Psalms
Ecclesiastes	Baruch	Job
Song of Songs	Lamentations	Proverbs
Wisdom of Solomon	Letter of Jeremiah	Ecclesiastes
Sirach	Ezekiel	Song of Songs
Job	Daniel	Wisdom of Solomon
		Sirach
		Psalms of Solomon

very similar to the one from which the Septuagint was translated: not only in small details, but also where the Greek Bible differs markedly from the Masoretic Text. In fact, 4QJer[b] and 4QJer[d] and the Septuagint present a version of Jeremiah that is about 13 percent shorter than the longer one found in modern Bibles. In addition to such major examples, many scrolls preserve readings that are found in the Septuagint but not the Masoretic Text.

THE SEPTUAGINT AND THE EARLY CHURCH

Although the Septuagint originated in Jewish communities where Greek was the main language and Hebrew and Aramaic were less well known, it was ultimately preserved by Christianity and became the Bible of the early church. Many distinctive readings found in New Testament quotations of the Old are from the Septuagint, and in some cases the Hebrew forms of these readings are preserved in the scrolls.

Other Early Translations

Besides the Hebrew and Greek Scriptures discussed above, scholars make use of other early translations or "versions" of the Hebrew Bible or Old Testament. The most important of these versions are (1) the Aramaic Targums (begun before the common era; *targum* means *translation* or *paraphrase*); (2) the Syriac Peshitta (second–third century CE); (3) the Old Latin (begun in the late second century CE); and (4) the Latin Vulgate (390–405 CE, which was translated by Jerome and became the Bible of the Church).

Examination and comparison of the biblical texts from the Judean Desert suggest that among these versions, significant ancient readings are occasionally preserved, especially in the Peshitta and the Old Latin. However, the Masoretic Text, Samaritan Pentateuch, and Septuagint remain our most significant witnesses to the biblical text or texts of antiquity.

Select Bibliography

Several articles that were especially helpful for this chapter appear in

Freedman, David Noel, ed. *The Anchor Bible Dictionary.* 6 vols. New York: Doubleday, 1992:
  Peters, M. K. H. "Septuagint." 5.1093–1104.
  Sanders, J. A. "Canon: Hebrew Bible." 1:837–52.
  Revell, E. J. "Masoretes." 4:593–94.
  ———. "Masoretic Text." 4:597–99.
  Waltke, B. K. "Samaritan Pentateuch." 4:932–40.

A detailed and up-to-date treatment of the text of the Hebrew Bible is

Tov, E. *Textual Criticism of the Hebrew Bible.* 2d ed. Assen/Maastricht: Van Gorcum;
  Minneapolis: Fortress Press, 2001.

CHAPTER **6**

The Biblical Scrolls and the Text of the Hebrew Bible/Old Testament

THERE ARE ALMOST 900 DEAD SEA SCROLLS, which are divided by scholars into two broad groups. The first of these, by far the larger, is the approximately 670 nonbiblical scrolls, which will be discussed in Chapter 9. The other group is the biblical scrolls, which number 222 and are the subject of the present chapter. A number of writings called the Apocrypha, which are accepted as Scripture by some churches, as well as the Pseudepigrapha, are surveyed separately in Chapter 8.

The distinction between *nonbiblical scrolls* and *biblical scrolls* is made from a modern standpoint; it cannot be presumed that every book in our modern Bibles was regarded as biblical (or, rather, scriptural) by the Qumran community. This question will be examined in Chapter 7, on the scrolls and the canon of the Hebrew Bible or Old Testament.

Scholars divide the scrolls into these two broad categories because readers approach the nonbiblical scrolls and the biblical scrolls with different questions in mind. Since the first group contains writings that are unfamiliar to most readers, the two main questions addressed in Chapter 9 are, What are the contents of these writings? and What is their significance?

The books of the Bible, however, are familiar or at least accessible to most readers, and their contents can easily be checked with recourse to any English Bible. So readers approach the biblical scrolls with different questions in mind. Four of these, which are addressed in this chapter, are, (1) How much of a particular biblical book is preserved in the scrolls? (2) How many scrolls contain text from this book? (3) To what extent, if any, does the form of this book in the scrolls differ from the traditional form found in my Bible? and (4) Do the scrolls preserve any interesting readings that will solve problems or help my understanding of particular biblical books?

In order to answer these questions more effectively, a few comments on the different editions of biblical books will be helpful. It was shown in Chapter 5 that several forms or editions of the Old Testament have been in existence since early times. The most important of these are the Proto-Masoretic Text (the forerunner of today's Masoretic Text), the Septuagint (Greek Bible), and the Samaritan Pentateuch. We shall discuss each book with two general questions in mind:

Can individual scrolls be placed in one of four textual categories (a) similar to the Masoretic Text; (b) similar to the Septuagint (i.e., with a Hebrew text similar to the one used by the Greek translator); (c) similar to the Samaritan Pentateuch; or (d) non-aligned texts (showing no consistent alignment with any of the other three)?

Can we identify distinct literary editions of various individual books in the scrolls? These categories will be explained and discussed later in the chapter.

The Scrolls and the Pentateuch

GENESIS

The book of Genesis[1] opens with the creation of the heavens and earth, describes the primeval history ending with the Tower of Babel, and presents the saga of the patriarchs Abram (later called Abraham), Isaac, and Jacob, Jacob's twelve sons, and their extended families. Not surprisingly, this book of beginnings—both cosmic and national—was very popular among the Qumranites, which is evidenced in the many biblical scrolls of Genesis and other documents that retell its compelling stories.

The remains of some twenty Genesis manuscripts were discovered at Qumran: one each from Cave 1, Cave 2, Cave 6, and Cave 8,[2] and as many as sixteen from Cave 4.[3] Fragments of another Genesis scroll were found to the south at Masada, and pieces of two or three more copies in a cave at Wadi Murabba'at, which was used as a hideout by rebels in the Bar Kokhba Revolt (132–35 CE).[4] The precise number and place of origin of the Murabba'at manuscripts is not quite certain, owing to the secrecy of their Bedouin discoverers, and the fact that pieces of the same scroll (MurGen and Sdeir 1) were obtained at different times from the Bedouin.

The oldest scroll of Genesis is 4QpaleoGen[m], which is dated to the middle of the second century BCE. This manuscript is written in the ancient Hebrew script known as *paleo-Hebrew,* which is rare among the biblical scrolls (see later, "the Paleo-Hebrew Biblical Scrolls"). Another feature is the title of Genesis, which is preserved in 4QGen[h-title]. Of the almost 900 manuscripts found in the Dead Sea caves, only this scroll and three others (1QS, 4Q249, 4Q504) preserve the title of the book involved. Since the fragment with the title has been separated from the rest of the manuscript, it is not clear if this is the only surviving piece or if it belongs to another scroll (most likely 4QGen[k]).

Did any of the Genesis scrolls contain more than one book? Parts of both Genesis and Exodus are preserved in two scrolls (4QGen-Exod[a] and 4QpaleoGen-Exod[l]), and one more (4QExod[b]) most likely contained both books, which shows that some biblical writings were physically found together and affirms the traditional order for these two important books. This is supported by the scroll from Murabba'at, which preserves portions of Genesis, Exodus, and Numbers (although it could be more than one manuscript) and may have originally contained the entire Pentateuch.

Despite their large number, the twenty-four Genesis scrolls are mostly fragmentary, with only thirty-four of the fifty chapters of Genesis represented (1–6, 8, 10, 12, 17–19, 22–24, 26–27, 32–37, 39–43, 45–50). It appears that the text of Genesis had become generally stable by the Qumran period, since these manuscripts reveal a text generally close to the traditional Masoretic Text and the Samaritan Pentateuch (see Box 6.1). Beyond minor variations or differences in spelling, only eleven Genesis scrolls contain any variants worth noting (a possible exception being the book's chronological system) and may be classified

Box 6.1	*Genesis 1:9*

Dead Sea Scrolls Bible	*Masoretic Text (NRSV)*
And God said, "Let the waters *underneath*[1] the heavens be gathered together in one *gathering*,[2] and let the dr[y land] appear." And it was so. [*And the waters under the heavens gathered to their gatherings*] *and the dr[y land] appeared.*[3]	And God said, "Let the waters under the sky be gathered together into one place, and let the dry land appear." And it was so.

1. 4QGen[g]. *under* MT, SP. 2. 4QGen[h1], LXX. *place* MT, SP, 4QGen[b]. 3. 4QGen[k], LXX. Not in MT, SP, 4QGen[b].

Comment: The Hebrew word *gathering (mikveh)*, which is translated by the Septuagint (LXX), is found in 4QGen[h1], rather than the traditional Hebrew *place (maqôm)*. In addition, the accomplishment of God's command, again found in the Greek, is evident in 4QGen[k]. Although most variants from the scrolls are not necessarily better, both readings here may represent the original form of the text.

(Adapted from AFU, 5–6)

as *mixed* or *non-aligned*. Other manuscripts, notably the two (or possibly three) from Wadi Murabba'at, copied at the beginning of the second century CE, are virtually identical to the Masoretic Text.

EXODUS

In Exodus,[5] the Israelites are set free from bondage in Egypt and are led by Moses to Mt. Sinai, where God makes a covenant with them. Much of the later part (chaps. 19–40) deals with the covenant, laws, the tabernacle, and instructions for worship. In view of these themes and its emphasis on Moses the lawgiver, Exodus was a popular book among the members of the Qumran community. This is confirmed by the large number of Exodus manuscripts found there: one each from Caves 1 and 7, three from Cave 2,[6] and twelve more from Cave 4,[7] for a total of seventeen. The oldest is 4QExod-Lev[f], which dates to the mid-third century BCE and is one of the two earliest scrolls (the other is 4QSam[b]) found at Qumran. One more scroll that contains Exodus is Mur1, which was found in a cave at Wadi Murabba'at. Between them, these eighteen manuscripts preserve parts of all forty chapters of this, the second book of the Pentateuch.

As already seen with Genesis, some Exodus scrolls offer evidence that several books of the Torah or Pentateuch were viewed as a collection, perhaps even all copied together in the same scroll. Two manuscripts from Qumran (4QGen-Exod[a], 4QpaleoGen-Exod[l]) preserve parts of Genesis and Exodus, a third (4QExod[b]) most likely contained at least both books, a fourth (4QExod-Lev[f]) shows that Exodus was followed by Leviticus, and what appears to be a single scroll from Wadi Murabba'at (Mur 1) includes fragments of Genesis and Numbers in addition to Exodus. This evidence suggests that the five books of the Torah were established as a collection well before the coming of Jesus.

Figure 6.1
A biblical scroll written in Paleo-Hebrew. 4QpaleoExod^m was written in the ancient paleo-Hebrew script, which was common before the Exile (587–539 BCE), rather than the square script in which the vast majority of the Dead Sea Scrolls were copied (PAM 41.386).
Courtesy of the Israel Antiquities Authority

Most of the Exodus manuscripts contain a text very much like that in the traditional Hebrew Bible (the Masoretic Text), including pap7QLXXExod, a scroll written on papyrus and in Greek. Moreover, the text of the Wadi Murabba'at scroll (Mur 1), which was copied in the early second century CE, conforms closely to the traditional text. At least two scrolls, 4QpaleoExod^m and 4QExod–Lev^f, are closer to the Samaritan Pentateuch, while 4QExod^b seems closer to the Septuagint.

4QpaleoExod^m, which was written in the archaic Hebrew script, is the most extensive scroll found in Cave 4, with the preserved text beginning at Exod. 6:25. In view of its closeness to the Samaritan Pentateuch, 4QpaleoExod^m provides a clear example of a different edition of a biblical book. The Samaritan Pentateuch has been known in the West since the seventeenth century (see Chapter 5) and is used to this day by the Samaritan community. Before the scrolls were discovered, some scholars dismissed the major differences found in the Samaritan Pentateuch as simply the work of the marginalized Samaritans. 4QpaleoExod^m now shows us that the book of Exodus circulated in early Judaism in two editions: the first close to the text found in the Masoretic Text and translated in the Septuagint, and the second as an intentionally expanded version with most of the features characteristic of

Box 6.2	*Exodus 7:18*

Dead Sea Scrolls Bible	*Masoretic Text (NRSV)*
"[And the fish] *in the mi[dst][1] of the Nile shall die, [and the Nile shall stink; and] the Egyptians shall weary of drinking water from the Nile.*" [*And Moses and Aaron went to Pharaoh] and [s]aid to him, The Lo[RD God of the Hebrews sent us to you saying], "Let my people go that [they] may serve [me in the wilderness." And behold, you have not listened until now]. Thus the LORD has said, "By [this you shall know that I am the LORD. Behold I am] s[trikin]g [the water which is in the Nile] with the rod that [is in my land and it shall be turned to blood] and [the f]ish that are in the mi[dst of the Nile shall die and the river shall stink and the] E[gy]ptians [shall weary] of dri[nking water from the Nile."[2]*	"The fish in the river shall die, the river itself shall stink, and the Egyptians shall be unable to drink water from the Nile."

1. 4QpaleoExod^m. *in* MT, SP, LXX. 2. 4QpaleoExod^m SP. Not in MT, LXX, 4QGen-Exod^a, 4QExod^c.

Comment: In an expansion of v. 18, 4QpaleoExod^m and the Samaritan Pentateuch repeat God's command from Exod. 7:16–18, but with Moses and Aaron reporting the words to Pharaoh. Such embellishments are characteristic of this scroll and the Samaritan Pentateuch.

(Adapted from AFU, 34)

the Samaritan version (see Box 6.2). Two specifically *Samaritan* features, however, are not included in 4QpaleoExod^m: the addition of an eleventh commandment to build an altar on Mt. Gerizim, and the use of the past tense, rather than the future, in the formula *the place that the Lord has chosen* (not *will choose*).

LEVITICUS

Leviticus[8] contains laws and regulations for worship, sacrifices, the ordination of priests, and religious festivals. The name given to Leviticus by the *tannaim,* or early rabbis, is very appropriate: *Torat Kohanim,* or the *Manual of the Priests,* especially the sons of Levi and the sons of the high priest Aaron. Its overall theme is holiness: "You shall be holy for I am holy" (Lev. 11:45). The importance of this book for the Qumran community is underscored by the fact that every chapter of Leviticus is referenced at least once in the nonbiblical scrolls.

A total of sixteen (or seventeen) Leviticus scrolls were found at two locations in the Judean Desert. Fourteen were unearthed in the vicinity of Wadi Qumran: one each from Caves 1, Cave 2, and Cave 6,[9] nine (or ten) from Cave 4,[10] and two from Cave 11.[11] Two more Leviticus scrolls were discovered in the ruins atop Masada.[12] As already mentioned, the oldest manuscript is 4QExod-Lev^f (mid-third century BCE), which is one of the two earliest scrolls found at Qumran. Between them these sixteen damaged manuscripts preserve at least a portion of all twenty-seven chapters of Leviticus, with the exception of chapter 12.

Figure 6.2

A Greek biblical scroll. Relatively
few scrolls are written in Greek,
the majority of them biblical and
from the Pentateuch, including
pap4QLXXLev[b], which is shown
here (PAM 40.575).

Courtesy of the Israel Antiquities Authority

No less than four Leviticus scrolls (1QpaleoLev, 2QpaleoLev, 6QpaleoLev, and 11QpaleoLev[a]) were written in paleo-Hebrew script, and two more were written in Greek (4QLXXLev[a] and pap4QLXXLev[b]). As already observed among the Genesis and Exodus scrolls, two or three Leviticus manuscripts (1QpaleoLev?, 4QExod-Lev[f], and 4QLev-Num[a]) each preserve portions of more than one book, thereby confirming the traditional order of Exodus–Leviticus–Numbers, suggesting that the Pentateuch was viewed as a collection at Qumran, and even hinting that all five books from Genesis to Deuteronomy were written on a single scroll.

Although most Leviticus scrolls contain some variant readings from the traditional Hebrew text and the Samaritan Pentateuch, the form of this book seems to have stabilized early, perhaps because it was a work containing specific cultic regulations. A single textual tradition is preserved in the sixteen manuscripts, although some variant readings have been described as *mixed* or *non-aligned*. The two Masada scrolls—which were copied about the mid-first century CE—are particularly close to the traditional Masoretic Text, suggesting that this textual form had become fixed, and was even becoming normative, during this century. To the best of our knowledge, none of the variant readings found in the Leviticus manuscripts have so far been accepted by modern Bible translators, although this may change as the readings are carefully analyzed and weighed. The nature of some of

Box 6.3	*Variants in Leviticus*
Dead Sea Scrolls Bible	*Masoretic Text*
1:17b: [And the priest shall burn it on the altar, on the wo]od that is on [the fir]e; it is a *burnt offering*,[1] of a pleasing odor to the L[ORD].	**1:17b:** Then the priest shall burn it on the altar, on the wood that is on the fire; it is a burnt offering, an offering by fire of pleasing odor to the LORD.
3:11: And the priest shall *burn*[2] on the altar; it is the f[ood, *for a pleasing od*]*or*,[3] [of the offering made by fire to the LORD].	**3:11** Then the priest shall burn these on the altar as a food offering by fire to the LORD.

1. 4QLev[b]. *burnt offering, an offering by fire* MT, SP, LXX. 2. 4QLev[b] SP, LXX. *burn it* MT. 3. pap4QLXXLev[b], LXX. Not in MT, SP.

(Adapted from AFU, 79, 81)

these variants becomes evident in the accompanying examples from Leviticus 1 and 3 (see box 6.3).

One of the three targums (translations into Aramaic) among the scrolls is of Leviticus (the other two are of Job). Found in Cave 4 (and thus abbreviated 4QtgLev or 4Q156), the Targum of Leviticus was copied about 150 BCE. Only Lev. 16:1–15 and 16:18–21 are preserved, but the manuscript may have contained all of Leviticus or a ritual text for the Day of Atonement. (For a translated sample of a targum, see under Job.)

NUMBERS

Numbers[13] opens with the Israelites in the Sinai desert, covers their forty years of wandering, and ends with the people in the plains of Moab, poised to cross over the river Jordan into the land that God had promised to give them. A total of eleven Numbers scrolls were discovered in the Judean Desert. Eight of these were found at Qumran: one in Cave 1, four in Cave 2, and three in Cave 4.[14] Three more manuscripts were found at sites farther to the south: two at Naḥal Ḥever, and one at Murabbaʿat.[15] Although none of these scrolls is complete, of the thirty-six chapters of Numbers only chapters 6 and 14 are not represented in at least one of them.

Three of the Numbers manuscripts deserve special mention. The first is 1QpaleoLev, which, as its abbreviated title shows, was written in the paleo-Hebrew script. Although listed as a Leviticus scroll, 1QpaleoLev also preserves at least two passages from Numbers (1:48–50 and 36:7–8[?]) somewhere between Leviticus 23 and 27. The second unusual scroll is 4QLev-Num[a], which originally also contained the book of Leviticus (note also the scroll from Murabbaʿat [Mur 1], which preserves portions of Genesis, Exodus, and Numbers). This manuscript and others containing more than one book of the Pentateuch have already been discussed under Genesis, Exodus, and Leviticus above. Such evidence affirms the traditional order for Leviticus and Numbers and suggests that the five books of the Pentateuch were viewed as a collection at Qumran.

Box 6.4	*Numbers 27:22–23: A Speech of Moses*

Dead Sea Scrolls Bible (4QNum^b)	*Masoretic Text (NRSV)*
22 And [Moses did as the LORD commanded him; and he took] Joshua *the son of Nun,*[1] and set him before Eleazar t[he priest, and before all the congregation; 23 and he lai]d his hands on him, and commissioned him as the LORD spoke by Moses. [*And Mose*]s [*said*] *to him, "Your eyes have seen that which the* LORD *your God has done to* [*these*] *two k*[*ings; so shall the* LORD *do to all the kingdoms into which you are going. You shall not fear them; for the* LORD *your God, he is the one who fights for you*]."[2]	22 So Moses did as the LORD commanded him. He took Joshua and had him stand before Eleazar the priest and the whole congregation; 23 he laid his hands on him and commissioned him—as the LORD had directed through Moses.

1. 4QNum^b. Not in MT, SP, LXX.   2. 4QNum^b SP. Not in MT, LXX.

Comment: Num. 27:12–23 informs us that Joshua has been chosen by God to succeed Moses. In the Masoretic Text and Septuagint the passage ends with Moses laying hands on Joshua. 4QNum^b, however, then inserts a passage taken from Deut. 3:21–22, in order to emphasize Joshua's need to have courage: "for the LORD your God, he is the one who fights for you."

Note: Four more examples, all of them speeches, are Moses' plea to enter Canaan (Deut. 3:24–28, interpolated into Num. 20:13b); God's prohibition to fight Moab (Deut. 2:9, interpolated into Num. 21:12a); the prohibition to fight Ammon (Deut. 2:18–19, interpolated into Num. 21:13a); and God's command to fight the Amorites (Deut. 2:24–25, interpolated into Num. 21:21a).

(Adapted from AFU, 133)

The third special Numbers scroll is 4QNum^b, which is the best preserved, contains material from chapters 11–36, and may be described as an early Jewish Living Bible, since it features many interpolations (insertions of other material) and expansions of the biblical text. The book of Deuteronomy contains several speeches that are not found in the Masoretic Text of Numbers, but which were uttered during events also recounted in Numbers. So where these speeches are not included in the traditional book of Numbers, 4QNum^b imports them from Deuteronomy into the appropriate place in the narrative (see Box 6.4).

Many of the longer readings included in 4QNum^b are not found in the Masoretic Text and the Septuagint, but are preserved in the Samaritan Pentateuch. (A lesser number are present in the Greek Bible but not in the Masoretic Text or Samaritan Pentateuch, and yet other readings are independent, since they are found in none of the three textual traditions.) This important scroll was copied about 30 BCE, which was a critical time in the history of the transmission of the biblical text. It shows there were at least two editions of Numbers circulating in Judaism during the Second Temple period. Within a few decades rabbinic circles were actively striving to establish for the books of the Hebrew Bible a standardized form known as the Proto-Masoretic text (see Chapter 5). This effort included the elimination or suppression of textual forms that deviated from the preferred text. The Samaritans, however, chose the expanded version of Numbers (represented by 4QNum^b) for inclusion in their Pentateuch, making only a few changes in accordance with their characteristic beliefs.

DEUTERONOMY

Deuteronomy[16] contains a series of addresses delivered by Moses to the people of Israel in the land of Moab, as they were preparing to enter the Promised Land. Its final chapters feature the last words and death of Moses, the prophet, wonder-worker, and deliverer (Deut. 34:1–12). Since Deuteronomy also features the authoritative law and covenant made by God through Moses with Israel, themes that are prominent in several scrolls specific to Qumran, it is not difficult to see why it was one of the most popular books among the Qumranites. Only Psalms is represented by a greater number of manuscripts (thirty-nine altogether, thirty-six at Qumran).

There is a total of thirty-three Deuteronomy scrolls, of which thirty were discovered at Qumran: two in Cave 1, three in Cave 2,[17] twenty-two in Cave 4,[18] and one each in Caves 5, 6 and 11.[19] Three more manuscripts were found at sites farther to the south: one at Naḥal Ḥever, one at Murabbaʿat, and one at Masada (XḤev/SeDeut, MurDeut, MasDeut). Although none of these scrolls is complete, at least a portion of all thirty-four chapters of the book is represented in them.

The list of Deuteronomy manuscripts contains some interesting features. First, two scrolls (4QpaleoDeut^r and 4QpaleoDeut^s) were written in the paleo-Hebrew script, not the far more common square script. Second, a copy of Deuteronomy in Greek (4QLXXDeut) was used at Qumran, which means that at least some of the community there spoke Greek, as well as Hebrew and Aramaic. Third, one manuscript (pap6QDeut) was written on papyrus, which is much more fragile than the leather on which most of the scrolls were written. Finally, the confusing symbols 4QDeut^k1, 4QDeut^k2, and 4QDeut^k3 remind us just how difficult it is to categorize fragments of ancient writing, piece them together, and identify the manuscript to which each belongs. When earlier editors first identified these fragments as belonging to the book of Deuteronomy, they believed all were part of a single scroll, which they termed 4QDeut^k. But when it was later discovered that the pieces actually belong to three different scrolls, it was too late to assign the following symbols (*l* and *m*) to the two newcomers, since these symbols had already been allocated to other scrolls. For this reason the symbol *k* is now shared by three different manuscripts of Deuteronomy!

It is not easy to offer a precise account of the textual nature of Deuteronomy in the scrolls, but many are close to the text of the traditional Hebrew Bible (the Masoretic Text) and the Samaritan Pentateuch. Some manuscripts, however, seem to be textually independent (e.g., 4QDeut^b and 4QDeut^c), and at least one (4QDeut^q) contains readings also found in the Septuagint of Deuteronomy. Another type of variant appears in Box 6.5, which features a scroll, in this case 4QDeut^n, with a reading (following Deut. 5:15) that is not found elsewhere. An additional interesting passage appears in 4QDeut^j, where Deut. 8:20–21 is directly followed by material from another biblical book (Exod. 12:43–46). Since this scroll preserves text that seems to be from another book, an interesting question arises: Should this be classified as a biblical (or, rather, scriptural) manuscript, or as one that contains scriptural excerpts used for liturgical purposes? Since this feature also appears in scrolls such as 4QNum^b and *Reworked Pentateuch,* it appears that we are dealing here with different forms or editions of scriptural books (see chapter 9).

Box 6.5   *Deuteronomy 5:15*

Dead Sea Scrolls Bible	*Masoretic Text (NRSV)*
And you shall remember that you were a servant in the land of Egypt, and the LORD your God brought you out from there with a mighty hand and an outstretched arm. Therefore the LORD your God commanded you *to keep*[1] the sabbath day *to hallow it.*	Remember that you were a slave in the land of Egypt, and the LORD your God brought you out from there with a mighty hand and an outstretched arm; therefore the LORD your God commanded you to keep the sabbath day.
For in six days the LORD made heaven and earth, the sea, and all that is in them and rested the seventh day; so the LORD blessed the sabbath day and hallowed it.[2]	

1. 4QDeut[n], LXX. *to perform* MT, SP. 2. 4QDeut[n]. Not in MT, SP, LXX.

Comment: In the shorter, traditional version of Deut 5:15, which appears in the Masoretic Text, Samaritan Penta-teuch, and Septuagint, the LORD has commanded the Israelites *(you) to perform* the sabbath day (the Septuagint reads *to keep*). But the longer version, found only in 4QDeut[n], enjoins them *to keep* and *to hallow* the sabbath day and then provides two reasons for this observance as found in the Exodus version of the Fourth Commandment: "the Lord rested . . . and blessed the sabbath day. . . ." (Exod. 20:11). Another very early manuscript known as the Nash Papyrus has both reasons, but in the reverse order.

(Adapted from AFU, 154)

The Scrolls and the Historical Books

JOSHUA

The book of Joshua[20] describes the conquest of Canaan by the Israelites under Joshua's leadership, the division of the land among the tribes, and the renewal of the covenant at Shechem. Only two scrolls of Joshua were recovered in the Judean Desert (both from Cave 4 at Qumran).[21] The earlier is 4QJosh[a], which is dated to about 100 BCE. Of the twenty-four chapters in the traditional text of Joshua, only nine (2–8, 10, and 17) are represented in 4QJosh[a] and 4QJosh[b]. Another relevant scroll is *4QpaleoParaJoshua* (4Q123); although the contents are difficult to identify, the text is more reminiscent of Joshua than of any other known work.

Before the discovery of the scrolls, Joshua was already known to exist in two different literary editions. As also occurs with Jeremiah, the Septuagint (Greek) text of Joshua is an earlier, shorter edition of the book, which later developed into the fuller edition that appears in the traditional Masoretic Text. 4QJosh[a], however, now presents yet an earlier version of the text, with a shorter text in places. The Greek text is somewhat longer than the form found in 4QJosh[a], and the Masoretic Text is longer than the Greek text. The individual textual variants found in 4QJosh[a] (and also 4QJosh[b]) sometimes agree with the Sep-tuagint, sometimes with the Masoretic Text, and on occasion have their own distinctive readings. 4QJosh[a], then, contains an intentionally different order of the narrative and thus presents a third literary edition of Joshua. It is also feasible that yet another textual form or edition of this biblical book is found in *4QpaleoParaJoshua*.

4QJosh^a and the First Altar in the Promised Land

In the traditional narrative found in the Masoretic Text, Joshua leads the Israelites across the Jordan, fights the battle for Jericho, and gains another victory over the city of Ai (8:1–29). Soon afterward, he marches some 20 miles (32 kilometers) north to Shechem to build an altar on a mountain named Ebal. Ebal is opposite Mt. Gerizim, which was to become the holy mountain of the Samaritans (8:30–35). Joshua then unexpectedly journeys back south, abandoning his newly built altar in enemy territory. For many years scholars have puzzled over Joshua's apparently unwise movements; note that the Septuagint places the events on Mt. Ebal after Josh. 9:2, which hints that the passage Josh. 8:30–35 in the traditional text may have once belonged elsewhere in the book (see Box 6.6).

A relevant text for this passage is Deut. 27:4, in which Moses commands the building of the first altar *on Mount Ebal*. The Samaritan Pentateuch and the Old Latin, however, have the reading *on Mount Gerizim*. This shows that *on Mount Ebal* in the Masoretic and Greek traditions is a later Jewish polemical change from the Samaritan claim that the first altar was built *on Mount Gerizim*. A three-stage history in the development of this command-fulfillment passage has been proposed:

> First, the altar was simply to be built at the unspecified place—wherever the people crossed the Jordan. Secondly, northerners, perhaps the Samaritans, specified the site of the first altar as *on Mount Gerizim*. Finally, Jewish scribes discounted that claim by changing *Mount Gerizim* anomalously to the otherwise insignificant *Mount Ebal*.[22]

JUDGES

The book of Judges[23] spans the history of Israel from the invasion of Canaan to just before the establishment of the monarchy and features national leaders called *judges,* most of whom were military heroes. Only three scrolls of Judges were discovered at Qumran, one from Cave 1 and two from Cave 4,[24] preserving parts of just five chapters (6, 8?, 9, 19, and 21) of the twenty-one found in the traditional form of the book. The earliest scroll is 4QJudg^a, which was copied about 50–25 BCE. The Judges manuscripts confirm the patterns of growth of the biblical text that are provided by some other biblical scrolls. 4QJudg^a reveals an earlier text that is shorter than the Masoretic and Septuagint forms, since it does not yet include a theological passage (Judg 6:7–10) that was inserted into the later versions; this scroll may thus represent a separate edition of the book. It is also possible that 4QJudg^b had a shorter text, although evidence for the missing material is no longer preserved but can be deduced by reconstructing the original manuscript.

RUTH

Set in the time of the Judges, the charming story in this book[25] features Ruth, a Moabite woman whose loyalty to her mother-in-law, Naomi, and devotion to God lead her to follow Naomi back to Israel after the death of her husband. There she finds a new husband, Boaz, and becomes the great-grandmother of King David. This little work survives in fragments from four manuscripts found at Qumran, two from Cave 2 and two from

| Box 6.6 | *Joshua's First Altar* |

Dead Sea Scrolls Bible	*Masoretic Text (NRSV)*
Josh. 4:1: [When the whole nation had finished crossing the Jordan, the LORD said] to Josh[ua, 2 "From the people select one from each tribe 3 and give them this command: 'Pick up] for yourselves [twelve stones] *from the middle of the* [*Jordan,*[1] *and carry them over wi*]th you, and s[e]t t[hem] down [in the place where you camp tonight],...'"	**Josh. 4:1:** When the entire nation had finished crossing over the Jordan, the LORD said to Joshua: 2 "Select twelve men from the people, one from each tribe, 3 and command them, 'Take twelve stones from here out of the middle of the Jordan, from the place where the priests' feet stood, carry them over with you, and lay them down in the place where you camp tonight.'"
Josh. 4 (= 8 MT):34: [After this he read all the words of the law, the blessing and the curse, just as it is written in the book of] the [l]aw. 35 There was not a word of *all*[2] Moses commanded [*Jo*]*shua*[3] which Joshua did not read before all [......] *the Jorda*[*n,*[4] *and*] the women and children, and the stra[ngers] living among them.	**Josh. 8:34:** And afterward he read all the words of the law, blessings and curses, according to all that is written in the book of the law. 35 There was not a word of all that Moses commanded that Joshua did not read before all the assembly of Israel, and the women, and the little ones, and the aliens who resided among them.
Josh. 5:X: *After they had removed* [*their feet from the Jordan, ...*] *the book of the law. After that, the ark-bearers*[5] [..............................]	**Josh. 5:1:** When all the kings of the Amorites beyond the Jordan to the west, and all the kings of the Canaanites by the sea, heard that the LORD had dried up the waters of the Jordan for the Israelites until they had crossed over, their hearts melted, and there was no longer any spirit in them, because of the Israelites.
5:2: [At] that [time] the LORD said to Josh[ua, "Ma]k[e yourself flint knives, and again circumcise the children of *Israel.*" 6 So Jo]shua [made flint] kn[ives] for [himself, and circumcised the children of Israel at the hill of the foreskins.... *(text preserved through v. 7)*	**5:2:** At that time the LORD said to Joshua, "Make flint knives and circumcise the Israelites a second time." 3 So Joshua made flint knives, and circumcised the Israelites at Gibeath-haaraloth....

1. 4QJosh[b], LXX. *from here, from the middle of the Jordan* MT. 2. 4QJosh[a]. *all that* MT, LXX. 3. 4QJosh[a], LXX. MT lacks *Joshua*. 4. 4QJosh[a]. MT, LXX lack *the Jordan*. 5. 4QJosh[a] (with X denoting a different verse than the traditional v. 1). MT, LXX have the secondary traditional wording of 5:1 in its place.

(Adapted from AFU, 203–4)

Cave 4,[26] which preserve parts of all four chapters. The earliest Ruth scrolls are 2QRuth[a] and 4QRuth[b], which date from the middle of the first century BCE.

All four manuscripts contain a text very much like the one recorded in the Masoretic Text and in the Septuagint and include only minor variant readings. One example is in Ruth 2:18, where 2QRuth[a] reads that Ruth brought out the barley she had gleaned and gave Naomi what was left over *after she had eaten her fill,* whereas the Masoretic Text and the Septuagint tell us that she did so *from eating her fill.*

1 AND 2 SAMUEL

1 and 2 Samuel,[27] which are treated as a single book in the traditional Hebrew Bible, present Israel's history from the time of Samuel to the later events in David's reign. Beginning with the circumstances leading to his birth, 1 Samuel recounts the career of Samuel, the last great judge, and then focuses on the first two kings of Israel, Saul and David. 2 Samuel continues the story of David from the time he learns of Saul's death to his kingship over Judah and then all Israel, and then on to his setbacks and later years.

Four scrolls of Samuel were discovered at Qumran, one from Cave 1 and three from Cave 4.[28] The oldest of these is 4QSam[b], which was copied about 250 BCE, making it one of the two earliest scrolls (the other being 4QExod-Lev[f]). 4QSam[c], which dates to roughly 100–75 BCE, is rather unique since the idiosyncratic scribe who copied it has also been identified as responsible for copying two other scrolls—the *Rule of the Community* (1QS) and the *Testimonia* (4Q175)—and for a correction in the Great Isaiah Scroll (1QIsa[a]). The most significant Samuel manuscript is 4QSam[a], which was copied about the middle of the first century BCE. This is one of the largest biblical scrolls from Qumran, preserving text ranging from the first chapter of 1 Samuel to the final chapter of 2 Samuel (thus containing both parts of the book of Samuel). With the exception of six chapters (1 Samuel 13, 22, and 29; 2 Samuel 1, 9, and 17), the four Samuel manuscripts preserve text from all thirty-one chapters of 1 Samuel and all twenty-four chapters of 2 Samuel.

It is not clear if there were two separate editions of the entire book in antiquity or only of specific passages. Two examples are the events leading to Samuel's birth in 1 Samuel 1, and the narrative of David and Goliath in 1 Samuel 17–18. Two of the scrolls (1QSam, 4QSam[b]) are very close to the Masoretic Text, but 4QSam[a] contains many agreements with the Septuagint as well as several independent readings. Although it contains some errors, this important manuscript preserves some original or superior readings that often help correct problems in the traditional text. Moreover, several agreements with 1 and 2 Chronicles show that this was the type of Samuel manuscript that the Chronicler used in composing his books (or, rather, book).

Some of the variant readings in 4QSam[a] involve individual words, phrases, or even entire sentences that were left out of the Masoretic Text or added as supplementary material. The most dramatic example occurs in 4QSam[a] at the end of 1 Samuel 10, where an entire paragraph that was missing from our Bibles for two thousand years has now been restored in the New Revised Standard Version, published in 1989. (The existence of the passage was already footnoted in the New American Bible of 1970). This paragraph describes the atrocities perpetrated by King Nahash of the Ammonites, and thus explains his otherwise unusual behavior in the first two verses of chapter 11. It is interesting to note that the Jewish historian Josephus, writing in the second half of the first century CE, recounts the same details in his account of the history of the Jewish people, the *Jewish Antiquities*:

> However, a month later, [Saul] began to win the esteem of all by the war with Naas, king of the Ammonites. For this monarch had done much harm to the Jews who had settled beyond the river Jordan, having invaded their territory with a large and warlike army. Reducing their cities to servitude, he not only by force and violence secured their subjection in the present, but by cunning and ingenuity weakened them in order that they might never again be able to revolt and escape from servitude to him; for he cut out the right eyes of all who either surrendered to him under oath or were captured by right of war. This he did with intent—since the left eye was covered by the buckler—to render them

utterly unserviceable. Having then so dealt with the people beyond Jordan, the Ammanite king carried his arms against those called Galadenians. Pitching his camp near the capital of his enemies, to wit Jabis, he sent envoys to them, bidding them instantly to surrender on the understanding that their right eyes would be put out: if not, he threatened to besiege and overthrow their cities: it was for them to choose, whether they preferred the cutting out of a small portion of the body or to perish utterly. (6.68–71), translated by H. St. J. Thackeray and R. Marcus)

This passage shows that the longer account found at the end of chapter 10 in 4QSam[a] was also in the Greek Bible used by Josephus. Thus our two most ancient witnesses attest that the longer ending was present in at least some ancient biblical manuscripts. In Box 6.7, the traditional, shorter Masoretic Text is represented by the King James Version, and the longer text found in 4QSam[a] is represented by the *Dead Sea Scrolls Bible* and the New Revised Standard Version.

The Samuel scrolls also help us to reassess the ancient Septuagint translation. Until the last decades of the twentieth century, many scholars attributed differences between the Greek Bible and the Masoretic Text to a free style, or a paraphrase, or even error on the part of the Septuagint translator. Scrolls such as 4QSam[a], however, frequently agree with the Septuagint when it differs from the Masoretic Text, which shows that the Greek translator was using a Hebrew text similar in form to some of the Qumran manuscripts.

1 AND 2 KINGS

As with Samuel, 1 and 2 Kings[29] form a single book in the traditional Hebrew Bible. Its chapters recount the history of the Israelite monarchy from the end of David's reign to the reigns of Jehoshaphat of Judah and Ahaziah of Israel (1 Kings), and then from the prophet Elisha to the fall of Jerusalem and the release of the exiled King Jehoiachin from prison (2 Kings). Only three manuscripts containing Kings were discovered in the Judean Desert, all of them at Qumran: one each from Caves 4, 5, and 6.[30] The oldest of these are 5QKings and pap6QKings, which were copied in the late second century BCE. Over ninety-four fragments of pap6QKings—which was written on fragile papyrus instead of the more common leather—were found; only seventeen have been identified and placed, since most preserve only a few letters each. Between them the three Kings manuscripts preserve portions of six chapters (1, 3, 7, 8, 12, and 22) of the twenty-two in 1 Kings, and six chapters (5, 6, 7, 8, 9, and 10) of the twenty-five in 2 Kings.

Besides numerous small variant readings, which are sometimes in agreement with the Greek text, the Qumran scrolls preserve more significant variants. Some of these are superior readings, but in other cases the Masoretic Text has the best text. One example of a superior reading is in 4QKings, a scroll that is generally close to the traditional text. In 1 Kings 8:16, however, 4QKings preserves a passage that was lost from the Masoretic Text when a scribe's eye skipped from one phrase to a similar phrase below (see Box 6.8).

1 AND 2 CHRONICLES

1 and 2 Chronicles,[31] which also form a single book in the traditional Hebrew Bible, are mostly a retelling of the events recorded in Samuel and Kings, but from a different viewpoint. Written after the Exile, these books show that, despite the destruction of the kingdoms of Israel and Judah, God was still keeping his promises and working out his plan for those who were living in Judah. Another prominent theme is the worship of God and

Box 6.7	*1 Samuel 10:25–11:2*

King James Version (1611)	*Dead Sea Scrolls Bible*	*NRSV (1989)*
25 Then Samuel told the people the manner of the kingdom, and wrote it in a book, and laid it up before the LORD. And Samuel sent all the people away, every man to his house. 26 And Saul also went home to Gibeah; and there went with him a band of men, whose hearts God had touched. 27 But the children of Belial said, How shall this man save us? And they despised him, and brought him no presents. But he held his peace.	25 [Then Samuel explained to the people the or]dinances of [the kingship and wrote them in a book, and deposited it in the LORD's presence. Then Samuel dismissed all the peo]ple; each *went*[1] to [his] *pla*[*ce*.[2] 26 S]aul [al]so [went to his house in Gibeah]. The valiant *men*[3] [wh]ose hearts the LO[RD][4] had touched [went] with *Saul*.[5] 27 But certain worthless men s[aid, "How will this man save us?" And] they despise[d] him and brought him no *gift*.[6] X [*Na*]*hash king of the* [*A*]*mmonites oppressed the Gadites and the Reubenites viciously. He put out the right* [*eye*] *of a*[*ll*] *of them and brought fe*[*ar and trembling*] *on* [*Is*]*rael. Not one of the Israelites in the region be*[*yond the Jordan*] *remained* [*whose*] *right eye Naha*[*sh king of*] *the Ammonites did n*[*ot pu*]*t out, except seven thousand men* [*who escaped from*] *the Ammonites and went to* [*Ja*]*besh-gilead.*[7] 11:1 Then *after about a month,*[8] Nahash the Ammonite went up and besieged Jabesh-[gilead]. So all the people of Jabesh said to Nahash, "[Make a covenant] with [us, and we will serve you." 2 But] Nahash [the Ammonite said t]o [th]em, "I will ma[ke it with you on this condition: that I gouge out the right eye of every one of you and so disgrace all Israel]."	25 Samuel told the people the rights and duties of the kingship; and he wrote them in a book and laid it up before the LORD. Then Samuel sent all the people back to their homes. 26 Saul also went to his home at Gibeah, and with him went warriors whose hearts God had touched. 27 But some worthless fellows said, "How can this man save us?" They despised him and brought him no present. But he held his peace. Now Nahash, king of the Ammonites, had been grievously oppressing the Gadites and the Reubenites. He would gouge out the right eye of each of them and would not grant Israel a deliverer. No one was left of the Israelites across the Jordan whose right eye Nahash, king of the Ammonites, had not gouged out. But there were seven thousand men who had escaped from the Ammonites and had entered Jabesh-gilead. 11:1 About a month later, Nahash the Ammonite went up and besieged Jabesh-gilead; and all the men of Jabesh said to Nahash, "Make a treaty with us, and we will serve you." 2 But Nahash the Ammonite said to them, "On this condition I will make a treaty with you, namely that I gouge out everyone's right eye, and thus put disgrace upon all Israel."
11:1 Then Nahash the Ammonite came up, and encamped against Jabesh-gilead: and all the men of Jabesh said unto Nahash, Make a covenant with us, and we will serve thee. 2 And Nahash the Ammonite answered them, On this condition will I make a covenant with you, that I may thrust out all your right eyes, and lay it for a reproach upon all Israel.		

1. 4QSamᵃ, LXX. Not in MT.　2. 4QSamᵃ, LXX. *House* MT.　3. 4QSamᵃ, LXX. Not in MT.　4. 4QSamᵃ, LXX. *God* MT.
5. 4QSamᵃ, LXX. MT has *with him* earlier in the sentence, after *went*.　6. 4QSamᵃ, LXX. MT adds *But he kept silent*.
7. 4QSamᵃ; cf. Josephus. Not in MT, LXX.　8. 4QSamᵃ, LXX. Not in MT.

Comment: 4QSamᵃ contains a longer text and provides two important pieces of information. First, it was Nahash's practice to gouge out people's right eyes. Second, we are told that 7,000 men who had fled from the Ammonites had actually sought refuge in Jabesh-gilead. This information provides a logical explanation for the otherwise strange and cruel behavior of Nahash in 1 Sam. 11:1–2.

(Adapted from AFU, 225.)

| Box 6.8 | 1 Kings 8:16–18 |

Dead Sea Scrolls Bible	*Masoretic Text (NRSV)*
16 "[From the day I brought my people Israel out from Egypt, I have not chosen a city from among the tribes of Israel to build a house for my name to be there, *nor did I choose any one*] *to be a leader over* [*my*] *people* [*Israel, but I have chosen Jerusalem for my name to be there,*[1] and I have chosen David]* to be over my people, *over*[2] [Israel." 17 Now David my father had it in mind to build a house for the name of the LORD, the God of I]srael. 18 But [the LORD] said [to David my father, "Because you had a mind to build a house for my name, you did well; for it was your intention]."	16 "Since the day that I brought my people Israel out of Egypt, I have not chosen a city from any of the tribes of Israel in which to build a house, for my name to be there; but I chose David to be over my people Israel." 17 My father David had it in mind to build a house for the name of the LORD, the God of Israel. 18 But the LORD said to my father David, "You did well to consider building a house for my name;"

1. 4QKings (= 2 Chron 6:5b–6a). MT omits, having skipped from the first occurrence of *my name to be there* to the second. LXX omits the first clause but retains the second, having skipped from *but I chose (Jerusalem)* to *but I chose (David)*. The MT of Chronicles retained the entire reading intact.   2. 4QKings. Not in MT, LXX.

(Adapted from AFU, 264)

organization of rituals in the Temple at Jerusalem, which was really founded by David, although it was built by his son Solomon.

Among the scrolls, only one small fragment of Chronicles was discovered in Cave 4 (4QChron; see Figure 6.3). Dated about 50–25 BCE, this piece preserves parts of a mere four verses from two chapters (2 Chron. 28:27 and 29:1–3) out of the sixty-five chapters of 1 and 2 Chronicles. It could be argued that 1 Chronicles was never among the scrolls in their complete state, but it seems that 4QChron originally contained 1 and 2 Chronicles, since the Chronicler's work traditionally forms a single book. The scarcity of Chronicles at Qumran could be by chance, with several other manuscripts simply being lost. More likely, however, the small number of scrolls is by design, since Chronicles has a strong focus on Jerusalem and the Temple, from which the Qumran community had removed itself.

The text preserved in 4QChron is close to the traditional Masoretic Text, with only three minor variants. Preceding the verses from 2 Chron. 28:27–29:3, however, are the remains of a few letters in the previous column. These do not match the traditional text of Chronicles within a chapter or two before the recognizable verses, which suggests that at this point 4QChron varies from the traditional text. Alternatively, the fragment may not be from a manuscript of Chronicles itself, but from another work that quotes Chronicles.

EZRA AND NEHEMIAH

Ezra and Nehemiah,[32] which constitute one book in the traditional Hebrew Bible, deal with the return of some exiles to Jerusalem from Babylon and the process of starting over. The book of Ezra includes the rebuilding of the Temple and the restoration of true wor-

Figure 6.3
A tiny fragment representing all that remains of Chronicles in the Dead Sea Scrolls (PAM 41.785).
Courtesy of the Israel Antiquities Authority

ship, while Nehemiah focuses on the rebuilding the city walls and the carrying out of religious and social reforms.

Only one scroll of Ezra (4QEzra), and none of Nehemiah, was found in the Judean Desert at Qumran. There is thus no evidence for the book of Nehemiah among the scrolls, but it may have been part of the Ezra scroll if Ezra-Nehemiah was a single book at this early stage (which is not certain). Copied around the middle of the first century BCE, 4QEzra survives in only three small fragments containing material from three chapters (4, 5, and 6) of the ten in Ezra. The small amount of preserved text is almost identical to the same passage in the Masoretic Text, with only four minor variant readings.

The book of Ezra provides one of the terms that the Qumran community appropriated for itself: the *yaḥad* (*community,* Ezra 4:3). Unfortunately, the word itself is no longer preserved in 4QEzra. This designation features in the title of the foundation document named the *Rule of the Community* (*Serek HaYaḥad*), which is discussed in Chapter 9.

ESTHER

With the possible exception of Nehemiah, Esther[33] is the only book in the traditional Hebrew Bible not represented among the manuscripts found at Qumran, Masada, and other sites near the Dead Sea. It could be argued that the Qumran community did include Esther scrolls in its library and that the absence of these writings is simply due to chance and the relatively small size of the book (ten chapters). Research and evidence from certain nonbiblical scrolls, however, show that Esther was rejected by the Qumran community for theological reasons. But what is the correct explanation for its decision not to include this book?

One possibility is the secular nature of the work, which makes no mention of God at all. Another is that the story concerns the marriage of Esther, who was a Jew, to a gentile Persian king, which would have been offensive to conservative Jewish groups such as the Essenes. A third possibility is the emphasis on retaliation in the later chapters (7–9) of Esther, which conflicts with some of the Qumran community's own writings. The *Rule of the Community,* for example, exhorts:

> To no man shall I return evil for evil, I shall pursue a man only for good; for with God resides the judgment of all the living, and He shall pay each man his recompense. (10:17–18)

Although there may be some truth in these explanations, the Qumran community's decision to reject Esther almost certainly arose from a different, overriding concern. The book of Esther introduces a new festival named Purim (Esth. 9:20–32), which is not mentioned in the books of Moses. This most likely caused the Qumranites to exclude this book from their library of sacred writings. That the community *did* reject this feast is confirmed by the Qumran calendrical texts, which chart festivals and holy days in their 364-day year. These documents do not include the festival of Purim, which has its beginnings in the story of Esther. We may conclude, then, that the Qumran community objected to this new festival and to the book that inaugurates it for the Jewish people.

The Scrolls and the Poetical Books

JOB

The book of Job[34] deals with the problem of undeserved suffering and disaster and why good people often experience great adversity. After losing his children and property and being afflicted with a terrible disease, Job struggles to find answers, first from his friends and then from God himself. The Hebrew text of this book is one of the most difficult found in the Hebrew Bible, partly because it contains poetry of high dramatic quality and partly because it may be modeled on an earlier drama that was not Israelite in origin.

The remnants of only four Job manuscripts were discovered at Qumran: one in Cave 2, and three in Cave 4.[35] Only eleven chapters (8, 9, 13, 14, and 31–37) are represented of the forty-two that make up this large book. The largest scroll, with more than twenty-two small fragments preserved, is 4QJob[a]. The oldest manuscript is 4QpaleoJob[c], which was copied at a very early date (ca. 225–150 BCE) in the paleo-Hebrew script (for comments on this ancient script, see "The Paleo-Hebrew Biblical Scrolls" later).

In addition, two Aramaic translations, or targums, of Job were found: one in Cave 4 (4QtgJob, or 4Q157) and another in Cave 11 (11QtgJob, or 11Q10). There is only one other targum among the scrolls: 4QtgLev, or 4Q156, which preserves portions of Leviticus in Aramaic. Of the Job targums, the Cave 11 scroll (copied in the early first century CE) is far more extensive, preserving portions of text from Job 17–42. The portion that appears in Box 6.9[36] illustrates how the translation is quite literal, but also how the translator did not always understand the Hebrew text before him in ways that modern scholars do.

Unfortunately, the small amount of text preserved in the Job scrolls and targums from Qumran offers only limited help for better understanding the difficult Hebrew of the traditional text (to which 4QJob[a] is the closest). Most of the variant readings are quite minor; in Job 33:26, for example, 4QJob[a] uses a form of the word *God (El)* that is more familiar than the form found in the Masoretic Text *(Eloah)*. It is also significant that the *Targum of Job* ends with lines corresponding to Job 42:9–11, whereas the Masoretic Text has an additional passage dealing with the restoration of Job's fortunes (42:10–17). The Job scrolls also show that the Elihu speeches (chaps. 32–37), which many scholars believe were not part of the original composition, were included in this book before the common era.

PSALMS

The book of Psalms,[37] or the Psalter, has been called the "Hymn Book of the Second Temple Period" and for Jews and Christians alike is the hymn book and prayer book of the Bible. The Masoretic Text contains 150 Psalms divided into five books, or collections, most

Box 6.9	*Job 42:9–12*

11QtgJob	*Masoretic Text* (NRSV)
(So Eliphaz the Temanite and Bildad) **Col. 38,** [1] [the Shuhite and Zophar the Naamathite went and] did [what they had been told by] [2]God. *And G[o]d listened to the voice of Job and forgave* [3]*them their sins because of him.*	[9]So Eliphaz the Temanite and Bildad the Shuhite and Zophar the Naamathite went and did what the LORD had told them; *and the LORD accepted Job's prayer.*
Then God turned back to Job in compassion	[10]And the LORD restored the fortunes of Job when he had prayed for his friends;
[4]and gave him twice what he once had possessed. There came to [5]Job all his *friends and brethren* and those who had known him, and they ate bread [6]with him in his house. They consoled him	and the LORD gave Job twice as much as he had before. [11]Then there came to him all his *brothers and sisters* and all who had known him before, and they ate bread with him in his house; they showed him sympathy and comforted him
for all the evil that [7]God had brought upon him, and each man gave him *one sheep* [8]and one gold ring.	for all the evil that the LORD had brought upon him; and each of them gave him *a piece of money* and a gold ring.
[9]So God blessed J[ob's] latt[er days, and h]e [had] [10][fourteen thousand] sh[eep . . .]	[12]The LORD blessed the latter days of Job more than his beginning; and he had fourteen thousand sheep,

---

Comment: The translator's interpretative approach is clear by his treatment of Job 42:9 in l. 2 (MT: *and the LORD accepted Job's prayer*); of Job 42:11 in l. 5 (MT: *brothers and sisters*); and of Job 42:11 in l. 7 (MT: *a piece of money;* in this case the Hebrew word that he translated as *sheep* can also mean *money*).

(adapted from WAC, 453)

---

likely in imitation of the five books of Moses that constitute the Pentateuch. The Greek Psalter has an additional Psalm *(Psalm 151)* not found in the traditional Hebrew text. Seventy-three Psalms are associated with David, especially by their headings, and several more are attributed to other groups (e.g., twelve to the Sons of Asaph) or figures (e.g., two to Solomon) or are untitled (the thirty-four "orphan" Psalms).

There are no fewer than thirty-nine Psalms scrolls, plus at least one that incorporates a Psalm, ranging in date from the mid-second century BCE (4QPs[a]) to about 50–68 CE (e.g., 4QPs[c] and 11QapocrPs). Thirty-seven manuscripts were found at Qumran: three in Cave 1,[38] one each in Caves 2, 3, 5, 6, and 8,[39] twenty-three in Cave 4,[40] and six in Cave 11.[41] Three more were discovered farther south along the Dead Sea: one at Naḥal Ḥever and two at Masada.[42] Of all the works found in the Dead Sea Scrolls, the Psalms are represented by the greatest number of manuscripts. Although none is complete, several scrolls are very substantial, notably 11QPs[a], followed by 4QPs[a], 5/6ḤevPs, 4QPs[b], 4QPs[c], and 4QPs[e] in descending order.

Of the 150 Psalms found in the traditional Hebrew Psalter, 126 are preserved in the Psalms scrolls and a few other manuscripts such as the *pesharim,* or commentaries. The remaining twenty-four Psalms were most likely included, but are now lost due to deterioration and damage. Of Psalms 1–89, nineteen no longer survive, but of Psalms 90–150 only five are not represented, since the beginnings of scrolls are usually on the outside and are thus more prone to deterioration.

In addition to these Psalms at least fourteen "apocryphal" Psalms or similar compositions are also distributed among four manuscripts (4QPs^f, 11QPs^a, 11QPs^b, and 11QapocrPs). Six of these compositions were previously familiar to scholars;[43] five will be discussed among the Apocrypha and Pseudepigrapha in Chapter 8. The other eight or nine compositions were completely unknown prior to the discovery of the Dead Sea Scrolls. These are described in some detail below, since they do not feature in Chapters 8 or 9 later in this book. The presence of these other psalms or compositions in some of the Psalms scrolls reminds us that the book of Psalms at Qumran should not automatically be equated with the Psalter that appears in our Bibles.

Different Psalters in the Psalms Scrolls

What form or forms of the Psalter are found in the Psalms scrolls? For Psalms 1–89 or so, the Psalms scrolls contain material very much in the sequence familiar in Jewish and Christian Bibles. In 4QPs^a and 4QPs^q, however, Psalm 31 is followed directly by 33, and in 4QPs^a Psalm 38 is followed directly by 71. But for Psalms 91 onward—90 is not preserved—the form of the Psalter is considerably different. The most substantial evidence is in the Great Psalms Scroll from Cave 11 (11QPs^a), which was copied in about 50 CE and preserves forty-nine compositions in the following order (the siglum → indicates that the second composition directly follows the first):

> Psalm 101→102→103; 109; 118→104→147→105→146→148 [+ 120]→121→122
> →123→124 →125→126→127→128→129→130→131→132→119→135→136
> (with Catena)→145 (with postscript)→154→Plea for Deliverance→139→137→
> 138→ Sirach 51→Apostrophe to Zion→Psalm 93→141→133→144→155→
> 142→143→149→150→Hymn to the Creator→David's Last Words→David's
> Compositions→Psalm 140→134→151A→151B→blank column *[end]*

This arrangement differs greatly from the one found in the Masoretic and Septuagint Psalters, both because of the different order of the material and the presence of additional compositions. For Psalms 91 onward, then, five different arrangements are evident in the Psalms scrolls.

The most prominent is the one found in 11QPs^a, 11QPs^b, and 4QPs^e, which together may be termed the *11QPs^a-Psalter* (i.e., Psalms 1–89 plus the arrangement found in 11QPs^a). The second arrangement is conveniently termed the *MT-150 Psalter*, as found in the Masoretic Text. None of the Psalms scrolls from Qumran *unambiguously* confirms the arrangement of this Psalter, but it is evident in the second scroll from Masada (MasPs^b), which ends with Psalm 150.

The other three arrangements are much smaller. One is the *Four Psalms Against Demons* in 11QapocrPs, consisting of three previously unknown psalms followed by Psalm 91. Another is found in 4QPs^b, which preserves material from Psalms 91–118, but with Psalm 103 followed directly by 112 (thus excluding Psalms 92–111). The final arrangement is in 4QPs^f, which contains Psalms 22, 107, and 109, followed by three previously unknown psalms: the *Apostrophe to Zion, Eschatological Hymn,* and *Apostrophe to Judah.*[44]

This evidence suggests that at least two major editions of the book of Psalms are preserved in the scrolls: the *MT-150 Psalter*, which is found in the Masoretic Text and the Septuagint (although the Greek Bible has several variant readings and ends with Psalm 151); and the *11QPs^a-Psalter* (Psalms 1–89 plus the arrangement found in 11QPs^a). It should be pointed out, however, that scholars are divided as to whether the Psalms scrolls contain more than one edition of the book of Psalms. For M. H. Goshen-Gottstein, Shemaryahu Talmon, Patrick Skehan, Menahem Haran, and Emanuel Tov, the Psalms scrolls basically contain an early form of the Psalter as found in the Masoretic Text (i.e., the Proto-Masoretic form). For these scholars, the *11QPs^a-Psalter* is not an edition of the book of Psalms, but rather a secondary collection, based on the *MT-150 Psalter,* for liturgical or instructive purposes. In contrast, for James A. Sanders, Gerald Wilson, Peter Flint, and Eugene Ulrich, the *11QPs^a-Psalter* is a genuine edition, indeed the foremost edition, of the book of Psalms in the Dead Sea Scrolls.

New Readings in the Psalms Scrolls

There are dozens of readings in the Psalms scrolls that offer new insights into the meaning of specific passages in the Psalter and help clear up difficulties in the Masoretic Text. Some of these readings are already included in most modern Bible translations, and several more will be incorporated as the impact and importance of the scrolls become more widely appreciated.

A MISSING VERSE FROM PSALM 145

Scholars agree that a verse is missing from Psalm 145 in the Masoretic Text for a very good reason: this is an acrostic Psalm, with each verse beginning with a successive letter of the Hebrew alphabet. Although there are twenty-two letters in this alphabet, the Psalm contains only twenty-one verses, because a verse beginning with *nun* should come between v. 13 (the *mem* verse) and v. 14 (the *samek* verse). The missing verse is very evident in the Masoretic Text and the King James Version (see Box 6.10).

Box 6.10	*Psalm 145:12–14*

Masoretic Text (NRSV)	*King James Version*
12 לְהוֹדִיעַ ׀ לִבְנֵי הָאָדָם גְּבוּרֹתָיו וּכְבוֹד הֲדַר מַלְכוּתוֹ׃	12 To make known to the sons of men his mighty acts, and the glorious majesty of his kingdom.
13 מַלְכוּתְךָ מַלְכוּת כָּל־עֹלָמִים וּמֶמְשַׁלְתְּךָ בְּכָל־דּוֹר וָדוֹר׃	13 Thy kingdom is an everlasting kingdom, and thy dominion endureth throughout all generations.
14 סוֹמֵךְ יְהוָה לְכָל־הַנֹּפְלִים וְזוֹקֵף לְכָל־הַכְּפוּפִים׃	14 The LORD upholdeth all that fall, and raiseth up all those that be bowed down.

It is interesting to note that the Septuagint supplies an additional verse (which we shall call 13b) following v. 13 (which we shall call 13a):

> 13a Your Kingdom is a kingdom of all the ages, and your dominion is through all generations.
> 13b The Lord is faithful in all his words, and gracious in all his deeds.

This suggests that the Hebrew text used by the Greek translator had the missing *nun* verse. Among the Dead Sea Scrolls, 11QPs^a is the only scroll to preserve Psalm 145, including a recurring refrain. For v. 13 this manuscript contains not only the *mem* verse but the missing *nun* verse as well! In lines 2–3 of column 7, the *nun* verse is found in its expected place. There we read: נאמן אלוהים בדבריו וחסיד בכול מעשיו (*God is faithful in his words, and gracious in all his deeds);* see Box 6.11.

Box 6.11   *Psalm 145:12–14 in the Dead Sea Scrolls Bible*

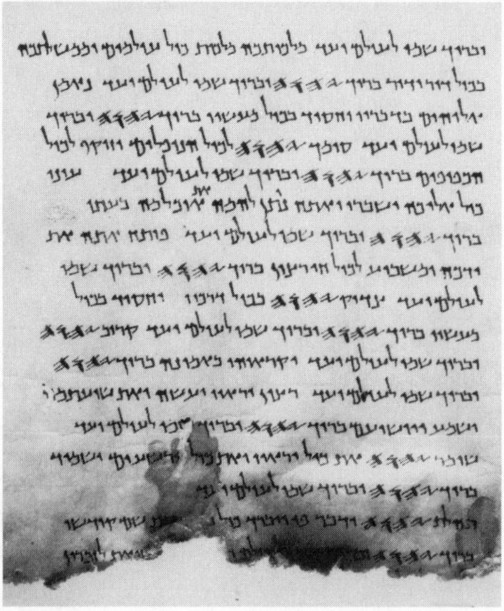

Figure 6.4
Part of column 7 of Psalm 145 in 11QPs[a]. The missing *nun* verse that has fallen out of the Masoretic Text is preserved in lines 2–3 (PAM 43.786).
Courtesy of the Israel Antiquities Authority

12 [. . . *Blessed be the* LORD] *and blessed be his name forever and ever.*[1] 13 Your kingdom is an everlasting kingdom, and your dominion endures throughout all generations. *Blessed be the* LORD *and blessed be his name forever and ever. God*[2] *is faithful in his words, and gracious in all his deeds.*[3] *Blessed be the* LORD *and blessed be his name forever and ever.* 14 The LORD upholds all are falling, and raises up all who are bowed down. *Blessed be the* LORD *and blessed be his name forever and ever.* . . .

1. A constant refrain at the end of each verse in 11QPs[a]. Not in MT, LXX.
2. 11QPs[a]. *The* LORD LXX; not in MT.
3. *God is faithful in his words, and gracious in all his deeds* 11QPs[a], MT[ms], LXX. Not in MT.

(AFU, 571)

This reading is so convincing that the *nun* verse has been included in many modern English Bibles, including the New Revised Standard Version, the New American Bible, the New International Version, and the Good News Bible. This is an important example of how the Dead Sea Scrolls sometimes preserve material that has fallen out of the Masoretic Text during the process of transmission (although it is preserved in one medieval Hebrew manuscript classified as Kennicott no. 142).

THE ORIGINAL READING OF PSALM 22:16

Psalm 22 begins as follows: "My God, my God, why have you forsaken me? Why are you so far from helping me, from the words of my groaning?" This familiar piece has proved significant in both Jewish and Christian exegesis, and is quoted by Jesus as he suffers on the cross (Mark 15:34; Matt 27:46). When we turn to v. 16 (Heb. v. 17) in the Masoretic Text, however, a difficult and puzzling reading is found:

> [15]My strength is dried up like a potsherd; and my tongue cleaves to my jaws; and you have brought me into the dust of death. [16] For dogs have surrounded me; the assembly of the wicked have encompassed me; *like a lion* are my hands and my feet.

Box 6.12	Psalm 22:15–16 (16–17)	
5/6ḤevPs	*Dead Sea Scrolls Bible*	*Septuagint*
16 [יבש כחרס כחי] [ולשוני מדבק מלקוחי] ולעפר מות תשפתני 17[כי סבבוני כלבים] עדת מרעים הקיפוני כארו ידיה ורגלי	15 [My strength is dried up like a potsherd], and my tongue *melts in* [my mouth][1] [They] have placed [me][2] *as the dust of death.*[3] 16 [For] dogs are [all around me]; a gang of evil[doers] encircles me. *They have pierced*[4] my hands and my feet.	16 ἐξηράνθη ὡς ὄστρακον ἡ ἰσχύς μου, καὶ ἡ γλῶσσά μου κεκόλληται τῷ λάρυγγί μου, καὶ εἰς χοῦν θανάτου κατήγαγές με. 17 ὅτι ἐκύκλωσάν με κύνες πολλοί, συναγωγὴ πονηρευομένων περιέσχον με, ὤρυξαν χεῖράς μου καὶ πόδας.

1. Probable meaning 4QPs[f]. *sticks to my palate* MT, LXX 2. Probable meaning 4QPs[f]. *and you have laid me* MT, LXX.
3. 4QPs[f]. *in the dust of death* MT, LXX. 4. 5/6ḤevPs, MT[ms], LXX. *Like a lion are* MT.

(AFU, 519)

The different reading in v. 16 depends on a single word: *k'ry* (כארי), which means *like a lion*. The Gospel writers quote from the Greek Bible, which reads; "*They have pierced* my hands and feet." Some scholars have suggested that the Septuagint reading represents a modification of the Hebrew *like a lion*, perhaps because it was difficult to make sense of the Hebrew. Another suggestion is that early Christian editors changed the Greek text in order to find evidence for Jesus' crucifixion in the Hebrew Bible.

Among the Dead Sea Scrolls, the reading in question is not preserved at Qumran, but in the Psalms scroll from Naḥal Ḥever (5/6ḤevPs), which is textually very close to the Masoretic Text. In line 12 of column 10 we read: "*They have pierced* my hands and feet"! For the crucial word (כארו) the Hebrew form is grammatically difficult; but it is clearly a verb, not a noun, and means *they have bored* or *they have dug* or they *have pierced*. A fuller picture, together with the relevant footnotes, appears in the *Dead Sea Scrolls Bible* (see Box 6.12).

New Compositions in the Psalms Scrolls

In addition to the six "apocryphal" psalms or similar compositions that were previously known to scholars (see Chapter 8), several more pieces were completely unknown prior to the discovery of the scrolls. These compositions are the *Apostrophe to Zion*, the *Eschatological Hymn* and the *Apostrophe to Judah*, the *Catena, David's Compositions*, the *Hymn to the Creator*, the *Plea for Deliverance*, and *Three Songs Against Demons*. Although ten titles are listed, the precise number may be as low as eight, since the *Apostrophe to Judah* and the *Eschatological Hymn* may in fact be a single work, and the *Catena* forms a longer ending to Psalm 136, but has been classified by some scholars as a separate piece.

THE *APOSTROPHE TO ZION*

Like several other Psalms (e.g., 46, 48, 76, and 87), the *Apostrophe to Zion* focuses on Jerusalem, in this case invoking blessing on her, affirming the defeat of her enemies, and looking forward to her salvation and everlasting righteousness. This is an acrostic composition, with each successive verse beginning with the next letter of the Hebrew alphabet. The *Apostrophe* is found in two collections: the *11QPs^a-Psalter* (col. 22 of 11QPs^a) and in 4QPs^f (cols. 7–8).[45]

Eschatological Hymn

[4]many . . .
And let them praise [5]the name of the LORD. [F]or he comes to judge [6]every ac[ti]on, to remove the wicked [7]from the earth, [so that the children of] iniquity will not [8]be found. [And] the hea[v]ens [will give] their dew, [9]and there will be no searing dro[ught within] their borders. And the earth [10]will yield its fruit in its season, and will not [11]cheat of its [pro]duce. The [12]fruit trees [will ...] their vines, and [...] will not cheat of its [... [13] ...] The [14] oppressed will eat, and those who fear the Lord [will be satisfied] . . .

Apostrophe to Judah

[5]. . . Then let heavens and earth give praise together; [6]then let all the stars of twilight give praise! [7]Rejoice, O Judah, in your joy; [8]be happy in your happiness, and dance in your dance. [9]Celebrate your pilgrim feasts, fulfill your vows, for no longer is [10]Belial in your midst. May your hand be lifted up! [11]May your right hand prevail! See, enemies will [12]perish, and all [13]evildoers will be scattered. But you, O Lord, are forev[er]; [14]your glory will be forev[er and ev]er. [15]Praise the Lord!

(AFU, 588–89)

THE *ESCHATOLOGICAL HYMN* AND THE *APOSTROPHE TO JUDAH*

These two compositions were unknown to scholars prior to the discovery of the Dead Sea Scrolls, but are now available to us in 4QPs^f. The *Eschatological Hymn* offers praise to God, but with an eschatological emphasis (i.e., with a view to the end times). The *Apostrophe to Judah* is also eschatological, but with a special focus on Judah. It is also highly anthological, containing many words and phrases known from other parts of the Hebrew Bible. Early editors of the scrolls, followed by most scholars, have treated these as two separate works. Some scholars, however, view both pieces as parts of a single acrostic poem.

THE *CATENA*

In column 16 of 11QPs^a and in 11QPs^b this longer ending to Psalm 136 contains material that is also found in Psalm 118. Scholars originally termed it the *Catena* (i.e., a connected series of verses). Since Psalm 118 itself is found earlier in 11QPs^a, this cannot be a different form of that Psalm. Some scholars have suggested that the *Catena* is in fact a separate composition altogether, but it is more likely a longer ending to Psalm 136 since it follows Ps. 136:26 with virtually no break in 11QPs^a (elsewhere this scroll typically has spaces between successive compositions or starts them on the next line). Because almost all its contents are found in Psalm 118, the verses of the *Catena* are numbered accordingly (vv. 1, 15, 16, 8, 8, X, and 29, with X denoting an unknown verse).

DAVID'S COMPOSITIONS

This important piece is really a prose epilogue to the *11QPs^a-Psalter,* although it is found in the second to last column (27) of 11QPs^a. *David's Compositions* clearly asserts that David is the author of the Great Psalms Scroll (and thus also of the *11QPs^a-Psalter*), thereby claiming that its arrangement and compositions were inspired by God himself. Note especially line 11: "All these he composed through prophecy . . ." The numbers (e.g., 364, 52, and 30) show that this Psalter was arranged in accordance with the year, weeks, and months of the 364-day solar calendar, which was followed by the Qumran community, rather than the lunar calendar, which has 354 days. The text appears in Box 6.13.

> ### Box 6.13   David's Compositions
>
> [2]And David, the son of Jesse, was wise, and a light like the light of the sun, and literate, [3]and discerning and perfect in all his ways before God and men. And the LORD gave [4]him a discerning and enlightened spirit. And he wrote [5]3,600 psalms; and songs to sing before the altar over the whole-burnt [6]perpetual offering every day, for all the days of the year, 364; [7]and for the offering of the Sabbaths, 52 songs; and for the offering of the New [8]Moons and for all the Solemn Assemblies and for the Day of Atonement, 30 songs. [9]And all the songs that he spoke were 446, and songs [10]for making music over the stricken, 4. And the total was 4,050. [11]All these he composed through prophecy which was given him from before the Most High.
>
> (AFU, 583)

THE *HYMN TO THE CREATOR*

Preserved only in 11QPs[a], this composition may be classified as a wisdom psalm praising God as Creator. It has clear affinities with Psalm 104, since both compositions draw on cosmic and creation themes from Genesis 1. The text appears in Box 6.14.

THE *PLEA FOR DELIVERANCE*

The *Plea* is mainly found in 11QPs[a], with a few lines also preserved in 11QPs[b]. This fascinating composition features a prayer for deliverance and appeals for God's forgiveness and protection. Embedded within the prayer are praise and thanksgiving for God's kindness and faithfulness. About twenty verses are preserved, but the first four or five verses are now lost.[46]

THREE SONGS AGAINST DEMONS

The manuscript known as *11QApocryphal Psalms* (11QapocrPs, or 11Q11), is dated about 50–70 CE and most likely contains four psalms for use in exorcisms against demons. Many

> ### Box 6.14   Hymn to the Creator
>
> [1]Great and holy is the LORD, the holiest of holy ones for every generation. [2]Majesty precedes him and following him is the rush of many waters. [3]Grace and truth surround his presence; truth and justice and righteousness are the foundation of his throne. [4]Separating light from deep darkness, he established the dawn by the knowledge of his mind. [5]When all his angels had witnessed it they sang aloud; for he showed them what they had not known: [6]Crowning the hills with fruit, good food for every living being. [7]Blessed be he who makes the earth by his power, establishing the world in his wisdom. [8]In his understanding he stretched out the heavens, and brought forth [wind] from his st[orehouses]. [9]He made [lightning for the rai]n, and caused mist[s] to rise [from] the end [of the earth].
>
> (AFU, 582–83)

> **Box 6.15**   *The Third Song Against Demons*
>
> Col. 5.4A Psalm of David. Again[st . . . An incanta]tion in the name of the Lor[D. To be invoked at an]y time 5the heav[ens. When] he comes to you at nig[ht], you will [say] to him: 6"Who are you? [Withdraw from] humanity and from the offspring of the ho[ly one]s! For your appearance is one of 7[delu]sion, and your horns are horns of [illu]sion. You are darkness, not light, 8[wicked]ness, not righteousness [. . .] the commander of the army, the Lord [will send] you [down 9into] deepest [Sheo]l, [. . . the] two bronze [ga]tes th[rough which n]o 10light [can enter], and [the] sun [will] not [shine for you] tha[t rises 11upon the] righteous to [. . . And] then you shall say: [. . . 12 . . . the right]eous, to come [. . .] for a de[mon] to harm him, [. . . 13 . . . of tr]uth from [. . . because] he has [righ]teousness to [. . .] 14 [. . .] and . . .
>
> (AFU, 540–41)

scholars believe these to be the "four songs for playing over the stricken" that are mentioned in *David's Compositions,* part of the Great Psalms Scroll (11QPs^a). The first three of these exorcism songs were unknown until the discovery of the Dead Sea Scrolls, but the fourth is found in modern Bibles as Psalm 91. Psalm 91 has brought comfort and hope to Jews and Christians over the centuries. Not only does it evoke God's help and protection against physical and human dangers, this psalm has been connected with exorcisms of demonic forces in both rabbinic and church traditions.[47]

Box 6.15 contains the third of these songs. Attributed to David, this psalm is uttered against a demon or evil spirit. The reference to the demon's horns in line 7 is particularly interesting in view of popular depictions of the devil as having horns.

PROVERBS

As a collection of moral and religious teachings, the book of Proverbs[48] was an important book in Israel for training in wisdom, prudence, and moral character. Its authorship was traditionally attributed to Solomon, Israel's wisest king (Prov. 1:1). It is surprising that scraps from only two Proverbs scrolls were found at Qumran, both in Cave 4,[49] and both copied in the late first century BCE or early first century CE. Of the thirty-one chapters in this major wisdom book, only six are represented (1, 2, 7, 13, 14, and 15) in the Proverbs scrolls.

There are major differences between the Masoretic Text and the Septuagint of Proverbs, which represent two different editions of the book. The fragments from Qumran, however, seem to agree with the traditional Hebrew edition. Just a few variant readings are preserved, involving only single letters but producing noticeable differences in meaning. One example is in Prov. 1:32, where 4QProv^a reads: "For the *narrow-mindedness* (Hebrew *mwškt*) of [simpletons shall kill them. . . . ," whereas the Masoretic Text reads: "For the *turning away* (Hebrew *mšwbt*) of simpletons shall kill them. . . ." A second example is in Prov. 14:32, where 4QProv^a agrees with the Masoretic Text: ". . . but the right]eous [have refug]e *in their death* (Hebrew *bmwtw*)." The Septuagint, in contrast, reads ". . . *in their piety* (τῇ ἑαυτοῦ ὁσιότητι, from the Hebrew *btwmw*)."

A verse of Proverbs is quoted explicitly in one of the foundational works of the Qumran community, the *Damascus Document* (CD). In CD 11:19–21 the command is given not to send an "offering to the altar through anyone impure . . . ; for it is written, 'The sacrifice of the wicked is detestable; but the prayer of the righteous is like a proper offering.'" This quotation from Prov. 15:8 has some interesting variants from the Masoretic Text, which reads, "The sacrifice of the wicked is detestable *to the* LORD, but the prayer of *the upright* is *his delight*."

ECCLESIASTES

The book of Ecclesiastes (Qohelet)[50] contains the words of the Teacher or the Philosopher, traditionally held to be Solomon. This was a man who reflected deeply about life: its transitory nature, contradictions, and injustices. Only two manuscripts of Ecclesiastes were discovered at Qumran,[51] the older being 4QQoh^a, which dates to about 175–150 BCE and is thus among the oldest scrolls at Qumran. 4QQoh^a is currently housed at the Amman Museum in Jordan, rather than at the Rockefeller Museum in Jerusalem, where 4QQoh^b and virtually all the other Cave 4 scrolls reside. Between them, these two manuscripts preserve text from four chapters (1, 5, 6, and 7) of the twelve that make up the book of Ecclesiastes.

Like the Masoretic Text and the Septuagint, the two Ecclesiastes scrolls generally exhibit a single edition of this book, although 4QQoh^a in particular preserves several variant readings. Most of these variants are minor, but a few are more significant. One example is at Eccles. 7:6, where 4QQoh^a has "[Extortion makes] the wise [foolish], and [a bribe] *perverts* [the heart]," as opposed to ". . . and a bribe *destroys* the heart" in the Masoretic Text and Septuagint. In Eccles. 7:19, the same scroll agrees with the Septuagint by reading "[Wisdom] *helps* [the wise more than ten rulers] who [are] in a city," whereas the Masoretic Text reads "Wisdom *strengthens* the wise . . ."

SONG OF SONGS

The Song of Songs (whose title means "The Greatest of All Songs"), or Canticles,[52] is a collection of love poems, several of which are very erotic and romantic. Some of the early rabbis and early church fathers, disturbed by this book's celebration of sexual love, tried to prevent its acceptance into the canon of the Hebrew Bible and Christian Old Testament. Others, however, recognized the Song of Songs as Scripture and understood it in different ways. Some Jewish sages interpreted the Song in terms of the relationship between God (the Bridegroom) and Israel (the Beloved, or Bride), while many church fathers understood it as depicting the relationship between Christ and his Church. In more recent times, however, both Jews and Christians have increasingly come to recognize and appreciate the sexual and romantic nature of the Song of Songs.

Four manuscripts of this little book were discovered at Qumran: three in Cave 4 and one in Cave 6.[53] All were copied in the Herodian period (between 30 BCE and 68 or 70 CE), the latest being 6QCant (ca. 50 CE). Between them these scrolls preserve text from seven of the Song's eight chapters.

Two of these manuscripts deserve special mention, both because they are the best preserved and because each has a number of interesting features. The first is 4QCant^a, in which the text between Cant. 4:7 and 6:11 is completely missing. Since in the traditional Masoretic Text Cant. 4:7 forms the *end* of a content unit and Cant. 6:11 is at the *beginning* of another unit, it appears that the absence of Cant. 4:8–6:10 was no mere accident. In other words, this material was deliberately omitted or was not part of the text being copied by the scribe.

Box 6.16	*Song of Songs 4:1–7*

Dead Sea Scrolls Bible	*Masoretic Text (NRSV)*
4:1 [How beautiful you are], my lo[ve]. O ho[w beauti]ful! Your eyes are like doves behind your veil; like a flock of go[ats is your hair, descend]ing from Mount Gilead. 2 Like a flock of newly-shorn ewes are your teeth (that) have come up from the [washing], all of which bear twins, and not one among them has lost its young. 3 Your lips are like a scarlet ribbon and your mouth is lovely. *Your chin is like a piece of pomegranate*[1] and is behind your veil.	4:1 How beautiful you are, my love, how very beautiful! Your eyes are doves behind your veil. Your hair is like a flock of goats, moving down the slopes of Gilead. 2 Your teeth are like a flock of shorn ewes that have come up from the washing, all of which bear twins, and not one among them is bereaved. 3 Your lips are like a crimson thread, and your mouth is lovely. Your cheeks are like halves of a pomegranate behind your veil.
4 [Your neck is like the tower of David, built in ripples]; on it hang a thousand bucklers, all the shields of the mighty men. 5 [Your twin breasts are like two fawns, like the twins of a gazelle] (which) feed among the lilies. 6 Until [the day] breathes [and the shadows flee, I will make my way to the mountain of myr]rh, *to the hill*[2] of incense. 7 [You] are altogether [beautiful, my love; there is no flaw in you]!	4 Your neck is like the tower of David, built in courses; on it hang a thousand bucklers, all of them shields of warriors. 5 Your two breasts are like two fawns, twins of a gazelle, that feed among the lilies. 6 Until the day breathes and the shadows flee, I will hasten to the mountain of myrrh and the hill of frankincense. 7 You are altogether beautiful, my love; there is no flaw in you.

1. 4QCant[a] (most likely *your chin*). *Your cheeks are like pomegranate-halves* 4QCant[b], MT, LXX.   2. 4QCant[a], MT[mss]. *and to the hill* MT, LXX.

Comment: In 4QCant[a], the text between Cant 4:7 and 6:11 was omitted by the scribe or not part of the text he was copying. In 4Cant[b], chap. 4:4–7 was omitted by the scribe or not part of the text he was transcribing, perhaps because of the beloved's breasts mentioned in v. 5.

(Adapted from AFU, 615–16)

When compared with the size of the book as a whole, the section missing in this scroll is very large (about 30 percent). One explanation is the sensual language and erotic imagery found in much of the missing passage; the Song of Songs was evidently a controversial, even disturbing, book to many readers before the time of Jesus (see Box 6.16).

The second noteworthy scroll is 4QCant[b], which features several scribal errors and, although written in Hebrew, contains several Aramaic word forms and several unusual scribal markings. Two large segments (3:6–8 and 4:4–7) are missing in the scroll, which possibly ended at 5:1. 4QCant[b] probably contained only the first half of the Song of Songs as found in modern Bibles. It is interesting to note that 4QCant[a] and 4QCant[b] each lack a section at exactly the same point (Cant 4:7). But whereas 4QCant[a] omits a large piece of text *starting* after 4:7, 4QCant[b] omits the three verses *ending* with 4:7.

When these two scrolls were copied, the Song of Songs as a work may well have contained all eight chapters, with 4QCant[a] and 4QCant[b] deliberately omitting large blocks of text or containing only excerpts from the larger book. Another possibility is that the text of the Song was not settled by the late first century BCE, or that these two scrolls may point to alternative editions of this little book.

The Scrolls and the Prophets

ISAIAH

For both Jews and Christians, Isaiah[54] is an important book in view of its message of judgment and comfort and its visions of the end times and the coming Kingdom of God. Many scholars believe that chapters 1–36 (or 1–39) are the work of Isaiah of Jerusalem (who lived in the second half of the eighth century BCE), that chapters 40–55 record the prophecies of Second Isaiah (an unnamed prophet who ministered after the fall of Jerusalem in 587 BCE and during the exile that followed), and that chapters 56–66 were written by Second Isaiah or other prophets in a similar style. The Isaiah scrolls found in the Judean Desert are of special interest, both because of their contents and because the Great Isaiah Scroll (1QIsa[a]) is the best known of all the Dead Sea Scrolls and the only one to preserve a biblical book virtually intact.

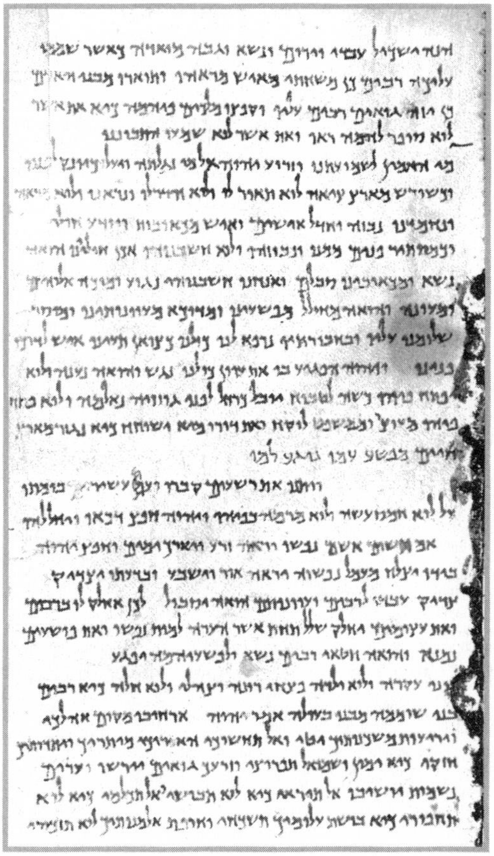

Isaiah was one of the three most popular books at Qumran, with twenty-one manuscripts recovered. The only books represented more often are the Psalms, with thirty-six scrolls, and Deuteronomy, with thirty. At Qumran, two Isaiah scrolls were found in Cave 1,[55] eighteen in Cave 4,[56] and one in Cave 5 (5QIsa). One more manuscript was discovered farther south at Wadi Murabbaʿat (MurIsa). Although only 1QIsa[a] survives intact, a few others are quite substantial (1QIsa[b], 4QIsa[b], and 4QIsa[c]); together, the fragmentary Isaiah scrolls preserve generous portions of the book. These manuscripts were copied over the course of nearly two centuries, from about 125 BCE (1QIsa[a]) to about 60 CE (4QIsa[c]).

The most famous of all the scrolls, the Great Isaiah Scroll (1QIsa[a]) was the only one to emerge virtually complete from the caves of Qumran (see Figure 6.5). The orthography (spelling) is very full, and paleographic analysis shows that the manuscript was copied in about 125 BCE. In its fifty-four columns, 1QIsa[a] preserves all sixty-six chapters of Isaiah, except for small gaps resulting from leather damage (notably in cols. 1–9). The text of this scroll is generally in agreement with the Masoretic Text, but it contains many variant readings and corrections, which are of great interest to scholars.

Figure 6.5
The Great Isaiah Scroll (1QIsa[a])
Courtesy of John C. Trever

For the book of Isaiah the scrolls and other ancient witnesses preserve apparently only one edition, with no consistent patterns of variant readings or rearrangements. Some manuscripts are especially close to the Masoretic Text: 1QIsa[b], 4QIsa[a], 4QIsa[b], 4QIsa[d], 4QIsa[e], 4QIsa[f], and 4QIsa[g]. Other scrolls, most notably 1QIsa[a] (and 4QIsa[c]), contain many highly instructive variants from the traditional form of the Hebrew text, which offer valuable insights on the late stages of the book's composition and provide many improved readings. These variant readings fall into four categories.

First, some variants are major or otherwise distinctive since they involve one or more verses that are present in some texts but absent from others. A contrasting pair of examples can be seen in chapter 2. On the one hand, the second half of v. 9 and all of v. 10 are not in 1QIsaᵃ. These appear to be an addition to the text of Isaiah by some unknown scribe, made early enough to be recorded in 4QIsaᵃ, 4QIsaᵇ, the Masoretic Text, and the Septuagint. On the other hand, v. 22 was not yet in the Hebrew text translated by the Septuagint, but was inserted later into 1QIsaᵃ and the Masoretic Text. Numerous similar examples are scattered throughout the Isaiah scrolls.

A second category involves errors on the part of the scribe or in the text he was copying. These are often difficult to identify as real errors, since a reading that to some scholars appears incorrect represents for others an alternative reading or a different textual tradition. But even with all due caution, we find that some scribes were careless or wrote down variants that are better explained as errors than as viable alternative textual forms. One example is found in Isa. 16:8–9, where the Masoretic Text and the Septuagint have a much longer passage than 1QIsaᵃ (see Box 6.17).

A third category involves thousands of differences in spelling, the forms of names, the use of the plural versus the singular, and changes in word order, to name a few. Although these are quite minor variants that are usually meaningless for purposes of interpretation, they provide rich evidence for the use of Hebrew, different spelling systems, and scribal conventions during the late Second Temple period.

Box 6.17   *Isaiah 16:8–9*

Dead Sea Scrolls Bible	*Masoretic Text* (NRSV)
8 For the fields of Heshbon and the vineyards of *Sibmah* languish.	8 For the fields of Heshbon and the vineyards of *Sibmah* languish. The leaders of the nations have broken down its choice branches, which reached as far as Jazer and extended into the wilderness; its shoots were spread and wide, even crossing the sea. 9 Therefore I will weep with the crying of Jazer for the vine of *Sibmah*.
9 I will water you with my tears, Heshbon and Elealeh, for the battle-cry has fallen upon your summer fruits and upon your harvest.	I will water you with my tears, Heshbon and Elealeh, for the battle-cry has fallen upon your summer fruits and upon your harvest.

Comment: The scribe's eye skipped from *Sibmah* (which precedes *languish* in the Hebrew) in v. 8 to *Sibmah* in v. 9, resulting in the omission of the intervening text. Since there are several more such examples, both larger and smaller, in 1QIsaᵃ, our scribe was evidently careless and responsible for many of the errors in this large scroll.

(Adapted from AFU, 294–95)

The final category includes a wide spectrum of variant readings, usually a single word or two, on a lesser scale than the compositional variants described in the first category, yet more important than the mostly insignificant variants in the third. One example is found at Isa. 1:15, which in 4QIsa[f] and the Masoretic Text concludes with *your hands are filled with blood,* while 1QIsa[a] completes the parallelism with *your fingers with iniquity.* Another example is at Isa. 2:20, where the idols of silver and of gold are described in the Masoretic Text as *which they have made for themselves to worship,* but in 1QIsa[a] as w*hich their fingers have made to worship.* A particularly interesting reading is found in Isa. 53:11. Here a difficult reading in the traditional text ("*He shall see* of the travail of his soul") is transformed by an additional word in three Isaiah scrolls ("Out of the suffering of his soul *he will see light*"); see Box 6.18.

Isaiah was one of the most influential books and the one quoted most among the Dead Sea Scrolls; this provides evidence of its impact on authors both of other Jewish works imported to Qumran and of works that were specifically composed by the Qumran covenanters. Five commentaries, or *pesharim,* on Isaiah were found in Cave 4 and another in Cave 3. With their system of quoting a base text and commenting on it, these commentaries underscore the authoritative and scriptural status of the book of Isaiah at Qumran.

With its emphasis on prophecy and the end times, it is not surprising that Isaiah was so popular among the Qumranites, just as it was among New Testament authors. In fact, Isa. 40:3 is quoted in the *Rule of the Community* and in all four Gospels for purposes of self-identity. The Qumran covenanters understand Isaiah's prophecy as signaling their own separation from the Jerusalem Jews and their departure for the wilderness in order to prepare the way of the Lord through study of the Torah. In contrast, the Gospel passages proclaim Isa. 40:3 as describing John the Baptist in the wilderness, calling his audience to prepare for the arrival of Jesus. In these two different, self-defining uses of the same scriptural passage, the Qumran covenanters view Isa. 40:3 as fulfilled in themselves, while the Evangelists present it as about to be fulfilled not in John, but in Jesus the Messiah.

Box 6.18	*Isaiah 52:13–53:12: A Reading from the Fourth Servant Song*

Masoretic Text (KJV)	*Dead Sea Scrolls Bible*
53:11 *He shall see of the travail of his soul;* he shall be satisfied: by his knowledge shall my righteous servant justify many; for he shall bear their iniquities.	**53:11** *Out of the suffering of his soul he will see light,*[1] *and*[2] *find satisfaction. And*[3] *through his knowledge* my servant, the righteous one, will make many righteous, and he will bear their iniquities.

1. 1QIsa[a], 1QIsa[b], 4QIsa[d]; cf. LXX. *He will see of the suffering of his soul* MT.   2. 1QIsa[a]. Not in 4QIsa[d], MT.   3. 1QIsa[a]. Not in MT.

Comment: In the traditional Masoretic Text, the first part of v. 11 is difficult to understand, since *he shall see* would normally take a direct object, not be directly followed with a preposition *(out of).* Some scholars suggest that the Hebrew verb *he shall see* (יראה) should read *he shall be filled* (ירוה; cf. Jer. 31:14), which involves the change of one consonant. For this verse, however, the additional word *light* is found in no fewer than three Isaiah scrolls (1QIsa[a], 1QIsa[b], and 4QIsa[d]), a reading that is supported by the Septuagint (φῶς). This shows that the early Hebrew text used by the Septuagint translator actually contained the word *light,* and provides a new reading for exegesis of the passage.

(Adapted from AFU, 358–59)

JEREMIAH

The prophet Jeremiah[57] preached during the closing years of the Kingdom of Judah and survived the destruction of Jerusalem and the Temple by the Babylonians in 587 BCE. After many Jews were exiled to Babylon, he chose to stay in Jerusalem in order to help those who had remained to start over. But a few years later this prophet was forced to flee to Egypt, and soon afterward is heard of no more. Six Jeremiah scrolls were found at Qumran: one in Cave 2 and five in Cave 4.[58] Although these manuscripts preserve much material, of the book's fifty-two chapters portions of only thirty-one are preserved: chapters 4, 7–15, 17–22, 25–27, 30–33, 42–44, and 46–50. The Jeremiah manuscripts were copied over approximately two hundred years, ranging from about 200 BCE (4QJer[a], one of the oldest scrolls) to the latter part of the first century BCE (4QJer[c]).

Two manuscripts of Jeremiah (4QJer[a] and 4QJer[c]) are close to the Masoretic Text, but two others (4QJer[b] and 4QJer[d]) contain a Hebrew text that is noticeably different. The biblical text in these scrolls is very similar to the Hebrew text from which the Septuagint was translated: not only in small details, but also where the Greek Bible differs markedly from the Masoretic Text. In fact, 4QJer[b] and 4QJer[d] and the Septuagint present a version of Jeremiah that is about 13 percent shorter than the longer version found in modern Bibles! Most scholars recognize two literary editions of Jeremiah, with an earlier, shorter edition documented in 4QJer[b], 4QJer[d], and the Septuagint, and a subsequent longer edition found in 4QJer[a], 4QJer[c], and the Masoretic Text.

One example of this shorter text is in Jer. 10:3–11, which presents a satire on idols. While the Masoretic Text has all nine verses, the Greek Bible and 4QJer[b] lack vv. 6–8 and 10, which extol the greatness of God (see Box 6.19).

Box 6.19	*Jeremiah 10:9–10*

Dead Sea Scrolls Bible	*Masoretic Text (NRSV)*
9 [Hammered silver is brought from Tarshish and gold from Uphaz, the work of the craftsman and of the hands of the goldsmith] with blue and purple [for their clothing; they are all the product of skilled workers. 10 *But the* LORD *is the true God; he is the living God and]* the everlasting King; at [*his a*]nger [*the earth quakes, and the nations cannot endure his wrath*].[1]	9 Beaten silver is brought from Tarshish, and gold from Uphaz. They are the work of the artisan and of the hands of the goldsmith; their clothing is blue and purple; they are all the product of skilled workers. 10 But the LORD is the true God; he is the living God and the everlasting King. At his wrath the earth quakes, and the nations cannot endure his indignation.

1. 4QJer[a], MT. Entire verse not present in 4QJer[b], LXX.

Comment: Jer. 10:3–11 presents an entertaining satire on idols. The Masoretic Text, supported by 4QJer[a] (which only preserves vv. 9–11) has all nine verses. 4QJer[b] and the Greek Bible, however, lack v. 6–8 and 10, which extol the greatness of God. In this extract, vv. 9–10 are found in 4QJer[a] and the Masoretic Text, but are absent from 4QJer[b] and the Septuagint.

(Adapted from AFU, 388)

A particularly fascinating manuscript is 4QJer[a], which contains more corrections than any other scroll in proportion to the length of the document. The most noticeable example is in column 3, which contains additions made by a second scribe after the original scribe had written Jer. 7:28–9:2, but had omitted a long section (Jer 7:30–8:3). The second scribe's attempt to insert so much missing text has resulted in a most unusual format: he squeezed Jer. 7:30–31 into the gap between Jer. 7:29 and 8:4 in the main text, then filled in 7:32–8:3a sideways along the left margin, and wrote chap. 8:3b upside down at the bottom of the page (see Figure 6.6).

LAMENTATIONS

Lamentations[59] consists of five poems dealing with the destruction of Jerusalem and the Temple in 587 (or 586) BCE. For people living in Judah in the sixth century, these traumatic events gave rise to a plaintive cry: "How did this happen?" a *How* that appears as the first word in three of the five laments (1:1; 2:1; and 4:1) and is the Hebrew title for the book (*'eykah* [איכה]). For the Qumran community, which considered itself in exile, these poems must have been profoundly significant.

Four scrolls—between them containing text from all five chapters of Lamentations— were found in the caves at Qumran: one in Cave 3, another in Cave 4, and two more in

Figure 6.6

A creative insertion in 4QJer[a]. In column 3, the original scribe omitted Jer. 7:30–8:3. A second scribe was most creative by inserting the missing text in the gap between Jer. 7:29 and 8:4 and in the margins! (PAM 4.792)

Courtesy of the Israel Antiquities Authority

Cave 5.[60] The oldest manuscript is 4QLam, which was copied in the early Herodian period (ca. 30 BCE–1 CE). One special feature of this book is that chapters 1–4 each contain an acrostic poem (each group of verses begins with a successive letter of the Hebrew alphabet). The scribe of 3QLam laid out his text as *cola* (poetic units), making it clear that this scroll contains poetry, but the scribes of 4QLam, 5QLam[a], and 5QLam[b] did not do so, giving the appearance of prose. The distinction made here is not on the level of the text of Scripture, but rather the layout of poetic units.

These manuscripts generally contain a form of Lamentations similar to the traditional Hebrew text, but 4QLam and 5QLam[a] preserve several distinctive readings that do not agree with either the Masoretic Text or the Septuagint. According to the editor of 4QLam, Frank Moore Cross, this scroll preserves several readings that are superior to those in the traditional text. The nature of several variant readings found in 4QLam is evident in Box 6.20.

Box 6.20	*Lamentations 1:7–9*

Dead Sea Scrolls Bible	*Masoretic Text (NRSV, Adapted)*
7 *Remember, O LORD,*[1]	7 Jerusalem remembers,
	in the days of her affliction and wandering,
all *our pains*[2]	all her precious things
that were from the days of old;	in days of old.
when her [people] fell into the hand of the adversary,	When her people fell into the hand of the foe,
and none did *help;*	and there was no one to help her,
her *adversaries*[3] mocked	the foe looked on mocking
at [*al*]*l her calamities.*[4]	over her downfall.
8 Jerusalem has sinned grievously,	8 Jerusalem sinned grievously,
there[fore] she has become *one who shows grief;*[5]	so she has become a mockery;
all that honored her *despise,*[6]	all who honored her despise her,
because they have seen her [nak]edness.	for they have seen her nakedness;
[She] also [sighs	she herself groans,
and turns] away.	and turns her face away.
9 Her uncleanness was in [her] sk[irts;	9 Her uncleanness was in her skirts;
she did not consider her end,	she took no thought of her future;
therefore she has come down *ap*]*pallingly;*[7]	her downfall was appalling,
and[8][she] has no [comforter.	with none to comfort her.
"O LORD, see my affliction;	"O LORD, look at my affliction,
for the enemy] has magnified himself."	for the enemy has triumphed!"

1. 4QLam. *In the days of her affliction and of miseries Jerusalem remembers* MT, LXX. 2. 4QLam. *her precious things* MT, LXX. 3. 4QLam. *help her; the adversaries saw her, they* MT, LXX. 4. 4QLam. *her desolations* MT, LXX. 5. 4QLam. *an unclean thing* MT, LXX. 6. 4QLam. *despise her* MT, LXX. 7. 4QLam. feminine. Masculine MT. 8. 4QLam. Not in MT, LXX.

Comment: The poetic layout here follows that of the traditional Masoretic Text. In 4QLam the text of Lamentations is not written in this format, but in prose, that is, without verses beginning successive lines or having spaces between them.

(Adapted from AFU, 624)

A final question—one that is important for a later book such as Lamentations—is whether it was quoted or used as Scripture in other writings found at Qumran. Lam. 1:1 is quoted in *A Lament for Zion* (4Q179; see Appendix III); moreover, *A Prayer for Deliverance* (4Q501) capitalized on the genre of lament, and material from Lamentations may be alluded to in the unidentified work 4Q282 (the fragments involved were previously grouped under 4Q241).

EZEKIEL

Ezekiel,[61] who was both priest and prophet, lived most of his life in exile in Babylon during the period before and after the fall of Jerusalem in 587 BCE. His message, addressed to both the people of Jerusalem and the exiles in Babylonia, includes prophecies of judgment, words of consolation and hope, and details of a future restored Temple and nation.

The Judean Desert has yielded the remains of seven scrolls containing text from Ezekiel. Six were found at Qumran: one each in Caves 1, 3, and 11 and three in Cave 4.[62] One more Ezekiel scroll (MasEzek) was discovered in the ruins of Masada. It is possible that 4QEzek[b], which preserves material only from chapter 1, never contained the complete book of Ezekiel, but perhaps simply the prophet's inaugural vision or a few episodes. The oldest manuscript is 4QEzek[c], which dates between the early and mid first century BCE. Of the forty-eight chapters in Ezekiel, the scrolls preserve portions of eighteen (1, 4, 5, 7, 10, 11, 13, 16, 23, 24, 31–37, and 41). However, since the preserved fragments range over the course of the entire work, it may be assumed that the complete book of Ezekiel was familiar to the Qumran community.

In the seven Ezekiel manuscripts, the textual form of the book is very similar to that of the Masoretic Text (especially 11QEzek). Relatively few variant readings are clearly preserved. Reconstruction, however, suggests that two of the scrolls had shorter readings in comparison with our Bibles. First, for Ezek. 5:13, 11QEzek may have had a shorter text than the traditional one (note that the Septuagint omits *and I will be comforted*). Second, 4QEzek[a] lacks space for all of Ezek. 23:16–17, which suggests here a shorter passage than in the Masoretic Text.

DANIEL

Most scholars agree that the book of Daniel[63] was written during a time of great persecution for the Jewish people under a pagan king. The stories of Daniel and his friends, set in Babylon during the Exile, encouraged readers to remain faithful to God and to refuse compromise, and offered the prospect of triumph over wickedness and idolatry. These themes must have brought encouragement to the Qumran covenanters, who also felt persecuted by other Jews and threatened by Hellenism.

A total of eight Daniel scrolls were discovered at Qumran: two in Cave 1, five in Cave 4, and one in Cave 6.[64] None is complete due to the ravages of time, but between them they preserve text from eleven of Daniel's twelve chapters. This does not mean that the book lacked the final chapter at Qumran, since Dan. 12:10 is quoted in the *Florilegium* (4Q174),[65] which tells us that it is "written in the book of Daniel the Prophet" (frags. 1–3 2.3–4). All eight manuscripts were copied in the space of 175 years, ranging from about 125 BCE (4QDan[c]) to about 50 CE (4QDan[b]). Of all the biblical scrolls found at Qumran, 4QDan[c] has the distinction of being closest in date to when the book itself was composed (about 165 BCE). It also shows that Daniel was being read at Qumran only forty years after being written.

What form of Daniel is found in these manuscripts: the twelve-chapter version preserved in the Masoretic Text or the longer version found in the Greek Bible (on the Additions to Daniel, see Chapter 8)? Seven of the eight scrolls originally contained the entire book of Daniel in the shorter form found in the received text, not the longer form preserved in the Septuagint. (In 1QDan[b] and 4QDan[d], for example, Dan. 3:23 is followed by 3:24, not the Prayer of Azariah and the Song of the Three Young Men as found in the Greek Bible.) It is possible that the eighth manuscript, 4QDan[e], is an abbreviated text that included only the Prayer of Daniel (Dan. 9:4b–19), since it preserves text only from chapter 9. If this is the case, 4QDan[e] does not strictly qualify as a copy of the book itself.

With respect to the text of Daniel, all eight scrolls reveal no major disagreements against the Masoretic Text, although 1QDan[a] is closest to the traditional text. Some variant readings are of interest. For instance, 4QDan[b] reads [*then*] *he wrote down the* [*dream*], but has no space for the awkward words *he related the sum of the words* at the end of Dan. 7:1. The shorter reading is accepted by the New Revised Standard Version, which simply has *then he wrote down the dream,* in line with the Qumran scroll and not with the Masoretic Text. A second example is in Dan. 10:16, where the Hebrew Bible reads *one in the form of a human* (literally, *one like the sons of man*), but the reconstructed form of pap6QDan shows that it most likely read *something in the form of a human hand* (as does the Septuagint). In this case, the editors of the New International Version decided to retain the reading of the Masoretic Text (as do other English translations), but considered the variant reading in pap6QDan important enough to merit an extensive footnote.

A final question concerns the bilingual nature of Daniel, which in the Hebrew Bible opens in Hebrew, switches to Aramaic at 2:4b, and then reverts to Hebrew at 8:1. The four scrolls that preserve material from the relevant sections (1QDan[a], 4QDan[a], 4QDan[b], and 4QDan[d]) support the same transitions from Hebrew to Aramaic and back again. Although the reasons for having Hebrew and Aramaic sections in the same book are complex, the scrolls show us that Daniel existed in this form very early on and was thus most likely compiled in Hebrew and Aramaic. This is not really surprising in the case of such a late book, which was written at a time when Aramaic was widely spoken by Jews in Palestine.

THE TWELVE MINOR PROPHETS

The Minor Prophets[66]—the term was coined by St. Augustine (*City of God* 18.25)—make up twelve books in the Septuagint and Christian Bibles, but the single Book of the Twelve in the traditional Hebrew Bible. This collection contains warnings of judgment and words of comfort from many men, some prophesying in the Northern Kingdom (Hosea, Amos), some in the Southern Kingdom of Judah (Joel, Micah, Nahum, Habakkuk, Zephaniah), and some during or after the Exile (Obadiah, Jonah, Haggai, Zechariah, Malachi). Several of these books may be small in size, but the message of each is profound.

Ten manuscripts of the Minor Prophets were found in the Judean Desert. Eight of these were from the caves at Qumran: seven in Cave 4 and one in Cave 5,[67] the dates of which range from 150 BCE (4QXII[a] and perhaps 4QXII[b]) to 25 BCE (4QXII[g]). Two more scrolls were found at locations used as hideouts by Jewish rebels during the uprising against Rome known as the Bar Kokhba Revolt (132–35 CE): one at Wadi Murabba'at, and the other at Naḥal Ḥever.[68] These manuscripts were copied in the later first century BCE (8ḤevXII gr) and between approximately 75 and 100 CE (MurXII). Of the sixty-seven chapters found in the twelve books, the Minor Prophets scrolls preserve parts of sixty-three, with only four not represented at all (Zechariah 7 and 13, Malachi 1 and 4).

Two questions may be asked of the Minor Prophets scrolls. First, do they confirm that these twelve prophetic books were copied together in ancient times? Seven manuscripts indicate this to be so; the other three (4QXII^d, 4QXII^f, 5QAmos) are so fragmentary that each contains parts of only one book.

Second, do the Minor Prophets scrolls support the order found in the Septuagint (Greek Bible), or the traditional Hebrew order found in the Masoretic Bible?

Hebrew Bible	Septuagint
Hosea	Hosea
Joel	*Amos*
Amos	*Micah*
Obadiah	*Joel*
Jonah	*Obadiah*
Micah	*Jonah*
Nahum	Nahum
Habakkuk	Habakkuk
Zephaniah	Zephaniah
Haggai	Haggai
Zechariah	Zechariah
Malachi	Malachi

On the whole these manuscripts follow the traditional Hebrew order, which has been adopted by modern English translations. Even the Minor Prophets scroll from Cave 8 at Naḥal Ḥever (8ḤevXII gr), written in Greek, displays the traditional Hebrew order, not that of the Septuagint. However, the oldest manuscript of all, 4QXII^a, suggests a third order in which Jonah follows Malachi as the last book in the collection. Thus the Minor Prophets scrolls suggest there was perhaps more fluidity in this ancient collection than was previously recognized.

The text of the books in the Minor Prophets scrolls is generally close to the traditional Hebrew one. Even the Greek manuscript from Naḥal Ḥever contains a Septuagint text that has been systematically corrected to correspond more closely to the proto-Masoretic Text (i.e., the ancient form of the medieval Masoretic Text). Yet there are also many variant readings, especially in 4QXII^a, 4QXII^c, 4QXII^e, and 4QXII^g. This suggests that the text of several Minor Prophets scrolls is mixed: quite close to the traditional form of the Hebrew Bible, but also showing some agreement with the Septuagint, as well as some readings that are unique. In the first example (Hos. 13:4), the longer text found in the seventh copy of the Minor Prophets scroll from Cave 4 (4QXII^g) also occurs in the Greek Bible, but not in the Masoretic Text. The second example shows that, for the second half of Mal. 2:13, 4QXII^a contains wording that is very similar to the Greek Bible, but differs from the Masoretic Text (see Box 6.21).

Box 6.21	*Variants in Hosea and Malachi*

Dead Sea Scrolls Bible	*Masoretic Text (NRSV)*
Hos. 13:4: [Yet I am the LORD yo]ur [God] *who fortifies heaven* [*and creates the earth, whose hands made the whole host of heaven, but I did not show them to you to go after them, but*] *I brought you up*[1] [from the land of Egypt; and you were not to know any god but me, and besides me there is no savior].	**Hos. 13:4:** Yet I have been the LORD your God ever since the land of Egypt; you know no God but me, and besides me there is no savior.
Mal. 2:13: And this again [yo]u do: You cover [the alt]ar of the LORD [with tears], *and*[2] with weeping, and with sighing *because of troubles; does he still regard* [*the offering and accept*[3] it with favor from] your [han]d?	**Mal. 2:13:** And this you do as well: You cover the LORD's altar with tears, with weeping and with groaning because he no longer regards the offering or accepts it with favor at your hand.

1. 4QXII^g, LXX. Not in MT.   2. 4QXII^a, LXX. Not in MT.   3. 4QXII^a; cf. LXX *(because of troubles; is it worthy to regard the offering and accept . . . ?).* because he no longer regards the offering and accepts MT.

(AFU, 426, 477)

The Minor Prophets were quite popular among the Qumran covenanters. Besides the ten scrolls already discussed, seven or eight *pesharim* (commentaries) were written on several Minor Prophets: two on Hosea (4Q166, 4Q167), two on Zephaniah (1Q15, 4Q170), one or two on Micah (1Q14, 4Q168?), and one each on Nahum (4Q169) and Habakkuk (1QpHab). (For more details on the *pesharim*, see Chapter 9.)

The Scrolls and the Text of the Hebrew Bible/Old Testament

The introduction to this chapter stated that several forms or editions of the Old Testament have been in existence since early times, the most important of which are the Proto-Masoretic Text, the Septuagint (Greek Bible), and the Samaritan Pentateuch. It was also pointed out that many biblical scrolls can be placed in one of four textual categories: (a) similar to the Masoretic Text, (b) similar to the Hebrew text translated by the Septuagint, (c) similar to the Samaritan Pentateuch, and (d) mixed or non-aligned (showing no consistent alignment with any of the other three). As individual biblical books and scrolls were examined in the preceding pages, their relationship to one or more of these categories was mentioned in many cases.

THEORIES OF TEXTUAL DEVELOPMENT

The Theory of Local Texts

As the biblical manuscripts from Qumran and other locations near the Dead Sea were coming to light, a theory of textual development began to crystallize. This was developed mainly by Frank Moore Cross,[69] building on the earlier work of his mentor, William

Foxwell Albright, who had recognized the great antiquity and diversity of the Dead Sea Scrolls in 1948. For a number of years, this theory stood alone as offering the clearest light available on the new discoveries from the Judean Desert. According to Cross, for the first five books of the Bible three main *text types,* which he termed *local texts* (see Figure 6.7), can be identified in the biblical scrolls and other ancient manuscripts:

(1) *The Palestinian Text:* The Hebrew Bible—or most of it—was written in Palestine, where it continued to be studied and copied for many centuries. The prime representative of this text is the Samaritan Pentateuch, which remains the Bible of the small group of Samaritan Jews to this day. To a very large extent, the ancient Palestinian text is found in this Pentateuch, but some specifically sectarian passages were later added (notably those asserting that God's holy mountain is at Shechem rather than at Jerusalem). Examples of this textual form include 4QpaleoExod[m], 4QExod-Lev[f], and 4QNum[b].

(2) *The Babylonian Text:* Jews carried the Palestinian text to other places, notably Babylonia when they went into exile in 587 BCE. As the text was copied by hand over the centuries, variations and different readings arose, some due to decisions made by scribes, others due to error. Although we have no early information about the development of this text, Cross concluded that the proto-Masoretic Text is the result of copying and finalization that took place among Babylonian Jews. Examples include 4QGen-Exod[a], 4QSam[b], 4QJer[a], and 4QPs[c].

(3) *The Egyptian Text:* Following the conquests of Alexander the Great, many Jews took up residence in Egypt; their descendants spoke Greek fluently, perhaps even as a first language. Because many of these Jews had assimilated much of Greek culture and knew little Hebrew, an urgent need arose for a Greek translation of the Hebrew Bible. Beginning with the Pentateuch in the third century BCE, a group of Jewish residents in Egypt translated a Hebrew text from Palestine into Greek. (For further details on this translation, known as the Septuagint, see Chapter 5.) Examples of this textual form include 4QLev[d], 4QJer[b], and 4QJer[d].

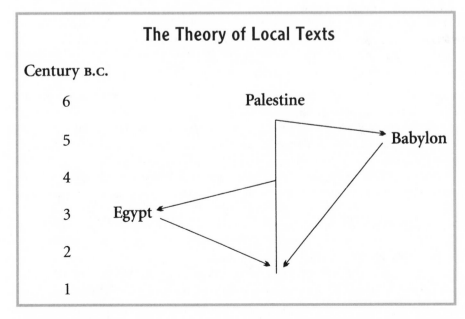

Figure 6.7

The three text types according to Frank Moore Cross. The Palestinian text is represented by the Samaritan Pantateuch, the Babylonian by the Masoretic Text, and the Egyptian text by the Septuagint.

From J. C. VanderKam, *The Dead Sea Scrolls Today* (Grand Rapids, MI: Eerdmans; London: SPCK, 1994) 133.

The local-texts theory maintains that examples of all three text types were present in Palestine or had been brought there well before the Christian era. According to Cross, this explains why many of the biblical scrolls from Qumran can be placed in one of these three categories.

Many Texts, and Creative Authors and Copyists

After surveying the great amount of variation in the biblical scrolls, Shemaryahu Talmon offered a different perspective. Rather than seeing distinct textual types or families, Talmon considered both the textual and sociological aspects of the biblical scrolls. Textually, he eliminated the distinction between authors and copyists:

> In the Qumran material coalesce the phase of creative authoring of biblical literature with the ancillary phase of text transmission[;] . . . in ancient Hebrew literature no hard and fast lines can be drawn between authors' conventions of style and tradents' and copyists' rules of reproduction and transmission.[70]

Sociologically, Talmon pointed out that the Masoretic Text, the Samaritan Pentateuch, and the Septuagint were salvaged from a much larger pool of textual forms, simply because the rabbis, the Samaritans, and the Christians each preserved their own particular collection of texts. Other forms of these texts also existed, but perished together with the groups that held them sacred.

A Theory of Textual Variety

Emanuel Tov differs from Cross by finding greater textual diversity among the biblical scrolls. Because of this variety, Tov asserts, the biblical scrolls do not fall neatly into one of Cross's three categories, but represent a large number of different textual forms. Nevertheless, each text can be placed into one of five broad groups, three of them according to the degree of closeness to the Masoretic Text, the Samaritan Pentateuch, or the Septuagint. Tov recognizes that the principle of grouping texts according to the degree of closeness to later textual witnesses, especially medieval ones like the Masoretic Text and Samaritan Pentateuch, is surprising, but states that this comparison is necessary since these texts already existed in the last centuries before the common era. In an important article published in 2002,[71] Tov outlines five principles in arriving at his more recent conclusions:

> In the calculation of the percentages for the various groups of texts, the numbers are based on a list of 128 biblical texts (the remaining 72 texts are too fragmentary for textual analysis). In this calculation, the following principles are employed: (1) Questionable attributions to textual groups are counted as regular ones. (2) In accord with statistical probability, texts that are equally close to MT and SP in the Torah and to MT and the LXX in the other books are counted as MT. (3) Texts written according to the Qumran practice (group *a*) are not included separately in the statistics, since these texts are counted in other groups in accord with their textual affiliation. (4) Texts that are characterized as both "independent" and close to the LXX or the SP are counted as "independent." (5) Since the texts like the SP are not evidenced for books other than the Torah, statistics for the Torah are separated from those of the other books, but they are rather similar.
>
> In the 46 Torah texts sufficiently large for analysis (out of a total of 52 such texts), 24 texts (52 percent) reflect MT (or are equally close to the MT and SP), 17 are independent

Table 6.1	*Textual Groups in the Biblical Scrolls (E. Tov)*				
Texts Eligible for Analysis	**Texts Used for Analysis**	**Texts That Reflect MT**	**Non-Aligned Texts**	**Texts Close to the SP**	**Texts Close to the LXX**
Torah: 52	Torah: 46	24 (52%)	17 (37%)	3 (6.5%)	2 (4.5%)
Other: 76	Other: 75	33 (44%)	40 (53%)		2 (3%)
Total: 128	Total: 121	57 (47%)	57 (47%)	3 (2.5%)	4 (3.3%)

(37 percent), 3 reflect the SP (6.5 percent), and 2 the LXX (4.5 percent). In the remainder of the Bible, in the 75 texts that are sufficiently large for analysis (out of a total of 76 such texts), 33 texts (44 percent) reflect MT (or are equally close to the MT and LXX), 40 are independent (53 percent), 2 reflect the LXX (3 percent). The preponderance of the Masoretic and independent texts in the Qumran corpus is thus evident.

See Table 6.1.

Tov's omission of percentages for texts written according to the "Qumran practice" represents an important departure from much of his earlier work, in which he presented statistics for each of the five broad groupings. The order of these groupings has been changed here to correspond with Cross's list:[72]

(1) *Pre-Samaritan (or Harmonistic) Texts:* These reflect the textual form (Cross: *Palestinian*) found in the Samaritan Pentateuch, although the Samaritan Bible itself is later and contains additional material not included in these earlier scrolls. The Qumran witnesses are characterized by orthographic corrections and harmonizations with parallel texts elsewhere found in the Pentateuch. Tov estimates the Pre-Samaritan scrolls at no more than three (6.5 percent) of the forty-six Qumran pentateuchal texts large enough for analysis.[73]

(2) *Proto-Masoretic (or, preferably, Proto-Rabbinic) Texts:* This form (earlier termed *Babylonian* by Cross) is characterized by a stable text and preserves the consonantal framework and distinctive readings found in the Masoretic Text. For Tov, 57 (47 percent) of the 121 Qumran biblical scrolls sufficiently large for analysis fall into this category. Of the 46 Torah texts that qualify, 24 (52 percent) reflect the Masoretic Text, and of the 75 texts that qualify from the rest of the Bible, 33 (44 percent) reflect the Masoretic Text.

It should be noted, however, that of the 24 pentateuchal texts that Tov classifies as Proto-Masoretic, 20 are equally close to the Samaritan Pentateuch. Moreover, of the 33 texts from elsewhere in the Bible that Tov classifies as Proto-Masoretic, 13 are equally close to the Hebrew source of the Septuagint. In other words, of the 57 analyzable texts that Tov lists as Proto-Masoretic, only 24 are definitely in this category.

(3) *Texts Close to the Presumed Hebrew Source of the LXX:* This form (Cross: *Egyptian*) is close to the Hebrew source from which the Septuagint was translated. Several other manuscripts also share distinctive individual readings with the Septuagint, although they do not fall in this category. According to Tov's analysis, there is a total of four texts in this category, representing 3.3 percent of the 121 biblical texts large enough for analysis. Of the 46 Torah texts that qualify, 2 (4.5 percent) are close to the Hebrew source of the Septuagint, and of the 75 analyzable texts from elsewhere in the Bible, 2 more (3 percent) are so aligned.

(4) *Non-Aligned Texts:* Many Qumran texts show no consistent closeness to the Masoretic Text, the Samaritan Pentateuch, or the Septuagint. On occasion they agree with the Masoretic Text over against the others, sometimes with the Samaritan Pentateuch, and sometimes with the Septuagint (e.g., 2QExod[a], 4QExod[b], 11QpaleoLev[a], 4QDeut[b], 1QIsa[a], 4QIsa[c], 4QPs[a], 11QPs[a], 4QCant[a], and 4QDan[a]). In addition, scrolls in this group often contain readings that diverge significantly from other texts (e.g., 4QJosh[a], 4QJudg[a], and 4QSam[a]). Tov estimates the non-aligned Qumran manuscripts at 57 (47 percent) of the 121 Qumran scrolls large enough for analysis. Of the 46 Torah scrolls that qualify, he places 17 (37 percent) in this category, and of the 75 analyzable texts from elsewhere in the Bible, he places 40 (53 percent) here.

(5) *Texts Written in the "Qumran Practice":* According to Tov, these scrolls were copied by scribes from the Qumran community in accordance with the "Qumran practice," which denotes manuscripts with distinctive long orthography (spelling) and morphology (such as word endings), frequent errors and corrections, and a free approach to the text. (Tov notes that virtually all the nonbiblical scrolls known to have been authored by members of the Qumran community reflect this combined set of features.) He identifies twenty-seven examples in this category, including 4QExod[b], 4QDeut[j], 1QIsa[a], 4QIsa[c], and 11QPs[a]. Departing from earlier studies, Tov gives no percentage for this group within the corpus of Qumran biblical texts, since the great majority are included in statistics for the other four categories. Most are characterized as textually independent, and thus fall into the non-aligned group.

Successive Literary Editions

Eugene Ulrich has proposed a theory of successive literary editions as a model for tracing and classifying the development of the biblical text of the various books. These different literary editions occurred later in the compositional process of the Scriptures, which took place in several stages that were different for each book or set of books. Each new edition resulted from the creative efforts of some author or scribe who intentionally revised the edition (or passages) current in his time in the light of a new religious outlook or national challenge.

Usually, the newer edition eventually replaced the older one(s), but this was not always the case; sometimes the newer edition was not well enough established, was known to be too recent, or clashed with deeply held beliefs. Two examples are 4QpaleoExod[m] and 4QNum[b], which share common features with the Samaritan Pentateuch—an edition not accepted by rabbinic Judaism. Two other editions that were not widely adopted are 11QPs[a] and the book of *Jubilees,* which support a 364-day calendar instead of the 354-day calendar practiced by the rabbis.

As they developed over time (i.e., *diachronically*) Ulrich labels the variant editions *text traditions,* and when considered at the same time (i.e., *synchronically*), he calls them *text types.* These variant editions are identified by large-scale *patterns* of variants. Within the same text tradition or text type, Ulrich also speaks of *text families,* which contain patterns of smaller-scale, individual variant readings.

Ulrich proposes two steps to help discern these variant literary editions: (1) Ignoring purely orthographic (spelling) differences, since the orthography of a manuscript is seldom related to any particular edition of that work; Ulrich also disagrees with Tov's assertion that scrolls written in the "Qumran practice" were copied by scribes from the Qumran community. (2) Ignoring individual variant readings that are not related to the *pattern of variants* by which an author or scribe reworked an existing edition of a work into a revised edition.

One obvious example of a book found in different literary editions is Jeremiah, with the longer version found in the Masoretic Text, 4QJer[a], and 4QJer[c] and the shorter version found in the Septuagint, 4QJer[b] and 4QJer[d]. In a recent evaluation of the biblical manuscripts from Qumran,[74] Ulrich identifies variant literary editions for at least six of the twenty-four books of the Masoretic canon in the late Second Temple period. He then suggests possible variant editions for four more books, bringing the total at Qumran to ten. When the the Septuagint (LXX) and the Samaritan Pentateuch (SP) are also taken into consideration as witness, Ulrich identifies six or seven more variant literary editions of books:

Variant Literary Editions Found at Qumran	Possible Variant Editions Found at Qumran	Variant Literary Editions in the LXX or SP
Exodus	Judges	Genesis (chaps. 5, 11)
Numbers	Samuel	Kings
Joshua	Twelve Prophets	Ezekiel
Jeremiah	Lamentations	Twelve Prophets
Psalms		Job (?)
Song of Songs		Proverbs
		Daniel

On the basis of the manuscript evidence, then, Ulrich concludes that during the closing centuries of the Second Temple period, Judaism knew variant literary editions for half or more of what later became the Tanakh (Hebrew Bible): at least twelve, and as many as seventeen, of the traditional twenty-four books.

THE SCROLLS AND THE DEVELOPMENT OF THE BIBLICAL TEXT

Each of the above four approaches to the biblical text has its merits, as well as possible shortcomings. On the positive side: (1) The identification of local texts by Cross is seminal to the discussion and was a great leap forward in our understanding of the development of the text of the Hebrew Bible.

(2) Talmon has made an essential contribution by showing that the Masoretic Text, Samaritan Pentateuch, and Septuagint are only three forms of the biblical text, and that many other forms—most of which are now lost—also existed. Also significant is his reminder that the finalization of various biblical books continued long after the initial authors had finished their work.

(3) Tov's method of grouping the biblical scrolls is more nuanced than the local-texts theory and provides more categories. It should be noted that Tov finds in the biblical scrolls from Qumran a great number of different textual forms, not just four or five. His first three categories (Pre-Samaritan, Proto-Masoretic, Texts Close to the Presumed Source of the LXX) must be understood as broad, and his fourth grouping (Non-Aligned) includes numerous forms of the biblical text; in this respect Tov's approach has some affinities with that of Talmon. By stressing such textual variety, Tov's work shows the biblical texts from Qumran are not to be divided into recensions (i.e., revisions of earlier texts).

(4) Ulrich's emphasis on successive literary editions and how to recognize them is to be welcomed. His identification of variant literary editions for at least twelve, and as many as seventeen, of the traditional twenty-four books of the Tanakh during the closing centuries of the Second Temple period is the culmination of three decades of study of the biblical text.

Some cautious words of constructive criticism are also in order: (1) Cross's division of the biblical scrolls from Qumran into three categories seems too restrictive, since several more different textual forms are found. However, Cross developed his theory at an early time, so it would inevitably be challenged and modified as more scrolls and further research became available.

(2) Although Talmon correctly recognizes the existence of many texts, his approach downplays the existence of distinct groupings or families of texts that have been identified.

(3) Tov's category of texts written in the "Qumran Practice" has not been accepted by all scholars (e.g., Eugene Ulrich). However, his more recent decision not to include these texts as a group with a separate textual affiliation—but instead to count the scrolls involved in one of the other four groups—is to be welcomed and may lead to wider acceptance of this category.

More problematic is Tov's principle that texts that are equally close to the Masoretic Text and the Samaritan Pentateuch, as well as to the Masoretic Text and the Septuagint, are listed in his Proto-Masoretic group (see Table 6.2). Tov justifies this decision as being "in accord with statistical probability," which has the effect of decreeing that Qumran biblical texts that are close to two or more of the ancient forms are Proto-Masoretic unless otherwise proven—which is problematic, to say the least. In fact, of the fifty-seven (47 percent) analyzable Qumran biblical scrolls that supposedly fall into this category, only twenty-four (20 percent) are strictly close to the traditional text, while the other thirty-three (58 percent) are as close to the Masoretic Text and either the Samaritan Pentateuch or the Hebrew source of the Septuagint. If this criticism is valid, Tov's total percentage for the Proto-Masoretic group (47 percent) will have to be adjusted sharply downward, and those for the Pre-Samaritan group (6.5 percent of the analyzable pentateuchal scrolls) and the group close to the source of the Septuagint (3.3 percent) will both need to be increased.

(4) Although Ulrich's emphasis on literary editions is most significant, his identification of variant editions for as many as seventeen of the traditional twenty-four books of the Tanakh will no doubt be challenged. Ulrich may be proved correct, but some scholars will question whether some of the books he lists as containing variant readings, even pat-

Table 6.2	*Qumran Biblical Texts That Reflect MT (E. Tov)*			
Texts Used	Tov's Number	Exclusively Close to MT	Equally Close to SP	Equally Close to LXX
Torah: 46	24 (52%)	4	20	Some?
Other: 75	33 (44%)	20 (14 + probably 6)	(Nil)	13
Total: 121	57 (47%)	24 (20%)	20 (17%)	13+ (11%+)

terns of variants, actually qualify as different literary editions. All would agree that there are two editions of Jeremiah, for instance, but the evidence for some books in Ulrich's list is not as clear (e.g., Genesis and Judges).

As stated at the outset of this chapter, we have approached the biblical scrolls with two general questions in mind: (1) Can the individual scrolls be placed in one of four textual categories: (a) similar to the Masoretic Text, (b) similiar to the Hebrew text translated by the Septuagint, (c) similar to the Samaritan Pentateuch, or (d) non-aligned texts? (2) Can we identify distinct literary editions of various individual books in the scrolls? The approach we have adopted takes into account the contributions of all four scholars discussed above, but especially those of Tov and Ulrich.

OBSERVATIONS ON THE BIBLICAL SCROLLS

The Number of Manuscripts

With reference to Tables 6.3 and 6.4, the grand total of all the biblical scrolls from all sites in the Judean Desert is 222, comprising 205 from Qumran and 17 from other sites (5 from Naḥal Ḥever, 5 from Murabbaʿat, 1 from Sdeir, and 6 from Masada). The numbers for Qumran include the Greek biblical scrolls and the three Aramaic targums (4QtgLev, 4QtgJob, 11QtgJob). For the Pentateuch, totals have been adjusted to read eight less, since six scrolls from Qumran (4QGen-Exod^a, 4QpaleoGen-Exod^l, 4QExod^b, 4QExod-Lev^f, 1QpaleoLev, 4QLev-Num^a) preserve parts of two books and so have been counted twice, and the Murabbaʿat scroll (Mur 1) preserves portions of three books and so has been counted three times.

Table 6.3 shows that for the four-part Christian Old Testament, the Pentateuch has the highest number of scrolls (95, with 84 at Qumran), followed by the Prophets (56, with 53 at Qumran), the Poetical Books (53, with 50 at Qumran), and then the Historical Books (18, all found at Qumran).

Table 6.4 shows that for the three-part Hebrew Bible, the Torah has the highest number of manuscripts (95, with 84 at Qumran), followed by the Writings (71, with 68 at Qumran), and then the Prophets (56, with 53 at Qumran).

According to Table 6.5, the book represented by the most manuscripts is Psalms (39 scrolls, with 36 at Qumran), followed by Deuteronomy (33, with 30 at Qumran), Genesis (24, with 20 at Qumran), Isaiah (22, with 21 at Qumran), Exodus (18, with 17 at Qumran), and Leviticus (17, with 15 at Qumran). Those with no representation are Esther and Nehemiah (but see the discussion under Nehemiah), while the remnants of one scroll each were found for Ezra and Chronicles.

Although these figures are as accurate as possible, the final count is not assured since the status of some manuscripts is not assured. (a) As seen above, some texts classified as biblical may in fact be abbreviated or excerpted compositions (e.g., 4QPs^g, 4QPs^h, 5QPs, 4QCant^a, 4QCant^b, and 4QDan^e). (b) *4QReworked Pentateuch* probably qualifies as an edition of the Pentateuch (see Chapter 7), in which case the five scrolls involved (4QRP^{a-e}) should be added to the totals in Tables 6.3, 6.4, and 6.5. (c) 4QGen^{h1} and 4QGen^{h2} may be one or two scrolls. (d) 4QJer^b, 4QJer^d, and 4QJer^e could be parts of the same manuscript, not three separate ones. (e) It is not altogether clear whether the Deuteronomy and Exodus segments of 4QDeut^j are part of the same scroll. (e) Mur 1 (MurGen, MurExod, MurNum) most likely constitutes a single manuscript, but could be two or three.[75]

Table 6.3	*Books of the Old Testament in the Scrolls*				
Book	**4Q**	**1–11Q**	**Qumran**	**Other**	**Total**
Pentateuch					
Genesis	16		20	4	24
Exodus	12		17	1	18
Leviticus	10		15	2	17
Numbers	3		8	3	11
Deuteronomy	22	1	30	3	33
Total	63	27	90	13	103
Adjusted	58	26	84	11	95
Historical Books					
Joshua	2		2		2
Judges	2		3		3
Ruth	2		4		4
1 & 2 Samuel	3		4		4
1 & 2 Kings	1	1	3		3
1 & 2 Chronicles	1		1		1
Ezra	1		1		1
Nehemiah					
Esther					
Total	12	6	18	0	18
Poetical Books					
Job	5		6		6
Psalms	22	1	36	3	39
Proverbs	2		2		2
Ecclesiastes	2		2		2
Song of Songs	3		4		4
Total	34	16	50	3	53
Prophets					
Isaiah	18	1	21	1	22
Jeremiah	5		6		6
Lamentations	1	2	4		4
Ezekiel	3		6		6
Daniel	5		8		8
12 Minor Prophets	7	1	8	2	10
Total	39	14	53	3	56
Grand Total	**143**	**62**	**205**	**17**	**222**

Table 6.4	Books of the Hebrew Bible in the Scrolls				
Book	**4Q**	**1–11Q**	**Qumran**	**Other**	**Total**
Torah					
Genesis	16		20	4	24
Exodus	12		17	1	18
Leviticus	10		15	2	17
Numbers	3		8	3	11
Deuteronomy	22	1	30	3	33
Total	63	27	90	13	103
Adjusted	58	26	84	11	95
Prophets					
Joshua	2		2		2
Judges	2		3		3
1 & 2 Samuel	3		4		4
1 & 2 Kings	1		3		3
Isaiah	18		21	1	22
Jeremiah	5		6		6
Ezekiel	3	1	6		6
12 Minor Prophets	7		8	2	10
Total	41	12	53	3	56
Writings					
Psalms	22	6	36	3	39
Job	5		6		6
Proverbs	2		2		2
Ruth	2		4		4
Song of Songs	3		4		4
Ecclesiastes	2		2		2
Lamentations	1		4		4
Esther					
Daniel	5		8		8
Ezra	1		1		1
Nehemiah					
1 & 2 Chronicles	1		1		1
Total	44	24	68	3	71
Grand Total	**143**	**62**	**205**	**17**	**222**

Table 6.5	Books Ranked According to Number of Mss.		
Book	Qumran	Other	Total
Psalms	36	3	39
Deuteronomy	30	3	33
Genesis	20	4	24
Isaiah	21	1	22
Exodus	17	1	18
Leviticus	15	2	17
Numbers	8	3	11
12 Minor Prophets	8	2	10
Daniel	8	0	8
Jeremiah	6	0	6
Ezekiel	6	0	6
1 & 2 Samuel	4	0	4
Job	6	0	6
Ruth	4	0	4
Song of Songs	4	0	4
Lamentations	4	0	4
Judges	3	0	3
1 & 2 Kings	3	0	3
Joshua	2	0	2
Proverbs	2	0	2
Ecclesiastes	2	0	2
Ezra	1	0	1
1 & 2 Chronicles	1	0	1
Nehemiah	0	0	0
Esther	0	0	0
Total	211	19	230
Adjusted	205	17	222

The Pentateuch and Other Collections

As already discussed, six scrolls from Qumran contain the remains of more than one book (4QGen-Exod[a], 4QpaleoGen-Exod[l], 4QExod[b], 4QExod-Lev[f], 1QpaleoLev, 4QLev-Num[a]). In addition, the Murabbaʿat scroll (Mur 1) preserves portions of Genesis, Exodus, and Numbers (although this could be more than one manuscript). On the basis of their large parameters, Emanuel Tov adds several more Torah scrolls that most likely contained two or more books: 4QGen[b], 4QGen[e], SdeirGen, 4QExod[e], and MasDeut, which brings the total up to twelve.[76] This evidence confirms the traditional order of at least Genesis–Deuteronomy and suggests that the Pentateuch was viewed as a collection at Qumran. In several of these examples, it is very possible that that all five books from Genesis to

Deuteronomy were written on one scroll, in which case they would have measured about 80–98 feet, or 25–30 meters. It is interesting to note that according to later Jewish tradition (*Soferim* 3.4) two books of the Torah should not be combined without the intention of adding the other three books; we have no indication if this principle was followed or even known with respect to the Qumran scrolls.

The Minor Prophets: According to the Babylonian Talmud (*Baba Batra* 13b), the twelve books of the Minor Prophets are to be combined as a single collection. Seven of the scrolls confirm that these twelve prophetic books were copied together in ancient times and that they follow the traditional Hebrew order, not the order found in the Septuagint. However, in the oldest manuscript, 4QXII^a, Jonah follows Malachi as the last book in the collection, which suggests more fluidity than was previously recognized.

The Five Scrolls: In Jewish tradition, five of the Writings are grouped together as the Five Scrolls, or Five Megillot: the Song of Songs, Ruth, Lamentations, Ecclesiastes, and Esther. In Christian Bibles, however, these books are arranged very differently, with Ruth and Esther among the Historical Books, Ecclesiastes and the Song of Songs among the Poetic Books, and Lamentations among the Prophets (for a comparison of the different listings of Scripture, see Table 7.1 in the next chapter). The scrolls offer few clues on whether these ancient books were grouped together or stood alone. If—as we have suggested—the book of Esther was deliberately excluded from the Scriptures used at Qumran, the Five Scrolls could not have existed there as a collection.

Some intriguing evidence is offered by 4QLam, in which the first preserved writing appears at the top of a column, beginning with the seventh Hebrew word of chapter 1. Lamentations must have begun at the bottom of the previous column, which means that it was not the first work in this scroll. But what was the book that preceded Lamentations: Ruth as in the Hebrew Bible, or Jeremiah as in the Old Testament? The Jewish historian Josephus, writing near the end of the first century CE, describes the Jewish Scriptures as containing twenty-two books (*Against Apion* 1.8), whereas modern Jewish Bibles contain twenty-four. Although he gives no specific details, Josephus's number may suggest that Ruth was included as an appendix to Judges, and Lamentations as an appendix to Jeremiah. (For more information on Josephus's list, see Chapter 7). On balance, then, the Qumran fragments suggest that the Five Megillot were not written together on a single scroll, but more likely on separate manuscripts. Lamentations, however, was grouped with at least one other book; the most plausible suggestion so far is Jeremiah.

The Paleo-Hebrew Biblical Scrolls

Eleven or twelve biblical scrolls are written in paleo-Hebrew, rather than the square script in which the vast majority of the Dead Sea Scrolls were copied. Ten or eleven are from the Pentateuch (4QpaleoGen^m, 6QpaleoGen, 4QpaleoGen-Exod^l, 4QpaleoExod^m, 1QpaleoLev, 2QpaleoLev, 6QpaleoLev, 11QpaleoLev^a, 1QpaleoNum [same scroll as 1QpaleoLev?], 4QpaleoDeut^r, and 4QpaleoDeut^s), and the final manuscript is of Job (4QpaleoJob^c). The paleo-Hebrew script, which was common before the Exile (587–539 BCE), was most likely used for books that were considered especially important, of great antiquity, and attributed to Moses. The inclusion of Job may well reflect the rabbinic tradition that Moses wrote this book (see the Babylonian Talmud, *Baba Batra* 14b, 15a). Four more Qumran texts written in this script are 4Q124, 4Q125, 11Q22 (each listed as *Unidentified Text*), and 4Q123 *(paleoParaJoshua),* which contains portions of Joshua 21. Besides the Qumran copies, only two texts in this script, both of them nonbiblical and written on papyrus, were found at Masada *(paleoText of Sam. Origin [recto] and paleoUnidentified Text [verso])*.

What was the purpose of writing scrolls in this ancient script? Emanuel Tov suggests that the paleo-Hebrew texts from Qumran may derive from the Sadducees, since writing in this script was forbidden by the Pharisees (see the Mishnah, *Yadayim* 4:5; Babylonian Talmud, *Sanhedrin* 21b; and cf. Babylonian Talmud, *Megillah* 9a; Tosefta, *Sanhedrin* 5:7; and Jerusalem Talmud, *Megillah* 1:71b–c).[77] He also observes that these scrolls display virtually no scribal intervention, and that the Qumran scribes may have been influenced by the Sadducean tradition of using paleo-Hebrew characters for writing divine names in biblical and nonbiblical texts to ensure that their sanctity would be recognized and thus not erased.

The Greek Biblical Scrolls and the Aramaic Targums

Relatively few scrolls were written in Greek. The majority are biblical manuscripts and from the Pentateuch: Exodus (pap7QLXXExod), Leviticus (4QLXXLev[a] and pap4QLXXLev[b]), Numbers (4QLXXNum), and Deuteronomy (4QLXXDeut). An important Greek scroll of the Minor Prophets is 8HevXII gr, which was found in Cave 8 at Naḥal Ḥever. Also noteworthy are a Greek paraphrase of Exodus (4Q127), the Letter of Jeremiah (pap7QEpJer gr), *1 Enoch* (pap7QEn gr), and the fascinating *Unidentified Greek Scroll* (4Q126).

For details on the three targums (4QtgLev, 4QtgJob, and 11QtgJob), see the comments on the biblical books involved. The statistics presented in Tables 6.3, 6.4, and 6.5 count these manuscripts as biblical scrolls. In light of the tradition that Moses wrote Job (Babylonian Talmud, *Baba Batra* 14b, 15a), it appears that only books of Moses were eligible for translation into Aramaic.

Excerpted or Abbreviated Biblical Texts

It is well known that many of the Dead Sea Scrolls are very fragmentary. When dealing with the remains of a biblical book, scholars tend to assume that the original scroll contained the entire work, but this is not always the case. Several scrolls have been identified as containing excerpted or abbreviated biblical texts, often for liturgical use.[78] Some examples are 4QDeut[j] and 4QDeut[n] (both containing Deuteronomy 31, on the Covenant), 4QDeut[q] (containing the Song of Moses in Deut. 32:1–44), 1QPs[a], 4QPs[g], 4QPs[h], and 5QPs (all containing Psalm 119), and 4QDan[e] (perhaps only the Prayer of Daniel in Dan. 9:4b–19).

Biblical Scrolls Written on Papyrus

The Dead Sea Scrolls, especially the biblical ones, were almost always written on leather parchment, while letters, bills, and documents were written on papyrus. Some one hundred papyri were discovered at Qumran, of which only eight contain biblical books: four of the Pentateuch (pap4QGen, pap7QLXXExod, pap4QLXXLev[b], and pap6QDeut?), one of the Historical Books (pap6QKings), one of the Poetic Books (pap6QPs), and two of the Prophets (pap4QIsa[p] and pap6QDan). To these may be added a ninth scroll, a possible biblical text from Cave 7 that was written in Greek: pap Biblical Text gr (7Q3).

The scarcity of biblical texts written on papyrus is partly due to the expense and scarcity of this material, which had to be imported from Egypt. More significant, perhaps, is that parchment was prepared from ritually pure animals. This would have been more acceptable to the Qumran community, and Jewish scribes in general, for copying biblical texts than papyrus, which was made by non-Jews in Egypt and thus was considered by many to be impure.[79] Compare the later Jewish tradition that biblical scrolls were to be written on parchment (the Mishnah, *Megillah* 2:2; the Jerusalem Talmud, *Megillah* 1:71d).

Select Bibliography

Sources that were especially used for this chapter:

Abegg, M. G., Jr., P. W. Flint, and E. Ulrich. *The Dead Sea Scrolls Bible*. San Francisco: Harper-SanFrancisco, 1999.

Tov, E. "The Biblical Texts from the Judean Desert—An Overview and Analysis of All the Published Texts." In *The Bible as Book: The Hebrew Bible and the Judaean Desert Discoveries.* Proceedings of the Conference Held at Hampton Court, Herefordshire, 18–21 June 2000. Edited by E. D. Herbert and E. Tov. London: The British Library, 2002. pp. 139–65.

Ulrich, E., *The Dead Sea Scrolls and the Origins of the Bible.* Studies in the Dead Sea Scrolls and Related Literature. Grand Rapids, MI: Eerdmans; Leiden: Brill, 1999. Especially chaps. 2–6 (pp. 17–120).

Several other informative articles are to be found in

Schiffman, L. H., and J. C. VanderKam, eds. *The Encyclopedia of the Dead Sea Scrolls.* 2 vols. New York and Oxford: Oxford University Press, 2000.

Other books and articles:

Albright, W. F. "New Light on Early Recensions of the Hebrew Bible." *Bulletin of the American Schools of Oriental Research* 140 (1955): 27–33.

Cross, F. M. *The Ancient Library at Qumran.* 3d ed. Sheffield: Sheffield Academic Press, 1995.

Cross, F. M., and S. Talmon, eds. *Qumran and the History of the Biblical Text.* Cambridge, MA: Harvard University Press, 1975.

Flint, P. W. *The Dead Sea Scrolls and the Book of Psalms.* Studies on the Texts of the Desert of Judah 17. Leiden: Brill, 1997.

Sanders, J. A. *The Dead Sea Psalms Scroll.* Ithaca, NY: Cornell University Press, 1967.

Talmon, S. "The Textual Study of the Bible—A New Outlook." In F. M. Cross and S. Talmon, eds. *Qumran and the History of the Biblical Text.* Cambridge, MA: Harvard University Press, 1975. Pp. 321–400.

Tov, E. *Textual Criticism of the Hebrew Bible.* 2d ed. Assen/Maastricht: Van Gorcum; Minneapolis: Fortress Press, 2001.

Ulrich, E. *The Qumran Text of Samuel and Josephus.* Harvard Semitic Monographs 19. Missoula, MT: Scholars Press, 1978.

VanderKam, J. C. *The Dead Sea Scrolls Today.* Grand Rapids, MI: Eerdmans; London: SPCK, 1994.

CHAPTER 7

The Dead Sea Scrolls and the Canon of the Hebrew Bible/Old Testament

THE TERM *CANON* IS NOT EASILY UNDERSTOOD with respect to Scripture for at least three reasons. First, this is a technical word with more than one meaning, so any proper definition must take several components into account. Second, different groups have different canons of Scripture. The most obvious distinction is between Jews, for whom Scripture is the Hebrew Bible, and Christians, whose Bible includes both the Old and New Testaments. This became very apparent to a young Ph.D. student of the Christian faith visiting Jerusalem for the first time to participate in an academic conference, when he was asked by an Israeli student: "What are you specializing in? Bible or New Testament?" This question—which was sincerely posed—highlights the different paradigms or suppositions held by each student: Jews and Christians have very different understandings of the term *Bible* and the books that a Bible contains.

Third, we all have a tendency to define earlier traditions—especially religious ones—in terms of what we know now or what we are used to. It is not difficult for Protestants to assume that Catholics have "added" books to the Bible, or for Catholics to maintain that Protestants have "omitted" books from the Bible, or for Jews to believe that Christians have "changed" the order and text of the Hebrew Bible with recourse to later translations used by the Church. This tendency is not special to one group; it is part of human nature, and we all act in this way at one time or another. It becomes destructive, however, when we declare that the beliefs of other groups (in this case, on the canon of Scripture) are wrong and have no ancient basis, whereas the canon of our own group is correct and is based on the decisions of ancient and eminent authorities (whether Moses or Ezra or Jesus or Paul). Most scholars now agree that the canons of Jews, Protestants, Catholics, and Orthodox Christians all derive from ancient evidence and were fixed by early councils of religious leaders. So readers will find this chapter more profitable and enjoyable by realizing that different canons of Scripture do exist, and that in the following pages we explore these canons in relation to the Dead Sea Scrolls without trying to prove which canon is "right" and which ones are "wrong."

What about the New Testament? Since the Dead Sea Scrolls were written and copied too early to provide much information on the New Testament canon, only the canon of the Old Testament or Hebrew Bible is discussed in the present chapter. It has been suggested, however, that some New Testament writings were actually found among the Greek scrolls in Cave 7. We shall, therefore, investigate this fascinating question in a later section of the book, Chapter 14.

Our discussion of scrolls and canon is divided into five parts: (1) defining the term *canon;* (2) appropriate terms for sacred or authoritative writings before the canon was fixed; (3) the Jewish, Protestant, Roman Catholic, and Orthodox canons of the Hebrew Bible/Old Testament; (4) ancient evidence apart from the Dead Sea Scrolls; and (5) the evidence from scrolls found at Qumran.

The Definition of *Canon*

The basic meaning of *canon* is a *reed,* but its two extended meanings in classical Greek, *norm* and *list,* are relevant for biblical Studies. A helpful verse is Gal. 6:16, which says that Christians are to live by a single *kanōn,* or normative rule, of life. In later Christian theology, the term *canon* has a twofold meaning: a *norm* for the church, and a *list* of sacred writings of the Old and New Testaments. This implies a reflexive judgment on the part of church authorities and compilers who declared certain lists to be normative and sacred.

TECHNICAL DETAILS
Canon

The term *canon* transliterates the Greek κανών *(kanōn),* which in turn derives from a Semitic word for *reed.* Compare the Greek κάννα *(kanna),* the Hebrew קָנֶה *(qaneh),* and the Arabic *qanāh,* as well as the English term *cane.* In classical usage, the basic sense of *reed* is then extended to that of *straight rod* or *bar,* with the literal meaning of a measuring tool (as used, for example, in building). Metaphorically, the term then becomes a *norm, ideal,* or *standard* of excellence (for instance, to denote the perfect human figure in sculpture, or the basis for knowing what is true or false in philosophy). Finally, the term can signify a *table* or *list* (e.g., a chronological timetable or a mathematical series).[1]

In the early fourth century (in his letter to Carpian) the church father Eusebius uses the plural term *kanones* for chronological timetables and for lists of Gospel references. However, in his *Ecclesiastical History* (3.25; 6.25) Eusebius refers to his own listing of New Testament books as a *katalogos.*

Our earliest surviving list of books is in the Muratorian Fragment (late second century), but it is only with lists from the later fourth century—by Athanasius and Augustine, and from the councils of Hippo (393) and Carthage III (397)—that general agreement with respect to their contents becomes clear for most of the church. Athanasius, for instance, distinguishes between the *kanonizomena,* or canonical books, and the Apocrypha.

1. See R. E. Brown and R. F. Collins, "Canonicity," in the *New Jerome Biblical Commentary,* §66.1–101, esp. §66.5; and H. W. Beyer, "κανών," in the *Theological Dictionary of the New Testament* 3:596–602.

A proper definition of *canon* should thus include the distinct components of norm, list, and reflexive judgment; we propose the following:

> A canon is the closed list of books that was officially accepted retrospectively by a community as supremely authoritative and binding for religious practice and doctrine.[1]

This definition allows for the fact that different groups have different canons, whether in the ordering of materials (Jewish versus Christian) or in the inclusion or exclusion of specific books (the canons of Roman Catholics, Orthodox, Protestants, Jews). Four canons of the Hebrew Bible/Old Testament are presented later (see Table 7.1).

Appropriate Terminology

The term *canon* belongs to the postbiblical period and should not be used for collections of sacred books, whether Jewish or Christian, before the second or third centuries CE. However, finding more fitting terms for sacred or authoritative writings in the Second Temple period is no simple task. The word *Bible*[2] usually denotes a book consisting of writings that are generally accepted by Jews or Christians as inspired by God and thus of divine authority, although more general, narrow, or technical meanings are also found. The problem with using this term for writings prior to the second century CE is that it implies the completion of the Jewish Scriptures and their existence in one book or collection at that time. This assumption, however, pertains only to a later date, since no completed Bible existed during the Qumran period or that of the New Testament writers.

Although the terms *canon, canonical, Bible,* and *biblical* should not be used with reference to the Dead Sea Scrolls and other Second Temple literature, the ancient sources suggest several others that are more appropriate:[3]

1. "What is read" (Neh. 8:8)
2. "As it is written" (1QS *[Rule of the Community]* 5.17; 8.14; 4QFlor *[The Last Days: A Commentary on Selected Versus]* 1.2, 12, 15, 16; 4QCatena A *[The Last Days: An Interpretation of Selected Verses]* frags. 5–6, l. 11; frag. 7, l. 3; frags. 10–11, l. 1)
3. "What is written" (11QMelch *[The Coming of Melchizedek]* 2.19)
4. "The holy writings" (Mishnah, *Yadayim* 4:6; see also *1 Clement* 53:1; 2 Tim. 3:15; Rom. 1:2)
5. "The books" (Dan. 9:2) or "the book" (1QS 7.2)
6. "The holy books" (1 Macc. 12:9; Alexander Polyhistor [according to Eusebius, *Preparatio Evangelica* 9.24])

These terms suggest that sacred material was contained in three loci, or activities: reading, writing, and books. At Qumran, "writing" features most often with respect to sacred truth or teaching, with passages from holy and authoritative works regularly introduced by *as it is written* or a similar phrase. Accordingly, the term *Scripture* (with its adjective *scriptural*) seems most fitting for uniquely sacred or authoritative writings in the Second Temple period.

It must be emphasized that *Scripture* here means a writing that was considered divinely revealed, uniquely authoritative, and believed to be of ancient origin (even if it was actually quite recent). In other words, while the Scriptures have much in common with other authoritative writings, they are unique. This distinction is illustrated by the *Commentary (Pesher) on Habakkuk* (1QpHab) from Qumran, in which the scriptural text is quoted and then followed by an interpretation. Both the scriptural base text (e.g., Hab. 2:1–2) and the interpretation were considered to be revealed and authoritative:

> So I will stand on watch and station myself on my watchtower and wait for what He will say to me, and [what I will reply to] His rebuke. Then the LORD answered me [and said, "Write down the vision plainly] on tablets, so that with ease [someone can read it]." (Hab. 2:1–2, quoted in 1QpHab 6.12–16)
>
> [This refers to . . . . . .] then God told Habakkuk to write down what is going to happen to the generation to come; but when that period would be complete He did not make known to him. When it says, "so that with ease someone can read it," this refers to the Teacher of Righteousness to whom God made known all the mysterious revelations of his servants the prophets. (1QpHab 6.16–7.5 [WAC, 119][4])

This passage indicates that for the Qumran community both the scriptural text and the interpretation were of divine origin and authoritative; nevertheless, there seems to be a distinction between the older revealed prophecy and the later revealed interpretation. In other words, the term *Scripture* can be used only for the excerpt from Habakkuk 2, not for the *pesher* that follows.

The Jewish, Protestant, Roman Catholic, and Orthodox Canons of the Hebrew Bible/Old Testament

The canon of the Hebrew Bible/Old Testament and its development are complex because of the different faith communities involved. With reference to Table 7.1, we shall discuss the similarities and differences between these canons under three headings: structure, contents, and form.

STRUCTURE OF THE CANONS

The overall structure of the various Christian Old Testaments follows the pattern given in Table 7.1, but more variety is evident in Jewish tradition. According to Jack Lightstone,[5] the twenty-four books of the tripartite rabbinic Bible were arranged somewhat differently in the medieval period, with Samuel, Kings, and Chronicles each counted as two books; with Ezra and Nehemiah each counted as one book; and with the Song of Songs, Ruth, Lamentations, Ecclesiastes, and Esther counted as a single collection (the Five Scrolls). Under this arrangement, the twenty-four books are as follows:

The Pentateuch, or *Torah*

(1) Genesis, (2) Exodus, (3) Leviticus, (4) Numbers, (5) Deuteronomy

The Prophets, or *Nebi'im*

The Former Prophets:

(6) Joshua, (7) Judges, (8) 1 Samuel, (9) 2 Samuel, (10) 1 Kings, (11) 2 Kings

The Latter Prophets:

(12) Isaiah, (13) Jeremiah, (14) Ezekiel, and (15) The Twelve Minor Prophets

Table 7.1			The Jewish, Protestant, Roman Catholic, and Greek Orthodox Canons

Jewish Tanakh [Total: 24 Books]	Protestant Old Testament [Total: 39 Books]	Roman Catholic Old Testament [Total: 46 Books +2 Additions]	Greek Orthodox Old Testament [Total: 48 Books +3 Additions]
Torah (5)	**Pentateuch** (5)	**Pentateuch** (5)	**Pentateuch** (5)
Genesis	Genesis	Genesis	Genesis
Exodus	Exodus	Exodus	Exodus
Leviticus	Leviticus	Leviticus	Leviticus
Numbers	Numbers	Numbers	Numbers
Deuteronomy	Deuteronomy	Deuteronomy	Deuteronomy
Nebi' im [Prophets] (8)	**Historical Books** (12)	**Historical Books** (16)	**Historical Books** (17)
Joshua	Joshua	Joshua	Joshua
Judges	Judges	Judges	Judges
Samuel	Ruth	Ruth	Ruth
Kings	1–2 Samuel	1–2 Samuel	1–2 Kingdoms (1–2 Samuel)
Isaiah	1–2 Kings	1–2 Kings	3–4 Kingdoms (1–2 Kings)
Jeremiah	1–2 Chronicles	1–2 Chronicles	1–2 Paraleipomena (1–2 Chronicles)
Ezekiel	Ezra	Ezra	1 Esdras
Book of the 12 Prophets	Nehemiah	Nehemiah	2 Esdras (Ezra-Nehemiah)
Hosea		Tobit	Tobit
Joel		Judith	Judith
Amos	Esther	Esther + Additions	Esther + Additions
Obadiah		1–2 Maccabees	1–3 Maccabees
Jonah			
Micah	**Poetry/Wisdom** (5)	**Poetry/Wisdom** (7)	**Poetry/Wisdom** (8)
Nahum	Job	Job	Job
Habakkuk	Psalms	Psalms	Psalms + Psalm 151
Zephaniah			Prayer of Manasseh

(continued)

The Writings, or *Kethubim*

(16) Psalms, (17) Proverbs, (18) Job, (19) The Five Scrolls (Song of Songs, Ruth, Lamentations, Ecclesiastes, Esther), (20) Daniel, (21) Ezra, (22) Nehemiah, (23) 1 Chronicles, (24) 2 Chronicles

When we compare the Jewish canon with the three Christian canons, a basic difference at once becomes evident: the arrangement of the books involved. All these canons begin with

Table 7.1	*(continued)*		
Jewish Tanakh *[Total: 24 Books]*	**Protestant** **Old Testament** *[Total: 39 Books]*	**Roman Catholic** **Old Testament** *[Total: 46 Books* *+2 Additions]*	**Greek Orthodox** **Old Testament** *[Total: 48 Books* *+3 Additions]*
Haggai	Proverbs	Proverbs	Proverbs
Zechariah	Ecclesiastes	Ecclesiastes	Ecclesiastes
Malachi	Song of Songs	Song of Songs	Song of Songs
		Wisdom of Solomon	Wisdom of Solomon
		Ecclesiasticus	Ecclesiasticus
Kethubim [Writings] (11)	**Prophets** (17)	**Prophets** (18)	**Prophets** (18)
Psalms	Isaiah	Isaiah	Isaiah
Proverbs	Jeremiah	Jeremiah	Jeremiah
Job	Lamentations	Lamentations	Lamentations
Song of Songs		Baruch + Letter of Jeremiah	Baruch + Letter of Jeremiah
Ruth	Ezekiel	Ezekiel	Ezekiel
Lamentations	Daniel	Daniel + Additions	Daniel + Additions
Ecclesiastes	Hosea	Hosea	Hosea
Esther	Joel	Joel	Joel
Daniel	Amos	Amos	Amos
Ezra-Nehemiah	Obadiah	Obadiah	Obadiah
Chronicles	Jonah	Jonah	Jonah
	Micah	Micah	Micah
	Nahum	Nahum	Nahum
	Habakkuk	Habakkuk	Habakkuk
	Zephaniah	Zephaniah	Zephaniah
	Haggai	Haggai	Haggai
	Zechariah	Zechariah	Zechariah
	Malachi	Malachi	Malachi

(Layout adapted from *The Folio* 11/1 [1991]:3.)

the five books of the Pentateuch (Torah), but then the Jewish or Hebrew Bible places Joshua through the book of the Twelve Prophets in a second category (the Nebi'im, or Prophets), and Psalms through Chronicles in a third division (the Kethubim, or Writings).[6] In contrast, Christian Bibles place the books after the Pentateuch in three different groups: the Historical Books, Poetry or Wisdom, and the Prophets.

Because it ends with Ezra-Nehemiah and Chronicles, the Hebrew Bible culminates with a clear theological message: the people's return to the land of Israel after the Exile, in fulfillment of God's covenant promises to Abraham and later Israelite leaders. With the religion, city walls, and Temple being rebuilt by Ezra, Nehemiah, and Zerubbabel, and with Israel's history being recounted to the returned exiles by the Chronicler, the culminating message of the Hebrew Bible is very evident.

In contrast, the Old Testament of Christian Bibles ends not with a return, but with prophecies of judgment and the promise of the messianic age. This theological message is also clear: Jews and the nations must forsake wickedness, be aware of coming judgment, and prepare for the advent of the Messiah. For Christian readers, the coming of Jesus and the reference to John the Baptist as preparing the way of the Lord flow quite naturally from the expectations and future orientation of the final books of the Old Testament.

With respect to structure, then, the Jewish Hebrew Bible and the Christian Old Testament are quite different. These two terms are not interchangeable, which is why we sometimes use the rather awkward term *Hebrew Bible/Old Testament* in this book. An interesting, and perhaps more suitable, alternative has been proposed by James Sanders: the First Testament. However, it seems best to retain the traditional terms, since "Hebrew Bible" and "Old Testament" are so familiar to readers.

CONTENTS OF THE CANONS

First, we may account for some of the differences between the four canons presented above in terms of simple arithmetic. Most notably, the Jewish canon of twenty-four books contains precisely the same writings as the Protestant canon of thirty-nine books. The total in the Jewish canon is far lower because Jews count each of the following groups as forming a single book: 1 and 2 Samuel, 1 and 2 Kings, the Twelve Minor Prophets, Ezra and Nehemiah, and 1 and 2 Chronicles. In contrast, most Christian canons reckon each of these writings as a separate book, thus yielding the higher total.

Second, while the Protestant Old Testament contains thirty-nine books, Roman Catholic Bibles contain an additional seven books, for a total of forty-six: Tobit, Judith, 1 and 2 Maccabees, the Wisdom of Solomon, Ecclesiasticus (also known as Sirach, or the Wisdom of Jesus ben Sira), and Baruch (of which chapter 6 is known as the Letter of Jeremiah). Catholic Bibles also contain "additions" or longer endings to Esther (in eight sections) and to Daniel (in three sections: the Prayer of Azariah and Song of the Three Young Men; Susanna; and Bel and the Dragon). (See Table 7.2.)

Third, Greek Orthodox Bibles include all the writings found in the Catholic canon, plus an additional three books for a total of forty-nine (1 Esdras, 3 Maccabees, and the Prayer of Manasseh), as well as a longer ending to the Psalter *(Psalm 151)*. Furthermore, in this tradition the books usually designated 1 and 2 Samuel are known as 1 and 2 Kingdoms, 1 and 2 Kings as 3 and 4 Kingdoms, 1 and 2 Chronicles as 1 and 2 Paraleipomena, and Ezra-Nehemiah together as 2 Esdras.

Finally, we should note that the Old Testament canons of other Orthodox churches contain additional differences. For example, the Slavonic Orthodox Church also includes 3 Esdras (called 4 Ezra in the Latin Vulgate), while the Ethiopian Church apparently recognizes *1 Enoch* and *Jubilees* as part of the Old Testament. (For further details, see Chapter 8.)

FORM OF THE CANONICAL BOOKS

Although the question of contents or structure involves entire books and their arrangement, the question of form is very different. In Chapter 6, which dealt with the scrolls and

Table 7.2	*Apocryphal Books in Various Bibles*

All Orthodox and Catholic Bibles

Tobit

Judith

Additions to Esther

Wisdom of Solomon

Ecclesiasticus (Sirach)

Letter of Jeremiah

Additions to Daniel

1 Maccabees

2 Maccabees

Greek Orthodox Bible	**Slavonic Orthodox Bibles**
Prayer of Manasseh	Prayer of Manasseh
Psalm 151	Psalm 151
1 Esdras	2 Esdras
3 Maccabees	3 Esdras
4 Maccabees (in appendix)	3 Maccabees

Adapted from *The HarperCollins Study Bible: New Revised Standard Version* (New York: HarperCollins, 1993) 1435.

the text of the Hebrew Bible/Old Testament, it became clear that different forms of several biblical books have been handed down in the Masoretic Text, the Samaritan Pentateuch, and the Septuagint. (Examples include Exodus, Jeremiah, Samuel, and the Psalms.) In light of this evidence, it is reasonable to ask: What form of the Scriptures or individual scriptural books should be translated? For modern Judaism, the answer is straightforward: the Masoretic Text, including the vowels and other Masoretic signs, since this is the authoritative text established and handed down by rabbinic Judaism. (An exception is the Samaritans, a Jewish group numbering a few thousand, for whom the Samaritan Pentateuch with its five books is the authoritative form of Scripture.)

For Christians, the issue is more complex. For most Protestants and Roman Catholics, the Masoretic Text is very authoritative. This view is shared by many biblical scholars, for whom the "final form" of the Hebrew text of Old Testament books is almost perfectly preserved in the Masoretic Text. However, most Christian groups and scholars are also open to including readings based on other ancient documents such as the Septuagint. In fact, the very order of books in all Christian Old Testaments follows most Greek Bibles (Genesis to Malachi), not the Masoretic Bible (Genesis to Chronicles). Furthermore, the first Testament of most modern Christian Bible translations contains many readings not found in the Masoretic Text, but in the Dead Sea Scrolls, the Septuagint, or other ancient versions. These include the Revised Standard Version, the New Revised Standard Version, the New International Version, the Jerusalem Bible, the New American Bible, and the Good News Bible.

Although the majority of Christian groups accept the Masoretic Text as the "Old Testament," but include readings from other ancient sources as representing the original or preferred text, there are notable exceptions. For some, the Masoretic Text—especially as translated in the Authorized (King James) Version—is supremely authoritative. For others, notably the Greek Orthodox Church, the Septuagint is the canonical and inspired Old Testament. This view is generally shared by all Orthodox confessions, such as the Russian Orthodox Church, for whom the Slavonic translation—which was made from the Septuagint—is viewed as the authoritative form of the Old Testament.

Ancient Evidence Outside Qumran

Passages and references found in ancient Jewish writings from about 200 BCE to about 100 CE show that most or all Jewish people considered certain books as divinely revealed and uniquely authoritative—in other words, as Scripture. Not surprisingly, none of these writings uses the word *canon* in the sense of a closed list of books that was officially accepted by a group as supremely authoritative (see "The Definition of *Canon*" earlier). The passages discussed below, from ancient writings other than the Dead Sea Scrolls, show that there was widespread agreement among Jewish groups on the scriptural or authoritative status of many books, and less agreement on others.

FROM THE SEPTUAGINT APOCRYPHA

Passages in Sirach

Among the Apocrypha is the wisdom book Sirach (also known as Ecclesiasticus, or the Wisdom of Jesus ben Sira), which was written in Hebrew about 190 or 180 BCE (see Chapter 8). Several passages furnish evidence about which books were considered by Ben Sira as authoritative in his day. One of these describes the activity of the scribe:

> How different the one who devotes himself to the study of **the law** of **the Most High!** He seeks out **the wisdom of all the ancients**, and is concerned with **prophecies**; he preserves the **sayings** of the famous and penetrates the subtleties of **parables**; he seeks out the hidden meanings of **proverbs** and is at home with the obscurities of **parables**. (Sir. 38:34–39:3)

It has been proposed that this passage points to "a tripartite structure of the canon,"[7] or even to the sequence of Law, Wisdom Writings, and Prophets as found in Greek and Latin Bibles.[8] These suggestions seem speculative by going beyond the evidence, but the passage shows that for our author *the law of the Most High, the wisdom of all the ancients, prophecies,* and *sayings, parables, and proverbs* were very authoritative.

More significant is the famous poem in praise of famous men from biblical times in chapters 44–50.[9] The order in which Ben Sira praises Israel's ancestors reveals the sources he drew upon and the sequence in which he found them. Our author refers to events in the five books of Moses, Joshua, Judges, 1–2 Samuel, 1–2 Kings (with some parallel material from Chronicles and Isaiah), Jeremiah, Ezekiel, possibly Job,[10] the Twelve Prophets, Ezra, and Nehemiah. If Chronicles and Job are removed from this list, it corresponds with the order of books in the first two divisions of the Hebrew Bible (the Torah and Prophets). Virtually all the books in the third division (the Writings) are absent: Psalms, possibly Job, Proverbs, Ruth, the Song of Songs, Ecclesiastes, Lamentations, Esther, Daniel, Ezra, and Nehemiah.

Half a century later, in about 132 BCE, the author's grandson translated Ben Sira's book into Greek, adding a prologue of his own. This prologue mentions three series or divisions of books that were apparently considered Scripture by himself and his audience:

> Many great teachings have been given to us through **the Law** and **the Prophets** and **the others that followed them**, and for these we should praise Israel for instruction and wisdom. Now, those who read **the scriptures** must not only themselves understand them, but must also as lovers of learning be able through the spoken and written word to help the outsiders. So my grandfather Jesus, who had devoted himself especially to the reading of **the Law** and **the Prophets** and **the other books of our ancestors**, and had acquired considerable proficiency in them, was himself also led to write something pertaining to instruction and wisdom, so that by becoming familiar also with his book those who love learning might make even greater progress in living according to the law.
>
> You are invited therefore to read it with goodwill and attention, and to be indulgent in cases where, despite our diligent labor in translating, we may seem to have rendered some phrases imperfectly. For what was originally expressed in Hebrew does not have exactly the same sense when translated into another language. Not only this book, but even **the Law** itself, **the Prophecies**, and **the rest of the books** differ not a little when read in the original. (NRSV)

The passage points to *the Law* and *the Prophets* (or *the Prophecies*) as Scripture, together with an apparent third series *(the others that followed them, the other books of our ancestors, or the rest of the books)*. It has been suggested that for the author's grandson—and even for Ben Sira himself—the Writings already "formed a closed collection."[11] The evidence, however, does not support such a proposal: the third series of old books is very vaguely defined, and was possibly not as authoritative for the translator as the other two.

1 Maccabees 1:56–57

Another apocryphal book is 1 Maccabees, which was written in the late second or early first century BCE. There we read that during the persecutions of the Jews by Antiochus IV "the books of the law that they found they tore to pieces and burned with fire. Anyone found possessing the book of the covenant, or anyone who adhered to the law, was condemned to death by decree of the king" (1:56–57). The following chapter refers to *the law* and *the deeds of the ancestors,* and mentions Abraham, Joseph, Phinehas, Joshua, Caleb, David, Elijah, the three Israelites in the fiery furnace, and Daniel (2:50–60). Although not very specific, this passage may point to the books of the law (Moses), some of the historical books, and the book of Daniel. Furthermore, 1 Macc. 7:17 quotes Ps. 79:2b–3 after introducing it with "in accordance with the word that was written," which indicates that for this author the book of Psalms was acknowledged as Scripture.

2 Maccabees 2:2–3, 13–14; 15:9

The apocryphal book 2 Maccabees, which deals with the events leading up to and following the Jewish revolt under Judas the Maccabee, was completed in 124 BCE. After *the law* is mentioned in 2:2–3, a significant passage follows in vv. 13–14:

The same things are reported in the records and in the memoirs of Nehemiah, and also that he founded a library and collected **the books about the kings and prophets**, and **the writings of David and letters of kings about votive offerings**. In the same way Judas [the Maccabee] also collected all the books that had been lost on account of the war that had come upon us, and they are in our possession. (NRSV)

Here *the books about the kings and the prophets* may mean the historical books (1–2 Samuel, 1–2 Kings, perhaps even Chronicles)[12] together with the prophetic books, *the writings of David* denotes the Psalms, and *letters of kings about votive offerings* may denote Ezra (which contains royal letters concerning offerings in the Temple). This proposal, however, is not certain, since our author does not clearly state which books he is describing.

Later on, 2 Maccabees mentions only two series of books: "Encouraging them from the law and the prophets, and reminding them also of the struggles they had won, [Judas] made them the more eager" (15:9). Again, the contents of these books, especially *the prophets,* is not specified; so these statements cannot be used to support a precise division of the biblical books into laws and prophecies.

FROM THE PSEUDEPIGRAPHA

4 Ezra *14:23–48*

This book, which is often included as chapters 3–14 of *2 Esdras,* was written after 70 CE, the year the Romans destroyed the Temple, and finalized in about 100. Some historic churches (e.g., the Russian Orthodox) include *4 Ezra* in their Old Testament canon (as *3 Esdras*). The author offers a profound meditation on the issues raised by the destruction of the Temple and adds that the Scriptures were lost in this terrible event. Ezra, the putative hero of the book, prays that God's Holy Spirit will inspire him to write down all that had been recorded in God's *Law* (here meaning all the Scriptures). By divine inspiration Ezra dictates ninety-four books, without a break, to five scribes over a forty-day period:

And when the forty days were ended, the Most High spoke to me, saying, "Make public **the twenty-four books** that you wrote first, and let the worthy and the unworthy read them; but keep **the seventy** that were written last, in order to give them to the wise among your people. For in them is the spring of understanding, the fountain of wisdom, and the river of knowledge." And I did so. (14:45–48, NRSV)

In this passage the number twenty-four is one way—based on the Greek alphabet—of counting the books of the Hebrew Bible (compare the twenty-two books in Josephus below). The fact that they were transcribed first gives these books priority, and they are meant for a general audience *(the worthy and the unworthy).* This is a significant passage, since it shows that by about 100 CE (perhaps earlier) the books that make up the Jewish canon were already assembled and accepted by many Jews as a distinct collection of scriptural writings. It also suggests that this collection was near to being closed, since it could not be expanded to include the other seventy inspired writings, which seem to form a separate group. Yet the collection falls shy of being a Bible or a canon, since the passage does not confirm that the twenty-four books were accepted by all Jews as supremely authoritative.

But what is meant by the other *seventy books* that were written last and are reserved for an exclusive audience *(the wise among your people)?* These seem to be esoteric books, possibly apocalyptic ones,[13] which needed special insight to be interpreted properly. In the quoted example, which is later than all the others mentioned in this section on evidence outside Qumran, the writer does not limit the inspired writings to the twenty-four found in the Hebrew Bible. It is difficult to decide, however, if he believes that many books besides the twenty-four should also be regarded as Scripture. It is equally plausible that he is advocating a brand of Judaism not followed by all Jews (such as Enochic Judaism, with its emphasis on apocalyptic themes), or that he may be distinguishing between older revealed Scripture and later revealed prophecy (see the comments on the *Habakkuk Pesher* in "Appropriate Terminology" earlier).

4 Maccabees *18:10*

Composed sometime in the first century BCE or the first century CE, *4 Maccabees* includes the following passage: "While he was still with you, he taught you the law and the prophets" (18:10). This is followed by references to the narratives in the Pentateuch and the books of Daniel, Isaiah, "the psalmist David," Proverbs, and Ezekiel. It is possible, but by no means certain, that here *the prophets* includes David's Psalter, the book of Daniel, and, surprisingly, the book of Proverbs.

FROM HELLENISTIC JEWISH WRITINGS

Philo, On the Contemplative Life *25*

The Jewish philosopher Philo lived in Alexandria, Egypt, from about 20 BCE until around 50 CE. In his treatise *On the Contemplative Life*, Philo describes a Jewish group called the Therapeutae, who shared several traits with the Essenes who lived at Qumran:

> In each house there is a consecrated room which is called a sanctuary or closet and closeted in this they are initiated into the mysteries of the sacred life. They take nothing into it, either drink or food or any other of the things necessary for the needs of the body, but **laws** and **oracles delivered through the mouth of prophets**, and **psalms and anything else which fosters and perfects knowledge and piety**. (*On the Contemplative Life* 25)[14]

Philo seems familiar with the series or categories of books that were mentioned earlier by Ben Sira's grandson. The philosopher's *laws and oracles . . . of prophets* sound similar to the grandson's *Law and Prophets,* while his *psalms and anything else which fosters and perfects knowledge and piety* may correspond to the grandson's even less specific *the others, the other books of our ancestors,* or *the rest of the books.* As Philo phrases it, the third category is rather vague, but *the psalms* (presumably the book of Psalms) is considered the most prominent of the nonlegal, nonprophetic works. If his third series does denote an early form of the Writings, Philo's quotations of Scripture show that it must have contained books besides those found in the present Hebrew canon. Whereas the Jewish philosopher quotes almost exclusively from the Pentateuch, he sometimes cites the books of Ben Sira and Wisdom of Solomon, thereby going beyond the limits of the traditional Kethubim.[15]

Josephus, Against Apion *1.37–42 (and* The Jewish War *10.35)*

Written by the historian Josephus in the 90s CE, *Against Apion* includes a defense of the veracity of the ancient records in which the history of the Jewish people is presented. In contrast, Josephus points out, the records of Greek history are less reliable and contradict one another:

> We do not possess myriads of inconsistent books, conflicting with each other. Our books, those which are justly accredited, are but two and twenty, and contain the record of all time.
>
> Of these, **five are the books of Moses**, comprising the laws and the traditional history from the birth of man down to the death of the lawgiver. This period falls only a little short of three thousand years. From the death of Moses until Artaxerxes, who succeeded Xerxes as king of Persia, **the prophets** subsequent to Moses wrote the history of the events of their own times **in thirteen books. The remaining four books contain hymns to God and precepts** for the conduct of human life.
>
> From Artaxerxes to our own time the complete history has been written, but has not been deemed worthy of equal credit with the earlier records, because of the failure of the exact succession of the prophets.
>
> We have given practical proof of our reverence for our own Scriptures. For, although such long ages have now passed, no one has ventured either to add, or to remove, or to alter a syllable; and it is an instinct with every Jew, from the day of his birth, to regard them as the decrees of God, to abide by them, and, if need be, cheerfully to die for them. (1.38–42)[16]

At first glance, this evidence seems the most complete and explicit of all our examples, but its interpretation is by no means transparent. One clear feature is that Josephus's listing of twenty-two books is another way of counting the books in the complete Hebrew Bible, most likely based on the Hebrew alphabet, which has twenty-two letters. There can also be little doubt that his first section comprises the five books of Moses (Genesis to Deuteronomy, ending with the *death of the lawgiver* in Deuteronomy 34).

The next two categories, however, are not straightforward. The second section contains the "thirteen" books written by the prophets, which contrasts markedly with the eight prophetic books of the Jewish canon outlined earlier. The mention of the Artaxerxes as the end point of prophetic succession offers a strong indication that Ezra, Nehemiah, and Esther were included in this prophetic group, since he is the latest Persian king mentioned in these books. Nevertheless, more than one grouping has been proposed for Josephus's thirteen prophets, as listed below:[17]

St. John Thackeray (1926)	Roger Beckwith (1985)	James VanderKam (1994)
Joshua	Joshua	Joshua
Judges + Ruth	Judges (+ Ruth?)	Judges
Samuel	Samuel	1 Samuel
		2 Samuel
Kings	Kings	1 Kings
		2 Kings
Chronicles	Chronicles	
Ezra-Nehemiah	Ezra-Nehemiah	Ezra-Nehemiah
Esther	Esther	Esther
Job	Job	

Isaiah	Isaiah	Isaiah
Jeremiah + Lam	Jeremiah (+ Lamentations?)	Jeremiah
Ezekiel	Ezekiel	Ezekiel
Daniel	Daniel	Daniel
Twelve Minor Prophets	Twelve Minor Prophets	Twelve Minor Prophets

In the *Jewish War,* however, Josephus mentions Isaiah and *also others, twelve in number,* which do not correspond with the thirteen books of the prophets referred to in *Against Apion.* This passage most likely refers to the books of Isaiah and Twelve Prophets:

> As for the prophet [Isaiah], he was acknowledged to be a man of God and marvellously possessed of truth, and, as he was confident of never having spoken what was false, he wrote down in books all that he had prophesied and left them to be recognized as true from the event by men of future ages. And not alone **this prophet, but also others, twelve in number,** did the same. (10.35)[18]

The compositions in Josephus's third section, *the remaining four books* that *contain hymns to God and precepts* have also found different identifications, all of them from what are now termed the Writings:[19]

St. John Thackeray (1926)	Roger Beckwith (1985)	James VanderKam (1994)
Psalms	Psalms (+ Ruth?)	Job
Proverbs	Proverbs	Psalms
Ecclesiastes	Ecclesiastes	Proverbs
Song of Songs	Song of Songs	Ecclesiastes

Although the passage from *Against Apion* hints at an emerging third series or section of Scriptures, another possibility is that Josephus has in mind literary forms that do not correspond to canonical divisions:[20] the books of Moses *comprising the laws and the traditional history,* the prophets presenting *the history of the events of their own times,* and the remaining four books containing *hymns to God and precepts for the conduct of human life.* If this is so, Josephus's text may indicate that the Scriptures derive from either of two sources, Moses or the prophets, which provides evidence for an essentially twofold division of Scripture.[21]

FROM THE NEW TESTAMENT

Matthew 23:34–35

Matt. 23:34–35 (= Luke 11:49–51) might be interpreted as showing that by Jesus' day the Scriptures ended with the book of Chronicles, since Jesus begins with an example of murder found in Genesis (Abel, Gen. 4:8) and ends with one from Chronicles (Zechariah, who was slain by Joash, 2 Chron. 24:20–22):

> Therefore I send you prophets, sages, and scribes, some of whom you will kill and crucify, and some you will flog in your synagogues and pursue from town to town, so that upon you may come all the righteous blood shed on earth, from the blood of righteous Abel to the blood of Zechariah son of Barachiah, whom you murdered between the sanctuary and the altar. (NRSV)

According to this view, Jesus' words have canonical significance since he chose examples from the first and last books of the Bible to show that such murderous conduct permeated the Scriptures. The reference, however, may simply be to the last murder mentioned in the historical books of Scripture, without necessarily implying that that Chronicles was the last book of the Bible.[22]

Another difficulty is that in the Chronicles passage Zechariah is called the son of Jehoiada. It is thus possible that Matthew is referring to the prophet Zechariah son of Berechiah (Zech. 1:1), or to Zechariah the son of Baris in Jerusalem during the first Jewish revolt as related by Josephus (*Jewish War* 4.334–44).[23]

Luke 24:44

The New Testament often features the expression *the law (of Moses) and the prophets,* for example: Matt. 5:17; 7:12; 22:40; Luke 16:16, 29, 31 *(Moses and the prophets);* John 1:45; Acts 13:15; 28:23; and Rom. 3:21. Luke also mentions *Moses and all the prophets* (24:27), but a few verses later this Gospel contains a longer and intriguing expression, in a scene where the resurrected Jesus appears to his followers:

> Then [Jesus] said to them, "These are my words that I spoke to you while I was still with you—that everything written about me in **the law of Moses, the prophets, and the psalms** must be fulfilled." (24:44)

In this passage *the psalms* most likely refers to the book of Psalms. It has been proposed that the term also encompasses additional books found in the Writings, but this identification extends beyond the evidence. A similar expression *(Davi[d)* is found in the Qumranic work known as 4QMMT; for comment on the passages from Luke 24 and 4QMMT and a third series of sacred writings, see "The Evidence from Qumran" below.

ASSESSMENT OF THE EVIDENCE OUTSIDE QUMRAN

Several Series of Scriptures

The texts featured in this section offer valuable insights into Jewish perceptions of Scripture outside Qumran from about 200 BCE to around 100 CE. The evidence indicates that already in the second century BCE many Jews were familiar with two series or sections of Scriptures and with others besides.

(1) The first series was variously known as *the law, the laws, Moses, the law of Moses,* or *the books of Moses.*

(2) The second series was variously termed *the Prophets, (the) prophecies,* or *oracles delivered through the mouth of prophets.*

(3) Additional books were also regarded as Scripture, but it is not clear if an actual third series was familiar to most authors. In one case (*4 Macc.* 18:15; cf. v. 10), *the psalmist David* seems to be among the prophets. Two other sources, however, refer to *the writings of David* (2 Macc. 2:13) or *the psalms* (Luke 24:44) separately from the prophets.

(4) Other terms suggest that many Jews viewed certain books beyond the Psalms as Scripture. Sometimes these writings are generally or vaguely designated: *the others that followed them, the other books of our ancestors,* and *the rest of the books.* Others seem to be poetic or wisdom books: *psalms and anything else which fosters and perfects knowledge and piety; the remaining four books [which] contain hymns to God and precepts;* and *sayings, para-*

bles, and proverbs. Two references in 2 Macc. 2:13 probably refer to writings of a narrative nature: *the books about the kings and prophets,* and *the letters of kings about votive offerings.*

The Books Included

Most scholars understand the *books of Moses* to be the five books of the Pentateuch (Genesis through Deuteronomy), which applies to most or all of the examples given above. Although this could mean that the first part of what was to become the Jewish Bible had been fixed by the second century BCE, evidence from Qumran indicates that at least some Jews believed that the *book(s) of Moses* contained more than the five books of the Pentateuch (see below).

The sources are not clear as to just how many and which books made up the second series of Scriptures, the *Prophets.* There is no firm evidence that this section contained the same list of prophets found in the Jewish canon (Joshua through the Twelve Minor Prophets), although Isaiah, Jeremiah, Ezekiel, Daniel, and the Minor Prophets are obvious candidates.

The Psalms could be included among the Prophets, yet were separate from them in the eyes of some Jewish communities. There is insufficient evidence to tell whether a distinct third series containing the Psalms and other books was emerging. If this were the case, the infant series did not contain all the books now preserved in the Writings (Psalms through Chronicles).

Several more books containing poetic and narrative material were also recognized as Scripture, but these do not belong to the second series or the possible third series.

By the close of the first century CE, then, there was as yet no canon in the sense of a closed list of books that was accepted retrospectively by all Jewish people as supremely authoritative. But the ancient sources do bear witness to the canonical process, or a canon in the making.

The Evidence from Qumran

The writings that featured in the evidence outside Qumran were written or have been preserved in Greek, even if some (e.g., Ben Sira) were originally composed in Hebrew. The Dead Sea Scrolls, however, were mainly written in Hebrew and Aramaic, the languages of the Hebrew Bible. What light do the scrolls, especially those published during the last decade of the twentieth century, shed on the growth of the canon of Scripture? What do they tell us about the arrangement of the Hebrew Bible/Old Testament? And were any of the apocryphal books accepted as Scripture by the Qumran community? The relevance of these ancient manuscripts for understanding the canon is discussed under two headings, structure and contents.

THE SCROLLS AND THE STRUCTURE OF THE HEBREW BIBLE/OLD TESTAMENT

Is there any evidence in the scrolls for the threefold division of Scripture as found in the Jewish Bible or the fourfold arrangement found in the Christian Old Testament? At least three relevant readings are found in the third section (C) of the *Sectarian Manifesto* (4QMMT; see Figure 7.1), which was composed in the mid-second century BCE by leaders of the Qumran community, perhaps before they migrated to Qumran.[24]

Figure 7.1
Manuscript 4Q396 of
4QMMT, plus several
fragments (PAM 43.490).
Courtesy of the Israel Antiquities
Authority

And so we see that some of the blessings and curses have already come that are written in **the b[ook of Mo]ses**. (section C, lines 20–21, from 4Q398 frags. 11–13 [WAC, 364])

[It is also written in **the book of] Moses** and in the [**books of the prophet]s** that [the blessings and curses] shall come [upon you. . .]. (C, lines 17–18, from 4Q398 frags. 11–17, col. i [WAC, 364])

[And] we have [also written] to you so that you may have understanding in **the book of Moses [and] in the book[s of the Pr]ophets** and in **Davi[d** and in **the events] of ages past** . . . (C, lines 9–11, from 4Q397 frags. 14–21)[25]

These readings suggest that up to four groupings of Scripture were accepted by the authors and their audience. First, all three excerpts (two partly reconstructed) refer to the *book of Moses*. This expression is equivalent to the *law of Moses,* which also occurs in a *Juridical Text* (2Q25) and even earlier as a doublet in 2 Kings 14:6: *the book of the law of Moses.* Second, two of the excerpts (one largely reconstructed) mention the *books of the Prophets,* which suggests two categories of Scripture. Similar terminology appears in the *Rule of the Community* (1QS) and in the *Damascus Document* (CD):

[The Instructor] is to teach them to seek God with all their heart and with all their soul, to do that which is good and upright before Him, just as He commanded through **Moses** and **all His servants the prophets**. (1QS 1.1–3 [WAC, 126–27])

The books of the Law are the tents of the king, as it says, "I will re-erect the fallen tent of David" (Amos 9:11). The king is <Leader of> the nation and the "foundation of your images" is the **books of the prophets** whose words Israel despised. (CD 7.15–18 [WAC, 57–58])

Third, the final excerpt from 4QMMT seems to denote [the *book of*] *Moses,* the *book[s of the Pr]ophets, Davi[d,* and *the events] of ages past.* Assuming that the placement of fragments is correct,[26] this reading may well have parallels in the passages from 2 Maccabees and Luke that were discussed earlier:

> The same things are reported in the records and in the memoirs of Nehemiah, and also that he founded a library and collected **the books about the kings and prophets**, and **the writings of David** and **letters of kings about votive offerings**. (2 Macc. 2:13–14)

> Then [Jesus] said to them, "These are my words that I spoke to you while I was still with you—that everything written about me in **the law of Moses, the prophets**, and **the psalms** must be fulfilled." (Luke 24:44)

It seems reasonable to equate 4QMMT's *David* with Luke's the *psalms.* (In both cases we take this to signify not the Writings or even the wisdom books as a whole, but only the Psalter.) An interesting picture then emerges: David (the Psalms) was considered prophecy, yet was emerging as a book distinct from the Prophets and as the forerunner of a third section of the Scriptures as early as the mid-second century BCE. Although the editors of 4QMMT propose that this passage is "a significant piece of evidence for the history of the tripartite division of the Canon,"[27] the excerpt suggests three series of the Scriptures for at least some Jews (in this case the Qumran community and its audience) in the second century BCE. For Julio Trebolle, "the book of Psalms becomes the key element in this discussion, seeing that it is a book at the borderline between Prophets and Writings."[28]

The words following *Davi[d* in the MMT passage are intriguing, though incomplete due to the broken text. The official editors suggest [*and in the events*] *of ages past* (Qimron and Strugnell),[29] while others have proposed [*. . . all*] *the generations* (Wise, Abegg, Cook), or [*and the annals of eac*]*h generation* (F. García Martínez), or [*and all the events*] *of every age* (G. Vermes).[30] In view of the key term *of each generation (dor w^{e}dor)* in line 11 of 4Q397 fragment 18, the missing and preserved words apparently refer to ages past, and thus probably denote writings of a narrative nature such as annals.[31]

Such language may refer to the historical books Joshua to Kings—perhaps even to these plus the books of Chronicles, Ezra, and Nehemiah. If this proposal is valid, 4QMMT suggests that, for some Jews at least, what are now the Former Prophets in modern Hebrew Bibles were grouped together as historical books (as in the Septuagint). Whether this is so, the absence of the nonhistorical wisdom books that were later included in the Writings (e.g., Proverbs) should be noted. The suggestions made here are admittedly speculative, so caution is advised. We can state, however, that in the mid-second century BCE 4QMMT seems to indicate an emerging third series of scriptural books that contained at least the Psalms, and possibly an emerging fourth series that contained historical writings.

To summarize: As was the case with several other Jewish writings, the evidence from the scrolls points to at least two series or sections of Scriptures for the Qumran community in the second century BCE: (1) *Moses* or *the book of Moses*, and (2) *the Prophets* or *the books of the Prophets*. Less conclusive, but of great interest, is the evidence in 4QMMT for an emerging third series: (3) *David* (i.e., the Psalms); and (4) possibly an emerging fourth series that contained historical writings.

With respect to *structure,* then, the evidence from Qumran is mixed. On the one hand, the sequence of Moses–Prophets supports the arrangement of Scripture as found in modern Jewish Bibles; on the other hand, the apparent grouping of historical writings lends support to the arrangement in the Septuagint and Christian Old Testament. It could be argued that some scrolls (notably those written in Greek) may support a different arrangement, but since these manuscripts are mostly fragmentary, this proposal is speculative.

(It is worth noting that in the most extensive Greek scroll from the Judean Desert, the Minor Prophets Scroll from Naḥal Ḥever, the sequence of books follows that of the Masoretic Text, not of the Septuagint.[32])

These series of Scriptures do *not* mean that for the Qumran community *Moses* or *the book of Moses* necessarily contained only the five books of the Torah (Genesis through Deuteronomy) as in modern Hebrew Bibles. Neither does it follow that *the Prophets* or *the books of the Prophets* contained the books of the Prophets (Joshua through the Twelve Minor Prophets), nor that *Davi[d* contained the books of the Writings (Psalms through Chronicles), nor that *the events] of ages past* contained the historical books (Joshua through Esther). The issue of *contents*—that is, which books were viewed as Scripture by the Qumran community—will be explored below.

THE SCROLLS AND THE CONTENTS OF THE HEBREW BIBLE/OLD TESTAMENT

We cannot assume that the Qumran community regarded as Scripture all the books found in traditional Hebrew Bibles or in a particular Christian Old Testament; any such decision must be based upon hard evidence found in the scrolls. Which criteria, then, are to be used for deciding whether specific books were viewed as Scripture by the Qumran community? No single approach is sufficient for deciding the scriptural status of individual books or groups of books, and so we propose the following nine criteria, with one or two examples for each. (Though many more can be given, we will try to provide examples from books whose authority at Qumran may not be obvious, i.e., books represented by few scrolls or books that are found among the Apocrypha or Pseudepigrapha.)

Statements Indicating Scriptural Status

Certain terms or statements in the community's own writings show that the Qumranites regarded particular writings as authoritative or sacred Scripture. Among the Prophets, for instance, Ezek. 44:15 is specified in the *Damascus Document:* "as God promised them by Ezekiel the prophet, saying . . ." (CD 3.20–4.2). The authoritative and prophetic status of Daniel is indicated in the *Florilegium* (WAC: *The Last Days: A Commentary on Selected Verses*), which quotes Dan. 12:3 and states: "As it is written in the Book of Daniel the Prophet" (4Q174 2.3).

Two other relevant passages are in *4QText with a Citation of Jubilees* (4Q228). Although this document is poorly preserved, fragment 1 1.1 seems to denote the book of *Jubilees* by its Hebrew title "[In the *Divisi]ons of the Times*," and fragment 1 1.9 introduces the first word of the title by a citation formula: "For thus it is written in the *Divisions [of the Times]*."[33] Finally, *Jubilees* is also specified as the source of information (the precise passage is not clear) in the *Damascus Document*, concerning the times when Israel would be blind to the law of Moses:

> But the specification of the times during which all Israel is blind to all these rules is laid
> out in detail in the *Book of Time Divisions by Jubilees and Weeks*. (CD 16.2–4 [WAC, 66])

The Appeal to Prophecy

Associating a book or writing with prophecy points to authoritative or scriptural status. An important New Testament example occurs in Jude 14–15, which tells us that Enoch *prophesied,* and then quotes from *1 Enoch* 1:9. A comparable case occurs in *David's Compositions,* the extended prose "epilogue" found in 27.2–11 of the Great Psalms Scroll (11QPs^a):

> And David, the son of Jesse, was wise, and a light like the light of the sun, and literate, and discerning and perfect in all his ways before God and men. And the LORD gave him a discerning and enlightened spirit. And he wrote 3,600 psalms; and songs to sing before the altar over the whole-burnt perpetual offering every day, for all the days of the year, 364; . . . **All these he composed through prophecy** which was given him from before the Most High.[34]

The key statement "all these he composed through prophecy[35] which was given him from before the Most High" clearly implies that all the compositions found in 11QPs^a are products of Davidic prophecy. As discussed in Chapters 6 and 8, these include works such as the canticle in Sir. 51:13–30, Psalms 151A, 151B, 154, and 155, and nine previously unknown compositions. The passage quoted from 11QPs^a provides striking evidence that its compiler and, most likely, its readers viewed the entire Psalter represented by 11QPs^a as authoritative Scripture.

Claims of Divine Authority

Besides obvious candidates such as Exodus or Isaiah, some writings found at Qumran are attributed to the forefathers and/or claim their message to be from God or from an angel. Two prominent examples are *1 Enoch* (1:2; 10:1–11:2) and *Jubilees* (1:5–18, 22–28, 26–29; 2:1), both of which also contain material that was written on heavenly tablets (see *1 Enoch* 81:1–2; 93:1; *Jub.* 3:8–14, 31). *Jubilees,* in fact, "advertises itself as divine revelation."[36] Two other very influential books that claim to be divine revelation should be mentioned. First, *Reworked Pentateuch* is nearly a verbatim quotation of material from Genesis through Deuteronomy; and the *Temple Scroll* presents itself as a new Deuteronomy directly from God, spoken in the first person (for more on these works, see Chapter 9).

Davidic Superscriptions

One function of Davidic superscriptions (headings; see Figure 7.2) in the book of Psalms is to associate particular compositions with David, the psalmist par excellence. There are very few examples among the scrolls of Davidic titles given to psalms not found in our traditional Psalter, which shows that adding such titles for purposes of lending authority was not practiced among the compilers of the different Psalters found at Qumran. Two rare examples of titles given to psalms absent from the traditional Psalter are the autobiographical Psalms 151A and 151B, whose titles are clearly Davidic and thus denote the scriptural status of the two psalms:

> A Hallelujah of David the Son of Jesse. (Ps. 151A:0)

> At the beginning of David's power after the prophet of God had anointed him.
> (Ps. 151B:1)

Quantity of Manuscripts Preserved

Works that are represented by a large number of manuscripts were extensively used at Qumran, which indicates their popularity and most likely their authoritative status. Of all

Figure 7.2
Davidic Superscriptions in
Col. 28 of 11QPsª (11Q5):
Psalms 151A and 151B
(PAM 43.792).
Courtesy of the Israel Antiquities
Authority

the scrolls discovered at Qumran, the books represented by the greatest number are—in descending order—the Psalms (thirty-six scrolls), Deuteronomy (thirty), Isaiah (twenty-one), Genesis (twenty), Exodus (seventeen), *Jubilees* (about fifteen), Leviticus (fifteen), and *1 Enoch* (twelve). On the number of manuscripts preserved for other books, see Table 6.5 in Chapter 6.

Translation into Greek or Aramaic

Comparatively few Qumran scrolls were written in Greek, but the translation of a Hebrew work into Greek may indicate its importance and authoritative status for its scribe or users. Several Greek scrolls were found in Caves 4 and 7 at Qumran, including Exodus (pap7QLXXExod), Leviticus (4QLXXLevª and pap4QLXXLevᵇ), Numbers (4QLXXNum), Deuteronomy (4QLXXDeut), the Letter of Jeremiah (pap7QEpJer gr), and *1 Enoch* (pap7QEn gr). In addition, the large Greek scroll containing the Book of the Twelve Minor Prophets (8 ḤevXII gr) was discovered at Naḥal Ḥever.

Moreover, only books that were regarded as Scripture—specifically as "books of Moses"—seem to have been translated into Aramaic. For further details on the three targums (4QtgLev, 4QtgJob, 11QtgJob) and the tradition that Moses wrote Job (Babylonian Talmud, *Baba Batra* 14b, 15a), see under the relevant books as well as Chapter 6 ("The Scrolls and the Text of the Hebrew Bible/Old Testament").

Pesharim *and Other Commentaries*

Books on which commentaries were written must have been viewed as Scripture by the commentators and their audiences. This category includes the *pesharim,* in the form of textual citation followed by interpretation *(pesher).* At least seventeen *pesharim* are found among the scrolls: six on Isaiah (3QpIsa and 4QpIsaª⁻ᵉ), two each on Hosea, Micah, and Zephaniah (4QpHosª, 4QpHosᵇ, 1QpMic, 4QpMic?, 1QpZeph, 4QpZephª), one each on Nahum and Habakkuk (4QpNah, 1QpHab), and three on the Psalms (1QpPs, 4QpPsª, 4QpPsᵇ). Two more works are *Apocryphal Malachi* from Cave 5 (5Q10), which was earlier classified as a *pesher,* and another unidentified *pesher* from Cave 4 called *4QpUnidentified* (4Q172). (For further details on the *pesharim,* see Chapter 9.)

Other types of commentary were found at Qumran, including *A Commentary on Genesis and Exodus* (4Q422), which may be classified as "rewritten Bible," and *A Commentary on the Law of Moses* (4Q251), which features passages concerning the law of damages (Exod. 21:19, 28–29), firstfruits (Exod. 22:29), and proper sacrifice. It has also been suggested[37] that the *Pesher on the Apocalypse of Weeks* (4Q247) may be a commentary on a section of *1 Enoch*. Caution is advised, however, since 4Q247 is very fragmentary.

Books Quoted or Alluded to as Authorities

Ways in which a book is used in later writings often point to its special authority or scriptural status. This category is very large, and its components are sometimes difficult to determine because the difference between definite allusion and general scriptural imagery is not always clear. With reference to the *Hodayot (Thanksgiving Psalms),* for example, Bonnie Kittel proposes four degrees of the use of scriptural language, ranging from definite quotations to the "free use of biblical idiom and vocabulary."[38] A few examples are discussed below. For an extensive list of quotations of, or clear allusions to, scriptural passages in the nonbiblical scrolls, see Appendix III.

MIDRASHIC TEXTS

Two examples are the *Florilegium* (4Q174), which includes Ps. 1:1 and Ps. 2:1 as base texts, and *Catena A* (4Q177), which contains quotations from several psalms (11:1–2; 12:1, 7; 5:10(?); 13:2–3, 5; 6:2–5, 6; 16:3; 17:1, apparently in that order).

QUOTATIONS WITH INTRODUCTORY FORMULAE

In many cases the quoted passage is preceded by a special phrase, especially *as he said* or *as it is written,* which suggests that the writer viewed the passage as especially authoritative or scriptural. Some examples are[39]

> *As God said.* The *Damascus Document* uses this phrase and refers to Mal. 1:10 (CD 6.13–14).

> *As David said.* In *4QCatena A* (4Q177), this formula introduces Ps. 6:2–5 (frags. 12–13 1.2).

> *As he said.* In the *Florilegium* (4Q174), this phrase introduces 2 Sam. 7:11, with God as the subject (3.7).

> *It is written.* In the *Damascus Document,* this formula introduces Prov. 15:8 (CD 11.19–21).

> *As it is written.* The *Isaiah Pesher* (4Q163) introduces a passage, apparently from Jeremiah, with this phrase (frag. 1, l. 4). Another important usage is found in the *Rule of the Community,* where Isa. 40:3 is quoted in relation to the self-identity and mission of the Qumran desert community:

>> They shall separate from the session of perverse men to go to the wilderness, there to prepare the way of truth, *as it is written* (Isa. 40:3): "In the wilderness prepare the way of the LORD, make straight in the desert a highway for our God." (1QS 8.13–14)

QUOTATIONS OR ALLUSIONS WITHOUT INTRODUCTORY FORMULAE

Some examples of texts that are quoted or alluded to are from the following books:

Genesis: In criticizing the polygamy of the Pharisees, the *Damascus Document* argues on the basis of Gen. 1:27 ("male and female he created them") and Gen. 7:9 ("went into the ark two by two") that one wife was the biblical norm (CD 4.19–5.1).

Leviticus: The key to understanding the Qumran community's emphasis on purity is found in Lev. 15:31: "You must keep the people of Israel separate from their uncleanness, so that they might not die in their uncleanness by defiling my tabernacle which is in their midst." See the *Ritual of Purification B* (4Q512) fragment 69, line 2 and the *Temple Scroll* (11QTª) 51.4b–10.

Jubilees: Jub. 3:8–14—which grounds the legislation of Leviticus 12 (concerning a woman's impurity) in the story of Adam and Eve—may be the source for the same material in the *Miscellaneous Rules* (4Q265 frag. 7 2.11–17). Moreover, a passage in the *Damascus Document* seems to be based on *Jub.* 23:11, which refers to people's loss of knowledge in their old age:

> No one above the age of sixty shall hold the office of judge of the nation, because when Adam broke faith, his life was shortened, and in the heat of anger against the earth's inhabitants, God commanded their minds to regress before their life was over. (CD 10.7–10 [WAC, 68])

Isaiah: The *Rule of the Community* refers to the *precious cornerstone* of Isa. 28:16 (1QS 8.7).

Jeremiah: The first column (1.1–11) of the *Apocryphon of Jeremiah C* (4Q385b) draws on Jeremiah 40–44, although lines 4–6 recall the fall of Jerusalem as found in Jer. 52:12–13.

Psalms: The *Hodayot* cite Ps. 26:12, but with some modification (1QHª 2.30).

Proverbs: Prov. 1:1–6 is echoed in *4QBeatitudes* (4Q525): "[to kno]w wisdom and disc[ipline], to understand [. . .]" (frag. 1, l. 2). Two texts that treat the biblical figures of Lady Wisdom and Dame Folly at Qumran are the *Wiles of the Wicked Woman* (4Q184) and *Sapiential Work* (4Q185). For example, Prov. 7:12 seems to be quoted in 4Q184, where Lady Folly "lies secretly in wait [. . .] in the city streets" (frag. 1, ll. 11–12).[40]

Lamentations: A Lament for Zion (4Q179), which appears to be patterned after Lamentations, quotes Lam. 1:1 (frag. 2, l. 4). *A Prayer for Deliverance* (4Q501) capitalized on the genre of lament, although in this case the enemy was not a foreign people, but rather unbelieving Jews.

Dependence on Earlier Books

Several Qumran texts show a more general dependence on particular earlier works, which suggests that those works were authoritative for the later writers:

Genesis: Retelling portions of Genesis occupied more than one Qumran scribe. For example, the *Genesis Apocryphon* is an Aramaic work that rehearses the lives of Enoch, Lamech, Noah and his sons, and Abraham.

Exodus and Leviticus: Exodus 22–35 and Leviticus, as well as Numbers and Deuteronomy, form the foundation of the largest nonbiblical manuscript, the *Temple Scroll.* This work presents itself as a new Torah for the last days in which God speaks to Israel—evidently through Moses—in the first person.

Leviticus: Of the approximately two dozen rulings found in 4QMMT, more than half are based on legal issues concerning ritual purity from the text of Leviticus. Furthermore, most of the laws in the *Damascus Document* are retellings of various Levitical commands, and the assorted legal discussions in *A Commentary on the Law of Moses* (4Q251) are largely Levitical in origin.

Jubilees: This work may well be the source for dating covenants to the third month, especially the fifteenth day, as well as the Qumranic idea that the covenant was to be renewed on the Festival of Weeks.

Ezekiel: At least five scrolls, possibly representing three separate compositions, contain rewritten versions of the book of Ezekiel: *4QPseudoEzekiel*[a–e] (4Q385–88, 5Q391).

1 Enoch: This book details a lunisolar calendar that combines a 364-day solar year with a schematic 354-day one and served as the model for the Qumran calendars.

Psalms: The *Hodayot* and some other collections of hymns found among the Dead Sea Scrolls are largely modeled on the Psalms.

Kings: At least one of the Dead Sea Scrolls contains a narrative retelling of some Elijah stories and other events that are described in 1 Kings: *4Qpap paraKings et al.* (4Q382), which was copied in the first half of the first century BCE. Another relevant scroll is the *Apocryphon of Elisha* (4Q481a), which presents a version of 2 Kings 2:14–16 and other material.

Ezra: This book provided one of the terms that the Qumran community appropriated for itself, the *yaḥad* ("community"); see Ezra 4:3. The designation also forms the title of one of its foundation documents, the *Serek HaYaḥad* or *Rule of the Community* (WAC, 123–43).

Summary

The evidence offered above, together with the list of quotations of and allusions to scriptural passages given in Appendix III, indicates that many books were viewed as Scripture by the Qumran community. In Tables 7.3–5, for convenience we place these books in three general groupings: *Books Associated with Moses, Books of the Prophets, David and the Other Books.*

Of course, not all of the nonbiblical scrolls were authored by the Qumran community, which means that a quotation in a particular work does not necessarily mean that the book cited was viewed as Scripture by the Qumranites. However, a quick survey of several of the best preserved or distinctive writings of the community itself provides a general but fairly accurate picture of just which books they regarded as scriptural.[41] These distinctive works are

RC: the *Rule of the Community* (1QS, 4Q255–264a, 5Q11)

DD: the *Damascus Document* (CD, 4Q266–73, 5Q12, 6Q15)

WS: the *War Scroll* (1QM, 1Q33, 4Q491–96)

1QH[a]: the *Hodayot* (1QH[a])

4QFlor: the *Florilegium* (4Q174; WAC: *The Last Days: A Commentary on Selected Verses*)

4QTest: the *Testimonia* (4Q175; WAC: *A Collection of Messianic Proof Texts*)

11QMelch: the *Melchizedek* Scroll (11Q13)

Table 7.3	Quantities of Scrolls and Citations at Qumran: Books Associated with Moses					
Name of Book	Used in Distinctive Works	Manuscripts	Certain	Uncertain	Not	
Genesis	DD (3)	20	Genesis			
Exodus	RC, DD, 4QFlor, 4QTestim	17	Exodus			
Leviticus	RC, DD (20), 11QMelch (2)	14	Leviticus			
Numbers	RC, DD (12), WS (2), 4QTestim	8	Numbers			
Deuteronomy	RC, DD (18), WS, 4QFlor (3),					
	4QTestim (3), 11QMelch	30	Deuteronomy			
Reworked Pentateuch	Possibly	5	*R. Pentateuch*			
Jubilees	DD (2) (see also 4Q228, 4Q265)	ca. 15	*Jubilees*			
Temple Scroll	???	ca. 5		*Temple Scroll*		

To these may be added the *pesharim: Pesher Isaiah* (3Q4, 4Q161–65), *Pesher Hosea* (4Q166–67), *Pesher Micah* (1Q14, 4Q168), *Pesher Nahum* (4Q169), *Pesher Habakkuk* (1QpHab), *Pesher Zephaniah* (1Q15, 4Q170), and *Pesher Psalms* (1Q16, 4Q171, 4Q173). Also worth noting are *Apocryphal Malachi* (5Q10) and the *Pesher on the Apocalypse of Weeks* (4Q247).

In Tables 7.3–5, the second column lists the number of times that a particular book is quoted or referred in one of these distinctive works; for example, Genesis is cited three times in the *Damascus Document*. (The exact references are found in Appendix III: in this case, Gen. 1:27 is cited in CD 4.21, Gen. 7:9 in CD 5.1, and Gen. 41:40 in CD 13.3.) When a book is not cited in one of the works listed above but in another document found at Qumran, such references are presented in parentheses. For example, the book of Lamentations is cited once (Lam. 1:1 in 4Q179 frag. 2, l. 4).

On the basis of the nine criteria listed above, including the number of citations (second column) and the number of manuscripts (third column), the scriptural status of each book at Qumran is given in one of three categories: *Certain, Uncertain,* or *Not*.

Comment on Table 7.3: All the listed books fall in the *certain* column and were thus viewed as Scripture by the Qumran community. In two cases, deciding on the correct category proved difficult. *Reworked Pentateuch* is included as Scripture on the grounds that it comprised the entire Pentateuch in a form close to the early Samaritan Pentateuch. The *Temple Scroll* is in the Uncertain column, but just might qualify as Scripture since it features claims of divine authority and may be loosely viewed as a new Deuteronomy, just as the books of Chronicles largely retell large parts of Samuel and Kings. The status of *Jubilees* was easy to decide: this book presents itself as revelation, is preserved in many copies, and is quoted or referred to in other writings. Finally, it should be noted that these three works featured among the books of Moses at Qumran—but not in the Torah. Since several manuscripts indicate that Genesis–Deuteronomy were grouped together, sometimes even written on a single scroll (see Chapter 6), it seems that these five books formed

Table 7.4	Quantities of Scrolls and Citations at Qumran: Books of the Prophets				
Name of Book	**Used in Distinctive Works**	**Manuscripts**	**Certain**	**Uncertain**	**Not**
Isaiah	RC (4x), DD (16), WS, 4QFlor (2x), PesherIsa (51), 11QMelch (6x)	21	Isaiah		
Jeremiah	(yes, e.g., 4Q177, 4Q396, 4Q397)	6	Jeremiah		
Lamentations	(yes, 4Q179)	4	Lamentations		
Letter of Jeremiah	(no)	1			Letter of Jer.
Ezekiel	DD (4x), 4QFlor	6	Ezekiel		
12 Minor Prophets		8	12 Prophets		
Hosea	DD (6x), PesherHos (18)		Hosea		
Joel	DD (4x)		Joel		
Amos	DD (2x), 4QFlor		Amos		
Obadiah	(no)		Obadiah		
Jonah	(no)		Jonah		
Micah	DD (7x), PesherMic (8)		Micah		
Nahum	DD (2x), PesherNah (24)		Nahum		
Habakkuk	PesherHab (44)		Habakkuk		
Zephaniah	RC, PesherZeph (3x)		Zephaniah		
Haggai	(no)		Haggai		
Zechariah	DD (2x), PesherIsa		Zechariah		
Malachi	DD (4x), ApocrMal (2x)		Malachi		
1 Enoch	PesherApocWeeks(?)	12	*1 Enoch*		
Daniel	4QFlor, 11QMelch	8	Daniel		

a complete unit (the Pentateuch, or the Book of Moses). If our classification is correct, *Reworked Pentateuch, Jubilees,* and the *Temple Scroll* were viewed as other books of Moses by the Qumranites.

Comment on Table 7.4: As we would expect, Isaiah, Jeremiah, Ezekiel, and Daniel were definitely viewed as Scripture at Qumran *(certain)*. The same is true of the Minor Prophets; although not all of them are referred to in other writings, this collection was treated as a single book at Qumran. The book of *1 Enoch* is also classified as *certain,* since it is presented as revelation, is preserved in many copies, served as the model for the Qumran calendars, and may be quoted in the *Pesher on the Apocalypse of Weeks* (4Q247). The book of Lamentations is likewise classified, since it is represented by four copies and is quoted once (4Q179 frag. 2, l. 4). The Letter of Jeremiah is found only in one manuscript (pap7QEpJer gr) and is apparently not alluded to elsewhere, hence its *uncertain* scriptural status at Qumran.

Table 7.5	Quantities of Scrolls and Citations at Qumran: David and the Other Books				
Name of Book	**Used in Distinctive Works**	**Manuscripts**	**Certain**	**Uncertain**	**Not**
Psalms	DD (2x), IQHᵃ, 4QFlor (3x), PesherPs (42x), 11QMelch (3x)	36	Psalms		
Proverbs	DD (2x)	2	Proverbs		
Job	DD (cf.)	4	Job		
Song of Songs	(no)	4		Songs	
Ecclesiastes	(no)	2		Ecclesiastes	
Ben Sira	(no)	2		Sirach	
Joshua	4QTestim	2	Joshua		
Judges	(cf. 4Q522)	3	Judges		
Ruth	(no)	4		Ruth	
1 Samuel	DD?, WS (cf.)	4	1 Samuel		
2 Samuel	4QFlor (3)	3	2 Samuel		
1 Kings	(cf. 4Q504)	3	1 Kings		
2 Kings	(no)	1	2 Kings		
1 Chronicles	(cf. 4Q522)	0		1 Chronicles	
2 Chronicles	(cf. 4Q522)	1		2 Chronicles	
Ezra	(the *yaḥad,* Ezra 4:3)	1	Ezra		
Nehemiah	CD (cf.)	0		Nehemiah	
Esther	(no, but cf. 4Q550)	0			Esther
Tobit	(no)	4		Tobit	

Comment on Table 7.5: Several books in the *uncertain* category are represented by comparatively few manuscripts at Qumran and are apparently not referred to in the community's other writings: the Song of Songs, Ecclesiastes, Sirach, Ruth, 1 and 2 Chronicles, and Tobit. Some or all of these *may* have been viewed as Scripture by the community, but the mere existence of manuscripts of these works at Qumran is insufficient to ensure their authoritative status. As many scholars have noted, the single book that was not viewed as authoritative Scripture by the Qumran community is Esther, most likely because it features a festival (Purim) that was not included in the Qumran calendar (see Chapter 6).

Select Bibliography

Articles that were especially helpful for this chapter:

Lightstone, J. N. "The Rabbis' Bible: The Canon of the Hebrew Bible and the Early Rabbinic

Guild." In L. M. McDonald and J. A. Sanders, eds. *The Canon Debate: The Origins and Formation of the Bible.* Peabody, MA: Hendrickson, 2002. Pp. 163–84.

Trebolle, J. "Origins of a Tripartite Old Testament Canon." In L. M. McDonald and J. A. Sanders, eds. *The Canon Debate: The Origins and Formation of the Bible.* Peabody, MA: Hendrickson, 2002. Pp. 128–45.

Ulrich, E. "Canon." In L. H. Schiffman and J. C. VanderKam, eds. *Encyclopedia of the Dead Sea Scrolls.* 2 vols. New York and Oxford: Oxford University Press, 2000. 1:117–20.

Note also the important early study:

Eybers, I. H. "Some Light on the Canon of the Qumran Sect." In S. Leiman, ed. *The Canon and Masorah of the Hebrew Bible: An Introductory Reader.* New York: KTAV, 1974. Pp. 23–36.

Other books and articles:

Barton, J. "The Significance of a Fixed Canon of the Hebrew Bible." In *Hebrew Bible/ Old Testament: The History of Its Interpretation.* Edited by Magne Saebo. Vol. I/1. Göttingen: Vandenhoeck & Ruprecht, 1996. Pp. 67–83.

Beckwith, R. *The Old Testament Canon of the New Testament Church and Its Background in Early Judaism.* London: Clowes, 1985.

Kooij, A. van der. "The Canonization of Ancient Books Kept in the Temple of Jerusalem." In *Canonization and Decanonization.* Edited by A. van der Kooij and K. van der Toorn. Leiden: Brill, 1998. Pp. 17–40.

Sanders, J. A. "The Scrolls and the Canonical Process." In P. Flint and J. VanderKam, eds. *The Dead Sea Scrolls After Fifty Years: A Comprehensive Assessment.* 2 vols. Leiden: Brill, 1998–99. 2:1–23.

Ulrich, E. *The Dead Sea Scrolls and the Origins of the Bible.* Studies in the Dead Sea Scrolls and Related Literature. Grand Rapids, MI: Eerdmans; Leiden: Brill, 1999. Pp. 51–78.

VanderKam, J. "Questions of Canon Viewed Through the Dead Sea Scrolls." *Bulletin for Biblical Research* 11 (2001): 269–92.

CHAPTER 8

Apocrypha and Pseudepigrapha in the Dead Sea Scrolls

APOCRYPHA AND *PSEUDEPIGRAPHA* EACH HAVE more than one meaning, which gives rise to some confusion for both scholars and general readers, and so these key terms are examined in this chapter before we examine these writings in the scrolls.

Defining the Apocrypha

Apocrypha is a plural word (singular: *apocryphon*) that originally denoted *hidden* or *secret* writings, to be read only by initiates into a given Christian group. The term was eventually used for works that were similar to biblical books in content, form, or title, although not accepted into a particular canon of Scripture.[1]

APOCRYPHA IN THE TRADITIONAL (NARROW) SENSE

The most common use of *Apocrypha* is the narrow one, denoting *books or parts of books that appear in Roman Catholic Bibles, but not in Jewish or Protestant ones*. These books derive from the Septuagint (Greek Bible), but were not accepted by the rabbis who finalized the Jewish canon or by the church leaders who fixed the Protestant canon during the Reformation (see Chapter 7). For Catholics and Orthodox Christians, these writings qualify as Scripture and are known as the *Deuterocanonicals*. The seven complete books are Tobit, Judith, 1 and 2 Maccabees, the Wisdom of Solomon, Ecclesiasticus (also known as Sirach or the Wisdom of Jesus ben Sira), and Baruch (which includes the Letter of Jeremiah). The Apocrypha also include the Additions to Esther (in eight sections) and to Daniel (in three sections: the Prayer of Azariah and Song of the Three Young Men; Susanna; and Bel and the Dragon). Approximate dates for these works are[2]

Tobit	fourth or third century BCE
Judith	second or first century BCE
Additions to Esther	second or first century BCE
1 Maccabees	late second or early first century BCE
2 Maccabees	124 BCE

Wisdom of Solomon	ca. 40 CE or earlier
Ecclesiasticus (Sirach)	ca. 180 BCE; prologue ca. 132 BCE
Baruch	between 200 and 60 BCE
Letter of Jeremiah (Baruch 6)	fourth to late second century BCE
Additions to Daniel	third to second century BCE

APOCRYPHA IN THE BROADER SENSE

When we add additional books found in the Septuagint and those used by the various Orthodox churches (see Table 7.1), a broader definition of Apocrypha becomes possible—one that includes several books usually classified as Pseudepigrapha. The longer canons (or lists of scriptural books) of these churches not only incorporate works that are quite unfamiliar to most readers (such as the *Prayer of Manasseh*), they also have differing names for the same books (e.g., the *1 Esdras* of English Bibles is known as *3 Ezra* in the Latin Vulgate and as *2 Esdras* in the Slavonic Bible). These works[3] and their dates[4] are

Prayer of Manasseh	probably first century BCE
Psalm 151	Hellenistic period
1 Esdras (or *2 Esdras*)	probably second century BCE
2 Esdras (or *3 Esdras*)	late first to third centuries CE
3 Maccabees	Roman period (30 BCE–70 CE)
4 Maccabees	first century BCE to late first century CE
1 Enoch	third century BCE to late first century CE
Jubilees	second century BCE

When these books are included, the term *Apocrypha* may be more broadly defined as *Jewish works of the Second Temple period that are excluded from the Hebrew Bible, yet included in the Old Testaments of some but not all churches.*

Apocrypha in the broader sense necessarily excludes later writings, since the books involved must be Jewish works of the Second Temple period, and thus of ancient origin. Even if they were later altered or interpolated by Christian editors, this proviso prevents originally Christian or other late writings from being included among the Old Testament Apocrypha. For example, the wider Ethiopian canon includes the *History of the Jews and Other Nations* by Joseph ben Gorion (or Pseudo-Josephus), which was composed only in the tenth century CE. According to our broad definition, this work must be excluded from the Apocrypha.

APOCRYPHA IN A MORE SPECIALIZED SENSE

Before we consider the various apocryphal books among the scrolls, a third use of the term *Apocrypha* must be observed: for denoting the names of certain books found at Qumran, such as the *Genesis Apocryphon* or the *Apocryphal Psalms*. Works such as these are similar to their biblical namesakes, but were virtually all unknown before the discovery of the Dead Sea Scrolls.

This chapter is organized with the traditional and narrower definition of Apocrypha in mind, since most readers and scholars are familiar with it.

Survey of the Apocrypha in the Dead Sea Scrolls

Bibliographical Note: For an index of passages in the scrolls from writings traditionally regarded as Apocrypha and Pseudepigrapha, see Appendix II. For details of volumes in the series "Discoveries in the Judaean Desert," see Appendix IV.

TOBIT

The dramatic tale of Tobit,[5] a Jewish exile from the Northern Kingdom, Israel, opens as follows: "I, Tobit, have walked in the ways of truth and righteousness all the days of my life" (Tob. 1:3). Tobit lived in Nineveh, the capital of ancient Assyria, where he rose to prominence but then suffered several reverses, which included poverty and culminated in blindness. His son, Tobias, was sent to recover the family fortune, which had been hidden with a relative. Although both father and son were not aware of it, Tobias's traveling companion, Azariah, was actually the angel Raphael in disguise. After many adventures, Tobias rescued and married a relative named Sarah, found a remarkable cure for his father's blindness, and secured his fortune. With several similarities to Job, the book of Tobit emphasizes the virtues of faithfulness in times of distress, ministering to the hungry and destitute, and honoring one's parents. The book was most likely written in the fourth or third century BCE.

Five manuscripts of Tobit were discovered in Cave 4 at Qumran, four of them written in Aramaic (the first on papyrus) and the other in Hebrew.[6] The oldest scroll is 4QTobit[d] ar, copied about 100 BCE, and the latest is 4QTobit[e], copied between 30 BCE and 20 CE. Because of damage and deterioration, none of these five scrolls is fully preserved, but all fourteen chapters of Tobit are represented; see Figure 8.1. The best-preserved manuscript is 4QpapTobit[a] ar, which contains portions of chapters 1–7 and 12–14. In contrast, very little text is preserved in 4QTobit[c] ar (14:2–6, 10?) and 4QTobit[d] ar (7.11; 14.10).

In which language was Tobit originally written? Before copies were discovered at Qumran, the earliest surviving manuscripts were in Greek, which caused scholars to debate whether it was composed in Greek or a Semitic language (Hebrew or Aramaic). Many authorities now regard the original language as Aramaic. J. T. Milik, for instance, points to the tendency at Qumran—as part of a literary and nationalist renaissance—of translating

Figure 8.1
Fragments of Tobit: Portions of Tob 6:12–7:10 in 4QTobit[b] ar (4Q197) (PAM 43.181).
Courtesy of the Israel Antiquities Authority

works that were originally composed in Aramaic into Hebrew, but not vice versa.[7] Another indication that the Aramaic text of Tobit was most likely earlier and that the Hebrew was translated from it, is that the Aramaic text is attested from about 100 BCE in the scrolls— whereas the only Hebrew copy is dated at about 30 BCE at the earliest. An Aramaic original is also supported by Aramaic influences in the only Hebrew copy, which seems to suggest that the Hebrew translator was using an Aramaic base text. We thus have in Cave 4 one of the earliest examples of a book in its original language (Aramaic), used alongside a translation into another language (Hebrew).

Does the form of Tobit in the scrolls differ from the form found in later Greek and Latin manuscripts? In his edition of the Qumran copies, Joseph Fitzmyer observes that both the Aramaic and Hebrew forms generally agree with the longer edition preserved in Greek and Latin manuscripts that were copied centuries later.[8] He concludes, however, that neither the Greek nor the Latin is directly translated from an Aramaic form such as the one in the Qumran texts. This is because both the Greek and Latin versions contain inverted phrases, expanded expressions, and words that were misunderstood by the translators.

THE WISDOM OF JESUS BEN SIRA

Jesus ben Sira was a Jewish teacher who compiled a book of wise sayings and instructions in Hebrew somewhere between 190 and 180 BCE. The author's grandson later translated this work into Greek and added a preface of his own. The traditional form of the Wisdom of Jesus Ben Sira (also known as Sirach or Ecclesiasticus)[9] is based on the grandson's Greek translation, which is found in the Septuagint. Sirach is included in the Old Testament of Roman Catholic and Orthodox Christians, whereas Protestants and Jews group it among the Apocrypha. The traditional title is Sirach or Ecclesiasticus, while the Wisdom of Jesus Ben Sira, or simply Ben Sira, is increasingly preferred by scholars who recognize the Hebrew origins of the book. Strictly speaking, Sirach or Ecclesiasticus is more appropriate for the traditional form, which is based on the Greek, whereas the (Wisdom of) Jesus Ben Sira better describes the original Hebrew form, which is somewhat different.

Although scholars have been aware of Sirach for several hundred years in ancient Greek, Latin, and Syriac versions, the quest for the original Hebrew text has proved formidable. Ben Sira/Sirach was excluded by the rabbis from their list of scriptural books, but the Hebrew text was known during the early centuries of the common era, since it is discussed in some Jewish writings; the book then fell into disuse and was not recopied for a long time. In the late nineteenth century, substantial Hebrew texts of Ben Sira/Sirach, copied in the eleventh and twelfth centuries CE, were discovered in the Cairo Genizah. This term denotes a storeroom attached to a synagogue in Cairo, which was used for old and damaged manuscripts, since in Jewish tradition these cannot simply be discarded or burned. None of the Cairo copies is complete, but when combined they provide the Hebrew text for approximately two-thirds of the book.

In contrast to the Genizah manuscripts, it is surprising that for such a long book (fifty-one chapters in all), only three copies containing text from Ben Sira were found among the scrolls. Two of these, preserving portions of just three chapters, were discovered at Qumran. The third manuscript, with six chapters represented, was found at Masada.[10]

The Qumran evidence is particularly interesting. The Cave 2 scroll (2QSir) apparently contained the Hebrew text of some or all of Sirach as found in later Greek manuscripts. The Cave 11 text, however—which originally contained the entire second canticle after the epilogue (Sir. 51:13–30)—is not from a Ben Sira manuscript at all, but part of the Great Psalms Scroll and was copied later than 2QSir. This composition is clearly presented as a distinct work in columns 21–22 of 11QPs^a, where it is separated from the preceding Psalm (138) and from the one that follows (the *Apostrophe to Zion*) by substantial intervals. Its inclusion in a collection of Psalms shows that the canticle was still being used as an independent unit in the first century CE, long after its presumed incorporation in the book of Ben Sira. The fact that it is found in two different books suggests that this canticle was a "floating piece" and that where it originally belonged is now open to question.

The canticle was previously known in the Greek, Latin, and Syriac versions, and a large amount of a medieval Hebrew copy was found in the Cairo Genizah. In contrast to these, 11QPs^a presents the original Hebrew and shows this to be an acrostic poem. Such compositions, in which each successive verse begins with a new letter of the twenty-two letter Hebrew alphabet, are well known elsewhere in the Hebrew Bible, especially the Psalms (e.g., Psalm 145). Strangely, however, in 11QPs^a this acrostic poem concludes with an additional twenty-third verse (beginning with *pe*).[11] A translation of the surviving text is presented in Box 8.1, using verse numbers based on the Qumran scroll (the traditional numbering is vv. 13–30, following the Septuagint).

Comparison with the Greek reveals interesting differences, including the blurring of the canticle's acrostic nature in later translations and Hebrew transcriptions (e.g., the

---

| **Box 8.1** | *Sirach 51:13–30 in 11QPs^a (with line numbers)* |

[1]I was a young man before I had erred
   when I looked for her.
[2]She came to me in her beauty
   when finally I sought her out.
[3]Even (as) a blossom drops in the ripening of grapes, making glad the heart,
[4](So) my foot trod in uprightness;
   for from my young manhood have I known her.
[5]I inclined my ear a little,
   and great was the persuasion I found.
[6]And she became for me a nurse;
   to my teacher I give my ardor.
[7]I purposed to make sport:
   I was zealous for pleasure, without pause.
[8]I kindled my desire for her
   without distraction.
[9]I bestirred my desire for her,
   and on her heights I do not waver.
[10]I opened my hand [...]
   and I perceive her unseen parts.
[11]I cleansed my hand
   [. . . . .]
[23][. . . . .]
   [. . .] your reward in his due season.

(Adapted from AFU, 606)

Greek has no text corresponding to the second parts of the Hebrew *ḥet* and *ṭet* verses; and for the second part of the *'alep* verse, the Greek has a longer, more pietistic text). The Greek translation—followed by the other versions and the medieval Hebrew text—has revised the original poem by substituting pious ideas to replace the many erotic images in the canticle still preserved in 11QPsᵃ.[12] For instance, lines 9–10 from 11QPsᵃ contain highly erotic sexual imagery: "I bestirred my desire for her, and on her heights I do not waver. I opened my hand . . . and I perceive her unseen parts." In this verse the Hebrew word *hand* can also mean *penis*, and *unseen parts* can also be translated *nakedness*. The Greek translator, however, has clearly downplayed such erotic imagery by substituting pious language, in line with his overall purpose of pursuing wisdom in a more spiritual or philosophical sense: "I directed my soul towards her, and in my deeds I was exact. I stretched my hands on high, and perceived her secrets" (vv. 21–22).

The most substantial scroll containing text from Ben Sira was found at Masada, the fortress where, according to Josephus, over 900 Jewish defenders took their own lives in 73 or 74 CE. The fragments, discovered by Yigael Yadin's team at Masada on April 8, 1964, preserve text from chapters 39–44 and form the oldest of all the Ben Sira scrolls. If, as scholars believe, this book was composed in the first third of the second century BCE, the Masada scroll is only about a hundred years later than the original. Moreover, this form of the text confirms that the medieval manuscripts of Ben Sira that were discovered in the Cairo Genizah basically represent the original Hebrew version, but with numerous corruptions and later changes.[13]

THE LETTER (OR EPISTLE) OF JEREMIAH

The Letter of Jeremiah,[14] a work of one chapter, is addressed to Jews deported to Babylon by King Nebuchadnezzar, presumably in 597 BCE, and contains ten warnings emphasizing the helplessness of idols and condemning idolatry. The Letter is represented by a single scroll from Qumran that was copied about 100 BCE. This manuscript is unusual in view of the material on which it was inscribed (papyrus) and the language in which it was written (Greek)—hence the rather awkward abbreviation pap7QEpJer gr. The Letter of Jeremiah was originally an independent work that appears as chapter 6 of Baruch in the Latin Vulgate, but is separated in the Septuagint from Baruch by Lamentations. It is probable that pap7QEpJer gr contained only the Letter and not the first five chapters of Baruch (none of which have been found at Qumran or other Judean sites). The book itself was most likely written in Greek sometime between the late fourth and late second century BCE.

For pap7QEpJer gr very little text has survived: only two complete words (*therefore* and *them* in v. 44) and parts of seven others. Identifying this fragment is thus difficult, but it appears to contain text from the Letter of Jeremiah in view of the relative positions of letters in successive lines. The lineup of words requires an interesting textual variant in v. 44: "So how can anyone *suppose them to be gods, or claim them as gods?*" as opposed to the Septuagint's "So how can anyone *suppose or claim that they are gods?*" The fragment is translated as follows:

> [And when one of them is drawn away by one of the passers-by and is lain with, she reviles the woman next to her, because she was not as attractive as herself nor was her cord] br[ok]en. Everything which is don]e [for] th[em is false]. Therefore, [h]ow [can anyone] su[ppose] *them* [*to be*] g[*ods, or claim th*]e[*m as gods*]? (vv. 43–44; adapted from AFU, 629)

Pseudepigrapha

The two most familiar collections of Pseudepigrapha are R. H. Charles's *The Apocrypha and Pseudepigrapha of the Old Testament* (1913) and James Charlesworth's *The Old Testament Pseudepigrapha* (1983–85). The term *Pseudepigrapha* is even more complex than *Apocrypha*. In the most general sense it denotes virtually all ancient Jewish works—outside the Old Testament, the Apocrypha, and a few other major writings (notably Philo and Josephus)—that were known to us prior to the discovery of the Dead Sea Scrolls. A useful definition of *Pseudepigrapha* in this sense has been proposed by Moshe Bernstein: "Jewish and Christian writings dating from the last centuries BCE to the first centuries CE which did not become part of the canon in either religion."[15]

But when we consider the entire corpus of Second Temple Jewish literature, including the Dead Sea Scrolls, a quite different sense emerges: *Pseudepigrapha* as a literary genre, or group, of falsely attributed writings. This corresponds with the literal meaning of the term as "writings that are falsely attributed to ancient authors." Biblical scholars, of course, are familiar with this category in the Old Testament itself, where the primary example is Daniel. So when discussion extends, for example, to the *Pseudo-Ezekiel* documents at Qumran, this is no great surprise. But readers should be aware that a shift in meaning has taken place here: *Pseudepigrapha* no longer refers to previously known writings, but to the genre of later writings that are falsely attributed (in this case, to the biblical prophet Ezekiel).

The problem of terminology in this area has been investigated by Michael Stone, who concludes that "there is no simple formula according to which we may categorize the Jewish literature of the Second Temple period."[16] Stone proposes that the term *Pseudepigrapha* be used in a loose sense, as encompassing both traditional *Apocrypha* and *Pseudepigrapha,* and suggests that previous criteria for determining these categories may have to be abolished and replaced with others:[17]

> We may question, however, whether this is a sensible way of thinking about the Jewish literary production of the Greco-Roman period at all. Another option, for example, would be to abolish these categories determined by the chance of transmission, and to classify the works by genre, time or place of origin, source, or some other group of criteria.

There is thus an urgent need for clarity and stricter terminology with respect to the terms *Apocrypha* and *Pseudepigrapha*. It is helpful to note that both share several common elements. First, both terms have arisen in Western scholarship, not from Hebrew tradition; Jewish writers refer to all of this literature as the *exterior books* (ספרים חיצונים, i.e., books exterior to the canon of the Hebrew Bible). Second, virtually all the compositions involved have been transmitted by Christian sources, since they were not accepted into the rabbinic canon of Scripture. Third, in view of this means of transmission, we should not be surprised that the surviving forms of virtually all these books have been altered by later Christian editors.

How, then, are we to define the Pseudepigrapha? In both scholarly and more popular writings the term is being used in two very different senses: as a large group of nonbiblical Jewish works that were *previously known* (before the discovery of the Dead Sea Scrolls) and as a literary genre, or group, of *falsely attributed writings*.

Because of the way in which this book is organized, the main focus in this section is on Pseudepigrapha in the traditional sense: Jewish works outside the Old Testament and the

Apocrypha that were known to us before the discovery of the scrolls. Since this approach excludes the second meaning of Pseudepigrapha as a group of falsely attributed writings, we also offer some comments on the many books that would qualify under this definition. Most of these texts will be treated separately in Chapter 9.

Pseudepigrapha as Previously Known Writings in the Scrolls

According to the traditional definition of Pseudepigrapha, the first five books or parts of books discussed below fall into this category: *Psalm 151, Psalm 154, Psalm 155, 1 Enoch,* and *Jubilees.* But according to the broader definition of Aprocrypha, they would also fall under the heading Apocrypha, since they are included in the Old Testament canon of at least one ancient Orthodox church.

There are nine Pseudepigrapha in the traditional sense (previously known writings) among the Dead Sea Scrolls. The last of these, the *Damascus Document,* was discovered only toward the end of the nineteenth century.

PSALMS 151A AND 151B

It is well known that in the Septuagint (Greek Bible) the Psalter ends not with Psalm 150 but with *Psalm 151,* which also concludes the Psalter used by Orthodox Christians today. Before the discovery of the Dead Sea Scrolls, *Psalm 151* was known as a single composition in the Septuagint and in the Latin and Syriac translations, which are based on the Greek. Many scholars were thus intrigued to find a Hebrew form of this psalm preserved in column 28 of 11QPs[a], which was copied about 30–50 CE and discovered in 1956 (see the survey of biblical scrolls in Chapter 6).

When the Greek and Hebrew versions are compared, several striking differences emerge. First, although *Psalm 151* is a single composition in the Septuagint, 11QPs[a] contains two distinct psalms (*151A* and *151B*[18]), each with its own superscription (heading) and with the second psalm beginning on a new line. It seems that the Great Psalms Scroll represents the original Hebrew with its two originally separate psalms. *Psalm 151A* is a poetic midrash on the events on David's life found in 1 Sam. 16:1–13, and *Psalm 151B* covers the events reported in 1 Sam. 17:17–54. The Greek translator reworked and synthesized all this material into a single composition, with *Psalm 151A* condensed into Greek vv. 1–5, and *Psalm 151B* into Greek vv. 7–8.[19]

Second, *Psalms 151A* and *151B* are the only truly "autobiographical" psalms because they unequivocally relate to actual events in David's life. The following excerpts, for example, tie these Psalms directly to David:

> He made me shepherd of his flock and ruler over his little goats. (*Psalm 151A:*1)

> He sent his prophet to anoint me, Samuel to make me great; my brothers went out to meet him. (*Psalm 151A:*6)

> Then I [saw] a Philistine uttering defiances from the r[anks of the enemy].
> (*Psalm 151B:*2)

Although similar statements are found in some superscriptions to canonical Psalms (e.g., 51, 52, 54, 57, 60), such direct references to David never appear in the actual text of Psalms

| Box 8.2 | Psalm 151 |

11QPs^a	*Septuagint*

11QPs^a

(*Psalm 151A*) A Hallelujah of David the Son of Jesse.

[1]Smaller was I than my brothers,
      and the youngest of my father's sons,
so he made me shepherd of his flock
      and ruler over his little goats.
[2]My hands fashioned a reed pipe,
      and my fingers a lyre;
and I gave glory to the Lord.
      I said within my soul:
[3]The mountains cannot witness to him,
      nor can the hills proclaim about him;
nor the trees my words,
      nor the flock my compositions.
[4] For who can relate, and who can tell,
      and who can recount the deeds of the Lord?
Everything has God seen,
      everything has he heard—and he has given heed.
[5] He sent his prophet to anoint me,
      Samuel to exalt me.
My brothers went out to meet him,
      handsome of figure, handsome in appearance.
[6] Though they were tall of stature
      and handsome because of their hair,
the Lord God did not choose them.
[7] But he sent and took me from behind the flock
      and anointed me with the holy oil,
and he made me prince of his people
      and ruler over the sons of his covenant.
(*Psalm 151B*) At the beginning of power for David,
after the prophet of God had anointed him.
[1]Then I [saw] a Philistine,
      heaping scorn from the r[anks of the enemy].
[2]. . . I . . . the . . .

(Adapted from Sanders, *The Dead Sea Psalms Scroll*, 97, 99)

Septuagint

This psalm is ascribed to David as his own composition (though it is outside the number), after he had fought in single combat with Goliath.
[1]I was small among my brothers,
      and the youngest in my father's house;
I tended my father's sheep.

[2]My hands made a harp;
      my fingers fashioned a lyre.

[3]And who will tell
                              my Lord?

      The Lord himself; it is he who hears.
[4a]It was he who sent his messenger

[5]My brothers
                    were handsome
                                        and tall,

but the Lord was not pleased with them.
      [4b]And he took me from my father's sheep,
[4c]and anointed me with his anointing oil.

[6]I went out to meet the Philistine,
      and he cursed me by his idols.
[7]But I drew his own sword; I beheaded him,
      and took away disgrace from the people of Israel.

1–150. Furthermore, when the superscriptions are compared, in the scroll found at Qumran *Psalm 151* is seen to be more Davidic than in the Septuagint, which downplays this psalm by declaring it to be "outside the number" (i.e., outside the book of Psalms). The heading found in the Greek Bible seems to reflect the concerns of later editors about the place of *Psalm 151* in the Greek Psalter at a time when the Proto-Masoretic Psalter (i.e., the earlier textual form now represented by the Masoretic Psalter) of 150 compositions was becoming or had become normative for Judaism:

A Hallelujah of David, son of Jesse.	*Psalm 151A* (11QPs^a)
This Psalm is truly written by David, although it is outside the number, after he had fought with Goliath in single combat.	*Psalm 151:1* (LXX)
At the beginning of David's power, after the prophet of God had anointed him.	*Psalm 151B* (11QPs^a)

Third, as in the case of the Greek version, the Psalter represented by 11QPs^a ends not with Psalm 150, but with *Psalm 151*. Although the Hebrew text comprises two psalms and differs from the Greek in other ways, this "Qumran Psalter" shows that in the first century BCE some Jews used a collection of Psalms that also ended with *Psalm 151*. This has important implications for our understanding of the finalization of the book of Psalms; see the discussion of the scrolls and the text of the Hebrew Bible/Old Testament in Chapter 6.

Finally, in combining the two psalms, the translator (or the Hebrew text he was translating) introduced several changes, including a different order of verses and the omission of material in the original Hebrew version. The extent of these changes is clear when the accompanying translations of the Hebrew and Greek texts are compared (see Box 8.2).[20]

PSALMS 154 AND 155 (SYRIAC *PSALMS II* AND *III*)

Psalms 154 and *155*[21] were known as *Syriac Psalms I* and *II* in the *Book of Discipline* by the tenth-century Nestorian bishop Elijah of al-Anbar (with *Psalm 151* as Syriac *Psalm I*), but as *Psalms 154* and *155* in the Mosul manuscript, the oldest surviving Syriac version of the book of Psalms.[22] Comparison with the Qumran evidence shows that for *Psalms 154* and *155* the Mosul copy is the most faithful Syriac version of the psalms that we have, although it contains significant variant readings against later manuscripts. 11QPs^a represents the Hebrew text used by the translator of the Syriac version preserved in this medieval manuscript, since there is a 95 percent, or better, correspondence in wording. *Psalms 154* and *155* are found only in the Great Psalms Scroll, 11QPs^a, which was copied about 30–50 CE.

Psalm 154 is written in excellent biblical-style poetry and may be classified as a call to worship. One interesting feature of this well-crafted sapiential psalm is the personification of Wisdom as a woman (vv. 5ff.), which also occurs in the Hebrew Bible (notably Prov. 8:34) and in the book of Sirach (1:15). In the translation given in Box 8.3, vv. 3–19 are from column 18 of 11QPs^a, and the remaining verses are based on the Syriac.

Although the Qumran covenanters identified with several themes in this lovely composition (such as praise and wisdom), there is no evidence that it was actually composed by them. It should also be noted that vv. 17–20 of this psalm seem to be incorporated in the first column of a fascinating nonbiblical composition discovered in Cave 4, *A Prayer for King Jonathan* (4Q448[23]).

Psalm 155 has been described as a psalm of thanksgiving with a plea for deliverance embedded in it.[24] The text contains a large amount of biblical vocabulary, reminiscent of Psalms 22 and 51, and seems to be a broken acrostic psalm that ended in column 24 with the *pe* verse instead of the expected *taw* verse. Opening with the psalmist's cry for deliverance, the composition asks for God's protection from overwhelming situations (v. 11) and from the "evil scourge" (v. 13), and asserts with confidence God's positive response and his ability to save the psalmist (vv. 15ff.). The phrase in v. 11, "Remember me and forget me

Box 8.3   Psalm 154

¹[With a loud voice glorify God;   *(from the Syriac)*
      in the congregation of the many proclaim his majesty.
²In the multitude of the upright glorify his name,
      and with the faithful recount his greatness.]
³[Bind] your souls with the good ones,   *(11QPsᵃ)*
      and with the pure ones to glorify the Most High.
⁴Form an assembly to proclaim his salvation,
      and be not lax in making known his might
      and his majesty to all simple folk.
⁵For to make known the glory of the LORD
      is wisdom given,
⁶and for recounting his many deeds
      she is revealed to man:
⁷to make known to simple folk his might,
      to explain to senseless folk his greatness,
⁸those far from her gates,
      those who stray from her portals.
⁹For the Most High is the LORD of Jacob,
      and his majesty is over all his works.
¹⁰And a man who glorifies the Most High,
      he accepts as one who brings a meal offering,
¹¹as one who offers he-goats and bullocks,
      as one who fattens the altar with many burnt offerings,
      as a sweet-smelling fragrance from the hand of the righteous.
¹²From the gates of the righteous is heard her voice,
      and from the assembly of the pious her song.
¹³When they eat with satiety she is cited,
      and when they drink in community together,
¹⁴their meditation is on the law of the Most High,
      their words on making known his might.
¹⁵How far from the wicked is her word,
      from all haughty men to know her.
¹⁶Behold the eyes of the LORD
      upon the good ones are compassionate,
¹⁷and upon those who glorify him he increases his mercy;
      from an evil time will he deliver [their] soul.
¹⁸[Bless] the LORD
      who redeems the humble from the hand of stran[gers
      and deliv]ers the pure from the hand of the wicked;
¹⁹[who establishes a horn out of Ja]cob
      and a judge [of peoples out of Israel];
²⁰[He will spread his tent in Zion   *(from the Syriac)*
      and abide forever in Jerusalem.]

(See AFU, 572–73)

Box 8.4   **Psalm 155**

[1]O Lord, I called unto you, give heed to me.
[2]I spread forth my palms toward your holy dwelling.
[3]Incline your ear and grant me my plea,
[4]and do not withhold my request from me.
[5]Edify my soul and do not cast it down,
[6]And abandon (it) not in the presence of the wicked.
[7]May the Judge of Truth remove from me the rewards of evil.
[8]O Lord, judge me not according to my sins;
    for no man living is righteous before you.
[9]Grant me understanding, O Lord, in your law,
    and teach me your ordinances,
[10]That many may hear of your deeds
    and peoples may honor your glory.
[11]Remember me and forget me not,
    and lead me not into situations too hard for me.
[12]Cast far from me the sins of my youth,
    and may my transgressions not be remembered against me.
[13]Purify me, O Lord, from the evil scourge,
    and let it not turn again upon me.
[14]Dry up its roots from me,
    and let its leaves not flourish within me.
[15]You are my glory, O Lord.
    Therefore my request is fulfilled before you.
[16]To whom may I cry and he would grant (it) me?
    And the sons of man—what more can [their] pow[er] do?—
[17]My trust, O Lord, is befo[r]e you.
    I cried "O Lord," and he answered me,
    [and he healed] my broken heart.
[18]I slumbered [and sl]ept,
    I dreamt; indeed [I awoke].
[19][You supported me, O Lord,
    and I invoked the Lo]rd, [my deliverer].
[20][Now I shall behold their shame;   *(from the Syriac)*
    I have trusted in you and I shall not be abashed,
    (Render glory forever and ever!)
[21]Deliver Israel, O Lord, your faithful ones,
    and the house of Jacob, your chosen ones.]

(See AFU, 579–80)

---

not, and lead me not into situations too hard for me," is reminiscent of similar language in the Lord's Prayer: "Lead us not into temptation."

Even less than *Psalm 154,* there is no real evidence to link the Qumran community with the composition of this moving piece. Most of the composition is preserved in column 24 of 11QPs[a]; in the translation in Box 8.4, vv. 1–19 are from the Hebrew and the final two verses are reconstructed from the Syriac.

ENOCH OR *1 ENOCH*

1 Enoch (or *Ethiopic Enoch*)[25] is one of the most fascinating compositions from ancient times. Containing 108 chapters in present form, this long work is not known to most general readers and biblical scholars and is often difficult to understand for those who are familiar with it. Until Richard Laurence published the first English translation in 1821 and the text of one Ethiopic manuscript in 1838,[26] the very existence of this book was known to most Western readers only because the Epistle of Jude cites one verse from it (*1 Enoch* 1:9 in Jude 14–15). *1 Enoch* survives in full only in Ethiopic, and some Greek fragments are cited by ancient authors or known from papyri.

As preserved in the Ethiopic tradition, the complete work consists of five units, or "booklets": the Book of the Watchers (chaps. 1–36), the Similitudes or Parables (37–71), the Astronomical Book (72–82), the Book of Dreams (83–90), and the Epistle of Enoch (91–108). Each of these booklets contains revelations supposedly given to Enoch, son of Jared in the seventh generation from Adam (Gen. 5:21–24). Genesis tells us, rather mysteriously, that Enoch "walked with God; then he was no more, for God took him away" into

Figure 8.2

Portions of *1 Enoch* in 4QEn^c ar (4Q204) (PAM 43.202).

Courtesy of the Israel Antiquities Authority

heaven (Gen. 5:24). This explains why the later book centers on Enoch rather than another biblical character; because he was now in heaven, Enoch became the ideal recipient of the revelations that are described in the five booklets. Since the author has clearly assumed the identity of a famous ancient figure, *1 Enoch* is clearly a pseudepigraphic writing in form, in addition to the sense of being previously known.

A prominent theme throughout is the story of angels who came down from heaven, married earthly women, and produced gigantic offspring. According to *1 Enoch,* these giants were the cause of the great evil that made God send the Flood to punish them and destroy the world. Such ideas are based on the key text Gen. 6:1–4, which describes the *sons of God* who married the daughters of men; not unreasonably, *1 Enoch* takes these *sons of God* to mean angels (cf. Job 8:37). With Gen. 6:1–4 coming just before the Flood story, for the authors of *1 Enoch* it was the evil resulting from the angels' gigantic offspring—far more than the story of Adam, Eve, and their descendants—that explains the explosion of human sin that caused God to send the devastating flood.

A second major theme in *1 Enoch* is judgment. The Flood story, which is called the first judgment, highlights the divine response to great evil and serves as a warning of judgment to come. In his exhortations, Enoch himself refers to this example several times; it is interesting to note that some New Testament writers do so as well (e.g., 2 Pet. 3:5–6). Other features of this fascinating and composite book are that it apparently contains the earliest Jewish examples of apocalypses, in which human history is surveyed from beginning to end, and that it includes the earliest Jewish text on astronomical matters (*1 Enoch* 72–82).

Material from *1 Enoch* is preserved in twelve scrolls from Qumran, eleven from Cave 4,[27] and one from Cave 7.[28] A welcome addition—only recently identified—is a Greek scroll of *1 Enoch* that some scholars had erroneously identified as several fragments containing New Testament texts from Qumran. Since this topic is covered separately in Chapter 14, it is not dealt with here at any length. The evidence detailed there is that 7Q4.1, 7Q8, 7Q12, and 7Q14 contain material from *1 Enoch* 103:3–8, 12; that 7Q4.2 contains text from 98:11 or 105:17; that 7Q11 contains text from 100:12; and that 7Q13 contains text from 103:12. The likely identification of these fragments is significant since it affirms the existence of a Greek copy of *1 Enoch* at Qumran and provides a new classification (pap7QEn gr) for the previously unidentified fragments 7Q4, 7Q8, 7Q11, 7Q12, 7Q13, and 7Q14.

The Qumran evidence clarifies or solves several questions surrounding *1 Enoch.* First, most if not all of this book was originally written in Aramaic, was subsequently translated into Greek, and from the Greek it was rendered into Ethiopic and perhaps other languages.

The second question concerns the earliest form of *1 Enoch.* According to the first editor, J. T. Milik,[29] the Qumran Enochic corpus comprised a "pentateuch" modeled after the five books of Moses, to which the complier then added chapters 106 and 107. Milik also observed that of the eleven Aramaic manuscripts from Qumran, five preserve 50 percent of the Book of the Watchers,[30] four scrolls contain 30 percent of the Astronomical Book,[31] four more preserve 26 percent of the Book of Dreams,[32] and two contain 18 percent of the Epistle of Enoch.[33] (These numbers are inflated, however, since they include Milik's large restorations.) It is interesting indeed that nothing is preserved from the Similitudes or Parables of Enoch (chaps. 37–71). For scholars of the New Testament, the Similitudes are of special import because they feature someone called *the son of man,* who is eventually identified as Enoch himself. One important question is whether this messianic son of man as found in *1 Enoch,* who will play a role in the final judgment, was an early source on which the New Testament Gospel writers drew for their descriptions of Jesus as the Son of Man. Milik, followed by some scholars, concluded that the Similitudes are absent at Qumran—while the other four parts of *1 Enoch* are present—because the Similitudes were written much later, probably even after the Gospels themselves. Other scholars, however, believe that the Similitudes were written before the Christian era, but represent a type of Judaism different from that practiced at Qumran. Whichever view is correct, it is very probable that the Similitudes, unlike the other four booklets of *1 Enoch,* were never included in any of the Qumran manuscripts.

It is likely, although not assured, that in place of the Similitudes the version of *1 Enoch* known at Qumran contained a separate composition known as the *Book of Giants.* This work, which is found in nine or ten Qumran scrolls, including at least one of those listed above,[34] concerns the giants who were the sons of the angels described elsewhere in *1 Enoch.* If it was the third unit in the Qumran version of *1 Enoch,* this booklet was later replaced by the Similitudes.[35] The history of the *Book of Giants* is intriguing. Centuries later, it was rewritten by a religious leader from Babylonia named Mani, who synthesized various elements of Zoroastrianism, Judaism, and Christianity to form a religion known as Manichaeism. It was this reworked *Book of Giants* that became a central document, in fact a canonical work, for Mani and his followers.

A third question concerns the accuracy of the later translations in the light of the Qumran evidence. When the Enoch scrolls are compared with the Ethiopic and Greek translations, we find that these later versions are basically faithful and reflect the original. One exception, of course, is the Similitudes (chaps. 37–71), which were not found in any of the scrolls. Another is the Astronomical Book (chaps. 72–82), which was substantially longer in the scrolls than in the Ethiopic version. All four of the relevant Qumran texts provide exhaustive details such as the positions of the sun and moon on various days of the months and years. Most significantly, this longer, original form of the booklet describes a solar calendar that had 364 days, but also a lunar calendar containing 354 days.

Fourth, it appears that the Enochic literature was more influential in the earlier period of the Qumran community's history than in the latter part. According to Milik, apart from 4QEnastr[b] ar and some copies of the *Book of Giants,* the dates of all the Enochic scrolls are relatively early, with none written "in the beautiful 'classical' writing of the Herodian era or from the last period of the Essene occupation of Ḥirbet Qumrân."[36] This leads to the reasonable conclusion that Qumran scribes and readers gradually lost interest in compositions attributed to Enoch, or at least that the booklets were not extensively used at Qumran in the first century CE. One scholar, Gabriele Boccaccini, proposes that the Essenes were an offspring of Enochic Judaism—specifically as a radical and minority group that then split from the main Enochic heritage just before the composition of the Qumran sectarian texts.[37]

One final issue: It is very likely that *1 Enoch* was viewed as Scripture by the Qumran community, at least in the earlier part of its history. Furthermore, although *1 Enoch* is not included in the Bibles of modern Jews, Protestants, or Roman Catholics, it is regarded as Scripture by one Christian tradition, the Ethiopian Orthodox Church (see Chapter 7).

JUBILEES

The book of *Jubilees*[38] is a fascinating ancient Jewish work that is unfamiliar to most modern readers, including many biblical scholars. *Jubilees* survives in full only in Ethiopic and about two-fifths remains in a Latin translation, both of which were translated from the Greek, which is now lost. The book presents itself as a revelation from God, delivered through an angel of his presence (i.e., an angel serving in God's presence) to Moses during his forty days on Mt. Sinai (Exod. 24:18). The angel presents an overview of the history of humankind and of God's chosen people, beginning with the creation (Genesis 1) and ending with the exodus from Egypt (Exodus 7–14) and details of the Passover (Exod. 12:1–28) and the sabbath (Exod. 20:8–11). Written about 160 BCE, perhaps shortly before the Qumran community was founded, *Jubilees* gets its name by dividing the history that it covers into fifty units of forty-nine years each. Thus the author took the term *jubilee* to mean not the fiftieth year, which is the case in Leviticus 25, but rather the forty-nine-year period that is marked off by the fiftieth year.

This book is usually categorized as "rewritten Bible," since it retells many of the events that are described in the biblical books of Genesis and Exodus. Because the author offers his retelling via a famous ancient figure (in this case Moses), *Jubilees* is clearly pseudepigraphic in form. The fifty chapters may be grouped in seven sections:

An introduction (chap. 1), describing the apostasy of God's people and their future restoration

A primeval history (chaps. 2–4), dealing with the creation and Adam

Stories about Noah (chaps. 5–10)

Stories about Abraham (chaps. 11–23:8)

Thoughts on Abraham's death (chap. 23:9–32)

Stories about Jacob and his family (chaps. 24–45)

Stories about Moses (chaps. 46–50)

The author follows the general outline of Genesis and the early part of Exodus, but in the process of retelling the biblical narratives he at times omits, condenses, expands, supplements, or alters the biblical accounts. In this way the author presents his own distinctive views on historical, theological, and legal matters. For example, the long account of the plagues in Exodus 7–10 receives only a few verses in *Jub.* 48:4–11, while Reuben's apparent incest (Gen. 35:22) is extensively explained in *Jub.* 33:2–20.

Five caves at Qumran yielded many copies of *Jubilees,* all of which were written in Hebrew, and at least one on papyrus. The oldest is 4QJub[a], copied 125–100 BCE (see Figure 8.3), and the latest is probably 11QJub (about 50 CE). A total of fifteen scrolls is suggested, two each from Caves 1 and 2,[39] one from Cave 3,[40] nine from Cave 4,[41] and one from Cave 11.[42] The precise number may be as low as thirteen or as high as sixteen, since 1QJub[a] and 1QJub[b] may belong to the same scroll, the Cave 3 fragments may represent more than one manuscript, and the precise identification of 4Q217 (pap 4QJub[b]?) is uncertain.[43]

At least five more manuscripts are related in some way to this book, but in some cases this link is speculative. These scrolls are *4QPseudo-Jubilees*[a, b, c] (4Q225–27); *4QText with a Citation of Jubilees* (4Q228); and a *Work Similar to Jubilees* from Masada (Mas 1j). The last-mentioned text is viewed by its editor, Shemaryahu Talmon, as possibly part of a *Pseudo-Jubilees* composition.[44] One more relevant scroll is *pap4QJubilees?* (4Q482), but the text is ambiguous since it covers either *Jub.* 13:29 or Gen. 14:22–23.

The abundant material relating to *Jubilees* raises several issues and solves some problems. First, is the original form of this book as found in the scrolls similar to the one

Figure 8.3

Fragments of *Jubilee* from Qumran:
4QJub^a (4Q216) (PAM 43.185).
Courtesy of the Israel Antiquities Authority

preserved in the Ethiopic and Latin translations? On comparing the Judean Desert fragments with these later versions, we see that—in marked contrast to parts of *1 Enoch*—the ancient translators of *Jubilees* carried out their task with great care and literalness. As might be expected, of course, there are some exceptions to this statement.

Second, both the large number of copies and several related works show that *Jubilees* was much used and very popular at Qumran; of all the books found among the scrolls, only the Psalms, Deuteronomy, Isaiah, and Genesis are represented by more manuscripts (see Chapter 6). As an influential pre-Qumranic writing, *Jubilees* has frequently been compared by scholars to *1 Enoch*. The surviving copies are distributed over five caves (as well as Masada), whereas the Enochic fragments, apart from the *Book of Giants,* are all from Cave 4. It is also interesting to note that none of the *Jubilees* manuscripts is as early as two of *1 Enoch* (4QEn^a ar and 4QEnastr^a ar), and those that are preserved range in date from about 125–100 BCE to 50 CE. We have already suggested that Qumran scribes and readers gradually lost interest in compositions attributed to Enoch, or that the Enochic booklets were not extensively used at Qumran in the first century CE. The reverse statement may well be true with respect to *Jubilees*—that the sort of exegesis and biblical interpretation represented in this book became increasingly important to the Qumran community during its later history.

Third, *Jubilees* was most likely viewed as Scripture by the Qumran community. As with *1 Enoch,* this book does not feature in the Bibles of modern Jews, Protestants, or Roman Catholics, but it is regarded as Scripture by one Christian confession, the Ethiopian Orthodox Church. (For further details, see the discussion of the scrolls and canon in Chapter 7.)

Finally, scholars find *Jubilees* significant in view of its relationship to several texts that were composed by the Qumran community itself. Prominent themes include its division of the course of history into forty-nine-year jubilee periods; its practice of dating covenants to the third month (especially the fifteenth day), which may have inspired the practice at Qumran of renewing the covenant annually on the Festival of Weeks; and this book's espousal of the solar calendar. The author of *Jubilees* makes it clear that the true annual calendar is a solar one that contains 364 days, a system that also features in the Astronomical Book of *1 Enoch* (chaps. 72–82). Since this calendar (not the lunar one with its 354-day year) is prominent in several of the writings produced by the Qumran community itself, e.g., 4QMMT (WAC: *A Sectarian Manifesto*), their ready acceptance of *Jubilees* is not difficult to understand.

MATERIAL RELATED TO THE *TESTAMENTS OF THE TWELVE PATRIARCHS*

The term *testaments* refers to works that either "mention their speakers as figures from Israel's ancestral period or can be logically assigned to such persons."[45] Such works were quite prominent in both ancient Judaism and Christianity, since they contained edifying teaching and prophetic words that were supposedly offered by patriarchs or other godly heroes shortly before their deaths. Perhaps the most popular collection was the *Testaments of the Twelve Patriarchs (T12P),* which presents the imagined last words of Jacob's twelve sons, the forefathers of the twelve tribes of Israel.

Although the *Testaments of the Twelve Patriarchs*[46] is preserved in Greek and languages such as Armenian, most scholars now agree that this is an originally Jewish work (written in Aramaic or Hebrew), of which the surviving later copies have been reworked by Christian editors. No copy of *T12P* itself or of any single testament in its later form has come to light among the scrolls. Several fragmentary scrolls from Qumran, however (notably of *Aramaic Levi*), seem related to *T12P* or to traditions about the patriarchs upon which the compiler drew. One scroll is from Cave 1, one from Cave 3, and eight from Cave 4.[47] Paleographical evidence suggests that the earliest manuscript is 4QLevi[f] ar (150–30 BCE) and the latest is pap4QTJudah? (mid-first century CE).

It is often impossible to identify the contents of these scrolls in relation to some "standard" document such as the *Testaments of the Twelve Patriarchs,* since the correspondences are often confusing or nonexistent.[48] Several correspondences in content, however, may be identified with greater or lesser certainty; these are listed in Appendix II.

The main group of scrolls is from a work known as the *Aramaic Levi Document,* in which the speaker or central character is Levi, the third of Jacob's twelve sons. Understanding this composition is difficult since it is preserved in three different forms. The first two forms are in the fragments discovered at Qumran and several portions found in the Cairo Genizah (for more on the Genizah, see the Wisdom of Jesus Ben Sira in the section on Apocrypha earlier). A comparison shows that, although much of the Qumran

Box 8.5	*Outline of* Aramaic Levi

1. The Prayer of Levi
2. Levi's Vision
3. Levi Installed as Priest
4. The Instructions of Isaac
5. Levi's Children and Later Life
6. Levi's Teaching in Praise of Wisdom
7. The Prophecy of Levi
8. A Priest Who Is to Appear in the Future
9. This Priest's Great Wisdom, Insight, and Power
10. Books or Scrolls Entrusted to Levi's Descendants

material overlaps with the Genizah copy, some fragments contain text from previously unknown parts of the document. The third form consists of several passages that were inserted into a manuscript of the Greek *Testament of Levi* (one of the *T12P*), from the Monastery at Mt. Athos in Greece. Comparison with the Qumran material shows that these Greek passages had been translated directly from the *Aramaic Levi Document*.

The Aramaic fragments found at Qumran reveal striking differences between *Aramaic Levi* and the Greek *Testament of Levi*. For instance, *Aramaic Levi* possibly never included a testament and contained only one vision, not the two now found in the later Greek composition. The Qumran evidence now suggests that *Aramaic Levi* was composed in the third century BCE and is a source for the exaltation of Levi that features in both the Greek *Testament of Levi* and *Jubilees* 30–32.[49]

An Excerpt from Aramaic Levi

After a long life serving God, Levi passes on to his sons the duty to pursue wisdom. Levi's praise of wisdom echoes similar themes in other Jewish literature, particularly the poem commending wisdom in Sirach (Ecclesiasticus) 51:13–30. An outline of *Aramaic Levi* appears in Box 8.5.

Although he was the forefather of the Levitical tribe that included all the priests, in Genesis the patriarch Levi avenged the rape of his sister, Dinah, by joining his brother Simeon in massacring the men of Shechem while they were recovering from the effects of circumcision (34:1–29). Not surprisingly, their father Jacob criticized them for giving him and his family an odious reputation among the surrounding peoples (Gen. 34:30)—sentiments that were repeated in the patriarch's dying words to the two brothers (Gen. 49:5–7). In later compositions such as *Aramaic Levi* and *Jubilees,* however, Levi's reputation improved markedly. In both texts, for example, the Shechem incident helps explain why Levi became a priest (cf. Mal. 2:4–7) and was given the promise of an eternal priesthood for his descendants. Box 8.6 contains an excerpt from this fascinating pseudepigraphical book, Levi's "Teaching in Praise of Wisdom."

Other Testaments

In addition to the *Aramaic Levi* scrolls, two very fragmentary Hebrew texts are alleged to be from the *Testament of Judah*: 3QTJudah? and pap4QTJudah?, the latter written on papyrus. Though this identification is possible, both manuscripts are so fragmentary that any positive identification is uncertain.

Box 8.6	*Levi's "Teaching in Praise of Wisdom"*

In the 118th year of my life, the year that my brother Joseph died, I called together my sons and their sons and I began to command them everything that was in my mind. I raised my voice and said to my sons, "Listen to your father Levi's speech, pay heed to the precepts of God's friend. I will instruct you, my sons, I will tell you what is right, my dears. The whole of your actions must be right, so may goodness remain forever with you, and the right [...] a blessed yield. Whoever sows goodness will reap goodness; but whoever sows evil, his seed will return to him.

"So now, my sons, teach writing and discipline and wisdom to your children, so that wisdom may be their perpetual glory, for the one who learns wisdom shall have glory through it. But whoever disdains wisdom becomes an object of scorn. Consider, my sons, my brother Joseph, who teaches writing and discipline and wisdom.

[. . .] Do not ignore the teaching of wisdom, [for] every man who learns wisdom, his days [will be long], and his reputation will grow in every land and nation that he goes to. He will be like a brother there, and will be recognized, and will not seem like a foreigner or a half-breed, for all of them will give him honor, and all will want to learn from his wisdom. His friends will be many, his well-wishers numerous, and they will make him sit in the chair of honor to hear his words of wisdom. So wisdom is a great fortune of glory, and a fine treasure for all who possess it.

If mighty kings come with many people, and an army, horsemen, and many chariots with them, and if they seize the wealth of lands and nations, plundering everything in them, they still could not plunder the storehouses of wisdom, nor could they find its hidden riches.

They could not enter its gates, nor could they [. . .] could not overrun its walls [. . .] nor [. . .] would they see her treasure ruined [. . .] for there is no price equal to it [. . . he who] seeks wisdom, [will find] wisdom ... and [nothing will] be hidden from him [. . .] he will lack nothing [. . .] in truth [. . .] from all who seek wisdom [. . .] reading and discipline [...] you will inherit them [. . .] great [honor] you shall give [. . .] honor. Tr[uth . . .] in the books [. . .] rulers and judges [...] and servants [. . .] priests and kings [. . .] your kingdom [. . .] there shall be no end [. . . the priesthood shall never] pass from you until all [. . .] in great honor."

(Cambridge Genizah Text col. E + 4Q213 frag. 1 1.3–23, col. F + 4Q213 frag. 1 1.1–23, 4Q213 frag. 1 2.1–20; adapted from WAC, 257–58)

Three fragments of a Hebrew text (4Q215) that parallels part of the *Testament of Naphtali* were published in 1996.[50] In his summary, editor Michael Stone states that the eleven surviving lines deal with two separate narrative units and are separated by a blank line. The first unit (ll. 1–5) describes the birth and naming of Bilhah, and the second (ll. 7–11) deals with Laban's giving of Hannah (Bilhah's mother) to her husband, and with the birth of Dan. Although the first of these sections is very similar to the Greek *Testament of Naphtali* (1:6–8), the second section has no counterpart in the Greek text. However, the eleventh-century work *Midrash Bereshit Rabbati* includes both the first section and details of the second.

Several more Aramaic scrolls have titles that are reminiscent of one or another of the Testaments: 4Q537 (*Testament of Jacob?* ar); 4Q538 (*Testament of Judah* ar); 4Q539 (*Testament of Joseph* ar); 4Q542 (*Testament of Qahat* ar); and 4Q543–48 (*Visions of Amram* ar).[51]

THE DAMASCUS DOCUMENT

The final text in this section is the *Damascus Document*, whose mention here will be surprising to some readers. This work falls in the traditional category of Pseudepigrapha as "previously known" writings other than Scripture or the Apocrypha, since it was familiar to scholars long before the Qumran copies came to light. Well over fifty years earlier, in 1896, the Jewish scholar Solomon Schechter had found medieval copies of this composition in the Cairo Genizah, which he published in 1910. The *Damascus Document* is one of the most important Dead Sea Scrolls and will be discussed in Chapter 9.

Pseudepigrapha as Falsely Attributed Writings in the Scrolls

When it denotes a group of falsely attributed writings, the term *Pseudepigrapha* may be defined narrowly or broadly. Moshe Bernstein gives the narrow sense as "texts falsely ascribed to an author (usually of great antiquity) in order to enhance their authority and validity."[52] Preferring the term *pseudepigraphy* over *Pseudepigrapha*, Bernstein distinguishes between works that are genuinely pseudepigraphic and those more loosely so in that their editors have attached to them the term *pseudo-*. His broader definition has three categories:[53]

1. *Authoritative pseudepigraphy*, in which the speaker of the work is a purported ancient figure.
2. *Convenient pseudepigraphy*, where the work is anonymous but individual pseudepigraphic voices are heard within it.
3. *Decorative pseudepigraphy*, where the work is associated with a name without particular regard for content or to achieve a certain effect.

Pseudepigrapha as a group of writings falsely attributed to an ancient figure treats pseudepigraphy as a type of writing among all the writings found at Qumran. The compositions involved are all relatively late and may be listed under four headings: biblical texts, apocryphal texts, traditional Pseudepigrapha, and new Pseudepigrapha.

BIBLICAL TEXTS

Most scholars agree that the book of Daniel is pseudepigraphic, since it is attributed to Daniel in the Babylonian period, although it was written and describes events in Hellenistic times (for more on Daniel at Qumran, see Chapter 6).

APOCRYPHAL TEXTS

Apocryphal works qualifying as Pseudepigrapha in the sense of falsely attributed writings are Tobit (featuring a pious Jewish exile from the Northern Kingdom who remains faithful to God in the face of suffering) and the Letter of Jeremiah (purportedly written by the prophet to the exiles).

TRADITIONAL PSEUDEPIGRAPHA

Traditional Pseudepigrapha that are also pseudepigraphical in form include *Psalms 151A and 151B* (with Davidic superscriptions and references to events in David's career); *Psalms 154* and *155* (as part of a Davidic Psalter); *1 Enoch* (attributed to this figure mentioned in Gen. 5:18–24); *Jubilees* (retelling biblical events via a famous ancient figure, in this case Moses); and compositions related to the *Testaments of the Twelve Patriarchs* (most notably *Aramaic Levi*).

NEW PSEUDEPIGRAPHA

The scrolls also preserve a large number of Pseudepigrapha that were previously unknown to scholars. These may be grouped in several ways. Moshe Bernstein, for example, places such writings under four headings: Rewritten Bible (narrative and legal), Prayers, Other Moses Pseudepigrapha, and Prophetic Pseudepigraphy.[54] Another method is to group these texts around the biblical figures that feature in them, which is followed in this book. The texts involved are only listed below, since they are discussed more fully among the nonbiblical scrolls in Chapter 9 ("Rewritten Scriptures").

1. The *Genesis Apocryphon* (1QapGen); see WAC, 74–84 *(Tales of the Patriarchs)*.

2. Texts featuring Noah: 1Q19 *(Noah)* and possibly 4Q534 *(Noah* ar). In WAC, 427–29, 4Q534 is combined with 4Q535–36 to form *The Birth of the Chosen One*.

3. A text featuring Jacob: 4Q537 *(Testament of Jacob?* ar); see WAC, 429–30 *(A Vision of Jacob)*.

4. A text featuring Judah or Benjamin: 4Q538 *(Testament of Judah* ar); see WAC, 430–31 *(An Apocryphon of Judah)*.

5. Texts featuring Levi: Besides *Aramaic Levi,* there is 4Q540–41 *(Apocryphal Levi* ar); see WAC, 258–59 (as part of *The Words of Levi)*.

6. A text featuring Rachel: 4Q474 *(Text Concerning Rachel and Joseph);* not in WAC.

7. Texts featuring Joseph: 4Q371–73 *(Apocryphon of Joseph);* see WAC, 331–35 *(Stories About the Tribes of Israel).* Also 4Q539 *(Testament of Joseph* ar); see WAC, 431 *(The Last Words of Joseph)*.

8. A text featuring Qahat (Aramaic form of the Hebrew Kohath): 4Q542 *(Testament of Qahat* ar); see WAC, 432–33 *(The Last Words of Kohath)*.

9. Texts featuring Amram: 4Q543–48 *(Visions of Amram* ar); see WAC, 433–36 *(The Vision of Amram)*.

10. Texts featuring Moses: (a) *Reworked Pentateuch* (4Q158, 4Q364–67); see WAC, 199–204 *(A Reworking of Genesis and Exodus)* and 325–28 *(An Annotated Law of Moses).* (b) The *Temple Scroll* (11Q19–20); see WAC, 457–92. (c) *Jubilees* (see above). (d) 1Q22 *(An Apocryphon of Moses);* see WAC, 172–74 *(Words of Moses).* (e) 1Q29, 4Q375–76 *(Three Tongues of Fire);* see WAC, 178–79. (f) 4Q368 *(Apocryphal Pentateuch A)* and 4Q377 *(Apocryphal Pentateuch B);* see WAC, 337–38 *(A Moses Apocryphon).* (g) 2Q21 *(Apocryphon of Moses?);* not in WAC. (h) The legal text 4Q249 *(Midrash Sefer Moshe);* not in WAC. (i) 4Q374 *(Exodus/Conquest Traditions);* see WAC,

335–36 *(Discourse on the Exodus and Conquest).* (j) 4Q408 *(Apocryphon of Moses[c]?);* see WAC, 377 *(Prayer of Praise).*

11. Texts featuring Joshua: 4Q123 *(Paraphrase of Joshua);* not in WAC; 4Q378–79 *(Apocryphon of Joshua);* see WAC, 339–42 *(Psalms of Joshua);* and 4Q522 *(Prophecy of Joshua);* see WAC, 422–23 *(A Tale of Joshua).*

12. Texts featuring Samuel: 4Q160 *(Vision of Samuel);* see WAC, 207–9 *(An Account of the Story of Samuel);* and 6Q9 *(Apocryphon of Samuel-Kings);* not in WAC.

13. Texts featuring David: 2Q22 *(Apocryphon of David?);* see WAC, 331–35; 4Q380–81 *(Noncanonical Psalms A and B);* see WAC, 342–47 *(A Collection of Royal Psalms).*

14. A text featuring Jonathan? 4Q523 *(Unclassified);* not in WAC.

15. A text featuring Solomon? 11Q11 *(Apocryphal Psalms);* see WAC, 453–54 *(Songs to Disperse Demons).*

16. A text featuring Elijah: 4Q382 *(Paraphrase of Kings);* see WAC, 347–48 *(An Apocryphon of Elijah).*

17. A text featuring Elisha: 4Q481a *(Apocryphon of Elisha);* not in WAC.

18. Texts featuring Jeremiah and Ezekiel: 4Q383–91; see WAC, 349–56 *(Prophetic Apocryphon).*

19. A text featuring Malachi: 5Q10–11 *(Apocryphon of Malachi);* see WAC, 414–17 *(The Songs of the Sage for Protection Against Evil Spirits).*

20. A text featuring Esther? 4Q550 *(Proto-Esther[a] ar);* see WAC, 437–39 *(The Tale of Bagasraw).*

21. Texts featuring Daniel: (a) 4Q242 *(Prayer of Nabonidus* ar); see WAC, 265–66 *(The Healing of King Nabonidus).* (b) 4Q243–44 and 4Q245 (two *Pseudo-Daniel* ar compositions); see WAC, 266–68 *(The Vision of Daniel).* (c) 4Q246 *(Apocryphon of Daniel* ar); see WAC, 268–70 *(A Vision of the Son of God).* (d) 4Q552–53 *(Four Kingdoms* ar); see WAC, 439–41 *(The Vision of the Four Trees).* (e) Possible 4Q489 *(Apocalypse* ar), not in WAC.

22. A text featuring Suzanna? 4Q551 *(Daniel-Suzanna?* ar), not in WAC.

These twenty-two new texts or groups of new texts, which will be discussed more fully in Chapter 9, present many biblical characters in transformed settings. It is interesting to note that several major Qumranic writings do not feature in this list since they are not pseudonymous works. For example, the *Rule of the Community,* the *War Scroll,* and the *Damascus Document* are better classified as anonymous compositions.

Select Bibliography

See the entries for the individual books in

Schiffman, L. H., and J. C. VanderKam, eds. *Encyclopedia of the Dead Sea Scrolls.* 2 vols. New York and Oxford: Oxford University Press, 2000.

Also helpful for this topic:

Abegg, M. G., Jr., P. W. Flint, and E. Ulrich. *The Dead Sea Scrolls Bible.* San Francisco: HarperSanFrancisco, 1999.

VanderKam, J. C. *The Dead Sea Scrolls Today*. Grand Rapids, MI: Eerdmans; London: SPCK, 1994.

Wise, M., M. Abegg, Jr., and E. Cook, *The Dead Sea Scrolls: A New Translation*. San Francisco: HarperSanFrancisco, 1996.

For translations of the Pseudepigrapha:

Charles, R. H. *The Apocrypha and Pseudepigrapha of the Old Testament*. 2 vols. Oxford: Clarendon Press, 1913.

Charlesworth, J. H., ed. *The Old Testament Pseudepigrapha*. 2 vols. Garden City, NY: Doubleday, 1983–85.

For a more technical survey of the works in this chapter:

Flint, P. W. "'Apocrypha,' Other Previously-Known Writings, and 'Pseudepigrapha' in the Dead Sea Scrolls." In P. Flint and J. VanderKam, eds. *The Dead Sea Scrolls After Fifty Years: A Comprehensive Assessment*. 2 vols. Leiden: Brill, 1998–99. 2:24–66.

Other books and articles:

Bernstein, M. "Pseudepigraphy in the Qumran Scrolls: Categories and Functions." In E. G. Chazon and M. Stone, eds., with the collaboration of A. Pinnick. *Pseudepigraphic Perspectives: The Apocrypha and Pseudepigrapha in Light of the Dead Sea Scrolls*. Proceedings of the International Symposium of the Orion Center for the Study of the Dead Sea Scrolls and Associated Literature, 12–14 January, 1997. Studies on the Texts of the Desert of Judah 36. Leiden: Brill, 1999. Pp. 1–26.

Dimant, D. "Apocrypha and Pseudepigrapha at Qumran." *Dead Sea Discoveries* 1 (1994): 151–59.

Fitzmyer, J. "The Aramaic and Hebrew Fragments of Tobit from Qumran Cave 4." *Catholic Biblical Quarterly* 57 (1995): 655–75.

Hollander, H. W., and M. de Jonge. *The Testament of the Twelve Patriarchs. A Commentary*. Studia in Veteris Testamenti pseudepigraphica 8. Leiden: Brill, 1985.

Kugler, R. A. *From Patriarch to Priest: The Levi-Priestly Tradition from* Aramaic Levi *to* Testament of Levi. Society of Biblical Literature, Early Judaism and Its Literature 9. Atlanta: Scholars Press, 1996.

Milik, J. T. *The Books of Enoch: Aramaic Fragments of Qumran Cave 4*. Oxford: Clarendon Press, 1976.

Sanders, J. A. *The Dead Sea Psalms Scroll*. Ithaca, NY: Cornell University Press, 1967.

Stone, M. "Categorization and Classification of the Apocrypha and Pseudepigrapha." *Abr-Nahrain* 24 (1986): 167–77.

Stuckenbruck, L. T. *The Book of Giants from Qumran*. Texte und Studien zum antiken Judentum 63. Tübingen: Mohr Siebeck, 1997.

Talmon, S. "Hebrew Written Fragments from Masada." *Dead Sea Discoveries* 3 (1996): 168–77.

VanderKam, J. "The Apocrypha and Pseudepigrapha at Qumran." In J. Charlesworth et al., eds. *The Bible and the Dead Sea Scrolls: Proceedings of the Dead Sea Scrolls Jubilee Symposium Held at Princeton University, November 1997*. N. Richland Hills, TX: Bibal, forthcoming.

PART THREE

The Nonbiblical Scrolls and Their Message

CHAPTER 9

A Survey of the Nonbiblical Scrolls

THE 222 "BIBLICAL" SCROLLS WERE DISCUSSED in Chapter 6, and the copies of books traditionally classified as Apocrypha and Pseudepigrapha were surveyed in Chapter 8. In this chapter we examine the remaining texts—about three-quarters of the total—that have been identified in the Qumran library. As with the "biblical" and apocryphal or pseudepigraphal books, they belong to several different literary categories. It is helpful to divide texts by content, but we should keep in mind that there are uncertainties involved, as we are dealing in almost every case with very fragmentary remains.

Did the people associated with Qumran classify their literature? We do not know whether they did; at least we can say that there is no evidence they distributed them by type, with Cave 1 containing one kind of scroll, Cave 2 another, and so on. The caves where many texts were found, especially Caves 1, 4, and 11, include scrolls that belong to the three large categories we are calling Bible, Apocrypha or Pseudepigrapha, and the others. The one cave with a unified collection in a certain sense is Cave 7, which housed only texts written on papyrus and in the Greek language. The few Greek texts found there, however, fall into at least the first two of the three kinds listed above.

There are grounds for thinking the Qumran collection of manuscripts was purposeful, not haphazard. The works belong to a variety of literary categories, but not an endless variety, and although they include much, they exclude much as well. Devorah Dimant, in assessing the entire collection, has written:

> Not only is the Qumran collection characteristic in the use it makes of a well-defined range of genres and styles, but it is also remarkable in its exclusion: none of the Jewish Greek works were found there (such as the Wisdom of Solomon), nor, for that matter, works such as the Psalms of Solomon. Nor is there any remnant of the pro-Hasmonean 1 Maccabees, or the Book of Judith. No precursor to the later tannaitic literature has surfaced at Qumran, nor the New Testament. One cannot, then, escape the conclusion that the collection was intentional and not a haphazard assemblage of disparate works.[1]

Dimant surveyed all the texts known at the time she wrote and drew some important conclusions about the distribution of texts in the caves. Many more scrolls were found in

Cave 4 (about 600) than in any of the others, but when one examines the nature of the manuscripts found in the other caves, the proportions resemble those of Cave 4. Accordingly, Dimant speaks of:

> the uniform character of the entire collection. All the caves contain the same types of works in more or less the same proportions. In fact, on a smaller scale most of the minor caves mirror the picture of cave 4. The links between cave 4 and the minor caves are also indicated by the presence in both of copies of the same works. Being an integral part of the Qumran site, cave 4 as the center of the library also establishes a close link between the entire collection and the site.[2]

As we look at the "nonbiblical" texts, we should note that some are sectarian and others presumably are nonsectarian. Here *sectarian* means texts that express distinctive views of the Qumran community and its associates, while *nonsectarian* refers to ones that embody ideas held by a larger circle of Jews, not ones unique to the people of Qumran. It is tempting to use the sectarian/nonsectarian distinction as the basic division of the "nonbiblical" texts, but there are so many instances in which one cannot be sure, that the division frequently proves unworkable.

The pages that follow survey the "nonbiblical" texts under seven headings: legal texts; interpretation; calendars, liturgies, and prayers; poetic texts; wisdom texts; eschatological texts; and documentary texts (?).[3]

Legal Texts

Laws were an integral part of Israel's covenant with the Lord. A set of works found in the Qumran caves are legal in character in one of two senses: (a) they devote a significant amount of space to setting forth the teachings of books such as the latter half of Exodus, Leviticus, Numbers, and Deuteronomy as the group understood and enhanced them; or (b) they spell out rules that governed the life of the community—rules that are also related in some cases to a biblical base. We call the first type *works of law*[4] (setting forth "biblical" laws), while the second we label *rules*. A number of texts not included here contain legal material but belong predominantly in other categories (e.g., *Jubilees*).

WORKS OF LAW

In the case of the Qumran texts treated here, the order in which material appears in the biblical text does not necessarily determine that of the scrolls' presentation.

Longer Texts

Two extensively preserved works stand in a closer relationship to the scriptural base than do other texts in the category, the *Reworked Pentateuch* and the *Temple Scroll.*

REWORKED PENTATEUCH

There may be five fragmentary copies of the *Reworked Pentateuch,*[5] which is nearly a verbatim quotation of material from the first five books of the Bible. It is likely that the work included the entire Pentateuch. There are only a few small additions (i.e., additions relative to the familiar form of the Pentateuch), such as a song of Miriam in Exodus 15 or references to the festivals of wood and oil after Lev. 24:2 (festivals that are mentioned in the *Temple Scroll* and in some calendaric texts); there are also some differences in the order of sections. In it we see some harmonizing or blending of passages—separated in the Masoretic Pentateuch—that deal with the same subject. For example, it brings together parallel material from Deuteronomy into passages from Exodus, just as the Samaritan Pentateuch does. As for the wording of the text, *Reworked Pentateuch* is nearest to the presectarian form of the Samaritan Pentateuch as attested in some copies of pentateuchal books at Qumran. The composition is interesting for a number of reasons, one of which is that it raises the question of whether, when scrolls writers refer to the Torah of Moses, they include *Reworked Pentateuch*. It is difficult to tell whether this was meant as a scriptural text (an authoritative Pentateuch, a Torah) or whether it should be seen as a slight reworking of the books of Moses familiar to us and thus an example of Rewritten Scriptures (see later).

THE *TEMPLE SCROLL*

11Q19, which is more than 8 meters, or 26 feet, in length, with remains of sixty-six columns, offers most of the surviving text, while four more fragmentary copies parallel and/or supplement it.[6] The first preserved part has Moses at Mt. Sinai (Exodus 34), where God gives him instructions about building the sanctuary and altar (cols. 2–13), the festivals and their sacrifices (13–29), the courtyards of the Temple complex and various buildings in them (30–45), and other matters such as purity (45–51); material paralleling the law code in Deuteronomy 12–23 occupies columns 52–66. It seems that the text moves from the center (the sanctuary) outward to include laws about the Temple courts, Jerusalem, and other towns.

The *Temple Scroll* is a re-presentation of biblical law, and almost always presents those laws as being spoken by God in the first person to Moses, who is not even named but whose identity must be inferred from the phrase "your brother Aaron" (44.5). Where the Pentateuch speaks of the Lord in the third person ("the Lord said"), in this text he speaks in the first person ("I say to you"). The scroll's list of festivals and their dates presupposes a 364-day year as in *Jubilees* and the Qumran calendars.

The *Temple Scroll* appears to be an authoritative *interpretation* of the Torah of Moses, not a *replacement* for it. The editor harmonizes passages, solves problems in them, and brings the scattered laws (e.g., laws about festivals and their sacrifices) into a more ordered arrangement. Its pseudepigraphic framework (direct speech by God) clearly stakes a claim of authority and raises the question whether this text, too, was considered scriptural at Qumran—*the* proper interpretation of the Torah. The Temple it describes is one that humans will construct in the future, but its massive dimensions would have posed a prodigious problem for anyone trying to situate it at the appropriate site in Jerusalem.

We do not know who compiled the *Temple Scroll* from the sources evident in it. Experts have been tempted to see in this text the hand of the Teacher of Righteousness as he records his revealed understanding of the Mosaic Torah. That would be exciting, but we have no convincing evidence about the matter, although a Psalms commentary from Cave 4 mentions a "Law" that the Teacher wrote (4Q171 4.8–9 [WAC, 223]). The section about the king (based on Deut. 17:14–20) in cols. 56.12–59.21 mentions mercenaries and subordinates the king to the high priest; this has been understood as anti-Hasmonean, but the point is uncertain. If 4Q524 is a copy of the *Temple Scroll*, then it was composed no later than 150–125 BCE (the paleographical date of the manuscript) and probably antedated the group's arrival at Qumran. Y. Yadin, the original editor, ascribed the *Temple Scroll* to the time of John Hyrcanus (134–104 BCE), possibly a little earlier.[7]

4QMMT

In 4QMMT,[8] the abbreviation MMT stands for a phrase appearing in the text and meaning *Some of the Works of the Law (Miqṣat Ma ʿaśe Ha-Torah)*. In the official publication,[9] the editors presented the text as though it began with a calendrical list spelling out the sabbaths and festivals in a year. It is clear that there was material about a 364-day calendar early in the text, but the full calendar seems to be from a separate scroll (4Q327). (See Figure 9.1.)

4QMMT looks like a letter, though the senders do not identify themselves, nor do they say who the recipients were. It is commonly thought that leaders of the Qumran community, perhaps before they migrated to Qumran, sent it to priestly authorities in Jerusalem in the hope that the latter would see the error of their ways and change accordingly. The body of the text centers on a set of over twenty legal issues on which the writers disagree with the recipients of the work. The laws in dispute (after the calendrical statement) concern matters of sacrifice, priestly gifts, purity, forbidden marriages, and persons prohibited from entering the sanctuary.

Among the legal rulings is one that explains how the writers transformed scriptural provisions (see Lev. 17:3–9) that referred to the desert tabernacle and camp of Israel in order to make them applicable to later times when the Temple stood in Jerusalem:

> We have determined that the sanctuary is [the "tabernacle of the tent of meeting," that Je]rusale[m] is the "camp," and that outside the camp [is "outside of Jerusalem]," in other

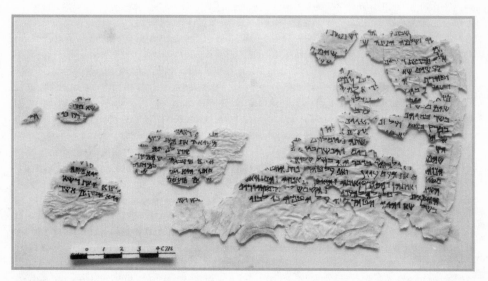

Figure 9.1
4QMMT fragments 3–7, columns 1–2. (PAM 43.492)
Courtesy of the Israel Antiquities Authority

words the "camp of their citie[s]." Outside the c[amp . . . the sin offe]ring, [and] they take out the ashes of [the] altar and bur[n the sin offering there. For Jerusalem] is the place which [He chose] from all the tri[bes of Israel to make His name to dwell . . .]. (sec. B, ll. 29–33 [WAC, 361])

Another paragraph that has attracted scholarly attention is also in section B:

[Co]ncerning streams of liquid, we have determined that they are not intrinsically [p]ure. Indeed, streams of liquid do not form a barrier between the impure and the pure. For the liquid of the stream and that in its receptacle become as one liquid. (ll. 55–58 [WAC, 362])

Though this law may not appear significant, we know that it was an issue on which Pharisees and Sadducees clashed, with the Sadducees adopting the position advocated in our scroll—that impurity passes through a stream of liquid from an impure to a pure container (see Mishnah, *Yadayim* 4:7). This and similar points have given rise to the theory that, in legal practice, the people of Qumran and the Sadducees represented the same, more demanding approach, which, in turn, differed from the more moderate ways of the Pharisees (see Chapter 10).

The composition concludes with a firm but remarkably gentle appeal to the recipients. The authors mention that they have separated from others so as not to share in the practices rejected in the letter and claim they want the recipients to understand the Scriptures, which warn of evil befalling the disobedient. To support their case, they cite examples of blessing (Solomon) and punishment (Jeroboam). They end by saying:

Now, we have written to you some of the works of the Law, those which we determined would be beneficial for you and your people, because we have seen [that] you possess insight and knowledge of the Law. Understand all these things and beseech Him to set your counsel straight and so keep you away from evil thoughts and the counsel of Belial. Then you shall rejoice at the end of time when you find the essence of our words to be true. And it will be reckoned to you as righteousness, in that you have done what is right and good before Him, to your own benefit and to that of Israel. (C 26–32; WAC, 364)

Does this reflect a time just after the community separated from the Temple establishment and still held out hope for reconciliation? We do not know, but this may be the case.

Other Texts

Sizable parts of the preceding works have survived, but about others we know very little because only small pieces are available.

4Q251 (HALAKHA A)

4Q251 *(Halakha A)*[10] is a set of fragments touching on several points of law. For example, fragments 1–2 contain a prohibition of carrying an object from within a house to the outside or bringing something from outside into a house (see Exod. 16:29; CD11.7–8; 4Q271 frag. 5 1.4). It goes on to deal with other laws attested in Exodus (e.g., fragment 8 gives the rule for an ox that gores from Exod. 21:28) and Leviticus (fragment 9 prohibits eating different kinds of produce before the priest offers the firstfruits, using various passages including Lev. 23:17).

Among the other topics treated in 4Q251 is a ruling that was disputed among Jewish parties in antiquity. Fragment 17 (12 in WAC) deals with forbidden degrees of marriage. Such laws are stated in most detail in Lev. 18:7–20, where they are introduced with this heading: "None of you shall approach anyone near of kin to uncover nakedness; I am the Lord" (18:6). This subject was of obvious practical import and was later elaborated because the list in Leviticus did not name all possible cases. Among the possibilities not mentioned in Leviticus is marriage to one's niece. Lines 2–3 of our fragment read: "Let no one take] his brother's daughter or the daughter of [his] si[ster . . ." The same law is stated in two other texts from Qumran—the *Temple Scroll* 66.16–17 and CD 5.7–11. The latter not only provides the ruling, but adds the way in which it was related to a scriptural text:

> Furthermore they marry each man the daughter of his brothers [or: brother] and the daughter of his sister, although Moses said, "Unto the sister of your mother you shall not draw near; she is the flesh of your mother" (Lev. 18:13). But the law of consanguinity is written for males and females alike, so if the brother's daughter uncovers the nakedness of the brother of her father, she is the flesh <of her father>.

The opponents mentioned in this text are thought to be Pharisees, and the Babylonian Talmud indicates that the rabbis permitted niece marriages (*Yebamot* 62b; *Giṭṭin* 83a; *Sanhedrin* 76b).

4Q264A (HALAKHA B)

4Q264a (not in WAC) treats sabbath laws in fragment 1. Lines 6–8 deal with what may be said on the sabbath: "let him not talk] about any matters of work, or property, or [. . .] on the Sa[bba]th day, and let him not sp[eak wo]rds, except to [talk of holy things as is lawful, and to ut]ter blessings of God. Yet, one may talk (in order) to eat and to dr[ink."[11] The same subject surfaces in *Jub.* 50:8 and CD 10.19. This particular ban was related to Isa. 58:13–14:

> If you refrain from trampling the sabbath, from pursuing your own interests on my holy day; if you call the sabbath a delight and the holy day of the Lord honorable; if you honor it, not going your own ways, serving your own interests, or pursuing your own affairs [literally, speaking a word]; then you shall take delight in the Lord, . . .

In this case rabbinic law offers a similar teaching—speaking of one's own affairs is prohibited, but those of heaven are permitted on the sabbath (Babylonian Talmud, *Shabbat* 113a–b; 150a).

4Q265 (MISCELLANEOUS RULES)

The contents of 4Q265[12] are remarkably diverse. The few fragments surviving from it give rules for the sabbath (including the distance that one may walk to graze animals), prohibit a boy or woman from eating the paschal sacrifice, explain laws in Leviticus 12 regarding a woman's time of impurity after giving birth to a boy or girl as arising from the different times when Adam and Eve were brought into the garden (*Jubilees* 3 does the same; see also 4Q266 frag. 6 2.5–11), and detail penalties for infractions like the ones in the *Rule of the Community* and the *Damascus Document*.

OTHER TEXTS

Some texts focus on a single topic such as purity/impurity. The texts called *Tohorot (Purities) A–C*[13] deal with people who have gonorrhea, women who are menstruating, men with emissions of semen, unclean vessels, and rules about purity and impurity in connection with the red cow ritual (see Numbers 19). Another set of texts, labeled officially as *Ordinances*,[14] includes rules about produce for the poor, bringing the half-shekel tax once in a lifetime, not annually (as the Pharisees argued), not selling an Israelite to a non-Jew, not dressing like the opposite sex (see Deut. 22:5), marriages of priests' daughters, sabbath, purity, and others. *Purification Liturgy*[15] legislates regarding periods of purification; *Harvesting*[16] speaks of purity in connection with liquids from crops such as figs and olives; and *Ritual of Purification A*[17] details ceremonies and prayers for people going through purification (a seven-day procedure involving bathing at set points). As the battered remains of these texts suggest, issues of purity were highly significant for the people of Qumran.

RULES

In distinction from *works of law,* other texts legislate for the life of a community by explaining the regulations governing how to join the group, meetings of the membership, meals, and similar topics. There is some overlap between these and the first category above (e.g., for sabbath laws), but the focus is different.

The Damascus Document

In 1896 Solomon Schechter of Cambridge University, working with texts from a genizah in Cairo, identified a full copy (16 columns) and a smaller one (two columns paralleling to some extent columns 7–8 in the longer one) of a work that he called *Fragments of a Zadokite Work.*[18] Then in the 1950s, fragmentary remains of the same work were found at Qumran: eight copies in Cave 4, one in Cave 5, and one in Cave 6.[19] Some of these copies preserve the beginning and end of the text, which are missing from the genizah versions. How this work reached the Cairo Genizah, a storage place for discarded scrolls in a Karaite synagogue in Cairo, is not known, although the Karaites, a medieval Jewish group, also opposed the pharisaic-rabbinic approach to law. The presence of so many copies at Qumran (ten) implies that the *Damascus Document* was important to the group associated with the site, and in fact the penal code in it closely resembles the one found in the *Rule of the Community* (see below). Yet its contents suggest that this text was addressed to a community with members in various towns in Israel.

The *Damascus Document* falls into two principal parts (see Box 9.1). First is a scripturally based admonition in which a teacher urges the *sons of light* to separate from the wicked, speaks of the origins of the group 390 years after Jerusalem's destruction by Nebuchadnezzar, draws lessons from biblical history, warns about the *three nets of Belial* (fornication, wealth, defilement of the sanctuary), and threatens punishments for those who prove unfaithful to the new covenant. The second part is a legal section in which one finds a list of transgressors; rules about Zadokite priests, skin diseases, and feminine kinds of impurity; and laws connected with crops, purity and impurity, oaths, marriages, business transactions, purification, the sabbath, the Temple and Temple city, blasphemers, Gentiles, and foods. Some of these laws are introduced by rubrics such as *concerning the*

Box 9.1	*An Outline of the* **Damascus Document** *(Genizah A + B, 4Q266–72)*

A. The Exhortation

1. Introduction and epigraph
2. Israel's sin, the Man of Mockery, the willful heart
3. Belial and the punishment of sin
4. An addendum on marriage
5. On prophecy and faithfulness
6. The need to remain faithful

B. The Laws or Rules

1. For the priests
2. On skin diseases, bodily discharges, childbirth
3. For business and betrothal
4. On measurements, offerings, Gentile meat
5. On oaths, becoming a member of the Yahad community, making vows
6. On property and restitution
7. On witnesses and judges
8. On purification, sabbath, sacrifices, holiness of the sanctuary and city
9. On the demon-possessed, Gentiles, impure foods
10. Rules for those in camps, for the overseer, for relationships with outsiders
11. Punishments for breaking rules

C. Conclusion of the Rule

"This is the exposition of the regulations that they shall follow during the era of wickedness [. . . so that they can] stand firm during all the times of wrath and the stages of the journey made by those [who live in camps and all their cities. All of] this is on the basis of the most recent interpretation of the Law."

(See WAC, 49–74: A, 51–61; B, 61–74; C, 74)

Sabbath. To this section is added one that gives rules more specifically for the community (the roles of priests and the overseer, punishments for offenses); it also describes a ritual for expelling unfaithful members, apparently at the annual ceremony for renewal of the covenant held in the third month. The admonition serves to introduce the laws, which take up the larger part in the work. The laws, the reader learns, are to be followed during "the era of wickedness" (apparently the present evil age) and are said to be in agreement with "the most recent interpretation of the law" (4Q266 ends with these comments [WAC, 74]).

The community for which the *Damascus Document* legislates involves men who have families, earn wages, and own property. These people are said to live in *camps*—apparently communal cells in the villages and towns of the land. The Qumran copies show that the text did contain a penal code, as in the *Rule of the Community,* but the one in the *Damas-*

cus Document differs in some ways from the version in the *Rule of the Community*—for example, by not including in the penalties reductions in food rations.

Scholars have eagerly scoured the opening part of the work for clues to the origin and early leadership of the group. According to it, a community of penitents arose 390 years (cf. Ezek. 4:5) after Jerusalem's destruction and wandered about leaderless for twenty years. At that time God raised up for them a Teacher of Righteousness to lead them in his way. The Teacher and his group were opposed by someone called the *man of mockery* and his followers (Pharisees?), and eventually they went into their own exile in the land of Damascus, where they entered into an agreement called "the new covenant." Whether this was an actual migration to the city of Damascus (see Amos 5:26–27) or a more symbolic reference is not known. The death of the Teacher seems to be mentioned in 20.1, 14.

The Rule of the Community

One of the first scrolls removed from Cave 1 in 1947 was a lengthy (11 cols.), almost complete copy of what may be termed a constitution for the Qumran community. Later, ten fragmentary copies were identified in Cave 4 and one in Cave 5 (5Q13 quotes from it).[20] This text legislates for a withdrawn group, seemingly all male; presumably the group in question was the Qumran community and possibly others like it. Although the Cave 1 scroll is the best preserved among the twelve copies of the work, comparison with the Cave 4 copies suggests that it contains a later, more developed form of the text.

The Cave 1 copy (1QS) begins with a statement about the nature and purpose of the community (1.1–15), continues with a ritual for entry into the covenant community (1.16–2.18), instructions for the yearly renewal of the covenant (2.19–25), a section on sincere repentance (2.25–3.12), an explanation of the community's dualistic, predestinarian views (3.13–4.26), regulations for communal organization (5.1–7.25 [including rules for meetings and admission of new members, punishments for breaking rules]), a section regarding the nature of the community (8.1–10.5 [going into the wilderness, the community as a temple, spiritual sacrifice, duties of the Instructor and times for praise]), and ends with a hymn of praise offered by the Instructor (10.5–11.22; see Box 9.2).

Two of the Cave 4 copies (b [4Q256] and d [4Q258]) preserve shorter versions of columns 5–7, and it may be that copy d began with what is column 5 in the Cave 1 copy; that is, it may have lacked 1QS 1–4. Several of the copies preserve additional material at the end. The Cave 1 scroll also contains, after the *Rule of the Community*, a text called the *Rule of the Congregation* (WAC: *A Charter for Israel in the Last Days*) and one called the *Rule of the Blessings* (WAC: *Priestly Blessings for the Last Days*). Copies b and d from Cave 4 had more material at the end, but it is not clear what that material was. Copy e from Cave 4 (4Q259) had a calendrical text called *Otot (Signs),* perhaps in the place where 1QS has columns 10–11; copy e may also have lacked 1QS 1–4 and does not have 8.15b–9.11. These differences have given rise to a theory about the evolution of the text: perhaps the now lost original text consisted of a shorter form of columns 5–9 (lacking, e.g., 8.15b–9.11) and the *Otot* text; then the text was lengthened with scriptural justifications for the regulations; and later still columns 1–4 were prefaced and the form of columns 10–11 in 1QS replaced the *Otot* section. An oddity is that the latest form of the text is preserved in perhaps the earliest copy (1QS) and that earlier forms are found in later copies (with the dates established paleographically).[21]

Box 9.2   *An Outline of the* **Rule of the Community**
(1QS, 4Q255–264a, 5Q11)

The covenant and the role of the teacher (1.1–15)
Initiation of new members, annual review of membership, exclusion of some (1.16–3.12)
The two spirits and the problem of good and evil (3.13–4.26)
General rules for conduct of the community (5.1–20)
Specific rules for conduct of the community (5.20–7.25)
    Initiates
    Superiors/inferiors
    Joint meals, scriptural study, meetings
    Initiates
    Violations and penalties
An inner council or an early manifesto (8.1–9.2)
Purpose, prophet, two messiahs (9.3–11)
Rules for the Instructor (foremost priest?) (9.12–10.5)
A sample prayer (10.5–11.22)
    Solar calendar
    Ethical behavior
    Use of the tongue
    God the source of goodness
    God's greatness and human unworthiness
(See WAC, 123–43)

The text calls the community a *yaḥad,* a *unity,* and provides the information necessary for understanding the fellowship and living as a member of it. The picture it furnishes of the community and its ways has played a major part in the argument that the people of Qumran were members of the larger Essene movement (see Chapter 10). They were led by an Instructor who may have been a priest; the membership consisted of priests, Levites, and Israelites, each of whom was ranked annually according to his obedience to the Torah.

THE *RULE OF THE CONGREGATION*

As noted above, the Cave 1 copy includes at the end two other works. The first of these is called the *Rule of the Congregation.*[22] Until recently this appeared to be the only copy of either work, but it has now been claimed that some fragments written in a cryptic script belong to nine additional copies of the *Rule of the Congregation* (4Q249[a–i]).[23] This is still uncertain, but possible. However many copies there may be, the text identifies itself as "the rule for all the congregation of Israel in the Last Days" (1.1) who will live according to the community's law. The assembly of the end times (1.1–6) includes not only men (as apparently the *Rule of the Community* does), but women and children as well, as one might expect. All members receive instruction in the law. The training of a young man is detailed (1.6–19), from the beginning of his instruction to the point where he, at twenty years of age, joins the ranks and is eligible to marry. Additional rights and duties follow at ages twenty-five and thirty. When one becomes elderly, his duties are reduced to make them commensurate with his abilities. The text envisions a community led by priests and including Levites and the remainder of the membership; it is organized militarily (1.22–25). No one with an impurity, a physical blemish, or a handicap is allowed in the *yaḥad*, "[f]or the holy angels are [a part of] their congregation" (2.8–9; see all of 1.25–2.10).

The last section of the text describes a banquet (2.11–22). The line "When [God] has fa[th]ered(?) the Messiah (or, when the Messiah has been revealed) among them" (2.11–12) has sparked interest. As one can see from the punctuation and alternative translation, the text is very uncertain, but the preferred reading is "when the Messiah has been revealed among them." A priest (not called a messiah here) presides over the meal. He and his fellow priests enter first, followed by the messiah of Israel and his commanders and troops. Heads of clans and of the wise are also in attendance. The priest first extends his hand to bless the bread and wine (in that order) and only then do the others present do so. The text concludes with "[t]his procedure shall govern every me[al], provided at least ten me[n are ga]thered together" (2.21–22). It should come as no surprise that this banquet has reminded people of the Lord's Supper in the New Testament.

THE *RULE OF BLESSINGS*

The *Rule of Blessings*[24] is the second work appended to the Cave 1 copy. No other copy of this text has been located. It, like the previous text, may be for the final days. The Instructor first blesses those who hold fast to the covenant (1.1–7). In the benediction one reads "[m]ay He [gra]ce you with every blessing [of the heavenlies]; [may He teach] you the knowledge of the holy angels!" (1.5). The angelic theme continues elsewhere in the text (as in the *Rule of the Congregation*). The second blessing (2.22–3.21) seems to be for the high priest, although the place where the recipient is identified has not survived. There is reference to an eternal covenant with which God will grace him (2.25), and the words "[m]ay He choose all who abide in [your] pries[thood]" (3.1) seem to have the leading priest in mind. This high priest appears to have military functions.

The next blessing (3.22–5.19) falls upon "the Sons of Zadok, the priests" (3.22). The Instructor compares them to the highest-ranking angels: "May you [abide forever] as an Angel of the Presence in the holy habitation, to the glory of the God of host[s. May you] serve in the temple of the kingdom of God, ordering destiny with the Angels of the Presence, a society of the *yaḥad* [with the Holy Ones] forever, for all the ages of eternity" (4.24–26). The final blessing (5.20–29) is for "the Leader of the nation" (5.20). In it words for the future Davidic king from Isa. 11:2, 4 are applied to him: he will not only rule over all peoples, but his administration will be marked by justice for all.

The War Rule

Another of the first scrolls from Cave 1, the *War Rule* or *War Scroll* (nineteen fairly well preserved columns; see 1Q33 for remains of another column), offers detailed instructions for and predictions about the final war between the *sons of light* and the *sons of darkness*. In Cave 4, fragments from six additional copies have been identified;[25] 4Q497, once considered a seventh copy, is now called *War Scroll–like Text A* (4Q471 is *War Scroll–like Text B*).

The Cave 4 copies retain some evidence of a shorter version in places, but that is not consistently the case.

1QM 1.1–2.15 contains summary statements about the final conflict, but not all of them are easy to follow. Lines 1–7 predict an escalating conflict pitting the attacking sons of light, who are said to be the "sons of Levi, the sons of Judah, and the sons of Benjamin, those exiled to the wilderness" (1.2), against the sons of darkness, who at first are Israel's neighbors (Edom, Moab, Ammon, Amalek?, Philistia) with the "Kittim of Asshur [Assyria]." The war spreads to include the Kittim of Egypt and the kings of the north.

> [Then the]re shall be a time of salvation for the People of God, and a time of dominion for all the men of His forces, and eternal annihilation for all the forces of Belial. There shall be g[reat] panic [among] the sons of Japheth, Assyria shall fall with no one to come to his aid, and the supremacy of the Kittim shall cease, that wickedness be overcome without a remnant. There shall be no survivors of [all the Sons of] Darkness.
>
> Then [the Sons of Rig]hteousness shall shine to all ends of the world, continuing to shine forth until [the] end of the appointed seasons of darkness. (1.5–8 [WAC, 151–52])

Later in the first column we learn that the war will proceed as follows:

> In three lots the Sons of Light shall stand firm so as to strike a blow at wickedness, and in three the army of Belial shall strengthen themselves so as to force the retreat of the forces [of Light. And when the] banners of the infantry cause their hearts to melt, then the strength of God will strengthen the he[arts of the Sons of Light]. In the seventh lot the great hand of God shall overcome [Belial and al]l the angels of his dominion, and all the men of [his forces shall be destroyed forever]. (1.13–15 [WAC, 152])

A section about the organization of the congregation follows (1.19–2.6). It is evident here that the service of the Temple was expected to continue during the eschatological war. The next part (2.6–15) includes some indications about the number of years that the war will last: a forty-year period is envisaged, but during it there would be five sabbatical years in which no fighting would take place. The other thirty-five years are divided so that in six of them the entire congregation fights the foe, while in the remaining twenty-nine there is a "war of divisions" (2.10), during which they will fight against specific enemies who are named (a listing based on the genealogies of Noah's sons in Genesis 10).

These segments are followed by several others that, in great detail, give information about the trumpets used in battle (2.15–3.11), the banners and shields (3.12–5.2), arming and deploying the divisions (priests and Levites are also involved), with indications of ages required for various roles (5.3–9.16; here, too, no blemished or impure person is permitted, "for holy angels are present with their army" [7.6]), and a lengthy section with priestly prayers reciting God's victories for Israel in the past and blessings pronounced by leaders (9.17–15.3). In 15.4–18.8 we return to the course of the war; as in column 1, the seven battles of the last day are described (although the sections on battles 4–6 are lost). Once again the priests offer encouragement when soldiers in the congregation are killed "by God's mysteries and to test by these mysteries all those appointed for battle" (16.11). Beginning around 18.10 and continuing to the end of the preserved text (19.14), there is a section with rituals of thanksgiving on the day after the decisive victory.

The *War Rule* sketches a dualistic picture of the final conflict, when the forces of evil under Belial and his spirits will be annihilated. In that war God and his angels fight on the side of the sons of light. The parts of the text that resemble ancient military treatises are encased within a strongly theological and liturgical setting. The final war is a ritual in which, although there are setbacks, the conflict reaches its predestined end in the victory of God and his hosts.

A work called the *Book of War*[26] may preserve parts of the lost ending of the *War Rule*. In the fragments someone is brought before the prince of the congregation (a messianic title) and executed (see frags. 6 + 4, l. 10; frag. 5, l. 4); there is also reference to the corpses of the Kittim (5.6). Since the fragments do not overlap with any of the extant text of the *War Rule*, it is safer to view this work as an independent but related composition.

For further discussion on the *War Rule*, including a table of contents, see "The Eschatological War" in Chapter 17.

Interpretation

A second major category among the Qumran texts may be called *interpretation*. Almost all of the texts found in the Qumran caves are works of scriptural exposition, since they so often deal with scriptural passages and characters or resort to "biblical" language; but a set of texts may be characterized as especially devoted to interpretation in that representing "biblical" material seems to be the essence of their message.

COMMENTARIES ON AUTHORITATIVE TEXTS

The Qumran caves preserved evidence that the group led an active exegetical life. The *Rule of the Community,* as it deals with some basic aspects of organization, stipulates:

> In any place where is gathered the ten-man quorum, someone must always be engaged in study of the Law, day and night, continually, each one taking his turn. The general membership will be diligent together for the first third of every night of the year, reading aloud from the Book, interpreting Scripture, and praying together. (1QS 6.6–8 [WAC, 134])

It sounds from these words as if scriptural interpretation was a daily, communal responsibility, something done in a religious or liturgical context. The scrolls that may be labeled commentaries on authoritative texts can be divided into two categories.

Continuous Commentaries

Continuous commentaries are works that explain consecutive, extended stretches of text. One of the first seven scrolls discovered in Cave 1 comments on the initial two chapters in the prophetic book of Habakkuk.[27] Since this manuscript is well preserved, it has dominated discussion of the continuous commentaries. The term used in the commentary to introduce interpretations is the Hebrew word *pesher;* as a result, the texts in this category are labeled *pesharim* (the plural of *pesher*). Whether the *pesher* on Habakkuk is typical of the category is a different question; however, as the other examples are far less well preserved, we cannot say much about the issue.

The *pesharim* are the oldest surviving examples of the practice, familiar from modern commentaries, of citing a scriptural verse or section and then offering an explanation of it, before proceeding to the next verse or section and exegeting it. These works reveal an approach to prophetic texts that can be found in many modern commentaries written by conservative authors: they assume that the prophet was predicting events in the commentator's time. The writer of the *Habakkuk Pesher* believed that the prophet, who was active in the late 600s BCE, wrote about the Teacher of Righteousness and his opponent, the Wicked Priest, both of whom lived, it seems, in the second century BCE. While commenting on Hab. 2:1–2 the expositor makes a claim about interpretive authority:

> So I will stand on watch and station myself on my watchtower and wait for what He will say to me, and [what I will reply to] His rebuke. Then the Lord answered me [and said, "Write down the vision plainly] on tablets, so that with ease [someone can read it]." (Hab 2:1–2) [This refers to . . .] then God told Habakkuk to write down what is going to happen to the generation to come; but when that period would be complete He did not make known to him. When it says, "so that with ease someone can read it," this refers to the Teacher of Righteousness to whom God made known all the mysterious revelations of his servants the prophets. (1QpHab 6.12–7.5 [WAC, 119])

This passage asserts much: Habakkuk did not know when the period of which he spoke would be complete, but the Teacher of Righteousness, to whom the passage refers, received revelation from God so that he could understand those mysterious words that the prophets themselves did not grasp. Moreover, the age predicted by the prophets—the last days—was the one in which the community was living.

Because the interpreters understood the ancient prophets to be predicting what was happening in their time, the *pesharim* contain a significant number of references to historical persons and events. These have played a large part in discussions of dating the community. It is a pity for us that some key individuals, such as the Teacher of Righteousness and the Wicked Priest, are never named. For groups, other vague designations are used, such as "the Men of Mockery who are in Jerusalem" (*Commentary on Isaiah*[b] 2.6–7).

Several types of interpretative techniques are at work in the continuous commentaries, but they often read as if decoding a cryptic or mysterious text, much as a dream or vision would require some such unraveling. The community's expositors had the advantage of interpreting authoritatively, while in their opinion other Jews failed to grasp the prophetic message because they lacked the exegetical key to unlock its secrets.

A total of seventeen or eighteen *pesharim* have been identified, and they comment on passages from seven scriptural books:

Isaiah	(6) 3Q4, 4Q161–65
Hosea	(2) 4Q166–67
Micah	(1 possibly 2) 1Q14, 4Q168?
Nahum	(1) 4Q169
Habakkuk	(1) 1QpHab
Zephaniah	(2) 1Q15, 4Q170
Psalms	(3) 1Q16, 4Q171, 4Q173
4QpUnidentified	(1) 4Q172

The fact that at least some of the Psalms received *pesher* treatment implies that this book, too, was believed to contain prophecies. Two examples will illustrate the sort of material found in the continuous commentaries. The first passage is from the *Commentary on Habakkuk* 1.16–2.10 (commenting here on Hab. 1:5):

> "[Look, traitors, and see, and be shocked—amazed—for the Lord is doing something in your time that you would not believe it if] told" (Hab. 1:5).
>
> [This passage refers to] the traitors with the Man of the Lie, because they have not [obeyed the words of] the Teacher of Righteousness from the mouth of God. It also refers to the trai[tors to the] New [Covenant], because they did not believe in God's covenant [and desecrated] His holy name; and finally, it refers [to the trai]tors in the Last Days. They are the cru[el Israel]ites who will not believe when they hear everything that [is to come upon] the latter generation that will be spoken by the Priest in whose [heart] God has put [the ability] to explain all the words of His servants the prophets, through [whom] God has foretold everything that is to come upon His people and [His land]. (WAC, 116)

Here the prophetic word *traitors* is understood to include three groups: devotees of the Teacher's opponent called *the Man of the Lie,* individuals who had proved unfaithful to the group's new covenant, and other Israelites who did not believe interpretations by the Teacher (here called *the Priest*) of prophecy, although he received them from God.

The second passage is from the *Commentary on Psalms* (4Q171) 4.7–10 (commenting on Ps. 37:32–33):

> "The wicked man observes the righteous man and seeks [to kill him. But the Lo]rd [will not leave him in his power and will not co]ndemn him when he comes to trial" (Ps. 37:32–33).
>
> This refers to the Wicked [Pri]est who ob[serv]es the [Teach]er of Righteous[ness and seeks] to kill him [. . .] and the Law that he sent to him, but God will not le[ave him in his power] and will not [condemn him when] he comes to trial. But to the [wicked God will give] his just [de]serts, by putting him into the power of the cruel Gentiles to do with him [what they want]. (WAC, 223)

The commentator sees in the words *wicked* and *righteous* (both are singular) references to the Wicked Priest and the Teacher of Righteousness. Here there is evidence that the Wicked Priest tried to kill the Teacher. In the broken context *the Law that he sent to him* is tantalizing: perhaps the Teacher sent it to the Wicked Priest. Though we do not know what text that might be and whether we have it, one suggestion is that the *Temple Scroll* or 4QMMT is meant.

Thematic Commentaries

Another set of texts comment on scripture, but not on continuous stretches of one work as the *pesharim* do. The procedure in thematic commentaries is to gather and interpret passages drawn from several scriptural works and understood to deal with a common theme or group of themes. The authors believed passages in one scriptural book could be clarified by ones found in other books—that all of these books were interrelated in some way. At least three manuscripts may be listed here: *4QFlorilegium* (4Q174), *4QCatena A* (4Q177), *11QMelchizedek* (11Q13).[28] Others exhibit similar techniques, but center on a single book: 4Q252 *(Commentary on Genesis)* explains selected passages from Genesis in order, but skips large chunks of the text; and the *Commentary on Isaiah^c* (4Q163) is a *pesher*, but introduces into its commentary material from Jeremiah, Hosea, and Zechariah.

4Q174 (*FLORILEGIUM*)

The first legible, connected parts of *4QFlorilegium*[29] cite and comment on several of the blessings Moses pronounced over the tribes in Deuteronomy 33: Levi (33:8–11), Benjamin (33:12), and Gad (33:20–21). The broken section after the blessing of Gad speaks of the house of Judah (apparently the author's community) and the trials to which Belial subjects them. The notion of a house brings in its wake the prophetic words of 2 Sam. 7:10–11, where God promises his people a place where no one will harm them. The author understands this place to be the house that someone will build for God in the last days, as noted in Exod. 15:17–18. He continues with 2 Sam. 7:11, which mentions rest for Israel; this rest the writer explains as the deliverance God will give from the evil caused by Belial and his followers. He quotes 2 Sam. 7:11–14, which promises David a son who will have an eternal kingdom. For the writer this is the messianic Shoot of David, and he cites Amos 9:11 as clarification (it promises that the fallen booth of David will be raised).

Without further explanation, the text then moves to the Psalms. Ps. 1:1, which speaks of those who do not follow the advice of the wicked, is explained from Isa. 8:11 and Ezek. 37:23 as pointing to the sons of Zadok and their men who "pu[rsue righ]teousness and follow them to join the *Yahad*." The last surviving parts of the text cite Ps. 2:1 (persecution in the last days, with survival of a remnant who will perform the law), which is clarified by Dan. 12:10, and Ps. 5:2–3, which relate to the last days and are elaborated through the promise in Isa. 65:22–23.

4Q177 (*CATENA A*)

4QCatena A[30] may be another part of the text represented by the preceding example. It is so badly damaged that the order of the few surviving pieces is not certain, but from what remains it appears that citations of various verses from the Psalms are the connecting link. These are explained as referring to the last days and clarified through citations of other scriptures. The order seems to be: material from Ps. 10:2, 7–11? (with Isa. 37:30; 32:7), Ps. 11:1–2 (with Mic. 2:10–11), Ps. 12:1 (with Isa. 27:11; 22:13), Ps. 12:7 (with Zech. 3:9; Isa. 6:10), Ps. 13:2–3, 5 (with Ezek. 25:8), Ps. 16:3 (with Jon. 2:2; Nah. 2:11), Ps. 17:1 (with Zeph. 3:4; Hos. 5:8), and Ps. 6:2–6. A number of the terms we are accustomed to finding in sectarian texts appear here: the *Flattery-Seekers* (literally, *those who look for smooth things*), the *Interpreter of the Law,* the *Yahad, Belial,* and the *children of light.* By combining and interpreting passages, the writer assures the community that though the last days will be difficult, God will save them from Belial and his assistants.

11Q13 (*MELCHIZEDEK*)

In Gen. 14:18–20, Melchizedek, a king of Salem and priest of God Most High, met Abram as the patriarch returned from battle. He brought bread and wine and blessed Abram, while Abram gave him a tenth of the military spoils. Ps. 110:4 mentions someone who is a priest forever after the order of Melchizedek. This royal priest, every expression about whom is intriguing and begging for comment, became the subject of speculation. One familiar book that makes him prominent is Hebrews, in which Jesus is an eternal heavenly high priest after Melchizedek's order.

In the Qumran text,[31] Melchizedek is an exalted figure who is seen as the referent of several biblical passages. Where the text becomes legible and somewhat connected, it cites Lev. 25:13 (the year of jubilee, when all return to their ancestral land) and Deut. 15:2 (debts are remitted in the sabbatical year). The author reads these passages as referring to the last days and involving captives—a term that may have brought to mind Isa. 61:1 (release of captives in the year of the Lord's favor). The sense is that the captives are the community and the remitted debts are their sins that will be forgiven. The writer also uses *jubilee* in the sense of a forty-nine-year period, divided into seven "weeks" of seven years each (as in the book of *Jubilees*); he says that release will occur in the first week of the tenth jubilee period. Since a jubilee year begins on the Day of Atonement, he begins to reflect on that topic: "Then the 'D[ay of Atone]ment' shall follow af[ter] the [te]nth [ju]bilee period, when he shall atone for all the Sons of [Light] and the peopl[e who are pre]destined to Mel[chi]zedek" (2.7–8). The writer substitutes Melchizedek's name for that of the Lord in Isa. 61:2: "the year of Melchiz[edek]'s favor" (2.9).

Furthermore, he is seen as the "god-like being" who will judge in Ps. 82:1 (Ps. 7:7–8 is also adduced). Ps. 82:2 is understood to refer to Belial and his forces; Melchizedek will free the captives from them. The messenger who brings good news in Isa. 52:7 is taken to be the anointed one of Dan. 9:26; he proclaims the year of favor and comforts the mourners (Isa. 61:2). Thus Melchizedek will deliver the community from the clutches of Belial at a fore-ordained time.

REWRITTEN SCRIPTURES

A sizable number of texts found at Qumran are re-presentations of scriptural material, often centering around a famous or not so famous character. We have examined some of these in Chapter 8, where *1 Enoch* and *Jubilees,* texts that predate the Qumran community, were studied. Both are reworkings of parts of the Scriptures: *Enoch* of Genesis 5–9, and *Jubilees* of Genesis 1–Exodus 24. *Aramaic Levi* can be similarly categorized; it builds upon the slim scriptural givens about Jacob's third son, but elaborates extensively on them. Other works should also be listed here.

The Genesis Apocryphon

The *Genesis Apocryphon,*[32] one of the first seven scrolls removed from Cave 1, is large but badly damaged; it has never been fully deciphered. It is written in Aramaic and retells and expands upon stories in Genesis. The first recoverable parts deal with the time before the Flood and, like *1 Enoch,* are concerned with the angels who mated with women. There is a long section on Noah (cols. 2–17 [3–18 in WAC]) formulated in the first person, including a story about how luminous and precocious he was at birth (there is a parallel in *1 Enoch* 106–7). This led his father, Lamech, to suspect adulterous relations between his wife, Batenosh, and the angels and that the child was supernatural. Enoch confirmed that Noah was the child of Lamech and Batenosh, but added that his spectacular traits portended astonishing events, particularly the Flood. The Noah stories include the Flood, of course, and the division of the earth after the Flood, much of this being parallel to the Noah stories in *Jubilees*. There is more (e.g., a vision with interpretation in cols. 13–15 [14–16]), but the text is very broken and difficult to read. The stories about Abram occupy the last surviving columns of the scroll (19–22 [20–23]) and correspond to Genesis 12–15 (see Figure 9.2).

Figure 9.2

The *Genesis Apocryphon* column 21 (SHR 3862)
Courtesy of the Israel Museum

Judging from its contents, the *Genesis Apocryphon* belongs very much in the tradition that produced the Enoch booklets and *Jubilees*. For example, it suggests to the reader that the children of Shem intermarried among themselves and not with the children of his brothers, thus preserving the purity of the chosen line (12[13].9–12). In the Abram stories, the "lie" about Sarai's identity is placed in context: in a dream Abram was warned of the trouble that would occur in Egypt, Sarai's beauty is praised at length and in anatomical detail, and Abram exorcises from the pharaoh and his household the evil spirit the Lord had sent upon them at the prayer of Abram (19 [20].9–20, [21].32). In a number of places the author solves problems in the biblical text. For example, at 22 (23).17 the text supplies *Abram* as the one who gave a tithe to Melchizedek, whereas in Gen. 14:20 only a pronoun is used, leaving one unsure who tithed to whom (the NRSV adds *Abram*).

Other Rewritten Scriptures

A lengthy series of works focus on one or two biblical characters, or so it seems from what survives of them.

NOAH

We have seen that the *Genesis Apocryphon* devotes a large amount of space to the Flood hero. A few other texts are related to him. 1Q19 (not in WAC) mentions the evil times before the Flood (frag. 1) and the radiance of Lamech's child (frag. 3). The fragments are in Hebrew and are therefore not from the *Genesis Apocryphon*. Scholars often claim that the Aramaic text 4Q534 (*Noah* ar) is another text describing Noah's birth. It speaks of characteristics of someone (red hair and moles, according to 1.1) who will apparently have great understanding already in his youth and is called *the chosen one of God*. The Watchers are mentioned in the second column. If 4Q535–36 are added to this text,[33] then perhaps the same person weighed 350 shekels at birth (4Q535 2.3). There seems to be no convincing reason, however, to see Noah in this text, and at the very least he is not named in the surviving fragments.

JACOB

It is possible that 4Q537 (*Testament of Jacob?* ar)[34] is a version of a second vision granted to Jacob at Bethel as recounted in *Jub.* 32:21. One clue is the tablets that the person narrating this text is told to read (1.3). The years of his lifetime were also specified but only the last part of the number survives; it is, however, consistent with Jacob's 147 years (1.4). A building (the subject in *Jubilees* 32) is described in fragment 2.

A TEXT FEATURING JUDAH (OR BENJAMIN)

4Q538 (*Testament of Judah* ar)[35] may be related to Judah, though Benjamin is also a possibility. The broken text reflects the scene where Joseph reveals his identity to his brothers after Judah's emotional appeal to him. In favor of connecting the text with Benjamin is the fact that Gen. 45:14 says Joseph embraced him by the neck, and our text says, "He fe]ll [up]on my neck and kissed me" (frags. 1 + 2, l. 6).

TEXTS FEATURING LEVI

Besides the copies of *Aramaic Levi* (see Chapter 8), several other texts may be associated with him. Most notably, 4Q540–41 (*Apocryphal Levi* ar)[36] may contain predictive words spoken by Levi to his descendants; they say that opposition will come to a future leader.

A TEXT FEATURING NAPHTALI

4Q215 *(Testament of Naphtali)*[37] offers a few lines that parallel part of the Testament of Naphtali, known from the *Testaments of the Twelve Patriarchs*. The parallel lines deal with the genealogy of Bilhah, a wife of Jacob and mother of Dan and Naphtali.

A TEXT FEATURING RACHEL

4Q474 (*Text Concerning Rachel and Joseph;* not in WAC) at least mentions a beloved son and the name of Rachel; it has therefore been named *Text Concerning Rachel and Joseph*. Almost nothing of it survives.

TEXTS FEATURING JOSEPH

Several texts involve Joseph, some of which were mentioned above. In the official lists, 4Q371–73 is called the *Apocryphon of Joseph*,[38] and 4Q539 (written in Aramaic) is called the *Testament of Joseph*.[39] 4Q371–72 speak of punishment and destruction, mention Joseph, and recall his being in a foreign land. 4Q372 preserves his prayer of distress that is nevertheless full of praise for God. Whether all the words in fragments 2–3 are also those of Joseph is difficult to decide. 4Q373 mentions the giant king Og. A connection with Joseph is unclear, as it overlaps with 2Q22, which has tentatively been identified as an *Apocryphon of David*.

A TEXT FEATURING QAHAT

Qahat (Aramaic form of the Hebrew *Kohath*) was a son of Levi and grandfather of Moses and Aaron (see Exod. 6:16–20). In 4Q542 (*Testament of Qahat* ar),[40] Qahat commands his children to be careful with their patrimony, defined as "truth, good deeds, honesty, perfection, purity, holiness, and priesthood" (1.12–13). In the future they will be blessed and will give judgment. The speaker is Qahat, because he refers to *Amram, my son* (2.9). Within this genealogical line the sacred books were to be preserved; they had been given to Levi and he had transmitted them to Qahat, who was now handing them to Amram.

TEXT FEATURING AMRAM

Son of Qahat and father of Aaron and Moses, the priest Amram is the subject of a single work preserved in six copies (4Q543–48, *Visions of Amram* ar).[41] The beginning of the text survives on fragment 1 of 4Q543:

> A copy of the book "The Words of the Vision of Amram [son of Levi." It contains everything that] he told his sons and everything that he commanded them on [the day he died, in the] one hundred thirty-sixth year, that is the year of [his death, in the one hundred] and fifty-second year of [Israel's sojourn in Egypt . . .]. (ll. 1–4 [WAC, 434])

Amram blesses his son Aaron, who was to become the ancestor of Israel's priests. The text relates other incidents in Amram's life, such as burying ancestors in Canaan and not being able to return to Egypt because of war between Egypt and Philistia (4Q544; see *Jub.* 46:6–7). Amram saw in a vision two individuals fighting over him, one hideous, the other delightful and pleasant. The hideous one is identified as Malki-Resha, the ruler of wickedness; the other may be Melchizedek, whose name is an antonym of Malki-Resha. This leads to talk about the children of darkness and those of light and their just rewards. In this work we have the third in a series of three Aramaic texts that contain the teachings of the three ancestral priests Levi, his son Qahat, and his grandson Amram.

TEXTS FEATURING MOSES

As we might expect, the great prophet and lawgiver attracted a lot of attention. Besides the name of Moses being used in connection with the Torah, large works such as the *Reworked Pentateuch* (4Q158, 4Q364–67),[42] the *Temple Scroll* (11Q19–20),[43] and *Jubilees* may be classified as Moses texts, as well as several others in more fragmentary form:

1Q22 *(An Apocryphon of Moses)*[44] reworks material in Deuteronomy, including Moses' final address to the people, and is set on the date given in Deut. 1:3. God orders him to tell the priestly leaders and the people "the words of the Law that I have commanded [you] on Mt. Sinai to command them in their hearing" (1.4). The deity predicts that Israel will serve the gods of the nations and violate sabbaths and festivals (as in *Jubilees* 1). In his address Moses urges the people to obey, but forecasts disobedience (col. 2).

1Q29, 4Q375–76 *(Apocryphon of Moses)*[45] are copies of what may be one work that centers around the Urim and Thummim (stones in the high priest's breastplate) and their connection with prophecy. The text appears to claim that one of the two stones would be lit with tongues of fire, depending on the divine answer to a question posed by the priest. 4Q375 describes a procedure for consulting God when there is a disagreement about whether someone is a true prophet.

4Q368 *(Apocryphal Pentateuch A; not in WAC)* consists of several fragments that parallel biblical material about Moses (e.g., Exod. 33:11–13; 34:11–20, 29–35; Numbers 20). It appears to be a work with narratives about Moses, conversations between him and God, and exhortations and warnings that Moses delivers to the people.

4Q377 *(Apocryphal Pentateuch B)*[46] declares that anyone who does not obey the Lord's commands through Moses, his anointed, is cursed (frag. 2 2.5). The text praises God who spoke face-to-face with Israel at Sinai and describes how Moses was on the mountain with God where "God would speak through his mouth as though he were an angel; indeed, what herald of glad tidings [better: who of flesh] was ever like him?" (frag. 2 2.11).

Other possible Moses texts include 2Q21 *(Apocryphon of Moses?)*, the legal text 4Q249 *(Midrash Sefer Moshe)*, 4Q374 *(Exodus/Conquest Traditions)*,[47] and 4Q408 *(Apocryphon of Moses^c?)*.[48]

TEXTS FEATURING JOSHUA

4Q123 *(Paraphrase of Joshua; not in WAC)* is a text written in paleo-Hebrew letters. Just four small fragments remain and they contain words similar to but not identical with parts of Joshua 21. 4Q378–79 *(Apocryphon of Joshua)*[49] deal with the conquest but add other material such as speeches and prayers. 4Q379 fragment 22 is especially interesting because it is quoted along with passages from the scriptures in 4Q175 (*A Collection of Messianic Proof Texts*; see under thematic commentaries above). It deals with the rebuilding of Jericho and the evil that will come from this. The text mentions the death of Moses, and threats are given by someone else. An exhortation is reminiscent of Joshua's words in Joshua 1; there are also prayers and an account of the crossing of the Jordan River. 4Q522 (*Prophecy of Joshua*)[50] contains a list of cities and places, many of which are mentioned in Joshua 13–21 (col. 1), while column 2 speaks of the choice of Zion and the future building of the temple there, where Amorites and Canaanites now dwell.

TEXTS FEATURING SAMUEL

4Q160 (*Vision of Samuel*)[51] has a section much like 1 Sam. 3:14–18 (Samuel receives God's message, and Eli tells Samuel to divulge what God has revealed to him), a prayer calling on God to help his people, and apparently a report from Samuel about his life while Eli was still alive. Another relevant text is 6Q9 (*Apocryphon of Samuel–Kings*).

TEXTS FEATURING DAVID

2Q22 (*Apocryphon of David?*) may be a text related to David, but is very difficult to identify, although the context is military. A connection with Joseph is also possible, since it overlaps with 4Q373, and thus could be included among the *Stories About the Tribes of Israel*.[52] The relatively well preserved scrolls 4Q380–81 contain *Noncanonical Psalms A and B*,[53] which resemble biblical psalms and in some cases may presuppose Davidic authorship.

A TEXT FEATURING JONATHAN?

4Q523 (officially listed as *Unclassified*; not in WAC) mentions a certain Jonathan, Gog and Magog, and treasure houses. This is most likely not the biblical character who befriended David; perhaps another Jonathan, such as Jonathan the Maccabee, is meant.

A TEXT FEATURING SOLOMON?

The absence of pseudepigraphal texts attributed to Solomon, despite the tradition of his authorship of Proverbs and Ecclesiastes, is noteworthy. An exception is the incantation against demons attributed to Solomon in 11Q11 (*Apocryphal Psalms*).[54]

A TEXT FEATURING ELIJAH

4Q382 (*Paraphrase of Kings*)[55] consists of a large number of fragments most of which are too small to yield a connected sense. The few useful ones tell stories about Elijah and his conflicts with Ahab and the removal of Elijah; others predict the rise of a strong person and contain a prayer (if this fragment belongs to the work).

A TEXT FEATURING ELISHA

4Q481a (*Apocryphon of Elisha*; not in WAC) preserves few words that can be read. The document apparently tells the story of Elisha's coming to Jericho after receiving the spirit from Elijah and his encounter with the sons of the prophets living there.

TEXTS FEATURING JEREMIAH AND EZEKIEL

A series of fragmentary copies deal with Jeremiah and Ezekiel or material found in the books by those names. Scholars debate whether more than one work is involved in 4Q383–91.[56] Both prophets are mentioned by name, and places and events in their lives are reflected. So, for instance, Ezekiel's vision of the valley of dry bones figures in 4Q385 fragment 2, 4Q386, and 388; it was shown to him in answer to his question when the Lord would redeem his people—an issue that arises in other fragments as well (e.g., 4Q386 frag. 1, col. 2). His chariot vision is the subject of 4Q385 fragment 4. Jeremiah's experiences with the exiles are told in 4Q385 fragment 16; included are references to his traveling with them to a river where he instructed them and mention of his relations with the exiles in Egypt. Other fragments offer predictions of difficult times for Israel and the rise of one called Gadfan *(blasphemer)*, who will apparently oppress disobedient Israel (4Q387 frag. 3, col. 2). The predictions express time units in the language of jubilees of years, as in the book of *Jubilees* and a number of Qumran texts. The future wickedness of the sons of Aaron when they reign in Israel forms the subject of 4Q390 fragment 1 and perhaps fragment 2, column 1. These texts appear to adapt prophetic material in order to apply it to more recent times.

A TEXT FEATURING MALACHI

5Q10–11 *(Apocryphon of Malachi)*[57] contains a few words cited from Mal. 1:14 and an apparent interpretation of them. The text may well be a *pesher*.

A TEXT POSSIBLY RELATED TO ESTHER

Though no copy of the book of Esther has turned up at Qumran, a number of fragments grouped under 4Q550 have been identified as copies of a work named *Proto-Esther* ar,[58] which includes mention of the Persian king Darius. Much is conjectural but one Patireza apparently did a favor for the Persian king (here Darius is named). Later, Darius's son learns from the records, read to him one sleepless night, that Patireza had done the deed, and belatedly rewards Patireza's son, who may be Bagasraw. Bagasraw seems to have come to high honor after overcoming opposition. The fragments show a number of similarities with parts of the book of Esther, though they plainly do not tell the same story.

TEXTS FEATURING DANIEL

Several texts preserve themes or other items that remind one of Daniel. 4Q242–46 all fall into this category:

4Q242 *(Prayer of Nabonidus* ar)[59] is the Babylonian king's first-person narrative about his suffering from a seven-year inflammation while he was in Teima. He mentions that his sins were forgiven (apparently after he prayed), at which point a Jewish exorciser told him to credit his recovery to God. The text reminds one of the story about Nebuchadnezzar in Daniel 4 and uses some of the same language.

4Q243–44 (the first *Pseudo-Daniel* ar composition)[60] locate Daniel in the presence of King Belshazzar. He presents an overview of biblical history (again the chronological unit "jubilee" is used) until the Babylonian exile (the seventy years prophesied by Jeremiah appear here), after which the holy kingdom will be established.

4Q245 (the second *Pseudo-Daniel* ar composition), in a frustratingly broken section, makes reference to a writing, a list of high priests that includes the Hasmoneans Jonathan and Simon, and a list of kings from David to Ahaziah and possibly Joash. Eventually the extermination of wickedness and a return are predicted.

4Q246 (*Apocryphon of Daniel* ar)[61] pictures someone before a king and interpreting his vision. The vision alludes to difficult times coming, referring specifically to the king of Assyria and Egypt (1.6). The text then says that someone will be named "*The Great,* and be designated by his name. He will be called the *Son of God,* and they will call him the *Son of the Most High*" (1.9–2.1; see Luke 1:32–33). Many scholars regard these titles as attributed to an oppressive ruler during a time of suffering and war, a period followed by victory for the people of God, who establish an eternal kingdom of peace under divine rule. Other scholars, however, understand the titles as being attributed to a messianic figure at the end times (for more on 4Q246, see Chapter 15).

4Q552–53 (*Four Kingdoms* ar)[62] presents a seer's narration of his vision of an angel and four trees, which symbolize four kingdoms.

4Q489 (*Apocalypse* ar). A connection with the book of Daniel has been proposed, but this text is too fragmentary for any firm relationship to be established

A TEXT FEATURING SUZANNA?

The story of Susanna (Daniel 13 in the Greek version) is one of the Additions to Daniel in the Apocrypha; it has been suggested that such a story may lie behind 4Q551 (named *Daniel-Suzanna?* ar; not in WAC). Any such relationship, however, is uncertain; the account in the Qumran text sounds more like the story of Lot and the men of Sodom (Gen. 19:1–11).

As this survey indicates, there are many texts that deal with biblical characters and use the stories and other kinds of texts in new settings. It is frustrating, indeed, that so many of them are reduced to shreds.

Calendars, Liturgies, and Prayers

The third major division of Qumran texts includes three categories; they are related in that the holidays, marked by liturgies and prayers, are regulated by the calendars of the community.

CALENDARS

We have already seen that *1 Enoch* 72–82 describes the workings of a 364-day solar calendar, along with a 354-day lunar arrangement; the details of both were revealed to Enoch by the angel Uriel. *Jubilees,* unlike *1 Enoch,* rejects lunar calendars and staunchly defends a 364-day solar calendar, which, it claims, was revealed to Enoch. The Qumran calendars, most fully visible in about twenty different texts but evident in others, side with *1 Enoch* in presenting both a solar calendar (364 days) and a lunar calendar (354 days).

We can classify the calendaric texts under several rubrics (for further details on the calendars, see Chapter 11).[63]

Schedules

Some texts enumerate days, weeks, months, seasons, and/or the festivals and sabbaths in the 364-day system. An example is 4Q327,[64] which some claim is the first part of 4Q394 (4QMMT), though it seems to be a separate work. It lists the dates, apparently for an entire year, on which sabbaths and festivals fall.

There are also texts that give schedules for sequences in a lunar month. For example, 4Q317 (*Phases of the Moon* [65]) tabulates the amount of the lunar surface that is illuminated each night. During the period of waxing, each night another one-fourteenth of the surface is lit, while during the time of waning each night another one-fourteenth is darkened.

Priestly Courses

According to 1 Chronicles 24, King David divided the priestly families into twenty-four groups, all of whom are listed in vv. 7–18. As we know from later sources, one priestly group would serve at the Temple for one week, after which it was succeeded by the next in the list. The twenty-four names are used often in Qumran calendars as, in effect, names for weeks. Since there were twenty-four courses, or shifts, each group would serve two weeks in a year and thus provide the name for those weeks, and four would serve three weeks and be the name of three weeks in a fifty-two-week year. After six years every one of the groups would have served three weeks in a year ($4 \times 6 = 24$).

At Qumran there are texts that simply list the dates when the courses would begin their week of duty (4Q322–24 are examples[66]), while others correlate the periods of service with other items such as sabbaths and festivals (e.g., 4Q325[67]). We also have calendars that apparently list which course would be on duty for a six-year rotation, although we have only small fragments from them (see 4Q328–29[68]).

Synchronizing Texts

Several texts provide an extra level of information: they correlate dates in a solar calendar with a lunar calendar. These equivalences are at times also supplemented with the names of the priestly course on duty at the time. 4Q320 fragment 1 1. 6–7 reads:

> [On the fifth day (Thursday) of the course of Jedaia]h is the twenty-ninth day of the lunar month, on the thirtieth day of the first solar month. [On the Sabbath of the course of Ha]kkoz is the thirtieth day of the lunar month, on the thirtieth day of the second solar month. (WAC, 310)

(Here the words "day of the lunar month" and "day of the solar month" are not in the text but are supplied to help understand it.)

Otot

Otot, the Hebrew word meaning *signs,* is the name for a text that presents a very complicated set of data. It correlates jubilee periods (forty-nine-year units), conjunctions of the beginning of a lunar month with the beginning of the solar year, which happened after every three-year period, the priestly course that would be on duty on that date (only two, Gamul and Shecaniah, are possible in this system), and sabbatical years. 4Q319,[69] which belongs to the fifth Cave 4 copy of the *Rule of the Community* (4Q259), calculates for a six-jubilee-year period, or 294 years (6 × 49). It hardly makes for exciting reading but reveals a remarkable interest in calendrical and chronological systems by some writers of the Qumran community.

Some texts found at Qumran reveal a divinatory use of astronomical information. 4Q186 *(A Horoscope Written in Code)*[70] correlates physical characteristics with the parts of a person's spirit that are in light or in darkness. 4Q318 *(A Divination Text [Brontologion])*[71] lists the dates of the month and the sign of the zodiac in which the moon appears, and predicts the events that will happen if thunder occurs in a particular sign of the zodiac (see also 4Q561, *An Aramaic Horoscope*[72]).

PRAYERS IN LITURGIES

Although they had removed themselves from the Jerusalem Temple and its rituals, the Qumran community continued to worship. Several texts furnish the words and actions for days, sabbaths, and festivals.

Some liturgical texts are meant for daily occasions. 4Q503 *(Daily Prayers)*[73] includes blessings of God recited in the evenings and mornings of each day in the month. The preserved part seems to be from the first month. The luminaries are prominent, and these texts also mention the amount of the lunar surface that is illuminated each night, using one-fourteenth as the division (see the calendric texts above). 4Q504–506 *(Words of the Luminaries)*[74] record communal blessings for each day of the week. The individual blessings consist of a historical review, a petition for forgiveness (and the like), and a blessing, concluding with a double "amen." The form for the sabbath involves hymns of praise. God's covenant with Israel is an important theme in these prayers.

This is an appropriate place to mention the *Songs of the Sabbath Sacrifice* (4Q400–407, 11Q17, WAC 365–77), a copy of which was also found at Masada. The songs presuppose that the earthly and heavenly communities join in worship on sabbaths. The sabbaths mentioned (their dates are given) are the first thirteen of a year, that is, exactly one-quarter of the year in the 364-day calendar, which underlies the text. Lavish descriptions of the heavenly worship with its numerous angelic participants form the center of the detailed accounts in the text, and the visions of Ezekiel 1 and 10 were major biblical inspirations for the chariot imagery used for God's throne. However great the angels are, God himself is far greater and worthy of their praise. These songs, like the rules treated earlier, are said to be for the Instructor.

Several other texts preserve prayers to be used on festivals. On 1Q34–34bis and 4Q507–509 *(Festival Prayers)*[75] a set of poorly preserved prayers can be recognized. It is likely that several of them relate to the Day of Atonement (called *a festival of fasting* in 4Q508 2.3), while 4Q508 13.2–3 refers to festivals and mentions wine and oil, holidays known from Qumran holiday lists.

4Q409 *(A Liturgy)*[76] also calls for praise and blessing of God on festivals. It mentions (the festival of) wood, the day of remembrance, and branches—perhaps meaning the Feast of Tabernacles.

A final set of manuscripts is called *Berakhot* (*Blessings*, 4Q286–90, with perhaps 4Q280).[77] The text may provide the liturgy for the annual covenant renewal ceremony described more briefly in the *Rule of the Community* 1–2. The ritual called for both blessings and curses, and both figure in the text. God is the recipient of blessings for his power in creation and in history, while Belial, his lot, and Malki-Resha are the objects of curses. The term *yaḥad* is used several times.

Poetic Texts

There are more copies of the book of Psalms among the scrolls than of any other scriptural book. In addition to copying the scriptural poems, Jewish authors continued to write in this vein during the later Second Temple period, although the forms and sentiments changed somewhat to reflect new situations and views. Poems appear in a number of the scrolls (e.g., the last columns of the Cave 1 copy of the *Rule of the Community*), but some works are entirely poetic. Prominent among these are the *Hodayot* and the *Noncanonical Psalms*.

THE *HODAYOT*

A long scroll from Cave 1 (1QH[a], with perhaps twenty-eight columns of text) preserves poems that are regularly introduced with the formula "I give thanks to You, O Lord"; for this reason E. Sukenik called them *Hodayot*,[78] a Hebrew noun related to the verb "to give thanks." Fragments from a second copy surfaced in Cave 1 (1QH[b] = 1Q35) and six fragmentary copies were housed in Cave 4 (4Q427–32). Although they resemble the biblical psalms in many ways, these poems show a development of literary forms and express the theology of the Qumran group. They speak often of the psalmist's suffering, including attacks by Belial's people, and of God's grace to him despite his own unworthiness.

In the relatively long history of scholarship on the *Hodayot*, it has been the practice to divide the psalms into two types: those of the Teacher and those of the community. That is, some of the poems have been identified as first-person expressions by the Teacher of Righteousness himself, while the others are seen as expressing the feelings and views of ordinary members of the community. The theory was developed on the basis of the longer copy from Cave 1, where the Teacher hymns are concentrated in columns 10–17 and are thus surrounded by hymns of the community. In the Teacher hymns the speaker stresses the trials he has endured, God's grace in saving him from them, and the knowledge revealed to him so that he could teach it to the community. It has been claimed that among the Cave 4 copies, 4QH[c] (4Q429) had only Teacher poems, while 4QH[a] (4Q427) had only community hymns. Other copies from Cave 4 contain both types.

It is true that in some of these poems, regardless of whether they should be attributed to the Teacher of Righteousness, we do find especially strong personal assertions with confessions of human powerlessness and divine grace to save. Here is an example:

> But by me You have illumined the face of many (*or* the general membership) and have strengthened them uncountable times. For You have given me understanding of the mysteries of Your wonder, and in Your wondrous council You have confirmed; doing wonders before many (*or* the general membership) for the sake of Your glory, and making known Your mighty deeds to all living. (12.27–29 [WAC, 96])

In one of the poems of the community one reads these words:

> Blessed are You, O God of compassion and grace in accordance with your grea[t pow]er and the abundance of Your truth, and the profusion of Your mercy for all Your creatures.

> Gladden the soul of Your servant with Your truth and cleanse me in Your righteousness. For just as I waited for Your goodness, so I hope in Your mercy and Your forgiveness. You have relieved my adversities and in my grief You have comforted me, for I depended upon Your compassion. (19.29–32 [WAC, 108])

Even if there is a distinction between the two types of these first-person poems, both kinds express many of the same ideas.

Mention should also be made of highly fragmentary texts labeled *Hodayot-like* (4Q433, 4Q433a, 4Q440; not in WAC). It is not impossible that these preserve pieces of *Hodayot* manuscripts, with which they do share some formal features and vocabulary. 4Q433a is copied on the back of 4Q255, the first Cave 4 copy of the *Rule of the Community*.

NONCANONICAL PSALMS

The poems in *Noncanonical Psalms* (4Q380–81)[79] also resemble biblical psalms (even the word *selah* appears) and may in some cases presuppose Davidic authorship. One preserved rubric identifies a poem as "the Prayer of Manasseh, king of Judah, when the king of Assyria imprisoned him" (4Q381 33.8). This is another attempt (see the *Prayer of Manasseh* in the Apocrypha) to supply a prayer for the penitent king who, according to 2 Chron. 33:10–13, prayed to God from his place of Assyrian imprisonment. 2 Chronicles does not reproduce the words of his prayer; it says only that God accepted it and restored him to his place. In this text he recognizes his sinfulness and divine deliverance. Praise of God is a prominent theme throughout these psalms; there are also pleas for his help and a wisdom poem.

Wisdom Texts

Together with a few copies of biblical wisdom books like Proverbs, the Qumran caves yielded fragments of other, previously unknown sapiential works.

The composition with the largest amount of preserved text is called *4QInstruction* (1Q26, 4Q415–18a, 418c, 423).[80] In good wisdom form, a sage instructs a person called "one who understands," and topics met often are finances, relations in society, and family issues. Although these subjects are familiar from older wisdom writings, in this text there are also differences relative to the scriptural examples. One phrase met frequently can be translated "the secret of the way things are" or "the secret/mystery that is/will be." It points to knowledge available only to those with the right kind of insight. That knowledge has to do with the nature of the created order and with God's plan in history and the goal toward which it is moving. Accordingly there is an eschatological dimension to the teaching. The person with understanding grasps the times of God—apparently the ages into which history is divided. The special knowledge is revealed by God (4Q416 fragment 2 3.17–18; 4Q418 fragment 123 2.2–4; 1Q26 1.4):

> The God of knowledge is the confidant of Truth, and in the secret of the way things are He has made plain its basis [. . .] what is its nature and the governing principle of its deeds, for every [. . .] He has made plain to the mind of every [man] how to live by the nature of His understanding; and He has made plain [. . .] and by the faculty of understanding [He revealed] the enigmas of His purpose with blameless conduct [in all] His deeds. Inquire into these things at all times, give careful thought to all their effects, and

> then you will know [eternal] glory with His wonderful secrets and His mighty deeds.
> (4Q417 frag. 2 1.8–13 [WAC, 381])

If one understands the nature of reality and acts accordingly, one can gain contentment in life and eternal reward. God will favor those who do the truth but will judge the wicked (see 4Q416 frag. 1, ll. 10–16, where this follows a statement about God's creation of the world).

A number of other works have been identified as wisdom texts. One with the title *Mysteries* (1Q27, 4Q299–301)[81] also mentions the secret/mystery of what is/will be and speaks of the reward of the good and punishment of the wicked who did not live in accord with this mystery. *The Wiles of the Wicked Woman* (4Q184, 240–41) presents a memorable Dame Folly who reminds one of her counterpart in the book of Proverbs. 4Q185 *(Sapiential Work)*[82] calls on people to seek wisdom and remember God's deeds for his own people in the past. Two other texts, 4Q420–21 *(Ways of Righteousness)*[83] and 4Q424 *(Instruction-like Work)*,[84] offer instructions about wise and foolish conduct and the sorts of people to be sought out and those to be avoided. See also 4Q298 *(The Sage to the "Children of Dawn")*,[85] 4Q525 *(Beatitudes)*,[86] and 4Q510–11 *(Songs of the Sage)*.[87]

Eschatological Texts

Many, perhaps most, of the Qumran texts could be labeled eschatological. This is true because the people of Qumran believed they were living in the final age of world history, the end of days, and wrote accordingly. So, for example, the *pesharim* are eschatological in that they view prophecies about the last days as being fulfilled in their time. Or, the *War Rule* describes the final conflict between the sons of light and the sons of darkness. A few texts, however, seem to fit best under this heading and will be mentioned here.

THE *NEW JERUSALEM TEXT*

The *New Jerusalem Text* (1Q32, 2Q24, 4Q554, 554a–55, 5Q15, 11Q18)[88] was written in Aramaic and takes the form of a guided tour like the one in Ezekiel 40–48. An anonymous guide shows unnamed individual features of the city (which are never identified) and the Temple, offering great detail about many items and specifying their measurements. The rectangular wall around the city (ca. 20 by 14 miles) and its gates named after the twelve sons of Jacob come first; this section is followed by descriptions of the city inside the wall, with its streets and ordered blocks of houses; last comes the Temple, again described from the outside moving inward and noting the cultic objects and activities. 4Q554 fragment 2, column 3 preserves a few words about the Kittim, about Babylon, Edom, Moab, and Ammon, and a promise that they will not harm someone's descendants until a certain time. Possibly these hints concern the eschatological war; they may therefore say something about the setting of the composition.

For further discussion on the *New Jerusalem Text,* including an outline of its contents, see Chapter 17.

THE *MESSIANIC APOCALYPSE*

The broken text of the *Messianic Apocalypse* (4Q521)[89] contains some words of reproof (frag. 1), but the largest amount of extant text (frags. 2 + 4, col. 2) speaks of the future. It predicts that "the hea]vens and the earth shall listen to His Messiah [and all w]hich is in them shall not turn away from the commandments of the holy ones. Strengthen yourselves, O you who seek the Lord, in His service" (ll. 1–3). It goes on to forecast the care the Lord will show to the pious and those in various kinds of need: "the Lord shall do glorious things which have not been done, just as He said. For He shall heal the critically wounded, He shall revive the dead, He shall send good news to the afflicted . . ." (ll. 11–12). (For more on the significance of "revive the dead," see Chapter 10, and on the relevance of 4Q521 for New Testament studies, see Chapter 15.)

Documentary Texts(?)

In the official lists of the Qumran texts there are several items that are not literary but documentary in character; that is, they are contracts, receipts, records, and so forth. The most famous of these is the *Copper Scroll* (3Q15).[90] This remarkable text, named for the material on which it is etched, offers a list of sixty-five places where treasures are supposed to be hidden. The first unit illustrates the contents: "In the ruin that is in the Valley of Achor, under the steps, with the entrance at the east a distance of forty cubits: a strongbox of silver and its vessels—seventeen talents by weight" (1.1–4; followed by some Greek letters whose meaning is unknown). There has been a spirited debate about whether the list records real treasures, and, if so, whose treasures. One theory is that it itemizes temple valuables hidden during the war against Rome in 66–70 CE. A supporting argument is that some of the treasures may have priestly connections, and priests are mentioned. An example:

> At the cairn by the ford of the High Priest, d[ig down] nine [cubits: twenty-] two (?) talents of silver coins. In the aqueduct of [. . .] the [. . .] northe[rn] reservoir [. . .] having four si[des], measure out from its [ri]m twent[y-fo]ur cubits: four hundred talents of silver coins. In the cave that is next to the cold-chamber belonging to the family of Hakkoz [a priestly clan], dig down six cubits: six jars of silver coins. (6.14–7.10 [WAC, 194])

Whatever the treasures were—real or fictitious, priestly or other—no one has been able to find them. If they were real, they may have been discovered long ago.

The *Copper Scroll* is not the only Qumran text that can be called documentary. One that has attracted much attention in recent years was found only in 1996, and for that reason does not appear in WAC. This is an ostracon that is a deed of gift and has been interpreted as a document in which one who is becoming a member of the community (the word *yaḥad* may be in the text) is deeding his property to it.

Another set of texts also falls into this category. 4Q342–60a, all of which are exceedingly fragmentary, seem to be fragments from documentary texts. It has been argued, however, that they are not from Qumran, but were actually found in the Wadi Seiyal. Ada Yardeni claims that 4Q347 is a fragment from Wadi Seiyal text 32 and that a name in 4Q359 is reminiscent of one found in Seiyal text 7, so that it, too, comes from this site. The name argument is weak, but if 4Q347 were a fragment of Seiyal text 32, there would be good reason for saying it did not come from Qumran. Yet a look at the photographic plate where the two are placed close together shows that the argument is implausible. 4Q347 does not seem to belong with text 32.[91] At present, therefore, these texts do appear to have come from Qumran, and add a little to its small inventory of documentary texts.

CHAPTER 10

Identifying the Group Associated with Qumran

IN ATTEMPTING TO UNDERSTAND THE DEAD SEA SCROLLS in their historical context, scholars have tried diligently to identify the group that was responsible for the texts. Although we know that the Qumran covenanters did not copy all of the manuscripts found in the caves—some of them, for instance, were written before the community went to the Judean wilderness—the presence of several inkwells at the site makes it likely that some were written or copied there. However many scrolls may have been copied at Qumran, presumably the collection was in the care of the group of people associated with the site. Who were they and how can we tell? There are several possible answers to these questions:

The scrolls were associated with a Jewish group known to us from ancient sources. Those groups are primarily the Pharisees (with the Zealots as a subset), the Sadducees, and the Essenes.

The scrolls were associated with a Jewish group unknown to us from ancient sources.

The scrolls were not associated with a single group, but with the nation.

The scrolls were not associated with a Jewish group, but a Christian one.

Although all of these possibilities should be considered, it is only fair to say that identification of the group as Essene has received the largest amount of support and so will receive the bulk of our attention. After the arguments for and against it have been reviewed, the others will be taken up more briefly.

Before doing that we should be aware that we know very little about the Jewish groups that existed in late Second Temple times. We should also keep in mind how slippery party labels can be in modern times and recall that words such as Democrat and Republican or liberal and conservative can mean different things in different times and places. Presumably words like *Essene* and *Pharisee* were also somewhat flexible, and this should warn us to be careful in attempting to apply names to ancient groups.

239

The Scrolls Were Associated with a Group of Essenes

From the beginning of scrolls studies to the present, the most widely adopted view has been that the Qumran community was a small branch of the larger Essene movement. The first expert to voice the hypothesis was Eleazar Sukenik, whose crucial role in acquiring, studying, and publishing the first scrolls was described in Chapter 1. He made the suggestion when only a few scrolls from Cave 1 were available to him.

> We must, of course, await more thorough study to discover to whom the *genizah* cave belonged. Nonetheless, there is one point that seems very suggestive to me. On examining the scrolls owned by the Syrian Orthodox Metropolitan, I found one of them to contain a manual of discipline for a community or sect. I am inclined to believe that the *genizah* was instituted by the sect of Essenes who, as several ancient literary sources tell us, had their seat on the western side of the Dead Sea, in the neighborhood of 'Ein Gedi.[1]

The "manual of discipline" to which he referred is the *Rule of the Community* (1QS), a text that has been a central element in the Essene identification. Metropolitan Samuel also saw an Essene connection with the texts, as did the American scholars who issued the first press release about the scroll discoveries (see Chapter 1). In listing the scrolls of which they knew, they wrote: "Another seemed to be a manual of discipline of some comparatively little-known sect or monastic order, possibly the Essenes." This point of view has been championed by many in the intervening years, although there have always been some scholars who challenged it.

Rather than trace the history of scholarship on the subject, it is more advantageous to examine the data on which the inference is based. No matter how many adopt a position, its strength depends on the evidence. Two types of arguments have been marshaled in support of the Essene hypothesis.

INFORMATION FROM PLINY THE ELDER

The Roman author Pliny the Elder (23–79 CE), an administrator, military official, and scholar, wrote extensively, but his only surviving book is the thirty-seven-volume *Natural History,* which he finished around 77 CE. He informed readers that he compiled the work from many sources. The words that have interested students of the scrolls appear in book 5, which is part of his long section on the geography of the world in books 3–6. Pliny described the geography of Judea (paragraph 70) and included within it a treatment of the Jordan River and, of course, the Dead Sea (71–74). Among his comments about the Dead Sea area are these lines:

> To the west [of the Dead Sea] the Essenes have put the necessary distance between themselves and the insalubrious shore. They are a people unique of its kind and admirable beyond all others in the whole world, without women and renouncing love entirely, without money, and having for company only the palm trees. Owing to the throng of newcomers, this people is daily re-born in equal number; indeed, those whom, wearied by the fluctuations of fortune, life leads to adopt their customs, stream in in great numbers. Thus, unbelievable though this may seem, for thousands of centuries a race has existed which is eternal yet into which no one is born: so fruitful for them is the repentance which others feel for their past lives! Below the Essenes was the town of Engada [Engedi],

which yielded only to Jerusalem in fertility and palm-groves but is today become another ash-heap. From there, one comes to the fortress of Masada, situated on a rock, and itself near the lake of Asphalt. (5.17, 4 [73])[2]

The next words inform us that Pliny has finished his account of Judea, and he then moves on to deal with the Decapolis ("ten towns").

What may we conclude from this paragraph? One obvious point is that Pliny says there were Essenes (*Esseni* in Latin) at some place along the western shore of the Dead Sea. The place names that follow—Engedi and Masada—indicate that his description moves in a north-south direction; consequently, the Essenes were located somewhere north of Engedi. These Essenes were also located far enough from the shore of the Dead Sea that they did not have to inhale the unpleasant smell of the salty sea.

A second point is that Pliny attributed some remarkable traits to these Essenes: there were no women in the group, they lacked money, and, though no one was born into it, the group continued to exist owing to newcomers who joined. As we will see, all of these characteristics can be documented from Qumran texts and fit no other Jewish group mentioned in ancient sources.

That much seems clear enough, and a reasonable inference would be that Pliny (or his source) was referring to Qumran and the Essenes located there. But some scholars think this does not follow and suggest that Pliny is describing a different site. The term that has occasioned the debate is the Latin word *infra* in the phrase *infra hos* (translated "below the Essenes").[3] Scholars who advocate the Essene hypothesis say that *infra* here means *below* in the sense of *south of, downstream from;* those who think Pliny is not describing Qumran argue that the word means *below* in the sense of *at a lower altitude than.* Hence, they conclude that he was writing about a site located in the mountains above Engedi. The point is, however, not convincing in light of how the term is used in the *Natural History.* As Todd Beall puts it:

> There are two problems with this view. First, *infra hos* does mean "downstream" in nine of its seventeen occurrences in Pliny. . . . Second, despite extensive excavations in the early 1960s, archaeologists have not uncovered a trace of any ruins in the Roman period near 'Ein-Gedi. Recent claims to the contrary have been widely disputed.[4]

When all is said and done, it is more likely that Pliny or his source had an Essene settlement north of Engedi in mind when writing the paragraph in question. This does not entail that the statement is a fully accurate historical description because there are errors in the section (e.g., *Jerusalem* may be a mistake for *Jericho,* and the "thousands of centuries" are hyperbolic), but at least we have in this paragraph from the *Natural History* a claim that Essenes were present on the western coast of the Dead Sea north of Engedi, and there is no reason why Pliny or his source would have fabricated the report.

We may supplement Pliny's paragraph with another excerpt associating Essenes and the Dead Sea. Dio Cocceianus, who lived at the end of the first and the beginning of the second century CE and who was later called Chrysostomos, was an orator and philosopher. According to Synesius of Cyrene (ca. 370–413), who wrote a biography of him, Dio mentioned the Essenes: "Also somewhere he praises the Essenes, who form an entire and prosperous city near the Dead Sea, in the centre of Palestine, not far from Sodom."[5] Since the location of Sodom was disputed in ancient sources, reference to it does not pinpoint the location of the Essene city, but Dio is credited with placing them near the Dead Sea. As there is nothing in the short citation suggesting he borrowed the information from Pliny, he seems to be an independent witness.

AGREEMENTS BETWEEN THE SECTARIAN SCROLLS AND ANCIENT DESCRIPTIONS OF THE ESSENES

The second line of argument in support of the Essene identification is that the traits of the group as they emerge from the sectarian scrolls and the ones found in ancient accounts of the Essenes agree and that this is the case for no other group. There is a long list of parallels between these sources and a shorter one of discrepancies. The major classical descriptions of the Essenes are found in two writings of the Jewish historian Josephus (ca. 37–100 CE): the *Jewish War* (esp. 2.119–61) and the *Jewish Antiquities* (esp. 13.171–73; 18.18–22); and in two treatises by Philo of Alexandria (ca. 20 BCE–50 CE): *Every Good Man Is Free* (75–91) and *Hypothetica: Apology for the Jews*. There is no evidence that either of these authors was aware of the settlement on the shore of the Dead Sea; rather, they wrote about Essenes who were more a part of Jewish society. It is possible that their descriptions of the Essenes derive from a common source; if so, that source would have been written no later than the early part of the first century CE. Some important parallels are summarized below.

Same Theology

The sectarian texts from Qumran and the ancient descriptions of the Essenes attribute the same theology to the group. The early sources do not focus on this aspect of the Essenes; they devote more space to their practices. But what they do say about them agrees with what we find in the scrolls. Josephus, in a well-known statement, contrasts the views of the Jewish groups regarding what he calls fate:

> Now at this time [Josephus is writing about the rule of Jonathan, 152–142 BCE] there were three schools of thought among the Jews, which held different opinions concerning human affairs; the first being that of the Pharisees, the second that of the Sadducees, and the third that of the Essenes. As for the Pharisees, they say that certain events are the work of Fate, but not all; as to other events, it depends upon ourselves whether they shall take place or not. The sect of Essenes, however, declares that Fate is mistress of all things, and that nothing befalls men unless it be in accordance with her decree. But the Sadducees do away with Fate, holding that there is no such thing and that human actions are not achieved in accordance with her decree, but that all things lie within our power, so that we ourselves are responsible for our well-being, while we suffer misfortune through our own thoughtlessness. (*Antiquities* 13.171–73)[6]

Josephus makes a similar but briefer statement in *Antiquities* 18.18: "The doctrine of the Essenes is wont [literally, *likes to*] leave everything in the hands of God."[7]

The same picture emerges from Qumran sectarian texts. The most famous passage on the subject is found in the *Rule of the Community* 3.13–4.26, a section on the two spirits. (See Figure 10.1.) It may be that this part of the text did not belong in the earliest version of the *Rule of the Community*, but, however that may be, it is attested not long after 100 BCE in the copy from Cave 1. There one reads:

Figure 10.1
Col. 1 of the
Community Rule
(Trever, 1966)
Courtesy of John C. Trever

All that is now and ever shall be originates with the God of knowledge. Before things come to be, He has ordered all their designs, so that when they do come to exist—at their appointed times as ordained by His glorious plan—they fulfill their destiny, a destiny impossible to change. He controls the laws governing all things, and He provides for all their pursuits. (3.15–17 [WAC, 129][8])

The section proceeds to describe the two spirits—the one of truth and the other of falsehood—that God established for humans "in which to walk until the time ordained for His visitation" (3.18). They are the causes for the actions of the two kinds of people:

God has appointed these spirits as equals until the time of decree and renewal. He foreknows the outworking of their deeds for all the ages [of eternity]. He has granted them dominion over humanity, so imparting knowledge of good [and evil, de]ciding the fate of every living being by the measure of which spirit predominates in hi[m, until the day of the appointed] visitation. (4.25–26 [WAC, 131])

Other texts express the same deterministic theology. In the *Thanksgiving Psalms* the poet proclaims:

By Your wisdom [You have establish]ed the successive [generations] and before You created them You knew {all} their works for ever and ever. [For apart from You no]thing is done, and without Your will nothing is known. You have formed every spirit and [You determined their] de[eds] and judgment for all their works. (9.7–9 [WAC, 90–91])

The hymn in which these words figure is replete with predestinarian language. Note the following two examples:

In the wisdom of Your knowledge You determined their destiny before they came into existence and according [to Your will] everything come[s to pass], and nothing happens apart from You. (9.19–20 [WAC, 91])

What can I say that is not known and declare that is not told? Everything is engraved before You with the ink of remembrance for all the times of eternity, for the numbered seasons of eternal years in all their appointed times. Nothing is hidden, nor does anything exist apart from Your presence. (9.23–25; cf. 7.14 [WAC, 91])

These two sectarian works serve to establish the point, but it could be reinforced from a number of other texts. The *Damascus Document*, as it predicts the destruction of the ones who despise the law, says:

. . . for God had not chosen them from ancient eternity. Before they were created, He knew what they would do. So He rejected the generations of old and turned away from the land until they were gone. He knows the times of appearance and the number and exact times of everything that has ever existed and ever will exist before it happens in the proper time, for all eternity. (CD 2.7–10 [WAC, 53])

The writers of the *pesharim*, by assuming ancient prophecies were coming true in the commentators' time, presuppose that God had determined the course of history before events took place. Moreover, the wisdom texts (though one could argue they are not sectarian), with their teachings about "the secret of the way things are *[raz nihyeh]*," point in the same direction because the concept includes not only the nature of the created order but also the predetermined ages of history. Then, too, the *War Rule* is predicated on the idea that the pattern for the final struggle has already been determined and will transpire according to plan; the same may be said about the *Melchizedek* text, which calculates the chronology of the future in jubilees of years.

A belief such as this is not a minor matter like preferring decaffeinated coffee to regular; it affects one's approach to life, one's ethics, one's view of others, and more. If Josephus wrote the truth in his description of the Essene belief regarding fate as distinguished from the theories of the Pharisees and Sadducees and if the Qumran sectarian scrolls give an accurate expression of the group's convictions, important consequences follow. For one, the sectarian scrolls express a central Essene tenet; for another, this tenet distinguishes their theology from the views of the other major groups in Jewish society at the time.

Although Josephus and Philo deal more with Essene practices than with their beliefs, another theological doctrine attributed to them by Josephus is a set of teachings about the final destiny of the individual. This example may also serve to illustrate a problem in using our ancient sources. Josephus says on this topic:

It is a firm belief among them that although bodies are corruptible, and their matter unstable, souls are immortal and endure for ever; that, come from subtlest ether, they are entwined with the bodies which serve them as prisons, drawn down as they are by some physical spell; but when they are freed from the bonds of the flesh, liberated, so to speak, from long slavery, then they rejoice and rise up to the heavenly world. Agreeing with the sons of the Greeks, they declare that an abode is reserved beyond the Ocean for the souls of the just; a place oppressed neither by rain nor snow nor torrid heat, but always refreshed by the gentle breeze blowing from the Ocean. But they relegate evil souls to a dark pit shaken by storms, full of unending chastisement. (*War* 2.154–55)[9]

Although this statement seems clear enough in some respects—the Essenes believed the soul was immortal, with good and bad ones going to the opposite kinds of places—another ancient description of the Essenes' doctrine regarding the afterlife reads differently. Hippolytus of Rome (ca. 170–236), in his *Refutation of All Heresies,* offers a picture of the Essenes closely paralleling the one in *War* 2. It is likely that he and Josephus drew on the same source but unlikely that Hippolytus borrowed his description directly from Josephus. When sketching their eschatology, Hippolytus writes:

The doctrine of the resurrection has also derived support among them, for they acknowledge both that the flesh will rise again, and that it will be immortal, in the same manner as the soul is already imperishable. They maintain that when the soul has been separated from the body, it is now borne into one place, which is well ventilated and full of light, and there it rests until judgement. This locality the Greeks were acquainted with by hearsay, calling it "Isles of the Blessed."[10]

A few lines later he notes that they "affirm that there will be both a judgement and a conflagration of the universe, and that the wicked will be eternally punished" (paragraph 27). Although much of this echoes Josephus's account, the new factor is a belief that the body at the end, after having been separated from its soul following death, will rise and share the soul's immortality.

When we turn to the scrolls, we find a range of texts that speak, often in general terms, about the future state of people. This is not the place for a full discussion of Qumran eschatology (see Chapter 11), but specifically on the subject at hand we should note that some scrolls do in fact agree with Hippolytus's statement. 4Q385 and 4Q386[11] contain parallel texts offering an interpretation of Ezekiel's vision in the valley of dry bones (Ezekiel 37). The prophecy expresses a hope for national revival after exile (37:11). In the Qumran text, Ezekiel asks the Lord, who has just promised what he will do for Israel in the future, a question about timing:

"[And I said, "O Lord], I have seen many from Israel who have loved Your name and have walked in the ways [of God]. When will [th]ese things come to pass? How shall their faithfulness be rewarded?" And the Lord said to me, "I Myself take note of the Sons of Israel. And they shall know that I am the Lord." [And He said], "Son of man, prophesy to these bones, and you shall say, "Come together, bone to its bone and joint [to its joint." And it wa]s s[o]. And He said a second time, "Prophesy!" And sinews came upon them and skin covered them [and flesh grew back upon them]. And He s[ai]d, "Prophesy to the four winds of the heavens." And a wind [of heaven] blew [upon them and they revived] and stood up, a great many people. And they blessed the Lord of hosts . . . (4Q385 2.2–8 [WAC, 350–51])

Although the key word *revive* must be restored, the text closely mirrors Ezek. 37:10 where it is used. The passage appears in an eschatological setting and explains for Ezekiel what God will do for those who have been faithful. It does not seem to have the purely national meaning that Ezekiel 37 has, but speaks of those in Israel whom God will raise to life.

According to 4Q521,[12] "the Lord shall do glorious things which have not been done, just as He said. For He shall heal the critically wounded, He shall revive the dead, He shall send good news to the afflicted, . . ." (frags. 2 + 4 2.11–12). The words appear in a context dealing with the last times and announce what God himself will accomplish then. "Reviving the dead" implies more than a spiritual existence; in the context, where the parallel terms are "wounded . . . dead . . . afflicted," it refers to something physical, to a resurrection of bodies.

A few other texts offer intriguing tidbits suggesting a belief regarding resurrection of bodies, but they are so broken that one cannot be sure. So, for example, 4Q245 *(The Vision of Daniel)*[13] has "th]ese then shall arise" in an eschatological context, but whether this means resurrection or a more literal arising is not clear.

Some dispute exists as to whether texts such as 4Q385–86 and 4Q521 are sectarian. There is no strong contrary evidence, and the fact that they were found at Qumran suggests at least that some there found their teachings acceptable.

Same Practices

The sectarian texts from Qumran and the ancient descriptions of the Essenes attribute the same distinctive practices to them. The Essenes may have caught the attention of ancient writers because of their unusual practices—or so it seems from the amount of space they devote to them.

As an example, let us take the finances of the group. Josephus says:

They despise riches and their communal life is admirable. In vain would one search among them for one man with a greater fortune than another. Indeed, it is a law that those who enter the sect shall surrender their property to the order; so neither the humiliation of poverty nor the pride of wealth is to be seen anywhere among them. Since their possessions are mingled, there exists for them all, as for brothers, one single property. (*War* 2.122)[14]

A few lines later the Jewish historian adds:

They neither buy nor sell anything among themselves; each man gives what he has to whoever needs it, and receives in return whatever he himself requires. And they can even receive freely from whomsoever they like without giving anything in exchange. (*War* 2.127; see also *Antiquities* 18.20)[15]

Philo reinforces the point while speaking about the Essenes' fellowship:

First of all, then, no one's house is his own in the sense that it is not shared by all, for besides the fact that they dwell together in communities, the door is open to visitors from elsewhere who share their convictions. Again they all have a single treasury and common disbursements; their clothes are held in common and also their food through their institution of public meals. In no other community can we find the custom of sharing roof, life and board more firmly established in actual practice. And that is no more than one would expect. For all the wages which they earn in the day's work they do not keep as their private property, but throw them into the common stock and allow the benefit thus accruing to be shared by those who wish to use it. The sick are not neglected because they cannot provide anything, but have the cost of their treatment lying ready in the common stock, so that they can meet expenses out of the greater wealth in full security. (*Every Good Man Is Free*, 85–87;[16] see also *Hypothetica*, 8.11, 4–5, 10–13)

In the sectarian scrolls we meet the same ideal both as it was practiced in the withdrawn group at Qumran and among other Essene communities. The *Rule of the Community* deals with the practice of common ownership of property when treating the process for becoming a member of the group. After instruction and a first examination, if a candidate is allowed to continue the process leading to membership, "he must not touch the pure food of the general membership before they have examined him as to his spiritual fitness and works, and not before a full year has passed. Further, he must not yet admix[17] his property with that of the general membership" (*Rule of the Community* 6.16–17).

Once the candidate has completed that year and has sustained another examination,

Then he shall be initiated further into the secret teaching of the *Yahad*. They shall also take steps to incorporate his property, putting it under the authority of the Overseer together with that of the general membership, and keeping an account of it—but it shall not yet be disbursed along with that of the general membership. (6.19–20 [WAC, 135])

Upon passing another test at the end of that second year, he attains full membership, which included "admixture of property" (6.22).

The *Rule of the Community* allows one to infer the scriptural basis for the practice.

All who volunteer for His truth are to bring the full measure of their knowledge, strength, and wealth into the *Yahad* of God. Thus will they purify their knowledge in the verity of God's laws, properly exercise their strength according to the perfection of His ways, and likewise their wealth by the canon of His righteous counsel. (1.11–13 [WAC, 127]; see also 5.2)

Pooling personal property is related to the familiar scriptural injunction: "You shall love the Lord your God with all your heart, and with all your soul, and with all your might" (Deut. 6:5). The nouns *heart, soul,* and *might* are reflected in the *Rule*'s terms *knowledge, strength,* and *wealth*. Interpreting biblical *might* in Deut. 6:5 as *wealth* is attested in other sources.

The Essene ideal manifested itself somewhat differently in the non-Qumran communities, as we learn from the *Damascus Document*. For communal cells, or "camps," located in the cities and towns where members may have held jobs outside the community and where families were included, the practice was as follows:

This is the rule of the general membership for meeting all their needs: a wage of two days every month at least shall be given to the Overseer. Then the judges will give some of it for their wounded, with some of it they will support the poor and needy, and the [feeble] elder, the man with a skin disease, whoever is taken captive by a foreign nation, the girl without a near kinsman, the boy without an advocate; and the rest for the business of the entire community, so that the family of the community should not be excluded. (CD 14.12–17 [WAC, 72])

Another distinctive Essene practice related to the sharing of wealth is the procedure for becoming a member of the group. Josephus writes at some length on the subject in *War* 2.137–42. The process he describes takes three years before one attains full membership:

> Those desiring to enter the sect do not obtain immediate admittance. The postulant waits outside for one year; the same way of life is propounded to him and he is given a hatchet, the loin-cloth which I have mentioned, and a white garment. Having proved his continence during this time, he draws closer to the way of life and participates in purificatory baths at a higher degree, but he is not yet admitted into intimacy. Indeed, after he has shown his constancy, his character is tested for another two years, and if he appears worthy he is received into the company permanently. But before touching the common food he makes solemn vows before his brethren.[18]

Josephus's account sounds much like the one in the *Rule of the Community* (the sort of text one expects to deal with admission procedures). In column 6 it prescribes this method for entry. First there is an initiatory period when the aspirant receives instruction and must, after an unspecified time, be examined before the full membership. Second, should he pass the examination, the next stage appears to be a one-year period:

> If he does proceed in joining the society of the *Yahad*, he must not touch the pure food of the general membership before they have examined him as to his spiritual fitness and works, and not before a full year has passed. Further, he must not yet admix his property with that of the general membership. When he has passed a full year in the *Yahad*, the general membership shall inquire into the details of his understanding and works of the Law. (6.16–18 [WAC, 134–35])

If the candidate passes this test, he is instructed further in the secret teachings of the group and his property is taken over, though not yet used by the group. Third, another year within the fellowship must pass before he is allowed "to touch the drink of the general membership" (6.20). If a review by the membership after this year leads to a positive vote, he becomes a full member: "they shall enroll him at the appropriate rank among his brothers for discussion of the Law, jurisprudence, participation in pure meals, and admixture of property. Thenceforth the *Yahad* may draw upon his counsel and judgment" (6.22–23). The pattern seems to be a progressive movement from a state of ritual impurity to greater and greater levels of purity—with the levels within the fellowship marked by first being able to share in the food and finally in the drink of the community.

It seems that Josephus and the *Rule of the Community* describe the same three-part procedure, with one or the other source being more specific at one time or another: for Josephus, there is a period of one year outside the group followed by a two-year period when one is closer and finally admitted; in the *Rule of the Community* there is a period outside the group and then a year within the group, followed by a second when one is finally admitted. A possible discrepancy is the timing of the oaths, which Josephus next describes at considerable length (*War* 2.139–42). The *Rule of the Community* does not mention oaths at the end of the procedure, as Josephus does, but refers to them in an earlier context in column 5:

> Every initiant into the society of the *Yahad* is to enter the Covenant in full view of all the volunteers. He shall take upon himself a binding oath to return to the Law of Moses (according to all that He commanded) with all his heart and with all his mind, to all that has been revealed from it to the Sons of Zadok—priests and preservers of the covenant, seekers of His will—and the majority of the men of their Covenant (that is, those who have jointly volunteered for His truth and to live by what pleases Him). Each one who thus enters the Covenant by oath is to separate himself from all of the perverse men. (5.7–10 [WAC, 132])

Yet it seems likely, in view of the further clarification of the community requirements and the covenantal ceremony in columns 1 and 2, that this oath is associated with the end of the process, with full membership, and is the multifaceted one to which Josephus refers.

The Essenes were not the only Jewish group that had admission and membership requirements. In some ways the people called *haverim* resemble the Essenes: they had gradual entrance requirements, and issues of purity, especially as they involved food, were highly significant. We do not know as much as we would like about the *havurot*, or associations, of *haverim*, since our sources about them are much later and not very ample. Hence we do not know how long the admission process was or exactly what it involved.[19] Even if it was much like the one Josephus attributes to the Essenes, there are important differences between the Essenes of Josephus and the *haverim*. For one, the *haverim* were not required to give up their property to the association. As a result, the people described in the Qumran *Rule of the Community* seem more likely to be Essenes than *haverim*, because that text prescribes both the admission procedure and forfeiting of private property.

Josephus also writes about the meetings of the Essenes. He speaks of gatherings of no fewer than a hundred at which justice is dispensed. A line later he continues: "They make it their duty to obey their elders as well as the majority;[20] for example, when ten men sit together no man speaks if the other nine oppose it. In addition, they refrain from spitting in the middle of the company, or to the right" (*War* 2.146–47).[21] A number of points in these statements remind one again of the teachings of the *Rule of the Community*, where meetings of the community are described:

> This is the rule for the session of the general membership, each man being in his proper place. The priests shall sit in the first row, the elders in the second, then the rest of the people, each in his proper place. In that order they shall be questioned about any judgment, deliberation, or matter that may come before the general membership, so that each man may state his opinion to the society of the *Yahad*. None shall interrupt the words of his comrade, speaking before his brother finishes what he has to say. Neither should anyone speak before another of higher rank. Only the man being questioned shall speak in his turn. During the session of the general membership no man should say anything except by the permission of the general membership, or more particularly, of the man who is the Overseer of the general membership. If any man has something to say to the general membership, yet is of a lower rank than whoever is guiding the deliberations of the society of the *Yahad*, let him stand up. He should then say, "I have something to say to the general membership." If they permit, he may speak. (6.8–13 [WAC, 134])

The code, which gives penalties for violations occurring during sessions, includes this one: "A man who spits into the midst of a session of the general membership is to be punished by reduced rations for thirty days" (7.13).

The series of close parallels between classical descriptions of the Essenes and the evidence of the scrolls could be extended, but the point is clear. There are remarkably precise correspondences on fundamental beliefs and practices between the two types of sources. To be sure, there are some problems in trying to correlate the evidence. One has been the issue of marriage and celibacy. Philo said the Essenes "banned marriage at the same time as they ordered the practice of perfect continence. Indeed, no Essaean takes a woman because women are selfish" (*Hypothetica* 8.11, 14; there follows a long string of misogynist statements).[22] Josephus explains:

> The Essenes renounce pleasure as an evil, and regard continence and resistance to the passions as a virtue. They disdain marriage for themselves, but adopt the children of others. . . . It is not that they abolish marriage, or the propagation of the species resulting from it, but they are on their guard against the licentiousness of women and are convinced that none of them is faithful to one man. (*War* 2.120–21)

Later he mentions that there is a different group of Essenes who do marry, although they marry women only after they have "proved themselves capable of bearing children" (*War* 2.160–61).

Pliny says the Essenes on the shore of the Dead Sea were an all-male society that practiced continence. Some of the Qumran texts, however, refer to families: for example, the *Damascus Document,* 1Q28a *(Charter for Israel in the Last Days),* the *Temple Scroll* (45.11–12), and others. Furthermore, for a long time it was thought there were skeletons of women and children in the Essene cemeteries. It appears now that those graves with the bones of women are from a much later time than the Essene settlement at Qumran and are in fact Bedouin burials (see Chapter 3). The most economical solution to the various statements about marriage and nonmarriage is to say that the Qumran community, a small branch of the Essenes, was celibate but that its beliefs about the end of time quite understandably incorporated men, women, and children. Other Essenes who did not reside around Qumran adopted a more regular way of life (as in the *Damascus Document*) by marrying and having children. Seen in such a light, the evidence of the classical texts would not be in opposition on this point to the teachings of the scrolls.

There are items in the scrolls that the ancient sources about the Essenes do not mention (such as their 364-day calendar) and items in the ancient sources that the scrolls do not mention (their tendency to live a long time is one; *War* 2.151). Incomplete coverage in one or the other is not, however, a counterargument to identifying the people of Qumran as a branch of the Essenes.

The Scrolls Were Associated with Either the Sadducees or the Pharisees

The discussion here can be much shorter because there is little reason to adopt either identification and strong grounds for opposing them.

SADDUCEES

The Sadducees were probably an important group in Second Temple society, but the sources disclose little about them. Josephus describes them briefly, the New Testament mentions them several times, and rabbinic literature adds some data. It was proposed early in the history of scholarship on the scrolls that there were Sadducean elements in them, but in the 1980s the position took a new form when Joseph Baumgarten noticed that a ruling in 4QMMT agreed with a position identified in the Mishnah as a Sadducean one.[23] The scrolls passage is section B, lines 55–58 of *A Sectarian Manifesto:*

> [Co]ncerning streams of liquid, we have determined that they are not intrinsically [p]ure. Indeed, streams of liquid do not form a barrier between the impure and the pure. For the liquid of the stream and that in its receptacle become as one liquid. (WAC, 362)

The meaning is that a liquid poured from a container that is ritually pure into one that is not conveys the ritual impurity through the liquid back to the pure container. Mishnah *Yadayim* 4:7, which records a series of points disputed between the Pharisees and the Sadducees, begins: "The Sadducees say, We cry out against you, O ye Pharisees, for ye declare clean an unbroken stream of liquid. The Pharisees say, We cry out against you, O ye Sadducees, for ye declare clean a channel of water that flows from a burial ground."[24] The Pharisees clearly came to the opposite conclusion about the stream of liquid, saying that impurity was not conveyed through it, and they adduced an inconsistency they had found in the Sadducees, who failed to apply their own principle to a stream that flowed from an unclean source. This is a firm example of a legal stance in the scrolls that agrees with a Sadducean view.

Lawrence Schiffman, in particular, has employed such evidence to argue that the Qumran community may be called Sadducean. He thinks that after the Maccabean revolt, which occurred in the 160s BCE, some Sadducees remained in Jerusalem, but that "a small, devoted group of Sadducean priests probably formed the faction that eventually became the Dead Sea sect."[25] Over time, he believes, the group at Qumran developed its own legal positions while retaining a link with the Sadducean tradition.[26]

We should recognize both the valid and invalid aspects of the Sadducean identification. It is true that one can find legal points in the scrolls that agree with those attributed elsewhere to the Sadducees. Although an issue such as whether unbroken liquid streams convey impurity may seem a minor one, it is part of a larger teaching in the scrolls about the greater ability of liquids to communicate impurity. Moreover, the scrolls refer a number of times to Zadokite priests as leaders in the community[27] and the name *Zadok* may underlie the name *Sadducee* (= a Zadokian?). Yet the conclusion that the people of Qumran were Sadducees as described in the classical texts does not follow from such arguments. The fact that the Qumranites and the Sadducees agreed on some important *legal* views means only that they belonged to a similar legal tradition, apparently one noted for its literal and strict reading of the Torah.

It is important to know this, but when one turns to the *theological* beliefs of the Qumran community and those assigned to the Sadducees by the ancient texts, one meets a number of fundamental contradictions. Take, for instance, the two doctrines reviewed above—predestination and the afterlife. Josephus says the Essenes and the Sadducees took opposing stands on predestination, with the Essenes attributing everything to fate and the Sadducees denying fate altogether. If the Qumran scrolls teach a strong predestination, they are clearly not Sadducean in theology. Regarding the afterlife, we have noted the evidence from the scrolls for belief about survival after death, including a resurrection of the faithful. According to Acts 23:8, the "Sadducees say that there is no resurrection, no angel, or spirit; but the Pharisees acknowledge all three" (see also Mark 12:18). This contradicts what a text such as 4Q521 from Qumran says about resurrection; and, of course, the statement in Acts about angels and spirits would not at all fit the Qumran texts, which refer to many angels and spirits (e.g., the Enoch booklets, *Songs of the Sabbath Sacrifice*).

As a result, we may say that there are some agreements between Qumran texts and legal views of Sadducees, but disagreements in theological positions. This implies that the Qumran community was not Sadducean, if by that adjective we mean the people described by Josephus; they would be Sadducean according to some legal stances. The most economical way to handle the evidence is to conclude that the Essenes and Sadducees were two distinct groups that shared a similar approach to understanding the legal aspects of the Torah—an approach that distinguished both from the Pharisees.

PHARISEES

Few have identified the Qumran covenanters as Pharisees, and the reason is obvious. Although there are major disagreements between the Qumran texts and Pharisaic beliefs about theology and law, there is little that they share; indeed, it is more likely that the Pharisees were the key Jewish opponents for the community of the scrolls.

Long before the Qumran discoveries were made, Louis Ginzberg, a great authority on rabbinic literature, wrote an extensive study of the *Damascus Document*. In it he argued that the legal material in the text was Pharisaic. After reviewing the work's legal section, he concluded: "And since we have now adduced the entire content of the legal part, with the exception of a single passage, we may state the *certain result of this to be that in our document we have a Pharisaic book of law*."[28] As one reads this statement in context, one is struck not only by this admission of a passage that did not fit his theory, but also by his acknowledgment that several laws in the *Damascus Document* did not agree with what seems to have been the Pharisaic position. The one exception that Ginzberg mentioned was niece marriage, which, as we have observed, was a subject on which the scrolls and rabbinic practice (possibly inherited from the Pharisees) disagreed, with such marriages permitted by the rabbis and prohibited in the scrolls (see also Chapter 12). Ginzberg had to posit a *strict* Pharisee to account for the laws of the *Damascus Document*, but the Qumran scrolls have provided the evidence to show that his conclusion was wrong.

The Pharisees would not have accepted the teaching about fate or predestination in the scrolls; Josephus says they attributed some events to God but believed others were within human control. We have seen that some scrolls contain laws at variance with what was probably Pharisaic practice—liquid streams and niece marriages are examples.

It is likely that the writers of some scrolls refer to the Pharisees as opponents, calling them by different epithets. We will discuss this in more depth in Chapter 12, but here it may at least be said that when referring to the "those who look for smooth things" they probably are punning on the Pharisaic word for legal statements and are criticizing them in the process.

Some Other Views

A few scholars of the scrolls have adopted other positions. One option is to say that the scrolls are from no known Jewish group, but are instead from one not recorded in the sources. We should, therefore, simply call them by a name that they use for themselves—members of the renewed covenant. Shemaryahu Talmon, for one, has warned against methodological pitfalls and has encouraged scholars to examine the community from within before comparing and identifying it with a contemporary body. Any comparison that is eventually drawn must be holistic and recognize what groups shared because of their common biblical heritage.

> I insist on viewing the Community of the Renewed Covenant as a socio-religious phenomenon *sui generis* of Judaism at the height of the Second Temple period. A study of this group from within heightens the recognition of the internal multiformity which characterized Judaism in those days, showing it to have been more diversified than is suggested by the sources which were at our disposal prior to the Qumran discoveries. The Covenanters' community is another tessera in the mosaic-like composition of the Jewish people at the turn of the era, in addition to Samaritans, Hasidim, Sadducees, Boethusians, Zealots, Essenes, Pharisees, and nascent Christianity, to name only the more prominent factions.[29]

This seems a cautious position to adopt, but it really fails to do justice to the multisided evidence pointing clearly to an Essene identification.

Another view defended by a couple of experts is that no one group was responsible for the scrolls. Rather, the scrolls came from Jerusalem (from a library or libraries there) and were hidden in the caves to protect them from the invading Romans at some point between 66 and 70 CE. They do not, therefore, express the views of one sect but of a broad range of Jewish opinion at the time. This hypothesis was articulated in 1960 by K. H. Rengstorf and was later defended with some alterations by Norman Golb.[30] Golb, unlike Rengstorf, thinks the Qumran structures were a fortress and that the contents of the caves were not associated with the people in the fortress. This view has not commended itself because it clearly does not fit the evidence. It does not account for the fact that, where a scroll expresses a distinctive view, this is an Essene one, never, say, a distinctively Pharisaic one. That is unexpected if the Pharisees were supposed to be a major force in Jewish society in the last century BCE and the first century CE. The scrolls seem far from expressing the views of broader Judaism and appear to articulate those of one group within it—a group opposing itself to others. Also, that Qumran was a fortress is contrary to the conclusions of the archeologists who have worked there.

Finally, another small number of scholars have interpreted the scrolls as Christian texts. If this is so, they would be informing us about a type of Christianity that failed to carry the day. The epithets *Teacher of Righteousness* and *Wicked Priest* have been read as referring to New Testament characters such as John the Baptist, James the brother of Jesus, the apostle Paul, and Jesus himself.

To take one example, in several books Robert Eisenman has defended his understanding of the scrolls within an early Christian setting.[31] For him, James the brother of Jesus was the Teacher of Righteousness, who represented an anti-Hellenistic, anti-Roman kind of Judaism. His opponent, the Wicked Priest, was the Sadducean high priest Ananus who, according to Josephus, was responsible for the stoning of James (*Antiquities* 20.200). Although this Ananus was the Wicked Priest, a key enemy of James was the apostle Paul, who is the *Liar* and *Spouter of Lies* mentioned in some Qumran texts. Paul was allied with the high-priesthood and with the Roman occupying power; all were opposed to James, who led the lower priesthood. The New Testament book of Acts distorts the serious conflict between James and Paul, but one can still work behind the text (by using other early Christian literature) to discern what actually happened (the stoning of Stephen in Acts 7 is really the stoning of James). This short description obviously does not do justice to the full range of arguments Eisenman presents, but it gives some idea of his approach.

Although such identifications have often been argued with great ingenuity and at length (Eisenman's book is 1,074 pages long!), it is difficult to lend them credence because they run counter to so much evidence. Advocates of the Christian reading have had to oppose the findings of the paleographers who have dated the scripts of some texts that mention these characters to pre-Christian times (e.g., a copy of the *Damascus Document*, a text that names the Teacher several times); they must now also reject the conclusions of the scientists who have conducted the AMS tests on Qumran texts (see Chapter 2). If a manuscript dating from the first century BCE mentions the Teacher of Righteousness, the Teacher was not James the brother of Jesus.

When all is said and done, the Essene hypothesis is consistent with the evidence and provides the most economical explanation. All other identifications come face-to-face with too much counterevidence.

Select Bibliography

Baumgarten, J. "The Pharisaic-Sadducean Controversies About Purity and the Qumran Texts." *Journal of Jewish Studies* 31 (1980): 157–70.

Eisenman, R. *James the Brother of Jesus: The Key to Unlocking the Secrets of Early Christianity and the Dead Sea Scrolls.* London and New York: Penguin Books, 1997.

Golb, N. *Who Wrote the Dead Sea Scrolls? The Search for the Secret of Qumran.* New York: Scribner, 1995.

Schiffman, L. *Reclaiming the Dead Sea Scrolls.* Philadelphia and Jerusalem: Jewish Publication Society, 1994.

Talmon, S. "The Community of the Renewed Covenant: Between Judaism and Christianity." In *The Community of the Renewed Covenant: The Notre Dame Symposium on the Dead Sea Scrolls.* Edited by E. Ulrich and J. VanderKam. Christianity and Judaism in Antiquity 10. Notre Dame, IN: University of Notre Dame Press, 1994. Pp. 3–24.

Vermes, G., and M. D. Goodman, eds. *The Essenes According to the Classical Sources.* Oxford Centre Textbooks 1. Sheffield: JSOT Press, 1989.

CHAPTER **11**

The Theology or Belief System of the Qumran Group

WE HAVE SEEN THAT THERE ARE DIFFERENT THEORIES about how the manuscripts in the eleven caves around Khirbet Qumran came to be there, and the theory one follows affects to some extent how one reads their contents. The hypothesis accepted here is that a small group of Essenes occupied the area and was responsible for the scrolls, whether members copied or wrote them or the community simply possessed them. It is reasonable to think that the group hid the manuscripts in nearby caves to protect them when Roman attack seemed likely, perhaps in 68 CE. If all of the texts were associated with this group, we may use all of them as indicators of its beliefs or theological convictions. Even the presence of scrolls neither written nor copied at Qumran says something about which texts were read by the group. We should also recognize that the theology that comes to expression in the texts found in the caves overlaps in some respects with what we know about the theology of other Jewish groups. This is only natural since all of them shared a tradition, even though not all groups may have agreed about which ancient writings possessed greatest authority (see Chapter 7). Despite the shared heritage, each of the groups seems to have had its distinctive emphases. We will survey what the scrolls teach about God, law (for nature and for humans), and the future.

God

The starting point in the belief system of the Qumranites, as for all Jewish groups, was God himself. Their understanding of the created order, of history, and of the life beyond began with the confession that there is one God who is the creator of all. He is not only omnipotent and omniscient, but also continues to rule what he made, usually through angelic agents.

One set of texts that celebrates God as creator is the collection called the *Hodayot,* or *Thanksgiving Psalms.* In 1QHᵃ 18.8–11 the psalmist confesses:

> You are Chief of the gods and King of the glorious, Lord of every spirit and Ruler over every creature. Apart from You nothing is done, nor is there any knowing without Your

will. There is no one beside You and no one approaches You in strength. No one can compare to Your glory and as to Your strength, there is no price. Who among the celebrated creatures of Your wonder can maintain the strength to take a stand before Your glory? (WAC, 105)[1]

The same work has a poetic elaboration of God's creative acts of Genesis 1 in 9.7–20 (see also *Jubilees* 2). In the *Hodayot* the majesty and greatness of God are often contrasted with the lowliness and unworthiness of humans (e.g., 5.19–20; 18.12). In the first Psalms scroll from Cave 11, a unit known as the *Hymn to the Creator* reads:

> Blessed be He who by His might created the earth, who by His wisdom established the world. By His understanding He stretched forth the heavens and brought out [the wind] from [His] trea[sure stores]. He created [lightning for the ra]in and [from] the end of [the earth] made vapor[s] to rise. (11Q5 26.13–15 [WAC, 451]; see also the *War Scroll* 10.11–16; 4Q416 17–10; 4Q422 frag. 1 1.6–12; *1 Enoch* 9:5)

Though he created the universe and possesses infinite power and wisdom, God has chosen to place the day-to-day operation of his handiwork under the supervision of angels (see below).

Law

The almighty God established laws for his creation, whether the natural order or humanity. Obedience to the appropriate law ensures harmony, while disobedience disrupts the whole.

LAW FOR NATURE

The books of *Enoch* and *Jubilees* speak of divinely given laws by which the parts of nature operate (*1 Enoch* 2–5; *Jubilees* 5). The same idea underlies the understanding of nature in the sectarian texts.

In this theological tradition, God has appointed angels to rule over the immense system he created. We find the idea expressed in *1 Enoch* and *Jubilees* and in other works. In *1 Enoch* 20 there is a list of perhaps seven angels to whom God has assigned different supervisory roles over aspects of the creation. The *Astronomical Book of Enoch* (*1 Enoch* 72–82) identifies Uriel as the leader of all celestial luminaries and the revealer of the book's contents to Enoch (e.g., 72:1; 74:2; 75:3; 82:7–8). Beneath his command stand other angels who govern the various components of the luminaries such as the stars (75:1; 80:1; 82:10–20). The book of *Jubilees,* which presents itself as God's revelation to Moses through an angel of the presence (*Jubilees* 1), adds to Genesis's terse account of the first day of creation that the deity made the angels and appointed them to rule the many parts of the creation (2:2):

> the angels of the presence; the angels of holiness; the angels of the spirits of fire; the angels of the spirits of the winds; the angels of the spirits of the clouds, of darkness, snow, hail, and frost; the angels of the sounds, the thunders, and the lightnings; and the angels of the spirits of cold and heat, of winter, spring, autumn, and summer, and of all the spirits of his creatures which are in the heavens, on earth, and in every (place).[2]

The many calendrical scrolls presuppose the unchanging order of the luminaries as they go about their assigned courses in the heavens (see also the *Thanksgiving Psalms* 9.11–13). For them, all happens in a wondrous, schematic harmony. The calendrical texts feature a 364-day calendar that never changes its pattern, or at any rate this seems to be what the texts say.

Again *1 Enoch* and *Jubilees* are traditional texts that present such a calendar, which was later adopted by the people of Qumran. We can see from the information given above that in the listing of angels and their functions the two books show special interest in the heavenly lights. One reason is the importance their writers attached to the calendar. In the *Astronomical Book of Enoch* (*1 Enoch* 72–82) we read about the sun and moon, both of which serve as instruments to measure the year. The solar year lasts 364 days (72:2–32; v. 32 adds the word "exactly"; see also 74:10). The year by lunar reckoning adds up to 354 days. *1 Enoch* 74:10–16 provides some obvious figures for how many days the moon falls behind the sun during three (30), five (50), and eight (80) years (see also 79:4–5). The fact that they are compared for these numbers of years and that the two kinds of years are always 364 and 354 days shows that no intercalation was invoked to bring them into harmony. In *Jubilees* we also meet a year of 364 days (the precision of the number is emphasized in 6:38) and there, too, it is revealed first to Enoch (4:17, 18, 21). *Jubilees*, however, fulminates against the practice of using lunar calculations of the year (6:23–38). The author knows that a lunar sequence of twelve months amounts to 354 days and considers this evidence of "corruption" in that, if one tried to date festivals according to it, one would mix sacred and profane times (6:35–37). In fact, in his version of what God had created on the fourth day, the author omits any mention of a calendrical function for the moon (contrast *Jub.* 2:8–10 with Gen. 1:14–19). Like *1 Enoch, Jubilees* mentions no intercalary procedure. (See Figure 11.1.)

The Qumran calendaric texts follow the Enochic pattern of accepting two schematic years—a solar one of 364 days and a lunar one of 354 days—but they align themselves with *Jubilees* in dating festivals by the 364-day system. Though scholars had suspected that the festivals of Qumran were dated by the *Jubilees* calendar, the first explicit statement confirming this hunch came with the decipherment of the first Psalms scroll from Cave 11. In a paragraph about David's compositions it says:

> The Lord gave him a brilliant and discerning spirit, so that he wrote: psalms, three thousand six hundred; songs to sing before the altar accompanying the daily perpetual burnt offering, for all the days of the year, three hundred and sixty-four. (*Apocryphal Psalms of David* 27.3–6 [WAC, 452])

The same number is now attested in 4Q252 (*Commentaries on Genesis*), which, like *Jubilees*, attaches the details of the calendar to the story of the Flood: "On that day Noah went out from the ark, at the end of an exact year, three hundred and sixty-four days . . ." (see also 4Q394 frags. 3–7 1.2–3 [WAC, 320]).

The beautiful symmetry of the 364-day system (see Table 11.1) is evident in several ways, even if it fails to correspond with reality. Since 364 is an exact multiple of seven, the calendar has exactly 52 weeks, so that every date falls on the same day of the week every year. Each quarter of the year is arranged in exactly the same way, and the year begins on Wednesday, since God created the luminaries on the fourth day (Gen. 1:14–19).

With this pattern in mind we can read a short text like 4Q327, which lists dates on which sabbaths and festivals fall. The first legible lines read "On the twenty-third of the month is a Sabbath. [On the] thir[tie]th [of the month is a Sabbath]" (*The Sabbaths and Festivals of the Year*, frags. 1–2 1.4–8 [WAC, 319]). If the twenty-third of a month is a sabbath, it must be dealing with month 2, 5, 8, or 11.

Figure 11.1
Fragments of *Jubilees:*
4QJub^d (4Q219)
(PAM 43. 187)
Courtesy of the Israel Antiquities
Authority

Table 11.1			*A 364-Day Calendar*							
Day	**Months 1, 4, 7, 10**				**Months 2, 5, 8, 11**				**Months 3, 6, 9, 12**			
Wed.	1	8	15	22	29		6	13	20	27		4	11	18	25
Thurs.	2	9	16	23	30		7	14	21	28		5	12	19	26
Fri.	3	10	17	24		1	8	15	22	29		6	13	20	27
Sat.	4	11	18	25		2	9	16	23	30		7	14	21	28
Sun.	5	12	19	26		3	10	17	24		1	8	15	22	29
Mon.	6	13	20	27		4	11	18	25		2	9	16	23	30
Tues.	7	14	21	28		5	12	19	26		3	10	17	24	31

A series of calendar texts add a dimension to this system. These have recourse to the list of priestly groups or shifts in 1 Chron. 24:7–18. The passage credits King David with dividing the numerous priests into these groups, which were to rotate terms of duty at the Temple. As the practice developed, one group would serve for a week (from Sunday to Saturday) at the Temple and then be relieved by the next one in the list. The names of the groups thus could function as ways for naming weeks. In a nicely preserved fragment we read the following:

> The festivals of the first year: On the third day from Sabbath (Tuesday) of the course of the sons of Maaziah is the Passover. On the first day (Sunday) of the course [of] Jeda[iah] is the Waving of the [Omer]. On the fifth day (Thursday) of the course of Seorim is the [Second] Passover. On the first day (Sunday) of the course of Jeshua is the Feast of Weeks. On the fourth day (Wednesday) of the course of Maaziah is the Day of Remembrance. [On the] sixth day (Friday) of the course of Jehoiarib is the Day of Atonement, [in the] seventh [month]. [On the] fourth day (Wednesday) of the course of Jedaiah is the Feast of Booths. (*Synchronistic Calendars,* 4Q320 frag. 4 3.1–9 [WAC, 311])

All of this may sound confusing or worse, but armed with the list of priestly groups in front of us and with knowledge of when festivals were dated in the Bible, we can decode the lines with ease. Maaziah is the twenty-fourth priestly group, and Passover (the fourteenth of the first month; see Exod. 12:6) occurs on its third day; so its week of duty ran from 1/12 to 1/18.[3] Jedaiah, the next group mentioned, is second on the list in Chronicles, and the waving of the barley omer falls on its first day. So, if Maaziah's week of service lasted from 1/12 to 1/18, we have to add the seven days for Jehoiarib (the first name on the list), which would be 1/19 to 1/25. The first day of Jedaiah's shift would then be 1/26. The Bible mentions, but does not date, the waving of the omer, yet the date was important because the seven-week count to the Festival of Weeks was to begin from it (Lev. 23:9–16).

The next festival, the Second Passover, which Num. 9:9–11 places on 2/14, falls on the fifth day of Seorim, which is the fourth priestly course. Jedaiah's shift would have run from 1/26 to 2/2, the third shift (Harim) from 2/3 to 2/9, so that the fifth day of Seorim would be 2/14. The remaining data in the text put the Festival of Weeks (not dated in the Bible) on 3/15 (just as in *Jubilees*), the day of remembrance on 7/1, the Day of Atonement on 7/10, and the beginning of the Festival of Booths on 7/15 (these last three are in harmony with their biblical dates).

When we add together such texts and the information found in the *Temple Scroll,* we arrive at this list of festivals and dates:

Passover	1/14
Unleavened Bread	1/15–21
Omer Waving	1/26
Second Passover	2/14
Festival of Weeks	3/15 (50 days after the omer waving)
Festival of Wine	5/3 (50 days after the Festival of Weeks)
Festival of Oil	6/22 (50 days after the Festival of Wine)

Festival of Wood	6/23–29 (?)
Day of Remembrance	7/1
Day of Atonement	7/10
Booths	7/15–21

The festivals of Wine and Oil are extrabiblical holidays of firstfruits; their dates were calculated like that of the Festival of Weeks (see Lev. 23:15–16), counting 49 days from the previous holiday and celebrating the next day. It is no accident that the festivals of Purim and Hanukkah fail to appear in the list, as the book of Esther (the basis for Purim) is not attested at Qumran[4] and Hanukkah celebrated the triumph of the Maccabees, who were enemies of the Qumranites.

The priestly shifts were of great interest to the Qumran calendarists. As a result, we have texts that detail their times of service throughout a six-year period. Since there were twenty-four groups, but fifty-two weeks in a year, it would take six years for the first shift to revert to its original time of duty ($52 \times 6 = 312$; in 312 weeks each of the twenty-four groups would serve thirteen times).

Alongside the simple solar arrangement we find that the covenanters accepted a schematic lunar calendar, which they synchronized with the 364-day system. We find in 4Q317 *(The Phases of the Moon)* tables recording how much of the lunar surface was illuminated and how much was dark on successive nights (dividing the visible surface into fourteenths for the purpose, as in *1 Enoch*). Other texts correlate dates in the two calendars and even add which priestly group would be on duty for those dates. So, for example, in 4Q320 fragment 1 1.6 we read: "[On the fifth day (Thursday) in the course of Jedaia]h is the twenty-ninth day of the lunar month, on the thirtieth day of the first solar month" (WAC, 310).

The corpus of calendaric texts includes works with more advanced computations than these and longer time spans than six years,[5] but the ones that have been mentioned may serve in this context to document the covenanters' understanding of God's orderly creation in which the heavenly luminaries operate in perfectly predictable harmony in obedience to the law that God created for them. The fact that the cycles of Temple worship are correlated with the courses of the sun and moon has implications for the group's understanding of the connection between heaven and earth.

LAW FOR HUMANITY

All parts of creation are meant to operate according to the systems God made for them, but his law for people receives more attention. Of course, the law in question is the law of Moses, which God progressively revealed in ancient times and which people continued to study and interpret. Natural phenomena obey the laws ordained for them, but human beings more frequently disobey the ones instituted for them (see *1 Enoch* 2–5)—and this with disastrous results.

Some Qumran texts echo the account about human transgression in Genesis 3. An example is 4Q422 *(A Commentary on Genesis and Exodus)* fragment 1 1.9–12:

> They exercised their dominion to eat the frui[t of the earth . . .] [. . .] not to eat from
> the tree of the kn[owledge of good and evil . . .] [. . .] he arose against Him and they for-

got [His statutes . . .] [. . .] with an evil inclination, and for work[s of injustice . . .].
(WAC, 392)

But in the scrolls relatively little attention is paid to the story about the disobedience of Adam and Eve and more emphasis is placed, at least in texts such as *1 Enoch, Jubilees,* the *Genesis Apocryphon,* 4Q180, and the *Damascus Document,* on the evil introduced or augmented by the illicit marriages between angels and women (see especially *1 Enoch* 6–16, parts of which are closely related to Gen. 6:1–4). According to that story, angels, whose proper, created place was in heaven, saw women, desired them, and married them. They are charged not only with violating their created orders, but also with producing gigantic, evil, and violent offspring and with teaching illicit secrets to women. The resulting exponential growth in wickedness on the earth led God to send the Flood as punishment. Although the versions differ, both *1 Enoch* 12–16 and *Jubilees* 10 attribute the continuation of human wickedness after the Flood to the demons who were connected with the angels or giants and survived the Flood.

The Qumran teaching about human behavior that has attracted much attention is that there are two spirits, or angels, which God has created and under whose influence people necessarily live. The doctrine is set forth at the greatest length in the *Rule of the Community* 3.13–4.26, but is found in other texts as well. The relevant section in the *Rule of the Community* identifies itself as being for the Instructor

> who is to enlighten and teach all the Sons of Light about the character and fate of humankind: all their spiritual varieties with accompanying signs, all their deeds generation by generation, and their visitation for afflictions together with eras of peace. (3.13–15 [WAC, 129])

In the immediate continuation the basic perspective comes to the fore:

> All that is now and ever shall be originates with the God of knowledge. Before things come to be, He has ordered all their designs, so that when they do come to exist—at their appointed times as ordained by His glorious plan—they fulfill their destiny, a destiny impossible to change. He controls the laws governing all things, and He provides for all their pursuits. He created humankind to rule over the world, appointing for them two spirits in which to walk until the time ordained for His visitation. These are the spirits of truth and falsehood. Upright character and fate originate with the Habitation of Light; perverse, with the Fountain of Darkness. The authority of the Prince of Light extends to the governance of all righteous people; therefore, they walk in the paths of light. Correspondingly, the authority of the Angel of Darkness embraces the governance of all wicked people, so they walk in paths of darkness. (3.15–21 [WAC, 129–30])

This is the arrangement for the time before the judgment ("His visitation") when God will introduce a new order. The theologically rich section also explains that the angel of darkness is responsible for the sins of the righteous—a situation permitted by God "in His mysteries" (3.21–24). Lists of the traits produced by the good angel and the evil one and their results occupy 4.2–14. Included are everlasting life for the righteous and eternal damnation for the wicked. God allows this situation of competing spirits to continue until he destroys evil and gives the ultimate victory to the side of good (4.15–26). It is quite possible that this overarching understanding of human history, conduct, and eschatology is what is meant by the phrase "the mystery that is to be," which is used often in the Qumran wisdom texts.

As we can see from this section, the creator God was believed to have appointed angels to rule over humans, just as they govern the parts of creation. There are biblical precedents for angelic association with nations (Deut. 32:8–9; Dan. 10:10–14), but the idea that one spirit rules the "sons of light" and one the "sons of darkness" is not attested in the Hebrew Bible.

Within this general deterministic framework, the covenant between God and his chosen people and the law that lies at the heart of that ongoing relationship find their place. The book of *Jubilees* presents a picture of the *one* covenant that God has made with his own. It was inaugurated with Noah and all living beings after the Flood and was renewed with Abra(ha)m, Isaac, Jacob, and Moses (see *Jubilees* 6). With the renewals came further revelation of the divine laws. Also, texts such as *Jubilees, Aramaic Levi,* and 4Q265 trace the origins of some Mosaic laws back into patriarchal times, so that the ancestors already practiced central commandments such as the festivals and their sacrifices.

The Qumranites understood themselves and those who agreed with them, not all of Israel, as the people with whom God was in covenant and as the ones who accurately understood and implemented the laws of that agreement. The *Rule of the Community* has an important section about an annual ceremony in which the group renewed the ancient covenant and welcomed new members. We learn there that the Instructor is to "induct all who volunteer to live by the laws of God into the Covenant of Mercy, so as to be joined to God's society and walk faultless before Him, according to all that has been revealed for the times appointed them" (1.7–9 [WAC, 127]). The ceremony itself is handled in 1.16–2.25:

> All who enter the *Yahad*'s Rule shall be initiated into the Covenant before God, agreeing to act according to all that He has commanded and not to backslide because of any fear, terror, or persecution that may occur during the time of Belial's dominion. While the initiates are being inducted into the Covenant, the priests and the Levites shall continuously bless the God of deliverance and all His veritable deeds. All the initiates into the Covenant shall continuously respond "Amen, amen." (1.16–20 [WAC, 127])

The priests then bless (using an expanded form of the priestly blessing in Num. 6:24–26) those "foreordained to God, who walk faultless in all of His ways" (2.2), while the Levites curse (using an expanded and reverse form of the priestly blessing) those "foreordained to Belial" (2.4–5; see all of 1.21–2.10 [WAC, 127–28]). The Instructor warns against joining the covenant without true repentance (2.11–18) and indicates that the ceremony is to take place every year for "all the days of Belial's dominion" (2.19). The result was to be an ideal community: "So shall all together comprise a *Yahad* whose essence is truth, genuine humility, love of charity, and righteous intent, caring for one another after this fashion within the holy society, comrades in an eternal fellowship" (2.24–25 [WAC, 128]).

Though the covenantal ceremony took place each year, the *Rule of the Community* does not explain when it occurred. One of the Cave 4 copies of the *Damascus Document* may supply the needed information. A section belonging at the end of the text describes the procedure for expulsion of a member who has rebelled against the group's regulations. In it the priest blesses God, notes that he has cursed transgressors, and acknowledges that the obedient remain resolute. That is, the context sounds covenantal and reminds one of the

Rule of the Community 1–2. The text goes on to say: "The Levites and those who live in the camps shall convene on the third month and curse those who stray from the Law to the right [or to the left]" (4Q266 fragment 18 5.16–18 [WAC, 74]). Reference to the third month recalls the teaching in *Jubilees* that the Festival of Weeks, the holiday of the covenant, occurs in the middle of the third month. Evidence in the book allows one to date the holiday to 3/15, a date for the Festival of Weeks that is found in the Qumran calendars. So the annual renewal of the covenant may well have occurred on 3/15.

It is possible that the texts called *A Liturgy of Blessing and Cursing* (esp. 4Q286–90) are the liturgical words used in the annual covenant renewal ceremony. So, for example, in 4Q286 fragment 7, column 2, "The society of the *Yahad* shall say in unison, 'Amen, amen'" (WAC, 288); this is followed by curses on Belial and those of his lot (fragment 7 2.1–12).

Given the centrality of covenantal law to the belief system of the Qumranites (and other Essenes), it is understandable that proper interpretation and implementation of it were paramount. The Zadokite priests were apparently the authoritative interpreters, and their teachings probably come to expression in the many legal texts surveyed in Chapter 9. Emphasis on proper interpretation can be found in the *Damascus Document,* the *Rule of the Community,* and other texts. The covenanters distinguished between revealed laws and those they had learned through their special interpretive techniques. After a summary of Israel's disobedience, the author of the *Damascus Document* writes:

> But when those of them who were left held firm to the commandments of God, He insti-
> tuted His covenant with Israel for ever, revealing to them things hidden, in which all Is-
> rael had gone wrong: His holy Sabbaths, His glorious festivals, His righteous laws, His
> reliable ways. The desires of His will, which Man should carry out and so have life in
> them, He opened up to them. So they "dug a well," yielding much water. Those who reject
> this water He will not allow to live. (3.12–17 [WAC, 54]; see also 6.11–7.6; 15.7–10)

The *Rule of the Community* reinforces the point by legislating for one entering the community that he is to "take upon himself a binding oath to return to the Law of Moses (according to all that He commanded) with all his heart and with all his mind, to all that has been revealed from it to the Sons of Zadok—priests and preservers of the covenant, seekers of His will—and the majority of the men of their Covenant" (5.8–9 [WAC, 132]; see 8.11–12). Those outside the pact have neither discovered the hidden laws nor obeyed the revealed ones (5.11–12). 4QMMT, with its careful delineation of correct understandings of the Torah, provides evidence for what these people considered valid interpretation. It seems that disputes about such matters are what led them to leave the Temple community and forge their own way in a self-imposed exile.

The community, organized in several respects like Israel at Mt. Sinai and understanding themselves as recipients of renewed revelation about God's will, believed that they enjoyed a unique fellowship with the heavenly realm. As the priestly courses were in harmony with the circuits of the celestial luminaries, so the covenanters perceived themselves to be unified with the angels. The poet in the *Thanksgiving Psalms* professes about himself:

> The perverse spirit You have cleansed from great transgression, that he might take his
> stand with the host of the holy ones, and enter together (or in the *Yahad*) with the con-
> gregation of the sons of heaven. And for man, You have allotted an eternal destiny with
> the spirits of knowledge, to praise Your name together. . . . (11.21–23 [WAC, 94])

Later he adds: "For You have brought [Your] t[ruth and g]lory to all the men of Your council, in the lot together with the angels of the presence" (14.12–13 [WAC, 99]; see also 19.13–14). The *War Rule* pictures the sons of light fighting together with the angels against the sons of darkness and Belial's hosts (7.5–6;[6] 9.14–16; 12.1–9; see also *Priestly Blessings for the Last Days* 3.25–26; 4.23–26). The same association appears to be assumed in the *Songs of the Sabbath Sacrifice,* where heavenly worship is depicted in glorious detail. This takes place according to the same calendar followed by the covenanters, who apparently worship God on earth in tandem with his angels in heaven.

The Future

THE END OF DAYS

With this understanding of God's mysterious ways and the context in which they were living in this present evil age, the Qumranites attempted to order their ways in exact obedience to the will of God as they understood it. They also searched the prophetic Scriptures for clues to the meaning of what was happening in their time and how it fit into God's overall plan. Evidence for this we find in the *pesharim.* As all natural processes and human history have proceeded according to God's predetermined pattern, so would the future. The covenanters believed they could read off coming events from prophecies, because God had already decreed what was going to happen. In fact, the future, like the past, could be divided into defined periods, as it is in various passages in Daniel 7–12. Or, in the words of the *Commentary on Habakkuk* (1QpHab): "all the times fixed by God will come about in due course as He ordained that they should by His inscrutable insight" (7.13–14 [WAC, 119]). In the future as they envisaged it, we may distinguish more than one phase.

The Qumranites believed they were living in a segment of time called the end of days or the last days, the period that lay just before the decisive end or visitation. In it the forces of good and evil continued their age-old battle for control, but during this especially charged time the small chosen community was playing a decisive role not only for themselves, but also for others. They believed that their fellowship had assumed functions normally associated with the Temple in Jerusalem:

> When such men as these come to be in Israel, then shall the society of the *Yahad* truly be established, an "eternal planting" (*Jubilees* 16:26), a temple for Israel, and—mystery!—a Holy of Holies for Aaron; true witnesses to justice, chosen by God's will to atone for the land and to recompense the wicked their due. They will be "the tested wall, the precious cornerstone" (Isa. 28:16) whose foundations shall neither be shaken nor swayed, a fortress, a Holy of Holies for Aaron, all of them knowing the Covenant of Justice and thereby offering a sweet savor. They shall be a blameless and true house in Israel, upholding the covenant of eternal statutes. They shall be an acceptable sacrifice, atoning for the land and ringing in the verdict against evil, so that perversity ceases to exist. (1QpHab 8.4–10 [WAC, 137–38])

The concept of "the end of days" or "the last days," which is mentioned frequently in the scrolls, refers to the time period before that decisive end to history when some will experience judgment and others will receive salvation. The end of days seems to have, from the perspective of the covenanters, a negative and a positive side. Negatively, the last days will or already do involve a period of heightened testing or trial, when the forces of Belial redouble their efforts to defeat the ranks of the righteous. 4Q174 *(The Last Days: A Commentary on Selected Verses)* pictures the nations conspiring against Israel in the last days and predicts that it will be a time of persecution (3.18–4.1 [WAC, 228]). But some of these same passages indicate that it will also be a time of deliverance or purifying for the chosen (e.g., 4Q174 4.1–4). One passage making the point that this period will be longer than anticipated is found in the *Commentary on Habakkuk* where Hab. 2:1–3 is explained as referring to the coming generation. Regarding Hab. 2:3, which mentions a specific period, the expositor writes:

> This means that the Last Days will be long, much longer than the prophets had said; for God's revelations are truly mysterious. "If it tarries, be patient, it will surely come true and not be delayed" (2:3b). This refers to those loyal ones, obedient to the Law, whose hands will not cease from loyal service even when the Last Days seems long to them, for all the times fixed by God will come about in due course as He ordained that they should by His inscrutable insight. (7.7–14 [WAC, 119])

THE MESSIAHS

Within the context of the last days one meets messianic characters in the scrolls. 4Q174, in interpreting 2 Sam. 7:11–14 (the promise of a descendant for David who will have an eternal throne), says:

> This passage refers to the Shoot of David, who is to arise with the Interpreter of the Law, and who will [arise] in Zi[on in the La]st Days, as it is written, "And I shall raise up the booth of David that is fallen" (Amos 9:11). This passage describes the fallen **booth**[7] of David, [w]hom He shall raise up to deliver Israel. (4Q174 3.11–13 [WAC, 228])

The two titles, *the Shoot* (or *Branch*) *of David* and *the Interpreter of the Law*, point to two figures who are elsewhere in the scrolls considered messiahs. That the Qumran community anticipated the appearance of two messiahs, not just one, was known already when the first scrolls were published. The *Rule of the Community* says: "They shall govern themselves using the original precepts by which the men of the *Yahad* began to be instructed, doing so until there come the Prophet and the Messiahs of Aaron and Israel" (9.10–11 [WAC, 139]).[8]

We know little about the prophet who was anticipated,[9] but we can say more about the messiahs. The plural *messiahs*, followed by the explanatory names *Aaron* and *Israel*, points not only to two individuals, but indicates that one, possibly named first for a reason, will be a priest and the other a nonpriest. According to this passage, the advent of the prophet and the messiahs would mark the end of an age, the end of the time when they would live according to certain precepts. The plural *messiahs* in the *Rule of the Community* proved to be especially interesting because scholars were aware before this that the *Damascus Document* contained four instances of the same expression, but there the word *messiah* was always in the singular—the messiah of Aaron and (of) Israel (CD 12.23–13.1; 14.18–19; 19.10–11; 19.33–20.1). They had debated whether the phrase spoke of one or two messiahs, but the *Rule of the Community* from Qumran now favors understanding it as a plural expression. Perhaps more important, in the *Damascus Document* the phrase is also employed to designate the close of an age: "This is the rule for those who live in camps, who live by these rules in the era of wickedness, until the appearance of the Messiah of

Aaron and Israel" (12.23–13.1 [WAC, 70]). It is not said that the messiahs will come at the final judgment, but only that their arrival will define the end of the present evil age.

We meet these messiahs in several texts, though little is said about what they will do other than end an era by their appearance (atonement is mentioned in CD 19.11, but it is not clear whether the messiahs do the atoning). An especially interesting passage occurs in the second column of the *Rule of the Congregation* (1Q28a), where a meal is described in an explicitly eschatological text (WAC: *Charter for Israel in the Last Days*). There a priest and the messiah of Israel attend the meal, and the priest presides in the sense that, as a priest should, he blesses the meal:

> The procedure for the [mee]ting of the men of reputation [when they are called] to the banquet held by the society of the *Yahad,* when [God] has fa[th]ered(?) the Messiah (or, when the Messiah has been revealed)[10] among them: [the Priest], as head of the entire congregation of Israel, shall enter first, trailed by all [his] brot[hers, the Sons of] Aaron, those priests [appointed] to the banquet of the men of reputation. They are to sit be[fore him] by rank. Then the [Mess]iah of Israel may en[ter], and the heads of the th[ousands of Israel] are to sit before him by rank . . . (1Q28a 2.11–15 [WAC, 147]; the section about the blessings of the food follows)

Here we have one individual who is termed a messiah, and he is in the company of a priest. This is a pattern in the messianic texts—a nonpriest and a priest together.

The messiah of Israel is also called the *Branch of David* (as in the passage from 4Q174 quoted above) in 4Q252 fragment 1, 5.1–5 (commenting on Gen. 49:10):

> A ruler shall [no]t depart from the tribe of Judah when Israel has dominion. [And] the one who sits on the throne of David [shall never] be cut off, because the "ruler's staff" is the covenant of the kingdom, [and the thous]ands of Israel are "the feet," until the Righteous Messiah, the Branch of David, has come. For to him and to his seed the covenant of the kingdom of His people has been given for the eternal generations, because he has kept [. . .] the Law with the men of the *Yahad.* (WAC, 277)

4Q161 (*Commentary on Isaiah*[a]) 8 + 9 + 10, line 22 may say that he will stand at the end of days (see Figure 11.2). Another intriguing passage is 4Q285 (WAC: *The War of the Messiah*) fragment 5. It deals with Isa. 10:34–11:1 (which predicts a shoot from the stump of Jesse and a branch from its roots) and explains:

> [This is the] Branch of David. Then [all forces of Belial] shall be judged, [and the king of the Kittim shall stand for judgment] and the Leader of the **congregation**[11]—the Bra[nch of David]—will have him put to death. [Then all Israel shall come out with timbrel]s and dancers, and the [High] Priest shall order [them to cleanse their bodies from the guilty blood of the c]orpse[s of] the Kittim. (5.3–6 [WAC, 293])

Though too much must be filled in, the passage does mention the *Branch of David* and also supplies an additional title for him—the *Leader of the Congregation*. The Davidic messiah in a military context apparently executes the human leader of Belial's forces in a future war. This military association characterizes other uses of the title *prince* or *leader of the congregation*. In *Priestly Blessings for the Last Days* 5.20–29 he is described in the language of Isaiah 11, stressing his righteous rule and his victory over the wicked (and referring to the

Figure 11.2
Commentary on Isaiah: 4QIsaᵃ
(4Q161) (PAM 43.431).
Courtesy of the Israel Antiquities Authority

scepter forecast in Num. 24:17). CD 7.18–21 also connects Num. 24:17 with him and announces his victory over the enemy.

The same passage in the *Damascus Document* mentions the Interpreter of the Law, a title for the messianic priest. It understands the star predicted in Num. 24:17 as this priest. We should recall that 4Q174 also associates the Davidic messiah with the Interpreter of the Law. *Priestly Blessings for the Last Days* includes blessings on a high priest, although it is not clear exactly which lines of the text apply to him (in WAC, 2.22–3.21 is attributed to him).[12]

TWO PROPOSALS NAMING THE MESSIAH

It is worth underscoring that messianic figures are not mentioned very often in the scrolls. The topic has been, nevertheless, of immense interest for obvious reasons. In fact, within the last few years two scholars of the scrolls have published books in which they present differing cases for identifying a Qumran messiah by name. As these have attracted considerable attention, the two proposals are summarized and critiqued below. This will also allow us to examine another text that these writers think is messianic, though we have not studied it to this point.

The "First" Messiah

Michael Wise, of Northwestern College (St. Paul, Minnesota), argues in *The First Messiah: Investigating the Savior Before Christ* that the Qumran messiah may have been named Judah and that we meet him and learn about him primarily in the Teacher hymns in columns 10–17 of the *Thanksgiving Psalms*.[13] We should recall that a number of scholars have identified the poems in this section of the collection as containing the words of the Teacher of Righteousness himself. Wise accepts this reasonable conclusion and traces in detail what the Teacher says about himself and his community in them.

Wise thinks that the Teacher hymns in these columns appear in chronological order and that we can, therefore, trace the developments in his career by reading the poems one after another. The Teacher of Righteousness, according to Wise, rose to prominence as a wisdom teacher and advisor, beginning in about 110–105 BCE; he was an expert in the law, which included many rules about Temple procedures. His early career fell at a time when the Sadducees were the leading force in society, before the Pharisees usurped that role. The pharisaic takeover occurred in 76 BCE when Alexander Jannaeus died and his widow Alexandra, obeying her husband's dying request, entrusted control of affairs to the Pharisees. The change produced a crisis for the Teacher, who saw his world crumble as people who embraced what he considered erroneous views about God's law became dominant. Since he considered himself a prophet[14]—one who received revealed mysteries from God and who had knowledge about the times (a point clarified from the text called *The Secret of the Way Things Are* [WAC, 378–90])—he spoke out in protest. But by this time the Teacher's point of view was not welcome in Jerusalem, and the Pharisees were vigorously persecuting their opponents, including him. The authorities arrested the Teacher and subjected him to trial (we have no historical evidence of this; it is inferred from poetic statements). He was convicted as a false prophet and sent into exile. The place to which he and his followers went was the land of Damascus, more specifically the region of Trachonitis, where they became brigands! While there, he predicted, in line with the prophecy of Daniel 9 about the last week of years, that an invasion of Israel from the north (by the Seleucids) would occur within seven years (by 67 BCE).

When the Teacher was first in the land of Damascus, many of his followers deserted him, driving him to depression. In his despair, thoughts about the new Jerusalem that would come (as described in the text *A Vision of the New Jerusalem*) revived his spirits. Now he became conscious not only of his role as prophet, but also as messiah, who would rule in Jerusalem (see hymn 7 = 1QH^a 13.22–15.7). However, on the Teacher's Day of Atonement in 74 BCE, the high priest Hyrcanus II and his forces attacked him and his band. They chose this time not only because their observance of the Day of Atonement fell on a different day, but also because the Teacher's dangerous messianic pretensions had become known in Jerusalem. The attackers killed many of the exiled group, but the Teacher escaped. He was understandably discouraged, yet confident that he would still be vindicated and transformed in a glorious way.

The Teacher developed the idea that most of his contemporaries did not properly recognize him because this is the way God had always planned it; that is, his experience was like that of the "servant of the Lord" in Isaiah. The nation did not acknowledge the Teacher because he was God's hidden messiah. Judah died (we do not know how) in 72 BCE. This event did not induce his followers to reject his claims; rather, they developed a doctrine of multiple messiahs, including the Teacher (during his lifetime they had considered him alone to be the messiah). His death somehow energized his disciples, who redacted his hymns by surrounding them with their own (these are the hymns of the community at the beginning and end of the *Thanksgiving Psalms* scroll) and added what Wise calls the *Hymn of the Exalted One* in columns 25–26, a poem in which the Teacher is made to claim not only to have suffered as the servant of Isaiah 53, but to have been exalted to God's right hand.

Another text composed by the Teacher's devotees is the *Coming of Melchizedek*. It mentions the herald from Isa. 52:7 (translated *messenger* in WAC, 457), whom the author identifies as Daniel's (9:26) anointed one of the spirit (2.16–18). The Teacher is that herald (both are said to teach about the periods of history and the future and the statutes of truth); he is therefore actually called "anointed," that is, "messiah," in this passage. Wise also thinks the character named Melchizedek in the text is the Teacher. The *Damascus Document* predicts that the end would come about forty years after the Teacher's death; this would be 34 BCE on Wise's calculation. Though the Teacher had claimed that his followers could not go on without him, they composed the Manifesto in the *Rule of the Community* (it lies behind 8.1–16) showing how they would in fact continue in his absence. In the *Damascus Document* they presented a case that the Teacher had predicted the war of 63 BCE when the Romans took Jerusalem (actually, he was a few years off about this and thought the Seleucids would be the invaders); at the time other Jewish groups were unable to explain the catastrophe. Their successful explanation caused the number of the Teacher's followers to mushroom to more than 4,000. Wise makes the surprising claim that most of the sectarian manuscripts at Qumran were copied between 45 and 35 BCE, when the membership was at its peak. However, when the prediction of the end failed to materialize in 34 BCE, the group dwindled and eventually died out. That is why no historical events or characters postdating 34 BCE are mentioned in the texts. Wise's last chapter details what he takes to be extraordinarily close parallels between Judah and Jesus, including their atoning suffering.

We should commend Wise for articulating a creative understanding of the Teacher's messianic role, but his thesis is unconvincing for several reasons. First, though it is likely that the poems in *Thanksgiving Psalms* 10–17 are from the Teacher himself, there are no convincing reasons for seeing them as his chronologically ordered, autobiographical reflections. Rather, they are poetic compositions that return repeatedly to the same or similar topics—such as the Teacher's understanding of his role, his strong dislike for his enemies who responded in kind to him, his sufferings, God's deliverance of him, and his gratitude for divine rescue. The poems use much traditional language that is rich in ambiguity; to tease autobiographical details in chronological order from them seems implausible. Second, if the Teacher were a messiah, whether in his own estimation or that of his followers or both, he and the other scrolls authors are remarkably reticent about it. The Teacher is never termed a messiah. The herald/messenger in the *Coming of Melchizedek* does not appear to be the Teacher (and the herald is distinguished from Melchizedek); the claim that his functions are those of the Teacher assumes that the very fragmentary text is clearer than it is.

Third, Wise's claim that the Teacher's disciples composed the Manifesto in the *Rule of the Community* after his death raises a chronological problem. If the Teacher died in 72 BCE, as Wise says, then the *Rule of the Community* was composed no earlier than this date. However, there is at least one copy of the *Rule of the Community* (1QS) that was very likely written earlier and that contains the Manifesto material.[15] Fourth, it seems perverse to call the Teacher a messiah when the *Damascus Document* clearly distinguishes him from the two messiahs: "They shall not be reckoned among the council of the people, and their names shall not be written in their book from the day the Beloved Teacher dies until the Messiah from Aaron and from Israel appears" (19.35–20.1). And finally, though Wise makes much of the reflection of language drawn from Isaiah's servant songs in the Teacher hymns, there is no evidence in the Qumran texts that the suffering of the Teacher was vicarious, that it atoned for others.

The "Suffering" Messiah

The second and smaller book is by Israel Knohl of the Hebrew University of Jerusalem. In *The Messiah Before Jesus: The Suffering Servant of the Dead Sea Scrolls*,[16] he maintains that the messiah was named Menahem and that we meet him in some poems that are found in the *Thanksgiving Psalms,* especially one that some have called the Self-Glorification Hymn (Wise's Hymn of the Exalted One). The poem in question is attested in several manuscripts and, as all recognize, it constitutes an usual case. There are two versions: one is found in 1QH^a 25.35–26.10, 4QH^a (4Q427) fragment 7, 4QH^e (4Q431), and 4Q471b,[17] and the second is in 4Q491c fragment 1. The key point for Knohl is that the speaker in the poem utters two types of statements: ones in which he makes astonishing claims for himself, such as "who is like me among the gods [i.e., angels],"[18] and ones that sound like words about the suffering servant of the Lord in Isaiah 53. The former is seen in:

> . . . a mighty throne in the congregation of the gods. None of the ancient kings shall sit on it, and their nobles [shall] not [. . . There are no]ne comparable [to me in] my glory, no one shall be exalted besides me; none shall associate with me. For I dwelt in the [. . .] in the heavens, and there is no one [. . .] I am reckoned with the gods and my abode is in the holy congregation. [My] desi[re] is not according to the flesh, and everything precious to me is in the glory [of] the holy [habit]ation. (4Q491c frag. 11 1.12–15 [WAC, 171])

and the latter in: "Who shall [experience] troubles like me? And who is like me [in bearing] evil?" (l. 16). These words are so unusual that Knohl concludes the poem was inserted into the *Thanksgiving Psalms* at a later time; they are not like the others in the collection, claiming more than even the other Teacher hymns. On his view, the messianic concept in the text was influenced by claims made for the divinity of Augustus in Roman sources.

There have been several suggestions about who the speaker of these lines could be (the angel Michael, the priestly messiah, the Teacher, the community), but Knohl identifies him as a certain Menahem whom Josephus called an Essene. About this man, who was living at the time of King Herod (37–4 BCE), the historian tells a story in *Antiquities* 15.372–79. Josephus says that when Herod was a child, Menahem once greeted him as "king of the Jews" and predicted that, although he would enjoy wonderful success as monarch, he would forget piety and justice so that God's anger would fall on him. Later, when Herod did become king, Menahem predicted that he would rule for twenty or thirty years, but did not give an exact number:

> And from that time on he [that is, Herod] continued to hold all Essenes in honour. Now we have seen fit to report these things to our readers, however incredible they may seem, and to reveal what has taken place among us because many of these men have indeed been vouchsafed a knowledge of divine things because of their virtue. (*Antiquities* 15.378–79)[19]

Knohl surmises that Menahem became an advisor to King Herod, and, as one line in the Qumran hymn says that the poet is the "friend of the king" (4Q431 frag. 1, l. 6), Josephus's Menahem was the author of the Qumran poem. Knohl realizes that the word *king* here refers to *God* but thinks the reference must reflect historical reality as well. Thus Menahem led a double life: he was advisor to the king, but also the acknowledged messiah of his community, one devoted to the overthrow of the reigning order. For Knohl, this Menahem is also the one referred to in some rabbinic texts that pair him with Hillel but say he was eventually excommunicated for not properly honoring the majesty of God (as in the Qumran poem). The combination of Menahem's exalted claims and his expectation of suffering are clearly significant antecedents for Jesus' understanding of his mission as portrayed in the Gospels—a "catastrophic messianism" that Knohl finds to be historical.

Knohl appeals to two other texts to fill out the portfolio of the Qumran messiah in the remarkable poem. The first is the *Oracle of Hystaspes*, which he, following D. Flusser, thinks is a Jewish text. It speaks about one frightful king who will arise and later be defeated by another terrible monarch. This second king, who is also a false prophet, will kill the true prophet whom God sends and will leave his body lying unburied. God's sword will then come down from heaven and destroy the king and his army.[20] On the third day the true prophet will revive and be taken up to heaven. Knohl takes the first king to be Mark Antony, the second to be Octavian/Augustus, and the true prophet to be Menahem. The picture in the *Oracle of Hystaspes* reminds Knohl of the two beasts in Revelation 13 and of the two witnesses in Revelation 11. He thinks the Revelation of John, like the *Oracle*, was influenced by Qumran messianism about Menahem. The second beast of Revelation, which has two horns like a lamb, is Augustus, although Knohl has to adjust matters a bit here because Augustus was not associated with lamb imagery, but with goat imagery (he was born in Capricorn). The two witnesses of Revelation 11, like the prophet of the *Oracle*, are slain and their bodies left unburied for three and a half days before they revive and ascend. These are the royal and priestly messiahs whom we know from Qumran (cf. Zechariah 4).

All of this allows Knohl to create a scenario for Menahem the messiah and his execution in 4 BCE. When Herod died in that year, a revolt broke out. Menahem and his followers decided that this was the time to go public with their messianic secret and take up arms in what appeared to be the final war of redemption. But Roman troops who crushed the revolt killed Menahem and left his body exposed for three days. Thus were the Qumran messianic hopes dashed.

It is very difficult to accept this case, which involves some daring leaps between floating pieces of evidence. The poem in the *Thanksgiving Psalms* is truly a remarkable one, giving rise to various theories about who the speaker may be (see above). Even if we concede that the speaker could be a messianic figure, we would be far from agreeing with all of

Knohl's hypothetical reconstruction. Paleographical study suggests that all copies of the poem date from the period 50–1 BCE, although 4Q427 may be older (as old as 75 BCE, thus raising chronological problems for a messiah active in 4 BCE); but the leap from a poet who says "who is like me among the angels" to the Menahem of Josephus's story is almost too large to imagine. Josephus, although he tells the story only about Menahem, uses him as an example of many Essenes who were reputed to be able to predict. He says nothing about Menahem's advising the king, about messianic claims he or others may have made about himself, and certainly nothing about a connection between Menahem and Qumran. From Josephus we learn nothing about participation by Menahem and his followers in a revolt in 4 BCE and nothing about his death at this time amid the circumstances envisioned by Knohl.

In addition, Knohl's interpretation of the *Oracle of Hystaspes* and the book of Revelation is unconvincing. Whatever one thinks about his identification of the two kings in the *Oracle* and the two beasts in Revelation, the prophet in the *Oracle* is a prophet, not a messiah; and the witnesses in Revelation (they are reminiscent of Moses and Elijah) are witnesses, not messiahs. It may also be that the *Oracle* is too old to have been influenced by a first-century BCE idea from Qumran; it does not seem to be Jewish; and Knohl has taken evidence from it selectively.

There is one other problem with Knohl's thesis. As we have seen, a number of Qumran texts document an expectation that two messiahs would come. Knohl thinks that the Self-Glorification Hymn was a later text that was inserted into the *Thanksgiving Psalms* and reflects beliefs from the period of Herod's reign. This would mean that there had been a large change in Qumran messianic expectation—from anticipating the arrival of a priestly and a royal messiah to believing there was only one messiah who was living among them—something we do not see in the other texts.[21] In fact, it seems fair to charge both Wise and Knohl with largely ignoring the Qumran texts that do mention messiahs and focusing on ones that do not—something that hardly commends their approaches.

Returning to our survey of messianism in the scrolls, as several of the passages we have surveyed indicate, the covenanters expected a war in the future and that the Davidic messiah would lead the forces of good to victory and execute the leader of the armies of evil. This does appear to be the war described at length in the *War Rule*, which mentions in several passages the roles of the chief priest in that conflict (10.2; 15.4; 16.13; 18.5; 19.1; see cols. 10–12 for his address and prayer).

There is some evidence that the community tried to calculate the time of the end and whatever events it would bring. We know that, as they organized the past in terms of weeks of years (seven-year units) and jubilees of years (forty-nine-year units), so they arranged the future. The *Prophetic Apocryphon* contains hints about this. 4Q387 fragment 3, column 2 mentions a time of unfaithfulness that would last for ten jubilees (490 years), but whether this marks the end of the period of punishment is not clear (WAC, 353). 4Q390, another copy of this text, speaks of a time of wickedness in the seventh jubilee after the land was destroyed (1.7–12). A reasonable reading of the passage is that the ten-jubilee period was thought to begin with the Exile.

The *Melchizedek* text may offer other clues for this scenario. It uses jubilee language in discussing the release Melchizedek will effect for those enslaved to sin. The key time is the tenth jubilee period:

[He shall pro]claim this decree in the fir[s]t [wee]k of the jubilee period that foll[ows nine j]ubilee periods. Then the "D[ay of Atone]ment" shall follow af[ter] the [te]nth [ju]bilee period, when he shall atone for all the Sons of [Light] and the peopl[e who are pre]destined to Mel[chi]zedek. (2.6–8 [WAC, 456])

This ten-jubilee sequence is reminiscent of Daniel 9, which also speaks of a period of 70×7 years, or 490 years, beginning in the time of Babylonian exile and ending with the restoration of Jerusalem.

One more chronological sequence should be included. In the *Damascus Document* one finds a series of numbers that may be related, but that are difficult to interpret. As we have seen, in CD 1.5–11, 390 years after giving Israel into the hand of Nebuchadnezzar, God caused a "root of planting" (apparently the community) to spring up; then, after another twenty years, he raised up a Teacher of Righteousness for them. CD 20.13–14 seems to mention the death of the Teacher and measures some forty years after it: "Now from the day the Beloved Teacher passed away to the destruction of all the warriors who went back to the Man of the Lie will be about forty years" (WAC, 60). If we add these numbers ($390 + 20 + 40$), the total is 450 years. It has been suggested (though no text says this) that we should add another forty years for the Teacher's career (a number with good biblical precedent in the life of Moses, the reigns of kings such as David and Solomon, and other careers) and thus arrive at 490, or ten jubilees. This may be true, but we do not know what time it implies for the destruction of unfaithful warriors and whether this is an allusion to the final war.

We learn few specifics about the community's beliefs regarding what was to happen after the great victory. There are several copies of *A Vision of the New Jerusalem,* which pictures a large city with a temple; it seems to be one that will be present after the war against wickedness is completed, but that is not explicit in the text. There are also references to the temple that the Lord himself will establish—one that is apparently to replace the future gigantic complex described in the *Temple Scroll* (see *Temple Scroll* 29.7–10). How the teaching about resurrection fits into this we do not know, although one of the texts mentioning resurrection (4Q521) also refers to a messiah: "[. . . For the hea]vens and the earth shall listen to His Messiah" (frags. 2 + 4 2.1 [WAC, 421]). The future beyond the eschatological war will involve bliss for the righteous (see ll. 5–13 of the text just quoted) and destruction for the wicked (as in the *Rule of the Community* 4.18–23).

Select Bibliography

There have been a few attempts to synthesize the theology of the Qumran covenanters. An early example:

Ringgren, Helmer. *The Faith of Qumran: Theology of the Dead Sea Scrolls.* Philadelphia: Fortress, 1963. Reprint, New York: Crossroad, 1995. The Swedish original appeared in 1961.

A more recent effort can be found in

Collins, John, and Robert Kugler, eds. *Religion in the Dead Sea Scrolls.* Studies in the Dead Sea Scrolls and Related Literature. Grand Rapids, MI: Eerdmans, 2000.

Articles on most of the subjects surveyed in this chapter can be found in

Schiffman, L. H., and J. C. VanderKam, eds. *Encyclopedia of the Dead Sea Scrolls*. 2 vols. New York and Oxford: Oxford University Press, 2000.

The standard work on Qumran messianism remains

Collins, J. *The Scepter and the Star: The Messiahs of the Dead Sea Scrolls and Other Ancient Literature*. New York: Doubleday, 1995. As the title suggests, Collins places the Qumran teachings in the context of messianic references in other texts from the same period.

For other helpful surveys:

Collins, J. *Apocalypticism in the Dead Sea Scrolls*. The Literature of the Dead Sea Scrolls. London: Routledge, 1997.

Harrington, D. *Wisdom Texts from Qumran*. The Literature of the Dead Sea Scrolls. London: Routledge, 1996.

CHAPTER 12

The Qumran Group Within Early Judaism

THE DEAD SEA SCROLLS HAVE GIVEN US the most extensive documentation in Hebrew and Aramaic about Jewish phenomena in the last centuries BCE and the first century CE. They have the additional advantage that they were not only written then, but remained unaltered in subsequent centuries as they lay in the caves. There are pristine witnesses to their times, although, of course, they express a very definite point of view. Because of the scrolls' unique nature as primary witnesses, scholars have searched them for clues both about those who wrote, copied, and read them and about other groups of Jews living at the time.

The scrolls are frustratingly damaged, and the preserved texts are often concerned with internal or more general matters, but some of them do reveal information about other Jewish people. The community living at Qumran and the wider movement of which they were a part tried at least once to convince others of the rightness of their way (4QMMT), but they more often criticized others for their errors. It would have been helpful indeed if the writers, when speaking of others, employed names with which we are familiar, but they did not. Only in rare cases are known names used for groups or individuals; usually the writers resort to nicknames or epithets for others. At times we can decipher the nicknames; at times we are baffled by them.

The first part of this chapter examines references in the scrolls to other Jewish groups, while the second builds on this information, but zeros in on some individuals. From the combined data of these two sections, an attempt is made to sketch a history of the scrolls community within its ancient context.

Groups

We have seen that Josephus names three major Jewish groups or factions in the later Second Temple period: Pharisees (with whom the Zealots agreed almost entirely), Sadducees, and Essenes. Presumably there were more groups, but these were the ones Josephus chose to mention in his listing. In Chapter 10 we argued that the Qumran community was a small subset of the larger Essene party and that "camps" within the larger body are described in the *Damascus Document*. We then proceeded to study in Chapter 11 the teachings embedded in the Dead Sea Scrolls. Do the texts found at Qumran also contain information about the Pharisees and Sadducees? It seems likely that they do.

PHARISEES

A good case can be made that the Qumran scrolls tweak the Pharisees with a few nick-names.

"Those Who Look for Smooth Things"

In several texts a group of opponents is dubbed *doreshey (ha)halaqot, those who look for smooth things.*[1] The first word has to do with people searching, including searching or investigating the Scriptures. The second term means *smooth,* often with a negative connotation when connected with words or speech. So, for example, Prov. 26:28 speaks of a lying tongue in parallel with smooth speech and uses this word. Dan. 11:32 refers to Antiochus IV as one who will flatter with smooth words. The sense in our phrase may be not only flattering things, but also easy ones, as the epithet may connote interpreters who search for the easy way out rather than full, rigorous obedience to laws in the Torah.

Five texts mention the ones who look for smooth things. The *Damascus Document* associates them with an early juncture in the group's history. After the appearance of a "root of planting," an event dated 390 years after Nebuchadnezzar defeated the nation, and after another twenty years of uncertainty before the Teacher of Righteousness came on the scene, an opponent to the new group and its leader surfaced:

> When the man of mockery [*'ish hal-laṣon*] appeared, who sprayed on Israel lying waters, he led them to wander in the trackless wasteland. He brought down the lofty heights of old, turned aside from paths of righteousness, and shifted the boundary marks that the forefathers had set up to mark their inheritance so that the curses of the covenant took hold on them. Because of this they were handed over to the sword that avenges the breach of His covenant.
>
> For they had **looked for smooth things**, choosing travesties of true religion; they looked for ways to break the law; they favored the fine neck. They called the guilty innocent, and the innocent guilty. They overstepped covenant, violated law; and they conspired together to kill the innocent, for all those who lived pure lives they loathed from the bottom of their heart. So they persecuted them violently, and were happy to see the people quarrel. Because of all this God became very angry with their company [*ba-'adatam*]. He annihilated the lot of them because all their deeds were uncleanness to Him. (CD 1.14–2.1 [WAC, 52])

From this passage we see that issues regarding the Torah underlay a dispute between those around the Teacher of Righteousness and a congregation (perhaps of some size), with the former charging the latter with violating the covenant and inducing others to do the same. The opposition to the Teacher and his followers took on a violent form. That they "looked for smooth things" is included in a catalog of charges against these early opponents.

The image of a group misinterpreting the law and drawing others after them is reinforced in the *Thanksgiving Psalms* in two poems that are often identified as hymns of the Teacher. In the first (10.31–38) the psalmist thanks the Lord for rescuing him "from the jealousy[2] of the mediators of lies [*meliṣey kazav*] and from the congregation of those who look for smooth things" (10.31–32 [WAC, 93]). He goes on to charge them with trying to murder him and calls them "those who seek deceit" (l. 34). He also regards them as stronger than he is. The emphasis on misuse of language is again to the fore, as in the *Damascus Document,* and again the opponents are considered an organized group, a congregation.

The second passage is in the poem that begins at 12.5. The psalmist thanks God for revealing himself to him, but charges others with using smooth language (WAC: "flatter themselves with words") and with being "mediators of deceit" as they lead the people astray.

> But they are mediators of a lie and seers of deceit. They have plotted wickedness against me, so as to exchange Your Law, which You spoke distinctly in my heart, for **smooth things** directed to Your people. (12.9–11 [WAC, 95]; see ll. 12–20 for further accusations, including a reference to "their festivals" in l. 12)

The conflict revolves around a law revealed to the psalmist, and the opponents are condemned for their deceitful language, which entailed exchanging the revealed law for something else.

The next text in which we meet the ones who look for smooth things is *The Last Days: An Interpretation of Selected Verses* (4Q177). In a section citing Ps. 13:4, which refers to "enemies," we read: "they are the company of the **ones looking for smooth things**, who [. . .] who seek to destroy [. . .] in their zeal and in their hostility" (frags. 10 + 11 + 7 + 9 + 20 + 26, ll. 12–13 [WAC, 236]). The entire text deals with the end of days, so these people were considered latter-day enemies who had been predicted in the Scriptures.

The third copy of a *Commentary on Isaiah* (4Q163) talks about the ones looking for smooth things after citing Isa. 30:15–18, a text that mentions pursuers or persecutors. "This passage is for the Last Days and refers to the company of **ones who look for smooth things** who are in Jerusalem [. . .] in the Law and not [. . .] heart, for trample [. . .]" (frag. 23 2.10–13 [WAC, 213]). Once again they form a congregation, the law is mentioned, and they belong at the end of days. A new element is that they are in Jerusalem.

All of these passages supply useful clues toward formulating a profile of the group in question, but none of them is specific enough to allow us to identify them. In contrast, a set of references to them in the *Commentary on Nahum* (see Figure 12.1) holds enough clues to reveal who they were. The enemies put in their first appearance in the surviving parts of the text at the comment on Nah. 2:11b: "where the lion goes, and the lion's cubs, with no one to disturb them." The commentary reads:

> [This refers to Deme]trius, king of Greece, who sought to enter Jerusalem through the counsel of the **ones who look for smooth things**; [but it never fell into the] power of the kings of Greece from Antiochus until the appearance of the rulers of the Kittim; but afterwards it will be trampled [by the Gentiles . . . .]. (frags. 3–4 1.2–4 [WAC, 217])

Just a few words after these, while interpreting Nah. 2:12b ("he has filled his caves with prey and his dens with torn flesh"), the expositor continues:

> This refers to the Lion of Wrath [. . . ven]geance against the **ones who look for smooth things**, because he used to hang men alive, [as it was done] in Israel in former times, for to anyone hanging alive on the tree, [the verse app]lies: "Behold, I am against [you], [says the Lord of Hosts" (2:13a). (ll. 6–9 [WAC, 218])

Figure 12.1
From column 1 of the *Commentary on Nahum* (4Q169) (PAM 43.351)
Courtesy of the Israel Antiquities Authority

A third appearance of the group comes in the *Pesher on Nahum* 3:1 ("Ah! City of blood-shed, utterly deceitful, full of booty"): "The meaning of the passage: this is the city of Ephraim, the **ones who look for smooth things** in the Last Days, who conduct themselves in deceit and lies" (2.2 [WAC, 218]). The terms *Ephraim* and *the ones who look for smooth things* are in apposition and are associated with abuses of speech (2.2).

The sequel describes them at some length. Nah. 3:1–4 is understood as predicting the seekers. Where the scriptural lemma mentions spoils of war, sounds of battle, and heaps of bodies, the writer explains in part: "This refers to the rule of **those looking for smooth things**; never absent from their company will be the sword of the Gentiles, captivity, loot-ing, internal strife, exile for fear of enemies" (2.4–5 [WAC, 218]). He continues emphasiz-ing the bloody fate that will meet them before turning to Nah. 3:4, which describes a prostitute and her ways: "This refers to the deceivers of Ephraim, who through their decep-tive teaching, lying talk, and dishonest speech deceive many: kings, princes, priests, native and foreigner alike. Cities and clans will pass away through following their principles, nobles and rulers will perish through their [arrog]ant talk" (2.8–10 [WAC, 219]).

The next passage mentioning the seekers comments on Nah. 3:6–7a ("I will throw filth at you and treat you with contempt, and make you a spectacle. Then all who see you will shrink from you"). In the eyes of the commentator,

> This refers to the **ones looking for smooth things.** In the time to come their bad deeds will be made manifest to all Israel and many will perceive their wrongdoing and reject them and be disgusted with them because of their criminal arrogance; and when the glory of Judah is made manifest, the simple-hearted folk of Ephraim will withdraw from their company, abandon the ones who deceive them, and ally themselves to the true Is-rael. (3.3–5 [WAC, 219])

Their final appearance in the *Commentary on Nahum* is in the explanation of Nah. 3:7b, which predicts the ruin of Nineveh, a city that will be left without comforters: "This refers to the **ones who look for smooth things**, whose faction will pass away, and whose assembly will be abandoned. They will no longer deceive the congregation and the simple-hearted will no longer hold to their opinions" (3.6–8 [WAC, 219]).

The passages in the *Commentary on Nahum* not only repeat ideas in the other texts (the seekers are an organized group who mislead others with their lying teachings), but also associate the opponents with Ephraim and speak of their acting as rulers and deceiving leaders. The specific passages that allow us to identify these people are the references to Demetrius and the Lion of Wrath who hanged men alive. It seems likely that the Demetrius in question is the Seleucid king Demetrius III Eukerus (96–88/87 BCE), who was invited by the opponents of Alexander Jannaeus (103–76 BCE), a Hasmonean ruler who aroused powerful opposition among his subjects, to invade Judea. Josephus is our only source of information about the incident, and he tells the story and its sequel in both *War* and *Antiquities* (*War* 1.92–114; *Antiquities* 13.376–418). After Alexander Jannaeus had executed thousands of his Jewish opponents, his surviving enemies invited King Demetrius to assist them, and the Seleucid monarch accepted their offer in 88 BCE. Josephus does not attach a party label to Jannaeus's opponents as he narrates the event, but from the events that ensued we can infer who they were. After Demetrius defeated Alexander, he subsequently withdrew, yet inner-Jewish hostilities continued in the form of armed revolt. Alexander captured the powerful among his opponents and crucified 800 of them alive while their wives and children were slaughtered in front of them. The commentator on Nahum seems to have this event in mind when referring to the Lion of Wrath who hanged men alive.

It is only later in Josephus's narratives that we get a good idea of who these victims were. As he lay dying, Alexander urged his wife and successor, Alexandra, to give the Pharisees some power and allow them to deal with his body as they saw fit. The reason that the people were so hostile to him was, as he recognized, because of how badly he had treated them (*Antiquities* 13.402–3). It is interesting that the treatment of his body is so important in his last instructions regarding the Pharisees, considering what Alexander had done to the 800. Josephus does connect the 800 crucified Jewish opponents with the group who invited King Demetrius to come to their aid (*Antiquities* 13.381–82). Alexandra complied with her husband's dying request. When the Pharisees were in positions of authority, they urged Alexandra to kill those who had advised her husband to crucify the 800 and they carried out their revenge on a number of them—so much so that these opponents had to appeal to Alexandra's son Aristobulus for help against them (*Antiquities* 13.410–18). The earlier version in *War* is shorter, but tells largely the same story.

Given their concern with avenging the 800 whom Jannaeus had crucified, it seems likely that the Pharisees regarded them as part of their group. And, since the *Commentary on Nahum* identifies the people in question as the ones who look for smooth things, they are most likely Pharisees. It is interesting that the writer speaks of their "lying talmud" (2.8 [translated "their deceptive teaching"]) and that they conduct themselves (using a form of the verb *halak* [2.2]) in deceitful ways, since both terms may have connections with the Pharisees. In fact, the standard way of explaining the epithet "ones who look for smooth things" is that, rather than searching the Scriptures for the ways in which to conduct themselves *(halakhot)*, the Pharisees, in the opinion of the Qumranites, searched it for easy or smooth things, the easy way out *(ḥalaqot)*.

Ephraim

The *Commentary on Nahum* also provides us with a second name for the Pharisees—Ephraim—a term used in apposition with "ones who look for smooth things" in 2.2. The second copy of a commentary on Hosea may also allude to Alexander Jannaeus's treatment of the Pharisees when dealing with Hos. 5:14. The verse speaks of the Lord being like a lion to Ephraim and says this refers to the last priest (perhaps a play on the expression "lion of wrath"),[3] who will extend his hand to strike Ephraim (2.2–3; the lion of wrath is mentioned in l. 2). According to the first copy of a *Commentary on the Psalms* (4Q171), the wicked of Ephraim and Manasseh will try to harm the Teacher and his council in the period of testing, but God will save them and hand the opponents over to the Gentiles (frags. 1–2 2.17–19). The same group may be under consideration in the *Damascus Document 7.9–15*, where the separation of Ephraim from Judah mentioned in Isa. 7:17 is treated. The writer does not take this as the historical division of the Northern and Southern Kingdoms after the death of Solomon; rather, the names point to groups, one of which (Ephraim) consists of ones who reject the commandments and who will be judged for their wickedness. Judah appears to be a designation for the sect here because they are said to have migrated to Damascus—an event of sectarian lore (see, e.g., CD 6.5).

"Builders of the Wall"

One other possible nickname for the Pharisees appears in the *Damascus Document*—the *builders of the wall* (rendered curiously in WAC as the *Shoddy-Wall-Builders*). It occurs in a context in which these people are accused of falling into two of Belial's traps—fornication and violation of the sanctuary. *Fornication* the writer explains as taking two wives in one's lifetime.

> They also defile the sanctuary, for they do not separate clean from unclean according to the Law, and lie with a woman during her menstrual period. Furthermore, they marry each man the daughter of his brothers and the daughter of his sister, although Moses said, "Unto the sister of your mother you shall not draw near; she is the flesh of your mother" (Lev. 18:13). (5.6–9 [WAC, 55])

We saw earlier that the scrolls community differed from rabbinic (and hence Pharisaic?) practice by prohibiting niece marriages. Here the wall builders are accused of niece marriages. This suggests that behind the nickname stand the Pharisees. It is been suggested that the term *builders of the wall* may play on the famous saying about the rabbinic tradition—that they made a hedge or fence around the Torah with their oral law (see Mishnah, *Avot* 1.1).

The references to the legal teachings of these seekers–Ephraim–wall-builders should remind us that in 4QMMT the rejected position is in some cases identifiable as the Pharisaic one, so that in this text, too, the people of the scrolls are distancing their views from those of the Pharisees.

SADDUCEES

A far less likely case can be made that the Sadducees come under consideration in the scrolls. We should recall that their legal approach may well have been congenial to the

Qumranites because there is some agreement between Qumran legal decisions and stances attributed in the Mishnah to the Sadducees. But, as we have seen, there were fundamental, unbridgeable differences between the two in theology (e.g., on predestination), with the result that the scrolls may be expected to yield negative references to them as well.

One candidate for such a nickname is Manasseh. In the Bible the paired names Ephraim and Manasseh designate the Northern Kingdom; for this reason they were ciphers useful to the Qumran community, which considered itself the faithful kingdom—Judah (cf. CD 7.13). The other two were its enemies. The texts imply that the Pharisees were the more troublesome foe, but Manasseh comes in for criticism a few times. We saw earlier that in the first copy of the Psalms commentary the wicked people of Ephraim and Manasseh tried unsuccessfully to harm the Teacher of Righteousness.

The *Commentary on Nahum* mentions Manasseh several times in its treatment of Nah. 3:8–10. The city name *No-Amon* (= Thebes) in 3:8 is said to be Manasseh, possibly recalling that Amon was the son of King Manasseh (2 Kings 21:17–18), and her waters are interpreted as the noble men within Manasseh. Nah. 3:9 alludes to the allies of No-Amon, and these are decoded as "the wicked of [. . .], a divisive group [or: the house of Peleg] who ally themselves to Manasseh" (4.1 [WAC, 219]). Finally, the exile of No-Amon with her full population, including notables, is taken to mean: "Manasseh in the Last Days, for his kingdom shall be brought low in Is[rael . . .] his women, his infants, and his children shall go into captivity; his warriors and his nobles [shall be killed] with the sword [. . .]" (4.3–4 [WAC, 220]). We learn little from this other than that the group designated Manasseh seems to have been a socially prominent one; in fact Manasseh has a kingdom. Josephus says that the Sadducees were prominent people (*Antiquities* 18.16), and they were the dominant group in the time of Alexander Jannaeus. This is a characterization consistent with what the *Commentary on Nahum* says about Manasseh. It should be admitted, nevertheless, that the equation of Manasseh with the Sadducees rests on fragile, skimpy evidence.

This is a convenient place to mention one more term, this time for a non-Jewish group—the Kittim. The name is not really an epithet, but a historical designation for a people that took on a particular meaning or meanings in the scrolls. Depending on the scroll one is reading, it refers to either Greeks or Romans (the more common usage). The word originally meant people from the Cyprian city of Citium and later, by extension, came to refer to peoples who reached Israel from that direction, whether Greeks (see 1 Macc. 1:1; 8:5), Romans (e.g., Dan. 11:30 in the Septuagint), or others (see Josephus, *Antiquities* 1.128).

In the *War Scroll* it is reasonably clear that "the Kittim of Asshur" are the Seleucids (1.2; see 1.4), but in a text such as the *Commentary on Nahum* the Romans are meant. The claim that no Greek king entered Jerusalem from the time of Antiochus IV (175–164 BCE) until the rise of the Kittim (frags. 3–4 1.2–3) documents this, because it distinguishes the Greek kings from the Kittim, apparently alluding to the Roman conquest of Jerusalem in 63 BCE. The *Commentary on Habakkuk* 6.4, which says the Kittim sacrifice to their standards, also points to the Romans, who were known for this practice. The writer of *The War of the Messiah*, fragment 5 predicts that the king of the Kittim will be killed by the prince of the congregation in the last war (see also the *Commentary on Isaiah*ª frags. 8 + 9 + 10, l. 12).

Individuals

The scrolls characteristically designate groups with epithets; they do the same for individuals who were prominent, either as leaders or opponents of the group. A few notes about epithets for individuals follow.

THE TEACHER OF RIGHTEOUSNESS

Despite many attempts, no one has succeeded in identifying the Teacher with a person mentioned in our other sources. The Teacher figures, with some small variations in the forms of the title, in the *Damascus Document* and in a few *pesharim*. The *Damascus Document* speaks about his first appearance as a leader, about his importance, and about his death, while the *pesharim* refer to a few incidents in his life. The title *Teacher of Righteousness (moreh haṣṣedeq)* may emphasize the content of what the Teacher gives to his students—he teaches them the right lessons—or it may express primarily his authenticity as a teacher—he is the right or legitimate teacher. It is often suggested that the title was derived from a phrase in Joel 2:23: "O children of Zion, be glad and rejoice in the Lord your God; for he has given the early rain for your vindication *[ham-moreh li-ṣdaqah]*, he has poured down for you abundant rain, the early and the later rain, as before." The phrase "early rain" was understood as "the teacher" (they are spelled the same way in Hebrew), however unlikely the interpretation in the context, and the passage was taken as an expression of thanksgiving to God for giving the righteous teacher to the children of Zion: since he has given the teacher for righteousness.

We have examined the passage in the *Damascus Document* column 1, in which the Teacher first figures. Three hundred and ninety years after Nebuchadnezzar, a "root of planting" sprang up and struggled to find the right way for another twenty years. Then "God considered their deeds, that they had sought Him with a whole heart. So He raised up for them a teacher of righteousness to guide them in the way of His heart" (1.10–11 [WAC, 52]). In the immediate sequel, opposition from the "man of mockery" is mentioned—hardly the only violent foe the Teacher would face. That the Teacher founded or established a community follows from the *Commentary on Psalms*[a] 3.15–17 (Ps. 37:23–24): "This refers to the priest, the Teacher of R[ighteousness, whom] God [ch]ose to be His servant [and] ordained him to form Him a company [. . .] [his] way He smoothed for the truth" (WAC, 222).

Some incidents of his life are told in two *pesharim* in particular. The appearance of the Teacher in these texts means that the expositors found him predicted in the prophetic works being studied. That the Teacher experienced opposition from someone called *the liar* is confirmed in the *Commentary on Habakkuk* (see Figure 12.2): the traitors in Hab. 1:5 are taken as "the traitors with the Man of the Lie, because they have not [obeyed the words of] the Teacher of Righteousness from the mouth of God" (2.1–3 [WAC, 116]). Here the writer claims inspiration for the Teacher. Similarly, in 5.9–12 the traitors in Hab. 1:13b are

> the family of Absalom and the members of their party, who kept quiet when the Teacher of Righteousness was rebuked,[4] and they did not help him against the Man of the Lie, who had rejected the Law in the presence of their entire [company]. (WAC, 118; see also the first copy of a *Commentary on Psalms* 1.26–2.1, where the Man of the Lie appears, but not the Teacher)

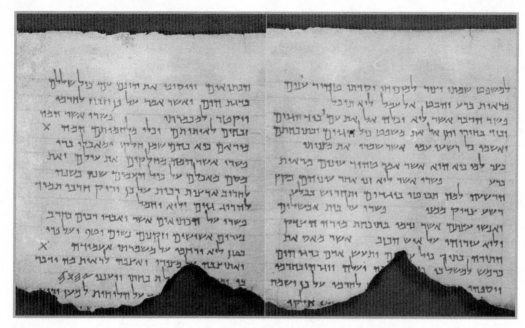

Figure 12.2
Columns 5–6 of the *Commentary on Habakkuk* (1QpHab) (Trever, 1966)
Courtesy of John C. Trever

The Teacher and his followers staked powerful claims for his relation to God and his inspired ability to read the Scriptures. The first column of CD traces his appointment to the deity himself. In the *Commentary on Habakkuk* the clearest assertion of his inspired exegesis comes in 7.1–5, the interpretation of Hab. 2:1–2:

> Then God told Habakkuk to write down what is going to happen to the generation to come; but when that period would be complete He did not make known to him. When it says, "so that with ease someone can read it," this refers to the Teacher of Righteousness to whom God made known all the mysterious revelations of his servants the prophets. (WAC, 119)

In light of this teaching, we may confidently view 2.6–10 as also a statement about his ability. Here he is called the priest (as in the *Commentary on Psalms*[a] 3.15):

> They are the cru[el Israel]ites who will not believe when they hear everything that [is to come upon] the latter generation that will be spoken by the Priest in whose [heart] God has put [the ability] to explain all the words of His servants the prophets, through [whom] God has foretold everything that is to come upon His people and [His land]. (WAC, 116)

It is little wonder that such claims aroused strong opposition from those who thought the Teacher was wrong. The future state of the Teacher's followers is even tied to their relation to him in the *Commentary on Habakkuk* 8.1–3 (interpreting Hab. 2:4b: "but the righteous live by their faith"): "This refers to all those who obey the Law among the Jews [literally: house of Judah] whom God will rescue from among those doomed to judgment, because of their suffering and their loyalty to the Teacher of Righteousness" (WAC, 119).

Besides from the Man of the Lie and his community, the Teacher suffered from a person called the Wicked Priest (for more on him, see below). In a famous passage, the commentator on Habakkuk writes:

> "Woe to the one who gets his friend drunk, pouring out his anger, making him drink, just to get a look at their holy days" (2:15). This refers to the Wicked Priest, who pursued the Teacher of Righteousness to destroy him in the heat of his anger at his place of exile. At the time set aside for the repose of the Day of Atonement he appeared to them to destroy them and to bring them to ruin on the fast day, the Sabbath intended for their repose." (11.2–8 [WAC, 121–22])

An attack of this sort may be the subject of the *Commentary on Psalms*[a] 4.7–9:

> "The wicked man observes the righteous man and seeks [to kill him. But the Lo]rd [will not leave him in his power and will not co]ndemn him when he comes to trial" (37:2–3). This refers to the Wicked Priest who observes the Teacher of Righteousness and seeks to kill him [. . .] and the Law that he sent to him, but God will not leave him in his power and will not condemn him when he comes to trial. (WAC, 223)

We have seen that the dispute with the Man of the Lie concerned law; the same seems to be the case with the Wicked Priest, to whom, it appears, the Teacher sent a "law" (which some understand as 4QMMT). If the Teacher wrote a revealed law, then, according to the *pesharim,* his inspiration extended to both the law and the prophets. The failure of the attack on the Teacher and his community is noted in the *Commentary on Habakkuk* 9.9–12, where the crime leads God to deliver the Wicked Priest "to his enemies, humiliating him with a consuming affliction with despair, because he had done wrong to His chosen" (1QpHab 9.10–12 [WAC, 120]).

It is likely that CD 20.13–15 mentions the Teacher's death: "Now from the day the Beloved[5] Teacher passes away to the destruction of all the warriors who went back to the Man of the Lie will be about forty years" (WAC, 60). The text is not quite this clear—"passes away" is literally "the being gathered"—but the death of the Teacher seems the most likely interpretation (see 19.35–20.1 for the same expression). The deaths of rebellious warriors, just like the generation that turned against Moses in the wilderness (see Num. 14:32–34; Deut. 2:14), will take place within a forty-year period, perhaps before what was anticipated to be a new entry into the land.

These (with the *Commentary on Psalms*[b] 1.4–5 [where he is perhaps called a priest]; 2.2; and the *Commentary on Micah* [1Q14] 8–10.6) are the preserved references to the Teacher of Righteousness. Some scholars think he was the author of one or more texts found at Qumran, with the strongest case being made for the so-called Teacher Hymns in the *Thanksgiving Psalms* (esp. those in cols. 10–17).

The facts that the Teacher was a priest, that astonishing claims were made for his legal and interpretive authority, and that he drew the attention of the Wicked Priest (probably a high priest; see below) have given rise to the theory that the Teacher was himself a high priest or, perhaps more plausibly, that he acted as high priest in the years 159–152 BCE when, according to the received list, there was no high priest in Jerusalem.

THE WICKED PRIEST

A person (or persons) called the Wicked Priest was a contemporary and violent opponent of the Teacher of Righteousness. Although the epithet expresses clearly the group's opinion of this priest, the individual thought worthy of such criticism is not named. It is quite likely that the title "the Wicked Priest" (in Hebrew *hak-kohen ha-rasha'*) is a pejorative play on one form of the title high priest—*hak-kohen ha-ro'sh*. If so, the Wicked Priest was a Jewish high priest. Since only a small number of them served at the times of which the texts speak, we have a much better chance of identifying this man than we have for some of the other characters in the scrolls.

Like the Teacher, the Wicked Priest is mentioned only a few times in the Qumran texts. The epithet fails to appear in works such as the *Damascus Document* and the *Rule of the Community;* it figures only in the *Commentary on Habakkuk* (five times) and the first copy of the *Commentary on Psalms* (once). There are several other passages in the *Commentary on Habakkuk* that may refer to him, but call him only "the priest" (three times). Since sections of the text of the commentary are in poor shape, he may have appeared at other points as well (e.g., 1.13).

The *Commentary on Habakkuk* 8.3–13 focuses on Hab. 2:5–6, which speaks about an arrogant person who insatiably acquires wealth, but is eventually subjected to the taunts of people from other nations:

> This refers to the Wicked Priest who had a reputation for reliability [literally: was called by the name of truth] at the beginning of his term of service; but when he became ruler over Israel, he became proud and forsook God and betrayed the commandments for the sake of riches. He amassed by force the riches of the lawless who had rebelled against God, seizing the riches of the peoples, thus adding to the guilt of his crimes, and he committed abhorrent deeds in every defiling impurity. (8.8–13 [WAC, 120])

We do not know what is meant by the priest's being called by the name of truth at first, but the passage clearly indicates that he was a ruler and thus was almost certainly a high priest from the Maccabean/Hasmonean family. The charge of amassing riches could be leveled at several of these priests.

It is probable that the Wicked Priest is considered the subject of Hab. 2:7–8a, which predicts that the person of the previous verses will be plundered by the nations he despoiled.

> [This refers to] the priest who rebelled [and violated] the commandments of [God . . . they mis]treated him [. . .] inflicting upon him the punishments due to such horrible wickedness, perpetrating upon him painful diseases, acts of retaliation against his mortal body. (8.16–9.2 [WAC, 120])

The graphic account of his sufferings at the hands of foreigners may supply a clue to his identity because the first Maccabean high priest, Jonathan (152–142 BCE), died at the

hands of his captors after being held by them for some time (1 Macc. 13:23, though no tor-
ture is mentioned there).

The commentator brings the Wicked Priest and the Teacher of Righteousness together
for the first time in the extant text at the *Commentary on Habakkuk* 9.9–12. Explaining
Hab. 2:8b (the verse charges someone with committing murder and injustice in the land),
the author says:

> This refers to the Wicked Priest. Because of the crime he committed against the Teacher
> of Righteousness and the members of his party, God handed him over to his enemies,
> humiliating him with a consuming affliction with despair, because he had done wrong to
> His chosen [singular]. (WAC, 120)

The passage is admittedly vague, but the priest had harmed the Teacher and his followers
and for this God condemned him to a horrible fate at the hands of his enemies.

It may be that the Wicked Priest, again called only "the priest," appears at 9.16, this
time as the hoarder of Hab. 2:9–11, but the next certain reference is in the explanation of
Hab. 2:15, which was quoted in the section about the Teacher of Righteousness. This is the
passage that treats the Wicked Priest's attack on the Teacher and his followers on their Day
of Atonement. The violence described shows how very hostile the priest was toward the
Teacher. The punishment that awaits the priest is described in 11.12–15 (Hab. 2:16); he is
also accused of living extravagantly at the expense of those who had little. The final references to him in this commentary connect him with Hab. 2:17 (punishment on someone
for crimes against Lebanon):

> The passage refers to the Wicked Priest, that he will be paid back for what he did to the
> poor, for "Lebanon" refers to the society of the *Yahad*, and "beasts" refers to the simple-
> hearted of Judah who obey the Law. God will condemn him to utter destruction, just as
> he planned to destroy the poor. As for the verse that says, "because of murder in the city
> and injustice in the land," this refers to Jerusalem, where the Wicked Priest committed his
> abhorrent deeds, defiling the Temple of God. "Injustice in the land" refers to the cities of
> Judah where he stole the assets of the poor. (12.2–10 [WAC, 122])

The *Commentary on Psalms*[a] mentions the Wicked Priest in 4.7–10, where it is explaining
Ps. 37:32–33 (the wicked person watches the righteous one and tries to kill him, but God
does not permit it): "This refers to the Wicked [Pri]est who ob[serv]es the [Teach]er of
Righteous[ness and seeks] to kill him [. . .] and the Law that he sent to him, . . ." (4.8–9
[WAC, 223]). God prevented him from carrying out his design; eventually the deity will
hand the wicked over to the Gentiles for abuse.

There are several theories about who the Wicked Priest was, although virtually everyone thinks he was one of the Hasmonean high priests. The most likely is that he was
Jonathan (152–142 BCE), who acquired wealth through his campaigns of conquest and,
though he was only a military leader at first, became the high priest despite not being from
the high-priestly family. We know nothing of how Jonathan may have handled dissidents,
but his death at enemy hands comes closest to matching what the *Commentary on
Habakkuk* says about the Wicked Priest's terrible end. One theory holds that the title "the
Wicked Priest" was used for a succession of Hasmonean high priests, not just one of them,
but there is no compelling evidence pointing in this direction. If Jonathan was the Wicked
Priest, then we have solid evidence that the Teacher of Righteousness was active in the
years 152–142 BCE.

THE LIAR

Several epithets, all of which have to do with lying or other misuses of speech, may refer to a single individual. He is called literally "the man of the lie," "the preacher of the lie," and "the man of scoffing/mockery." It is possible that the person so named was the founder and leader of "the ones who look for smooth things" who were described above and identified as Pharisees.

We have already examined CD 1.14–2.1 where the Man of Mockery is a contemporary of the Teacher of Righteousness. An influential man, he misled Israel by instructing them to depart from ancient ways. As a result, the curses of the covenant rested upon the people. A similar impression emerges from 4Q177 *(The Last Days: An Interpretation of Selected Verses),* where he is apparently understood to be the person in Isa. 32:7, who destroys the poor with falsehoods and the needy when they require justice (the word "man" must be restored; the actual passage—fragments 5–6, line 7—is not translated in WAC).

We meet not only a Man of Mockery, but also Men of Mockery, presumably the members of his community. The second copy of a *Commentary on Isaiah* explains that the people who are criticized so roundly in Isa. 5:11–14, 24–25 are the Men of Mockery. Isaiah castigates those who chase after luxuries but do not notice what God is doing and leave the people without knowledge:

> These are the Men of Mockery who are in Jerusalem. They are the ones "who have rejected the Law of the Lord, and the word of Israel's Holy One they have cast off. For this reason He became angry with his people, He stretched out his hand against them and struck them so that the mountains shook and the corpses lay like garbage in the middle of the streets. Even so, his anger [has not receded, his hand is still stretched out]" (5:24–25). This is the company of the Men of Mockery who are in Jerusalem. (2.6–10 [WAC, 211–12])

The word rendered *company* is the same as the one used for the congregation of those looking for smooth things (see also 4Q525 22.8 for a reference to the Men of Mockery in a broken context).

It seems that the Liar is also the person called "the man of the lie" in the *Damascus Document* and the *Commentary on Habakkuk.* In the former there is a passage that connects the two designations. In column 20, where the subject is members who have rejected the commandments of the community and have been expelled, we read:

> They have no part in the household of the Law. They will be condemned along with their companions who have gone back to the Men of Mockery, because they have uttered lies against the correct laws and rejected the sure covenant that they made in the land of Damascus, that is, the New Covenant. Neither they nor their families shall have any part in the household of the Law. Now from the day the Beloved Teacher passed away to the destruction of all the warriors who went back to the Man of the Lie will be about forty years. (20.10–15 [WAC, 60])

If these lines are referring to the same subject, the Men of Mockery are associated with the Man of the Lie. These are people who belonged to a faction opposed to the Teacher's group and with whom they differed on issues having to do with covenantal law.

If we may identify the Man of Mockery with the Man of the Lie, we should also be able to equate him with the person maligned as "the spreader of lies." The *Commentary on*

Habakkuk uses both "man of the lie" and "spreader of lies." While explicating Hab. 1:5, which mentions traitors, the commentator says:

> [This passage refers to] the traitors with the Man of the Lie, because they have not [obeyed the words of] the Teacher of Righteousness from the mouth of God. It also refers to the trai[tors to the] New [Covenant], because they did not believe in God's covenant [and desecrated] His holy name; and finally it refers [to the trai]tors in the Last Days. They are the cru[el Israel]ites who will not believe when they hear everything that [is to come upon] the latter generation that will be spoken by the Priest in whose [heart] God has put [the ability] to explain all the words of His servants the prophets. (2.1–9 [WAC, 116])

The dispute about law that is at the heart of this passage is reiterated in 5.8–12: "'How can you look on silently, you traitors, when the wicked destroys one more righteous than he?' (1:13b). This refers to the family of Absalom and the members of their party, who kept quiet when the Teacher of Righteousness was rebuked, and they did not help him against the Man of the Lie, who had rejected the Law in the presence of their entire [company]." Here the Man of the Lie is a contemporary of the Teacher, a person who rejected the Teacher's law—just the accusation the *Damascus Document* makes against the Man of Mockery. The same text mentions the Spreader of Lies in 10.5–13, which begins by citing Hab. 2:12–13:

> "Woe to you who build a city by bloodshed, who found a town by vice! Indeed this prophecy is from the Lord of Hosts: peoples will toil just for enough fire, nations will wear themselves out for nothing." This refers to the Spreader of Lies, who deceived many, building a worthless city by bloodshed and forming a community by lies for his own glory, making many toil at useless labor, teaching them to do false deeds. In the end, their toil will be for nothing. As a result they will undergo fiery punishments, because they blasphemed and reviled God's chosen ones. (WAC, 121; this individual may also be mentioned at the end of col. 10 and the beginning of col. 11).

The Spreader of Lies also formed a community and misled people in doing so. It may be that the city imagery is not meant literally, but refers to construction of a community.

An individual called by the same name may be brought into connection with the Teacher of Righteousness in the *Commentary on Micah* (1Q14; not in WAC). There he misleads the simple (see 8–10.4–9, interpreting Mic. 1:5–6).

An especially interesting passage about the "spreader of lies" is given in two parallel forms in CD 8 and 19. The passage deals with people who do not remain faithful to the laws of the group and who are charged with actions contrary to them (including accusations we have met in connection with those looking for smooth things). Against these the writer quotes from Deut. 32:33: "Their wine is venom of snakes, the cruel poison of vipers," which he then explains:

> "The snakes" are the kings of the Gentiles and "their wine" is their customs and "the poison of vipers" is the chief of the kings of Greece, who comes to wreak vengeance on them. But the "Shoddy-Wall-Builders" and "White-washers" understood none of these things, for one who deals in mere wind, a spewer [= spreader] of lies, had spewed on them. . . ." (8.9–13 [WAC, 58–59]; 19.25–26 rephrases the title "spewer of lies" slightly.)

Here the Spreader of Lies is the teacher of the wall-builders, a designation for Pharisees.

The Man of Mockery–Man of the Lie–Spreader of the Lie may have been the founder of the Pharisaic movement. He was a contemporary of the Teacher and came into sharp conflict with him regarding interpretation of the law. Some members of the Teacher's community were considered traitors for going over to his side. Who this person was we do not know.

THE LION OF WRATH

The *Commentary on Nahum* speaks of the angry young lion when dealing with the invasion by the Greek king Demetrius, who came on the advice of the ones who look for smooth things. It was maintained above that the event in question is Demetrius's incursion in 88 BCE; if so, the angry young lion, who is a ruler, must be Alexander Jannaeus (103–76 BCE), who hanged 800 of his opponents alive (see frags. 3–4 1.1–9).

History

Is it possible, on the basis of the scrolls and any other information at our disposal, to write a history of the scrolls community? The answer is clearly no. There is insufficient evidence, because the subject seems not to have been one on which they wrote much, and no one else supplied the missing information. Perhaps this is not surprising, because it must have been a small group. One can, however, discern some points in the group's history as they chose to present it, and archeological evidence provides a general chronological framework within which to place that history. Any attempt at sketching a history of the community requires guessing who characters, designated only by nicknames, might have been.

ORIGINS

We do not know when the group associated with the scrolls began, but the *Damascus Document* column 1, cited several times above, deals with the subject and supplies some chronological notes.

> In the era of wrath—three hundred and ninety years at the time He handed them over to the power of Nebuchadnezzar king of Babylon—He took care of them and caused to grow from Israel and from Aaron a root of planting to inherit His land and to grow fat on the good produce of His soil. They considered their iniquity and they knew that they were guilty men, and had been like the blind and like those groping for the way twenty years. But God considered their deeds, that they had sought Him with a whole heart. So He raised up for them a teacher of righteousness to guide them in the way of His heart. (CD 1.5–11 [WAC, 52])

The passage points to a penitential group, one realizing the error of its way, during the time when God was punishing Israel. The number 390 probably comes from Ezek. 4:5, where the Lord commands the prophet to lie on his left side and set the guilt of the house of Israel on it: "you shall bear their punishment for the number of the days that you lie there. For I assign to you a number of days, three hundred and ninety days, equal to the number of the years of their punishment" (4:4b–5a). As the number is used in the *Damascus Document*, it is not clear whether it points to the past (as the WAC translation may suggest) or, as seems more likely, to the period that began with Judah's defeat by Babylon in 587 BCE.

The meaning of the number 390 has been debated at length. In some Jewish texts the exact chronology of the post–587 BCE period is badly miscalculated; in others it is measured more accurately. But how our author meant it we do not know. If we take the number literally and assume the writer made a reasonably precise estimate of the length of time since Nebuchnezzar's victory, we would arrive at the early second century BCE (197 BCE to be exact). The passage in the *Damascus Document* appends a twenty-year period of uncertainty after the group began and before the Teacher arrived. The same problems attend an attempt to read this number. Taken in a straightforward sense it would, however, almost bring one to the beginning of the period when troubles with the Jewish high-priesthood began and when the high priest Jason lent official support to Hellenistic institutions and practices in Jerusalem. If the writer thought the post-587 period was shorter than we believe it was, the time to which his numbers point would be later. Above we have seen that the Teacher and the Wicked Priest were contemporaries. If Jonathan was the Wicked Priest, the Teacher was active during his term as high priest (152–142 BCE). It is worth adding that *1 Enoch* 90:6–10; 93:10; and *Jub.* 23:26 also allude to a reform or penitential movement apparently just before or around Maccabean times.

No scrolls passage associates these early years of the movement with Qumran. The *Commentary on Habakkuk* 11.6 refers to the place of exile for the Teacher and his band, but does not identify it by name. We should recall also that the *Damascus Document* speaks several times about going to Damascus and about a new covenant there. Whether the Teacher and his followers actually went to Damascus we do not know.

The Teacher is called a priest. He is never called the high priest, but we have already alluded to the suggestion that he was acting high priest in the seven-year period when there was no official high priest in Jerusalem. If the Teacher did serve in this capacity (and it is no more than a guess) Jonathan would have ousted him from the leading priestly position in 152 BCE (it is not one of the charges made against the Wicked Priest). Forceful removal from office could certainly account for the hostility between the two men and perhaps even for a decision by the Teacher and his followers to leave Jerusalem. But the archeological remains may suggest that the community did not settle at Qumran until around 100 BCE, long after any conflict with Jonathan. Where they were in the interval we cannot say.

Even though there are few events that we can situate in the group's history, it is possible that the covenanters refer in their texts to a series of Maccabean/Hasmonean rulers under different nicknames.

Jonathan (152–142 BCE): We have already met the argument for seeing Jonathan as the Wicked Priest. He may also be the Jonathan of 4Q523 fragments 1–2.2 (not in WAC). It is possible, too, that the end of his name has survived in 4Q245 *(The Vision of Daniel)* fragment 1 1.10 (rendered "Jo]hn" in WAC, 268). See on Simon below.

Simon (142–134): Some have identified Simon as the "man of Belial" in 4Q175 (see on John Hyrcanus below), who was in turn the Wicked Priest, although the two are never identified with each other. The name "Simon" does occur in 4Q245 fragment 1 1.10, after what may be the name Jonathan in a list of priests.

John Hyrcanus (134–104): John Hyrcanus may be the "man of Belial" who is mentioned in the *Testimonia* (*A Collection of Messianic Proof Texts,* 4Q175), which quotes from the *Psalms of Joshua* (4Q378–79, specifically 4Q379 frag. 22). The text offers an interpretation of Joshua's curse on Jericho—that the rebuilder would lay its foundation at the cost of his firstborn son and its gates at the cost of his youngest son. The text finds the prediction fulfilled in a cursed "man of Belial" (4Q175 l. 23). He will have two sons who will come after him and be

> instruments of wrongdoing. They shall rebuild [this city and s]et up for it a wall and towers, creating a stronghold of evil [and a great wickedness] in Israel, a thing of horror in Ephraim and Judah. [. . .] They shall [wo]rk blasphemy in the land, a great uncleanness among the children of [Jacob. They shall pour out blo]od like water upon the bulwark of the daughter of Zion and within the city limits of Jerusalem. (ll. 25–30 [WAC, 231]; the parallel in 4Q379 frag. 22 allows a number of the gaps to be filled.)

Hyrcanus developed the city and area of Jericho, where the Hasmoneans had palaces, and two of his sons died before the end of his reign. Whether he is the one meant is less than obvious (some think the man of Belial was Simon), but 4Q175, in addition to the words quoted above, contains scriptural citations promising an ideal prophet, ruler, and priest, and, according to Josephus, Hyrcanus exercised all of these functions (*Antiquities* 13.299–300). The text may have been compiled to counter such claims about Hyrcanus.[6] He may also be the person called Yohanan in 4Q331 fragment 1 1.7 (the word "priest" occurs in the previous line).

Alexander Jannaeus (103–76): As we have seen, he is called the Lion of Wrath in the *Commentary on Nahum* and in the second copy of a *Commentary on Hosea.* He may also be the king named in 4Q448 *(In Praise of King Jonathan).* This manuscript, which contains more than one composition, reads: "the holy city, for Jonathan, the king, and all the congregation of Your people Israel which have been dispersed to the four winds of the heavens, let peace be on all of them and Your kingdom" (B 1–8). Jonathan the king is also mentioned but in a broken context, in C 8. Alexander Jannaeus's Hebrew name was Jonathan, as we know from the coins he minted; consequently, he is probably the person intended in this text. This is most interesting, because the prayer for peace appears to include Jonathan, although there is solid reason for thinking that the people of Qumran were confirmed opponents of the Hasmonean rulers.[7] The translation in WAC for the beginning of the text is probably not correct. The editors rendered it as "Guard (or: Rise up), O Holy One, over King Jonathan (or: for King Jonathan) and all the congregation. . . ."[8] Another possibility is: "Rise up, O Holy One, against King Jonathan, but over all the congregation . . ."; in this case, the king would not be included in the prayer for peace (though the kingdom would). What the precise situation may be here is not clear, but at least we may say that Alexander Jannaeus is the most likely candidate for the King Jonathan of this text. Some scholars have proposed that he is Jonathan, the first Maccabean high priest, but, as far as we know, he was not called a king.

After Jannaeus we have no certain reference to a Hasmonean priest-king. Several fragmentary works from Cave 4 do mention the names of other historical individuals who lived in the first century BCE. The contexts are so broken that nothing can be concluded about the precise circumstances of the persons and events in question.

Salome Alexandra (76–67): The spouse and successor of Alexander Jannaeus is mentioned in 4Q331 fragment 1 2.7 and 4Q332 2.4 ("] foundation, Shelamzion entered [" [WAC, 314]).

Hyrcanus II and Aristobulus II: These two sons of Jannaeus and Alexandra competed for power in the next decades. Hyrcanus II may be the Hyrcanus who is said to rebel in 4Q332 fragment 2, line 6. The one against whom he rebelled was perhaps identified after the reference to Hyrcanus, but this part of the text is lost. Arabs may be mentioned in line 2, possibly pointing to the alliance between Hyrcanus II and the Nabateans against Aristobulus.[9] Aristobulus is not mentioned (despite the translation in WAC, 315 of what is numbered there as 4Q323 frag. 3, l. 6). The name *Hyrcanus* is also present in a strange text that seems to be a writing exercise; there it is simply included in an alphabetical series of names (4Q341 l. 7 [not in WAC]); whether any specific Hyrcanus was meant we cannot tell.

Two other names should be noted. *Aemilius* figures twice in 4Q333 1.4, 8, both times apparently as the subject of the verb "kill" (WAC, 316). This is Marcus Aemilius Scaurus, a Roman official who was involved in Pompey's conquest of Judea in 63 BCE and in the subsequent administration of the area. In 4Q468e line 3 is a name that is probably to be read as *Pytl'ws* (Peitholaus) and may well be the individual mentioned by Josephus in *War* 1.162, 172, 180; *Antiquities* 14.84, 93, 124. He was active on the Roman side in various military campaigns in the decade or so after Pompey's conquest.

In Chapter 3 we examined the archeological evidence from Qumran and saw that there may have been a short gap in occupation around the end of the first century BCE, but that the site was again occupied in the first century CE. It was finally destroyed as a sectarian center during the war against Rome (66–70 CE). It is possible that the year of destruction was 68 CE. What happened during the last century or so of the community's existence we cannot say.

Select Bibliography

Helpful, summary articles about most of the groups and individuals mentioned in this chapter are found in

Schiffman, L. H., and J. C. VanderKam, eds. *Encyclopedia of the Dead Sea Scrolls.* 2 vols. New York and Oxford: Oxford University Press, 2000.

CHAPTER 13

Biblical Interpretation in the Dead Sea Scrolls

The Interpretation of Scripture at Qumran

As we have seen in studying the problem of *canon* at Qumran, there were many older books that the scrolls writers regarded as authorities and cited in their compositions. The many cases in which they quote or allude to Scriptures demonstrate that they placed some books on the highest level. Such works they read, interpreted, and applied to the needs of their community. This process of using older writings had begun already in "biblical" times, as we can see from examples such as 1–2 Chronicles, which are based on and to some extent interpret 1–2 Samuel and 1–2 Kings; or Daniel 9, which provides a reading of Jeremiah's prophecy regarding the seventy years of exile.

The Qumran community labored earnestly and continually at the task of explaining the Scriptures. We read in the *Rule of the Community:*

> In any place where is gathered the ten-man quorum, someone must always be engaged in study of the Law, day and night, continually, each one taking his turn. The general membership will be diligent together for the first third of every night of the year, reading aloud from the Book, interpreting Scripure,[1] and praying together. (6.6–8 [WAC, 134])

We have evidence that the covenanters studied the law and the prophets with utmost care and that their exegetical concerns moved beyond these two categories to embrace others as well. The Instructor of the community had the duty "to teach them to seek God with all their heart and with all their soul, to do that which is good and upright before Him, just as He commanded through Moses and all His servants the prophets" (1QS 1.1–3).

The scriptural interpretation evidenced in the Qumran texts is not all of one type. It is important to notice what kind of text is being subjected to interpretation, because a legal text may call forth one kind of reading, while a predictive one could be handled differently. Hence it is not accurate to lump all biblical interpretation in the scrolls into a single category such as *pesher* interpretation. That kind was important, but it is not the only way in which the covenanters approached older texts. There are examples of what we could call straightforward, or simple-sense, exegesis. An instructive case appears in the *Commentary on Genesis* (4Q252), where we find:

> Timna was a concubine of Eliphaz, Esau's son; she bore Amalek to him, he whom Saul def[eated]. Just as he said to Moses, "In the Last Days, the remembrance of Amalek shall be blotted out from under heaven." (4.1–3 [WAC, 276])

The first part of the passage (through the words "Amalek to him") is a citation from the genealogy in Gen. 36:12. The reference to Amalek the commentator then explains in a simple fashion by noting that King Saul later defeated this Amalek's descendants (see 1 Sam. 15:1–9). In order to gloss the passage more fully, he adds a quotation from Deut. 25:19 and understands it, in good Qumran fashion, to be referring to the last days.

We should also realize that Scripture was employed for more reasons than exegesis, strictly speaking. In reading the scrolls one gets the impression that education for the authors involved becoming steeped in the Scriptures and in the cadences of its language. Thus virtually everything the members of the group wrote echoes biblical language in some way. The poems among the *Thanksgiving Psalms* supply readers with a heavy dose of scriptural language, even as their authors resort to different poetic forms and express their distinctive ideas. In this chapter we do not pursue this echo effect, but are concerned with explicit cases of biblical interpretation—where an older text clearly lies behind a scrolls passage that provides an explanation of it. The Dead Sea Scrolls contain many examples of exegesis, some of which may sound strange today, but as one scrutinizes the writers' interaction with the ancient works, one comes to appreciate that they were exceedingly knowledgeable and careful readers of the text, all of which was for them a unified statement of the divine will and plan.

Types of Interpretation

LEGAL INTERPRETATION

There is no doubt that the community studied the law of Moses with a disciplined and informed eye. Each member pledged himself to obey it completely, but the legislation had to be understood in the proper way. As we might expect by now, the Qumranites thought they had the right interpretation as God had revealed it to them. According to the *Rule of the Community*, the entrant into the covenantal community

> shall take upon himself a binding oath to return to the Law of Moses (according to all that He commanded) with all his heart and with all his mind, to all that has been revealed from it to the Sons of Zadok—priests and preservers of the covenant, Seekers of His will—and the majority of the men of their covenant (that is, those who have jointly volunteered for His truth and to live by what pleases Him). (5.8–10 [WAC, 132])

The *Damascus Document* mentions "the Interpreter of the Law" (6.7), who is identified as the "rod" named in Num. 21:18 and who may be the Teacher of Righteousness himself.[2] If so, this early leader or even founder of the group would have been distinguished by his ability to interpret the Torah.[3]

The claim that they possessed a revealed interpretation of the law must have made it difficult for outsiders to argue points of legal exegesis with the members of the community. They made it even more difficult for others by drawing a distinction between revealed aspects of the law—apparently ones that all understood or were at least available to every-one—and hidden ones. It was the hidden laws that the community thought they could uncover, while all the rest of Israel went off on the wrong path.[4] The distinction is expressed in the *Rule of the Community:*

> Each one who thus enters the Covenant by oath is to separate himself from all of the per-verse men, those who walk in the wicked way, for such are not reckoned a part of His Covenant. They "have not sought Him nor inquired of His statutes" (Zeph. 1:6) so as to discover the hidden laws in which they err to their shame. Even the revealed laws they knowingly transgress, thus stirring God's judgmental wrath and full vengeance: the curses of the Mosaic Covenant. (5.10–12 [WAC, 132]; see also 8.11–12)

The *Damascus Document* offers some clarification of these terms:

> But when those of them who were left held firm to the commandments of God, He insti-tuted His covenant with Israel for ever, revealing to them things hidden, in which all Is-rael had gone wrong: His holy Sabbaths, His glorious festivals, His righteous laws, His reliable ways. The desires of His will, which Man should carry out and so have life in them, He opened up to them. So they "dug a well," yielding much water. Those who reject this water He will not allow to live. (3.12–17 [WAC, 54])

Among the hidden laws, calendrical matters ("His holy Sabbaths, His glorious festivals") seem to loom large, though they are not the only ones.

As the term *hidden laws*—ones present in the law but only now revealed to the group—implies, the covenanters held that more legislation was revealed or became known over time. In the book of *Jubilees* the patriarch Reuben was excused for sleeping with Bilhah, his father's concubine-wife, because the relevant law had not been revealed in his time (*Jub.* 33:15–16); it was first disclosed to Moses (Lev. 20:11).[5] Also, the Instructor was to conduct himself in line with certain statutes and was to be

> guided by the precepts appropriate to each era and the value of each person. He is to work the will of God according to what has been revealed for each period of history, studying all the wise legal findings of earlier times, as well as every statute applying to his own time. (*Rule of the Community* 9.12–14 [WAC, 139])

But in other instances God revealed more of his law, not so much through fresh, direct dis-closures, but through inspired study of the revealed law by specially endowed individuals. That is to say, continued study of the scriptural laws produced new insights for the com-munity, insights that the rest of Israel lacked. This is the implication of regarding the Teacher as an inspired interpreter, and, as we have seen above, the priests in the commu-nity enjoyed the same privilege. "The hidden laws required the help of divinely guided exe-gesis to enable sect members to discover their correct interpretation. This process involved searching in the law, an activity not practiced by the sect's opponents. Hence, the oppo-nents did not have the correct views."[6]

At least some of the laws under which they lived were applicable, it seems, only for this present era:

> They shall deviate from none of the teachings of the Law, whereby they would walk in their willful heart completely. They shall govern themselves using the original precepts by

which the men of the *Yahad* began to be instructed, doing so until there come the Prophet and the Messiahs of Aaron and Israel. (*Rule of the Community* 9.9–11 [WAC, 139]; cf. CD 4.7–9; 6.8–11, 14–16)

We have had opportunity to see that the many legal texts found in the Qumran caves relate to their scriptural base in differing ways. For example, a text like *Reworked Pentateuch* (4Q364–67; *An Annotated Law of Moses* in WAC, 325–28) largely reproduces the text of the Pentateuch and raises the question whether it is itself a scriptural text (see also Chapter 7). Even this, however, illustrates a more common manner of handling legal material in Exodus through Deuteronomy: at times it harmonizes and combines passages that deal with the same subject but are separated in Exodus through Deuteronomy. One example is in fragment 4, column 1 of 4Q366 (not in WAC), where the laws for the Festival of Tabernacles from Num. 29:32–39 and Deut. 16:13–14 are combined. Such combining and harmonizing of passages may be regarded as a kind of problem solving: the different scriptural sections that deal with a topic (like the festivals) may not give the same information or may give conflicting instructions about how to celebrate them; they must accordingly be brought into unity with each other.

The *Temple Scroll* raises that practice to an art form. As Y. Yadin has written, the author of the *Temple Scroll* "arranged the main topics in the same order as they appear in the legislative books of the Pentateuch: Exodus, Leviticus, Numbers and Deuteronomy."[7] For an example of assembling texts treating the same subject, we may use a case that Yadin classified as an instance of "unifying duplicate commands (harmonization)." In 1 Sam. 30:24 David articulated a law about the spoils of warfare: "For the share of the one who goes down into the battle shall be the same as the share of the one who stays by the baggage; they shall share alike" (v. 25 calls this "a statute and an ordinance for Israel; it continues to the present day"). Another law about plunder occurs in Num. 31:27–30:

Divide the booty into two parts, between the warriors who went out to battle and all the congregation. From the share of the warriors who went out to battle, set aside as tribute for the Lord, one item out of every five hundred. . . . Take it from their half and give it to Eleazar the priest as an offering to the Lord. But from the Israelites' half you shall take one out of every fifty . . . and give them to the Levites who have charge of the tabernacle of the Lord.

With this information in mind, the compiler of the *Temple Scroll* wrote:

If they defeat their enemies, crushing them and putting them to the sword, and carry off their plunder, they are to give the king one-tenth of it. The priests shall receive one part per thousand and the Levites one percent of the total. The rest is to be divided equally between the warriors who fought the battle and their comrades who remained behind in their cities. (58.11–15 [WAC, 486])

This passage and the two biblical ones agree about a 50-50 division. The *Temple Scroll* takes from Numbers the figure for the priestly portion but expresses it differently: 1/500 of one-half is equal to 1/1000 of the whole; it does the same for the levitical share—1/50 of half the total is equivalent to 1/100 of the entire amount. But this command is placed in the section where the author of the scroll is explaining the law of the king in Deut. 17:14–20, and the writer was aware that the king, who is not mentioned in 1 Sam.

30:24–25 or Num. 31:27–30, also received a share. Yadin thinks he derived the idea that the king took one-tenth especially from Gen. 14:20, where Abram, on returning from battle, presents Melchizedek, the priest-king of Salem, with one-tenth of everything. He refers to the *Genesis Apocryphon* (WAC: *Tales of the Patriarchs*) 22.17, which explains that Abram gave Melchizedek (regarded in the text as the king of Jerusalem) a tenth of all the possessions of the people he had defeated. This principle is then incorporated into the calculations and the royal portion is removed before the other parts are allotted.[8]

The book of *Jubilees,* which, while retelling scriptural stories, attempts to solve problems raised by the biblical text, provides clear illustrations of a method that we could call antedating laws. The author tries to find occasions in the text of Genesis where he could anchor laws that do not appear in Scripture until the time of Moses and lack context or rationale. As he tells the story of the first couple, he separates the times when Adam and Eve were introduced into the Garden.

> In the first week Adam and his wife—the rib—were created, and in the second week he showed her to him. Therefore, a commandment was given to keep (women) in their defilement seven days for a male (child) and for a female two (units) of seven days. After 40 days had come to an end for Adam in the land where he had been created, we brought him into the Garden of Eden to work and keep it. His wife was brought (there) on the eightieth day. After this she entered the Garden of Eden. For this reason a commandment was written in the heavenly tablets for the one who gives birth to a child: if she gives birth to a male, she is to remain in her impurity for seven days like the first seven days; then for 33 days she is to remain in the blood of purification. She is not to touch any sacred thing nor to enter the sanctuary until she completes these days for a male. As for a female she is to remain in her impurity for two weeks of days like the first two weeks and 66 days in the blood of purification. Their total is 80 days. (3:8–11)[9]

The law noted here is from Lev. 12:2–5, where it is simply stated and no motivation is offered. *Jubilees* tries to explain it in connection with chronological details from Genesis 1–2 (in Gen. 2:7–8 the man is created outside the Garden and then put in it, while the woman is fashioned later). This unusual exegetical step is now attested in 4Q265 *(Portions of Sectarian Law),* where, in fragment 7 2.11–17, the same material is found. Both *Jubilees* and 4Q265 declare that the Garden of Eden was a sanctuary, and this allows the writers to attach the law of Leviticus 12, which deals with a woman's not being allowed to enter the sanctuary immediately after childbirth, to the Eden story.

At times writers of the scrolls explain the procedures they followed in applying Mosaic laws to their times. The work called 4QMMT (WAC: *A Sectarian Manifesto*) draws conclusions from legislation regarding the tabernacle and the Israelite camp in the desert for contemporary realities:

> [Concer]ning that which it [*sic*] is written: [anyone who slaughters in the camp or] outside the camp an ox, [a lam]b, or a goat, that [. . . to the n]orth of the camp. We have determined that the sanctuary is [the "tabernacle of the tent of meeting," that Je]rusale[m] is the "camp," and that outside the camp [is "outside of Jerusalem,"] in other words the "camp of their citie[s]." (B 27–31 [WAC, 360–61])

With these equivalences established, one can systematically translate legislation in the wilderness passages so that it applies to the Temple, Jerusalem, and surrounding areas.

Another case is found in the *Damascus Document*. As the author discusses some legal issues on which the community differed with its opponents (perhaps Pharisees), he cites Lev. 18:13, but extends its application:

> Furthermore, they marry each man the daughter of his brothers[10] and the daughter of his sister, although Moses said, "Unto the sister of your mother you shall not draw near; she is the flesh of her mother" (Lev. 18:13). But the law of consanguinity is written for males and females alike, so if the brother's daughter uncovers the nakedness of the brother of her father, she is the flesh <of her father>. (CD 5.7–11, WAC, 55)

The law in Leviticus concerns a male who marries his aunt; the commentator declares, however, that the law applies not only to this situation but also to the parallel one in which a niece would marry her uncle. Scripture is explicit only regarding males, but the rule applies to females as well.

The legal texts not only clarify scriptural laws, but also at times expand them. In the *Damascus Document*'s code of sabbath laws the first one is: "A man may not work on the sixth day from the time that the solar orb is above the horizon by its diameter, because that is what is meant by the passage, 'Observe the Sabbath day to keep it holy' (Deut. 5:12)" (CD 10.14–17). It is not immediately obvious from the Deuteronomy verse that it has anything to do with when the sabbath began, much less a specific amount of time before sunset when work must cease. However, we know that exegetes found a clue in the double imperative *(observe and keep holy)* that both the beginning of the sabbath and the end of it were in view. In rabbinic literature the same passage is taken in this sense, even though not all authorities agreed on how much time before sunset on Friday and after sunset on Saturday was implied by the commands.[11]

Another point worth noting about the Qumran legal exegesis is that laws could be based not only on the Torah of Moses, but also on prophetic writings—something not characteristic of rabbinic interpretation (see the example from the *Temple Scroll* above, in which 1 Sam. 30:24 is used). An example may be cited from the *Damascus Document*, where the requirement that a member should not enter the Temple to "light up His altar in vain" is documented by reference to Mal. 1:10 (6:11–14). Where the same text is treating the practice of rebuking fellow members of the group (see Chapter 15 for a more extensive analysis), the base law is Lev. 19:17–18 (against taking vengeance and bearing a grudge), but in the course of explaining the law the writer cites Nah. 1:2, which declares that God is the one who takes vengeance (CD 9.2–8). Hence a human is not allowed to usurp the divine prerogative. The examples are consistent with the statement in the *Rule of the Community* 8.15–16, which interprets the word *highway* in Isa. 40:3: "This means the expounding of the Law, decreed by God through Moses for obedience, that being defined by what has been revealed for each age, and by what the prophets have revealed by His holy spirit." See also 4Q264a *(Halakha B)* fragment 1, lines 6–8, which was presented in Chapter 9.

NARRATIVE INTERPRETATION

We have extensive examples in which narrative passages of Scripture are interpreted; in many cases the best term for describing the procedure is to call it "rewriting Scripture." In such works the writer may adhere more or less strictly to the text of Scripture, but will supplement or in other ways modify it, presumably to achieve some ends that he has in mind.

Lengthy examples are *Jubilees, Aramaic Levi* (WAC: *The Words of Levi*), and the *Genesis Apocryphon* (WAC: *Tales of the Patriarchs*). Some of the material in the Enoch booklets falls into the same category, although their adherence to the scriptural text is often looser. It may be that this type of work was common in the Qumran library, or so it would seem from the many very fragmentary texts that may have revolved around biblical characters (see the survey in Chapter 9). Rewritten Scripture is not the only way in which the writers related to narratives, but it is a prominent one. We should recall that some of these works, such as the Enoch booklets and *Jubilees,* may themselves have been considered Scripture at Qumran (see Chapter 7).

1 Enoch

A dominant theme in the Enochic literature is the marriages between angels and women that led to all manner of evil and eventually to the Flood. The story as presented in *1 Enoch* 6–11 is an instance of rewritten Scripture (see Box 13.1).

As one can see by comparing the two columns below, the writer of this part of *1 Enoch* has interpreted *the sons of God* as *angels* (see Job 38:7) and thus understands the passage as referring to marriages between angels and women. The offspring of the marriages he takes to be giants (as did the Greek translator of Genesis). In *1 Enoch* 6–16 the story is elaborated in great detail and brought into connection with the Flood. This reading of Genesis 6 may seem strange, but it was accepted more widely in late Second Temple times: for example, in *Jubilees,* the *Damascus Document* (CD 2.17–21), the *Genesis Apocryphon* (WAC: *Tales of the*

Box 13.1	*The Sons of God and the Daughters of Men in Genesis and 1 Enoch*

Genesis 6:1–2, 4 (NRSV)	1 Enoch 6:1–2; 7:1–2
When people began to multiply on the face of the ground, and daughters were born to them, the sons of God saw that they were fair;	. . . when the sons of men had increased, that in those days there were born to them fair and beautiful daughters. And the angels, the sons of heaven, saw them and desired them. And they said to one another: "Come, let us choose for ourselves wives from the children of men, and let us beget for ourselves children. . . ."

and they took wives for themselves of all that they chose.
 	
    The Nephilim were on the earth in those days—and also afterward—when the sons of God went in to the daughters of humans, who bore children to them. These were the heroes that were of old, warriors of renown.
	And they took wives for themselves, and everyone chose for himself one each.
	
	    And they began to go in to them and were promiscuous with them. . . . And they became pregnant and bore large giants . . .[1]

1. Knibb, trans., *The Ethiopic Book of Enoch,* 2:67, 76–77.

Figure 13.1
Fragments of *1 Enoch:* 4QEnᵃ
(4Q201) (PAM 43.198)
Courtesy of the Israel Antiquities Authority

Patriarchs), and 4Q180–81 (WAC: *The Ages of the World*). The Enochic *Book of Giants* represents another elaboration of the story, focusing on the children of the marriages.

Another of the Enoch booklets is called the Book of Dreams (*1 Enoch* 83–90), and parts of it have survived at Qumran. The Book of Dreams includes the Animal Apocalypse (*1 Enoch* 85–90), in which the scriptural story is retold, but with animals and birds representing individuals and nations and people standing for angels. The story of the angelic descent to earth is an important element in this text as well (*1 Enoch* 86–88, with other references). (For further details on *1 Enoch*, see Chapter 8 and Figure 13.1.)

Jubilees

Jubilees is a retelling of Genesis 1 to Exodus 24, one that adheres closely to the text of Genesis and Exodus. Because it is tightly wedded to the scriptural text, one can see more clearly the aspects of the rewriting that occur. Here are some examples.

PROBLEM SOLVING

We find instances in which the author solves a difficulty in the text, whether a minor or a major one. Take angels, for instance. Readers of Genesis may be puzzled about when angels were created. They are not mentioned in Genesis 1, but at the end of Genesis 3 cherubim who seem to be angels are stationed to guard the entry to the Garden; later angels appear to other characters such as Hagar (Gen. 16:7) and Abraham (in Genesis 18). The writer of *Jubilees* places the creation of angels on the first day and takes as his clue the presence of the word *spirit* in Gen. 1:2. So, angels were available from this time on to carry out important missions for God.

Another instance has to do with the time when God finished his work of creation. Does Gen. 2:2 ("on the *seventh* day God finished the work that he had done") imply that God violated the work ban on the very first sabbath? *Jub.* 2:16 reads: "He finished all his works on the *sixth* day." In reading *sixth*, the book of *Jubilees* agrees with several ancient versions of Gen. 2:2 (including the Samaritan Pentateuch and the Septuagint), but the reading seems theologically motivated and not the original one.

IMAGE ENHANCEMENT

Several passages in *Jubilees* show a desire to touch up the reputations of biblical characters. So the author omits inconvenient statements like Abram's claim in Gen. 12: 13, 19 that Sarai was his sister (see *Jub.* 13:11–13) or he rephrases Jacob's outright lie in Gen. 27:19 ("I am Esau your firstborn") so that the ancestor of Israel says only "I am your son" (*Jub.* 26:13). At other times the writer was concerned that God himself might appear in an unfavorable light. After all, in Gen. 22:2 God told Abraham to offer his son Isaac as a burnt offering. Did God approve of child sacrifice? The story is introduced differently in *Jubilees*, where the suggestion to sacrifice Isaac comes from Mastema, the leader of the forces of evil; God goes along with this test of Abraham's faith just to prove Mastema wrong (17:15–18:19). In other words, the story begins just as the story of Job does. The same approach is reflected in 4Q225 (WAC: *A Paraphrase of Genesis and Exodus*).

MAJOR ISSUES

Although there are many cases like these, *Jubilees* also handles larger problems raised by Genesis and at times by Genesis in connection with other texts. One nagging concern was why the Israelites thought they had a right to take the land of Canaan by force. There is evidence that some ancient people charged Joshua and the Israelites with stealing Canaan from its rightful owners—the Canaanites. *Jubilees* addresses the matter directly: after the flood when Noah divided the earth among his three sons, he gave to Shem the land incorrectly called Canaan at a later time. Noah's sons agreed under oath to honor the boundaries assigned by their father, but Canaan, a son of Ham (Noah's son), did not like the place assigned to him in West Africa and took Canaan for himself. He was cursed at the time he did this, and Joshua and the Israelites later simply reclaimed the land that was rightfully theirs (*Jub.* 8:8–9:15; 10:27–34). Much of the lengthy section about division of the earth in *Jubilees* is paralleled in the *Tales of the Patriarchs* 17–18.

LEVI

Another major problem suggested by other scriptural texts was the character of Levi, Jacob's third son and the ancestor of Israel's priests. In Genesis Levi is mentioned in lists of Jacob's children and in two other places, in both of which his father is very angry at him: Genesis 34, where he and his brother Simeon take revenge for the rape of their sister, Dinah, by slaughtering the men of Shechem after requiring them to be circumcised; and

Gen. 49:5–7, where Jacob curses both of them for their actions in Shechem. How did such a character become the ancestor of the priests? The Jubilean Levi looks very different. He is not criticized for his role at Shechem, but praised highly for it, since he saved his family from intermarrying with the people of Shechem (see Gen. 34:13–24). Also, he was divinely chosen for the priesthood, was blessed by his grandfather Isaac as a priest, and was installed by his father Jacob so that he served as priest already in his time (30:1–32:9). The author's procedure was not entirely arbitrary, because in Mal. 2:4–7 God spoke of Levi in highly positive terms:

> My covenant with him [Levi] was a covenant of life and well-being, which I gave him; this called for reverence, and he revered me and stood in awe of my name. True instruction was in his mouth, and no wrong was found on his lips. He walked with me in integrity and uprightness, and he turned many from iniquity. (vv. 5–6)

The writer of *Jubilees* was not the first to exalt Levi. This is done in the older work called *Aramaic Levi* (WAC: *The Words of Levi*) and in the later one called *The Testament of Levi*, which is part of the Greek work *The Testaments of the Twelve Patriarchs*. (See Chapter 8.)

Exegetical examples from *Jubilees* could be multiplied. The book leaves one with the strong impression that the author was an astute student of the text he was rewriting, an expert who was thoroughly familiar with all of Israel's ancient Scriptures.

A Commentary on Genesis *(4Q252)*

The calendar was important to the people of Qumran, as we know from the number of texts that employ it and give details about it. Both *1 Enoch* 72–82 and *Jubilees* 6 teach a 364-day solar calendar, and this calendar is reflected in a number of texts from Qumran. *Jubilees* attaches its most extended statement about the calendar to the story of the Flood—the story in Genesis with the largest number of specific dates. The Flood seems to last one year, making the story about it a convenient peg on which to hang calendrical teachings. 4Q252, one of the commentaries on Genesis, is interesting in this regard. The first preserved part of the text is an extended treatment of the Flood chronology, specifying dates and days of the week on which various events happened. It ends the account by saying: "On that day Noah went out from the ark, at the end of an exact year, three hundred and sixty four days, on a Sunday"[12] (frag. 1 2.2–3 [WAC, 275]). *Jubilees* also deals with the dates in the Flood story and repeats the biblical claim that the waters increased for 150 days, which appears to be a five-month period—from 2/17 to 7/17[13] (see Gen. 7:11, 24; 8:3–4). *Jubilees* even makes the point more directly than Genesis does: "The waters remained standing on the surface of the earth for five months—150 days" (5:27). Yet, in the calendar of *Jubilees* there would be not 150 days from 2/17 to 7/17, but 152 days (each month has 30 days, but months 3, 6, 9, and 12 have 31). 4Q252 deals with this very issue:

> The waters prevailed upon the earth one hundred and fifty days, until the fourteenth day of the seventh month, on Tuesday. And at the end of one hundred and fifty days, the waters decreased for two days—Wednesday and Thursday—and on Friday, the ark came to rest upon Mount Ararat. T[his was] the seventeenth day of the seventh month. (frag. 1 1.7–10 [WAC, 275])

Prophetic Interpretation

Over the years since the scrolls were found, the interpretation of prophetic texts in them has received a lot of attention. Sixteen or seventeen texts have been named *pesharim* (see Chapter 9) by scholars because the term *pesher* ("interpretation") regularly appears in the formulas with which the writers introduce their exegesis of scriptural texts. The pattern employed by them is to quote a short section of the scriptural work, insert a formula using the word *pesher*, and then contribute an interpretation that applies the scriptural text to present circumstances or people. The first scholar to write a book-length study of one of the *pesharim*, K. Elliger, wrote that two assumptions underlie *pesher* exegesis:

1. Prophetic proclamation has as its content the end.
2. The present is the end time.[14]

We may doubt whether these two statements cover all cases, but they are descriptive of the general approach taken by the commentator—of the thought world in which he operated. As he read the prophetic text, he believed firmly that it spoke of his times and addressed his community's deepest concerns. An oft-cited example of the thinking that may lie behind all of the *pesharim* appears in the *Commentary on Habakkuk*:

> Then God told Habakkuk to write down what is going to happen to the generation to come; but when that period will be complete He did not make known to him. When it says, "so that with ease someone can read it," this refers to the Teacher of Righteousness to whom God made known all the mysterious revelations of his servants the prophets. (1QpHab 7.1–5 [WAC, 119])

We have seen before that the *pesharim* may contain the inspired interpretations of the Teacher, with the result that in these texts we have both inspired prophetic texts and inspired explanations of them. We have also observed that the *pesher* technique was not confined to books we call prophetic, but included the Psalms, which the group associated with David, who composed them "through prophecy given him by the Most High" (*David's Compositions*, 11Q5 27.11).

   We should look at some examples of how the interpretation is done in the surviving texts. Some equivalences occur regularly in the *Commentary on Habakkuk* (1QpHab): the *Chaldeans* in Habakkuk are interpreted as the *Kittim*, apparently a name for the Romans, as we have seen. So, when Hab. 1:6 quotes God as saying that he is raising up the Chaldeans, the commentator says: "This refers to the Kittim" (2.12). After the identification he paraphrases the text: Hab. 1:6 calls the Chaldeans "brutal and reckless"; the commentator says the Kittim are "swift and mighty in war, annihilating" (2.12–13). Or, in commenting on Hab. 1:13 the exegete makes other identifications:

> "How can you look on silently, you traitors, when the wicked destroys one more righteous than he?" (Hab 1:13) This refers to the family of Absalom and the members of their party, who kept quiet when the Teacher of Righteousness was rebuked, and they did not help him against the Man of the Lie, who had rejected the Law in the presence of their entire [company]. (1QpHab 5.8–12 [WAC, 118])

Here the terms *traitors, wicked,* and *righteous* are assigned values, and the remainder of the verse is applied to the specific situation in which all these characters were present. Through equivalences like these, suggested to the expositor by words in the text, which he transposes into a new key, he is able to unfold the meaning of the text in light of his community and its experiences.

One feature of the *pesharim* that has intrigued scholars is the wording of the biblical citations in them. Though the text is quoted, the wording does not always agree in every detail with the traditional (Masoretic) text of the Hebrew Bible. The citations in the *pesharim* are themselves additional witnesses to the wording of the biblical text at that time. One interesting example is the section treating Hab. 2:15. In the *pesher*, the biblical text is cited as reading: "Woe to the one who gets his friend drunk, pouring out his anger, making him drink, just to get a look at their holy days" (11.2–3). The Masoretic Text reads: "Woe to the one who gets his friend drunk, pouring out his anger, making him drunk, in order to gaze on their nakedness" (the NRSV revised to fit the translation of Hab. 2:15 in WAC, 121). The Hebrew word for *their nakedness* is *me'orêhem,* while the word for *their holy days* is *mo'adêhem.*[15] The reading *their holy days* is important in the interpretation because the commentator takes the verse to be predicting the Wicked Priest's attack on the Teacher and his community as they were observing the Day of Atonement. It may be that the expositor works with another meaning of the letters *m'd* ("to totter") when he writes that the Wicked Priest intended "to bring them to ruin [literally, to make them stumble] on the fast day" (11.8).

A different phenomenon appears in the treatment of the next verse. Hab. 2:16 in the Masoretic Text reads: "Drink, you yourself, and be circumcised *[he' arel]."* The text as cited in the *pesher* reads: "Drink, you yourself, and stagger *[hera' el]"* (WAC, 122, modified toward the NRSV). The latter seems the more fitting reading in the context, but in the comment on the passage the pesherist indicates that, while the text he has cited reads *stagger,* he knows about the reading *be circumcised:* "This refers to the priest whose disgrace became greater than his honor, because he had not circumcised his heart's foreskin" (1QpHab 11.12–13).

In a few instances the commentator leaves one with the impression that the prophetic message, expressed in coded form, could be deciphered by playing with the text in ways such as regrouping letters. In Hab. 1:12 we meet the words "O Rock, you have made them for rebuke *[wṣwr lmwkyḥw ysdtw]"* (5.1). The letters of *wṣwr lmwkyḥw* appear almost exactly in the interpretation but are divided differently: *bṣr lmw ky' hw'* ("in the time of their distress, for that is" [5.6]).[16]

We have seen that because the pesherists regularly identified terms in the biblical text with contemporary persons and events, these texts are some of the few sources of historical information about the Qumran group (see Chapter 12). We have references in the *Commentary on Habakkuk* to the Teacher and his opponents such as the Wicked Priest and the Man of the Lie, while in the *Commentary on Nahum* we read about the Angry Lion's crucifying of opponents and, unlike the other *pesharim,* we find in it the names of historical rulers (Antiochus and Demetrius). Here, too, we encounter the terms *Ephraim* (Pharisees) and *Manasseh* (perhaps Sadducees).

The *pesharim* are not the only literary expression of Qumran exposition of prophetic books. One example of a different sort can be found in the text called *Prophetic Apocryphon,* preserved in a series of fragmentary copies; it centers its attention on Ezekiel and Jeremiah and their books. Fragments from three copies of this work include sections that recount Ezekiel's vision in the valley of dry bones (Ezekiel 37). In the prophetic book, the vision has a brief introduction. "He [God] said to me, 'Mortal, can these bones live?' I [Ezekiel] answered, 'O Lord God, you know'" (37:3). In the Qumran work the passage is set in a different context:

> [And I said, "O Lord], I have seen many from Israel who have loved your name and have walked in the ways [of God]. When will [th]ese things come to pass? How shall their faithfulness be rewarded?" And the Lord said to me, "I myself take note of the Sons of Israel, and they shall know that I am the Lord." (4Q385 frag. 2, ll. 2–4 [WAC, 350–51])

A summary of the vision follows these words. Although the summary is shorter than Ezekiel's account of the vision, it adds that the many people who stood up "blessed the Lord of hosts" (l. 8; WAC, 350–51). So here the famous vision is recontextualized as the divine answer to Ezekiel's eschatological question and is perhaps understood as predicting a resurrection of faithful individuals in Israel.

Another familiar prophetic passage, this time one that received both *pesher* and non-*pesher* interpretation, is Isaiah 11. There the prophet writes: "A shoot shall come out from the stump of Jesse, and a branch shall grow out of its roots" (11:1). He goes on to describe the glorious gifts of the divine spirit that will rest upon the descendant of David and the ideal rule he will exercise. Not only will he judge justly and treat the poor fairly, but "he shall strike the earth with the rod of his mouth, and with the breath of his lips he shall kill the wicked" (11:4). The first *Commentary on Isaiah* (4Q161) quotes Isa. 11:1–5 in fragments 8 + 9 + 10, lines 15–20; the *pesher* on the passage reads:

> [This saying refers to the Branch of] David, who will appear in the Las[t Days, . . .] [. . .] his enemies; and God will support him with [a spirit of] strength [. . .] [. . . and God will give him] a glorious throne, [a sacred] crown, and elegant garments. [. . . He will put a] scepter in his hand, and he will rule over all the G[enti]les, even Magog [and his army . . . all] the peoples his sword will control. As for the verse that says, "He will not [judge only by what his eyes see], he will not decide only by what his ears hear," this means that [he will be advised by the Zadokite priests], and as they instruct him, so shall he rule, and at their command [he shall render decisions; and always] one of the prominent priests shall go out with him, in whose hands shall be the garments of [. . .]." (ll. 22–29 [WAC, 211])

This passage nicely illustrates how the commentator reads the text eschatologically (in this case mentioning the last days and referring to a messiah of David's line—the Branch of David—and perhaps also a priestly messiah—one of the prominent priests). The reference to Magog (from Ezekiel 38–39) further documents the point, as Gog and Magog became names for an eschatological enemy. It also includes a re-citation—a re-quotation—of part of the scriptural passage, which the commentator then subjects to special treatment.

The same passage underlies 4Q285 *(The War of the Messiah)*, fragment 5. Although some have read the fragment as if it were talking about a slain messiah, it is probably a description of the last battle in which the Davidic messiah slays his enemy as Isa. 11:4 prophesies he will:

> [. . . just as it is written in the book of] Isaiah the prophet, "And [the thickets of the forest] shall be cut down [with an ax, and Lebanaon with its majestic trees w]ill fall. A shoot shall come out from the stump of Jesse [and a branch shall grow out of his roots" (Isa. 10:34–11:1). This is the] Branch of David. Then [all forces of Belial] shall be judged, [and

the king of the Kittim shall stand for judgment] and the Leader of the nation—the Bra[nch of David]—will have him put to death. [Then all Israel shall come out with timbrel]s and dancers, and the [High] Priest shall order [them to cleanse their bodies from the guilty blood of the c]orpse[s of] the Kittim. (5.1–6 [WAC, 293])

For more discussion of this document, see Chapter 15, where the issue of a suffering messiah is examined.

Other Texts

Although many examples of scriptural interpretation may be attached to specific books or types of literature, other cases transcend these bounds. When we surveyed the nonbiblical scrolls from Qumran (Chapter 9), we noted that there were, besides the continuous *pesharim* described above, other works that we may call thematic *pesharim*. Major examples are *The Last Days: A Commentary on Selected Verses* (4Q174), *The Last Days: An Interpretation of Selected Verses* (4Q177), and *The Coming of Melchizedek* (11Q13). In that survey we looked at the content of these works, so there is no need to repeat all of the information here. An example or two should suffice.

In the *Melchizedek* text (see Figure 13.2), that mysterious figure known from Gen. 14:17–24, where he plays a role in the story about Abram's returning property and people to the king of Sodom, is brought into relation with a series of biblical texts dealing with the jubilee and the sabbatical year. Although the text is broken, it is clear enough that Lev. 25:13 (regarding the jubilee year) is being cited in 2.2; this citation is followed by Deut. 15:2, which deals with the year of remission, or sabbatical year. The Leviticus passage speaks about the return of property to its rightful owners in the jubilee, and the Deuteronomy verse mentions remission of debts in the seventh year. The writer tells us that the passage (or passages) refers to the last days and concerns captives. "Melchize]dek, who will return them to what is rightfully theirs. He will proclaim to them the jubilee, thereby releasing th[em from the debt of a]ll their sins" (2.5–6 [WAC, 456]). So, *debts* in Deuteronomy is read here as debts in the sense of *sins;* these will be remitted at the appointed time when Melchizedek judges. The sequel shows that a future jubilee period is meant, and mention of a jubilee period brings in its train the notion of atonement, because the Day of Atonement marked the beginning of a jubilee period. These thoughts are then developed further in connection with Melchizedek's role in the future judgment. A work such as this shows a process of association carried out by a writer who was intimately acquainted with a range of scriptural passages, which he was able to combine through verbal and thematic connections. It, like so much of Qumran exegesis, is eschatological, assuming that texts in the Hebrew Bible that seem addressed to the authors' times actually pertain to the last days.

At the end of this survey we should remind ourselves that the Dead Sea Scrolls are not the only surviving examples of scriptural interpretation from antiquity. Not only are examples found already in the Hebrew Bible, but the works in the Apocrypha and Pseudepigrapha offer many examples, as do the writings of Philo, Josephus, the New Testament, patristic literature, and the vast corpus of rabbinic commentary. A number of scholars have compared the techniques found in the scrolls with those attested in these other works, but that sort of study lies beyond the confines of an introduction to the Dead Sea Scrolls. Suffice it

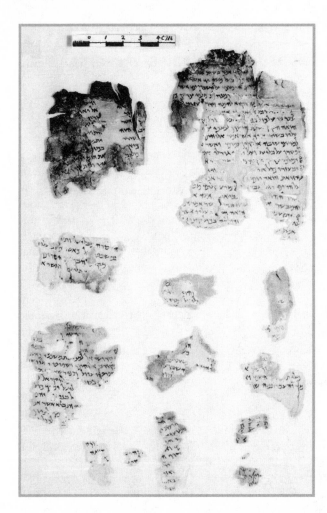

Figure 13.2
Fragments of *Melchizedek Text*
(11Q13) (PAM 43.979)
Courtesy of the Israel Antiquities Authority

to say that the Qumran exegetical practices would not have seemed strange in the late Second Temple period, although the remarkable claims to authoritative interpretation would have raised eyebrows—perhaps not so much because of the claims made, but because of who were making the claims.

Select Bibliography

For a survey of scriptural interpretation in the scrolls:

Fishbane, M. "Use, Authority and Interpretation of Mikra at Qumran." In M. J. Mulder, ed. *Mikra: Text, Translation, Reading, and Interpretation of the Hebrew Bible in Ancient Judaism and Early Christianity*. Compendia Rerum Iudaicarum ad Novum Testamentum 2.1. Assen: Van Gorcum; Minneapolis: Fortress, 1990. Pp. 339–77.

A vast compilation of interpretations of various pentateuchal passages as they appear in ancient sources is

Kugel, J. *The Bible As It Was.* Cambridge, MA, and London: Harvard University Press, Belknap Press, 1997.

————. *Traditions of the Bible: A Guide to the Bible As It Was at the Start of the Common Era.* Cambridge, MA, and London: Harvard University Press, 1998. An expanded version of the earlier book.

The standard work on the *pesharim*, giving texts, translations, and commentary:

Horgan, M. *Pesharim: Qumran Interpretations of Biblical Books.* Catholic Biblical Quarterly Monograph Series 8. Washington, DC: Catholic Biblical Association of America, 1979.

On the *Commentary on Habakkuk*, see

Brownlee, W. *The Text of Habakkuk in the Ancient Commentary from Qumran.* Journal of Biblical Literature Monograph Series 11. Philadelphia: Society of Biblical Literature, 1959.

————. *The Midrash Pesher of Habakkuk.* Society of Biblical Literature Monograph Series 24. Missoula, MT: Scholars Press, 1979.

Articles about the major texts treated in this chapter and their scriptural interpretation may be found in

Schiffman, L. H., and J. C. VanderKam, eds. *Encyclopedia of the Dead Sea Scrolls.* 2 vols. New York and Oxford: Oxford University Press, 2000. Especially:

   Bernstein, M. "Interpretation of Scriptures." 1:376–83.

Other studies include the following:

Bernstein, M. "Pentateuchal Interpretation at Qumran." In P. Flint and J. VanderKam, eds. *The Dead Sea Scrolls After Fifty Years: A Comprehensive Assessment.* 2 vols. Leiden: Brill, 1998–99. 1:128–59.

Brooke, G. *Exegesis at Qumran: 4QFlorilegium in Its Jewish Context.* Journal for the Study of the Old Testament, Supplement Series 29. Sheffield: JSOT Press, 1985.

Campbell, J. *The Use of Scripture in the Damascus Document 1–8, 19–20.* Beihefte zur Zeitschrift für die alttestamentliche Wissenschaft 228. Berlin and New York: DeGruyter, 1995.

Endres, J. *Biblical Interpretation in the Book of Jubilees.* Catholic Biblical Quarterly Monograph Series 18. Washington, DC: Catholic Biblical Association of America, 1987.

Knibb, M., trans. *The Ethiopic Book of Enoch.* 2 vols. Oxford: Clarendon Press, 1978. vol. 2.

Swanson, D. *The Temple Scroll and the Bible: The Methodology of 11QT.* Studies on the Texts of the Desert of Judah 14. Leiden: Brill, 1995.

VanderKam, J. "Biblical Interpretation in *1 Enoch* and *Jubilees*." In J. Charlesworth and C. Evans, eds. *The Pseudepigrapha and Early Biblical Interpretation.* Journal for the Study of the Pseudepigrapha, Supplement 14. Sheffield: Sheffield Academic Press, 1993. Pp. 98–117.

Vermes, G. "Bible Interpretation at Qumran." *Eretz Israel* 20 (1989): 184–91.

PART FOUR

The Scrolls and the New Testament

CHAPTER **14**

Were New Testament Scrolls Found at Qumran?

THE MATERIAL IN THIS CHAPTER DIFFERS FROM the rest of *The Meaning of the Dead Sea Scrolls* by including several Greek passages, which is necessary in view of the topic. Readers who have not studied Greek should nevertheless find the discussion of interest and fairly easy to follow.

Virtually all scholars agree that the scrolls found at Qumran were copied from about 250 BCE to 68 CE, when the Romans destroyed the community's settlement as they swept through Palestine on a campaign that was to include the destruction of Jerusalem and the catastrophe at Masada. Because several scrolls were copied during the lifetimes of Jesus and his apostles, many scholars have wondered whether any New Testament writings are preserved in the caves at Qumran. If such scrolls are preserved, the implications for long-held positions concerning the writing and development of the New Testament would be profound indeed.

The Proposal That New Testament Manuscripts Were Found at Qumran

In 1972 the Spanish scholar José O'Callaghan startled many biblical scholars with the announcement that he had identified several portions of New Testament documents in Cave 7 at Qumran.[1] This is a curious cave in that all the fragments found there were written on papyrus and in Greek, whereas the vast majority of the Dead Sea Scrolls were written on leather and in Hebrew or—to a lesser extent—in Aramaic (see Chapters 6, 8, and 9). O'Callaghan claimed that nine Greek fragments found in Cave 7 contain portions of six New Testament books: Mark, Acts, Romans, 1 Timothy, James, and 2 Peter. Dating eight of these fragments within the Qumran period (the exception being 7Q4 at about 100 CE), he described four identifications as certain, three as probable, and two as possible:

Manuscript	Contents	Identification	Date CE
7Q4	1 Tim. 3:16; 4:1, 3	Certain	ca. 100
7Q5	Mark 6:52–53	Certain	ca. 50
7Q6.1	Mark 4:28	Certain	ca. 50
7Q6.2	Acts 27:38	Probable	ca. 60
7Q7	Mark 12:17	Probable	ca. 50
7Q8	James 1:23–24	Certain	ca. 50–70
7Q9	Rom. 5:11–12	Probable	ca. 50–60
7Q10	2 Pet. 1:15	Possible	ca. 60
7Q15	Mark 6:48	Possible	ca. 50

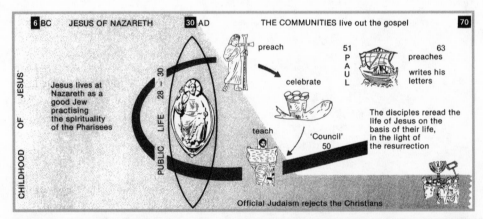

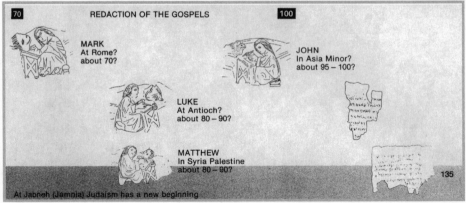

Figure 14.1

The Formation of the New Testament According to Most Scholars

Adapted from Etienne Charpentier. *How to Read the New Testament* (New York: Crossroad, 1982) 10–11. Used with permission.

If he is correct, O'Callaghan's identifications have far-reaching implications that pose enormous problems for scholars of early Christianity and the New Testament. First, they would mean either that early Christians had contact with the Qumran community, or that they hid their documents in one of the Qumran caves after the community had been dispersed in 68 CE. Second, it challenges long-held theories regarding the formation of the New Testament. If, as O'Callaghan alleges, parts of Mark, Acts, and several Epistles were found in Cave 7 and if his datings are correct, one may argue that many New Testament writings were completed far earlier than was previously supposed. This directly contradicts the findings of the vast majority of New Testament scholars, who conclude that most of the books listed were written some or many decades after 68 (see Figure 14.1).

Considering the Evidence More Closely

When we examine the Cave 7 fragments claimed by O'Callaghan to contain New Testament writings, several problems arise to challenge his proposal. First, we are dealing with very meager evidence, which is clear in Figure 14.2 below: the largest piece is fragment 7Q4.1, which measures a mere 6.8 by 3.4 cm. (2.7 by 1.3 ins.), while several more are tiny and preserve just a few letters. Furthermore, only five complete words clearly survive, none

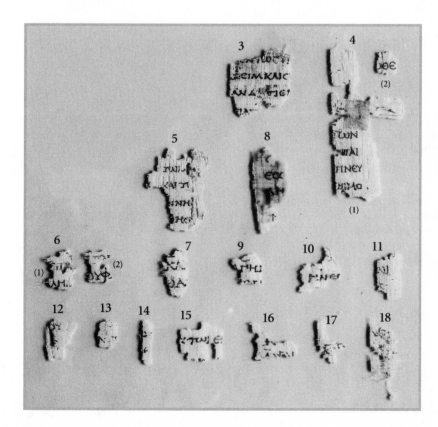

Figure 14.2

The Greek Fragments 7Q3–18 (PAM 42.961)

The photograph (plate xxx) and a transcription of the fragments (pp. 143–45) were published in 1962 by Maurice Baillet in DJD 3 (see Appendix IV). (Not included here are 7Q1 and 7Q2, which were earlier identified as containing parts of Exodus and the Epistle of Jeremiah, and 7Q19, which does not feature in O'Callaghan's identifications or the present discussion.)

Courtesy of the Israel Antiquities Authority

of which is distinctive enough to aid in identifying the passages involved. There are two cases of *and (kai)* on fragments 3 and 5, a single case of *what/something (ti)* on fragment 3, and two cases of *for the (tōi)* on fragments 5 and 15.

The second objection to O'Callaghan's thesis is his late dating of many manuscripts. The two Greek pieces from Cave 7 that were identified early on by scholars—7Q1 and 7Q2—are both dated at about 100 BCE (see below). Moreover, in the official edition of the fragments that O'Callaghan lists, one (7Q4) is dated at about 100 BCE and another (7Q5) at 50 BCE–50 CE (the others are not given dates since they preserve so few letters).[2] Like some other scholars who find alleged connections between the scrolls and the New Testament, O'Callaghan is obliged to date all the pieces listed by him to the mid-first century CE or later.

Third, the identifications made by O'Callaghan are tenuous and speculative. For example, his treatment of 7Q5, one of the largest fragments involved, relies on unconvincing evidence (see Figure 14.3).

In Box 14.1, the left column presents the Greek transcription of 7Q5 and a translation, with the extant letters in bold type and the reconstructed text in brackets. The standard text from Mark's Gospel and an English translation appears in the right column.[3] According to the traditional text, line 4 would be too long; O'Callaghan's reconstruction thus omits ἐπὶ τὴν γῆν *(to the land)* so that the words can line up correctly.[4] This variant reading is not supported by any significant manuscript of the New Testament, whether in Greek or in ancient languages.

Identifying the Greek Scrolls from Cave 7

LITTLE SUPPORT FOR O'CALLAGHAN'S VIEW

For many years, most scholars were quite mystified about the Greek fragments from Cave 7 at Qumran. O'Callaghan found few followers for his thesis; in 2000 the German scholar Stefan Enste even devoted an entire book on whether 7Q5 contains text from Mark

Figure 14.3
7Q5, one of the two largest fragments discussed by O'Callaghan.
Courtesy of the Israel Antiquities Authority

Box 14.1	*O'Callaghan's Reconstruction of 7Q5 Compared with Mark*

7Q5 (O'Callaghan)	Mark 6:52–54
[52οὐ γὰρ [συνῆκαν]ἐ[πὶ τοῖς ἄρτοις], [ἀλλ' ἦν α]ὐτῶν ἡ [καρδία πεπωρω-] [μέν]η. 53Καὶ τι[απεράσαντες] [ἦλθον εἰς Γε]ννησ[αρὲτ καὶ] [προσωρμίσ]θησα[ν. 54καὶ ἐξελ-] [θόντων αὐτῶν ἐκ τοῦ πλοίου εὐθὺς] [ἐπιγνόντες αὐτὸν]	52οὐ γὰρ συνῆκαν ἐπὶ τοῖς ἄρτοις, ἀλλ' ἦν αὐτῶν ἡ καρδία πεπωρω- μένη. 53Καὶ διαπεράσαντες ἐπὶ τὴν γῆν ἦλθον εἰς Γεννησαρὲτ καὶ προσωρμίσθησαν. 54καὶ ἐξελ- θόντων αὐτῶν ἐκ τοῦ πλοίου εὐθὺς ἐπιγνόντες αὐτὸν
[52For they did not] [understand] a[bout the loaves], [but t]heir [hearts were harden-] [e]d. 53And [when they had] cr[ossed over], [they came to Ge]nnes[aret and] [moored the] b]oa[t. 54And when they disem-] [barked from the boat, people straightaway] [recognized him.]	52For they did not understand about the loaves, but their hearts were harden- ed. 53And when they had crossed over, they came to the land at Gennesaret and moored the boat. 54And when they disem- barked from the boat, people straightaway recognized him.

6:52–53—and concluded that it does not.[5] Carsten Peter Thiede, however, embraced O'Callaghan's identification of several pieces from Cave 7 as containing text from the Gospels or the Epistles.[6] Most remained unconvinced, however—not only because of the challenges this theory posed to traditional views on the formation of the New Testament, but also because of the flimsy evidence on which it was based. To identify New Testament writings in tiny fragments such as 7Q6–7Q10 and 7Q15 seems speculative at best.

O'Callaghan's transcription of the larger fragment 5 has also been questioned, with some scholars offering different readings for certain lines. Graham Stanton lays out two varying transcriptions of the surviving Greek letters, shown in Box 14.2.[7]

It should be noted that 7Q5 is one of the larger fragments from Cave 7! With a grand total of five complete words preserved, none of which is distinctive, identifying the fragments 7Q3–18 is a formidable task indeed. Although many scholars have agreed what texts these fragments do *not* contain, it has proved a great challenge to say what they *do* contain.

PARTS OF THE GREEK BIBLE

The first two pieces from this cave, 7Q1 and 7Q2, were identified early on as containing excerpts from the Septuagint: Exod. 28:4–7 and the Epistle of Jeremiah 43–44.[8] Many scholars have reasonably concluded that most if not all the other fragments also preserve texts from the Greek Old Testament. Accordingly, in the edition of the Cave 7 fragments,[9] editor Maurice Baillet classified 7Q3–7Q5 as "biblical texts (?)," and Emanuel Tov has more recently suggested that all fragments from this cave are probably from the Septuagint.[10]

In 1992 the Spanish scholar Vittoria Spottorno proposed that 7Q5 preserves text from the book of Zechariah (7:3b–5),[11] and provided a transcription to support her view (see Box 14.3).

Box 14.2	**7Q5**

S. Pickering and R. Cook	*C. P. Thiede*
] . [	] ε [
] . τωι α . [	]υτωνη [
] η και τ. [	] η καιτι [
] ννη . [	] ννησ [
] θη . . [	] θησα [

Box 14.3	**7Q5**

Baillet (DJD 3, 1962)	*J. O'Callaghan (1972)*	*V. Spottorno (1992)*
] . [	] ε [	] τ [
] . τω α . [	] υτωνη [	] εγωνε [
] η και τω [	] η καιτι [	] ς και π [
εγε] ννησ [εν	] ννησ [	] ννησ [
] θηεσ [	] θησα [	] ωηεν [
		] ε [

Spottorno's identification, however, presents numerous problems, including doubtful readings of several Greek letters and variations from all known Greek texts of Zech. 7:3–5. These variants include: (a) In verse 4, her lineup of letters requires Spottorno to omit *of hosts* to produce the shorter reading *the Lord* (cf. LXX: *the Lord of hosts*). (b) In verse 5, her reconstruction requires a longer text: *the priests of the land* (LXX: *the priests*). (c) In the same verse, Spottorno proposes *in the fifth month* and *in the seventh month* (LXX: *in the fifth and the seventh months*).[12] Compare the translation based on Spottorno's reading of 7Q5 with the same passage translated from the Septuagint in Box 14.4.

PORTIONS OF *1 ENOCH*

A breakthrough was to come in the late 1980s and the 1990s—in a direction that few expected. It is fair to say that until then many scholars had focused on the New Testament or especially the Septuagint in the quest to identify the Greek fragments from Cave 7. In addition, most researchers had viewed individual fragments as representing different books or separate parts of books. New results, however, were achieved when other Jewish literature written in Greek was taken into account, and some fragments were pieced together or at least placed near each other in the original manuscript.

The German scholar Wilhelm Nebe and the French scholar Émile Puech concluded that several of the Cave 7 fragments are not from the New Testament or the Septuagint, but from the pseudepigraphical book of *1 Enoch*! Nebe proposed that 7Q4.1 is part of *1 Enoch* 103:3–4, that 7Q4.2 is from 98:11, and—with more reservation—that 7Q8 is from 103:7–8.[13] For his part, Puech reiterated that 7Q4.1 contains text from *1 Enoch* 103:3–4, but disagreed with Nebe's contention that 7Q4.2 is part of 98:11, preferring to place this fragment in *1 Enoch* 105:1. He further proposed that 7Q11 is part of *1 Enoch* 100:12, that 7Q13 belongs to 103:15, and that 7Q14 preserves traces of 103:12.[14] Some of these identifications were confirmed, and another was added, by the amateur American sleuth Ernest A. Muro, who succeeded in piecing together three tiny Greek fragments from Cave 7 (see below).

Building on the research of Nebe, Puech, and Muro with additional details, we may reconstruct 7Q4.1, 7Q8, and 7Q12 as preserving portions of *1 Enoch* 103:3–8 on two

---

Box 14.4	*Zechariah 7:3b–5*

Spottorno	*LXX*
[3]... "Should I mourn and practice abstinence in the fifth month, as I have done for so many years?" [4]Then the word of **the Lord** came to me: [5]Say to all the people of the land and to **the priests of the land**: When you fasted and lamented in **the fifth month and in the seventh month**, for these seventy years, was it for me that you fasted?	[3]... "The holy offering has come here in the fifth month, as it has already done for many years." [4]Then the word of **the Lord of hosts** came to me: [5]Say to all the people of the land and to **the priests**: Although you fasted or lamented **in the fifth and in the seventh months**, yes for these seventy years, was it for me that you fasted?

The Dead Sea Scrolls and Disney World

The contribution of Ernest A. Muro toward identifying the Greek scrolls from Cave 7 makes a fascinating story. Employed by the Disney company as a carpenter at Walt Disney World, Mr. Muro has confirmed the identification of the Greek fragments 7Q4.1, 7Q8, and 7Q12 as belonging to *1 Enoch* 103:3–8. As he studied the photographs of 7Q3–18, all written on papyrus (see Figure 14.4), Muro's expertise in different woods and their grain patterns caused him to focus on a distinctive feature common to some of the pieces: horizontal fibers with a characteristic downward slope to the right. By taking into consideration not only the Greek letters but the physical characteristics of the papyrus fragments themselves, Muro has played a significant role in solving the puzzle of the Cave 7 fragments. He writes:

> All previous efforts to identify these fragments had been hampered by the assumption that these fragments [i.e., 7Q4.1, 7Q8, and 7Q12] were originally from different scrolls. To the best of my knowledge no one had taken into consideration the unique characteristics of the papyrus fibers. The result was an impasse, as each fragment in itself was too small to identify with certainty. If it could be shown that these three fragments were originally related to each other in the scroll, then the impasse or difficulty would be resolved. . . . Because of the matching papyrus fibers, one should not attempt to identify three separate fragments but one ensemble that consists of three fragments. In essence, one is really dealing with one large fragment.[1]

1. Muro, "7QEnoch."

successive columns of a scroll. If Muro is correct in placing fragments 4.1 and 12 in one column and fragment 8 in the next one, the two columns must each have held about 17 lines, with about 24 letter spaces to the line. This calculation is made possible by the blank top margin on fragment 4.1, the right margins on fragments 4.1 and 12, and the left margin on fragment 8. A reconstruction is given in Figure 14.4; the Greek transcription and an English translation are provided in Box 14.5. In both cases the letters that are actually preserved on the Cave 7 fragments are printed in bold type. The identifications proposed by the three scholars all fall within the Epistle of Enoch (*1 Enoch* 91–107). This section of the pseudepigraphal book concerns the "two ways of the righteous and the sinner" and includes the Apocalypse of Weeks (91:12–17; 93:1–10).[15] (For further comments on *1 Enoch* at Qumran, see Chapter 8.)

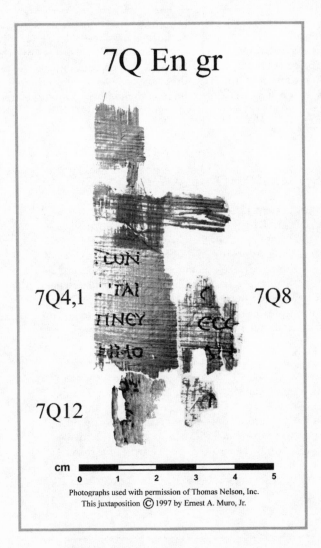

Figure 14.4
Reconstruction of 7Q4.1, 7Q8, and 7Q12 by Ernest A. Muro, Jr.
Used with permission.

Box 14.5	*7Q4.1, 7Q8, and 7Q12 Reconstructed (Muro)*

First Column (1 Enoch 103:3–7)	*Second Column* (1 Enoch 103:7–8)
[top margin]	[top margin]

First Column		Second Column	
[ται καὶ ἐγγέγραπται τ]**ῆ**	frag. 4.1	[τῶν ⁷αὐτοὶ ὑμεῖς γινώσκ-]	
[ς ψυχῆς τῶν ἀποθανόν]**τῶν**		[ετε ὅτι εἰς αἵδου κατάξου-]	
[εὐσεβῶν· ⁴καὶ χαιρήσο]**νται**		**σ**[ιν τὰς ψυχὰς ὑμῶν, ⁸καὶ ἐκεῖ]	frag. 8
[καὶ οὐ μὴ ἀπόλωται τὰ]**πνεύ-**		**ἔσο**[νται ἐν ἀνάγκηι μεγά-]	
[ματα αὐτῶν οὐδὲ τὸ μυ]**ημό-**		**λη**[ι καὶ ἐν σκότει καὶ ἐ-]	
[συνον ἀπὸ προσώπου]**τοῦ**	frag. 12	**ν**[παγίδα καὶ ἐν φλογὶ καιομένηι],	
[μεγάλου εἰς πάσας τὰς γ]**ε-**		[καὶ εἰς κρίσιν μεγάλην εἰσ-]	
[νεὰς τῶν αἰώνων. μὴ οὖν φο-]		[ελεύσονται αἱ ψυχαὶ ὑμῶν]	
[βεῖσθε τοὺς ὀνειδισμοὺς]		[ἐν πάσαις ταῖς γενεαῖς τοῦ]	
[αὐτῶν ⁵καὶ ὑμεῖς, οἱ νεκροὶ]		[αἰῶνος. οὐαὶ ὑμῖν, οὐκ ἔστ-]	
[τῶν ἁμαρτωλῶν, ὅταν ἀποθάν-]		[ιν ὑμῖν χαίρειν.]	
[ητε ἐροῦσιν ἐφ ὑμῖν, μακάρι-]			
[οι ἁμαρτωλοὶ πάσας τὰς ἡμέ-]			
[ρας αὐτῶν ὅσας εἴδοσαν ἐν]			
[τῆι ζωῆι αὐτῶν, καὶ ἐνδόξως]			
[⁶ἀπεθάνοσαν, καὶ κρίσις]			
[οὐκ ἐγενήθη ἐν τῆι ζωῆι αὐ-]			

English Translation: 1 Enoch 103:3–8

³[for good things and joy and honor have been prepared and written down for th]e [souls of the godly on]es who [have died. ⁴And **they** will rejo]ice, [and their] **spi**[rits will never perish, nor their me]**mo**[rial from the presence] **of the** [Great One for all g]e[nerations forever. So do not be afraid of their reproaches].

⁵[But as for you, you corpses of sinners, when you die, people will say concerning you: "Blessed are the sinners; they have seen all their days, so many, in their lifetime, and ⁶they have died in honor, and no judgment has been imposed in their lifetime." ⁷(But) you yourselves realize that] **th**[ey will drag your souls down to Hades. ⁸And there] they **w**[ill be in gr]**ea**[t anguish, and in darkness, and e]**n**[trapped and in a burning fire; and your souls will enter into the great judgment for all generations forever. Woe to you, (for) you are not able to rejoice]!

(Adapted from R. H. Charles, *The Apocrypha and Pseudepigrapha of the Old Testament.*)

Progress Made in Identifying the Fragments

The research of Nebe, Puech, and Muro suggests that 7Q4.1, 7Q8, 7Q12, and 7Q14 contain text from *1 Enoch* 103:3–8, 12; 7Q4.2 contains text from 98:11 or 105:1; 7Q11 contains text from 100:12; and 7Q13 contains text from 103:15. Although we are dealing with pieces of a damaged scroll, these three scholars make a reasonable case for identifying seven of the numbered Cave 7 fragments as containing text from *1 Enoch*.

If these identifications are correct, they show that a Greek copy of *1 Enoch* existed at Qumran and confirm the importance of this book for the Qumran community (as it was for Jude, who cites *1 Enoch* 1:9 in vv. 14–15 of his Epistle). The new classifications also yield a "new" scroll (pap7QEn gr) from a group of previously unidentified fragments. It should be noted, however, that in his recent commentary on *1 Enoch* one prominent scholar remains unconvinced that the text in these fragments is from the pseudepigraphical book.[16]

But what of other fragments discussed by O'Callaghan that were not dealt with by Nebe, Puech, and Muro? These three authors have suggested identifications for only two pieces listed by the Spanish scholar—7Q4 and 7Q8—but have made no proposals for 7Q5, 7Q6.1, 7Q6.2, 7Q7, 7Q9, 7Q10, and 7Q15. Could these fragments preserve words from New Testament writings? Until they can be identified with certainty, which may never be possible, it remains theoretically feasible that some pieces may contain tiny portions of early New Testament books such as Mark. It is far more likely, however, that the unidentified Greek fragments from Cave 7 preserve text from the Septuagint (as in frag. 1), the Apocrypha (frag. 2), or the pseudepigraphical book of *1 Enoch*.

Select Bibliography

Charles, R. H. *The Apocrypha and Pseudepigrapha of the Old Testament.* 2 vols. Oxford: Clarendon Press, 1913.

Flint, P. W. "'Apocrypha,' Other Previously-Known Writings, and 'Pseudepigrapha' in the Dead Sea Scrolls." In P. Flint and J. VanderKam, eds. *The Dead Sea Scrolls After Fifty Years: A Comprehensive Assessment.* 2 vols. Leiden: Brill, 1998–99. 2:24–66, esp. 42–43.

Isaac, E. "1 (Ethiopic Apocalypse of) Enoch." In Charlesworth, J. H., ed. *The Old Testament Pseudepigrapha.* 2 vols. Garden City, NY: Doubleday, 1983–85. 1:5– 89, esp. 72–89.

Muro, E. A. "7Q Enoch: A Synopsis of the Identification Process." http://www.breadofangels.com/7qenoch/synopsis.html.

———."The Greek Fragments of Enoch from Qumran Cave 7 (7Q4, 7Q8, & 7Q12 = 7QEn gr = Enoch 103:3–4, 7–8)." *Revue de Qumrân* 18/70 (1997): 307–12.

Nebe, G. W. "7Q4—Möglichkeit und Grenze einer Identifikation." *Revue de Qumrân* 13/49–52 (Carmignac Memorial, 1988): 629–33.

O'Callaghan, J. "¿Papiros neo–testamentarios en la cueva 7 de Qumrân?" *Biblica* 53 (1972): 91–100. English translation: W. L. Holladay. "New Testament Papyri in Qumrân Cave 7?" Supplement to the *Journal of Biblical Literature* 91 (1972): 1– 14.

Puech, É. "Notes sur les fragments grecs du manuscrit 7Q4 = 1 Hénoch 103 et 105." *Revue Biblique* 103 (1996): 592–600.

———."Sept fragments de la Lettre d'Hénoch (1 Hén 100, 103 et 105) dans la grotte 7 de Qumrân (= 7QHén gr)." *Revue de Qumrân* 18/70 (1997): 313–23.

Stanton, G. *Gospel Truth? New Light on Jesus and the Gospels.* Valley Forge, PA: Trinity, 1995. Pp. 20–32.

Thiede, C. P. *Rekindling the Word: In Search of Gospel Truth.* Leominster, UK: Gracewing; Valley Forge, PA: Trinity, 1995. Pp. 189–97.

CHAPTER 15

Jesus and the Dead Sea Scrolls: The Gospels and Qumran

WRITERS ON THE SUBJECT OF RELATIONS BETWEEN the scrolls and the New Testament, or between the people of the scrolls and the first Christians, have offered a range of views. On one side is a decided minority who say that the scrolls are in fact Christian texts—if only we knew how to read them properly—or that several of these documents contain references to Jesus and new revelations about his life. Those on the other side, one that is more heavily populated, claim that the scrolls are of indirect relevance to Jesus and early Christianity, but that they illuminate many aspects of Jesus' life and teaching and many events and doctrines of the New Testament.

Examination of the Dead Sea Scrolls shows that they never mention any Christian individuals by name and were not written by Christian authors. They do, however, throw welcome light on the Gospels by (1) providing helpful information about Jewish society, groups, practices, and beliefs at the time; (2) increasing our knowledge about early Judaism, which makes it clear that many aspects of the Gospel message are indebted to the mother religion; (3) helping us see in sharper outline some of the basic differences between the message of Jesus and that of other Jewish groups; and (4) providing new texts with wording similar to certain Gospel passages, which shows that some or much of Jesus' teaching was anticipated in earlier texts, rather than being the product of the later church.

Early Speculations

Long before the discovery of the Dead Sea Scrolls, several alleged links were identified between the Essenes—as described by Josephus, Philo, and Pliny the Elder—and Jesus. As early as 1790, a writer named Karl Bahrdt tried to account for the mysteries in Jesus' life by suggesting that he was a "secret agent" of the Essenes. Later, in 1863, the renowned biblical scholar Ernest Renan proposed that Jesus had been trained by the Essenes.

Such speculation was given added impetus when the scrolls came to light in 1947. Many scholars recognized that these ancient documents have several implications for our understanding of Jesus and his ministry and for several other aspects of New Testament studies (see Chapter 16). This is only to be expected, since the almost 900 texts that were discovered in the region of the Dead Sea date from about 250 BCE to the later first century CE, which, of course, includes the life of Jesus and the growth of the early church.

Since the discovery, several writers have sought to make connections between Jesus and the Essene movement. The journalist Edmund Wilson, for example, published several articles on the Dead Sea Scrolls in the *New Yorker* magazine, which maintained—among other things—that Jesus had spent his childhood years with the Essenes. These pieces were collected in 1955 in a slim volume entitled *The Scrolls from the Dead Sea,* and expanded in 1969 as *The Dead Sea Scrolls: 1947–1969.*[1] In 1962, Charles Francis Potter proposed that Jesus was a mere human whose teachings about God and his messianic ideas had been shaped by the Essenes.[2]

Perhaps the most brilliant early insights were offered by the French scholar André Dupont-Sommer. In 1950, when the contents of only a few scrolls were known, he argued that Jesus appeared to be an "astonishing reincarnation" of the Teacher of Righteousness:

> Everything in the Jewish New Covenant heralds and prepares the way for the Christian New Covenant. The Galilean Master, as He is presented in the writings of the New Testament, appears in many respects as an astonishing reincarnation of the Master of Justice [i.e., the Teacher of Righteousness]. Like the latter He preached penitence, poverty, humility, love of one's neighbour, chastity. Like him, He prescribed the observance of the Law of Moses, the whole Law, but the Law finished and perfected, thanks to His own revelations. Like him He was the Elect and the Messiah of God, the Messiah redeemer of the world. Like him He was the object of the hostility of the priests, the party of the Sadducees. Like him He was condemned and put to death. Like him He pronounced judgement on Jerusalem, which was taken and destroyed by the Romans for having put Him to death. Like him, at the end of time he will be the supreme judge.[3]

Although such lofty language gives the initial impression that Dupont-Sommer saw real connections between the Essenes of Qumran and early Christianity, this is not the case. He continues:

> The Master of Justice died about 65–63 B.C.; Jesus the Nazarene died about A.D. 30. In every case where the resemblance compels or invites us to think of a borrowing, this was on the part of Christianity. But on the other hand, the appearance of faith in Jesus—the foundation of the New Church—can scarcely be explained without the real historic activity of a new Prophet, a new Messiah, who rekindled the flame and concentrated on Himself the adoration of men.[4]

We should also note that several other early authors, whose writings on the subject were not as dramatic as those mentioned so far—and thus did not receive as much attention—discussed the similarities and differences between Jesus and the Teacher of Righteousness. One such writer was William LaSor, who wrote on this theme as part of a wider book on the contribution of the scrolls for understanding the Christian faith.[5]

Sensationalism, New Age Religion, and the Scrolls

Recognizing that different views exist on many issues, in *The Meaning of the Dead Sea Scrolls* we have tried to avoid unnecessary criticism of other scholars. Discussions of Jesus and the scrolls, however, have included several theories that can only be described as unfounded, even bizarre, and that are not accepted by recognized scholars in the field. We now describe and assess three such theories or approaches in this section.

JOHN ALLEGRO AND THE SACRED MUSHROOM

John Marco Allegro was part of the original team of Dead Sea Scrolls editors, which he joined in 1953, and was appointed to the faculty of the University of Manchester in 1954. He succeeded in bringing the *Copper Scroll* to the university for opening and quickly published the Cave 4 scrolls entrusted to him, first in journals, and officially in 1968.[6] Unfortunately, this edition contains so many errors that it must be used in conjunction with a 114-page article written by John Strugnell a few years later to provide the necessary corrections.[7] A revision of the British scholar's volume has since been assigned to a new team of scholars.[8] With respect to this carelessness on Allegro's part, Philip Davies generously writes: "The edition has been criticized as careless, and it is clear that Allegro was more interested in the wide dissemination of the contents of the scrolls."[9]

Allegro also conducted excavations at and near Qumran and took many photographs of the site and the texts. More than any other early editor, he made the contents of a great number of scrolls available to the public and sought to disseminate information about them. In addition to several books and many newspaper articles, he made a documentary on the Dead Sea Scrolls for the British Broadcasting Corporation (BBC), which was aired in 1959.

At one time a candidate for the Methodist ministry, John Allegro became increasingly agnostic and critical of traditional Christianity over the years. In his own popular book on the scrolls, which was published in 1956,[10] his conclusions about Jesus and the scrolls were quite nuanced and relatively restrained, for example:

> We should be wise at this stage to avoid too dogmatic assertions about the life of the Teacher or the manner of his death, or make too sweeping comparisons or contrasts with the Christian Master. . . .
>
> Some of the scrolls seem to have more relevance for urban Essenism than the ascetic life of the Qumran monastery. There must however have been considerable differences between these two branches of the movement, and Jesus would have been better acquainted with Essenes in the towns and villages than those in such monastic communities as Qumran. . . .
>
> My own opinion is that the scrolls prompt us increasingly to seek an eschatological meaning for most of Jesus' reported sayings: more and more become intelligible when viewed in the light of the imminent cataclysm of Qumran expectations, and the inner conflict in men's hearts as the time drew near.[11]

Allegro's views soon became increasingly vocal and radical. In 1956 he announced on a BBC program that he had found a text at Qumran describing the community as worshiping a crucified Messiah who they believed would return in glory. Allegro had in mind 1.4–9 of the *Commentary on Nahum*, which specifically mentions crucifixion; according to him, this passage teaches that the Angry Lion or Wicked Priest crucified the *seekers of smoothness* as well as the Teacher of Righteousness, who would rise again:

> [Jannaeus, that is, the Angry Lion] descended on Qumran and arrested its leader, the mysterious "Teacher of Righteousness," whom he turned over to his mercenaries to be

crucified. . . . When the Jewish king had left, [the Qumran sectarians] took down the broken body of their Master to stand guard over it until Judgment Day. . . . They believed their Master would rise again and lead his faithful flock (the people of the new testament, as they called themselves) to a new and purified Jerusalem. . . . What is clear is that there was a well-defined Essenic pattern into which Jesus of Nazareth fits.[12]

For the British scholar, these words summarize a common first-century Judean superstition, of which belief in the death, resurrection, and return of Jesus was but another example. Such sensational views, and the claim that the scrolls provided concrete evidence for them, caused several other members of the editorial team (de Vaux, Milik, Skehan, Starcky, and Strugnell) to write a letter to the London *Times,* denying that there was any "close connection between the supposed crucifixion of the 'teacher of righteousness' of the Essene sect and the crucifixion and resurrection of Jesus Christ."[13] According to these scholars, Allegro had "misread the texts, or he has built up a chain of conjectures which the materials do not support."[14] Allegro came to believe that he was being victimized for his views, and that publication of some scrolls was being suppressed by the other, Christian—notably Catholic—editors because they contained information which, if made public, would be disturbing and even prove dangerous for traditional Christianity.

But more was to come. In what can only be described as a notorious book, *The Sacred Mushroom and the Cross: A Study of the Nature and Origins of Christianity Within the Fertility Cults of the Ancient Near East* (1970),[15] Allegro proposed that early Christianity was a orgiastic fertility cult that made use of a hallucinogenic mushroom containing the drug psilocybin. Moreover, Jesus never actually existed, but was invented by early Christians under the influence of this drug. (Two additional tidbits: the name *Jesus* means "Semen, which saves," and *Peter* means "mushroom.") The absurdity of these allegations led fourteen prominent British scholars (including his mentor at Oxford, Godfrey Driver) to repudiate *The Sacred Mushroom and the Cross,* and the publisher apologized for issuing the book. Allegro resigned his university post and remained in academic and literary exile until his death at the relatively young age of sixty-five in 1988 (for further details, see Chapter 18).

John Allegro's ideas on Jesus and early Christianity are most fully articulated in *The Dead Sea Scrolls and the Christian Myth* (1979),[16] in which he claimed to identify a mystical tradition connected with the hallucinogenic mushroom out of which the myth of Jesus arose. He believed that the writers of the Gospels, who did not understand Essene thought, took the symbolic narratives found in many scrolls for literal truth, giving rise to traditional Christianity. Allegro also traced several key ideas and practices found in early Christianity and Gnosticism from texts found among the Dead Sea Scrolls. The following lengthy excerpt, from a chapter entitled "Will the *Real* Jesus Christ Please Stand Up?" clearly illustrates Allegro's view that (1) what he termed *Gnostic Christianity* arose from the Essene movement; (2) there was no historical person named Jesus Christ in first-century Palestine; and (3) the Jesus of the Gospels is an adaptation of the Teacher of Righteousness.

What is new, thanks largely to the Dead Sea Scrolls, is our ability now to recognize in the so-called intertestamental period . . . that the Essene movement produced just the right mix of early Canaanite folk-religion, prophetic Yahwism, Babylonian magic, and Iranian dualism to have produced Gnostic Christianity. What it could not produce, and never did, was an historical Joshua/Jesus Messiah living in Palestine during the first century AD and bearing any real resemblance to the benign, improbably naïve, not to say downright igno-rant, conjecturer-prophet that popular imagination has largely created out of the Gospels.

Behind the Jesus of western religious tradition there did exist in history an Essene Teacher of Righteousness of a century before. He was a leader of men, but not a magi-cian. . . . He led his followers into the desert and with them endured great privations and disappointments, not least with dissidents inside his own community. He believed that the suffering he shared with his people had a propitiatory role in the salvation of Is-rael. . . . He believed he was following in the footsteps of a previous Joshua/Jesus who had led the Israelites into the Promised Land, and, like him, he set out for the men of his Covenant a Way, based upon the Law which had first been revealed to Moses and which now must be reinterpreted to serve the new situation. Because we now have in our hands the literary record of that Way, thanks to the discoveries by the Dead Sea, we can see how the revelation became further adapted under the pressure of socio-political events of the first century to serve people on the fringes of Judaism, or completely outside that dis-pensation, as an expression of an intensely personal faith.

This was the religion that became characterized as messianism, or "Christianity" . . . [17]

Assessment: Surveying Allegro's legacy from the viewpoint of a new century, we may identify several positive aspects: his work on the *Copper Scroll;* his prompt publication of the manuscripts entrusted to him; making the contents of many scrolls available to the public; his conviction that these ancient documents were of vital relevance to the wider society, not just to scholars; and his realization that many scrolls were of great significance for our understanding of Jesus and Christian origins.

Yet it was Allegro's poor scholarship and bizarre views on Christian origins that resulted in his being forced to resign his academic position and lose his credibility. These negative aspects include the most careless and poorly produced volume among all the of-ficial editions of the Dead Sea Scrolls;[18] use of the scrolls to promote views that were extreme and far beyond legitimate differences between scholars; viewing Christianity as a fertility cult that made use of an hallucinogenic mushroom; proposing that Jesus never actually existed as a historical person; viewing the Jesus of the Gospels as an adaptation of the Teacher of Righteousness; and believing that a conspiracy existed to suppress publica-tion of some scrolls because they contained explosive information about the character of Jesus and other Christian doctrines.

One writer has called Allegro the "father of Scroll sensationalists,"[19] since his influence can be detected in the writings of several authors who have been critical of traditional views on Jesus (e.g., Edmund Wilson) or who maintain that the contents of the scrolls have been deliberately suppressed (e.g., Michael Baigent and Richard Leigh; the cover descrip-tion of their book, *The Dead Sea Scrolls Deception,* is particularly revealing: "Why a hand-ful of religious scholars conspired to suppress the revolutionary contents of the Dead Sea Scrolls").[20]

BARBARA THIERING'S PESHER TECHNIQUE FOR UNDERSTANDING THE GOSPELS

Like Allegro, the Australian scholar Barbara Thiering (lecturer at the Sydney University School of Divinity from 1967 to 1993) is trained in biblical studies and has done a con-siderable amount of research on the scrolls. As presented in her 1992 book, *Jesus and the*

Riddle of the Dead Sea Scrolls,[21] Thiering understands the Gospels as coded Essene documents, which can be read on two levels. The events depicted in the Gospels are on the surface level, which is meant "for babes in Christ," whereas the real events that took place are on a deeper level, which can only be understood by her *pesher technique.* Just as the *pesharim* explain to readers the true meaning of various biblical texts (see Chapter 9), Thiering maintains that her pesher technique is required to unlock the real meaning of the Gospels, thereby revealing the events that actually took place. This is because the New Testament was written in a cryptic code, with the aim of deliberately concealing historical events and persons.

Information from the Gospels that now becomes clear (according to the pesher technique) includes the following: *John the Baptist* is really the Teacher of Righteousness; *Jesus of Nazareth* is his opponent the Wicked Priest (also called the Man of the Lie); and the Essene group split into two factions, the first led by John (the Teacher) and the second by Jesus (the Wicked Priest). For Thiering, most of the personal names mentioned in the Gospels also have a deeper meaning; thus *Abraham* is really Hillel the Great, *Ananias* is the name used for Simon Magus, *Apostles* means John Mark (the plural is used because Mark represented a class), and *All* refers to King Herod Agrippa I.

Similarly, place-names in the Gospels must be understood as referring to geographical locations in the Qumran area; thus *Jerusalem* almost always denotes Khirbet Qumran, the *Sea of Galilee* is the Dead Sea, and the *Jordan River* is really a stream named Wadi Sekhakha (which flows into Wadi Qumran). Thiering places much of Jesus' activity at sites near Qumran, notably Ain Feshkha (where Qumran monks supposedly went when expelled for episodes of uncleanness), Mazin (associated with Essenes in the married state), Khirbet Mird (where the more Westernized Essenes met), and Mar Saba (a place on the pilgrim route that was frequented by ascetics).

Her reconstruction of Jesus' life can only be described as eccentric or bizarre, reading into the Gospels material that is simply not there: Jesus marries Mary Magdalene twice, he is crucified near the Qumran complex but does not die, his unconscious body is placed in Cave 8, and he later lives out his days in Rome as an old man (see Table 15.1). The following excerpt sufficiently illustrates Barbara Thiering's approach and method:

> Jesus did not die on the cross. He recovered from the effects of the poison, was helped to escape from the tomb by friends, and stayed with them until he reached Rome, where he was present in AD 64. This is not conjecture, but comes from a reading of the text by the pesher method. Its basic assumption is that nothing supernatural took place, no visions: these are the fictions for "babes."

Since Thiering situates much of the Gospel story and the life of Jesus at Qumran, it comes as no surprise that she challenges the conclusions of most scholars on when the scrolls were copied. There is now widespread agreement that the manuscripts discovered at Qumran (the vast majority of the Dead Sea Scrolls) were copied from about 250 BCE to 68 CE, when the Qumran settlement was destroyed by the Romans (see Chapter 2). Furthermore, most of the key manuscripts date from the first century BCE or earlier, with relatively few having been copied in the first century CE. In other words, many Dead Sea Scrolls describe events or ideas before the time of Jesus and are not contemporary with his message.

This presents an obstacle for Barabara Thiering, since her theory requires that the Teacher of Righteousness and his associates—whom she identifies with John the Baptist, Jesus, and others—lived under Roman rule in the first century CE. She thus goes to considerable lengths to show that the dates arrived at by other scholars by means of paleography are subjective, and misleadingly speaks of "uncritical reliance on paleography" being "trenchantly criticized by the new generation of scrolls scholars." If anything, the new generation of scrolls scholars inclines toward even earlier datings for the scrolls and supports the general findings of paleography in the light of carbon-14 methods of dating that include Accelerator Mass Spectrometry (AMS) testing (see Chapter 2). Thiering pays some attention to the results of AMS testing, but draws incorrect conclusions from them.

Assessment: As we have seen, despite John Allegro's poor editing skills and his strange views on Christian origins, there were several positive aspects to his research and writings. Unfortunately, the same cannot be said for Barbara Thiering, at least where the Dead Sea Scrolls are concerned. Her views and theories on Jesus and Christian origins have little basis in the scrolls, and even less in the New Testament. Her pesher technique misuses the concept of *pesher,* her datings of the scrolls are suspect and seem informed by an outside agenda, the connections she draws between Qumran and other nearby communities in the Judean Desert are highly questionable, and the links she finds between the scrolls and the New Testament are almost always without foundation.

THE DEAD SEA SCROLLS AND THE NEW AGE JESUS

Because of the mysterious origins of the Dead Sea Scrolls, the alleged secrecy surrounding their publication, and the esoteric nature of the Essenes, the scrolls have attracted a goodly share of intrigue and speculation. When we add to this the mystery of what Jesus did or where he went in the years before he was baptized in the Jordan, it comes as no surprise that some writers find in these ancient documents a Jesus very different from the Christ of faith and history. This has already become apparent in the cases of John Allegro and Barbara Thiering, but there is one crucial difference between them and the writers to whom we now turn. Whereas those two scholars were trained in Hebrew and biblical Studies, the authors mentioned below have had little or no training in the field, although they focus on the Essenes or make use of the scrolls to a greater or lesser extent.

In 1928 Edmond Bordeaux Székely founded the "International Biogenic Society" and published Book One of *The Essene Gospel of Peace.* Over the next half century, Books Two to Four appeared, with the subtitles *The Unknown Books of the Essenes, Lost Scrolls of the Essene Brotherhood,* and (published posthumously in 1982) *The Teachings of the Elect.* The contents of these works appear to be a mixture of New Age philosophy and Eastern religion; note two other works by Székely: *The Essene Book of Asha: Journey to the Cosmic Ocean,* and *Cosmotherapy of the Essenes: Unity of Man, Nature and the Universe.* Few of Székely's books contain any substantial discussion of the Dead Sea Scrolls; one exception would seem to be his *Teachings of the Essenes from Enoch to the Dead Sea Scrolls.*[22] This is evidently not the case, however, since the volume is billed as "one of the best introductions to the Essene Christianity," which "explores the Essene communions and meditation practice." Chapters include "The Essenes and Their Teaching," "The Essene Tree of Life,"

Table 15.1	*Jesus' Life According to Barbara Thiering*	
Date	**Event**	**Parallel References**
7 BCE (Sun., March 1)	Birth of Jesus.	Luke 1:56
5 BCE (Fri., Sept. 1)	Joseph comes out of hiding from Qumran *(Egypt).*	Matt. 2:15
6 CE (Mon., March 1)	Mary re-enacts her birth in a ceremony.	Rev. 12:1–2
29 CE (Tues., March 8)	At 6 AM, John the Baptist baptizes Jesus in running water at Qumran. A schism then breaks out.	John 1:35; Mark 1:9; Matt. 3:13–15
(Tues., March 8)	At 3 PM, Jesus is rebaptized by Jonathan Annas *(the Spirit),* who joins him in the schism.	Mark 10:1–11; Matt. 3:16–17
30 CE (Tues., June 6)	Betrothal of Jesus and Mary Magdalene at Ain Feshkha *(Cana).*	John 2:1–11
(Thurs., Sept. 21)	The wedding of Jesus and Mary at Ain Feshkha, with Simon Magus officiating as deacon.	Luke 7:36; cf. 7:44
31 CE (Wed., March 21)	Jesus leaves Ain Feshkha, arrives at Qumran.	John 2:13
(Fri., June 22)	Jesus baptizes at the southeast section of Qumran.	John 3:22
32 CE (Tues., Sept. 2)	Jesus stays at Ain Feshkha rather than Qumran (i.e., he does not profess full celibacy).	John 7:1–9
(Wed., Dec. 3)	Jesus arrives at Qumran, is told that Simon Magus–Lazarus is in Cave 4. He orders the release of Simon from the cave.	John 11:17–18, 38–44
33 CE (Thurs., March 19)	Second wedding of Jesus and Mary Magdalene at Ain Feshkha.	John 12:1–8; Mark 14:3–9
(Thurs., March 19)	The evening communal meal begins at Qumran.	Mark 14:17; Matt. 26:20; John 13:2–11
(Thurs., March 19)	Jesus prays to God in the grounds of the monastery at Qumran.	Mark 14:32–39; Matt. 26:36–42; Luke 22:41–42
(Fri., March 20)	The trial of Jesus before the high priest Caiaphas, and Peter's denial of Jesus.	John 18:12–27; Mark 14:53–65; Matt. 26:57–75; Luke 22:54–71

"The Essene Communions: Their Purpose and Meaning," "The Essene Communions: Their Actual Practice," and "The Sevenfold Peace."

Another figure who made pronouncements about the Essenes and New Testament characters was Edgar Cayce. Known as the "sleeping prophet," this famous psychic gave readings and uttered predictions on a variety of subjects while in a sleeplike trance. Although he died in 1945, well before the Dead Sea Scrolls were discovered, several of Cayce's statements on the Essenes locate them at places in the Holy Land. His pronouncements on this theme were collected in a 1970 volume called *Edgar Cayce on the Dead Sea Scrolls.*[23] According to Cayce, the group taught reincarnation and was headquartered on Mt. Carmel, where they had a temple. Mary, Elizabeth, and John the Baptist were members, and Joseph and Mary were married in the Essene temple. Furthermore, an "entity"

Table 15.1	*(continued)*

Date	Event	Parallel References
33 CE (Fri., March 20)	Pilate gives the order for Jesus' execution.	John 19:13–16
(Fri., March 20)	Jesus is crucified at Qumran "in the unclean area near the unstepped cistern" at Qumran, together with Simon Magus and Judas.	John 19:23–24; Mark 15:25–27; Luke 23:33–38; Matt. 27:36–38
(Fri., March 20)	In intolerable pain, Jesus drinks "snake poison"—which he earlier refused—and loses consciousness.	John 19:28–30; Mark 15:34–37; Luke 23:46–47; Matt. 27:46–51
(Fri., March 20)	The bodies of Simon Magus and Judas are placed in Cave 7. James leaves the unconscious Jesus in Cave 8, and departs through the opening above Cave 7.	John 19:42; Mark 15:42–46; Luke 23:54; Matt. 27:57–60
(Sat., March 21)	Peter and John enter Cave 8 and find Jesus able to walk.	*Gospel of Peter* 10:36–39
(Sat., March 21)	The evening common meal is held at Ain Feshkha; at the hour of the sacred wine or teaching, Jesus appears.	John 20:19–23
(Sun., March 22)	During his recovery from the crucifixion, Jesus is under the rule of the sick, and must stay outside Qumran for three days.	*Temple Scroll* 45.7–12
(Tues., March 24)	Jesus arrives back at Qumran.	*Temple Scroll* 45.9
58 CE (Wed., June 7)	Many years later, Jesus and Luke go to Qumran.	Acts 21:15–16
(Sat., June 24)	Jesus appoints Paul as bishop/martyr to Rome.	Acts 23:11
60 CE	Jesus journeys to Rome with Paul, Peter, and Luke.	Acts 27:1
64 CE	Jesus is now 70 years old.	
After 64 CE	Jesus probably dies of old age in seclusion in Rome.	

named Josie was chosen by the Essene Brotherhood to accompany Joseph and Mary on the flight to Egypt.

Several more figures could be mentioned who try to link the Essenes or the Dead Sea Scrolls with New Age philosophy, reincarnation, angels, and the like. One is Dolores Cannon, whose book *Jesus and the Essenes*[24] purports to offer fresh insights on Christ's ministry. Cannon is a regressionist and hypnotherapist who takes people back to earlier lives and specializes in the recovery and cataloging of "lost" knowledge. Since one of her clients was allegedly a member of the Qumran community in a past life, the book takes the form of direct dialogues between a modern researcher and this ancient Essene, who lived around the time of Christ. Among other features, *Jesus and the Essenes* describes the purpose of the community, offers new details surrounding the birth and upbringing of Jesus and John the Baptist, and provides Essene renderings of key Old Testament passages!

Another relevant name is Daniel Maziarz, a bishop in the Essene Foundation, which was founded by Edmond Székely, and a key figure in the "Essene Mystery School of Life." Maziarz has produced a manual called *The Angelic Way to Love: A Manual of Essene Angelology and Personal Growth*,[25] and in the School of Life's newspaper *(I Am News)* he offers frequent references to the Essenes and comments on the Dead Sea Scrolls. (A sampler: in "Highlights from the Dead Sea Scrolls" he writes, "[The word] Essene comes from the Greek and can be translated as 'sacred according to the natural order.' ")

CONCLUDING COMMENT ON SENSATIONALISM, NEW AGE RELIGION, AND THE SCROLLS

For many readers, the views that have been outlined above will seem novel or very strange. We have included them because books by authors such as John Allegro, Barbara Thiering, and Edmond Székely are popular in some circles and prominent in listings of books on the Dead Sea Scrolls (e.g., on the Web sites of on-line bookstores). Furthermore, both authors of *The Meaning of the Dead Sea Scrolls* have been approached several times by members of the public (especially in North America) who have been greatly moved and influenced by such views. Although we have no desire to criticize the individuals mentioned, we must make it clear that the theories or approaches described above are not supported by scholars of the Dead Sea Scrolls.

The Scrolls, Jesus, and the Gospels

Even though none of the Dead Sea Scrolls was written by or for a Christian as far as we know, these documents are of relevance for Christian origins. This is because several key texts among the scrolls contain information, ideas, or language very similar to that found in certain Gospel passages. In this section, we examine some of these texts in the light of the relevant Gospel portions.

THE DEAD SEA SCROLLS AND JOHN THE BAPTIST

Although there is no firm evidence linking John the Baptist with the Qumran community, many scholars believe that he had contact or even links with the Essenes during his ministry. There are four reasons for this assessment.

(1) John's *family background and lineage* fit with the beliefs of the Qumran covenanters. The report that he was born to elderly parents (Luke 1:7, 18) reminds some scholars of Josephus's comment about the Essenes' marriage practice: "Marriage they disdain, but they adopt other men's children, while yet pliable and docile, and regard them as their kin and mould them in accordance with their own principles" (*Jewish War* 2.120). Was John orphaned and then raised by Essenes? To this we may add that John came from a priestly family, while the Qumran group had a strong priestly component and seems to have been founded and led by priests.

(2) The *location of John's ministry* may have at times included the vicinity of Qumran, and his activity in the Judean wilderness near the Jordan may have brought him into con-

tact with the Essene settlement. Luke says that John was in the wilderness already in his growing years ("The child grew and became strong in spirit, and he was in the wilderness until the day he appeared publicly to Israel" [Luke 1:80]). The likelihood that he spent time not far from Qumran, where the Dead Sea Scrolls community resided, has contributed to the argument that he was once associated with this group. On the other hand, the Fourth Gospel tells us that John baptized "in Bethany across the Jordan" (1:28) and "at Aenon near Salim because water was abundant there" (3:23)—sites that were farther north. When we consider the main locations for John's ministry these do not provide sufficient evidence to relate him closely with the Qumran community. As J. Taylor has written:

> John's sphere of activity was mainly along the Jordan valley, Samaria, and Perea, not in the wilderness of Judea bordering on the Dead Sea. Therefore, he did not share the same desert with the community at Qumran. Even if he did, and even though he may have once baptized people in the Jordan at a point fairly close to the Dead Sea, this does not mean he was associated with the Qumran group.[26]

(3) John's *ministry* shared many features with that of the Qumran community. This includes (a) his urgent message that the time was at hand, that the axe was poised to strike the root (Luke 3:9), which is reminiscent of the Qumran belief that the final conflict would come soon, that the last days were nearly here; and (b) the prominent place of baptism or washings with water in John's ministry and in the life of the Qumran Essenes, which may suggest that John was at one time an Essene associated with the Qumran community. Compare the following passages from Luke's Gospel and the *Rule of the Community*[27] concerning baptism for the purpose of repentance:

> And [John] went into all the region about the Jordan, preaching a baptism of repentance for the forgiveness of sins. (Luke 3:3)

> For only through the spirit pervading God's true society can there be atonement for a man's ways, all of his iniquities; thus only can he gaze upon the light of life and so be joined to His truth by His holy spirit, purified from all iniquity. Through an upright and humble attitude his sin may be covered, and by humbling himself before all God's laws his flesh can be made clean. Only thus can he really receive the purifying waters and be purged by the cleansing flow. (*Rule of the Community* 3.6–9 [WAC, 129])

John, however, probably understood the baptisms he administered in a different way than the people of Qumran conceived of theirs. For one thing, he himself administered the baptisms; people who came to him apparently did not baptize themselves. At Qumran, however, the pools used for such a purpose had steps allowing a person who was ritually impure to walk down, enter the water himself, and come up from the pool cleansed—all seemingly without assistance from another. The washings at Qumran were a daily feature, not a one-time ceremony symbolic of repentance. In other words, although John and the Qumran community used water in ritual ways, the ceremonies involved often had different meanings.

(4) John's *interpretation of Scripture* was similar to that of the Qumran community. The significance of his ministry is expressed in all four Gospels through the words of Isa. 40:3: John was "the voice of one crying out in the wilderness: 'Prepare the way of the Lord, make his paths straight'" (Mark 1:3; Matt. 3:3; Luke 3:4; cf. John 1:23). In column 8,

lines 12–16 of the *Rule of the Community*, the Qumran covenanters used the same passage to explain their presence in the wilderness: they were preparing for the Lord's coming through the study of the Torah:

> When such men as these come to be in Israel, conforming to these doctrines, they shall separate from the session of perverse men to go to the wilderness, there to prepare the way of truth, as it is written, "In the wilderness prepare the way of the Lord, make straight in the desert a highway for our God" (Isa. 40:3). This means the expounding of the Law, decreed by God through Moses for obedience, that being defined by what has been revealed for each age, and by what the prophets have revealed by His holy spirit. (WAC, 138)[28]

To conclude: John the Baptist may well have had some contact with the Qumran community and the Essenes. It is also possible that he had closer links with them at one time; but if this was the case, he subsequently distanced himself from them. This is because John's ministry included "all the region around the Jordan" and a proclamation of repentance for the forgiveness of sins (Luke 3:3; cf. Mark 1:4; Matt. 3:1). The Qumran community, in contrast, did not actively seek converts.

THE COMING OF THE MESSIAH AND THE RESURRECTION OF THE DEAD IN 4Q521

One of the most important Qumran texts for better understanding Jesus and his ministry is 4Q521, which was introduced in Chapter 9. This work is officially known as the *Messianic Apocalypse* (WAC: *On Redemption and Resurrection;* see Figure 15.1). Copied in the first century BCE, it reveals much about Jewish messianism at the time and contains fascinating similarities to the New Testament's description of Jesus Christ. The scroll presents a "recipe," or list of characteristics, that at least some Jews expected would take place with the coming of the Messiah. In the main preserved section, 4Q521 associates several features with the messianic age (see Box 15.1).

Figure 15.1
The *Messianic Apocalypse* (4Q521) (PAM 43.604)
Courtesy of the Israel Antiquities Authority

Box 15.1   *The* **Messianic Apocalypse** *(4Q521)*

Col. 2[1][... For the hea]vens and the earth shall listen to His Messiah [2][and all w]hich is in them shall not turn away from the commandments of the holy ones. [3]Strengthen yourselves, O you who seek the Lord, in His service.

[4]Will you not find the Lord in this, all those who hope in their heart? [5]For the Lord seeks the pious and calls the righteous by name. [6]Over the humble His spirit hovers, and He renews the faithful in His strength. [7]For He will honor the pious upon the th[ro]ne of His eternal kingdom, [8]release the captives, open the eyes of the blind, lifting up those who are op[pressed]. [9]And for [ev]er I shall hold fast [to] the [ho]peful and pious [...] [10][...] shall not be delayed [...] [11]and the Lord shall do glorious things which have not been done, just as He said.

[12]For He shall heal the critically wounded, He shall raise the dead, He shall bring good news to the poor, [13]He shall [...], He shall lead the [hol]y ones, and the hungry He shall enrich (?). [14][...] and [...]

(Adapted from WAC, 421)

The quoted passage clearly refers to the Messiah (l. 1), whose coming is connected with the rule of heaven and earth (ll. 1–2). Among the wondrous signs that attend his coming are the release of captives, opening the eyes of the blind, raising up those who are oppressed (l. 8), raising of the dead, and bringing good news to the poor (l. 12).

Several of these features are found in Jesus' reading from the prophet Isaiah (portions of Isa. 61:1–2 and 58:6) in Luke 4:16–21:

> When he came to Nazareth, where he had been brought up, he went to the synagogue on the sabbath day, as was his custom. He stood up to read, and the scroll of the prophet Isaiah was given to him. He unrolled the scroll and found the place where it was written:
>
> "The Spirit of the Lord is upon me, because he has anointed me to bring good news to the poor. He has sent me to proclaim release to the captives and recovery of sight to the blind, to let the oppressed go free, to proclaim the year of the Lord's favor."
>
> And he rolled up the scroll, gave it back to the attendant, and sat down. The eyes of all in the synagogue were fixed on him. Then he began to say to them, "Today this scripture has been fulfilled in your hearing." (NRSV)

Comparison of these two texts reveals the following common elements: bringing good news to the poor, release for the captives, sight for the blind, and uplifting/freedom for the oppressed. Yet there are additional features in 4Q521 that are not found in the passage from Luke 4; for these we must turn to Luke 7:20–22 (= Matt. 11:2–5). In this passage, the disciples of John the Baptist—who is becoming discouraged or disillusioned—come to Jesus with an important question:

> When the [disciples of John] had come to [Jesus], they said, "John the Baptist has sent us to you to ask, 'Are you the one who is to come, or are we to wait for another?'" Jesus had just then cured many people of diseases, plagues, and evil spirits, and had given sight to many who were blind.

> And he answered them, "Go and tell John what you have seen and heard: the blind receive their sight, the lame walk, the lepers are cleansed, the deaf hear, the dead are raised, the poor have good news brought to them."

The New Testament passage contains seven distinctive features, three of which are prophesied in Isa. 35:5–6, and one more in Isa. 61:1–2. One feature associated with the Messiah's coming that is altogether absent from Isaiah is the dead being raised up (item 6). This idea, in fact, is very scarce in the Old Testament as a whole, since it is late development. The fact that 4Q521 includes raising of the dead among the list of characteristics expected with the coming of the Messiah constitutes an important agreement with Luke 7:21–22 (= Matt. 11:4–5). The following list compares the texts:

Luke 7:21–22 (= Matt. 11:4–5)	Isa. 35:5–6	Isa. 61:1–2	4Q521
1. Jesus cured many of diseases, plagues, evil spirits			1. Heal the wounded
2. The blind receive sight	2. Eyes of the blind opened		2. Open the eyes of the blind
3. The lame walk	3. The lame shall leap		
4. The lepers are cleansed			
5. The deaf hear	5. Ears of the deaf unstopped		
6. The dead are raised			6. Raise the dead
7. The poor have good news brought to them		7. Bring good news to the poor	7. Bring good news to the poor

According to John J. Collins, 4Q521 describes the expected activity of a prophetic Messiah,[29] which fits well with Isaiah 61 (on which the Qumran text is partially dependent). The remarkable similarity between 4Q521 and Luke 7:21–22 (= Matt. 11:4–5) supports the conclusion that in the New Testament passage Jesus "proclaims the kingdom of God, and through his ministry of healing and exorcism he proves that it is present; and he claims to be anointed and so qualified to proclaim the good news. 4Q521 significantly supports the traditional view that Jesus did indeed see himself as Israel's Messiah."[30]

SON OF THE MOST HIGH AND SON OF GOD IN 4Q246

4Q246, often referred to as the "Son of God" text, is officially called *Apocryphon of Daniel* ar (WAC: *A Vision of the Son of God;* see Chapter 9 and Figure 15.2). The surviving text consists of two columns of nine lines each, written in Aramaic; it was copied in the late first century BCE. Comparison with the Annunciation account in Luke 1:30–35 reveals interesting parallels between the two texts, including the titles *Son of the Most High* and *Son of God.*

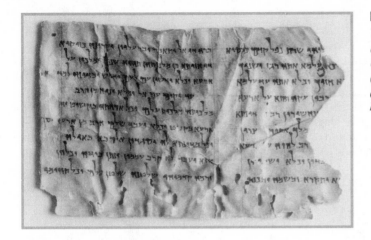

Figure 15.2
The Apocryphon of Daniel ar or *Son of God* text (4Q246)
(PAM 43.236)
Courtesy of the Israel Antiquities Authority

The angel said to her, "Do not be afraid, Mary, for you have found favor with God. And now, you will conceive in your womb and bear a son, and you will name him Jesus. He will be great, and will be called the Son of the Most High, and the Lord God will give to him the throne of his ancestor David. He will reign over the house of Jacob forever, and of his kingdom there will be no end."

Mary said to the angel, "How can this be, since I am a virgin?" The angel said to her, "The Holy Spirit will come upon you, and the power of the Most High will overshadow you; therefore the child to be born will be holy; he will be called Son of God."

Two translations of 4Q246 1.9–2.10 are presented in Box 15.2. Precisely who is being referred to in the Qumran text is not clear. We saw in Chapter 9 that many scholars regard these titles as attributed to an oppressive ruler during a time of suffering and war, a period followed by victory for the people of God who establish an eternal kingdom of peace under divine rule. Suggested identifications for this ruler are a historical king, Alexander Balas (J. T. Milik), the Antichrist (David Flusser), an angelic figure such as Melchizedek, Michael, or the Prince of Light (F. García Martínez), or the Jewish people collectively (Martin Hengel). The translation by Wise, Abegg, and Cook given in Box 15.2 accords with this interpretation of the passage.

Other scholars, however, understand the titles as being attributed to a messianic figure at the end times. Proponents of this view include Émile Puech and John Collins. The latter, for instance, observes that "the notion of a messiah who was in some sense divine had its roots in Judaism, in the interpretation of passages such as Psalm 2 and Daniel 7 in an apocalyptic context."[31] His translation in Box 15.2 reflects this interpretation of cols. 1.9–2.10 of 4Q246.

Whatever the identity of this ruler may be, three phrases correspond very closely in Luke and the Qumran passage: *will be great* (cf. Luke 1:32 and 4Q246 1.9); *he will be called son of the Most High* (cf. Luke 1:32 and 4Q246 2.1); and *he will be called Son of God* (Luke 1:35 and 4Q246 2.1). John Collins comments: "It is difficult to avoid the conclusion that Luke is dependent in some way, whether directly or indirectly, on this long lost text from Qumran."[32]

Box 15.2	4Q246 1.9–2.10

Collins (1995)	*Wise, Abegg, and Cook (1996)*
[9][. . .] will be called great, and be designated by his name. **Col. 2**[1]"Son of God" he shall be called, and they will name him "Son of the Most High." Like sparks [2]which you saw [or: of the vision], so will be their kingdom. For years they shall rule on [3]the earth, and they will trample all. People will trample on people and city on city, [*interval*] [4]until the people of God arises [or: until he raises up the people of God] and all rest from the sword. [5]His [or: its] kingdom is an everlasting kingdom and all his [or: its] ways truth. He [or: it] will judge [6]the earth with truth and all will make peace. The sword will cease from the earth, [7]and all cities will pay him [or: it] homage. The great God will be his [or: its] strength. [8]He will make war on his [or: its] behalf; give nations into his [or: its] hand [9]and cast them all down before him [or: it]. His [or: its] sovereignty is everlasting sovereignty and all the depths of [10][the earth are His].	[9][Also his son] will be called great, and be designated by his name. **Col. 2**[1]He will be called the Son of God, they will call him the son of the Most High. But like the meteors [2]that you saw in your vision, so will be their kingdom. They will reign only a few years over [3]the land, while people tramples people and nation tramples nation, [4]until the people of God arise; then all will have rest from warfare. [5]Their kingdom will be an eternal kingdom, and all their paths will be righteous. They will judge [6]the land justly, and all nations will make peace. Warfare will cease from the land, [7]and all the nations shall do homage to them. The great God will be their help, [8]He Himself will fight for them, putting peoples into their power, [9]overthrowing them all before them. God's rule will be an eternal rule and all the depths of [the earth are His].
(Adapted from *The Scepter and the Star,* 155.)	(WAC, 269–70)

A LIST OF BEATITUDES IN 4Q525

Another relevant text is 4Q525 (*Beatitudes;* called *The Blessing of the Wise* in WAC), which contains beatitudes similar to those found in the Sermon on the Mount (Matt. 5:1–12) and in the Sermon on the Plain (Luke 6:20–23). Besides being an interesting example of wisdom literature at Qumran, 4Q525 has some bearing on the relationship between the lists of beatitudes in Matthew and Luke. For many years, scholars have debated the relationship between these two lists: Was one set original and the other abbreviated (as in Luke) or expanded (as in Matthew)? Or are we dealing here with different groups of beatitudes that were spoken by Jesus on separate occasions? For many scholars, Luke's listing is more original, since the shorter reading is generally to be preferred. According to this theory, Luke's set has been expanded and supplemented in Matthew's longer listing. See the comparison of 4Q525, Matt. 5:1–12, and Luke 6:20–23 in Box 15.3.

According to the French scholar Émile Puech, 4Q525 originally contained nine beatitudes (8 short + 1 long).[33] If his reconstruction is correct, this text suggests that Matthew preserves an ancient listing—perhaps the original one—of the Gospel beatitudes, since Matthew's list then corresponds to a standard literary form that was found elsewhere (in this case, at Qumran). Luke's shorter list could then be regarded as an abbreviation of Matthew's longer one, although it remains possible that the two Gospel passages present beatitudes that were spoken by Jesus on separate occasions. The value of 4Q525 is not to confirm the actual words of Jesus, but to show that the structure of the beatitudes in Matthew 5 was probably familiar to some Jews in the first century BCE. This text also sheds

Box 15.3	*Beatitudes*

4Q525	Matthew 5:1–12 (NRSV)	Luke 6:20–23 (NRSV)
Col. 1 [1][The words of David (or Solomon son of David?) which he spok]e in the wisdom which God gave to him [...] [2][... to kno]w wisdom and disc[ipline], to understand [...] [3][...] to increase [...] [Blessed ....] [Blessed ....] [Blessed ....] [Blessed ....] [Blessed is the one who speaks truth] **Col. 2** [1]with a pure heart and does not slander with his tongue. Blessed are those who hold fast to its statutes and do not hold fast [2]to the ways of injustice. Ble[ssed] are those who rejoice in it, and do not burst forth on paths of folly. Blessed are those who seek it [3]with pure hands, and do not search for it with a deceitful [hea]rt. Blessed is the man who attains wisdom, and walks [4]in the law of the Most High: establishes his heart in its ways, restrains himself by its corrections, is continually satisfied with its punishments, [5]does not forsake it in the face of [his] trials, at the time of distress he does not abandon it, does not forget it [in the day of] terror, [6]and in the meekness of his soul he does not abhor it. But he meditates on it continually, and in his trial he reflects [on the law, ...]	[1]When Jesus saw the crowds, he went up the mountain; and after he sat down, his disciples came to him. [2]Then he began to speak, and taught them, saying: [3]"Blessed are the poor in spirit, for theirs is the kingdom of heaven. [4]"Blessed are those who mourn, for they will be comforted. [5]"Blessed are the meek, for they will inherit the earth. [6]"Blessed are those who hunger and thirst for righteousness, for they will be filled. [7]"Blessed are the merciful, for they will receive mercy. [8]"Blessed are the pure in heart, for they will see God. [9]"Blessed are the peacemakers, for they will be called children of God. [10]"Blessed are those who are persecuted for righteousness' sake, for theirs is the kingdom of heaven. [11]"Blessed are you when people revile you and persecute you and utter all kinds of evil against you falsely on my account. [12]Rejoice and be glad, for your reward is great in heaven, for in the same way they persecuted the prophets who were before you.	[20]Then he looked up at his disciples and said: "Blessed are you who are poor, for yours is the kingdom of God. [21]"Blessed are you who are hungry now, for you will be filled. "Blessed are you who weep now, for you will laugh. [22]"Blessed are you when people hate you, and when they exclude you, revile you, and defame you on account of the Son of Man. [23]Rejoice in that day and leap for joy, for surely your reward is great in heaven; for that is what their ancestors did to the prophets.

(Adapted from WAC, 423–24.)

welcome new light on the similarities and differences between two passages in the synoptic Gospels that seem to be related.

4Q525 also sheds light on our understanding of Jesus' beatitudes from a second angle. When we compare the wording of the Qumran document with the beatitudes in Matthew 5, several parallels may be noted:

Matthew 5	4Q525
Blessed are the pure in heart (v. 8).	[Blessed is the one who speaks truth] with a pure heart (2.1).
Blessed are you when men revile you . . . rejoice and be glad (vv. 11–12).	Blessed are those who rejoice in it (2.2).
Blessed are the meek (v. 5).	Blessed is the man who attains wisdom, . . . and in the meekness of his soul he does not abhor it (2.3–6).

There is of course no direct relationship between the two texts, but these parallels support the proposal by Ben Witherington that both the content and style of Jesus' teaching are right at home in Jewish wisdom tradition.[34] Although the beatitudes in Matthew 5 and Luke 6 (which are eschatological) differ from those in 4Q525 (which are sapiential), they also feature similarities. These show, according to Craig Evans, that "Jesus apparently took over a manner of speaking rooted in Israel's wisdom tradition and gave it his own eschatological spin."[35]

The evidence from the scrolls discussed here seems to undermine the theory of groups such as the Jesus Seminar that Jesus' teaching is best understood against the backdrop of Greco-Roman philosophy, notably Cynicism. The effect is to *authenticate* the words of Jesus in Matthew 5, not by demonstrating that he uttered them, but by showing that it is reasonable to believe he did so, since other Jews were using similar language in the century before his ministry.

REBUKING A FELLOW MEMBER: MATTHEW 18:15–17 AND THE DEAD SEA SCROLLS

One practice attested in both the Gospels and Qumran literature is rebuking a fellow member of the group when one has been offended or harmed by another. It is not surprising that the Qumran community, on the one hand, and the early Christians, on the other, had rules about this matter since it is based on teachings in Leviticus 19. Each group, however, developed the teachings of Leviticus in parallel ways.

In Matt. 18:15–17, Jesus offers a set of guidelines for church or fellowship practice, which may be summarized as follows (cf. Luke 17:3–4):

1. If one member sins against a second, the second is to point this out "when the two of you are alone." If this approach succeeds, then the matter is settled ("if he listens, you gain him").

2. If this private confrontation does not bring about the desired result, "take one or two with you so every word may be confirmed by two or three witnesses."

3. If the offender still persists after the private confrontation and the one before witnesses, the offended party is to take the matter to the entire assembly, here called the church.

4. If he still persists, he is to be considered in the same category as gentiles and tax collectors.

The Qumran covenanters' approach to such matters is outlined in 5.24–6.1 of 1QS, the *Rule of the Community:*[36]

1. It states the principle that the members "shall rebuke one another in truth, humility, charity. . . ." This was to be the spirit that prevailed when there was conflict.

2. An offended person is not to hate the offender, but "let him rebuke him on the very same day lest he incur guilt because of him."

3. A person is not to accuse another before the congregation without having first admonished him "in the presence of witnesses."

As nearly as we can tell, there are the same three successive stages here as in Matthew: personal confrontation, confrontation before witnesses, and bringing the matter before the entire group.

Something similar is found in CD 9.2–8, which quotes Lev. 19.17–18, one of the scriptural bases of the practice:

> As for the passage that says, "Take no vengeance and bear no grudge against your kinfolk" (Lev. 19:18), any covenant member who brings against his fellow an accusation not sworn to before witnesses or who makes an accusation in the heat of anger or who tells it to his elders to bring his fellow into disrepute, the same is a vengeance-taker and a grudge-bearer. It says only, "On his enemies God takes vengeance, against his foes he bears a grudge" (Nah. 1:2).
>
> If he kept silent day by day and then in anger against his fellow spoke against him in a capital case, this testifies against him that he did not fulfill the commandment of God which says to him, "You shall reprove your fellow and not bear the sin yourself" (Lev. 19:17). (WAC, 66–67).

An additional example is CD 7:2–3, which says: "reproving each his fellow according to the command, but not bearing a grudge day after day" (or "from one day to the next," see Num. 30:15).

Another relevant Qumran text is 4Q477 *(Rebukes of the Overseer; WAC: A Record of Disciplinary Action.)*[37] This document seems to contain a list of members of the community who were rebuked and records some of their transgressions. Parts of the fragmentary text are too broken for translation, but a substantial portion is included in *The Dead Sea Scrolls: A New Translation*:

> to [. . .] because [he . . . and also wh]o was acting with malice [. . . camps of] the general membership. [. . . And they chastised] Johanan ben Ma.[(?) . . .] he has a quick temper and an [evi]l eye and is also vainglorious [. . .] [. . .] and he [shall go] to the pi[t of hell]. They chastised Hananyah Nuthus because he [. . .] [. . .] to turn aside the spirit of the communi[ty and] also to intermingle [Isra]el [with . . .] [. . . Jo]seph they chastised, who has an evil [eye] and also does not [. . .] [. . .] and he also loves his blood relation [. . .]

[. . . They chastised] Hananyah ben Sim[on . . .] [. . . and al]so he loves the good [life . . .]. (2.1–10 [WAC, 406])

Finally, we turn once more to the *Damascus Document*. CD 9.16–20 describes the circumstances in which a sin in a capital matter is witnessed. This is to be reported to the overseer, and the witness is apparently the one who issues the rebuke in the presence of the overseer. The overseer then records this, in case this happens again and is witnessed once more. The process described here seems similar to the injunction found in Matt. 18:15–17, although the Gospel text does not mention the matter of keeping records.

A DISPUTE ON THE SABBATH:
THE SCROLLS, MATTHEW 12:11–12, AND PARALLELS

The following example involves the interpretation of Scripture and is from the legal sphere. It illustrates two different approaches to the same problem, thus illumining a fundamental difference between some New Testament authors and some writers of scrolls. In Matt. 12:11–12, before he heals a man with a withered hand on the sabbath, Jesus has a debate, apparently with some Pharisees who have asked whether it is lawful to heal on the sabbath:

> He said to them, "Suppose one of you has only one sheep and it falls into a pit on the sabbath; will you not lay hold of it and lift it out? How much more valuable is a human being than a sheep! So it is lawful to do good on the sabbath."

The Pharisees then make plans to destroy him. In his account of this incident, Mark does not reproduce the example of a sheep that falls into a pit, but in the same context he has the Pharisees consult with the Herodians about how to destroy Jesus (Mark 3:6). In Luke 14 the scene is Jesus' approach to a house belonging to a leader of the Pharisees. After he heals a man with dropsy, in the course of discussing with the lawyers and Pharisees whether to heal on the sabbath, Jesus says: "If one of you has a child [a variant New Testament manuscript reads: a donkey] or an ox that has fallen into a well, will you not immediately pull it out on a sabbath day?" (Luke 14:5).

The dispute evident in the Gospel passages can be clarified by turning to the *Damascus Document,* in particular CD 11.12–14, which is part of an extended series of sabbath laws (10.15–11.18). In the preceding legal statement the text stipulates that "No caregiver should carry a baby on the Sabbath, either going out or coming in" (11:10; see the Luke passage above). The pertinent law follows:

> No one should provoke his servant, his maid, or his employee on the Sabbath. No one should help an animal give birth on the Sabbath; and if it falls into a well or a pit, he may not lift it out on the Sabbath. (CD 11.12–14 [WAC, 69])

A little farther on, the *Damascus Document,* supported by a copy from Cave 4, adds that "[a]ny living human who falls into a body of water or a cistern shall not be helped out with ladder, rope, or instrument" (WAC, 69).

Another relevant text is 4Q265, *Miscellaneous Rules* (WAC: *Portions of Sectarian Law*), which combines aspects of the *Damascus Document* and the *Rule of the Community*. The principle here is that on the sabbath one must not get an instrument of rescue and carry it to the spot, but if one is wearing such an instrument it may be used for the rescue:

> Let no one raise up an animal which has fallen into the water on the Sabbath day. But if it is a man who has fallen into the water [on] the Sabbath [Day], one shall extend his garment to him to pull him out with it, but he shall not bear an implement [to pull him out with on the] Sabbath [day]. (frag. 7 1.6–9 [WAC, 280])

This example shows that the position that Jesus opposed was part of the legislation accepted by a contemporary group. It is interesting that Mark (3:6) mentions the Herodians as one of the groups opposing Jesus in this context, since some scholars (e.g., Harmut Stegemann) have identified them with the Essenes.

THE SUFFERING MESSIAH

One of the major differences between Judaism and Christianity is the latter's central belief in a messiah who would suffer and die for the sins of his people and, indeed, for the sins of the world. The Gospels and several other New Testament books contain many statements by Jesus and others indicating that he would be put to death as an atoning sacrifice. This outlook is very evident in Philip's meeting with the Ethiopian official in Acts 8:26–40, where the following details are recorded:

> So Philip ran up to it and heard him reading the prophet Isaiah. He asked, "Do you understand what you are reading?" He replied, "How can I, unless someone guides me?" And he invited Philip to get in and sit beside him. Now the passage of the scripture that he was reading was this:
>
> "Like a sheep he was led to the slaughter, and like a lamb silent before its shearer, so he does not open his mouth. In his humiliation justice was denied him. Who can describe his generation? For his life is taken away from the earth" (Isa. 53:7–8).
>
> The eunuch asked Philip, "About whom, may I ask you, does the prophet say this, about himself or about someone else?" Then Philip began to speak, and starting with this scripture, he proclaimed to him the good news about Jesus. (vv. 30–35; NRSV)

The question of whether the Dead Sea Scrolls contain evidence of a suffering or dying messiah has been investigated by several scholars. In this section, we briefly survey the evidence, using material that has appeared in earlier chapters, but focusing on the issue at hand.

4Q285: A Dying or Conquering Messiah?

In Chapter 9 we briefly discussed the *Book of War* (WAC: *The War of the Messiah*),[38] which consists of 4Q285 and 11Q14, and described it as an independent composition related to the *War Rule*. In the early 1990s, heated discussion centered around one tiny piece (frag. 5) of 4Q285. This began with an announcement by Professor Robert Eisenman of California State University, via a press release in 1991, that he had identified a Qumran text, which referred to a suffering or dying messiah. According to Eisenman, this fragment refers to the killing or execution of the messiah, which means that the Qumran community and the early church shared the belief in a slain messiah. Shortly after this, Geza Vermes (Professor

Box 15.4	*Two Translations of 4Q285 Fragment 5*

A Dying Messiah (Eisenman, 1991)	*A Conquering Messiah (Vermes, 1992)*
1.]Isaiah the prophet[	1.]Isaiah the prophet, And they shall be cut down
2.]the staff shall go forth from the root of Jesse	2. w]ill fall, and shoot shall spring from the root of Jesse
3.]Branch of David and they shall be judged	3.]Branch of David and they shall be judged
4.]and they put to death the leader of the community, the B[ranch of David	4.]and the Prince of the community will have him put to death, the B[ranch of David
5.]with wounds, and the (High) Priest shall order	5. timbrel]s and dancers, and the (High) Priest shall order
	6. the c]orpse[s of] the Kitians[

Emeritus of Jewish Studies at Oxford University) convened a seminar to discuss this new document. The conclusion of the approximately twenty scholars who attended was that in 4Q285 the messiah is not slain, but does the killing himself.[39] According to Martin Abegg (WAC, 292), even Eisenman no longer holds the view that a dying messiah is mentioned in 4Q285 fragment 5.

Two contrasting translations of 4Q285 fragment 5, which appear in Box 15.4, are mostly dependent on a single word in line 4: והמיתו *(whmytw)*. Depending on the vocalization (i.e., which vowels are used), this word can mean either "*and they put to death* the leader of the community, the Branch of David . . ." (Eisenman) or "and the Prince of the community, the Branch of David, *will have him put to death* . . ." (Vermes, adapted).

Following the discussion that took place in the 1990s, scholars are now in broad agreement on several features of fragment 5 of 4Q285: (1) The text refers to Isa. 10:34–11:1, which says that the forces of evil will be cut down by the messianic *shoot from the stump of Jesse*. (2) The branch that will grow out of his roots is the Branch of David. (3) Someone will be brought before the Leader of the Congregation (frags. 6 + 4, l. 10) or the Leader of the Nation (frag. 5, l. 4)—both messianic titles—and executed. (4) All Israel will rejoice with timbrels and dancers (frag. 5, l. 5). (5) There is also reference to the corpses of the "Kitians" (Kittim, frag. 5, l. 6):

> [1][. . . just as it is written in the book of] Isaiah the prophet, "And [the thickets of the forest] shall be cut down [2][with an ax, and Lebanon with its majestic trees w]ill fall. A shoot shall come out from the stump of Jesse [3][and a branch shall grow out of his roots" (Isa. 10:34–11:1). This is the] Branch of David. Then [all forces of Belial] shall be judged, [4][and the king of the Kittim shall stand for judgment] and the Leader of the nation—the Bra[nch of David]—will have him put to death. [5][Then all Israel shall come out with timbrel]s and dancers, and the [High] Priest shall order [6][them to cleanse their bodies from the guilty blood of the c]orpse[s of] the Kittim. [Then all the people shall . . .] (WAC, 293)

The First Messiah

At least two other attempts to identify a suffering or dying messiah in the Dead Sea Scrolls have been made, but both have proved unsuccessful. Only a few details are provided here with reference to the theme under discussion; for a fuller discussion, see "The First Messiah" and "The 'Suffering' Messiah" in Chapter 11.

In his 1999 book *The First Messiah: Investigating the Savior Before Christ*,[40] Michael Wise proposes that the Qumran messiah may have been named Judah and that our information about him derives especially from the Teacher hymns in columns 10–17 of the *Thanksgiving Psalms*. (Several scholars, including Wise, think the poems in these columns of the *Thanksgiving Psalms* contain the very words of the Teacher of Righteousness.) According to this theory, the Teacher came to believe that most of his contemporaries did not fully recognize him because that was God's plan. In other words, the Teacher's experience was similar to that of the suffering servant of the Lord in Isaiah. His contemporaries did not discern who the Teacher was since he was the hidden messiah.

According to Wise, after this Judah died, his followers came to believe that there was more than one messiah. The Teacher was one of them, although while he was alive they had thought he was the only one. His death moved his disciples to edit the Teacher hymns by placing their own hymns (the hymns of the community) before and after them. They also added the Hymn of the Exalted One in which the Teacher says he not only suffered like Isaiah's servant but also was raised to God's right hand. In the last chapter of his book, Wise draws out the close parallels between this kind of messiah and Jesus, both of whom atoned through suffering.

We may conclude, however, that although Wise bases much on the reflection of Isaiah's language about the servant in the Teacher hymns, the scrolls do not appear to describe the Teacher's suffering as offering atonement for others. (For further discussion and an evaluation of this theory, see Chapter 11.)

The Messiah Before Jesus

We have also discussed Israel Knohl's *The Messiah Before Jesus: The Suffering Servant of the Dead Sea Scrolls*.[41] According to the Israeli scholar, we meet a messiah (named Menahem) in some of the *Thanksgiving Psalms*, notably the poem that Wise calls the Hymn of the Exalted One. In this poem he says both "who is like me among the gods [i.e., the angels]" and uses words that derive from the poem about the suffering servant of the Lord in Isaiah 53: "Who shall [experience] troubles like me? And who is like me [in bearing] evil?" (l. 16).

Commentators have proposed several possible identifications of the person who utters such sentiments (see Chapter 11). Knohl thinks the speaker is the Menahem whom Josephus labeled an Essene. This Menahem, in Knohl's view, served as an advisor to King Herod and yet was also the author of this remarkable hymn; hence he led a double life as royal counselor and messiah of his own followers. The lofty personal claims made by Menahem and his sufferings serve as precedents for the way in which Jesus is presented in the Gospels where one also meets such a "catastrophic messianism." As explained in Chapter 11, Knohl also thinks the two witnesses in Revelation 11, individuals who were killed and whose bodies were exposed for three and a half days before they revived and ascended to heaven, are the royal and priestly messiah familiar from the Qumran texts.

Knohl places the execution of Menahem the messiah in 4 BCE. When Herod died in that year, disturbances broke out in the realm. Menahem and his followers chose that moment to disclose their secret about him as messiah. They armed themselves and fought in what they took to be the eschatological war of redemption. The Romans, however, quelled the uprising, executed Menahem, and left his body lying in public for three days. The hopes centered on him ended in this way.

Although Knohl may be correct that the speaker in the Qumran hymns is a messianic figure, identifying him as Menahem and as a suffering messiah is speculative to say the least. For additional comments on Knohl's approach and his theory, see Chapter 11.

Concluding Comment

The relevance of the Dead Sea Scrolls for better understanding Jesus and the Gospels is a controversial topic. In this chapter, we have emphasized that there is no direct relationship between Jesus and the scrolls, and none of these ancient documents was written by or for Christians as far as we know. Attempts have been made to find direct connections, but in many cases these are speculative, sensational, or bizarre (e.g., John Allegro and the sacred mushroom, Barbara Thiering's pesher technique, and the scrolls and the New Age Jesus).

Yet these ancient documents, which are roughly contemporary with the earliest New Testament texts, reveal to us a Jewish community and the way it lived and thought, thus throwing welcome light on aspects of the world of the first Christians. Moreover, several key texts are of relevance for Christian origins, since they illuminate many Gospel passages, and in some cases present significant parallels or even the same wording. As we have seen, there is no firm evidence linking John the Baptist with the Qumran community, but it is possible that he had contact or even links with the Essenes. Some documents (notably 4Q246, 4Q521, 4Q525) preserve language very similar to that found in certain Gospel passages, and one (4Q521) supplies a missing link between the Old and New Testaments by showing that, for at least some Jews in the first century BCE, one of the signs to accompany the messiah's coming would be raising of the dead. Other documents offer important parallels to practices among the early Christians, such as rebuking a fellow member, or to disputes about the sabbath.

The overall effect of several such texts is to *authenticate* the words or actions of Jesus and the New Testament account in several instances. By the term *authenticate* we do not mean that certain scrolls prove that Jesus said the words or performed the actions reported in the Gospels. Such conclusions are beyond the scope of evidence of this kind. What we do mean is that specific sayings and actions attributed to Jesus in several Gospel passages may now reasonably be viewed as authentic, since similar sayings or actions are recorded in certain key scrolls that predated him. These include Jesus' claim to be the messiah in Luke 4:16–21 and 7:20–22 (= Matt. 11:2–5) in the light of 4Q521; *Son of the Most High* and *Son of God* as Jewish terms, possibly messianic ones, in the light of 4Q246; the list of nine beatitudes in Matt. 5:1–12 in the light of 4Q525 (if Émile Puech's reconstruction is correct); and rebuking a fellow member in Matt. 18:15–17 in the light of several scrolls. Such evidence runs counter to the views of some scholars, notably those associated with the Jesus Seminar, who view much of what Jesus is reported to have said or done against the backdrop of Greco-Roman philosophy, or attribute his supposed words and actions to later church writers.

One feature that has not emerged in the scrolls is a suffering or dying messiah, despite the valiant attempts of several scholars to find evidence for it. It is very likely that this element has its origins in Jesus himself and in the early church's understanding of his life and mission.

Select Bibliography

Summary articles about several of the scholars and texts mentioned in this chapter appear in

Schiffman, L. H., and J. C. VanderKam, eds. *Encyclopedia of the Dead Sea Scrolls.* 2 vols. New York and Oxford: Oxford University Press, 2000.

Other helpful works:

Charlesworth, J. H., ed. *Jesus and the Dead Sea Scrolls.* Anchor Bible Reference Library 4. New York: Doubleday, 1992.

Collins, J. J. *The Scepter and the Star. The Messiahs of the Dead Sea Scrolls and Other Ancient Literature.* Anchor Bible Reference Library 10. New York: Doubleday, 1995.

Evans, C. A. "Jesus and the Dead Sea Scrolls from Qumran Cave 4." In C. A. Evans and P. W. Flint, eds. *Eschatology, Messianism, and the Dead Sea Scrolls.* Studies in the Dead Sea Scrolls and Related Literature. Grand Rapids, MI, and Cambridge: Eerdmans, 1997. Pp. 91–100.

Fitzmyer, J. A. *The Dead Sea Scrolls and Christian Origins.* Studies in the Dead Sea Scrolls and Related Literature. Grand Rapids, MI, and Cambridge: Eerdmans, 2000.

CHAPTER 16

The Dead Sea Scrolls and Other New Testament Books: Acts and the Letters

BECAUSE THE SUBJECT IS POTENTIALLY VERY LARGE and much has been written about it, this chapter contains only a selection of topics that illustrate how the additional information from the Qumran scrolls allows us to gain perspective in reading the Acts of the Apostles and the New Testament Letters. We lodge no claim here that the scrolls writers or the scrolls themselves directly influenced the authors of Acts and the New Testament Letters. Rather, we assert only that these New Testament writings are understood better because of the information that has come to light in the Dead Sea Scrolls. Although all of the New Testament books are in the Greek language and often reflect different concerns than does the Qumran literature, a comparison shows that Acts and the Letters have connections with Jewish ideas and events of the first century CE. This is hardly surprising, since Christianity began as a purely Jewish movement and the apostle Paul speaks with pride of his Jewishness (Phil. 3:4–6).

The Book of Acts

The book of Acts presents itself as a second volume to the Gospel of Luke. Like that Gospel, it was written late in the first century by an author whose name is not given, but who has been understood traditionally to be Luke, Paul's traveling companion. The story begins with Jesus' ascension and with the activity of his followers in Jerusalem and the immediately surrounding areas; it later narrates the spread of the movement by focusing on Paul and his many travels to proclaim the gospel in Cyprus, Asia Minor, Greece, and finally Rome itself. So the book describes the transformation of Jesus' followers from a small Jewish group in Jerusalem to a vigorous missionary movement to Jews and non-Jews throughout the Roman Empire. In depicting Christians as a proselytizing group, Acts portrays a body vastly different from the Qumran community, which did not engage in a mission of this kind. Nevertheless, there are some intriguing similarities between the first Christian community in Jerusalem as described in Acts and the Essene fellowship as pictured in the Qumran scrolls.

WEALTH-SHARING COMMUNITIES

After Jesus' ascent to heaven and the reconstitution of the apostles to the number twelve through the election of Matthias (chap. 1), Acts turns in chapter 2 to the famous story about the Pentecost celebration when the Spirit descended miraculously on the group and empowered them to speak the many languages of the world. Close scrutiny of this chapter and some of the following passages yields some features that may be illuminated by the Qumran texts.

The term *Pentecost* is derived from the Greek name *pentēkostē*, given to the Jewish Festival of Weeks. It means *fiftieth* and was chosen because this holiday falls on the fiftieth day after the waving of the barley omer, an event that happened around the time of Passover and the Festival of Unleavened Bread (see Lev. 23:15–16). Since it was one of the pilgrimage festivals (see, e.g., Exod. 23:14–17), not only Jews in the land but also diaspora Jews traveled to Jerusalem and its Temple to celebrate the holiday, which took place at the beginning of the wheat harvest. This accounts for the presence there of people from the many places listed in Acts 2:5–11; they were the ones in whose languages the followers of Jesus were enabled to speak the gospel.

Acts 2:14–36 presents Peter's address to the crowd of interested onlookers who were witnesses of the unusual event. In his message he showed from various Scriptures that the gift of the Spirit was a fulfillment of prophecy, as were Jesus' life, death, and resurrection. Once he had spoken, 3,000 people were added to the group (2:41). The notice about astonishing growth leads to a description of the fellowship that prevailed among them:

> All who believed were together and had all things in common; they would sell their possessions and goods and distribute the proceeds to all, as any had need. Day by day, as they spent much time together in the temple, they broke bread at home and ate their food with glad and generous hearts, . . . (2:44–46)

A similar point is made in Acts 4:32–35:

> Now the whole group of those who believed were of one heart and soul, and no one claimed private ownership of any possessions, but everything they owned was held in common. With great power the apostles gave their testimony to the resurrection of the Lord Jesus, and great grace was upon them all. There was not a needy person among them, for as many as owned lands or houses sold them and brought the proceeds of what was sold. They laid it at the apostles' feet, and it was distributed to each as any had need.

Acts 4:35–37 mentions Barnabas's donation of the proceeds from selling a field, and 5:1–11 tells the story about Ananias and Sapphira, who withheld part of the proceeds from a sale of property and lied about doing so. In the latter episode Peter asked Ananias: "While it remained unsold, did it not remain your own? And after it was sold, were not the proceeds at your disposal?" (5:4)

The practice of pooling resources has been, since the scrolls first were studied, a prominent point of comparison between the Qumran community and the Jerusalem church. The practices of the two fellowships respecting property are similar in that the wealth of individuals was put at the disposal of the entire group so that the needs of all could be met. At Qumran, merging one's resources with the community funds was required; this does not seem to have been the case in the Jerusalem church where, as Peter says, Ananias still had the money from the sale at his disposal after the transaction. Ananias met his death not because he failed to donate the money to the communal coffers, but because he misrepresented what he had done. The practices of the two communities also seem to be similar in that individuals may still have had some control over their funds even after they had contributed them to the group. But the important point is that at Qumran and in the Jerusalem church we see the same pooling of resources for the community's needs—something the ancient sources do not mention for other Jewish groups at the time.

It is helpful to see, however, that this shared practice is part of a larger scenario in both literatures. The Qumran community modeled itself after Israel in the desert under Moses' leadership, especially Israel as it encamped before Mt. Sinai and entered into covenant with the Lord. We know from several Jewish sources that the nation of Israel at Sinai (Exodus 19–24) was understood to be an ideal society. The people had been complaining about their plight before their arrival at the mountain, and Moses had become exasperated with them (Exod. 14:10–12; 15:22–25; 16:1–3; 17:1–7), but, once they had pitched their tents at the mountain, they changed dramatically. Even before they had heard the covenantal law, which the Lord revealed to Moses (in Exodus 20–23), the Israelites declared: "Everything that the Lord has spoken we will do" (Exod. 19:8). And, once they had heard the law, they reiterated their affirmation (24:3). The covenant between God and his people at the mountain was concluded in the third month of the year (Exod. 19:1), and, as a result, it became associated with the festival of the third month—the Festival of Weeks.[1] We see this clearly at the beginning of the book of *Jubilees,* which dates the Sinai covenant to the fifteenth day of the third month, its date for the Festival of Weeks. In *Jubilees* all covenantal ceremonies take place in the third month, and almost all of them (Noah's is the exception) fall on the Festival of Weeks. This is also the time when the covenant renewal ceremony took place at Qumran and when new members were welcomed into the fellowship.

The essence of the laws of the covenant was, "You shall love the Lord your God with all your heart, and with all your soul, and with all your might" (Deut. 6:5). We saw in Chapter 10 that the third term of Deut. 6:5 *(might)* was understood in the *Rule of the Community* (see Figure 16.1) to mean "money, possessions" and that this offers some background for the Qumran practice of merging one's funds with those of the community. In the Gospels, Jesus quotes this commandment and couples it with Lev. 19:18b: "You shall love your neighbor as yourself" (see Matt. 22:36–40; Mark 12:28–34; Luke 10:25–28). Whether the two commandments were combined in pre-Christian Jewish sources is debated,[2] but Lev. 19:18, the first half of which deals with rebuking one's fellow, could be seen as a complement to Deut. 6:5, especially if *might* in this verse were understood as *possessions.* Sharing one's wealth would demonstrate a person's love for a neighbor. We do find the Leviticus passage reflected in the *Damascus Document* 6.20–7.3 (see also 9.2–8), and the *Rule of the Community* discusses the rebuking command in a context where regulations about property are enunciated (see 6.24–7.9). At any rate, the teachings of Deut. 6:5 and Lev. 19:18 were basic for defining community life, and, it seems, sharing of property was an inference from them.

A NEW OR RENEWED COVENANT

We have seen that the Qumran community renewed the covenant annually on the Festival of Weeks. On the same occasion the book of Acts says that the Spirit was given to the Christians in Jerusalem, and the ideal society in which possessions were held in common

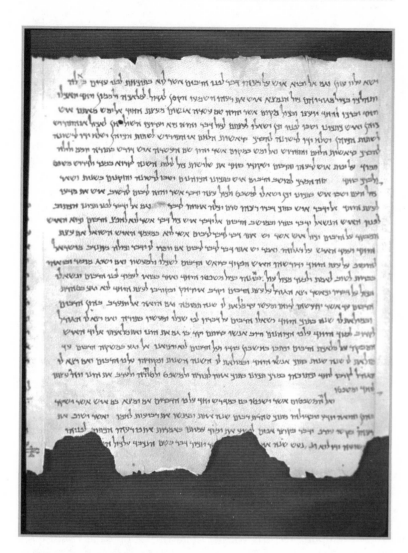

Figure 16.1
Column 6 of the *Rule of the Community* (1QS) (Trever, 1966).
Courtesy of John C. Trever

was established. We thus have a similar understanding of fellowship in the two literatures, with both tied to biblical traditions about the covenantal scene at Sinai. It is probably no accident that Acts 1 has Jesus, like Moses, climb a mountain before his ascent to heaven and that the Spirit is presented as the gift that the ascended Jesus has sent to his people below (Acts 2:33), just as Moses brought the covenantal law down to the Israelites.

INTERPRETATION OF SCRIPTURE

In this context we should also notice that the way in which Peter interprets the Scriptures would be at home among the Qumran exegetes. The apostle cites passages from the prophets and from the Psalms—the texts on which the Qumranites composed their *pesharim*. Peter almost sounds like a Qumran Essene when he defends his fellow believers against the charge of being drunk. He quotes Joel 2:28–32, and the citation begins "'In the last days it will be,' God declares, 'that I will pour out my Spirit upon all flesh . . .'" (Acts 2:17). In other words, the prediction about giving the divine Spirit to all peoples will come true in the last days, and Pentecost that year was understood by Peter as part of the last days. Actually our Hebrew and Greek texts of the verse in Joel do not read *in the last days*; instead, they have *after this*, that is, after the return of divine favor detailed in the previous section (2:18–27). In Acts the words *after this* are made more specific in light of the context in Joel. This sort of scriptural reading continues in Acts 2, where several Psalms are understood as referring to Jesus, just as in the *pesharim* this sort of contemporizing exegesis is the norm. The implication is transparent: both the Qumranites and the Jerusalem followers of Jesus considered themselves eschatological communities and constituted themselves as ideal fellowships on the model of Israel at Sinai.

VIEWS ON MARRIAGE

A difference between the two communities in this context has to do with marriage. Unlike the people of Qumran, who were most likely among the nonmarrying kind of Essene mentioned by Josephus,[3] there is no evidence that the Jerusalem church encouraged or mandated celibacy. The Qumran practice may have been understood as a logical inference from Exod. 19:15, where the Israelites refrain from sexual relations before making the Sinai covenant, or as necessary for those walking "in the perfection of holiness" (see CD 6.11–7.6);[4] apparently the earliest Christians did not draw the same conclusion.

Paul

The apostle Paul presents a curious situation when compared with the Essenes from Qumran. He tells us and Luke confirms that he was a Pharisee (Phil. 3:5; see 2 Cor. 11:22; Rom. 11:1; Acts 23:6). Membership in a group that the Qumran community considered its arch-opponents *(the ones who look for smooth things)* makes it seem unlikely that Paul would have been influenced by Essene thinking or language. Furthermore, the apostle is famous for proclaiming a law-free salvation through grace and faith—a message that appealed especially to non-Jews, while some texts from Qumran advocate a strict interpretation of the Mosaic law and insist upon precise obedience to it, without the same concern for the non-Jewish world. Despite such deep disagreements, there is much in Paul's Letters, all addressed to groups or individuals outside Judea, that seems clearer after reading the Qumran scrolls.

INTERPRETATION OF SCRIPTURE

In the Pauline corpus, as elsewhere in the New Testament, the ways in which Scripture is interpreted remind one of Qumran exegetical methods. For example, pericopes in which Paul adduces a string of citations centering around a subject recall the thematic *pesharim* at Qumran. In Rom. 3:10–18 he brings together words from seven passages in the Scriptures to demonstrate that all people, whatever their nationality, are sinful, just as texts like 4Q175 *(A Collection of Messianic Proof Texts)* or 11Q13 *(The Coming of Melchizedek)* associate scattered verses around a theme. The points being made in Romans and the Qumran commentaries are different, but the technique is the same.[5]

"WORKS OF THE LAW" IN 4QMMT AND PAUL

As we saw in Chapter 9, an important document specific to the Qumran community is 4QMMT, with the letters MMT abbreviating a Hebrew phrase meaning *Some of the Works of the Law (miqṣat maʻaśe ha-torah)*. The phrase *works of the law* apparently occurs nowhere else[6] in ancient writings other than once in MMT (C 26–27) and eight times in Paul's Letters (in the Greek form *erga nomou*: Rom. 3:20, 28; Gal. 2:16 [3 times]; 3:2, 5, 10).[7] The works of the law referred to in MMT include over twenty legal issues on which the writers disagree with the recipients of the text and which were detailed earlier in the document. The laws in dispute concern matters of sacrifice, priestly gifts, purity, forbidden marriages, and persons prohibited from entering the sanctuary. The relevant passage is found in section C of MMT:

> Now, we have written to you some of the works of the Law, those which we determined would be beneficial for you and your people, because we have seen [that] you possess insight and knowledge of the Law. Understand all these things and beseech Him to set your counsel straight and so keep you away from evil thoughts and the counsel of Belial. Then you shall rejoice at the end time when you find the essence of our words to be true. And it will be reckoned to you as righteousness, in that you have done what is right and good before Him, to your own benefit and to that of Israel. (4QMMT C 26–32 [WAC, 364])

An additional point of contact between 4QMMT and Paul has been suggested by J. D. G. Dunn: the Deuteronomic pattern of blessings and curses.[8] Just as Paul declares that "those who believe are *blessed* with Abraham who believed," and "all who rely on the works of the law are under a *curse*" (Gal. 3:9), 4QMMT introduces David the righteous one by quoting a passage that mentions blessings and curses:

> And it is writ[ten] "that when [al]l these thing[s happ]en to you in the Last Days, the *blessing* [and] the *curse*, [that you call them] to m[ind] and return to Him with all your heart and with [al]l [your] soul." (MMT C 12–16, quoting Deut. 30:1–2 [WAC, 363–64])

The occurrence of *works of the law* in both MMT and two of Paul's Letters, as well as the pattern of blessings and curses, has aroused scholarly interest as to whether there is some link or common outlook in these documents. Some scholars regard these as the same works of the law that Paul rejects in Galatians and elsewhere: for example, "No human being is justified by works of the law but only through faith in Jesus Christ" (Gal. 2:16).

N. T. Wright, however,[9] regards the works of the law in MMT as very different from those referred to by Paul and offers several reasons why the issues raised by the two ancient writers are distinct. For example, MMT defines one group of Jews over against other Jewish groups, while the works that Paul opposes define all Jews and proselytes over against Gentiles and pagans. Wright then proposes that "while MMT insists on certain postbiblical laws, Paul is battling those who wish to impose biblical regulations."[10]

For Martin Abegg, the evidence indicates a clear terminological connection between MMT and Paul's writings,[11] but he rejects the view that by these phrases Paul was challenging a theology which taught that good works earn salvation.

The scrolls indicate in a number of passages that, although obedience to the divine law as properly understood was crucial, the Qumran community also had a strong sense that their election and salvation came through God's grace. No less a person than the Instructor confesses in column 11 of the *Rule of the Community* his own sinfulness and inadequacy and the need for divine mercy. He acknowledges that he belongs among the company of wicked humans and that justification and atonement come not by works, but through God's loving-kindness and righteousness:

> Surely a man's way is not his own; neither can any person firm his own step. Surely justification is of God; by His power is the way made perfect. All that shall be, He foreknows, all that is, His plans establish; apart from Him is nothing done. As for me, if I stumble, God's loving-kindness forever shall save me. If through sin of the flesh I fall, my justification will be by the righteousness of God which endures for all time. Though my affliction break out, He shall draw my soul back from the pit, and firm my steps on the way. Through His love He has brought me near; by His lovingkindness shall he provide my justification. By His righteous truth has He justified me; and through His exceeding goodness shall He atone for all my sins. By His righteousness shall He cleanse me of human defilement and the sin of mankind—to the end that I praise God for His righteousness, the Most High for His glory. (1QS 11.10–15 [WAC, 143])

Similar sentiments appear frequently in the *Thanksgiving Psalms*. Naturally the ways out of the human predicament differ in the two literatures, but the recognition of human need for God's grace is common to both.

But what was the *purpose* of the law? E. P. Sanders concludes that the place of obedience in Qumranic literature, as for other branches of Palestinian Judaism, "is always the same: it is the *consequence* of being in the covenant and the *requirement for remaining* in the covenant."[12] In other words, obedience to the law is not the *entrance* into a relationship with God, but rather the *maintenance policy* to that relationship.[13]

In the light of MMT, then, several scholars are rethinking and rejecting the traditional Protestant understanding that by phrases such as *works of the law* Paul was challenging the theological teaching that salvation is earned by good works. Of Gal. 2:16 ("Yet we know that a person is justified not by the works of the law but through faith in Jesus Christ. And we have come to believe in Christ Jesus, so that we might be justified by faith in Christ, and not by doing the works of the law, because no one will be justified by the works of the law"), J. D. G. Dunn says:

> This [verse] has traditionally been understood as a denial that human beings, even the most religious of individuals, can achieve salvation by their own "works"; they cannot "work" their passage to heaven; they cannot earn salvation by their own efforts. Valid as that is as a theological insight of tremendous importance, it is doubtful whether it quite catches Paul's meaning here. Paul was evidently objecting to a current Jewish conviction. But so far as we can tell, the typical and traditional Jewish view of the time was *not* that anyone could earn God's favour.[14]

FAITH AND RIGHTEOUSNESS: ROMANS 1:17, GALATIANS 3:11, AND THE SCROLLS

As he defends and elaborates his understanding of how one becomes right with God, Paul quotes and interprets a number of texts from the Scriptures. One that he cites more than once and seems to have been important to him is Hab. 2:4b. In the ancient prophetic book the passage appears to be a call to faithfulness or fidelity, probably not an appeal for belief, during the time of crisis occasioned by the Chaldean invasion. Nevertheless, there has been much debate about the meaning of the Hebrew term *'emunato* in the verse (NRSV: "but the righteous live by *their faith*," with a footnote suggesting *faithfulness* as an alternative to *faith*). In Gal. 3:11 Paul quotes this passage as saying: "The one who is righteous shall live by faith" (so, too, in Rom. 1:17). Paul understands the prophet to be teaching that one is not justified before God through works of the law; rather, this is accomplished through faith, which for Paul means faith in Christ, who is the fulfillment of the promise to Abraham. In his teaching, the contrast is between doing works of the law and believing.

The same passage receives treatment in the Qumran *Commentary on Habakkuk* (see Figure 16.2). The pertinent words must have been quoted in the lost end of column 7, but the *pesher* on them has survived in full:

> This refers to all those who obey [literally: do] the Law among the Jews [literally: in the house of Judah] whom God will rescue from among those doomed to judgment, because of their suffering and their loyalty [*'emunatam*] to the Teacher of Righteousness. (8.1–3 [WAC, 119])

Figure 16.2
Column 7 of the *Pesher Habakkuk* (1QpHab) (Trever, 1966).
Courtesy of John C. Trever

It is intriguing that the Qumran expositor can begin his explanation of the verse with mention of all those who do the Law in the house of Judah. Judah, as we have seen, is a designation for the group in at least some Qumran texts, while "those who do [the Torah]" may be the Hebrew expression lying behind the word *Essene*.[15] This could hardly be more opposed to Paul's reading of the verse.

The pesherist, like Paul, understood the word *live* in Hab. 2:4b to mean more than normal day-to-day survival; it has to do with the life given to those who are saved or rescued by God from judgment. Following this explanation, the commentator uses two terms to explain the word *'emunato* in the verse: the word translated *suffering* and the one rendered *loyalty* (using the same Hebrew word as the one in the verse). Although the first term can point to *trouble* or *harm*, it may also mean *work* or *toil*. If so, it refers to what the doers of the law have carried out—quite the opposite of the way in which Paul read the verse. But what does *'emunatam* mean when followed by "to/in the Teacher of Righteousness"? Does it say that these Essenes have faith in the Teacher or does it express the idea that they are faithful to him? *Loyalty* may well the correct way to understand the term, but we cannot rule out that the meaning here is "their faith in the Teacher of Righteousness." If so, this would be along the lines in which Paul understood the term—belief in a person. The result would be that the Qumran commentator read the verse in two ways (reflecting the ambiguity in the meaning of *'emunato*), while Paul opted for only one of them.

BELIEVERS AND UNBELIEVERS:
2 CORINTHIANS 6:14–7:1 AND THE SCROLLS

Embedded in 2 Corinthians is a passage that, even in pre-Qumran days, had struck commentators as decidedly odd. 2 Cor. 6:14–7:1 uses language that is not attested elsewhere in Paul's Letters and sits uncomfortably in its context. The thought—if not much of the language—of 6:11–13 (encouragement to the Corinthian believers to open their hearts) is resumed in 7:2–4, leaving the passage in between looking very much like an awkward, poorly placed insertion:

> Do not be mismatched with unbelievers. For what partnership is there between righteousness and lawlessness? Or what fellowship is there between light and darkness? What agreement does Christ have with Beliar? Or what does a believer share with an unbeliever? What agreement has the temple of God with idols? For we are the temple of the living God; as God said, "I will live in them and walk among them, and I will be their God, and they shall be my people. Therefore come out from them, and be separate from them, says the Lord, and touch nothing unclean; then I will welcome you, and I will be your father, and you shall be my sons and daughters, says the Lord Almighty."[16] Since we have these promises, beloved, let us cleanse ourselves from every defilement of body and of spirit, making holiness perfect in fear of God.

As Joseph Fitzmyer explains the situation, there are especially five points on which the passage has affinities with Essene teachings as they are known from Qumran:

> (a) the triple dualism of righteousness and iniquity, light and darkness, Christ and Beliar,[17] together with the underlying notion of the "lot"; (b) opposition towards idols; (c) the temple of God; (d) separation from impurity; and (e) concatenation of Old Testament texts.[18]

The first of these (the dualisms) is particularly instructive. The language of light and darkness is familiar from texts such as the *War Rule* (see 1 Thess. 5:5; Eph. 5:8, where Christians are "sons of light"),[19] and Belial is a very frequently used name for the evil one in the scrolls. We should also note that the Qumran community thought of itself as a temple (*Rule of the Community* 8.4–10; 9.3–6),[20] and we have noticed the importance of purity issues in the legal texts (see Chapter 9). It is understandable, then, that some scholars see in 2 Cor. 6:14–7:1 an Essene text that Paul or someone else has inserted into his Letter; it is also understandable that no one has found a convincing reason why Paul or anyone else would have inserted the unit in this particular context.[21]

"HANGING ON A TREE": GALATIANS 3:12–13 AND THE SCROLLS

One more Pauline theme will illustrate the basis of at least some of his scriptural interpretation and argumentation in Jewish traditions of the time. As part of his argument about the way a person becomes right with God, Paul had to deal with the fact that the Scriptures do in fact present obedience to the covenantal law as a way to life:

> But the law does not rest on faith; on the contrary, "Whoever does the works of the law will live by them" [Lev. 18:5]. Christ redeemed us from the curse of the law by becoming a curse for us—for it is written, "Cursed is everyone who hangs on a tree" [Deut. 21:23]. (Gal. 3:12–13).

The full passage in Deuteronomy from which Paul quotes one sentence explains the punishment for someone found guilty of a serious offense:

> When someone is convicted of a crime punishable by death and is executed, and you hang him on a tree, his corpse must not remain all night upon the tree; you shall bury him that same day, for anyone hung on a tree is under God's curse. You must not defile the land that the Lord your God is giving you for possession. (Deut. 21:22–23)

It is generally thought that the law in Deuteronomy refers to someone who is first executed and then, after he is dead, his body is strung up to make a public display of him. The practice may be illustrated from Josh. 10:26–27 and 2 Sam. 4:12. If so, the passage does not speak about hanging as a method of execution, although that is the way in which Paul uses it.

The Deuteronomy passage comes up for consideration in two texts from Qumran. We have already studied the section in the *Commentary on Nahum* where the Lion of Wrath executed his enemies:

> This refers to the Lion of Wrath [. . . ven]geance against the ones who look for smooth things, because he used to hang men alive, [as it was done][22] in Israel in former times, for to anyone hanging alive on the tree, [the verse app]lies: "Behold, I am against [you], [says the Lord of Hosts" (2.13a). (*Commentary on Nahum* frags. 3–4 1.6–9 [WAC, 218])

This passage seems to allude to Deuteronomy 21, but it adds the important term "alive," indicating that hanging as a means of execution is meant. And if the *pesher* is reflecting the incident to which Josephus refers (as argued in Chapter 12), then crucifixion is definitely involved—the historian actually uses the word *crucifixion* for it (*anastaurogai; Antiquities* 13.380).

The *Temple Scroll* also includes a passage that speaks about crucifixion:

> If a man is a traitor against his people and gives them up to a foreign nation, so doing evil to his people, you are to hang him on a tree until dead. On the testimony of two or three witnesses he will be put to death, and they themselves shall hang him on the tree. (64.7–9 [WAC, 490])

The initial sentence makes clear that the traitor is first hanged and then dies. Yigael Yadin proposed that this law provides the backdrop for understanding the actions of Alexander Jannaeus in the incident mentioned in the *Commentary on Nahum:* he crucified the 800 opponents because they acted as traitors by inviting the foreign king Demetrius to invade Judea and by assisting him while there.[23] The following passage in the *Temple Scroll* treats a different kind of case and also appeals to Deuteronomy 21:

> If a man is convicted of a capital crime and flees to the nations, cursing his people and the children of Israel, you are to hang him, also, upon a tree until dead. But you must not let their bodies remain on the tree overnight; you shall most certainly bury them that very day. Indeed, anyone hung on a tree is accursed of God and men, but you are not to defile the land that I am about to give you as an inheritance. (64.9–13 [WAC, 490])

In light of these passages we may say that Paul, by applying Deut. 21:22 to Jesus' crucifixion, was explaining the passage in a way that some Jewish expositors would have accepted. This is not to say that the exact method of hanging envisaged in the two Qumran texts is the same as the one Jesus endured; but understanding Deut. 21:22 to mean hanging in order to execute is common to them and to Paul.[24]

SHARED LITERARY FORMS AND TERMS

Although the epistolary form to which Paul resorted is not frequent in the Qumran literature (only 4QMMT may be a letter), he does use some literary types also attested in the scrolls. One instance is Paul's list of contrasting qualities in Gal. 5:16–26 (see also Rom. 13:12–14). He begins the section in Galatians with some sentences that are reminiscent of columns 3–4 in the *Rule of the Community:* "Live by the Spirit, I say, and do not gratify the desires of the flesh. For what the flesh desires is opposed to the Spirit, and what the Spirit desires is opposed to the flesh; for these are opposed to each other, to prevent you from doing what you want" (5:16–17). According to the *Rule of the Community:*

> He created humankind to rule over the world, appointing for them two spirits in which to walk until the time ordained for His visitation. These are the spirits of truth and falsehood. Upright character and fate originate with the Habitation of Light; perverse, with the Fountain of Darkness. (3.17–19 [WAC, 129])

Paul follows his introductory comments with lists of traits, first of the "works of the flesh" (Gal. 5:19–21), then the "fruit of the Spirit" (vv. 22–24). In the *Rule of the Community,* the order is reversed, with the "operations" of the spirit of light first (4.2–6) and those of the spirit of darkness second (4.9–11; see Box 16.1).

Neither work is a copy of the other, but the texts do contain several similar qualities under their own rubrics. The qualities induced by the spirit of truth include a couple that

Box 16.1	*Contrasting Qualities in Galatians and the* Rule of the Community
### The Flesh	### The Spirit of Falsehood
Gal. 5:19–21: fornication, impurity, licentiousness, idolatry, sorcery, enmities, strife, jealousy, anger, quarrels, dissensions, factions, envy, drunkenness, carousing, and the like	1QS 4.9–11: greed, neglect of righteous deeds, wickedness, lying, pride and haughtiness, cruel deceit and fraud, massive hypocrisy, a want of self-control and abundant foolishness, a zeal for arrogance, abominable deeds fashioned by whorish desire, lechery in its filthy manifestation, a reviling tongue, blind eyes, deaf ears, stiff neck, and hard heart
### The Spirit	### The Spirit of Truth
Gal. 5:22–23: love, joy, peace, patience, kindness, generosity, faithfulness, gentleness, and self-control (NRSV)	1QS 4.3–6: humility, patience, abundant compassion, perpetual goodness, insight, understanding, and powerful wisdom ... a spirit knowledgeable in every plan of action, zealous for the laws of righteousness, holy in its thoughts and steadfast in purpose.... Plenteous compassion upon all who hold fast to truth, and glorious purity ... hatred of impurity ... humble deportment ... general discernment, concealing the truth, that is, the mysteries of knowledge (WAC, 130)

highlight the way preferred by the Qumranites, in which knowledge is emphasized and obeying laws, purity, and concealing knowledge from outsiders are also listed.

Finally, some terms in Paul's Letters have now turned up in their Semitic form in the scrolls. In 2 Cor. 2:5–7 Paul writes: "But if anyone has caused pain, he has caused it not to me, but to some extent—not to exaggerate it—to all of you. This punishment by the majority is enough for such a person; so now instead you should forgive and console him, so that he may not be overwhelmed by excessive sorrow." The phrase *the majority* resembles *the many* used for the Qumran community (see, e.g., the *Rule of the Community* 6–8, where the term is employed frequently; it is translated as "the general membership" in WAC). At least in 2 Cor. 2:6 one could debate whether the phrase designates the entire community when it meets to exercise a judicial function (as at Qumran) or only a majority in that community. It may be, though, that Paul uses *the majority* in parallel with *all of you* at the end of verse 5. If he does, then his usage would be the same as we find in the scrolls.[25]

Hebrews

The Letter to the Hebrews—not really a letter, but a homily that ends like a letter—offers a unique perspective on the position and work of Jesus Christ. Its author is unknown, as are its date, place of composition, and audience. The Letter offers a sustained argument about the superiority of Christ and his dispensation over the old system of the Jewish Scriptures, especially the levitical priesthood; on the basis of scripturally based arguments, the writer exhorts the recipients to firm up their sagging commitment to Christ. For students of Qumran, Hebrews would seem to offer valuable comparative material because it focuses its attention on the wilderness period of Israel's history—the model for the Qumran covenanters—and speaks at length about Melchizedek and a messianic high priest. In some respects, however, the book proves to have less comparative value than one might hope. In it the wilderness period serves a negative function and is certainly not viewed as an archetype for an ideal community (see chap. 3); and the understanding of Melchizedek, though it is not unrelated to the contents of the Qumran *Melchizedek* text, is decidedly different.

EXEGESIS OF SCRIPTURE

The methods of scriptural exegesis in parts of Hebrews remind one, as do sections in Paul's Letters, of the thematic commentaries from Qumran. The string of citations in Heb. 1:5–14 illustrates the point. Most of these come from what are called the Royal Psalms (such as Psalm 2), but the writer interprets them as referring not to the king or even to an angel, but to God's Son, Jesus Christ. "For to which of his angels did God ever say, 'You are my Son; today I have begotten you'?" (Heb. 1:5, quoting Ps. 2:7). The actualizing reading of the Royal Psalm documents the author's thesis that God's Son had "become as much superior to the angels as the name he has inherited is more excellent than theirs" (1:4). The author regards the present as the last days (1:2) and interprets the Psalms and 2 Samuel 7 messianically, as in 4Q174 (WAC: *The Last Days: A Commentary on Selected Verses*).

THE FIGURE OF MELCHIZEDEK

A strong theme in Hebrews is that Jesus is a high priest in the order of Melchizedek and is, for that reason, superior to the Jewish high priests who are descended from Levi. The idea of Jesus as high priest of a new and better covenant is prominent from Heb. 4:14–10:39, while the Melchizedek theme is developed especially in 5:1–10 and chapter 7. The connection between Melchizedek and Jesus is a natural consequence of the writer's way of reading royal psalms—they refer to Christ. Hence, when Ps. 110:4 quotes God as saying, "You are a priest forever, according to the order of Melchizedek," this is to be understood as being addressed to Jesus (5:5–6). His appointment as high priest in the Melchizedekian order was by God himself.

The writer attempts to show in various ways that membership in this order makes Christ a high priest superior to the ones from Levi's line. He argues that the priest-king was superior to Abram (the great-grandfather of Levi) from Gen. 14:19–20, where Melchizedek receives a tithe from Abram and blesses him. The author of Hebrews had a problem: he understood Jesus to be a heavenly high priest, but Jesus was from the tribe of Judah, not Levi, and priests came only from the tribe of Levi (see 7:13–14). For that reason, he had to explain Jesus' priestly status in a different way: it did not come through heredity but by divine appointment (7:16–17). After leading readers through study of a number of passages, he writes:

> Now the main point in what we are saying is this: we have such a high priest, one who is seated at the right hand of the throne of the Majesty in the heavens, a minister in the sanctuary and the true tent that the Lord, and not any mortal, has set up. (Heb. 8:1–2)

After describing the practice of the Jewish high priests, who alone could enter the Holy of Holies and that just once per year, our author pictures Jesus as carrying out the high-priestly function of entering the inner sanctuary behind the curtain on the Day of Atonement:

> But when Christ came as a high priest of the good things that have come, then through the greater and perfect tent (not made with hands, that is, not of this creation), he entered once for all into the Holy Place, not with the blood of goats and calves, but with his own blood, thus obtaining eternal redemption. (9:11–12; see also 6:19–20)

In the *Melchizedek* text found in Cave 11, the emphases are different. There, at least in the parts that can be pieced together from the manuscript, the context is set by references to liberty promised during the year of jubilee and the sabbatical year (Lev. 25:13 and Deut. 15:2 are cited). These passages speak about returning property to their original owners and remitting debts, but for our writer: "[the interpretation] is that it applies [to the L]ast Days and concerns the captives" (11Q13 2.4 [WAC, 456]). Isa. 61:1 may then be introduced (it speaks about release of captives) before we meet Melchizedek who "will return them to what is rightfully theirs. He will proclaim to them the jubilee, thereby releasing th[em from the debt of a]ll their sins" (2.6 [WAC, 456]). The sabbatical year and the jubilee were times when property reverted to its original owner, debts were cancelled, and slaves were released. In the *Melchizedek* text, these themes are transposed to the last days, when Melchizedek will release those who because of their sins are captive to Belial. He is pictured not only as the one who liberates, but also as the judge of the eschatological age. Ps. 82:1 and 7:7–8 are applied to him and the roles he will execute in "the year of Melchiz[edek]'s favor" (2.9 [WAC, 456]).

Though the overall presentations of Melchizedek in Hebrews and the Cave 11 text are different, they do share some points. For one, both deal with the Day of Atonement in connection with Melchizedek or his priesthood. In Hebrews, Jesus, the priest after Melchizedek's order, enters behind the curtain on the Day of Atonement as the high priest does in Jerusalem, but he, through sacrifice of himself, effects atonement for his people once for all. He does not have to repeat the act year after year. In the Cave 11 text, the time of Melchizedek's deliverance is explained as follows:

> Then the "D[ay of Atone]ment" shall follow af[ter] the [te]nth [ju]bilee period, when he shall atone for all the Sons of [Light[and the peopl[e who are pre]destined to Mel[chi]zedek. (2.7–8 [WAC, 456])

Both Jesus and Melchizedek are involved in the salvation of their people, but words like *atone* are rare in Hebrews (see 1:3, where the related term *purification* appears).

Hebrews is the only New Testament book that, among other titles, calls Jesus a high priest. The role that he plays as a priest after the order of Melchizedek he carries out in the heavenly sanctuary—an idea that would have been quite at home at Qumran. However, the presentation of Jesus as a priest reminds us of the covenanters' expectation that the lay or Davidic messiah would be accompanied by a priestly messiah. In Hebrews as elsewhere in the New Testament, Jesus' ancestry is traced to the tribe of Judah, but the priestly duties assigned to him show that the Qumranites were not the only ones who anticipated that messianic duties would include priestly ones. Jesus functions as both Davidic and priestly messiah in the New Testament, while at Qumran the roles are assigned to two separate individuals.

The Other Letters

Some parallels between certain Qumran scrolls and other New Testament Letters have been suggested (especially regarding types of scriptural interpretation), but it will suffice here to mention a thematic connection between some scrolls and the Letters of Jude and 2 Peter.

JUDE AND THE BOOK OF *1 ENOCH*

We saw in Chapter 9 that the Enochic literature, which is well represented at Qumran, traces the great growth of evil to the primordial sin of angels who descended to earth and married women. They passed along forbidden teachings to their wives, and their children, the giants, caused endless trouble and evil on the earth. Aspects of the different versions of this story appear in the various Enoch booklets (especially the Book of the Watchers and the Animal Apocalypse), the *Book of Giants, Jubilees,* the *Genesis Apocryphon,* the *Damascus Document,* 4Q180–81 *(The Ages of the World),* and elsewhere. The angel stories are a set of pre-Qumran traditions that were utilized by the Essenes (and are known to a lesser extent in some other texts).

The theme of the prediluvian sin of the angels is found in Jude and 2 Peter. It may be that Jude is the source of the information and that the writer of 2 Peter has borrowed it from him. In Jude the writer adduces a series of cases in which God judged sinners, some of whom had started out virtuously. He uses these examples as stimuli to goad the readers "to contend for the faith that was once for all entrusted to the saints" (v. 3) and to oppose certain "intruders" who "pervert the grace of our God into licentiousness" (v. 4). Jude mentions destruction of those who had experienced the Exodus and then writes:

> And the angels who did not keep their own position, but left their proper dwelling, he has kept in eternal chains in deepest darkness for the judgment of the great Day. Likewise, Sodom and Gomorrah and the surrounding cities, which, in the same manner as they, indulged in sexual immorality and pursued unnatural lust, serve as an example by undergoing a punishment of eternal fire. (vv. 6–7)

So the angels are accused both of leaving their position (i.e., being in heaven) and of sexual perversion and are being punished as a result. Divine judgment upon these quintessential violators of sexual propriety provides Jude with an excellent example to document his insistence that God punishes such actions severely. The section from *1 Enoch* that is under consideration is chapters 6–10; the punishment of binding and imprisonment in deep, dark places is recorded for Asael in 10:4–6 and for Shemihazah and his angels in 10:11–12.

Farther along in the little Letter, after additional words of condemnation, the author writes:

> It was also about these that Enoch, in the seventh generation from Adam, prophesied, saying, "See, the Lord is coming with ten thousands of his holy ones, to execute judgment on all, and to convict everyone of all the deeds of ungodliness that they have committed in such an ungodly way, and of all the harsh things that ungodly sinners have spoken against him." (vv. 14–15)

The quotation comes from *1 Enoch* 1:9, where it is set in an eschatological context—the end of history when God will descend to Sinai for judgment. Jude also regards the present as "the last time" (v. 18). The use to which the older prophecy is put in Jude is reminiscent of the Qumran *pesher* approach to words from the prophet—they were directed to present times and circumstances.

SECOND PETER AND THE LAST DAYS

In 2 Peter 2, the author warns his audience about those who will bring false teachings and be licentious; condemnation was pronounced against them long ago (2:1–3). He then adduces some examples of God's condemnation in the past to show that he is capable of dealing in a similar way with contemporary sinners: "For if God did not spare the angels when they sinned, but cast them into hell and committed them to chains of deepest darkness to be kept until the judgment . . ." (v. 4). He continues with the Flood and salvation of Noah and with Sodom and Gomorrah and the deliverance of Lot. The author concludes from these examples of God's actions: if he did all these things, "then the Lord knows how to rescue the godly from trial, and to keep the unrighteous under punishment until the day of judgment—especially those who indulge their flesh in depraved lust, and who despise authority." The actual term *hell* (a translation of Greek *tartaros*) is not found in the text of *1 Enoch* 6–10, but is an interpretive rendering (the word is used in *1 Enoch* 20:2, but in a different context). Like Jude, 2 Peter also regards the present time as the last days (see 2 Pet. 3:3).

Concluding Comment

In whatever way the material sketched in this chapter came to writers of the New Testament books, we can at least say that some ideas well known to us from Qumran literature left an imprint on others whose commitments took them in different directions than the ones followed by the Essenes. The early Christian writers shared much with advocates of Judaism, their mother religion, but developed the heritage in new ways dictated by their understanding of Jesus as the messiah and their eagerness to communicate that message to all.

Select Bibliography

Several articles on the books treated in this chapter are found in

Schiffman, L. H., and J. C. VanderKam, eds. *Encyclopedia of the Dead Sea Scrolls*. 2 vols. New York and Oxford: Oxford University Press, 2000:
>   Attridge, H. "Hebrews, Letter to the." 1:345–46.
>   Lim, T. "Paul, Letters of." 2:638–41.
>   Sterling, G. "Acts of the Apostles." 1:5–7.
>   Steudel, A. "Melchizedek." 1:535–37.

Another helpful article:

Fitzmyer, J. "Paul and the Dead Sea Scrolls." In P. Flint and J. VanderKam, eds. *The Dead Sea Scrolls After Fifty Years: A Comprehensive Assessment*. 2 vols. Leiden: Brill, 1998–99. 2:599–621.

CHAPTER 17

The Dead Sea Scrolls and the Book of Revelation

Introduction

For many readers, including not a few biblical scholars, the book of Revelation (also known as the Apocalypse of John) is a formidable document. With its visions, numbers, symbols, and description of a new heaven and new earth, Revelation forms a fitting finale to the New Testament and the Christian Bible. Except for the prologue or introduction (Rev. 1:1–3), the book has the framework of an ancient letter (Rev. 1:4–22:21; see Box 17.1).

Most studies or commentaries on Revelation explore questions of the book's authorship, the setting in which it was written, and different ways in which Revelation may be interpreted. These issues need not concern us here in any great detail; suffice it to say that the author identifies himself as John (1:1, 4, 9; 22:8), that the book was written toward the end of the first century CE, and that at this time Christians were being persecuted by the Roman authorities. Not surprisingly, Revelation has been interpreted in many ways. *Preterists* understand the book in its first-century setting, with most of the events already having taken place. *Historicists* interpret Revelation as outlining the story of the Church from the late first century to the end of history. *Futurists* situate the events in the end times. *Idealists* regard the events described as symbolic pictures of eternal truths, such as the eventual triumph of good over evil.

Most discussions of the relationship between the Qumran scrolls and the New Testament have placed little emphasis on the book of Revelation, focusing instead on particular themes (such as eschatology, messianism, and biblical interpretation), or figures (John the Baptist and Jesus of Nazareth), or texts (the Synoptic Gospels, the Fourth Gospel, the Pauline Letters).[1] This is somewhat surprising, in view of the relevance of documents such as the *War Rule* and the *New Jerusalem Text* for our understanding of the New Testament book. Although there are many references to the Dead Sea Scrolls in scholarly literature that throw light on the interpretation of specific passages in Revelation,[2] most studies and commentaries on the book of Revelation have not felt the full impact of the scrolls.[3]

Box 17.1	*Outline of the Book of Revelation*
Introduction	(1:1–3)
Greetings and Doxology	(1:4–8)
The Son of Man Among the Seven Churches	(1:9–20)
Messages to the Seven Churches	(2:1–3:22)
The Throne, the Scroll, and the Lamb in Heaven	(4:1–5:14)
The Seven Seals	(6:1–8:1)
The Seven Trumpets	(8:2–11:19)
Background of the Earthly Conflict	(12:1–14:20)
The Seven Bowls	(15:1–16:21)
Babylon, the Great Prostitute (Rome?)	(17:1–19:5)
Return of Christ and Judgment of the Dead	(19:6–21:8)
The New Jerusalem	(21:9–22:5)
Epilogue	(22:6–21)

The Last Days, Apocalypses, and the Qumran Community

As we saw in Chapter 11, the Qumran covenanters were an eschatological movement; in other words, they viewed themselves as living in a segment of time called *the end of days* or *the last days,* the period before the decisive end to history when some will experience judgment and others will receive salvation. The end of days would have a negative side, involving a time of heightened testing when the forces of Belial would redouble their efforts to defeat the righteous, and a positive side, when the chosen would be delivered or purified.

The Qumranites also believed they could read off coming events from prophecies, since God had already decreed what was going to happen. One group of writings that includes such prophecies is known as *apocalypses.* Since most scholars agree that the Qumran community was an apocalyptic or eschatological movement,[4] it is striking that there are very few apocalypses among the documents produced at Qumran, and that no true apocalypses originated within the Qumran community.[5] Nevertheless, many typically apocalyptic themes and motifs are evident in much of the literature that was produced by it (e.g., in *4QInstruction*).[6] Among previously known apocalypses found at Qumran are fragments of four of the five apocalyptic booklets making up *1 Enoch,* as well as fragments of Daniel, *Jubilees,* and the *Aramaic Levi Document* (for details on these, see especially Chapter 8). Although none of these apocalypses was composed by the Qumranites, the fact that they used them indicates that such writings were very much in tune with their eschatological outlook.

Several other texts that were found among the scrolls—all of them previously unknown—have been labeled apocalypses by various scholars. One of these is the *Four Kingdoms* (4Q552–53), which was discussed in Chapter 8. Four more compositions, which we met in Chapter 9, are the *Apocryphon of Daniel* (4Q246),[7] *Pseudo-Jeremiah and Ezekiel:* (4Q483–90), the *Vision of Amram* (4Q543–48), and the *Messianic Apocalypse* (4Q521).[8]

Apocalypses and Apocalypticism

The book of Revelation is among a group of writings known as *apocalypses*, which express an *apocalyptic* ideology. The term itself is from the opening sentence: *The Revelation* (Greek, *apokalypsis*) *of Jesus Christ* (Rev. 1:1), which describes the book's contents. *Apocalypse* is a type of literature in which an angel or other heavenly being discloses to a human recipient a revelation that includes the end of the world and coming salvation. In more popular use, however, the term is used for any work with a revelatory character, although many of these writings are not strictly apocalypses. Writings that deal with the end times without having the apocalyptic features described above are better described as *eschatological*.

The term *apocalypticism* is used for the belief systems found in the main apocalypses. Besides Revelation, these writings include Daniel 7–12 in the Old Testament, and early Jewish writings such as *1 Enoch, 2 Enoch, Jubilees, 2 Baruch, 4 Ezra*, and the *Apocalypse of Abraham*.

According to Devorah Dimant, ten of the Aramaic works found in Cave 4 are apocalypses or visionary narratives.[9] Yet although they all have some features of apocalypses, most of these works are very fragmentary, which makes it difficult to decide whether they included the other required features before they were damaged. For example, 4Q521—which the French scholar Émile Puech[10] terms a *Messianic Apocalypse*—refers to the idyllic eschatological future and the resurrection from the dead; the *Vision of Amram* includes a heavenly vision and a dialogue between Moses' father, Amram, and two angelic beings; and the *Four Kingdoms* text features an interpreted dream or vision. We are aptly reminded by David Aune that these texts are certainly eschatological, but lack the complete motif of a heavenly revealer who offers to a human figure supernatural revelations about heavenly secrets and final events.[11]

Three more works, which were discussed in Chapter 9, will be explored in some detail below. The first is the *War Rule,* or *War Scroll,* which—unlike the other texts—was produced by the Qumran community, since it shares terms that are distinctive to their writings. Although this document is dominated by eschatological and apocalyptic themes, including the final battles between the Sons of Light and the Sons of Darkness, it is not written in the style of an apocalypse, but rather as a rule book.[12] The second work is the *New Jerusalem Text,* which can be categorized as an apocalypse, since it does include the required features (e.g., a revelation to a human individual through a heavenly figure, the end of history, and details of the heavenly world). Finally, some comments will be made on the *Temple Scroll.* This text is not as significant as the other two for understanding the book of Revelation, since in John's description of the New Jerusalem there is no temple (Rev. 21:22).

The Eschatological War: Revelation and the *War Rule*

THE FINAL CONFLICT AND THE *WAR RULE*

A final, holy war at the end of time is found in many prophetic and apocalyptic descriptions of events that will bring the present age to a decisive end. This theme is prominent in

Figure 17.1
Columns 16–17 of the *War Rule* (SHR 3380 and 3381)
Courtesy of the Israel Museum

both the Old Testament (e.g., Ezek. 38:7–16; 39:2; Joel 3:2; Zech. 12:1–9; 14:2) and other, mostly later, Jewish writings (such as *1 Enoch* 56:5–7; 90:13–19; 99:4; *Jub.* 23:23; *4 Ezra* 13:33–34; and the *Sibylline Oracles* 3.663–68).

In early Jewish literature, by far the most detailed description of the final conflict is found in the *War Rule* (see Figure 17.1).[13] This text describes the eschatological war in which the Sons of Light, who belong on the side of God, are opposed by the Sons of Darkness, whose leader is Belial. The particular focus in the *War Rule* is on the final series of seven battles between the forces of God and Satan, which will last forty years. In the first three battles the Sons of Light will prevail, and in the next three the Sons of Darkness will have the advantage. With the two armies tied, in the seventh and final battle the hand of God will prevail and the Sons of Darkness will be completely destroyed (1QM 1.13–16; see Box 17.2). As Jean Duhaime and David Aune point out, although the *War Rule* contains many apocalyptic features, it is not a true apocalypse, but rather a rule book that closely resembles Greco-Roman tactical manuals on how a war should be conducted.[14] There are many similarities between the military features of the *War Rule* and those of 1–2 Maccabees (two books in the Apocrypha that detail the wars of the Maccabees in the second century BCE).

COMPARISON WITH THE BOOK OF REVELATION

The theme of war and combat is also evident in the Revelation of John.[15] Several short narratives describe the gathering of end-time armies with a view to destroying God's people and the decisive eschatological battle that eventually takes place (see Rev. 16:12–16;

Box 17.2   *Outline of the War Rule (1QM, 4Q491–96)*

1. Description of Eschatological War (1.1–15)
2. Annihilation of Sons of Darkness and Service to God During the War Years (1.16–2.15)
3. Description of the Trumpets (2.16–3.12)
4. Description of the Banners (3.13–4.17)
5. Description of the Shields (5.1–2)
6. Arming and Deployment of Divisions (5.3–6.7)
7. Deployment of the Cavalry (6.8–17)
8. Recruitment and Age of the Soldiers (7.1–7)
9. Ministry of the Priests and Levites (7.9–9.8)
10. Maneuvers of the Battle Divisions (9.10–18)
11. Addresses, Prayers and Blessings
    Address of the Chief Priest (10.1–8)
    Prayer of the Chief Priest (10.8–12.19)
    Blessings of the War Recited by the Leaders After the Victory (12.20–14.1)
    Blessings of the War Recited by the Leaders in the Morning
        Before Battle (14.2–15.3)
12. The Final Battle
    First Engagement (15.4–16.9)
    Second Engagement (16.11–17.9)
    Third Engagement (17.10–16)
    Fourth, Fifth, Sixth Engagements (Not preserved)
    Seventh Engagement (18.1–9)
13. Thanksgiving for Final Victory (18.10–19.8)
14. Ceremony After the Final Battle (19.9–14)

17:14; 19:11–21; and 20:8–9). According to Rev. 16:16, the location of this battle is Armageddon:

> Then I heard a loud voice from the temple telling the seven angels, "Go and pour out on the earth the seven bowls of the wrath of God." . . .
>
> The sixth angel poured his bowl on the great river Euphrates, and its water was dried up in order to prepare the way for the kings from the east. And I saw three foul spirits like frogs coming from the mouth of the dragon, from the mouth of the beast, and from the mouth of the false prophet. These are demonic spirits, performing signs, who go abroad to the kings of the whole world, to assemble them for battle on the great day of God the Almighty. ("See, I am coming like a thief! Blessed is the one who stays awake and is clothed, not going about naked and exposed to shame.") And they assembled them at the place that in Hebrew is called *Armageddon*. (16:1, 12–16, NRSV)

In Rev. 20:9 we are told that the enemy surrounds *the beloved city* (i.e., Jerusalem), where the *camp of the saints* is located. This reference is based on Ezek. 38:12, where Gog and his allies converge on the *center of the world* (Jerusalem). The enemy is described as the hosts of Gog and Magog (Rev. 20:9) and in several other ways. In the *War Rule*, the enemies of the Sons of Light are also given various names, which may stand for Israel's enemies during the Greco-Roman period, but are difficult to identify. Names for the enemy in the *War Rule* and Revelation are compared in Box 17.3.

Unlike Revelation, however, the enemies in the *War Rule* do not assemble and march in one vast body to the place of battle, but are confronted in various encounters by the armies of Israel. Another important difference is that in Revelation humans and angels never join forces in any eschatological battle, whereas in the *War Rule* the holy angels fight together with the Sons of Light (1QM 1.10; 7.6; 19.1):

> Then [the Sons of Rig]hteousness shall shine to all ends of the world, continuing to shine forth until end of the appointed seasons of darkness. Then at the time appointed by God, His great excellence shall shine for all the times of e[ternity]; for peace and blessing, glory and joy, and long life for all Sons of Light. On the day when the Kittim fall there shall be a battle and horrible carnage before the God of Israel, for it is a day appointed by Him from ancient times as a battle of annihilation for the Sons of Darkness. On that day the congregation of the gods and the congregation of men shall engage one another, resulting in great carnage. The Sons of Light and the forces of Darkness shall fight together to show the strength of God with the roar of a great multitude and the shout of gods and men; a day of disaster. (1QM 1.8–11 [WAC, 152])

Two additional passages in Revelation, both of which mention the 144,000 (7:1–8; 14:1–5), seem to presuppose the combat theme without actually describing a holy war. First, Rev. 7:1–8 reads like a military census of the tribes of ancient Israel (cf. Numbers 1–3), with 12,000 sealed from each of the twelve tribes, for a grand total of 144,000. The reference to all twelve tribes assumes their regathering at the end time, which is also the case in the *War*

Box 17.3	*Names for the Enemy*
War Rule	*Revelation*
All nations (15.1; 16.1)	The nations in the four quarters of the earth (20:8)
All the nations of wickedness (15.2)	The kings of the east (16:12, the Parthians?)
The Sons of Darkness	The kings of the whole world (16:14)
The Kittim	The ten kings (17:12–14)
Edom, Moab, the sons of Ammon, the Kittim of Asshur, the Kittim in Egypt, and the sons of Japhet (1.1–7)	The hosts of Gog and Magog (20:8)
Aram-Naharaim, the sons of Lud, the sons of Aram, Uz, Hul, Togal, Mesha, the sons of Arphaxad, the sons of Asshur and Persia, the Kadmonites, Elam, the sons of Ishmael, and Ketura, Ham, Japhet (2.10–14)	
Led by the king of the Kittim (15.2)	Led by the Devil, the Beast, the False Prophet (20:10)

Rule, where the twelve tribes participate in the final series of eschatological battles (1QM 5.1–2). Most scholars identify the group of Rev. 7:1–8 as the innumerable multitude of martyrs who are then described in Rev. 7:9–17. Others, however, see the first group as the remnant of Christians living at the end of days, who are chosen to participate in the final eschatological conflict. According to this view, the eschatological army of Rev. 7:1–8 consists not of martyrs, but of followers of Jesus whose participation in the final conflict is similar to the role of Israel in the *War Rule.*

The second passage, Rev. 14:1–5, depicts the Lamb on Mt. Zion together with the 144,000 and seems to be part of an eschatological battle narrative that focuses on Jerusalem (see also Rev. 20:9). The members of this group are identified as celibate males (v. 4), since sexual abstinence was required of holy warriors (see Deut. 23:9–14; 1 Sam. 21:5; 2 Sam. 11:9–13); an interesting comparison is the lifelong celibacy that was practiced by many Essenes. The precise location of the future battles narrated in the *War Rule* is not clear, but 1QM 1.1–7 indicates that the Sons of Light will return from the wilderness (probably Qumran) to encamp in the wilderness of Jerusalem (1.3), after which the armies of the Sons of Light will go forth from Jerusalem (3.11; 7.4).

The British scholar Richard Bauckham regards the Revelation of John as a *Christian War Scroll,* modeled on the *War Rule,* but with extensive revision of Jewish traditions about a final battle against evil, which has already been defeated by the witness and death of Christ.[16] According to this view, the author of Revelation reinterprets the metaphor of warfare associated with apocalyptic traditions about the final messianic war to present an image of Christian witness and martyrdom. In Rev. 5:5–6, for example, John depicts the Messiah as a military victor, but reinterprets this tradition in terms of his sacrificial death for the redemption of people from all nations (Rev. 5:9–10). The eschatological holy war tradition takes two forms: the *passive* model, in which the victory is won by God alone or with his heavenly armies; and the *active* model, in which the people of God physically participate in the warfare against their enemies (this is the model found in the *War Rule*). The view of Revelation as a *Christian War Scroll* understands several passages as using the language of holy war, but transforming its meaning to nonmilitary means of triumphing over evil. These passages include (1) the conquering Messiah (Rev. 5:5–6); (2) the messianic army (7:2–14); and (3) the Lamb and his army (14:1–5).

Other passages, however, specifically mention the coming eschatological battle. (1) In Rev. 16:12–16 the kings from the east or the kings of the world assemble at Armageddon "for the battle on the great day of the Lord Almighty" (v. 14). (2) In Rev. 17:14 a coalition of ten kings wages war on the Lamb, but are conquered by him. Those who are with the Lamb are "called and chosen and faithful" and most likely participate in the battle although this is not stated. (3) In Rev. 19:11–21 the Messiah appears as a rider on a white horse followed by the armies of heaven, who battle the kings of the earth with their armies (v. 19). Although the actual battle itself is not described, the beast and the false prophet are captured and the others are killed by the sword that came out of the rider's mouth (vv. 15, 21). The role of the rider on the white horse is emphasized, but no specific role is given to the heavenly forces. (4) In Rev. 20:8–9 the hosts of Gog and Magog besiege the camp of the holy ones and the beloved city, but are destroyed by fire from heaven. The Devil, their leader, is then thrown into the lake of fire and sulfur.

Only one of these texts, Rev. 17:14, reflects the *active* model, where those who are with the Lamb most likely take part in the battle. In contrast, the other three passages confirm the tendency of apocalyptic literature to highlight the *passive* model.[17] In other words, most of these texts feature the role of God and his angels in the eschatological battle and ignore any role of God's people in the conflict.

The *War Rule* is a striking and consistent example of the *active* model of the eschatological war, but the book of Revelation is more complex. The *active* model of the eschatological war is reflected (or at least presupposed) in Rev. 7:1–9; 14:1–5; and 17:14; but the *passive* model is evident in Rev. 16:12–16; 19:11–21; and 20:8–9.

The New Jerusalem

THE *NEW JERUSALEM TEXT* FROM QUMRAN

The relevance of the Qumran scrolls is especially evident in the parallels between the *New Jerusalem Text* and the Revelation of John. As described in Chapter 9, the *New Jerusalem Text*[18] was written in Aramaic and takes the form of a guided tour like the one in Ezekiel 40–48. An anonymous guide (most likely an angel) shows an unnamed visionary many features of the future city and temple and offers various details and measurements. The most striking aspect about the architectural features of the New Jerusalem in this text is their immense proportions. At least one part of the document is said to originate with a book or writing, which is shown to the visionary and read by the guide (11Q18 frag. 19, l. 5). Together with the *Temple Scroll,* this text is part of a tradition linking the description of the eschatological temple and city in Ezekiel 40–48 with that of the New Jerusalem in Rev. 21:9–22:9. The description of the New Jerusalem in the *New Jerusalem Text* has been described as being midway between Ezekiel's description of the future Jerusalem and the heavenly Jerusalem of Revelation 21–22.[19]

Although the terms *Jerusalem* and *New Jerusalem* do not actually occur in the surviving fragments of the *New Jerusalem Text,* this work clearly focuses on the eschatological city of Jerusalem and the temple. (It is interesting to note that the name *Jerusalem* also does not occur in Ezekiel 40–48 or in the *Temple Scroll.*) Like the *Temple Scroll* (11QT^a), the *New Jerusalem Text* is clearly dependent on Ezekiel 40–48, is opposed to the Jewish groups who controlled the Temple in the author's day, and shares common traditions of a future ideal city and temple. Seeing that it survives in six copies from five of the Qumran Caves (1, 2, 4, 5, and 11), the *New Jerusalem Text* was popular among the Qumran community. As we have already mentioned, this work is an apocalypse, since it includes most of the characteristic apocalyptic features.

The guided tour begins outside the New Jerusalem (see Box 17.4). The visionary is given the measurements of the walls enclosing the city, which form a rectangle. The wall has twelve gates, with three on each side (see Ezek. 48:33–34; 11QT^a 39.12–13; 40.11–14; 4Q554), and each gate is flanked by two towers and named for one of the twelve sons of Jacob. The author later describes the inside of the city, which is constructed like a chessboard with its 192 blocks, each consisting of a square row of houses and surrounded by a spacious street:

> Then he brought me into the city, and [measured all the] city blocks. Length and breadth, they measured fifty-one staffs by fifty-one staffs, [making a square], three hundred and fifty-seven cubits to each side. Each block had a sidewalk around it, bordering

Box 17.4	*Outline of the* New Jerusalem Text *(1Q32, 2Q24, 4Q554–55, 5Q15, 11Q18)*

1. The 12 gates of the city
    Description and naming of the gates
2. The city divided into square blocks
    Each block surrounded by a spacious street
    The city divided by larger streets
3. The guide shows the visionary:
    The structure of the outer walls
    Its gates and towers
    Stairs providing access to the towers
    Structure of the city blocks
    The houses within each block
    Description of the city towers
4. The priests in the temple
    Offerings, bread, incense
5. Concluding prophecy
    The kingdoms to come
    The final battle
    Israel triumphs over the Gentile nations

the street, three staffs, that is, twenty-one cubits. So he showed me the measurement of all the blocks, between each block was a street six staffs in width, that is, [forty-two cubits]. (4Q554 frag. 1 2.11–15 [WAC, 181])

The city streets intersect at right angles, a design that originated in ancient Egypt and was later used in Hellenistic town planning (see Figure 17.2). The city as a whole is divided by larger streets, three passing from east to west, and three passing from north to south. This network of streets divides the city into large blocks. Each street, and even the city itself, is paved in white stone:

The main streets that passed from east to west were ten [staffs]. The width of the street was seventy cubits, for two of them. A third street, which was on the [north] of the temple, he measured at eighteen staffs in width, that is, [one hundred twenty-four] cubits.

The width of the streets that go from south [to north, for two of them], nine staffs, with four cubits to each street, making [sixty-seven] cubits. He measured [the middle street in the] middle of the city. Its width was [thirteen staffs and one cubit, that is ninety-two cubits]. And every street and the city itself [was paved in white stone]. (4Q554 frag. 1 2.15–22 [WAC, 181–82])

The visionary is also given a detailed description of a typical block of houses, and then of the inside of a typical house (see Figure 17.3). According to one scholar, the sizes of the residential blocks and houses, as well as their structure, indicate that the city is organized so as to house large groups of pilgrims. This suggests that the heavenly model described here is to realize the prophets' visions of the eschatological Jerusalem to which all nations will

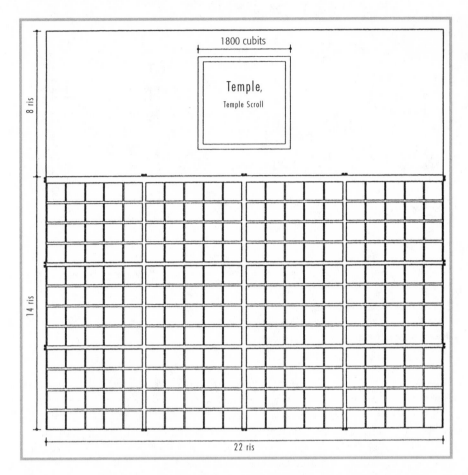

Figure 17.2

Plan of the New Jerusalem

Adapted from M. Chyutin, "The New Jerusalem: Ideal City," *Dead Sea Discoveries* 1 (1994): 83

Courtesy of Brill Academic Publishers

come at the end time.[20] The passage below features the housing block, which has a tower with a spiral staircase and four gates, one in the middle of each side:

> He then showed me the measurements of the gates of the city blocks. Their width was two staffs, fourteen cubits], and the width of the [. . .]s, its measurement in cubits. [He then measured] the width of each atrium: [two] staffs, 14 cubits, and the roof, one cubit. . . .
>
> Now a gate opposite the gate opened into the block and its measurements were like those of the outer gate. On the left of this entrance he showed me a spiral staircase [going up: its width] was a single measurement, two staffs by two, fourteen cubits; and [gates opposite the gates] were of a like measurement.
>
> There was a pillar that the stairs spiraled [around. Its width and its length was the same, six cubits by six, square]. The stairs that [went up around it] were four cubits wide and they spiraled upwards [to a height of two staffs until . . .]. (4Q554 frag. 1 3.12–4.2 = 5Q15 frag. 1 1.7–15 [WAC, 182])

A similar course is followed in the description of the eschatological temple. Apparently the visit to the temple proceeds from the outside courtyard to the inside, culminating in the

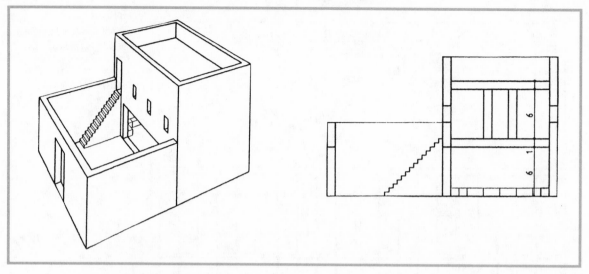

Figure 17.3
A Typical House in the *New Jerusalem Text*
Adapted from M. Chyutin, "The New Jerusalem: Ideal City," *Dead Sea Discoveries* 1 (1994): 90.
Courtesy of Brill Academic Publishers

description of the throne of God. Unfortunately, in the *New Jerusalem Text* the passages describing the architecture of the temple, its measurements, and the precious metals used for its construction are very fragmentary. The same is true for the description of the various utensils and furniture used in the temple and the vestments of the high priest. Better preserved are details of the priestly activities and rituals practiced in the temple, including the slaughtering of animals used for sacrifices and the celebration of Passover and other festivals.

The final preserved column of the *New Jerusalem Text* presents us with a prophecy of the kingdoms to come, leading up to the final apocalyptic battle between the gentile nations and Israel, with Israel being finally triumphant. This places the description of the New Jerusalem in the context of the final battle with the nations, which emphasizes the eschatological character of the entire composition:

> [... shall rise up] in place of it, and the kingdom of P[ersia ... and then shall rise up] the Kittim in place of it. All these kingdoms shall appear one after another [...] others numerous and lordly with them [...] with them Edom and Moab and the Ammonites [...] of the whole land of Babylon, not [...] and they shall do evil to your descendants until the time of [... shall come ... and then shall appear] among all the peoples the kingdom. (4Q554 frag. 2 3.14–21 [WAC, 184])

COMPARISON WITH THE BOOK OF REVELATION

When we compare the description of the New Jerusalem in the book of Revelation with the *New Jerusalem Text*, several similarities and contrasts emerge. Two other texts that must also be considered are Ezekiel 40–48 and the *Temple Scroll*. But first, we present here in full the key passage from the New Testament book (Rev. 21:9–22:7, NRSV):

> [9]Then one of the seven angels who had the seven bowls full of the seven last plagues came and said to me, "Come, I will show you the bride, the wife of the Lamb." [10]And in the spirit he carried me away to a great, high mountain and showed me the holy city Jerusalem coming down out of heaven from God. [11]It has the glory of God and a radiance like a very rare jewel, like jasper, clear as crystal. [12]It has a great, high wall with twelve gates, and at the gates twelve angels, and on the gates are inscribed the names of the twelve tribes of the Israelites; [13]on the east three gates, on the north three gates, on the south three gates, and on the west three gates. [14]And the wall of the city has twelve foundations, and on them are the twelve names of the twelve apostles of the Lamb.
>
> [15]The angel who talked to me had a measuring rod of gold to measure the city and its gates and walls. [16]The city lies foursquare, its length the same as its width; and he measured the city with his rod, fifteen hundred miles; its length and width and height are equal. [17]He also measured its wall, one hundred forty-four cubits by human measurement, which the angel was using. [18]The wall is built of jasper, while the city is pure gold, clear as glass. [19]The foundations of the wall of the city are adorned with every jewel; the first was jasper, the second sapphire, the third agate, the fourth emerald, [20]the fifth onyx, the sixth carnelian, the seventh chrysolite, the eighth beryl, the ninth topaz, the tenth chrysoprase, the eleventh jacinth, the twelfth amethyst. [21]And the twelve gates are twelve pearls, each of the gates is a single pearl, and the street of the city is pure gold, transparent as glass.
>
> [22]I saw no temple in the city, for its temple is the Lord God the Almighty and the Lamb. [23]And the city has no need of sun or moon to shine on it, for the glory of God is its light, and its lamp is the Lamb. [24]The nations will walk by its light, and the kings of the earth will bring their glory into it. [25]Its gates will never be shut by day—and there will be no night there. [26]People will bring into it the glory and the honor of the nations. [27]But nothing unclean will enter it, nor anyone who practices abomination or falsehood, but only those who are written in the Lamb's book of life.
>
> [22:1]Then the angel showed me the river of the water of life, bright as crystal, flowing from the throne of God and of the Lamb [2]through the middle of the street of the city. On either side of the river is the tree of life with its twelve kinds of fruit, producing its fruit each month; and the leaves of the tree are for the healing of the nations. [3]Nothing accursed will be found there any more. But the throne of God and of the Lamb will be in it, and his servants will worship him; [4]they will see his face, and his name will be on their foreheads. [5]And there will be no more night; they need no light of lamp or sun, for the Lord God will be their light, and they will reign forever and ever.
>
> [6]And he said to me, "These words are trustworthy and true, for the Lord, the God of the spirits of the prophets, has sent his angel to show his servants what must soon take place."
>
> [7]"See, I am coming soon! Blessed is the one who keeps the words of the prophecy of this book."

First, the *New Jerusalem Text* and Revelation, as well as the *Temple Scroll,* draw on Ezekiel 40–48, where the following features are found: the wall around the temple (Ezek. 40:1–47), the exterior and interior of the temple (40:48–42:20), the return of God's glory to the temple (43:1–27), admission to the temple and details of the priesthood (44:1–31), al-lotment of land (45:1–9), festivals, offerings and various regulations (45:10–46:24), life-giving water flowing from the temple (47:1–12), and further allotment of land (45:1–9 and 47:13–48:35). Revelation mentions that the names of the twelve tribes of Israel are written on the city gates, but does not list them, and—like the *New Jerusalem Text* and Ezekiel—specifies that there are three gates in each of the four walls (Rev. 21:12–13). The names of the gates are listed in the *New Jerusalem Text* (4Q554 frag. 1 1.12–2.9) and in Ezekiel (48:30–35), but in a different order. (The listing presented in the *New Jerusalem Text* generally conforms to the order found in the *Temple Scroll* [11QT^a 39.12–13; 40.11–14]):

Ezek. 48:30–34	*New Jerusalem Text*
North:	South:
Reuben	Simeon
Judah	[Levi]
Levi	Judah
East:	West:
Joseph	Joseph
Benjamin	[Benjamin]
Dan	Reuben
South:	North:
Simeon	[Issachar]
Issachar	[Zebulon]
Zebulun	Gad
West:	East:
Gad	Dan
Asher	Naphtali
Naphtali	Asher

The second feature common to all three texts is the guide who leads and informs the visionary: the angel of Revelation, the unnamed figure of the *New Jerusalem Text,* and the mysterious *man* of Ezekiel 40–48. In Rev. 21:9–22:9 this angel functions in three ways: (1) by measuring the architecture, (2) by offering occasional comments, and (3) by lead-ing the visionary from place to place. The same three functions are carried out by the guides in the *New Jerusalem Text* and in Ezekiel 40–48. One phrase found in two of the three writings is *then he showed me* (for Revelation, see Rev. 21:10 and 22:1; for the *New Jerusalem Text,* see 2Q24 1.3; 4Q554 frag. 1 2.15; 3.20; 4Q555 1.3; 5Q15 frag. 1 1.2, 15; 2.6; and 11Q18 16.6; 18.1).

Third, the dimensions of the ideal, eschatological city (and the temple in two cases) that are described in Ezekiel 40–48, the *Temple Scroll,* the *New Jerusalem Text,* and Revela-tion 21 are all enormous. The precise length of ancient measuring standards is not always clear; the standard length of the cubit, for instance, is about 17.5 inches, but this differs in Ezekiel (the royal cubit of 20.5 inches). The following statistics may be regarded as reasonably accurate:

> In Ezekiel 40–48, the outer court of the temple is surrounded by a square wall, measuring 850 feet (259 meters) on each side for a total of 3,400 feet (1,036 meters); see Ezek. 40:5; 42:15–20; 45:2. The walls of the city itself form a gigantic square of 1.45 miles (2.33 kilometers) on each side, for a total of 5.8 miles (9.33 kilometers); see Ezek. 48:30–35.

> In the *Temple Scroll,* the sanctuary complex consists of three concentric squares, with the outer court, or Court of Israel, measuring 2,860 feet, or 880 meters (1,700 cubits), per side, with a total perimeter of 11,450 feet, or 3,522 meters (6,800 cubits). Such a structure would equal the size of the entire city of Jerusalem in the Hasmonean period (150–30 BCE)!

> The *New Jerusalem Text* contains a rectangular city plan of approximately 20 by 14 miles (32 by 23 kilometers), for a total of 280 square miles (736 square km), with the temple inside.

> In Revelation, the dimensions reach fantastic proportions. Here the city is not square or rectangular, but in the shape of a cube, with an equal length, width, and height of 1,500 miles (about 2,400 kilometers) each!

Fourth, all three texts share a striking emphasis on the twelve tribes of Israel, whose names are associated with the gates of the New Jerusalem (Ezek. 48:30–35; 4Q554 frag. 1 1.9–2.9; Rev. 21:12; see also 11QT^a 39.12–13; 40.11–41.12). As David Aune reminds us,[21] this feature anticipates the final realization of a central concern of Jewish eschatology: the restoration of all Israel, which is repeatedly mentioned in Old Testament writings after the Exile and in other early Jewish literature.

Finally, the *New Jerusalem Text* and Revelation 21 (but not Ezekiel 40–48) share a common emphasis on the precious stones and metals used as building materials for the eschatological structures of the city. The earliest references to precious stones used in the rebuilding of Jerusalem are found in Isa. 54:11–12 and Tob. 13:16, and the historian Josephus reports that gold overlay was used on parts of Herod's Temple (*Jewish War* 5.201, 205, 207). In the *New Jerusalem Text,* the city is described as having buildings of electrum, sapphire, chalcedony, and gold (4Q554 frag. 2 2.15), and every street—indeed, the entire city—is paved with white stone, marble, and onyx (5Q15 frag. 1 1.6–7). In Revelation, the description of the New Jerusalem is even more dazzling. The city is described as having "a radiance like a very rare jewel, like jasper, clear as crystal" (21:11) or of "pure gold, clear as glass" (21:18). The city wall is built of jasper (21:18), and its twelve foundations are constructed of a variety of precious and semiprecious stones (21:19–20).

In Jewish writings the tradition of using precious stones and metals for holy buildings arises from the huge and costly stones that were used for the foundation of Solomon's Temple (1 Kings 5:17; 7:10). This theme, however, is also found in non-Israelite traditions. For example, in the second century CE the Roman author Lucian refers to a city of gold surrounded by an emerald wall with seven gates. Each gate is constructed of a single plank of cinnamon, with a river of myrrh running through it (*Verae Historiae* 2.11).

The Temple, Ritual Purity, and the *Temple Scroll*

In the book of Revelation, the New Jerusalem has no temple (Rev. 21:22), which is surprising since in Jewish writings of that time the eschatological expectation of a New Jerusalem usually included a new temple. But in this book, Jerusalem itself clearly functions as a temple-city: "I saw no temple in the city, for its temple is the Lord God the Almighty and the Lamb. And the city has no need of sun or moon to shine on it, for the glory of God is its light, and its lamp is the Lamb" (vv. 22–23).

The Essenes who formed the Qumran community had separated themselves from the Temple in Jerusalem because they believed that the religious authorities running it were lax in ritual purity and were using an unlawful ritual calendar (cf. CD 20:22–23 and 4QMMT). This does not mean that they rejected the basic validity of a Temple religion; indeed, they awaited its eschatological renewal. Before this end-time event, the Qumranites tended to describe their community as an eschatological temple, with *Israel* (the laymen) as the holy place and *Aaron* (the priests) as the Holy of Holies:

> When such men as these come to be in Israel, then shall the party of the *Yahad* truly be established, an "eternal planting" (*Jub.* 16:26), a temple for Israel, and—mystery!—a Holy of Holies for Aaron; true witnesses to justice, chosen by God's will to atone for the land and to recompense the wicked their due. They will be "the tested wall, the precious cornerstone" (Isa. 28:16) whose foundations shall neither be shaken nor swayed, a fortress, a Holy of Holies for Aaron, all of them knowing the Covenant of Justice and thereby offering a sweet savor. They shall be a blameless and true house in Israel, upholding the covenant of eternal statutes. They shall be an acceptable sacrifice, atoning for the land and ringing in the verdict against evil, so that perversity ceases to exist. (1QS 8.4–10 [WAC, 137–38]; see also 1QS 5.4–7; 9.3–6)

In Ezekiel 40–48, the destruction of the First Temple in 587 or 586 BCE gave rise to the prophet's vision of an ideal or eschatological temple. When the *New Jerusalem Text* and the *Temple Scroll* were written, the Second Temple was standing; however, the authors of these texts were opposed to the religious leaders who ran it, and so (like Ezekiel) envisaged an ideal or eschatological temple. Among the Qumran community, the negative view of the existing city and Temple found in the *New Jerusalem Text* and the *Temple Scroll* was welcome and positively received. In Revelation and the *New Jerusalem Text,* the emphasis is on the city, and Revelation calls attention to the absence of a temple from city's midst. In Ezekiel and the *Temple Scroll*, however, the main emphasis is on the temple complex itself.

Nothing unclean will enter this city, "nor anyone who practices abomination or falsehood" (Rev. 21:27). A longer list of those excluded from the city is given in Rev. 22:15: "Outside are the dogs and sorcerers and fornicators and murderers and idolaters, and everyone who loves and practices falsehood." Although these lists differ in detail, both seem to begin with a *ritual* category, followed by a list of *moral* transgressors.[22]

With respect to ritual, in the *Temple Scroll* the temple and the holy city form a temple-city unit, so that the purity requirements that normally apply to the temple are extended to the entire city. A pronouncement that closely parallels Rev. 21:27, with its exclusion of anything impure from the eschatological Jerusalem, is found in column 47:

> The city that I shall sanctify by establishing My name and temp[le] there must be holy and pure from anything that is in any way unclean, by which one might be defiled. Every-

thing inside it must be pure, and everything that enters it must be pure: wine, oil, edibles and any foodstuff upon which liquid is poured—all must be pure. (11QT^a 47.3–6 [WAC, 478])

In the Old Testament, the prediction that unclean persons or things will not enter the eschatological Jerusalem occurs in only two passages, both from Isaiah:

For the uncircumcised and the unclean shall enter you no more. (Isa. 52:1b)

A highway shall be there, and it shall be called the Holy Way; the unclean shall not travel on it, but it shall be for God's people. (Isa. 35:8)

The passage that was quoted from Rev. 21:27 most likely alludes to Isa. 52:1, but no such allusion is evident in 11QT^a 47.3–6. This suggests that the exclusion of unclean persons or things from the eschatological Jerusalem was a more widely held conviction, one not restricted to the exegesis of the two passages in Isaiah.

Select Bibliography

Two informative articles on the material in this chapter appear in

Schiffman, L. H., and J. C. VanderKam, eds. *Encyclopedia of the Dead Sea Scrolls*. 2 vols. New York and Oxford: Oxford University Press, 2000:
    Collins, A. Y. "Revelation, Book of." 1:772–74.
    García Martínez, F. "New Jerusalem." 1:606–10.

Another, advanced article helpful in compiling this chapter:

Aune, D. E. "Qumran and the Book of Revelation." In P. Flint and J. VanderKam, eds. *The Dead Sea Scrolls After Fifty Years: A Comprehensive Assessment*. 2 vols. Leiden: Brill, 1998–99. 2:622–48.

Other books and articles:

Bauckham, R. "The Apocalypse as a Christian War Scroll." In his *The Climax of Prophecy: Studies on the Book of Revelation*. Edinburgh: T & T. Clark, 1993. First appeared as "The Book of Revelation as a Christian War Scroll." *Neotestamentica* 22 (1988): 17–40.
Broshi, M. "Visionary Architecture and Town Planning in the Dead Sea Scrolls." In D. Dimant and L. H. Schiffman, eds. *Time to Prepare the Way in the Wilderness: Papers on the Qumran Scrolls by Fellows of the Institute for Advanced Studies of the Hebrew University, Jerusalem, 1989–1990*. Studies on the Texts of the Desert of Judah 16. Leiden: Brill, 1995. Pp. 9–22.
Chyutin, M. "The New Jerusalem: Ideal City." *Dead Sea Discoveries* 1 (1994): 71–97.
Collins, J. J. *Apocalypticism in the Dead Sea Scrolls*. London and New York: Routledge, 1997.
Davies, P. R. *1QM, the War Scroll from Qumran: Its Structure and History*. Biblica et Orientalia 32. Rome: Biblical Institute Press, 1977.
Dimant, D. "Apocalyptic Texts at Qumran." In E. Ulrich and J. VanderKam, eds. *The Community of the Renewed Covenant: The Notre Dame Symposium on the Dead Sea Scrolls*. Christianity and Judaism in Antiquity 10. Notre Dame, IN: University of Notre Dame Press, 1994. Pp. 175–91.
Draper, J. A. "The Twelve Apostles as Foundation Stones of the Heavenly Jerusalem and the Foundation of the Qumran Community." *Neotestamentica* 22 (1988): 41–63.

Duhaime, J. "The War Scroll from Qumran and the Greco-Roman Tactical Treatises." *Revue de Qumrân* 13/49–52 (Carmignac Memorial, 1988): 133–51.

García Martínez, F. *Qumran and Apocalyptic: Studies on the Aramaic Texts from Qumran.* Studies on the Texts of the Desert of Judah 9. Leiden: Brill, 1992.

García Martínez, F., and J. Trebolle Barrera. *The People of the Dead Sea Scrolls, Their Writings, Beliefs and Practices.* Leiden: Brill, 1995.

Licht, J. "The Ideal Town Plan from Qumran: The Description of the New Jerusalem." *Israel Exploration Journal* 29 (1979): 47–50.

PART FIVE

Controversies About the Dead Sea Scrolls

CHAPTER 18

Scroll Wars

The Early Years (1947–67)

The Dead Sea Scrolls have been a subject of keen interest from the time they first became known, and that interest has continued to the present. Not only have people been fascinated by the scrolls, they have also fought about them. In the early years one intensely debated subject was the authenticity of the scrolls. Did they really date to the turn of the eras or were they forgeries, texts from much later times mistaken by the gullible for ancient works?

ESTABLISHING THE AUTHENTICITY OF THE SCROLLS

Most experts who studied the scrolls became convinced at an early time that they did in fact come from the late Second Temple period, and they had several converging lines of evidence supporting this conviction, as we saw in Chapter 2. The paleographers and the archeologists came to the same general conclusions, and the carbon-14 date of a linen scroll wrapper was consistent with their understanding. One critic who persisted for years in denying the authenticity of the scrolls was Solomon Zeitlin of Dropsie College in Philadelphia. Long after other skeptics had dropped the argument, Zeitlin clung to his thesis that the scrolls were medieval in date or just plain forgeries. In a long series of articles, mostly in the *Jewish Quarterly Review,* of which he was the editor, he set forth his views. The titles of some pieces make entertaining reading: "Scholarship and the Hoax of Recent Discoveries," "The Fiction of the Recent Discoveries Near the Dead Sea," and "The Antiquity of the Hebrew Scrolls and the Piltdown Hoax: A Parallel."[1] A learned man with vast knowledge of Jewish texts, Zeitlin charged, for example, that the different stories told about the discovery contradicted each other; and expressions like the *Teacher of Righteousness* and the *house of judgment* betray their more recent date because they are unknown in the classical sources. In his opinion, this would be like introducing terms such as *automobile* and *telephone* into a work of Shakespeare, yet claiming it was written in Shakespeare's time. He also thought the handwriting in the scrolls did not look ancient. These arguments were not convincing when he raised them, and are even less so today, as the number of texts discovered has increased—whether from Qumran or elsewhere. Zeitlin, like several others who have held unusual views about the scrolls, was unimpressed with the arguments of paleographers like Albright.

PUBLISHING THE DEAD SEA SCROLLS: THE FIRST TEAM OF EDITORS

The great controversy that was to engulf the Dead Sea Scrolls at a later time did not concern their authenticity, but the pace at which they were published—or, rather, not published. To gain perspective on the issue, it will be useful for us to go back to the discovery of Qumran Cave 4 in 1952. The sudden presence of unprecedented numbers of texts in very fragmentary, tattered condition necessitated a fundamental change in the way in which the scrolls were handled. We saw in Chapter 1 that the first few scrolls taken from Cave 1 were all published within a short span of time. Beginning in 1948 when Sukenik made photographs and transcriptions of some of his texts available and ending in 1956 with the appearance of the *Genesis Apocryphon,* all of these texts reached the scholarly world in eight years. The editions of the texts consisted of photographs and transcriptions, with some brief introductory sections.

We should applaud the efficiency of the first editors, but we should also remember that they worked mostly with well-preserved manuscripts that presented relatively few reading problems. The *Genesis Apocryphon* is an exception. This took the longest to get into print (1956) because it was difficult to unroll, and when it did appear only small parts were made available.

Even the many fragments from Cave 1 were quite manageable. After the Bedouin and Syrians had removed the larger pieces from Cave 1, archeologists came along and salvaged hundreds of small scraps. These, too, were in print in a short time. Two scholars associated with the École Biblique, D. Barthélemy and J. T. Milik, edited the fragments in a large tome entitled *Qumran Cave 1* in 1955. This was the initial volume in a new series devoted to the scrolls and related finds, Discoveries in the Judaean Desert (DJD), published by the Clarendon Press in Oxford, England. (For three volumes, the series was called Discoveries in the Judaean Desert of Jordan [DJDJ].) Despite the English title of the first volume, it is written in French. The second publication in the DJD series was in two parts (one volume of texts, one of photographic plates) edited by P. Benoit, Milik, and R. de Vaux (1961). In it were the texts found in the nearby Murabba'at caves.

The Bedouin found Qumran Cave 2 in 1952, and Caves 3–6 came to light later in the same year; Caves 7–10 were discovered in 1955. The yield of manuscript fragments from Caves 2–3 and 5–10 was relatively small, so a decision was made to publish them together, again in two parts, with one volume for texts and one for photographic plates. The publication date for DJD 3 (*Les 'petites grottes' de Qumran*) was 1962; the editors were M. Baillet, Milik, and de Vaux. The manuscripts from Cave 11 (located in 1956), some of which were in a very good state of preservation, were handled differently. Several were purchased by foreign institutions, and major ones were published individually in the 1960s, 1970s, and 1980s. One of the longest manuscripts from the cave, the first Psalms scroll, saw print in 1965 as DJDJ 4 (*The Psalms Scroll of Qumrân Cave 11 [11QPs^a]*), edited by J. Sanders.

Cave 4, however, posed a problem of a different magnitude because of the many thousands of battered fragments preserved in it. As the nearly innumerable bits and pieces were being bought from the discoverers by the Jordanian government and collected at the Palestine Archaeological Museum in East Jerusalem, it soon became evident that the work of preparing them for publication would be slow and difficult, requiring the help of more experts than the few priests from the École Biblique who had worked on the other texts. In 1952 G. Lankester Harding, the director of the Jordanian Department of Antiquities, appointed de Vaux chief editor of the Judean Desert texts. With more and more fragments flooding into the museum, the authorities decided to appoint an international team of scholars to prepare the Cave 4 materials (see Figure 18.1). The directors of archeological schools in Jerusalem (they were members of the board of the Palestine Archaeological Museum) were asked to help in forming such a group; also, prominent scholars in England, the United States, and Germany were invited to suggest candidates. The ones chosen would not only need the relevant academic training, but would also have to be in a position to spend extended amounts of time in Jerusalem working at the museum. As a result, the appointees were quite young. The seven men who eventually formed the Cave 4 team, their nationalities, and religious affiliations, were, in the order of their appointments:

F. M. Cross: American, Presbyterian

J. T. Milik: Polish, Catholic (a priest at the time)

John Allegro: English, agnostic

Jean Starcky: French, Catholic (a priest)

Patrick Skehan: American, Catholic (a priest)

John Strugnell: English, Presbyterian, later Catholic

Claus-Hunno Hunzinger: German, Lutheran

A glaring omission from the team is the name of any Jewish scholar, despite the prominent role Jewish experts had already played in scrolls research. Under the auspices of the Jordanian government none could be included. As a result, some of the greatest students of Hebrew language and literature were unable to work with the Cave 4 fragments, unless team members happened to issue preliminary editions of texts in their allotment. The seven men who constituted the group, all appointed in 1953 and 1954, joined de Vaux, who was chair of the museum board, as the international team that would prepare the Cave 4 fragments for publication. This small group did not remain the same very long. In 1958 M. Baillet (a priest from the École) joined them, and Hunzinger eventually withdrew in 1971, leaving his material to Baillet.

The Cave 4 texts, once they were identifiable, were divided by kind among the committee members. Cross and Skehan received the biblical material, and the others took on the varied extrabiblical works. It was apparently understood that these scholars had the official right to first publication of the texts in their respective "lots," or assignments.

During the 1950s the team was able to spend extended stretches of time in Jerusalem because money was available to support their labors. J. D. Rockefeller, Jr., the founder of the Palestine Archaeological Museum where the scroll fragments were housed, donated funds sufficient to underwrite the work of several editors for six years (Milik and Starcky

Figure 18.1

Members of the
editorial team
outside the Palestine
Archaeological Museum

Courtesy of the Estate
of John Allegro

were supported by the Centre National de la Recherche Scientifique). Among the items covered by his funds were the costs of the many photographs taken of the scroll fragments. Under these circumstances, the group toiled away at the enormous challenge of cleaning, sorting, reading, identifying, and at times joining the thousands of pieces. One really has to see the fragments to begin getting an idea of what confronted the small band of scholars. Cross has written a description of the work:

> Unlike the several scrolls of Caves 1 and 11 which are preserved in good condition, with only minor lacunae, the manuscripts of Cave 4 are in an advanced state of decay. Many fragments are so brittle or friable that they can scarcely be touched with a camel's-hair brush. Most are warped, crinkled, or shrunken, crusted with soil chemicals, blackened by moisture and age. The problems of cleaning, flattening, identifying, and piecing them together are formidable.
>
> The fragments when they are purchased from tribesmen generally come in boxes; cigarette boxes, film boxes, or shoe boxes, depending on the size of the fragments. The precious leather and papyrus is delicately handled by rough Bedouin hands, for the value of

the material is all too keenly appreciated. Often cotton wool or tissue paper has been used by Bedouin to separate and protect the scraps of scrolls; and on occasion they have applied bits of gummed paper to pieces which threatened to crack apart or disintegrate. Not since the clandestine digs of Cave 1 have owners broken up large sheets or columns to sell them piecemeal.[2]

We should recall that the Bedouin were not the only ones to apply foreign materials and thus damage the scrolls. The scholars applied castor oil to pieces to make them easier to read and joined the backs of some fragments with cellulose tape. All of this, of course, has had to be undone in more recent times (see Chapter 4).

There were interruptions in the work that was being carried out in such a volatile part of the world. In September 1956, during the Suez War, the international team had to leave the area. At that time Jordanian authorities transported the scroll fragments in the museum to Amman; they were to remain there until early 1957.

GOOD PROGRESS IN THE PRELIMINARY WORK

In 1957 work began on compiling a concordance of all the words that occurred in the hundreds of texts that the team was identifying. This was done for the convenience of the editors, who would often need to check in what other fragments a word might occur, and for this reason the concordance was a tool for work at the museum and was not published at the time. The concordance was prepared for the team by other scholars: Raymond Brown, Joseph Fitzmyer, Willard Oxtoby, and later Javier Teixidor (for Caves 2–3, 5–10). It was entitled *A Preliminary Concordance to the Hebrew and Aramaic Fragments from Qumran Caves II–X*. This work will reappear later in our story. Any such work in the late 1950s had to be preliminary, because analysis of the thousands of fragments proceeded only gradually and fragments continued to arrive at the museum until the very late 1950s. When the Rockefeller support ran out in 1960, the team had done a large amount of the preparatory work and of the painstaking labor of identification and transcription. By this time they had identified more than 500 texts in the Cave 4 collection. The results of their study to that point were recorded in the concordance and on the photographs.

It seems in retrospect as if the time was ripe for rapid publication of the Cave 4 manuscripts, but that was not to be the case for most of them. The members of the team did prepare preliminary editions of some of their texts or parts of them, and these appeared in journals and as book chapters in the 1950s and early 1960s. During the 1960s, Clarendon Press published two more volumes in the Discoveries in the Judaean Desert series: DJDJ 4: *The Psalms Scroll of Qumran Cave 11 (11QPs^a)*, edited by J. Sanders; and DJDJ 5: *Qumran Cave 4.I (4Q158–186)*, edited by J. Allegro. The latter volume has the distinction of being the first in the series to offer Cave 4 texts—all of those in Allegro's lot of manuscripts. Despite this distinction, the volume was to experience a rocky reception.

Israel Gains Control of the Scrolls (1967)

In 1967, the Six-Day War broke out in the Middle East. Israel's conquests included East Jerusalem, and as a result the Palestine Archaeological Museum fell into its hands. At that time Israel took over control of the scrolls from Jordan (which had nationalized them in

1961 and had done the same to the museum in 1966), although the question of who the legal owners of the texts might be remains a thorny, if theoretical, problem. When Israel gained the museum (which was renamed the Rockefeller Museum) and its contents, the original Jordanian arrangement with the members of the Cave 4 team was honored. Strugnell recalls that

> between de Vaux, Yadin, and the Government's Director of Antiquities then, Avraham Biran, the pattern and outlines of the continuation of our work were agreed on (i.e., principally on the keeping of the Palestine Museum's manuscript collections in it, and physically separate from the Israeli collections, on the guarantee of our group's autonomy and on the maintenance of our exclusive rights to continue and to finish our project).[3]

It appears that only one new condition was stipulated—that the last two words be removed from what had become the full title of the series, Discoveries in the Judaean Desert *of Jordan* (a form that had appeared on DJD 3, 4, 5).[4]

THE SLOW PACE OF PUBLICATION

By the end of the 1960s, only the Allegro volume of Cave 4 texts had appeared in print—this despite the impressive progress in reading the fragments that had been made by 1960 and enshrined in the *Preliminary Concordance*. For financial and other reasons, team members were unable to spend as much time in Jerusalem as they had in the 1950s, and the disruption caused by the war naturally did not help. After Allegro's 1968 volume, the next number in the DJD series (vol. 6) did not see the light of day until 1977, when *Qumrân grotte 4.II.I: Archéologie, II: Tefillin, Mezuzot et Targums (4Q128–157)* appeared under the editorship of de Vaux (who had died in 1971) and Milik. Yet another five years passed before DJD 7 was published—*Qumrân grotte 4.III (4Q482–520)*, edited by Baillet (1982). True, there was a delay of several years between when the editors submitted their manuscripts to the press and the date of publication, but there is no denying the publication project by this time was merely limping along.

The DJD series is not the sole measure of progress in publishing Cave 4 texts. As in the early years, there continued to be major editions of texts issued outside the official series, but not many of them. In 1976 Milik published his landmark work *The Books of Enoch: Aramaic Fragments of Qumrân Cave 4* (also by the Clarendon Press), in which he presented editions, photographs, and extensive commentary on *most* of the Enoch manuscripts from Cave 4, as well as extended and at times controversial essays about the origins and development of the Enoch traditions. The next year saw publication in Hebrew of Yigael Yadin's *The Temple Scroll*, a three-volume edition of the long and important text thought to be from Cave 11. Yadin had acquired it from Kando by force after the Israeli victory in 1967 (an English translation and slight revision of the work was issued in 1983).[5] These amazing works by Milik and Yadin illustrate another development in the editorial process: scholars were no longer content to prepare transcriptions and brief treatments of the texts; they were now writing exhaustive commentaries in addition to doing the basic work of editing. The vast growth in the quantity of commentary hardly boded well for adhering to any publishing timetable that might have been in place.

TENSIONS AMONG THE TEAM
AND THE ADDITION OF NEW MEMBERS

Then, too, not all was going well for the team of scholars working on the Cave 4 manu-scripts. With the exception of Baillet, who was added, and Hunzinger, who left, the mem-bership of the group had remained constant since the 1950s, even though they did not actually work together very often at the museum. In the later 1950s and on into the 1960s tensions arose and marred relations among them. John Allegro, who, as we have just seen, was the only editor of Cave 4 manuscripts to publish his lot at all efficiently, had a falling out with his colleagues. The case of John Marco Allegro is decidedly strange. He won the gratitude of many people by getting his texts into print long before any of his fellows did, but speed in publication did not improve the quality of his work. Allegro's editions were spartan compared to others in DJD volumes (e.g., he reports nothing about paleographi-cal dates for the manuscripts and in fact gives no introductions to them), and many of his readings were debatable. One result was that Strugnell wrote a massive review of Allegro's volume (the review is longer than the book itself): in it he offered detailed corrections and suggestions for line after line in Allegro's work.[6] Such an exchange says something about the lack of collegiality that had grown up between these former teammates.

Allegro's relations with the group had been deteriorating for some time. From his study of the texts he had concluded that traditional views about the origins of Christianity were wrong and that Qumran texts supported his theory about close parallels between the scrolls and the New Testament. He gave three radio talks on such matters; these were broadcast in the north of England during three successive weeks in January 1956. Some of the talks received treatment in the *New York Times* and thus reached a wider audience. Allegro's colleagues on the team responded to his claims in a letter to *The Times* of Lon-don; in it they explained that they had seen all the texts he had studied and none of them supported his position. Allegro hardly enhanced his reputation when he went off hunting (unsuccessfully) for the treasures of the *Copper Scroll* (and, according to de Vaux, damaged Qumran ruins in the process). He also published a translation of the scroll without autho-rization, when he thought that Milik was taking too long to issue his official version (Milik's edition is in DJDJ 3). Allegro had been the one who arranged to have the *Copper Scroll* opened in Manchester (it had to be sawed into strips) and was eager to let people know the contents. He differed from Milik in thinking that the treasures mentioned in it were real treasures from the Jerusalem Temple. Later he tarnished his reputation irrepara-bly by writing *The Sacred Mushroom and the Cross* (1970), a book regretted by friend and foe alike. Even the publisher apologized for it, and Allegro's mentor, Sir Godfrey Driver, was one of the academics who repudiated its arguments. In this book Allegro traced the origins of Christianity to the effects of a hallucinatory drug named psilocybin. (For further details on Allegro, see Chapter 15.)

As mentioned above, Hunzinger resigned his position in 1971. De Vaux died on Sep-tember 10, 1971, and was succeeded as chief editor by P. Benoit who, as de Vaux had been, was Director of the École Biblique in Jerusalem and had been an editor of the Murabba'at texts in DJD 2. The team had nominated him, and his appointment was apparently con-firmed by Israeli and Jordanian authorities. Benoit tried to set a timetable for publication of the texts by the team members, but not everyone seems to have taken it very seriously. Patrick Skehan, however, had completed a large percentage of his editions and might have seen his volume into print within a few more years, had death not intervened. Shortly before he died on September 9, 1980, Skehan had transferred his materials to Eugene Ulrich of the University of Notre Dame, who in time also received some of Cross's texts for publication. After being ill for some time, Benoit resigned his position (he died on April 23, 1987), and John Strugnell, an original member of the team, became chief editor in September 1984. To this point, the practice was that, when one member was lost to the team, he was replaced by just one other person. So J. Starcky began working with Émile Puech of the École Biblique in 1982, and Puech inherited his texts when Starcky died (October 9, 1988). As a result, the number of people engaged in the large project did not grow.

THE STRUGNELL YEARS (1984–90)

One of the trademarks of John Strugnell's editorship was an effort to expand the original, small team of scholars and to involve Jewish experts in the work. It seems that having a small team was advantageous during the initial phases of the project, because it permitted more efficient interaction as the members worked together at the museum and consulted and helped one another with the fragments. But the initial editorial work was one phase; preparing the extensive and difficult materials for official publication was quite another matter. Here the system was obviously inadequate. Tens of thousands of fragments were more than eight experts, however skilled, could have handled, even if the Rockefeller money had continued. When the funds lapsed and were not renewed, the work slowed considerably. Yet no new scholars were brought on board to assist in completing the task. It is understandable that scholars who by this time had invested some thirty years in the work wanted to see it through to publication by themselves, not by others. But by the 1980s there was little evidence they would ever complete the task. During Benoit's tenure as editor in chief (1971–84) two DJD volumes appeared (vol. 6 in 1977 and vol. 7 in 1982); one DJD volume (vol. 8) was published during Strugnell's stint in office (1984–90), although at least one other was in an advanced state of preparation. The one volume that did appear was not an edition of Qumran texts, but of a large scroll from the Nahal Hever.[7]

It was not until Strugnell became chief editor that the small team was enlarged to about twenty members, although already in 1979 he had enlisted the young Israeli scholar Elisha Qimron for work on one of his texts (4QMMT). Strugnell himself was responsible for the expansion, as was Ulrich who, when offered some of Cross's texts for editing, accepted on condition that some established textual critics as well as some dissertationists working with Cross and Strugnell at Harvard University be added to assist in the work. Among the Jewish scholars who were brought on board during the 1980s were Devorah Dimant (who began working with Strugnell in 1985) and Emanuel Tov. Joseph Baumgarten, a Jewish scholar at Baltimore Hebrew College, was given the responsibility of finishing editions of some of Milik's texts (copies of the *Damascus Document*). James VanderKam was added to the team in 1989 when Milik allowed him to partner in completing editions of the fragments of the book of *Jubilees* and related texts; and Peter Flint was added in 1991 by Ulrich to complete Skehan's edition of Cave 4 Psalms scrolls. Strugnell also attempted to set up with the scholars a firm deadline for publication of their texts.

It was also during Strugnell's tenure as chief editor that both scholarly and public annoyance at the continuing delays in publishing the Cave 4 material increased and turned into a vocal, more visible protest. In the middle of Strugnell's editorship, the fortieth anniversary of the Cave 1 discoveries passed (1987). By this time there was a growing perception that the small team of scholars held a monopoly on the Cave 4 texts and refused to show them to others before official publication—an event that, of course, kept being pushed further into the future. There were cases when team members did share their texts with other scholars (e.g., committees preparing translations of the Bible received permission to use evidence from unpublished manuscripts). For a long time there had been an undercurrent of grousing in academic circles about what could be taking the team so long, but, as we recall, scholars generally, though somewhat miffed, were content to wait until the team members produced their editions of the Qumran texts. No one seemed to take the wild charges of people like Allegro very seriously. The vast majority of scholars continued waiting quietly year after year.

There were, however, some exceptions. Robert Eisenman of California State University, Long Beach, and Philip Davies of Sheffield University in England tried in 1989 to obtain access to some unpublished fragments. Both men had written several books on Qumran subjects and were quite independent in their viewpoints. Eisenman in particular had taken an unusual approach to the scrolls, which he considered Christian compositions. When they requested permission from Strugnell to examine fragments at the Rockefeller Museum, he turned down their application. Their case and the wider cause of free access to the many unpublished scrolls fragments caught the attention of a new player on the stage, Hershel Shanks, a Washington, D.C., attorney and lover of archeology who founded the Biblical Archaeology Society. Through one of his immensely popular journals, the *Biblical Archaeology Review,* he had begun a campaign (starting in 1985) to raise public awareness of the way in which the unpublished scrolls were being handled and why they were still not available some forty years after their discovery. In this way not only academics but the public became more interested in the subject, and suspicions began to grow about what the team was or was not doing with the scrolls. The rhetoric became more inflammatory as the language of monopoly gave way to talk of a scrolls cartel—a term with unpleasant associations from the worlds of drugs and oil and one not calculated to calm the waters.

With the mounting negative publicity, Israeli authorities began pushing for a specific timetable for publication to which the team members would be held. So, for example, when James VanderKam was working at the Rockefeller Museum in January 1990, Amir Drori, the director of the Israel Antiquities Authority (IAA), checked carefully about when VanderKam planned to publish the texts entrusted to him by Milik. Later that year, Peter Flint had a similar meeting with Drori with respect to the edition of the Psalms scrolls he was to publish in DJD 16 with Eugene Ulrich and the late Patrick Skehan.

Such concern was commendable, but a whole series of events soon occurred that changed the entire landscape of the Qumran world. The IAA had named a three-man Scrolls Advisory Committee in 1989 to help in monitoring the situation. In October 1990 the international team appointed Emanuel Tov of the Hebrew University to serve as editor alongside Strugnell, with the hope that his presence would speed up the process. The move did not please Strugnell, but he was soon to be ousted from his position in unfortunate circumstances. In the fall of 1990 he gave an interview to an Israeli journalist, Avi Katzman. When this was published in the Tel Aviv newspaper *Ha'aretz* on November 9, 1990, it caused an immediate sensation. In the interview Strugnell was quoted as saying, among other provocative comments, that Judaism was "a horrible religion." He was later to claim that his remarks were taken in an unintended sense. What is clear is that Strugnell was ill at the time of the interview.

The Tov Era (1990–)

It would not have been surprising if such an interview had caused Strugnell's dismissal as chief editor of Jewish texts, but the committee had apparently decided on the move even before this because Strugnell was not functioning effectively as editor-in-chief. The result was that in December 1990 Strugnell was removed from his post. Tov was appointed editor-in-chief by the IAA and later by the international team. Two others were appointed to make the transition easier: Eugene Ulrich and Émile Puech. Tov and Ulrich played leading roles in reorganizing the international team, with Tov concerning himself with the entire team and Ulrich focusing on editors for the biblical scrolls. Through their leadership and on the basis of the progress that Strugnell had made, the team was eventually enlarged to a more realistic size of about fifty and later even more members. Although this long overdue growth was newsworthy in itself, several other events soon grabbed the international headlines.

FORCING ACCESS TO THE SCROLLS

The first happened in the fall of 1991. On September 4, Ben Zion Wacholder, a senior scholar at the Hebrew Union College in Cincinnati and an expert who had been waiting throughout his career for the appearance of the hundreds of remaining scrolls, and Martin Abegg, at the time a graduate student at the Hebrew Union College who was hard at work on a dissertation dealing with some scrolls, came out with the first volume in their series, *A Preliminary Edition of the Unpublished Dead Sea Scrolls* (Washington, DC: Biblical Archaeology Society, 1991). The book immediately captured the popular fancy because it not only made unpublished scroll fragments available in transcribed form, but it also resulted from applying something so modern as computer technology to something so ancient as the Dead Sea Scrolls.

The project was born out of frustration at the long delay in publishing the scrolls, and involved bypassing the editorial team to get at the texts. Wacholder and Abegg used a copy of the handwritten *Preliminary Concordance* that had been compiled from the Cave 4 texts (see above; some thirty copies had been made in 1988). Copies of the concordance had been deposited in a few libraries around the world, and one was made for the Hebrew Union College. From the words and phrases in the concordance, the two scholars reconstructed the texts on the basis of which the concordance had been made in the first place. Their backward procedure was successful because in a concordance every word is recorded with its context; from such information whole texts could be reconstructed. Wacholder and Abegg were hailed by many for their end-around maneuver to avoid the blockade surrounding the texts that, so it was widely believed, had been erected by the official team. For some time their edition, which eventually included four volumes,[8] became the only source for previously unpublished scroll fragments. Some wondered, however, what legal right Wacholder and Abegg had to publish the work of others (i.e., the editors of the texts, who had established the readings, and those responsible for compiling the concordance from their transcriptions). Questions were also raised about the accuracy of their reconstructed texts, since they were based on pre-1960 versions. The scholars on the team had improved many of their earlier readings in the intervening thirty years. The Wacholder-Abegg volume included no photographs against which to check their readings.

The second event happened in the same month. On September 22, 1991, William A. Moffett, recently named director of the Huntington Library in San Marino, California, announced that a complete set of photographs of the scrolls owned by the library would be made available to anyone who wished to study them. Before his announcement, not many people were aware that the Huntington Library had a set of scrolls photographs, and in fact Moffett himself had learned about them only a short time earlier. Ten years before this, the library had received the photographic set from Elizabeth Hay Bechtel, whose generous support of scrolls research was well known. She had funded the creation of the Ancient Biblical Manuscript Center in Claremont, California, and had obtained permission to house a set of scrolls photographs on microfilm there. After a serious disagreement with the director of the Ancient Biblical Manuscript Center, she had another copy made and placed in the Huntington Library (Claremont and San Marino are both in the Los Angeles area). There they languished largely unnoticed until Moffett's announcement. Apparently the thought of free speech was much on the minds of the Huntington staff in September 1991 because the exhibition "The Sacred Fire of Liberty: The Creation of the American Bill of Rights" was then showing at the library (July 16, 1991–January 26, 1992). There were, it seems, some murky questions about who controlled the library's photographs. At any rate, the IAA was not pleased with Moffett's decision to make the photographs available and talk of a possible lawsuit floated about for a while.[9] Nevertheless, the praises of Moffett and the library echoed throughout the newspapers of the land. We were told that at last the scrolls were *liberated,* despite the best efforts of the editors to keep them in some sort of bondage. This liberation took a limited form—these were photographs of ancient fragments that only experts could read—but at least the texts were accessible.

STARTLING CONCLUSIONS FROM THE UNPUBLISHED SCROLLS?

One of the people who took advantage of the Huntington Library's offer to open its archives to interested parties was Robert Eisenman, the man who had done so much to publicize the inaccessibility of the scrolls. He worked with photographs at the library and soon thought he had made a momentous discovery. On November 1, 1991, the university where he teaches (California State Univerity, Long Beach) issued a press release in which Eisenman announced that he had found a text that was not only revolutionary, but also showed how wrong the official team had been about the scrolls:

> Robert Eisenman, the first scholar given access to the Huntington Library's collection of Dead Sea Scrolls microfilms, has announced the discovery of a text that refers to the execution of a Messianic leader. "This tiny scroll fragment puts to rest the idea presently being circulated by the Scroll editorial committee that this material has nothing to do with Christian origins in Palestine," said the California State University, Long Beach professor of Middle East religions.
>
> Leading scroll editors have been saying there is nothing interesting in the unpublished scrolls and that they have nothing to do with the rise of Christianity in Palestine.

Eisenman is also quoted as saying that the text (4Q285, *The War of the Messiah*)

> makes concrete reference to "the putting to death" or "the execution of the leader of the community, an individual the text appears to refer to as "the branch of David." . . . Though this passage can be read in either the past or future tense, the reading is not subject to doubt.

Not surprisingly, Eisenman's discovery was soon trumpeted abroad in the newspapers.

We should have empathy for people who work in university public relations offices and who must put out statements on varied and complicated topics and we can understand the excitement of discovery, but the press release and Eisenman's quoted statements make some unlikely claims. Eisenman, who reads the scrolls as Christian documents, thought he had found confirmation for some of his ideas in a fragment that no editor had issued, though it was known already in the 1950s when its readings were recorded in the *Preliminary Concordance*. As we have seen in discussing the beliefs about messiahs held by the Qumran community (Chapter 11), Eisenman's reading of the fragment is very much subject to doubt, since he opted for a less likely interpretation of the key line (the messianic figure probably does the killing rather than being executed) and failed to see its relation to Isaiah 11 (see also Chapter 15).

The press release gave the impression that the official editors had a monolithic view about the scrolls and that they were trying to distance them from Christian origins. Anyone who has read the varied opinions of the team members will know that they disagreed on many points and that not one of them tried to separate the scrolls from the beginnings of Christianity. The scrolls editorial committee had by no means claimed they had nothing to do with Christian origins; they held only that the scrolls, which clarify much about the circumstances when Christianity began, were Jewish texts, not Christian ones. All of them were quite aware of the significant parallels between the scrolls and the New Testament; they did not, however, draw the implausible conclusions that Eisenman did (e.g., that Jesus' brother James was the Teacher of Righteousness).

THE *FACSIMILE EDITION*

The quick pace of events continued. On November 19, 1991, the Biblical Archaeology Society published a two-volume work, *A Facsimile Edition of the Dead Sea Scrolls*. The title page says it was "Prepared with an Introduction and Index by Robert H. Eisenman and James M. Robinson." In these volumes were 1,785 photographs of Dead Sea Scroll fragments. The source of the photographs has not been divulged; we know only that they came through Eisenman. This publication, too, was a remarkable breakthrough because it made a very large number of the still unpublished texts readily available to those who could afford the volumes ($195 at time of publication) and read the texts on the photographs. The pictures are often small and in some instances illegible or nearly so; many are, however, very usable.

The first volume of *A Facsimile Edition* also contained a "Publisher's Foreword" (contributed by Hershel Shanks), in which a number of documents (such as photocopies of letters, newspaper articles, etc.) that had been generated by the recent scrolls controversies were printed. Among the items included was Figure 8, a Hebrew transcription of the 121-line *Halakhic Letter*, which was being edited by Strugnell and Qimron. Abbreviated

4QMMT, the text printed is a composite made from the six fragmentary copies, 4Q394–99; WAC call this *A Sectarian Manifesto* (pp. 358–64). For some years before this, photocopies of the transcription made by the editors had been circulating freely among interested scholars. It had even appeared in print in December 1990 in a journal published in Poland called *The Qumran Chronicle.* The journal's editor, Zadzislaw Kapera, a scholar of the scrolls, had informed readers that the source of the text was anonymous and asked them not to copy and circulate it. He even raised the possibility that the text was a hoax. A. Drori of the IAA, after Qimron learned of the publication and complained about it, warned Kapera in a letter of March 12, 1991, to stop the distribution of the journal issue.[10] Kapera apologized, complied, and that was the end of the matter.

Shanks, who had received a copy of the December 1990 issue of *The Qumran Chronicle,* thought the action of the IAA wrong, and he published the Hebrew transcription in the first volume of *A Facsimile Edition* (in the List of Figures on pg. xxiii, Figure 8 is called "Transcription of MMT from *The Qumran Chronicle*—12/90"). Nowhere in the book was Qimron acknowledged as one of the scholars who had produced the composite text of 4QMMT. Shanks wrote critically in the Foreword about the official policy of not allowing access to unpublished scroll fragments. Regarding the origin of the transcription he had printed, he wrote only:

> The text was assigned to John Strugnell for publication nearly 40 years ago. However, he did not even disclose its existence until 1984.[11] Then, with a colleague, Strugnell proceeded to write a 500-page commentary on this 120-line text. The commentary is still not published and no one knows when it will be. But Strugnell won't release the 120-line text until the commentary is published. He has, however, given copies of his transcription to friends and colleagues. (pp. xv–xvi)

Shanks was to write later, in explaining why he phrased the matter as he did, that at the time he regarded Strugnell as the "chief devil. It was he who was withholding MMT. I knew Elisha Qimron was working with him, but I did not know the extent of his contribution. And I did not want to be critical of a young untenured Israeli scholar."[12]

NEW POLICIES FOR ACCESS TO UNPUBLISHED SCROLLS AND PHOTOGRAPHS

That same month the annual meeting of the Society of Biblical Literature and the American Academy of Religion took place in Kansas City, Missouri. Among the sessions there that had to do with the scrolls was one in which Martin Abegg and William Moffett spoke to great applause, and Emanuel Tov addressed the audience, explaining recent events and the changes in the editorial team's makeup and procedures. At this meeting two societies, the Society of Biblical Literature and the American Schools of Oriental Research, worked on formulating policies regarding access to texts and other ancient artifacts.

As these events were swiftly unfolding, the IAA was reassessing its position about permitting access to the photographs of the scrolls. Copies of the photographs were housed in Jerusalem and in four other places: the Ancient Biblical Manuscript Center in Claremont, California; the Huntington Library; the Oxford Centre for Postgraduate Hebrew Studies; and Hebrew Union College in Cincinnati. The IAA had given permission (press release, October 27, 1991) for these centers to make their photographs available to interested parties, but at first the Israeli authorities wanted to require anyone who studied the photographs of unpublished texts to agree not to produce an edition of them, though they could use the texts in their research. On November 11 the IAA backed down from this impracticable position and relieved the four institutions holding the microfilm photographs of the need to obtain such a statement from users. Only a certain moral pressure was to be exerted on them so that team members would not be deprived of the right to first publication of the texts they had been studying for a long time, in some cases for over thirty-five years.

A "CONSPIRACY TO SUPPRESS THE SCROLLS"

Another publication from that fateful year grabbed headlines for a while and did much to spread misinformation. M. Baigent and R. Leigh authored a book called *The Dead Sea Scrolls Deception: Why a Handful of Religious Scholars Conspired to Suppress the Revolutionary Contents of the Dead Sea Scrolls.*[13] The subtitle expresses the slant the writers took. The first part of the book—in which they describe the scrolls, arrangements for publication, the so-called consensus that developed about them, and all the problems that resulted—makes for interesting and informative reading. Among the valuable evidence they cited are excerpts from letters of John Allegro; from these one can observe firsthand how his relations with the other team members were turning from bad to worse. But after a rather good start, the book quickly degenerated into a poorly informed attack on the official team, especially de Vaux, who had been dead for twenty years by this time. Baigent and Leigh tried to convince readers that the delay in scroll publication came about because the Catholic-dominated team was under the control of the Vatican, which, somehow fully aware of what was in the unpublished scrolls, was anxious to suppress all their contents that would undermine Christianity. Roland de Vaux, who according to those who knew him was a pleasant man, turns out to be a monster who masterminded and enforced the Vatican's conspiracy to suppress the scrolls. Baigent and Leigh followed up this entertaining effort by advancing a form of Eisenman's theory about the scrolls—one that somehow gave them satisfactory answers to the questions that the Essene hypothesis just could not handle.

Conspiracy theories tend to get a lot of attention, and Baigent and Leigh's book became a best-seller, both in English and in translation. Now that all of the scrolls are available in photographic form, in transcriptions, and in translations, one wonders what anyone thought might damage Christianity or what the Vatican would be interested in and capable of suppressing. One of the beneficial side effects of full access to the scrolls has been to show that the Baigent-Leigh conspiracy theory is without merit.

A CONTROVERSIAL NEW BOOK AND THE ETHICS OF PUBLICATION

The following year also witnessed ongoing controversies and tensions. Among the events that riled the little world of Qumran studies was publication of *The Dead Sea Scrolls Uncovered: The First Complete Translation and Interpretation of 50 Key Documents Withheld for Over 35 Years.*[14] The authors, Robert Eisenman and Michael Wise, published in it an introduction and editions of fifty Qumran texts. The texts themselves were introduced briefly, transcriptions in Hebrew or Aramaic given, translations supplied, and notes (especially bibliography) added. In fact, at least parts of many of the texts had been published before but not in the DJD series. The introduction to the book makes for intriguing read-ing. In it the authors explain that photographs of the scrolls were sent (we are not told by whom) to Eisenman, beginning in September 1989 and continuing until the fall of 1990;[15] these were the photographs that appeared in *A Facsimile Edition of the Dead Sea Scrolls.* Eisenman shared the photographs with Wise, then at the University of Chicago.

> Two teams immediately set to work, one under Professor Eisenman at California State University at Long Beach and one under Professor Wise at the University of Chicago. Their aim was to go through everything—every photograph individually—to see what was there, however long it took, leaving nothing to chance and depending on *no one else's work.*[16]

The efforts of the two teams continued from January 1991 to May 1992.

One of the texts included (they considered it to be two texts) was 4QMMT, the text on which Strugnell and Qimron were working, as we saw earlier. In the Eisenman-Wise book, the text is regarded as two *Letters on Works Reckoned as Righteousness.*[17] They wrote in the introduction about it:

> For our part, in line with our previously announced intentions in this work, we have gone through the entire corpus of pictures completely ourselves and depended on no one else's work to do this. We made all the selections and arrangements of plates our-selves, including the identification of overlaps and joins. The process only took about six weeks.[18]

Naturally, their six weeks made the thirty-five years or so Strugnell had the text seem rather long.

The book sold very well, again both in English and in translation. Users found the transcriptions and translations (as opposed to the introductions to the texts) to be help-ful—an easy way to access some texts that were not available. The book also contains twenty-five photographic plates. The work of transcription was carried out mostly at Chicago,[19] and, as anyone in the field knows, Wise is a superb reader of texts. That there were some mistakes is only to be expected; there are in the DJD editions, too. However, when scholars who were preparing DJD editions of texts that appeared in the Eisenman-Wise volume and others who were familiar with the texts saw the editions in *The Dead Sea Scrolls Uncovered,* they thought that in some cases they looked suspiciously like their own editions, not like completely independent readings of photographs alone.

One such case was 4QMMT. We have seen that Strugnell and Qimron had circulated some copies of their composite text to elicit reactions from experts. As it turned out, the text of 4QMMT in *The Dead Sea Scrolls Uncovered* was almost identical to the Strugnell-Qimron transcription, which, it was later divulged, Wise had at the time he was working on the photographs. One could argue that this was natural: experts looking at the same evidence are likely to come up with the same results. The problem was that the version in *The Dead Sea Scrolls Uncovered* agreed so closely with Strugnell-Qimron that it even included the same mistakes. An example that was cited had to do with their text 36 (the *Second Letter on Works Reckoned as Righteousness,* l. 9), where their transcription has ביתו *(bytw),* which they translate as "in His Temple," which is not quite accurate.[20] In the hand-written transcription of Strugnell-Qimron, the word is actually written correctly as בידנו *(bydnw),* but the letters דנ *(dn)* are written in such a way that they look a lot like ת *(t),* the letter that appears in *The Dead Sea Scrolls Uncovered*. On the photograph the reading is clearly בידנו *(bydnw)*. The work of Strugnell and Qimron is not mentioned explicitly, although the introduction to text 35 does say: "Parts of it have been talked about, written about and known about for over three decades. Particularly in the last decade, parts have circulated in various forms."[21] Scholars also lodged charges about unacknowledged borrowing for their edition of 4Q390 and 4Q448.

As a result of what was perceived to be a lifting of other people's work that contradicted Eisenman and Wise's outright denial of having done so, a group of nineteen scholars (including members of the official team) signed a letter documenting and protesting what the authors had done. The letter, dated December 9, was sent to the media and received plenty of attention. Although those who signed the letter saw it as pointing out cases of dishonesty and lapses in ethics and integrity, others saw this as yet another attempt by the official team to hinder publication of scrolls outside official channels—something the writers of the letter explicitly denied.

Just a few days later (December 14–17, 1992) the first international conference to be held since the scroll photographs had become available took place. The New York Academy of Sciences and the Oriental Institute of the University of Chicago co-sponsored a conference entitled "Methods of Investigation of the Dead Sea Scrolls and the Khirbet Qumran Site: Present Realities and Future Prospects." This was a truly international gathering with a commendably broad representation of viewpoints. Because it was held under tense circumstances at a time when the scrolls were regularly in the news and because scholars who had signed the letter as well as Eisenman and Wise were present, the media coverage was the most intense at an academic conference in our experience. Ironically, the sessions were held in New York City at a place called the Blood Center, and it is the closest we have ever seen scholars come to blows. Yet, despite the atmosphere of anger, many fine papers were presented and lively discussions ensued.

One of the conference sessions was called "Ethics of Publication of the Dead Sea Scrolls: Panel Discussion."[22] A number of issues were covered by the panel and audience, one of which was the problems raised by the Eisenman-Wise book. The speakers expressed their differing points of view. Wise admitted using handouts in two cases, but insisted that his team had made its own transcriptions first.[23] Specifically on the charge that his בידו *(bytw)* was a misreading of Strugnell's handwriting (something that L. Schiffman had pointed out to him just before the conference), he said:

> It caught me completely by surprise. I went back and checked the photos, and indeed he was right. There was no question that the reading is *biyadenu*. The only thing I could think at the time was that there was no way I could have claimed to have looked at these texts and worked from the photos. It would appear that there was nothing I could say even if that were true, because of this error. So, I called my colleague, Norman Golb, more or less in despair and told him about this instance. He told me that this exact same phenomenon has occurred repeatedly in the editing of manuscripts, where one scholar has read the edition of another but then subsequently goes to the photographs and produces his own edition. In fact, this happened to Norman himself, as he has said. He can give examples, which I don't recall off the top of my head.
>
> I believe it was necessary to state this. It doesn't invalidate what we've said. It is a psychological phenomenon in the editing of texts.[24]

During the conference, a number of us who were concerned about the tone of what had been happening and also about the effect all this might have on Wise, an untenured assistant professor at the time, set in motion a process of reconciling the two sides, that is, those who had signed the letter and Eisenman and Wise. The details of what happened over those several days need not detain us, but the result was two statements,[25] one by Wise, the other by "Qumran Scholars." Wise stated:

> Having been responsible with my team for the transcriptions in the volume, *The Dead Sea Scrolls Uncovered*, I wish to state that, after fruitful discussion with my colleagues, I have come to understand their position more fully. I regret the impression, unintended by me, which emerges from the introduction concerning the degree to which some parts of the work were done independently. I am sorry that the documentation for certain portions of the book for which I was responsible was incomplete, and that I did not more fully express indebtedness to colleagues whose work I consulted and whom I admire, including Professors Devorah Dimant, Émile Puech, Elisha Qimron, and Shemaryahu Talmon. It is moreover regrettable that I did not have adequate input into the final form of the book, and that is something that should not have happened. I hope that there will be future editions of the book so that these deficiencies can be corrected, and look forward to creative work with my colleagues in the months ahead.

The statement of the "Qumran Scholars" read:

> We wish to communicate the understanding which we, colleagues in the study of the Dead Sea Scrolls, have reached after publication of the Eisenman-Wise volume, *The Dead Sea Scrolls Uncovered*, the statement of protest by scholars, and further discussion at the New York conference on "Methods of Investigation of the Dead Sea Scrolls and the Khirbet Qumran Site."
>
> In light of Prof. Wise's statement and after obtaining additional information about the production of the book, those of us who were signatories to the statement of protest hereby retract the statement and all it implies. All those present at this conference join in supporting this agreement. We reaffirm the authors' right and that of all scholars to publish Qumran texts and to make properly acknowledged use of the work of others. We join together in the spirit of collegial friendship and look forward to future cooperation in the domain of studies on the Dead Sea Scrolls.

THE "GOLDEN YEARS" OF PUBLICATION (1990–2002)

In the 1990s the work of making the unpublished scrolls available to all who wished to examine them saw remarkable advances, especially compared with what had happened in the previous decades. Brill and IDC published a large work entitled *The Dead Sea Scrolls on Microfiche: A Comprehensive Facsimile Edition of the Texts from the Judaean Desert*;[26] this was edited by Tov with the collaboration of Stephen Pfann. On microfiche were photographs (about 6,000 in all) of the Qumran scrolls and those from other Judean Desert sites. Companion volumes provided a full list of all the manuscripts, the numbers assigned to the different photographs of them, and something of the history of scrolls study and photography.[27] Those companion volumes were updated in a second edition issued by Brill in 1995 under the title *Companion Volume to the Dead Sea Scrolls Microfiche Edition* (edited by Tov with Pfann). Although the edition is very expensive, this publication made virtually all the Dead Sea Scrolls truly available in one form (perhaps the best one for seeing what is on the fragments).

Since microfiche is not the most convenient medium (not everyone has a microform reader in the office), the *Microfiche Edition* was followed by the *Dead Sea Scrolls Electronic Reference Library* in two volumes (1997, 1999). These two reference collections offer ready access by scholars to virtually all the Dead Sea Scrolls on a desktop computer. For a detailed description of the *Electronic Reference Library,* see Chapter 4.

The progress made in the DJD series under Tov's leadership has been extraordinary. One of the most satisfying characteristics of the successful drive to finish the project has been the continued co-operation of the original editorial team members (Cross, Milik, Strugnell) with the new generation. The enlarged team (eventually about one hundred scholars took part) has almost finished the project, which seemed stalled in the 1980s. As related above, DJD 8 bears the date of 1990 and is the last volume published before Tov was named editor-in-chief. Between then and late 2002, volumes 9–16, 18–31, 33–36, and 38–39 have appeared in print—a total of twenty-eight volumes in eleven years, compared with eight in the previous thirty-five years. The only numbers yet to be published as of late 2002 are volume 17 (the copies of Samuel), which has been completed but is not out; volume 32 (the two Isaiah scrolls from Cave 1, both of which have been issued but never in critical editions); and volume 37 (4Q550–75). In 2002 the press released a large introductory or rather summary volume, edited by Tov and containing several compilations of data from all the texts in the series (DJD 39).[28] An additional volume in press is the official *Concordance to the Non-Biblical Scrolls,* edited by M. Abegg (not in the DJD series, but to be published by Brill of the Netherlands). It would be difficult for anyone to charge seriously that the quality of the more recent twenty-eight volumes falls below that of the first eight in the DJD series.

The effect of publishing the scrolls has been, not surprisingly, to revolutionize the field. After the initial burst of excitement when the scrolls were discovered (late 1940s, 1950s, early 1960s), there came a period in the late 1960s, the 1970s, and the early 1980s when the scrolls receded in interest as little more was appearing. Since the late 1980s not only have the publications of manuscripts taken a quantum leap forward, but the volume of secondary scholarly studies has mushroomed. International conferences have proliferated, dissertations have multiplied, and publishing outlets have increased—not to mention all of the newspaper, television, and radio coverage as well as the television documentaries that have been made.

A COSTLY AND CONTROVERSIAL LAWSUIT

Regrettably, not all has been cheery and bright in the world of the Qumran scrolls, despite the progress that has been made. Publication of the Strugnell-Qimron transcription of the composite text of the *Halakhic Letter* (4QMMT) by Shanks in *A Facsimile Edition* led to a lawsuit. On January 14, 1992, Qimron (not Strugnell and Qimron) brought suit against Shanks, Eisenman, Robinson, and the Biblical Archaeology Society, "complaining of infringement of copyright, material and moral. In this suit, he sought an injunction and also damages in the amount of NIS [New Israeli Shekels] 472,500."[29] One week later the Israeli court served a temporary injunction prohibiting the defendants from distributing the composite text. The defendants complied with this, so that in the second edition it is not included.[30] A question that immediately arises regarding the case is why an Israeli court should have been the place to file the suit when the defendants and the publisher are Americans; another question is why a foreign court should be thought to have such powers. As Shanks writes, Qimron's attorney, Y. Molcho, "successfully argued that it was sufficient that three copies of the book had been mailed to Israel and that it had also been advertised in *Biblical Archaeology Review,* which was mailed to some subscribers in Israel."[31] Shanks's side argued that the case should be tried according to U.S. copyright law (in most states there is no provision for "moral right" in copyright cases), but the judge ruled civilized countries had the same law and thus the case could be tried according to Israeli copyright law, which does include the moral-right provision. *Moral right* is defined as the right "that the creation be attributed to his [i.e., the author's or creator's] name and published with fidelity to the original, without distortion or falsification."[32]

A trial took place on February 1–2, 1993, with Qimron, Shanks, and a number of others offering testimony. The testimony raised a host of interesting issues in the area of copyright. What is copyrightable? It seems that if Strugnell and Qimron had read the text and filled in the missing parts just as it was worded when the ancient author composed it, their transcription would not be protected by copyright, just as reconstruction of a pot from a bunch of pieces to its original shape does not enjoy copyright protection. If copyright existed in such a text, it would belong to the author (Shanks suggested the Teacher of Righteousness held the copyright). Oddly, only if mistakes were made would the work of the modern editors be copyrightable.

Another issue discussed was why Qimron should be thought to have copyright on the composite text when Strugnell had been working on 4QMMT far longer than he. What was Qimron's involvement in compiling the composite text? Two examples of his work are mentioned in the judge's ruling: arranging fragments differently in one place, and restoring one letter when Strugnell preferred another.[33] Presumably he did more, but those are the examples cited. Y. Sussman, who advised Strugnell and Qimron on halakhic issues, testified regarding Qimron that "for years this was the subject that had interested him and this was the subject that engaged him. And it seemed to me that he did not read nor was interested in anything else but that which could somehow bring him nearer to the issues connected with the Scroll."[34]

Then on March 30, 1993, Judge Dalia Dorner issued her verdict. She ruled that infringement had taken place, holding all four of the defendants liable. As Shanks, however, had published the composite text and also had told Eisenman and Robinson he would accept full liability, he was the one to receive the penalties. She determined that loss of right to publish the text first and to have his name connected with it caused Qimron "financial damage and mental anguish." As for monetary damage, she found no material basis for the amounts Qimron was seeking, "and not one of the witnesses was able to ascertain a firm estimate of the effects that the publication of the composite text will have upon sales of the Plaintiff's book and on his lecturing honoraria." Statutory compensation was in order, nevertheless, and she imposed the maximum—NIS 20,000. As for nonpecuniary damages, she rejected the amount sought (NIS 100,000 for "mental distress and injury to reputation"), but did cite Qimron's testimony:[35]

> For years I worked on "miqsat ma'aseh ha-torah" almost without working on anything else.... The whole family lived thriftily.... If my wife complained, I would say: "Look, this is our life, we will become famous." This is perhaps more to be considered than money.

The judge decided that the proper compensation for his mental anguish was NIS 80,000. Hence, besides prohibiting the defendants from publishing or distributing the composite text, she wrote: "I find the Defendants, jointly and severally, liable to pay the Plaintiff NIS 100,000 plus differential indexation and legal interests, from the day of the filing of the suit (14th January, 1992) and until the actual payment." To this she added another NIS 50,000 for the fees of Qimron's lawyer plus legal expenses, again with differential indexation and legal interest until the payment would be made.[36] Shanks filed an appeal.

Judge Dorner's ruling and some of the testimony cited in it raise basic problems. Leaving aside whether lawsuits are at all appropriate in such situations, just how realistic were Qimron's expectations? Would publication of 4QMMT, on which he began collaborating late in the work (1979), have made him any better known than he was? Everyone in the field knew of his expertise in grammar and philology (*halakhah* is not his specialty),[37] but, even granting that 4QMMT is an interesting text, would it have been so captivating to scholars and the public that having his name on a DJD volume with the text in it would have transformed his image? To the best of our knowledge, no one has become famous because of publishing something in the DJD series. It is also not a way to become rich. Then, too, the suggestion made by a witness that one could get $10,000 for one lecture will come as a real surprise to almost all academics.[38]

Strugnell and Qimron did publish 4QMMT in DJD 10, which bears the date of 1994. Far from being a 500-page commentary plus text, the volume is one of the slimmest in the series: there are 14 introductory pages (paginated with roman numerals), 235 pages of text, and 8 photographic plates. The section presenting the six individual manuscripts is on pp. 3–42, the composite text with translation and notes is on 44–63. The remainder consists of a set of essays (including Sussman's famous article, pp. 179–200), a concordance, and a reverse index. Upon seeing the modestly sized volume, some wondered why we had to wait so long for this. But the most peculiar part of DJD 10 is a paragraph on the copyright page. It is unlike any other in the entire series. Besides the usual information on a copyright page, it reads:

> ©Elisha Qimron 1994, without derogating from any rights vested in the Israel Antiquities Authority with regard to the Scrolls' fragments, photographs, and any other material which is in the possession of the Authority, and which the Authority has permitted Qimron to use for the purposes of the Work, and its inclusion therein.

One wonders why Qimron alone, not Strugnell or the other contributors to the volume, is the copyright holder and why the matter of copyright was handled differently with this text than with any other.

A SYMPOSIUM ON INTELLECTUAL PROPERTY

The case of *Qimron vs. Shanks et al.* has attracted some attention in the legal world. On May 19, 1999, a symposium held at New College, Edinburgh, on intellectual property and cultural artifacts centered on the kinds of issues raised in the legal dispute regarding 4QMMT. Eight papers from the symposium and five others were later combined to make up a volume that has been referenced several times in this chapter: *On Scrolls, Artefacts and Intellectual Property*. In it are the text of Judge Dorner's decision translated into

English, Hershel Shanks's article, five essays by legal experts, contributions from three scrolls scholars (Strugnell, Geza Vermes, and Tov), two papers on problems arising from other projects, and an English translation of the Supreme Court of Israel's decision about the appeal of Dorner's decision. The papers by the legal experts are remarkably interesting reactions to the 1993 ruling (they were written before the Supreme Court rendered its verdict). Hector McQueen of the University of Edinburgh generally supports Judge Dorner's decision that copyright protection is afforded Qimron's work; Paul Torremans of the University of Leicester treats the issue of which country's copyright law to apply and when; and Wojciech Kowlaski of the University of Silesia argues that the reconstruction of texts involving restoring fragments of "nonexistent manuscripts" is not subject to copyright, though this does not preclude a moral right.

The other two lawyers, Cindy Alberts Carson of Whittier Law School and David Nimmer of Irell & Manella and the UCLA School of Law (he is the son of the expert who wrote the book on copyright), had authored long studies of the case, which were published elsewhere.[39] They wrote shorter articles for incorporation in the book. The former, insisting that American copyright law should have governed the case, argued that the kind of labor performed by Qimron did not meet the standards of originality for which a work receives copyright.[40] Nimmer concluded: "In sum, it would seem that Qimron's entire copyright claim is premised on the faulty foundation that the textual variants that he indirectly observed entitles him to copyright protection. That conclusion cannot stand."[41]

THE LAWSUIT IS APPEALED

On August 20, 2000, the Supreme Court of Israel issued its judgment on the appeal. Shanks, Robinson, and the BAS had asked for a cancellation of the judgment of the district court and of the financial penalties it imposed, and Eisenman, too, had asked that the part of the judgment that concerned him be cancelled. "In his counter-appeal Qimron petitions to determine that he is entitled also to compensation for pecuniary injuries that he claims were proven to have been caused to him and also to increase the amount of damages that were awarded to him." Justice Y. Türkel delivered the judgment and upheld application of Israeli law (the three copies brought to Israel were apparently enough, even though purchased in the United States). He wrote that Qimron had done most of the work and, despite the fact that he could cite nothing but the two examples adduced in the original trial, thought that Qimron's contribution exhibited the necessary originality. He draws a curious conclusion after citing the two examples:[42]

> From all [!] of these the picture of Qimron's original contribution is clearly seen. From this follows the conclusion that the "inspiration," the "added soul" that he imbued into the Scroll fragments by the force of his work make him the owner of copyright in the Deciphered Text.

Strugnell seems to have disappeared from the judge's radar screen. He found that Qimron's copyright had been infringed as had his moral right, but agreed that pecuniary injury to him was not proved. He upheld the award for statutory damages (NIS 20,000, at that time the equivalent of $4,956) and for infringement of moral right (80,000, or $19,826). He granted Qimron all remaining copies and printing blocks (etc.) used to make the offending edition, as he had requested and as the law allowed.[43] Judge Türkel refused to relieve Shanks of the bill for court costs for the first trial, and added to the bill NIS 40,000 (or $9,913) that Shanks was required to pay for Qimron's attorneys' fees, while the two editors (Eisenman and Robinson) were ordered to pay him attorneys fees of NIS 10,000 (or $2,478). Hence, the Supreme Court challenge changed nothing in the decision of the district court other than to add attorneys' fees and to give Qimron the extra copies of the book.

It is puzzling why Shanks published the composite text as he did; he should not have done so without at least full acknowledgment, and even then one may wonder whether he should have done so. That granted, the financial penalties imposed by the Israeli court seem out of touch with reality (a large chunk of the money is to pay lawyers). That Qimron took the matter to court also seems out of touch with reality. As G. Vermes wrote after the district court decision: "In the opinion of most European and American scholars the complaint could and should have been settled out of court."[44] It may be best to drop the unpleasant subject here, but there is a footnote to it. The Israeli courts were convinced that Qimron had done a lot of work on the text (most, according to Judge Türkel) and had contributed sufficient originality to the composite text to justify his having copyright on it. But, as we have seen, the legal decisions mention only two examples of his contributions.

Florentino García Martínez, whose edition with translation of the scrolls is a standard work in the field, took the trouble to check how much work Qimron had done.[45] This was possible because the series of photographs of the scrolls taken until 1961 allow one to examine what stage the work had reached by that time. As scholars sorted the scrolls and worked with them in the 1950s, the photographer Najib Albina would record each stage in photographs. Thus it is possible to look at photos of 4QMMT made in 1961 and see how far Strugnell (with advice from others) had advanced the work by then. It is also possible to ascertain how Strugnell read the different copies by looking at the readings recorded in *A Preliminary Concordance*, completed at about the same time. Photos taken in 1985 permit one to compare what progress had been made between 1961 (Strugnell's work to that point) and 1985 (the results of Strugnell's and Qimron's joint work). After going through all of this evidence, García Martínez drew two conclusions:

> 1. The selection of fragments belonging to each manuscript, putting separated fragments together, their transcription, translation (as one can deduce from the analysis of each word in the *Concordance*) as well as the correspondences between the different manuscripts were substantially completed in 1961.
>
> 2. The combination of the different manuscripts in a text more or less continuous (the reconstitution of the grand lines of the work later called MMT as it is represented by the composite text) was also substantially finished in 1961.[46]

The evidence led him to assert that Qimron's claim to the exclusive "paternity" of the composite text was both surprising and incomprehensible.

One wonders why such evidence, which has been available for a long time, was not introduced at the district court trial. It is transparently relevant and leads to quite a different conclusion than the one reached by the Israeli courts—that Qimron had done most of the work. Only of Strugnell could that have been said, whether regarding the individual texts or the composite text—the object of the suit.

Final Thoughts

Let us end this survey on a more positive note. A benefit of the publicity and controversies engendered by the scrolls is that learned societies have established positions regarding access to discoveries. Policy statements on the matter were adopted by the Society of Biblical Literature (SBL) in 1991 and the American Schools of Oriental Research (ASOR) in 1992. These societies have formulated the statements with the hope that, if members follow the guidelines and urge governmental institutions to do the same, the problems that have beset publication (or nonpublication) of the scrolls could be avoided when future discoveries are made. The statements of the two organizations, however, are not the same.

The SBL policy supports free access by all to discoveries and the right of anyone to publish editions of texts. It rejects the idea that any one person or group should have the sole right to publish an edition of a text for any number of years. The ASOR statement is more cautious because the society is different in character: it deals with the governments (which have their own policies) in whose lands it owns property and conducts expensive excavations. To cover the cost of the digs, funds must be raised from outside sources. ASOR therefore tries to ensure that the scholars who have found funding and done the work of discovery have rights to first publication for a reasonable amount of time. Nevertheless, both societies affirm the principle that discoveries must be made accessible to others in an expeditious way and not kept out of circulation for as long as they were in the case of the Cave 4 manuscripts. It is gratifying to learn that the SBL policy was used as a guide by the scholars who found texts at Petra several years ago.

Appendixes

Index of Passages in the Biblical Scrolls from the Judean Desert

FOR AN EARLIER LISTING, SEE EUGENE ULRICH, "Index of the Passages in the Biblical Scrolls," in P. W. Flint and J. C. VanderKam, eds., *The Dead Sea Scrolls After Fifty Years: A Comprehensive Assessment* (2 vols., Leiden: Brill, 1998–99) 2.649–65.

Note: (1) A question mark following a verse or manuscript (e.g., 10:6, 20? or 6QGen? ar) indicates that the identification is uncertain. (2) The siglum "X" denotes a verse that is found in one of the scrolls, but not in the traditional biblical text (e.g., Ps. 33:1–7, X, 8–14, 16–18). (3) A superscript "a" or "b" added to a verse (e.g., Exod. 7:29^b) indicates some additional text, usually from the Samaritan Pentateuch as numbered by A. von Gall (*Der hebräische Pentateuch der Samaritaner* [Giessen: Töpelmann, 1918; reprint, 1966]). (4) Occasionally, when the numbering differs in the Septuagint (LXX) or another source, the reading is also indicated in brackets (e.g., Exod. 8:1 [LXX 5], 12–18 [16–22]).

Genesis

1:1–28	4QGen^b
1:1–11, 13–22	4QGen^g
1:8–10	4QGen^{h1}
1:9, 14–16, 27–28	4QGen^k
1:18–27	4QGen^d
1:18–21	1QGen
1:28	pap4QGen?
2:1–3	4QGen^k
2:6–7 or 18 –19	4QGen^g
2:14–19	4QGen^b
2:17–18	4QGen^{h2}
2:18–19 or 6–7	4QGen^g
3:1–2	4QGen^k
3:11–14	1QGen
4:2–11	4QGen^b
5:13 or 14	4QGen^b
6:13–21	6QpaleoGen
8:20–21?	4QGen-Exod^a
10:6, 20?	6QGen? ar
12:4–5	4QGen$^{h\ para}$
17:12–19	8QGen

18:20–25	8QGen
19:27–28	2QGen
22:13–15	1QGen
22:14	4QGen-Exod[a]
23:17–19	1QGen
24:22–24	1QGen
26:21–28	4QpaleoGen[m]
27:38–39, 42–43	4QGen-Exod[a]
32:4–5, 30, 33	MurGen
33:1	MurGen
33:18–20	Mur(?)Gen
34:1–3	Mur(?)Gen
34:5–7, 30–31	MurGen
34:7–10	4QGen[n]
34:17–21	4QGen-Exod[a]
35:1, 4–7	MurGen
35:6–10, 25–29	SdeirGen
35:17–29	4QGen-Exod[a]
36:1–13, 19–27	4QGen-Exod[a]
36:1–2, 5–17	SdeirGen
36:6, 35–37	2QGen
36:43	4QGen[e]
37:1–2, 27–30	4QGen[e]
37:5–6, 22–27	4QGen-Exod[a]
39:11–23	4QGen-Exod[a]
40:1	4QGen-Exod[a]
40:12–13, 18–23	4QGen[c]
40:18?/19?–23	4QGen[e]
41:1–11	4QGen[c]
41:1–8, 35–44	4QGen[e]
41:15–18, 23–27, 29–36, 38–43	4QGen[j]
42:15–22, 38	4QGen[j]
42:17–19	4QGen[e]
43:1–2, 5–8	4QGen[j]
43:8–14	4QGen[e]
45:14–22, 26–28	4QGen[j]
45:23	4QGen-Exod[a]
46:7–11?	MasGen?
47:13–14	4QGen-Exod[a]
48:1–11	4QGen[f]
48:2–4, 15–17, 18–22	4QGen-Exod[a]
49:1–5	4QGen-Exod[a]
49:6–8	4QGen[e]
50:3	4QGen[n]
50:26?	4QpaleoGen-Exod[l]

Exodus

1:1–6, 16–21	4QExod[b]
1:1–5 (twice?)	4QpaleoGen-Exod[l]
1:3–17, 22	4QGen-Exod[a]
1:11–14	2QExod[a]
2:2–18	4QExod[b]
2:1–5	4QGen-Exod[a]
2:10, 22–25	4QpaleoGen-Exod[l]
3:1–4, 17–21	4QpaleoGen-Exod[l]
3:8–16, 18–21	4QGen-Exod[a]
3:13–21	4QExod[b]
4:1–8	4QExod[b]
4:4–9, 26–31	4QGen-Exod[a]
4:28–31	MurExod
4:31	2QExod[b]
5:1, 3–17	4QGen-Exod[a]
5:3–14	4QExod[b]
5:3–5	2QExod[c]
5:3	MurExod
6:3–6	4QExod[h]
6:4–21, 25	4QGen-Exod[a]
6:5–11	MurExod
6:25–30	4QpaleoExod[m]
7:1–19, 29[b]	4QpaleoExod[m]
7:1–4	2QExod[a]
7:5–13, 15–20	4QGen-Exod[a]
7:17–23, 26–29	4QExod[c]
7:29[b] (28–29?)	4QExod[j]
8:1[a–b] (1–2?)	4QExod[j]
8:1, 5–14, 16–18, 22	4QExod[c]
8:1[LXX 5], 12–18[16–22], 19[b]–22[24–26]	4QpaleoExod[m]
8:13–15, 19–21	4QpaleoGen-Exod[l]
8:20–22	4QGen-Exod[a]
9:5[b]–16, 19[b]–21, 35	4QpaleoExod[m]
9:8?	4QGen-Exod[a]
9:10–12, 15–20, 22–25, 27–35	4QExod[c]
9:25–29, 33–35	4QpaleoGen-Exod[l]
9:27–29	2QExod[a]
10:1–5, 7–9, 12–19, 23–24	4QExod[c]
10:1, 2[b]–12, 19–28	4QpaleoExod[m]
10:1–5	4QpaleoGen-Exod[l]
11:3–7	2QExod[a]
11:4–10	4QpaleoGen-Exod[l]
11:8–10	4QpaleoExod[m]

Leviticus

3:2–8	4QLev^e
3:4, 7, 9–14	pap4QLXXLev^b
3:16–17	4QLev^c
4:1–6, 12–14, 23–28	4QLev^c
4:3–4, 6–8, 10–11, 18–19, 26–28, 30	pap4QLXXLev^b
4:3–9	MasLev^a
4:24–26	11QpaleoLev^a
5:6, 8–10, 16–19	pap4QLXXLev^b
5:12–13	4QLev^c
6:1–5 [MT 5:20–24]	pap4QLXXLev^b
7:19–26	4QLev^g
8:12–13	6QpaleoLev
8:26–28	4QLev^c
8:31, 33–34	MasLev^b
9:1–10, 12–13, 15, 22–24	MasLev^b
9:23–24	11QLev^b
10:1–2	11QLev^b
10:1, 9–20	MasLev^b
10:4–7	11QpaleoLev^a
11:1–21, 24–40	MasLev^b
11:10–11	1QpaleoLev
11:22–29	2QpaleoLev
11:27–32	11QpaleoLev^a
13:3–9, 39–43	11QpaleoLev^a
13:32–33	4QLev-Num^a
13:58–59	11QLev^b
14:16–21, 52–57	11QpaleoLev^a
14:22–34, 40–54	4QLev-Num^a
14:27–29, 33–36	4QLev^d
15:1–5	11QpaleoLev^a
15:10–11, 19–24	4QLev-Num^a
15:20–24	4QLev^d
16:1–15, 18–21	4QtgLev
16:1–6, 34	11QpaleoLev^a
16:15–29	4QLev-Num^a
17:1–5	11QpaleoLev^a
17:2–11	4QLev^d
18:16–21	4QLev-Num^a
18:27–30	11QpaleoLev^a
19:1–4	11QpaleoLev^a
19:3–8	4QLev-Num^a
19:30–34	1QpaleoLev
19:34–37	4QLev^e
20:1–6	11QpaleoLev^a

20:1–3, 27	4QLev^e
20:20–24	1QpaleoLev
21:1–4, 9–12, 21–24	4QLev^e
21:6–12	11QpaleoLev^a
21:17–20, 24	4QLev^b
21:24	1QpaleoLev
22:1–6	1QpaleoLev
22:2–33	4QLev^b
22:4–6, 11–17	4QLev^e
22:21–27	11QpaleoLev^a
23:1–8, 10–25, 40	4QLev^b
23:1–3? (or Num 18:8–9?)	2QNum^{d?}
23:4–8	1QpaleoLev
23:22–29	11QpaleoLev^a
24:2–23	4QLev^b
24:9–14	11QpaleoLev^a
24:11–12	4QLev-Num^a
25:28–36	11QpaleoLev^a
25:28–29, 45–49, 51–52	4QLev^b
26:2–16	4QLXXLev^a
26:17–26	11QpaleoLev^a
26:26–33	4QLev-Num^a
27:5–22	4QLev-Num^a
27:11–19	11QpaleoLev^a
27:30–31?	1QpaleoLev

Numbers

1:1–5, 21–22, 36–40	4QLev-Num^a
1:48–50	1QpaleoLev
2:18–20, 31–32	4QLev-Num^a
3:3–19, 51	4QLev-Num^a
3:38–41, 51	2QNum^a
3:39?, 40–43, 50–51?	4QLXXNum
4:1–12, 40–49	4QLev-Num^a
4:1?, 5–9, 11–16	4QLXXNum
4:1–3	2QNum^a
5:1–9	4QLev-Num^a
7:88	2QNum^c
8:7–12, 21–22	4QLev-Num^a
9:3–10, 19–20	4QLev-Num^a
10:13–23	4QLev-Num^a
11:4–5, 16–22	4QLev-Num^a
11:31–35	4QNum^b
12:1–6, 8–11	4QNum^b
12:3–11	4QLev-Num^a

Reference	Scroll	Reference	Scroll
9:5–6, 21–23	XHev/SeDeut	19:17–21	4QDeut[f]
9:6–7	4QDeut[f]	19:21	4QDeut[h]
9:10	1QDeut[b]	20:1–6	4QDeut[f]
9:11–12, 17–19, 29	4QDeut[c]	20:6–19	4QDeut[k2]
9:12–14	4QDeut[g]	20:9–13	4QDeut[i]
9:27–28	1QDeut[a]	21:4–12	4QDeut[f]
10:1–2, 5–8	4QDeut[c]	21:8–9	1QDeut[b]
10:1–3	MurDeut	21:8–9? or 30:7–8?	4QpaleoDeut[r]
10:6? or 28:23? or 32:22?	4QpaleoDeut[r]	21:16?	4QDeut[k2]
10:8–12	2QDeut[c]	21:23	4QDeut[i]
10:11–12	4QpaleoDeut[r]	22:1–9	4QDeut[i]
10:12, 14–15	4QDeut[l]	22:3–6	4QpaleoDeut[r]
11:2–3	MurDeut	22:12–19	4QDeut[f]
11:3, 9–13, 18	4QDeut[c]	23:6–8, 12–16, 22–26	4QDeut[i]
11:4	4QLXXDeut	23:7, 12–15	4QpaleoDeut[r]
11:6–13	4QDeut[k1]	23:18–20	4QDeut[g]
11:6–10, 12–13, 21?	4QDeut[j]	23:21–26	4QDeut[f]
11:27–30	1QDeut[a]	23:22–26	4QDeut[k2]
11:28, 30–32	4QpaleoDeut[r]	23:26	4QDeut[a]
11:30–31	1QDeut[b]	24:1–8	4QDeut[a]
12:1–5, 11–12, 22	4QpaleoDeut[r]	24:1–3	4QDeut[k2]
12:18–19, 26, 31	4QDeut[c]	24:1	4QDeut[i]
12:25–26	MurDeut	24:2–7	4QDeut[f]
13:1–6, 13–14	1QDeut[a]	24:10–16	1QDeut[b]
13:5, 7, 11–12, 16	4QDeut[c]	24:16–22	4QDeut[g]
13:7–11	11QDeut?	25:1–5, 14–19	4QDeut[g]
13:19	4QpaleoDeut[r]	25:3–9	4QDeut[f]
14:1–4, 19–22, 26–29	4QpaleoDeut[r]	25:13–18	1QDeut[b]
14:21, 24–25	1QDeut[a]	25:19	4QDeut[k2]
14:29	MurDeut	26:1–5, 18–19?	4QDeut[k2]
15:1 or 2	MurDeut	26:1–5	4QDeut[g]
15:1–4, 15–19	4QDeut[c]	26:14–15	4QpaleoDeut[s]
15:5–6, 8–10	4QpaleoDeut[r]	26:18–19	4QDeut[f]
15:14–15	1QDeut[b]	26:19	4QDeut[c]
16:2–3, 6–11, 21–22	4QDeut[c]	26:19?	pap6QDeut?
16:4, 6–7	1QDeut[a]	27:1–2, 24–26	4QDeut[c]
17:1–5, 7, 15–20	4QDeut[c]	27:1–10	4QDeut[f]
17:5–6?	4QpaleoDeut[r]	27:1?	4QDeut[k2]
17:12–15	2QDeut[b]	28:1–14, 20, 22–25, 29–30, 48–50, 61	4QDeut[c]
17:16	1QDeut[b]	28:15–18, 20	4QpaleoDeut[r]
17:17–18	4QDeut[f]	28:15–18, 33–36, 47–52, 58–62	4QDeut[o]
18:1	4QDeut[c]	28:21–25, 27–29	4QDeut[g]
18:6–10, 18–22	4QDeut[f]	28:23? or 10:6? or 32:22?	4QpaleoDeut[r]
19:2–3	4QpaleoDeut[r]	28:44–48	1QDeut[b]
19:8–16	4QDeut[k2]		

28:67–68	4QDeut^l
29:2–4? or 7:19?	4QpaleoDeut^r
29:2–5	4QDeut^l
29:9–20	1QDeut^b
29:17–19	4QDeut^c
29:22–25	4QDeut^o
29:24–27	4QDeut^b
30:3–14	4QDeut^b
30:7–8? or 21:8–9?	4QpaleoDeut^r
30:16–18	4QDeut^{k3}
30:19–20	1QDeut^b
31:1–10, 12–13	1QDeut^b
31:9–11	4QDeut^h
31:9–17, 24–30	4QDeut^b
31:12	4QDeut^l
31:16–19	4QDeut^c
31:29	4QpaleoDeut^r
32:1–3	4QDeut^b
32:3	4QDeut^c
32:6–8, 10–11, 13–14, 33–35	4QpaleoDeut^r
32:7–8	4QDeut^j
32:9–10?, 37–43	4QDeut^q
32:17–18, 22–23, 25–27	4QDeut^{k1}
32:17–29	1QDeut^b
32:22? or 28:23? or 10:6?	4QpaleoDeut^r
33:1–2	4QDeut^l
33:2–8, 29	4QpaleoDeut^r
33:8–22	4QDeut^h
33:12–19, 21–24	1QDeut^b
33:17–21	MasDeut
34:1	4QpaleoDeut^r
34:2–6	MasDeut
34:4–6, 8?	4QDeut^l

Joshua

2:11–12	4QJosh^b
3:15–17	4QJosh^b
4:1–3	4QJosh^b
5:X, 2–7	4QJosh^a
6:5–10	4QJosh^a
7:12–17	4QJosh^a
8:3–14, 18?, 34–35	4QJosh^a
10:2–5, 8–11	4QJosh^a
17:1–5, 11–15	4QJosh^b

Judges

6:2–6, 11–13	4QJudg^a
6:20–22	1QJudg
8:1?	1QJudg
9:1–6, 28–31, 40–43, 48–49	1QJudg
19:5–7	4QJudg^b
21:12–25	4QJudg^b

Samuel

1 Samuel

1:11–13, 22–28	4QSam^a
2:1–6, 8–11, 13–36	4QSam^a
3:1–4, 18–20	4QSam^a
4:9–12	4QSam^a
5:8–12	4QSam^a
6:1–7, 12–13, 16–18, 20–21	4QSam^a
7:1	4QSam^a
8:9–20	4QSam^a
9:6–8, 11–12, 16–24	4QSam^a
10:3–18, 25–27	4QSam^a
11:1, 7–12	4QSam^a
12:7–8, 14–19	4QSam^a
14:24–25, 28–34, 47–51	4QSam^a
15:24–32	4QSam^a
16:1–11	4QSam^b
17:3–6	4QSam^a
18:17–18	1QSam
19:10–17	4QSam^b
20:26–42	4QSam^b
21:1–10?	4QSam^b
23:9–17	4QSam^b
24:4–5, 8–9, 14–23	4QSam^a
25:3–12, 20–21, 25–26, 39–40	4QSam^a
25:30–32	4QSam^c
26:10–12, 21–23	4QSam^a
27:8–12	4QSam^a
28:1–2, 22–25	4QSam^a
30:28–31	4QSam^a
31:2–4	4QSam^a

2 Samuel

2:5–16, 25–27, 29–32	4QSam^a
3:1–8, 23–29	4QSam^a
4:1–4, 9–12	4QSam^a

5:1–16 [omitted 5:4–5]	4QSam^a
6:2–9, 12–18	4QSam^a
7:23–29	4QSam^a
8:2–8	4QSam^a
10:4–7, 18–19	4QSam^a
11:2–12, 16–20	4QSam^a
12:4–5, 8–9, 13–20, 30–31	4QSam^a
13:1–6, 13–34, 36–39	4QSam^a
14:1–3, 18–19	4QSam^a
14:7–33	4QSam^c
15:1–15	4QSam^c
15:1–6, 27–31	4QSam^a
16:1–2, 11–13, 17–18, 21–23	4QSam^a
18:2–7, 9–11	4QSam^a
19:7–12	4QSam^a
20:2–3, 9–14, 23–26	4QSam^a
20:6–10	1QSam
21:1–2, 4–6, 15–17	4QSam^a
21:16–18	1QSam
22:30–51	4QSam^a
23:1–6	4QSam^a
23:7	11QPs^a
23:9–12	1QSam
24:16–20	4QSam^a

Kings

1 Kings

1:1, 16–17, 27–37	5QKgs
3:12–14	pap6QKgs
7:20–21, 25–27, 29–42, 51	4QKgs
8:1–9, 16–18	4QKgs
12:28–31	pap6QKgs
22:28–31	pap6QKgs

2 Kings

5:26	pap6QKgs
6:32	pap6QKgs
7:8–10, 20	pap6QKgs
8:1–5	pap6QKgs
9:1–2	pap6QKgs
10:19–21	pap6QKgs

Isaiah

1:1 to 66:24	1QIsa^a
1:1–31	1QIsa^a
1:1–6	4QIsa^b
1:1–6	4QIsa^j
1:1–3	4QIsa^a
1:4–8, 11–14	MurIsa
1:10–16, 18–31	4QIsa^f
2:1–22	1QIsa^a
2:1–4	4QIsa^e
2:1–3	4QIsa^f
2:3–16	4QIsa^b
2:7–10	4QIsa^a
3:1–26	1QIsa^a
3:14–22	4QIsa^b
4:1–6	1QIsa^a
4:5–6	4QIsa^a
5:1–30	1QIsa^a
5:1	4QIsa^a
5:13–14, 25	4QIsa^f
5:15–28	4QIsa^b
5:28–30	pap4QIsa^p
6:1–13	1QIsa^a
6:3–8, 10–13	4QIsa^f
6:4–8	4QIsa^a
7:1–25	1QIsa^a
7:14–15	4QIsa^l
7:16–18, 23–25	4QIsa^f
7:17–20	4QIsa^e
7:22–25	1QIsa^b
8:1–23	1QIsa^a
8:1, 4–11	4QIsa^f
8:1	1QIsa^b
8:2–14	4QIsa^e
8:11–14	4QIsa^l
9:1–20	1QIsa^a
9:3–12	4QIsa^c
9:10–11	4QIsa^b
9:17–20	4QIsa^e
10:1–34	1QIsa^a
10:1–10	4QIsa^e
10:16–19	1QIsa^b
10:23–33	4QIsa^c
11:1–16	1QIsa^a
11:4–11, 14–16	4QIsa^c
11:7–9	4QIsa^b
11:11–15	4QIsa^a
11:14–15	4QIsa^e
12:1–6	1QIsa^a

Reference	Scroll	Reference	Scroll
39:3? (or 41:25?)	5QIsa	51:1–23	1QIsa[a]
40:1–31	1QIsa[a]	51:1–10	1QIsa[b]
40:1–4, 22–26	4QIsa[b]	51:1–2, 14–16	4QIsa[b]
40:2–3	1QIsa[b]	51:8–16	4QIsa[c]
40:16, 18–19	5QIsa	52:1–15	1QIsa[a]
41:1–29	1QIsa[a]	52:2, 7	4QIsa[b]
41:3–23	1QIsa[b]	52:4–7	4QIsa[d]
41:8–11	4QIsa[b]	52:7–15	1QIsa[b]
41:25? (or 39:3?)	5QIsa	52:10–15	4QIsa[c]
42:1–25	1QIsa[a]	53:1–12	1QIsa[a]
42:2–7, 9–12	4QIsa[b]	53:1–12	1QIsa[b]
42:4–11	4QIsa[h]	53:1–3, 6–8	4QIsa[c]
42:14–25	4QIsa[g]	53:8–12	4QIsa[d]
43:1–28	1QIsa[a]	53:11–12	4QIsa[b]
43:1–13, 23–27	1QIsa[b]	54:1–17	1QIsa[a]
43:1–4, 16–24	4QIsa[g]	54:1–11	4QIsa[d]
43:12–15	4QIsa[b]	54:1–6	1QIsa[b]
44:3–7, 23	4QIsa[c]	54:3–5, 7–17	4QIsa[c]
44:1–28	1QIsa[a]	54:10–13	4QIsa[q]
44:19–28	4QIsa[b]	55:1–13	1QIsa[a]
44:21–28	1QIsa[b]	55:1–7	4QIsa[c]
45:1–25	1QIsa[a]	55:2–13	1QIsa[b]
45:1–13	1QIsa[b]	56:1–12	1QIsa[a]
45:1–4, 6–8	4QIsa[c]	56:1–12	1QIsa[b]
45:20–25	4QIsa[b]	56:7–8	4QIsa[i]
45:20	4QIsa[d]	57:1–21	1QIsa[a]
46:1–13	1QIsa[a]	57:1–4, 17–21	1QIsa[b]
46:1–3	4QIsa[b]	57:5–8	4QIsa[i]
46:3–13	1QIsa[b]	57:9–21	4QIsa[d]
46:8–13	4QIsa[c]	58:1–14	1QIsa[a]
46:10–13	4QIsa[d]	58:1–14	1QIsa[b]
47:1–15	1QIsa[a]	58:1–3, 5–7	4QIsa[d]
47:1–14	1QIsa[b]	58:13–14	4QIsa[n]
47:1–6, 8–9	4QIsa[d]	59:1–21	1QIsa[a]
48:1–22	1QIsa[a]	59:1–8, 20–21	1QIsa[b]
48:6–8	4QIsa[b]	59:15–16	4QIsa[e]
48:8–22	4QIsa[d]	60:1–22	1QIsa[a]
48:10–15, 17–19	4QIsa[c]	60:1–22	1QIsa[b]
48:17–22	1QIsa[b]	60:20–22	4QIsa[m]
49:1–26	1QIsa[a]	61:1–11	1QIsa[a]
49:1–15	1QIsa[b]	61:1–3	4QIsa[b]
49:1–15	4QIsa[d]	61:1–2	1QIsa[b]
49:21–23	4QIsa[b]	61:1, 3–6	4QIsa[m]
49:22	4QIsa[c]	62:1–12	1QIsa[a]
50:1–11	1QIsa[a]	62:2–12	1QIsa[b]
50:7–11	1QIsa[b]	63:1–19	1QIsa[a]

10:1–14	4QXIIg
11:2–11	4QXIIg
12:1–15	4QXIIg
13:1, 6–8?, 11–13	4QXIIg
13:3–10, 15	4QXIIc
14:1–6	4QXIIc
14:9–10	4QXIIg

Joel

1:10–20	4QXIIc
1:12–14	4QXIIg
2:1, 8–23	4QXIIc
2:2–13	4QXIIg
2:20, 26–27	MurXII
3:1–5	MurXII
4:1–16	MurXII
4:4–9, 11–14, 17, 19–20	4QXIIg
4:6–21	4QXIIc

Amos

1:3–15	4QXIIg
1:3–5	5QAmos
1:5–15	MurXII
2:1, 7–9, 15–16	4QXIIg
2:1	MurXII
2:11–16	4QXIIc
3:1–15	4QXIIc
3:1–2	4QXIIg
4:1–2	4QXIIc
4:4–9	4QXIIg
5:1–2, 9–18	4QXIIg
6:1–4, 6–14	4QXIIg
6:1?	MurXII
6:13–14	4QXIIc
7:1–4, 7–9, 12–16	4QXIIc
7:1, 7–12, 14–17	4QXIIg
7:3–17	MurXII
8:1–5, 11–14	4QXIIg
8:3–7, 11–14	MurXII
9:1–15	MurXII
9:1, 6, 14–15	4QXIIg

Obadiah

1–21	MurXII
1–5, 8–12, 14–15	4QXIIg

Jonah

1:1–16	MurXII
1:1–9	4QXIIg
1:1–5, 7–10, 15–16	4QXIIa
1:6–8, 10–16	4QXIIf
1:14–16	8HevXII gr
2:1–11	MurXII
2:1–7	8HevXII gr
2:1, 7	4QXIIa
2:3–11	4QXIIg
3:1–10	MurXII
3:1–3	4QXIIg
3:2–5, 7–10	8HevXII gr
3:2	4QXIIa
4:1–11	MurXII
4:1–2, 5	8HevXII gr
4:5–11	4QXIIg

Micah

1:1–16	MurXII
1:1–8	8HevXII gr
1:7, 12–15	4QXIIg
2:1–13	MurXII
2:3–4	4QXIIg
2:7–8	8HevXII gr
3:1–12	MurXII
3:5–6	8HevXII gr
3:12	4QXIIg
4:1–14	MurXII
4:1–2	4QXIIg
4:3–10	8HevXII gr
5:1–6 [LXX 2–7]	8HevXII gr
5:1–2	4QXIIf
5:1, 5–14	MurXII
5:6–7	4QXIIg
6:1–7, 11–16	MurXII
7:1–20	MurXII
7:2–3, 20	4QXIIg

Nahum

1:1–14	MurXII
1:7–9	4QXIIg
1:13–14	8HevXII gr
2:1–14	MurXII
2:5–10, 13–14	8HevXII gr
2:9–11	4QXIIg

Reference	Scroll	Reference	Scroll
18:26–29	MasPs^a	50:14–23	4QPs^c
19:3? or 60:9?	11QPs^d	51:1–5	4QPs^c
19:4–8	11QPs^c	51:2–6	4QPs^j
22:4–9, 15–21	5/6HevPs	52:6–11	4QPs^c
22:14–17	4QPs^f	53:1	4QPs^c
23:2–6	5/6HevPs	53:4–5, 7	4QPs^a
24:1–2	5/6HevPs	54:2–3, 5–6	4QPs^a
25:2–7	11QPs^c	56:4	4QPs^a
25:4–6	5/6HevPs	59:5–6, 8	11QPs^d
25:15	4QPs^a	60:9? or 19:3?	11QPs^d
26:7–12	4QPs^r	62:13	4QPs^a
27:1	4QPs^r	63:2, 4	4QPs^a
27:12–14	4QPs^c	66:16, 18–20	4QPs^a
28:1–4	4QPs^c	67:1–2, 4–8	4QPs^a
29:1–2	5/6HevPs	68:1–5, 16–18	11QPs^d
30:9–13	4QPs^r	69:1–19	4QPs^a
31:3–22	5/6HevPs	71:1–14	4QPs^a
31:23–24	4QPs^a	76:10–12	4QPs^e
31:24–25	4QPs^q	77:1	4QPs^e
33:1–7, X, 8–14, 16–18	4QPs^q	77:18–21	11QPs^b
33:2, 4–6, 8, 10, 12	4QPs^a	78:1	11QPs^b
34:21–22	4QPs^a	78:5–12	11QPs^d
35:2, 13–18, 20, 26–27	4QPs^a	78:6–7, 31–33	4QPs^e
35:4–5, 8, 10, 12, 14–15, 17, 19–20	4QPs^q	78:36–37	pap6QPs
35:27–28	4QPs^c	78:36–37?	11QPs^e?
36:1, 3, 5–7, 9	4QPs^a	81:2–3	4QPs^e
36:13	11QPs^d	81:2–3, 5–17	MasPs^a
37:1–4, 5?	11QPs^d	81:4–9	11QPs^d
37:18–19	4QPs^c	82:1–8	MasPs^a
38:2, 4–6, 8–10, 12, 16–23	4QPs^a	83:1–19	MasPs^a
39:13–14	11QPs^d	84:1–13	MasPs^a
40:1–2	11QPs^d	85:1–6	MasPs^a
42:5	4QPs^c	86:5–6, 8	1QPs^a
42:5	4QPs^u	86:10–11	4QPs^e
43:1–3	11QPs^d	86:11–14	11QPs^d
44:3–5, 7, 9, 23–25	1QPs^c	88:1–2, 4–5	4QPs^e
44:8–9?	4QPs^c	88:15–17	4QPs^t
45:6–8	11QPs^d	89:20–22, 23, 26, 27–28, 31	4QPs^x
45:8–11	4QPs^c	89:44–48, 50–53	4QPs^e
47:2	4QPs^a	91:1–14, 16	11QApocrPs
48:1–3, 5, 7, 9	4QPs^j	91:5–8, 12–15	4QPs^b
45:15	4QPs^c	92:4–8, 13–15	4QPs^b
49:1–17	4QPs^c	92:12–14	1QPs^a
49:6?, 9–12, 15, 17?	4QPs^j	93:1–3	11QPs^a
50:3–7?	11QPs^e?	93:3–5	4QPs^m
		93:5	4QPs^b

136:1–7, X, 8–16, 26	11QPs[a]
136:22–24	4QPs[n]
137:1, 9	11QPs[a]
138:1–8	11QPs[a]
139:8–24	11QPs[a]
140:1–5	11QPs[a]
141:5–10	11QPs[a]
141:10	11QPs[b]
142:4–8	11QPs[a]
143:1–8	11QPs[a]
143:3–4, 6–8	4QPs[p]
144:1–7, 15	11QPs[a]
144:1–2	11QPs[b]
145:1–7, 13, X, 14–21, X	11QPs[a]
146:1?	4QPs[e]
146:9, X, 10	11QPs[a]
147:1–4, 13–17, 20	4QPs[d]
147:1–3, 18–20	11QPs[a]
147:18–19	MasPs[b]
148:1–12	11QPs[a]
149:7–9, X	11QPs[a]
150:1–6	11QPs[a]
150:1–6	MasPs[b]
151A:1–7	11QPs[a]
151B:1–2	11QPs[a]
154:3–19	11QPs[a]
154:17–20	4Q448
155:1–19	11QPs[a]
Three Songs Against Demons	11QApocrPs
Apostrophe to Judah	4QPs[f]
Apostrophe to Zion 1–18	11QPs[a]
Apostrophe to Zion 1–2, 11–18	4QPs[f]
Apostrophe to Zion 4–5	11QPs[b]
David's Compositions	11QPs[a]
David's Last Words 7 (= 2 Sam 23:7)	11QPs[a]
Eschatological Hymn	4QPs[f]
Hymn to Creator 1–9	11QPs[a]
Plea for Deliverance	11QPs[a]
Plea for Deliverance	11QPs[b]

Job

3:5–6	4QtgJob
4:16–21	4QtgJob
5:1–4	4QtgJob
8:15–17	4QJob[b]
9:27	4QJob[b]
13:4	4QJob[b]
13:19–20, 24–27	4QpaleoJob[c]
14:4–6	4QJob[b]
14:13–17	4QpaleoJob[c]
17:14–16	11QtgJob
18:1–4	11QtgJob
19:11–19, 29	11QtgJob
20:1–6	11QtgJob
21:2–10, 20–27	11QtgJob
22:3–9, 16–22	11QtgJob
23:1–8	11QtgJob
24:12–17, 24–25	11QtgJob
25:1–6	11QtgJob
26:1–2, 10–14	11QtgJob
27:1–4, 11–20	11QtgJob
28:4–13, 20–28	11QtgJob
29:7–16, 24–25	11QtgJob
30:1–4, 13–20, X, 27–31	11QtgJob
31:1, 8–16, 26–32, 40	11QtgJob
31:14–19	4QJob[a]
31:20–21	4QJob[b]
32:1–3, 10–17	11QtgJob
32:3–4	4QJob[a]
33:6–16, 24–32	11QtgJob
33:10–11, 24–26, 28–30	4QJob[a]
33:28–30	2QJob
34:6–17, 24–34	11QtgJob
34:28–31	4QJob[a]
35:5–15	11QtgJob
35:16	4QJob[a]
36:7–16, 23–33	11QtgJob
36:7–11, 13–27, 32–33	4QJob[a]
37:1–5, 14–15	4QJob[a]
37:10–19	11QtgJob
38:3–13, 23–33	11QtgJob
39:1–11, 20–29	11QtgJob
40:4–14, 23–31	11QtgJob
40:5	11QtgJob
41:15–25, 25–26 [MT 7–17, 33–34]	11QtgJob
42:1–2, 4–6, 9–12	11QtgJob

Proverbs

1:27–33	4QProv^a
2:1	4QProv^a
7:9–11?	4QProv^b
13:6–9	4QProv^b
14:5–10, 12–13, 31–35	4QProv^b
15:1–8, 19–31	4QProv^b

Ruth

1:1–12	4QRuth^a
1:1–6, 12–15	4QRuth^b
2:13–23	2QRuth^a
3:1–8	2QRuth^a
3:13–18	2QRuth^b
4:3–4	2QRuth^a

Canticles

1:1–7	6QCant
2:9–17	4QCant^b
3:1–2, 5, 9–11	4QCant^b
3:4–5, 7–11	4QCant^a
3:7–8	4QCant^c
4:1–7	4QCant^a
4:1–3, 8–11, 14–16	4QCant^b
5:1	4QCant^b
6:11?–12	4QCant^a
7:1–7	4QCant^a

Ecclesiastes (Qoheleth)

1:10–14 (15?)	4QQoh^b
5:13–17	4QQoh^a
6:1, 3–8, 12	4QQoh^a
7:1–10, 19–20	4QQoh^a

Lamentations

1:1–18	4QLam
1:10–12	3QLam
2:5	4QLam
3:53–62	3QLam
4:5–8, 11–16, 19–22	5QLam^a
4:17–20	5QLam^b
5:1–13, 16–17	5QLam^a

Esther

[not represented]

Daniel

1:10–17	1QDan^a
1:16–20	4QDan^a
2:2–6	1QDan^a
2:9–11, 19–49	4QDan^a
3:1–2	4QDan^a
3:22–30	1QDan^b
3:23–25	4QDan^d
4:5?–9, 12–14	4QDan^d
4:29–30	4QDan^a
5:5–7, 12–14, 16–19	4QDan^a
5:10–12, 14–16, 19–22	4QDan^b
6:8–22, 27–29	4QDan^b
7:1–6, 11?, 26–28	4QDan^b
7:5–7, 25–28	4QDan^a
7:15–19, 21–23?	4QDan^d
8:1–8, 13–16	4QDan^b
8:1–5	4QDan^a
8:16–17?, 20–21?	pap6QDan
9:12–14, 15–16?, 17?	4QDan^e
10:5–9, 11–16, 21	4QDan^c
10:8–16	pap6QDan
10:16–20	4QDan^a
11:1–2, 13–17, 25–29	4QDan^c
11:13–16	4QDan^a
11:33–36, 38	pap6QDan

Ezra

4:2–6, 9–11	4QEzra
5:17	4QEzra
6:1–5	4QEzra

Nehemiah

[not represented]

Chronicles

2 Chron 28:27	4QChr
29:1–3	4QChr

Index of Passages from the Apocrypha and Pseudepigrapha in the Scrolls

FOR EARLIER LISTINGS, SEE PETER FLINT, "Appendix 2: Index of Passages in the Apocryphal and 'Pseudepigraphal' Scrolls," in A. Avery-Peck et al., eds. *Judaism in Late Antiquity,* Part 5, Vol. 2: *The Judaism of Qumran: A Systematic Reading of the Dead Sea Scrolls. World View, Comparing Judaisms* (Handbook of Oriental Studies, section 1: The Near and Middle East, vol. 57; Leiden: Brill, 2001) 101–3.

Note: (1) A question mark following a verse or manuscript (e.g., 3:3–4? or pap4QJub[b]?) indicates that the identification is uncertain. (2) Some passages relating to the *Testaments* are listed here on the understanding that the *Aramaic Levi Document* and similar texts are not the original Semitic texts used by the translator of the *Testaments of the Twelve Patriarchs.* Instead, these are Hebrew or Aramaic sources of the later composition that was extensively reworked by Christian editors.

Tobit

1:17, 19–22	4QpapTobit[a] ar
2:1–3, 10–11	4QpapTobit[a] ar
3:5, 9–15, 17	4QpapTobit[a] ar
3:6–8	4QTobit[b] ar
3:3–4?, 6, 10–11	4QTobit[e]
4:2, 5, 7	4QpapTobit[a] ar
4:3–9	4QTobit[e]
4:21	4QpapTobit[a] ar
4:21	4QTobit[b] ar
5:1, 9	4QpapTobit[a] ar
5:1, 12–14, 19–22	4QTobit[b] ar
5:2	4QTobit[e]
6:1–18	4QTobit[b] ar
6:6–8, 13, 15–19	4QpapTobit[a] ar
7:?	4QpapTobit[a] ar
7:1–6, 13	4QpapTobit[a] ar
7:1–10	4QTobit[b] ar
7:11	4QTobit[d] ar
8:17–19, 21	4QTobit[b] ar
9:1–4	4QTobit[b] ar
10:7–9	4QTobit[e]
11:10–14	4QTobit[e]
12:1, 18–22	4QpapTobit[a] ar
12:20–22	4QTobit[e]
13:1–4, 13–14, 18	4QTobit[e]
13:3–18	4QpapTobit[a] ar
14:1–2	4QTobit[e]

14:2–6, 10?	4QTobit^c ar
14:1–3, 7	4QpapTobit^a ar
14:10	4QTobit^d ar

Sirach (Ecclesiasticus, Ben Sira)

1:19–20? or 6:14–15?	2QSir
6:20–31	2QSir
39:27–28c, 29–32	MasSir
40:10–19, 28–30	MasSir
41:1–22	MasSir
42:1–25	MasSir
43:1–25 (omits 26–28), 29–30	MasSir
44:1–17	MasSir
51:1–11, 23 [LXX 13–20, 30]	11QPs^a

Epistle of Jeremiah

43–44	papEpJer gr

Apocryphal Psalms

Psalm 151A	
151A:1–7	11QPs^a
Psalm 151B	
151B:1–2	11QPs^a
Psalm 154	
154:3–19	11QPs^a
154:17–20	4Q448
Psalm 155	
155:1–19	11QPs^a

1 Enoch

1:1–6	4QEn^a ar
1:9	4QEn^c ar
2:1–3	4QEn^a ar
2:1–3	4QEn^c ar
3:1	4QEn^a ar
3:1	4QEn^c ar
4:1	4QEn^a ar
4:1	4QEn^c ar
5:1	4QEn^c ar
5:1–6	4QEn^a ar
5:9	4QEn^b ar
6:1–4, 7–8	4QEn^b ar
6:4–8	4QEn^a ar
6:7	4QEn^c ar
7:1–6	4QEn^a ar

7:1–6	4QEn^b ar
8:1, 3–4	4QEn^a ar
8:1–4	4QEn^b ar
9:1–3, 6–8	4QEn^a ar
9:1–4	4QEn^b ar
10:3–4, 21–22	4QEn^a ar
10:8–12	4QEn^b ar
10:13–19	4QEn^c ar
11:1	4QEn^a ar
12:3	4QEn^c ar
12:4–6	4QEn^a ar
13:6–10	4QEn^c ar
14:1–16, 18–20	4QEn^c ar
14:4–6	4QEn^b ar
15:11?	4QEn^c ar
18:8–12	4QEn^c ar
18:15?	4QEn^e ar
21:2–4	4QEn^e ar
22:3–7	4QEn^e ar
22:13–14	4QEn^d ar
23:1–4	4QEn^d ar
24:1	4QEn^d ar
25:7	4QEn^d ar
26:1–6	4QEn^d ar
27:1	4QEn^d ar
28:3	4QEn^e ar
29:1–2	4QEn^e ar
30:1–3	4QEn^c ar
31:1–3	4QEn^c ar
31:2–3	4QEn^e ar
32:1	4QEn^c ar
32:1–3, 6	4QEn^e ar
33:3–4	4QEn^e ar
34:1	4QEn^e ar
35:1	4QEn^c ar
36:1–4	4QEn^c ar
73:1–74:9 (similar)	4QEnastr^a ar
73:1–74:9 (similar)	4QEnastr^b ar
76:3–10, 13–14	4QEnastr^c ar
76:13–14	4QEnastr^b ar
77:1–4	4QEnastr^b ar
77:1–4	4QEnastr^c ar
78:6–8	4QEnastr^c ar
78:9–12, 17	4QEnastr^b ar
79:1, 3–5	4QEnastr^b ar
82:9–13	4QEnastr^b ar

after 82:20	4QEnastr^d ar
86:1–3	4QEn^f ar
88:3	4QEn^e ar
89:1–16, 26–30	4QEn^e ar
89:11–14, 29–31, 43–44	4QEn^d ar
89:31–37	4QEn^c ar
91:10?, 11–17, 18–19	4QEn^g ar
92:1–2, 5	4QEn^g ar
93:1–4, 9–11	4QEn^g ar
94:1–2	4QEn^g ar
98:11?	pap7QEn gr
100:12	pap7QEn gr
103:3–8, 12	pap7QEn gr
104:13	4QEn^c ar
105:1–2	4QEn^c ar
105:17?	pap7QEn gr
106:1–2, 13–19	4QEn^c ar
107:1–2	4QEn^c ar

Jubilees

Prologue	4QJub^a
1:1–2, 4–15, 26–28	4QJub^a
1:26–29?	pap4QJub^b?
2:1–4, 7–24	4QJub^a
2:14? or Gen. 1:28?	pap4QJub? (4Q483)
2:26–27	4QJub^c
3:25–27? or 14:4–6?	11QJub
4:6–11, 11–12 (or 16–17), 13–14, 17–18?, 29–30, 31	11QJub
4:17–24 (similar)	4QpseudoJub^c
5:1–2	11QJub
12:15–17, 28–29	11QJub
13:29? or Gen. 14:22–23?	pap4QJub? (4Q482)
14:4–6? or 3:25–27?	11QJub
21:1–2, 7–10, 12–16, 18–26	4QJub^d
21:5–10	4QJub^e
21:22–24	4QJub^f
22:1	4QJub^d
22:22, 30?	4QJub^f
23:6–7, 10, 12–13, 23a	3QJub
23:7–8	2QJub^a
23:21–23	4QTanh
23:30–31	4QTanh or 4QJub^f
23:10–13	4QJub^f

25:9–12	4QJub^g
27:6–7	4QJub^g
27:19–21	1QJub^a
32:18–21	pap4QJub^h
33:12–15	4QJub^f
34:4–5	pap4QJub^h
35:7–22	pap4QJub^h
35:8–10	1QJub^b
36:7–23	pap4QJub^h
36:12?	1QJub^b
37:11–15	4QJub^f
37:17–25	pap4QJub^h
38:1–13	pap4QJub^h
38:6–8	4QJub^f
39:4–9	4QJub^f
39:9–18	pap4QJub^h
40:1–7	pap4QJub^h
41:7–10, 28?	pap4QJub^h
46:1–3	2QJub^b
48:5?	4QJub^g

Material Related to the *Testaments of the 12 Patriarchs*

To the Testament of Levi

2:4 (similar)	4QLevi^b ar
8:11?	1QLevi ar
9:4 and elsewhere	1QLevi ar
chap. 8 (similarities)	4QLevi^b ar
12:7	4QLevi^a ar
13:1–4, 6, 8–9	4QLevi^a ar
19:1 (alleged)	Visions of Amram^f? ar

To the Testament of Judah

12:2 (similar)	pap4QTJudah?
25:1–2 (similar)	3QTJudah?
25:2 (similar)	pap4QTJudah?

To the Testament of Naphtali

1:6–8	4QTNaph

To the Testament of Joseph

17:1	4QTJoseph ar

APPENDIX III

Quotations and Allusions in the Nonbiblical Scrolls

THIS LISTING PRESENTS QUOTATIONS OF AND ALLUSIONS to Old Testament books in the nonbiblical scrolls. It is fairly comprehensive, following an extensive survey of the Qumran documents, but of course additional examples may be added as they are identified. Two resources that were especially helpful for this survey are M. Wise, M. Abegg, Jr., and E. Cook, *The Dead Sea Scrolls: A New Translation* (San Francisco: HarperSanFrancisco, 1996); and F. García Martínez and E. J. C. Tigchelaar, *The Dead Sea Scrolls Study Edition* (2nd ed., 2 vols.; Leiden: Brill; Grand Rapids, MI: Eerdmans, 2000).

Most of the quotations and allusions are definite or reasonably so. In cases where the identification is probable or involves a paraphrase of the source text, the reader is told to compare the two texts ("cf."). In a few cases, the identification is not clear, and so a question mark is added ("?"). On occasion, the form of text referred to is like the Samaritan Pentateuch, not the Masoretic Text, in which case the siglum "(Sam.)" is added. One final point: in some cases, the line numbering of editions and translations differs slightly. This is evident, for example, in the case of 4Q163 *(4QpIsa^c)*, where the two books listed above do no always agree with respect to lineation.

Genesis

1:16	1QSb 4.27	15:2–3	4Q225 frag. 2 1.3–4
1:27	CD 4.21	15:5	4Q225 frag. 2 1.5–7
1:27	6Q15 frag. 1, l. 3	15:6	4Q225 frag. 2 1.7–8
2:24	4Q416 frag. 2 4.1	15:13	4Q464 frag. 3 2.3–4
2:24	4Q418 frag. 10, ll. 4–5	18:20–21	4Q180 frags. 2–4 2.5–7
3:6	4Q423 frags. 1–2 1.1	22:2	4Q225 frag. 2 1.11–13
3:18	4Q423 frags. 1–2 1.3	22:4	4Q225 frag. 2 1.14
4:12	4Q423 frags. 1–2 1.3	22:7–8	4Q225 frag. 2 2.2–4
6:3	4Q252 1.2–3	22:11–12	4Q225 frag. 2 2.8–9
7:9	CD 5.1	25:18	4Q364 frag. 1a–b, ll. 1–2
9:27	4Q252 2.7	28:6	4Q364 frag. 3 2.7–8
		30:14	4Q364 frag. 4b,e 1.8
		32:25	4Q158 frags. 1–2, l. 13

427

41:40	CD 13.3
49:10	1QSb 5.27
49:10	4Q252 5.3

Exodus

4:22	4Q504 frags. 1–2R 3.6
4:27–28	4Q158 frags. 1–2, ll. 14–15
9:9–10	4Q365 frag. 3, ll. 21–22
14:10	4Q365 frag. 5, l. 1
14:12–20	4Q365 frag. 6a 1.1–10
15:17	4Q174 3.3
15:22–26	4Q365 frag. 6a, col. 2 + 6c, ll. 8–14
19:4	4Q504 frag. 6, ll. 6–7
19:6	4Q504 frag. 4, l. 10
20:6	CD 20.21–22
20:21 (Sam.)	4Q175 1.1–4
21:18	4Q251 frags. 4–7 1.5
21:19, 28–29	4Q251 frag. 4, ll. 1–6
21:29	4Q251 frag. 5, ll. 1–6
22:29–30	4Q251 frag. 7, ll. 1–7
23:7	1QS 5.15
24:18	4Q364 frag. 15, ll. 1–3
25:1–2	4Q364 frag. 15, l. 5

Leviticus

13:33	4Q266 frag. 6 1.9
13:33	4Q272 frag. 1 1.17–18
13:45	4Q274 frag. 1 1.3
18:5	CD 3.16 (cf.)
18:5	4Q504 frag. 6, l.17 (cf.)
18:13	CD 5.9
19:17	CD 9.7–8
19:17	4Q267 frag. 9 1.3
19:17	4Q270 frag. 6 4.1
19:17	5Q12 frag. 1, l.2
19:18	CD 9.2
19:18	4Q266 frag. 8 2.10
19:18	4Q270 frag. 6 3.17
19:19	4Q418 frag. 103 2.7
22:16	1QS 5.14–15
23:38	CD 11.18
23:38	4Q270 frag. 6 5.21
23:38	4Q271 frag. 5 1.12
23:42–24:2	4Q365 frag. 23, ll. 1–4
25:9	11Q13 2.25
25:13	11Q13 2.2

25:14	4Q271 frag. 3, ll. 4–5
26:25	CD 1.17–18
26:31	4Q266 frag. 11, ll. 3–4
26:31	4Q270 frag. 7 1.18
27:29	4Q266 frag. 8 2.8–9
27:31	4Q270 frag. 2 2.10

Numbers

4:47–47; 7:1	4Q365 frag. 28, ll. 1–5
6:24–26	1QS 2.2–4
6:24	4Q256 2.12
6:25	4Q374 frag. 2 2.8
6:26	1QSb 3.1
10:9	1QM 10.6–8
18:20	4Q418 frags. 81+81a, l. 3
21:18	CD 6.3–4
21:18	4Q266 frag. 3 2.10–11
21:18	4Q267 frag. 2, ll. 9–10
24:15–17	4Q175 1.11–13
24:17	CD 7.19–20
24:17	CD 7.20–21
24:17	1QSb 5.27
24:17, 19, 18	1QM 11.6–7
24:17	4Q266 frag. 3 3.20–21
24:17	4Q266 frag. 3 3.22
24:17	4Q269 frag. 5, l. 3
27:11	4Q365 frag. 36, ll. 1–3
30:9	CD 16.10
30:9	4Q271 frag. 4 2.10–11
30:17	CD 7.8–9
30:17	CD 19.5
36:1–2	4Q365 frag. 36, ll. 3–6

Deuteronomy

1:17	4Q364 frag. 21a–k, ll. 1–2
5:12	CD 10.16–17
5:12	4Q270 frag. 6 5.3
5:28b–29	4Q175 1.1–4
7:8	CD 8.15 (19.28)
7:9	CD 7.6 (19.1–2)
7:26	4Q397 frags. 14–21, l. 6
9:5	CD 8.14–15 (19.27)
10:16	4Q434 frag. 1 1.4
10:16	4Q435 frag. 1, l. 1
15:2	11Q13 2.2–3

17:17	CD 5.2
18:1–4	4Q524 frags. 6–13, ll. 4–7
18:5–14	11QT^a 60.10–21
18:18–19	4Q175 1.5–8
20:3–4	1QM 10.3–5
20:8	11QT^a 62.3–4
21:22–23	11QT^a 64.7–13
22:9–11	4Q270 frag. 5, l. 16 (cf.)
22:9–11	4Q271 frag. 3, l. 10 (cf.)
22:9–11	4Q418 frag. 103 2.7 (cf.)
22:11	4Q524 frag. 14, l. 5
22:19	4Q524 frag. 14, l. 6
23:24	CD 16.6
23:24	4Q270 frag. 6 2.19
23:24	4Q271 frag. 4 2.8
26:6	4Q461 frag. 1, l. 3 (cf.)
27:18	4Q269 frag. 9, l. 2
27:18	4Q270 frag. 5, l. 15
27:18	4Q271 frag. 3, l. 9
29:18–19	1QS 2.13–14
30:1–2	4Q397 frags. 14–21, ll. 13–14
30:1–2	4Q398 frags. 14–17 1. 5–8
31:29	4Q397 frags. 14–21, l. 12
31:29	4Q398 frags. 14–17 1.5
32:11	4Q504 frag. 6, ll. 7–8
32:24	4Q418 frag. 127, l. 3 (cf.)
32:28	CD 5.17
32:28	4Q266 frag. 3 2.4
32:33	CD 8.9–10
32:33	CD 19.22
33:8–11	4Q174 1.9–12
33:8–11	4Q175 1.14–20
33:12	4Q174 1.16–17
33:20–21	4Q174 2.3–4

Joshua

6:26	4Q175 1.22–23
6:26	4Q379 frag. 22 2. 8–9
13:3	4Q522 frags. 9, col. 1 +10, l. 8 (cf.)
13:3	4Q522 frags. 9, col. 1 +10, l. 9 (cf.)
15:24	4Q522 frags. 9, col. 1 +10, l. 11 (cf.)
15:28	4Q522 frags. 9, col. 1 i+10, l. 11 (cf.)
15:35	4Q522 frags. 9, col. 1 +10, l.12 (cf.)
15:44	4Q522 frags. 9, col. 1 +10, l. 12 (cf.)
15:51	4Q522 frags. 9, col. 1 +10, l. 16 (cf.)
15:57	4Q522 frags. 9, col. 1 +10, l. 13 (cf.)

21:21	4Q522 frags. 9, col. 1 +10, l 13 (cf.)
23:10	11Q11 3.11 (cf.)

Judges

1:30	4Q522 frags. 9, col. 1 +10, l. 14

1 Samuel

3:14–18	4Q160 frag. 1, ll. 1–7
2:10	4Q491 frag. 11 2.22 (cf.?)
19:22	4Q522 frags. 9, col. 1 +10, l. 14 (cf.)

2 Samuel

7:10–11a	4Q174 2.18–3.2
7:11b	4Q174 3.7
7:11c, 12b, 13b–14a	4Q174 3.10–11

1 Kings

5:18	4Q504 frags. 1–2R 4.12–13

Isaiah

1:1	3Q4 frag.1, ll. 1–4
1:1	3Q4 frag. 1, l. 4
2:22	1QS 5.17
5:5	4Q162 1.1
5:5	4Q162 1.3–4
5:9	4Q162 2.1 (cf.)
5:11–14	4Q162 2.2–6
5:20	4Q471a frag. 1, l. 8 (cf.)
5:24c–25	4Q162 2.7–10
5:29–30	4Q162 3.1–3
6:9	4Q162 3.7–8 (cf.?)
7:17	CD 7.11–12
7:17	4Q267 frag. 9 5.2–4
7:17	CD 13.23–14.1
7:17	4Q266 frag. 9 3.17–18
8:7–8	4Q163 frag. 2, ll. 1–3
8:11	4Q174 3.15–16
9:4 [Eng. 5]	4Q257 3.4
9:11–12 [Eng. 12–13]	4Q163 frags. 4–7, ll. 4–5
9:13–16 [Eng. 14–17]	4Q163 frags. 4–7, ll. 6–9
9:17–20 [Eng. 18–21]	4Q163 frags. 4–7, ll. 14–19
10:2	CD 6.16–17 (cf.)

10:2	4Q266 frag. 3 2.22 (cf.)
10:17–19?	4Q163 frags. 6–7 2.2–3
10:19	4Q163 frags. 6–7 2.1
10:19	4Q163 frags. 6–7 2.5
10:20–22	4Q163 frags. 6–7 2.10–13
10:22–23	4Q161 2.5 (cf.)
10:22–23 (?)	4Q163 frags. 6–7 2.14–17
10:24	4Q163 frags. 6–7 2.19
10:24–27	4Q161 2.10–15
10:28–32	4Q161 2.21–25
10:33–34	4Q161 3.5–7
10:34–11:1	11Q14 frag. 1 1. 11
10:34–11:1	4Q285 frag. 7, ll. 1–3
11:1–5	4Q161 3.15–20
11:4, 2, 5	1QSb 5.24–26
11:4	1QSb 5.21–22
11:11–12	4Q165 frag. 11, ll. 3–5
14:8	4Q163 frags. 8–10, ll. 1–3
14:19	4Q165 frag. 3, l. 1
14:26–27	4Q163 frags. 8–10, ll. 4–7
14:28–30	4Q163 frags. 8–10, ll. 11–14
15:4–5	4Q165 frag. 4.1–2
19:9–12	4Q163 frag. 11 2.1–5
19:14	4Q471a frag. 1, l. 6 (cf.?)
21:9–10	4Q165 frag. 5, ll. 1–2
21:11–15	4Q165 frag. 5, ll. 3–5
22:13	4Q177 1.15
24:17	CD 4.14
27:11	4Q266 frag. 3 2.4
27:11	CD 5.16
28:16	1QS 8.7
28:16	4Q259 2.14
29:10–12	4Q163 frags. 15–16, ll. 1–4
29:15–16	4Q163 frags. 17, l. 1
29:17	4Q163 frag. 21, ll. 1–2
29:18–23	4Q163 frags. 18–19, ll. 1–6
30:1–5	4Q163 frag. 21, ll. 9–15
30:15–18	4Q163 frag. 23 2.3–9
30:19–21	4Q163 frag. 23 2.15–19
30:20–21	4Q163 frag. 22, l. 1 (cf.)
30:23	4Q163 frag. 22, l. 4
30:30–32	4Q163 frag. 25, l. 1 (cf.)
31:1	4Q163 frag. 25, ll. 5–7
31:8	1QM 11.11–12
32:5–7	4Q165 frag. 6, ll. 2–6
32:7	4Q177 1.6
37:30	4Q177 1.2
38:19 (cf.)	11Q5 19.2
38:19 (cf.)	11Q6 frags. 4–5, l. 4
40:1–5	4Q176 frags. 1–2 1. 4–9
40:3	1QS 9.20
40:3	4Q259 3.5
40:3	4Q259 3.19–20
40:3	1QS 8.14
40:11	4Q165 frags. 1–2, l. 2
40:12	4Q165 frags. 1–2, ll. 3–4
40:12	4Q511 frag. 30, ll. 4–5
41:8–9	4Q176 frags. 1–2 1.9–11
42:16	4Q434 frag. 1 1. 9
42:16	4Q435 frag. 1 l. 8
43:1–2	4Q176 frag. 3, ll. 1–3
43:4–6	4Q176 frags. 4–5, ll. 2–4
49:2	4Q437 frag. 2 1.8–9
49:7, 13–17	4Q176 frag. 1–2 2.1–6
50:11	CD 5.13
50:11	4Q266 frag. 3 2.1
50:11	6Q15 frag. 2, l. 1 (cf.)
51:22–23	4Q176 frags. 6–7, ll. 1–3
52:1–3	4Q176 frags. 8–11, ll. 2–4
52:7	11Q13 2.15–16
52:7	11Q13 2.23
53:3?	4Q471b frag. 1a–d, ll. 1–2 (cf.?)
54:1–2	4Q265 frag. 1, ll. 4–5
54:4–10	4Q176 frags. 8–11, ll. 5–12
54:11	4Q164 frag. 1, l. 1
54:12a	4Q164 frag. 1, ll. 3–4
54:12b	4Q164 frag. 1, l. 6
54:16	CD 6.8
59:5	CD 5.13–14
59:5	4Q266 frag. 3 2.1–2
59:5	6Q15 frag. 2, ll. 2. 1–2 (cf.)
61:1	11Q13 2.4
61:1	4Q521 frags. 2, col. 2+4, l. 12
61:2	11Q13 2.19–20
61:2	11Q13 2.9 (cf.)
61:3	11Q13 2.14
65:22–23	4Q174 6.1–3

Jeremiah

2:3	4Q396 frags. 1–2 4.5
2:3	4Q397 frags. 6–13, ll. 11
5:7	4Q182 frag. 1, ll. 4–5

9:22 [Eng. 23]	4Q460 frag. 8, l. 2
14:22	4Q504 frags. 1–2R 4.3–4
18:18	4Q177 4.6
20:13	4Q434 frag. 1 1.1

Ezekiel

3:16	4Q385b frag. 1, l. 1 (cf.)
9:4	CD 19.12
20:11	4Q504 frag. 6, l. 17 (cf.)
20:35	4Q161 2.18
22:21	CD 20.3
25:8	4Q177 2.13–14
37:23	4Q174 3.16–17
39:3–4	4Q285 frag. 4, ll. 3–4
44:15	CD 3.21–4.2
44:15	4Q266 frag. 2 3.19–20

XII Prophets

Hosea

2:8 [Eng. 6]	4Q166 frag. 1 1.7–8
2:9 [Eng. 7]	4Q166 frag. 1 1.15–16
2:10 [Eng. 8]	4Q166 frag. 1 2.1–2
2:11–12 [Eng. 9–10]	4Q166 frag. 1 2.8–11
2:13 [Eng. 11]	4Q166 frag. 1 2.14–15
2:14 [Eng. 12]	4Q166 frag. 1 2.17–19
2:17 [Eng. 15]	4Q434 frag. 7b., l. 2
2:20 [Eng. 18]	4Q434 frag. 7b, ll. 2–3
3:4	CD 20.16
4:16	CD 1.13–14
4:16	4Q266 frag. 2 1.17
5:8	4Q177 3.13
5:10	CD 8.3
5:10	CD 19.15–16
5:10	4Q266 frag. 3 3.25–4.1
5:13	4Q167 frag. 2, l. 1
5:14	4Q167 frag. 2, ll. 2–3
5:15	4Q167 frag. 2, ll. 5–6
6:4	4Q167 frags. 5–6, l. 3
6:7	4Q167 frags. 7–8, l. 1
6:9	4Q163 frag. 23 2.14
6:9–10	4Q167 frags. 10+26, ll. 1–2
6:11	4Q167 frags. 10a+4+18+24, ll. 1–2
7:1	4Q167 frags. 10a+4+18+24, l. 6
8:6	4Q167 frags. 11–13, l. 3
8:6	4Q167 frags. 11–13, l. 5

8:7–8	4Q167 frags. 11–13, ll. 6–8
8:14	4Q167 frags. 15+33 2.1–2

Joel

Joel 2:12	4Q266 frag. 11, l. 5
Joel 2:13	4Q266 frag. 11, l. 5
Joel 2:13	4Q270 frag. 7 1.19
Joel 2:12	4Q270 frag. 7 1.19

Amos

5:26–27	CD 7.14–15
8:11	4Q387 frag. 3, ll. 8–9
9:11	CD 7.16
9:11	4Q174 3.12

Micah

1:2–5	1Q14 frags. 1–5, ll. 1–5
1:5	1Q14 frags. 8–10, ll. 1–3
1:6	1Q14 frags. 8–10, ll. 5–6
1:6	1Q14 frags. 8–10, ll. 10–11
1:8	1Q14 frags. 11, l. 2
1:9	1Q14 frags. 11, l. 3
2:6	CD 4.20
2:6	4Q269 frag. 3, l. 2
2:6	6Q15 frag. 1, l. 2
2:10–11	4Q177 1.10
4:13	1QSb 5. 26
6:14–16	1Q14 frags. 17–19, ll. 1–5
7:2	CD 16.15
7:2	4Q271 frag. 4 2.14–15
7:11	CD 4.12 (cf.)
7:11	4Q266 frag. 3 1.6 (cf.)

Nahum

1:2	CD 9.5
1:2	4Q270 frag. 6 3.19
1:3	4Q169 frags. 1–2, l. 1
1:4a	4Q169 frags. 1–2, l. 3
1:4b	4Q169 frags. 1–2, l. 4
1:4c	4Q169 frags. 1–2, l. 5
1:5–6	4Q169 frags. 1–2, ll. 9–11
2:11	4Q177 3.3
2:11a	4Q169 frags. 3–4 1.1
2:11b	4Q169 frags. 3–4 1.1–2
2:12a	4Q169 frags. 3–4 1.4
2:12b	4Q169 frags. 3–4 1.6
2:13a	4Q169 frags. 3–4 1.8–9
2:13b–c	4Q169 frags. 3–4 1.9–10

3:1a	4Q169 frags. 3–4 2.1
3:1b–3	4Q169 frags. 3–4 2.3–4
3:4	4Q169 frags. 3–4 2. 7
3:5	4Q169 frags. 3–4 2.10–11
3:6–7a	4Q169 frags. 3–4 3.1–2
3:7b	4Q169 frags. 3–4 3.5–6
3:8a	4Q169 frags. 3–4 3.8
3:8b	4Q169 frags. 3–4 3.10
3:9	4Q169 frags. 3–4 3.11–12
3:10	4Q169 frags. 3–4 4.1–3
3:11a	4Q169 frags. 3–4 4.4–5
3:11b	4Q169 frags. 3–4 4.6–7
3:12	4Q169 frags. 3–4 4.8–9

Habakkuk

1:1–2	1QpHab 1.1–2
1:3a	1QpHab 1.5
1:3b	1QpHab 1.7
1:4a	1QpHab 1.10–11
1:4b	1QpHab 1.12
1:4c	1QpHab 1.14–15
1:5	1QpHab 1.16–2.1
1:6a	1QpHab 2.10–11
1:6b	1QpHab 2.15
1:6b	1QpHab 3.2
1:7	1QpHab 3.2–3
1:8–9a	1QpHab 3.6–9
1:9b	1QpHab 3.14
1:10a	1QpHab 3.17–4.1
1:10b	1QpHab 4.3–4
1:11	1QpHab 4.9–10
1:11	1QpHab 4.13
1:12–13a	1QpHab 4.16–5.2
1:13a	1QpHab 5.6–7
1:13b	1QpHab 5.8–9
1:14–16	1QpHab 5.12–16
1:16a	1QpHab 6.2–3
1:16b	1QpHab 6.5
1:17	1QpHab 6.8–9
2:1–2	1QpHab 6.12–16
2:2	1QpHab 7.3
2:3a	1QpHab 7.5–6
2:3b	1QpHab 7.9–10
2:4a	1QpHab 7.14–15
2:4b	1QpHab 7.17
2:5–6	1QpHab 8.3–8

2:7–8a	1QpHab 8.13–15
2:8	1QpHab 9.3, 4, 7
2:8b	1QpHab 9.8
2:9–11	1QpHab 9.12–15
2:10	1QpHab 10.2
2:12–13	1QpHab 10.5–8
2:14	1QpHab 10.14–15
2:15	1QpHab 11.2–3
2:16	1QpHab 11.8–11
2:17	1QpHab 11.17–12.1
2:17b	1QpHab 12.6–7
2:18	1QpHab 12.10–12
2:19–20	1QpHab 12.14–13.1

Zephaniah

1:6	1QS 5.11
1:18	1Q15 frag. 1, ll. 1–2
2:1–2	1Q15 frag. 1, ll. 2–4
3:9	4Q464 frag. 3 1.9

Zechariah

3:9	4Q177 2.2
4:14	4Q254 frag. 4, l. 2
11:7	CD 19.9 (cf.)
11:11	4Q163 frag. 21, ll. 7–8
13:7	CD 19.7–9
13:9	4Q176 frag. 15, ll. 3–5

Malachi

1:10	CD 6.13
1:10	4Q266 frag. 3 2.19
1:14a	5Q10 frag. 1, l. 1
1:14b	5Q10 frag. 1, l. 3
2:10	4Q265 frag. 3, ll. 1–2
3:16	CD 20.19–20
3:16–18	4Q253a frag. 1 1.1–5
3:16	4Q418 frag. 43–45 1.12 (cf.)
3:18	CD 20.20–21

Psalms

1:1a	4Q174 3.14
2:1–2	4Q174 3.18–19
5:2–3a	4Q174 5.2
6:2–4	4Q177 4.7–8
7:7–8	11Q13 2.10–11
11:1–2	4Q177 1.7–8
12:1	4Q177 1.12

12:7	4Q177 2.1	68:12	1Q16 frags. 3–7, l. 3
13:2–3	4Q177 2.8–9	68:25–26	1Q16 frag. 8, l. 1
13:5	4Q177 2.11–12	68:29	1Q16 frags. 9–10, l. 1
16:3	4Q177 3.2	68:30	1Q16 frags. 9–10, ll. 2–3
17:1	4Q177 3.4	79:8	4Q504 frag. 4, l. 6
17:2	4Q177 3.6	82:1	11Q13 2.10
18:2	4Q381 frag. 24a+b, l. 7	82:2	11Q13 2.11
18:6	4Q381 frag. 24a+b, ll. 7–8	86:16	4Q381 frag. 15, l. 2
18:6–7	4Q381 frag. 24a+b, ll. 9–10	86:17	4Q381 frag. 15, ll. 2–3
26:12	1QH^a 10.29–30	89:7	4Q381 frag. 15, ll. 6–7
34:7	4Q434 frag. 1 1.12	89:10	4Q381 frag. 15, ll. 3–4
37:5	4Q171 frags. 1–10 1.11	89:11–12	4Q381 frag. 15, ll. 4–5
37:6	4Q171 frags. 1–10 1.12	89:14	4Q381 frag. 15, ll. 5–6
37:7	4Q171 frags. 1–10 1.17–18	94:21	CD 1.20
37:8–9a	4Q171 frags. 1–10 2.1–2	107:40	CD 1.15 (cf.)
37:9b	4Q171 frags. 1–10 2.4	127:2	4Q173 frag. 1, ll. 2–3
37:10	4Q171 frags. 1–10 2.5–6	127:3	4Q173 frag. 1, l. 7
37:11	4Q171 frags. 1–10 2.8	127:3	4Q173 frag. 2, l. 1
37:12–13	4Q171 frags. 1–10 2.12–13	127:5	4Q173 frag. 3, l. 1
37:14–15	4Q171 frags. 1–10 2.15–16	127:5	4Q173 frag. 3, l. 3
37:15	4Q437 frag. 2 1.3	129:7–8	4Q173 frag. 4, ll. 1–2
37:16	4Q171 frags. 1–10 2.21	146:7–8	4Q521 frag. 2 2+4.8
37:17	4Q171 frags. 1–10 2.23–24		
37:18	4Q171 frags. 1–10 2.24	**Job**	
37:19a	4Q171 frags. 1–10 2.26	12:24	CD 1.15 (cf.)
37:19b–20a	4Q171 frags. 1–10 3.2–3		
37:20b	4Q171 frags. 1–10 3.5	**Proverbs**	
37:20c	4Q171 frags. 1–10 3.7	15:8	CD 11.20–21
37:21–22	4Q171 frags. 1–10 3.8–9	15:8	4Q271 frag. 5 1.14–15
37:23–24	4Q171 frags. 1–10 3.14–15		
37:25–26	4Q171 frags. 1–10 3.17–18	**Lamentations**	
37:28	4Q171 frags. 1–10 4.1	1:1	4Q179 frag. 2, l. 4
37:29	4Q171 frags. 1–10 4.2		
37:30–31	4Q171 frags. 1–10 4.3–4	**Daniel**	
37:32–33	4Q171 frags. 1–10 4.7	9:26	11Q13 2.18
37:34	4Q171 frags. 1–10 4.10–11	12:10	4Q174 4.3–4
37:35–36	4Q171 frags. 1–10 4.13–14		
37:37	4Q171 frags. 1–10 4.16	**Nehemiah**	
37:38	4Q171 frags. 1–10 4.17–18	9:29	CD 3.15–16 (cf.)
37:39–40	4Q171 frags. 1–10 4.19–20		
45:1a	4Q171 frags. 1–10 4.23	**1 Chronicles**	
45:1b	4Q171 frags. 1–10 4.24–25	7:24	4Q522 frags. 9, col. 1+10, l. 15 (cf.)
45:2	4Q171 frags. 1–10 4.26–27		
51:17 (cf.)	4Q436 frag. 1a+b 1.1 (cf.)	**2 Chronicles**	
60:8–9	4Q171 frag. 13, ll. 3–4	28:18	4Q522 frags. 9, col. 1+10, l. 13 (cf.)
63:7	4Q437 frag. 2 1.16		

APPENDIX **IV**

Translations and Editions of the Dead Sea Scrolls

ALMOST ALL THE DEAD SEA SCROLLS ARE PUBLISHED IN THE SERIES "Discoveries in the Judaean Desert" (DJD) by Oxford University Press; in three of the earlier volumes (3, 4, and 5) the series was called "Discoveries in the Judaean Desert of Jordan" (DJDJ). The final volume contains a Concordance of the Non-Biblical Texts from Qumran, but is published by E. J. Brill in the Netherlands

A few other editions are outside the Oxford series. Two of these contain the documents from the Bar Kochba Period, published in the series "Judean Desert Studies" (JDS); and two more present the documents from Masada in "The Yigael Yadin Excavations," published by the Israel Exploration Society and the Hebrew University of Jerusalem. Also listed here are the Microfiche Edition, several Electronic Editions, and the Electronic Concordance of the Dead Sea Scrolls.

We are grateful to Professor Emanuel Tov for supplying bibliographical details, especially with respect to the volumes in the DJD series that were in preparation or in press as of late 2002.

English Translations of the Dead Sea Scrolls

The Biblical Scrolls

Abegg, M. G., Jr., P. W. Flint, and E. Ulrich. *The Dead Sea Scrolls Bible* (San Francisco: HarperSanFrancisco, 1999).

The Nonbiblical Scrolls

García Martínez, F. *The Dead Sea Scrolls Translated. The Qumran Texts in English* (2nd ed., Leiden: Brill; Grand Rapids, MI: Eerdmans, 1996).

Gaster, T. H. *The Dead Sea Scriptures* (3rd ed., New York: Doubleday, 1976).

Vermes, G. *The Complete Dead Sea Scrolls in English* (London: Penguin, 1997).

Wise, M., M. Abegg, Jr., and E. Cook. *The Dead Sea Scrolls* (San Francisco: HarperSanFrancisco, 1997).

Microfiche Edition

Tov, E., with the collaboration of S. J. Pfann. *The Dead Sea Scrolls on Microfiche: A Comprehensive Facsimile Edition of the Texts from the Judean Desert*, with a *Companion Volume* (2nd ed., Leiden: Brill and IDC, 1995).

Electronic Editions and the Electronic Concordance

Abegg, M. G, Jr. *Qumran Sectarian Manuscripts: Qumran Texts with Grammatical Tags* (Altamonte Springs, FL: Oak Tree Software, 2001).

Abegg, M. G, Jr. *Qumran Texts with Grammatical Tags: Concordance Module* (Altamonte Springs, FL: Oak Tree Software, 2002).

Lim, T., in consultation with P. Alexander. *The Dead Sea Scrolls: Electronic Reference Library* (Oxford: Oxford University Press; Leiden: Brill, 1997).

Tov, E., ed., prepared by the Foundation for Ancient Research and Mormon Studies (FARMS). *The Dead Sea Scrolls Database (Non-Biblical Texts)* (The Dead Sea Scrolls Electronic Reference Library, vol. 2; Leiden: Brill, 1999).

Judean Desert Studies

Lewis, N., et al. *The Documents from the Bar Kochba Period in the Cave of the Letters: The Greek Papyri* (N. Lewis); *Aramaic and Nabatean Signatures and Subscriptions* (Y. Yadin and J. C. Greenfield) (**JDS 2**; Jerusalem: Israel Exploration Society, the Hebrew University of Jerusalem, and the Shrine of the Book, 1989).

Yadin, Y., J. C. Greenfield, A. Yardeni, and B. A. Levine. *The Documents from the Bar Kochba Period in the Cave of Letters: Hebrew, Aramaic and Nabatean-Aramaic Papyri* (**JDS 3**; Jerusalem: Israel Exploration Society, Institute of Archaeology, the Hebrew University of Jerusalem, Shrine of the Book, Israel Museum, 2002).

Masada

Cotton, H. M., and J. Geiger. *Masada II, The Yigael Yadin Excavations 1963–1965, Final Reports: The Latin and Greek Documents* (Jerusalem: Israel Exploration Society, 1989).

Talmon, S., and Y. Yadin. *Masada VI, The Yigael Yadin Excavations 1963–1965, Final Reports* (Jerusalem: Israel Exploration Society and the Hebrew University of Jerusalem, 1999).

Discoveries in the Judaean Desert

Barthélemy, D., and J. T. Milik. *Qumran Cave 1* (**DJD 1**; Oxford: Clarendon Press, 1955).

Benoit, P., J. T. Milik, and R. de Vaux. *Les grottes de Murabbaat* (**DJD 2, 2a**; Oxford: Clarendon Press, 1961).

Baillet, M., J. T. Milik, and R. de Vaux. *Les 'petites grottes' de Qumrân* (**DJDJ 3, 3a**; Oxford: Clarendon Press, 1962).

Sanders, J. A. *The Psalms Scroll of Qumrân Cave 11 (11QPs^a)* (**DJDJ 4**; Oxford: Clarendon Press, 1965).

Allegro, J. M., with A. A. Anderson. *Qumrân Cave 4.I (4Q158–4Q186)* (**DJDJ 5**; Oxford: Clarendon Press, 1968).

Bernstein, M., and G. Brooke with the assistance of J. Høgenhavn. *Qumran Cave 4:I: 4Q158–186* (**DJD 5a**; Revised edition; Oxford: Clarendon Press [in preparation]).

de Vaux, R., and J. T. Milik. *Qumrân grotte 4.II: I. Archéologie; II: Tefillin, Mezuzot et Targums (4Q128–4Q157)* (**DJD 6**; Oxford: Clarendon Press, 1977).

Baillet, M. *Qumrân grotte 4.III (4Q482–4Q520)* (**DJD 7**; Oxford: Clarendon Press, 1982).

Tov, E., with the collaboration of R. A. Kraft. *The Greek Minor Prophets Scroll from Naḥal Ḥever (8ḤevXIIgr) (The Seiyâl Collection I)* (**DJD 8**; Oxford: Clarendon Press, 1990; repr. with corrections, 1995).

Skehan, P. W., E. Ulrich, and J. E. Sanderson. *Qumran Cave 4.IV: Palaeo-Hebrew and Greek Biblical Manuscripts* (**DJD 9**; Oxford: Clarendon Press, 1992).

Qimron, E., and J. Strugnell. *Qumran Cave 4.V: Miqṣat Maʿase ha-Torah* (**DJD 10**; Oxford: Clarendon Press, 1994).

VanderKam, J., and M. Brady, consulting eds. *Qumran Cave 4.VI: Poetical and Liturgical Texts, Part 1* (**DJD 11**; Oxford: Clarendon Press, 1998).

Ulrich, E., F. M. Cross, et al. *Qumran Cave 4.VII: Genesis to Numbers* (**DJD 12**; Oxford: Clarendon Press, 1994 [repr. 1999]).

VanderKam, J., consulting ed. *Qumran Cave 4.VIII: Parabiblical Texts, Part 1* (**DJD 13**; Oxford: Clarendon Press, 1994).

Ulrich, E., F. M. Cross, et al. *Qumran Cave 4.IX: Deuteronomy, Joshua, Judges, Kings* (**DJD 14**; Oxford: Clarendon Press, 1995 [repr. 1999]).

Ulrich, E., et al. *Qumran Cave 4.X: The Prophets* (**DJD 15**; Oxford: Clarendon Press, 1997).

Ulrich, E., et al. *Qumran Cave 4.XI: Psalms to Chronicles* (**DJD 16**; Oxford: Clarendon Press, 2000).

Cross, F. M., D. W. Parry, and E. Ulrich. *Qumran Cave 4.XII: 1–2 Samuel* (**DJD 17**; Oxford: Clarendon Press, 2002).

Baumgarten, J. M. *Qumran Cave 4.XIII: The Damascus Document (4Q266–273)* (**DJD 18**; Oxford: Clarendon Press, 1996).

VanderKam, J., consulting ed. *Qumran Cave 4.XIV: Parabiblical Texts, Part 2* (**DJD 19**; Oxford: Clarendon Press, 1995).

Fitzmyer, J. A., consulting ed. *Qumran Cave 4.XV: Sapiential Texts, Part 1* (**DJD 20**; Oxford: Clarendon Press, 1997).

Talmon, S., J. Ben-Dov, U. Glessmer. *Qumran Cave 4.XVI: Calendrical Texts* (**DJD 21**; Oxford: Clarendon Press: Clarendon Press, 2001).

VanderKam, J., consulting ed. *Qumran Cave 4.XVII: Parabiblical Texts, Part 3* (**DJD 22**; Oxford: Clarendon Press, 1996).

García Martínez, F., E. J. C. Tigchelaar, and A. S. van der Woude. *Qumran Cave 11.II: 11Q2–18, 11Q20–31* (**DJD 23**; Oxford: Clarendon Press, 1998).

Leith, M. J. W. *Wadi Daliyeh I: The Wadi Daliyeh Seal Impressions* (**DJD 24**; Oxford: Clarendon Press, 1997).

Puech, É. *Qumran Cave 4.XVIII: Textes hébreux (4Q521–4Q528, 4Q576–4Q579)* (**DJD 25**; Oxford: Clarendon Press, 1998).

Alexander, P., and G. Vermes. *Qumran Cave 4.XIX: 4QSerekh Ha-Yaḥad and Two Related Texts* (**DJD 26**; Oxford: Clarendon Press, 1998).

Cotton, H. M., and A. Yardeni. *Aramaic, Hebrew, and Greek Documentary Texts from Naḥal Ḥever and Other Sites, with an Appendix Containing Alleged Qumran Texts (The Seiyâl Collection II)* (**DJD 27**; Oxford: Clarendon Press, 1997).

Gropp, D. M. *Wadi Daliyeh II: The Samaria Papyri from Wadi Daliyeh*; J. VanderKam and M. Brady, consulting eds. *Qumran Cave 4.XXVIII: Miscellanea, Part 2* (**DJD 28**; Oxford: Clarendon Press, 2001).

VanderKam, J., and M. Brady, consulting eds. *Qumran Cave 4.XX: Poetical and Liturgical Texts, Part 2* (**DJD 29**; Oxford: Clarendon Press, 1999).

Dimant, D. *Qumran Cave 4.XXI: Parabiblical Texts, Part 4: Pseudo-Prophetic Texts* (**DJD 30**; Oxford: Clarendon Press, 2001).

Puech, É. *Qumran Cave 4.XXII: Textes araméens, première partie: 4Q529–549* (**DJD 31**; Oxford: Clarendon Press, 2001).

Flint, P. W., and E. Ulrich. *Qumran Cave 1.II: The Isaiah Scrolls* (**DJD 32**; Oxford: Clarendon Press [in preparation]).

VanderKam, J., and M. Brady, consulting eds. *Qumran Cave 4.XXIII: Unidentified Fragments* (**DJD 33;** Oxford: Clarendon Press, 2001).

Fitzmyer, J. A., consulting ed. *Qumran Cave 4.XXIV: Sapiential Texts, Part 2, 4QInstruction (Mûsār lĕ Mĕvîn): 4Q415 ff.* (**DJD 34;** Oxford: Clarendon Press, 1999).

Baumgarten, J. et al. *Qumran Cave 4.XXV: Halakhic Texts* (**DJD 35;** Oxford: Clarendon Press, 1999).

Pfann, S. J., J. VanderKam and M. Brady, consulting eds. *Cryptic Texts; Miscellanea, Part 1: Qumran Cave 4.XXVI* (**DJD 36;** Oxford: Clarendon Press, 2000).

Puech, É. *Qumran Cave 4.XXVII: Textes araméens, deuxième partie: 4Q550–575, 580–582* (**DJD 37;** Oxford: Clarendon Press [in press]).

VanderKam, J., and M. Brady, consulting eds. *Miscellaneous Texts from the Judaean Desert* (**DJD 38;** Oxford: Clarendon Press, 2000).

Tov, E., ed. *The Texts from the Judaean Desert: Indices and an Introduction to the* Discoveries in the Judaean Desert *Series* (**DJD 39;** Oxford: Clarendon Press, 2002).

Abegg, M. G., Jr. *Concordance of the Non-Biblical Texts from Qumran* (Leiden: E. J. Brill [2000]).

Notes

Chapter 1

1. Westwood, NJ: Revell, 1965. Trever refers to numerous interviews (between November 1961 and July 1964, i.e., about fourteen to seventeen years after the events in question) with the Bedouin involved. Specifically he mentions an interview with them conducted by Anton Kiraz (an individual whose name will appear in the story) and J. F. Docmac on November 24, 1961; the Bedouins' oral answers (tape recorded) to sixty-three questions formulated by Trever and put to them on November 25; Trever's interviews with them on July 29 and August 10, 1962, with Kiraz and Docmac as interpreters; and Kiraz's later questions to them and his report in letters about their answers.

2. *The Untold Story*, 103.

3. *The Untold Story*, 103–4.

4. *The Untold Story*, 104.

5. The scroll was called the *Manual of Discipline*, but is now named the *Rule of the Community*.

6. They were a second, more fragmentary copy of Isaiah, the *Thanksgiving Hymns*, and the *War Scroll*.

7. The word Mar is an ecclesiastical title of respect and means something like *Lord* or *Sir*.

8. This is the date Sukenik gives for the meeting (Sukenik, ed., *Dead Sea Scrolls of the Hebrew University* [Jerusalem: Magnes, 1955] 14). Trever implies it was November 24 (*The Untold Story*, 110).

9. Trever, *The Untold Story*, 110–11.

10. *Dead Sea Scrolls of the Hebrew University*, 17. A *genizah* is a storage place for old manuscripts no longer in use.

11. On December 21, 1947, Sukenik bought the third manuscript, the fragmentary Isaiah scroll, from Faidi Salahi.

12. *Dead Sea Scrolls of the Hebrew University*, 17.

13. Sukenik had earlier excavated some tombs found on property owned by Kiraz.

14. *Dead Sea Scrolls of the Hebrew University*, 16.

15. *The Untold Story*, 14.

16. *The Untold Story*, 25.

17. *The Untold Story*, 44. The famous picture can be seen in many places, such as opposite p. 129 in *The Untold Story*.

18. *The Untold Story*, 85.

19. *The Untold Story*, 94.

20. Note that this formulation differs from the one quoted above.

21. Burrows, *The Dead Sea Scrolls* (New York: Viking Press, 1955) 17–18.

22. *The Untold Story*, 121. Trever's article was "The Discovery of the Scrolls," *Biblical Archaeologist* 11 (1948) 46–57.

23. See *The Untold Story*, 203 n. 2, for a complete summary of the pieces of the individual manuscripts that were recovered in the cave.

24. "Introductory: The Discovery, the Excavation, Minor Finds," *Qumran Cave I*, ed. D. Barthélemy and J. T. Milik (DJD 1; Oxford: Clarendon Press, 1955) 6.

25. R. de Vaux, *Archaeology and the Dead Sea Scrolls* (The Schweich Lectures, 1959; rev. ed., London: Oxford University Press, 1973) 49.

26. "Introductory," DJD 1:6–7.

27. "La Poterie," DJD 1:11.

28. "Post-Scriptum: La cachette des manuscrits hébreux," *Revue Biblique* 56 (1949) 234.

29. "The Linen Textiles," DJD 1:18.

30. "The Linen Textiles," 19.

31. "The Linen Textiles," 24–27.

32. "La grotte des manuscrits hébreux," *Revue Biblique* 56 (1949) 586, n. 2 (translation here by J. VanderKam).

33. See his essay "Fouille au Khirbet Qumran: Rapport préliminaire," *Revue Biblique* 60 (1953) 89.

34. Both fascicles were published by the Mosad Bialik in Jerusalem.

35. See note 8 above. The edition was prepared for publication by N. Avigad. This is an English translation of a Hebrew volume published in 1954.

36. Millar Burrows, ed., with the assistance of John C. Trever and William H. Brownlee, *The Dead Sea Scrolls of St. Mark's Monastery*, vol. 1: *The Isaiah Manuscript and the Habakkuk Commentary* (New Haven, CT: American Schools of Oriental Research, 1950). The frontpiece has a photograph of Mar Athanasius Y. Samuel, and the volume is dedicated to him "in appreciation of the privilege of making these texts available to the world of scholarship."

37. Millar Burrows, ed., with the assistance of John C. Trever and William H. Brownlee, *The Dead Sea Scrolls of St. Mark's Monastery*, vol. 2, fascicle 2: *Plates and Transcription of the Manual of Discipline* (New Haven, CT: American Schools of Oriental Research, 1951). Although this was called fascicle 2, fascicle 1, which was to contain the *Genesis Apocryphon* (see vol. 1, p. x), has never appeared. This manuscript (then called the *Lamech Scroll*) had not been unrolled at that time because of its poor state of preservation.

38. Trever says that in an interview between himself and Sukenik in New York on March 21, 1949, Sukenik reported he was readying a document "to circulate to all libraries and universities which might consider purchasing the scrolls. In it he was warning them that such a purchase would be illegal and subject to antiquities laws, which could be invoked to return the scrolls to the country of their origin" (*The Untold Story*, 126). He was not the only one to challenge the Metropolitan's claim (see pp. 136–38).

39. On the Shrine of the Book, see A. Roitman, "Shrine of the Book," *Encyclopedia of the Dead Sea Scrolls*, ed. L. Schiffman and J. VanderKam (2 vols., New York and Oxford: Oxford University Press, 2000) 2:74–75. N. Avigad and Yadin published much of what could be deciphered on the fourth scroll, the only one of the Metropolitan's texts not issued by the Americans, as *A Genesis Apocryphon* (Jerusalem: Magnes Press and Heikhal ha-Sefer [Shrine of the Book], 1956).

40. "Archéologie," *Les 'petites grottes' de Qumran*, ed. M. Baillet, J. T. Milik, and R. de Vaux (DJDJ 3.1; Oxford:

Clarendon Press, 1962) 3. The thirty-three texts from Cave 2 were published in this volume.

41. *Archaeology and the Dead Sea Scrolls*, 51.

42. "Archéologie," *Les 'petites grottes*,' DJDJ 3,1:4.

43. See *Les 'petites grottes*,' 94–104. Milik's edition of the Copper Scroll is on pp. 201–302.

44. *Archaeology and the Dead Sea Scrolls*, 52.

45. De Vaux, "Archéologie," in R. de Vaux and J. T. Milik, eds., *Qumrân Grotte 4 II I. Archéologie, II Tefillin, Mezuzot et Targums (4Q128–4Q157)*, (DJD 6; Oxford: Clarendon Press, 1977) 3.

46. "Archeologie," *Qumrân Grotte 4 II*, 4 (translation here by J. VanderKam).

47. De Vaux, *Archaeology and the Dead Sea Scrolls*, 52.

48. Harding, *The Antiquities of Jordan* (London: Lutterworth Press, 1959) 201–2.

49. Allegro, *The Dead Sea Scrolls* (Harmondsworth, UK: Penguin, 1956) 37–38. While this was happening, there were reports in the press of fabulous sums—like $1 million—that Metropolitan Samuel was asking for his four scrolls.

50. He published the texts in *Les 'petites grottes*,' 167–97.

51. They were published by M. Baillet in *Les 'petites grottes*,' 105–41.

52. Baillet published the material in *Les 'petites grottes*', 142–64.

53. The Psalms scroll was published by J. Sanders, *The Psalms Scroll of Qumrân Cave 11 (11QPsᵃ)*, (DJDJ 4; Oxford: Clarendon Press, 1965). For the *Temple Scroll*, see Y. Yadin, *The Temple Scroll* (3 vols., Jerusalem: Israel Exploration Society, Institute of Archaeology of the Hebrew University of Jerusalem, and the Shrine of the Book, 1977 [Hebrew]). The English edition appeared in 1983. The remaining texts from Cave 11 appeared officially in F. García Martínez, E. J. C. Tigchelaar, and A. S. van der Woude, eds., *Qumran Cave 11 II: 11Q2–18, 11Q20–31* (DJD 23; Oxford: Clarendon Press, 1998).

Chapter 2

1. Other indicators of dates, such as coins (see Chapter 3), have been found at the site. Also, in some texts the names of known individuals are mentioned; for these, see Chapter 12.

2. See R. de Vaux, *Archaeology and the Dead Sea Scrolls* (The Schweich Lectures, 1959; rev. ed., London: Oxford University Press, 1973).

3. Meshorer, "Numismatics," in the *Encyclopedia of the Dead Sea Scrolls*, ed. L. Schiffman and J. VanderKam (New York and Oxford: Oxford University Press, 2000) 2:619–20.

4. "A Biblical Fragment from the Maccabaean Age: The Nash Papyrus," *Journal of Biblical Literature* 56 (1937) 145–76.

5. *The Qumrân [Dead Sea] Scrolls and Palaeography* (Bulletin of the American Schools of Oriental Research, Supplementary Studies 13–14; New Haven, CT: ASOR, 1952).

6. London: Palaeographica, 1954–57.

7. "The Palaeography of the Dead Sea Scrolls and Related Documents," in *Aspects of the Dead Sea Scrolls* (Scripta Hierosolymitana 4; Jerusalem: Magnes, 1958) 56–87.

8. It appeared in *The Bible and the Ancient Near East: Essays in Honor of William Foxwell Albright*, ed. G. E. Wright (New York: Doubleday Anchor, 1961) 133–202 (pp. 170–264 in the paperback edition of 1965, from which the page numbers below are taken). Cross had anticipated many of his conclusions in "The Oldest Manuscripts from Qumran," *Journal of Biblical Literature* 74 (1955) 147–72.

9. "Paleography," *Encyclopedia of the Dead Sea Scrolls*, 2:629–34; and "Palaeography and the Dead Sea Scrolls," in P. Flint and J. VanderKam, eds., *The Dead Sea Scrolls After Fifty Years: A Comprehensive Assessment* (2 vols., Leiden: Brill, 1998, 1999) 1:379–402.

10. "Development of the Jewish Scripts," 172.

11. "Development of the Jewish Scripts," 172.

12. "Development of the Jewish Scripts," 173.

13. "Development of the Jewish Scripts," 173.

14. "Development of the Jewish Scripts," 174.

15. "Palaeography and the Dead Sea Scrolls," 1:392; see plate 10 for the samples, the last of which, a contract from Murabbaʿat, bears a date equivalent to 133 CE.

16. The list appears in E. Tov, ed., *The Texts from the Judaean Desert: Indices and an Introduction to the Discoveries in the Judaean Desert Series* (DJD 39; Oxford: Clarendon Press, 2002) 371–75. (See Appendix IV.)

17. Libby, "Radiocarbon Dates, II," *Science* 114 (1951) 291.

18. "Date of Cloth from the ʿAin Fashkha Cave," *Biblical Archaeologist* 14 (1951) 29.

19. G. Doudna, "Dating the Scrolls on the Basis of Radiocarbon Analysis," in *The Dead Sea Scrolls After Fifty Years*, 1:432.

20. Zeuner, "Notes on Qumran," *Palestine Exploration Quarterly* 92 (1960) 27–36.

21. Zeuner explained the figures this way: "Since the log in question must have been long enough for its timber to serve as rafters, one arrives at an age of about 50 years ±35, i.e., the tree is likely to have been older than 15 years, but younger than 85. This allowance has to be taken into account when the radiocarbon age is considered" ("Notes on Qumran," 27).

22. Doudna, "Dating the Scrolls," 432–33. As Zeuner put it, "The figures represent the age of the wood and, according to what has been said, about 50 years have to be deducted to obtain the probable date of the burning. The analyses having been done in 1956, we obtain A.D. 66 or thereabouts for the date of the burning. Taking the standard deviation into account, a value within the first century A.D. is almost certain to be correct, and there is a remarkable approximation to the year of the Roman conquest, A.D. 68" ("Notes on Qumran," 27–28).

23. See G. Bonani, M. Broshi, I. Carmi, S. Ivy, J. Strugnell, and W. Wölfli, "Radiocarbon Dating of the Dead Sea Scrolls," *ʿAtiqot* 20 (1991) 27–32; and S. Ivy, W. Wölfli, M. Broshi, I. Carmi, and J. Strugnell, "Radiocarbon Dating of Fourteen Dead Sea Scrolls," *Radiocarbon* 34 (1992) 843–49.

24. A. Jull, D. Donahue, M. Broshi, and E. Tov, "Radiocarbon Dating of Scrolls and Linen Fragments from the Judean Desert," *Radiocarbon* 37 (1995) 11–19; "Radiocarbon Dating of Scrolls and Linen Fragments from the Judean Desert," *ʿAtiqot* 28 (1996) 85–91.

25. See his Table A in "Dating the Scrolls," 468–71. The year numbers in the "Paleographic dates" column are taken from statements by the editors of the texts.

26. "Dating the Scrolls," 445.

27. "Dating the Scrolls," 446.

28. "Dating the Scrolls," 447.

29. "Dating the Scrolls," 447.

30. "On the History of the Photographing of the Discoveries in the Judean Desert for the International Group of Editors," in the *Companion Volume to the Dead Sea Scrolls Microfiche Edition*, ed. E. Tov with S. Pfann (Leiden: Brill, 1995) 125.

31. Yardeni, in H. Cotton and A. Yardeni, eds. *Aramaic, Hebrew and Greek Documentary Texts from Naḥal Ḥever and Other Sites* (DJD 27; Oxford: Clarendon Press, 1997) 285.

32. *Aramaic, Hebrew and Greek Documentary Texts*, 289.

33. *Aramaic, Hebrew and Greek Documentary Texts*, 289.

Chapter 3

1. "Relation du voyage," *Voyage autour de la Mer Morte et dans les terres bibliques, exécuté de décembre 1850 à avril 1851* (Paris, 1853) 2:165–67.

2. *Voyage dans le Haouran et aux bords de la Mer Morte, exécuté pendant les années 1857 et 1858* (no date), 223, 227.

3. "Kumrân," *Archaeological Researches in Palestine During the Years 1873–1874* (2 vols., London: Published for the Committee of the Palestine Exploration Fund, 1896) 2:14–16.

4. His accounts may be read in the *Palestine Exploration Fund Quarterly Statements* from 1902–1913. See 1902, pp. 161–62; 1903, pp. 265–67 (aqueduct).

5. See his *Une Croisière autour de la Mer Morte* (Paris, 1911) 164-68 (Jan. 8, 1909, the last day of the cruise, involved visits to Ain Feshkha and Qumran).

6. See *Palästina-Jahrbuch* 10 (1914) 9–10; 16 (1920) 40.

7. *Das Buch Josua* (Handbuch zum Alten Testament 7; Tübingen: Mohr Siebeck, 1938) 72 (translation by J. VanderKam).

8. He mentioned this in the second edition of the commentary, published under the same title in 1953, p. 100.

9. See "Der alttestamentliche Name der Siedlung auf chirbet kumran," *Zeitschrift des deutschen Palästina-Vereins* 71 (1955) 111–23.

10. Cited by S. Pfann, "Sites in the Judean Desert Where Texts Have Been Found," in the *Companion Volume to the Dead Sea Scrolls on Microfiche Edition,* ed. E. Tov with S. Pfann (2d rev. ed., Leiden: Brill, 1995) 110.

11. Pfann, "Sites in the Judean Desert Where Texts Have Been Found," 110.

12. See de Vaux, "Fouille au Khirbet Qumrân: Rapport préliminaire," *Revue biblique* 60 (1953) 83–106.

13. "Fouille," 93–94.

14. "Fouille," 94.

15. "Fouille," 104 (translation by J. VanderKam).

16. For this text and a discussion of it, see Chapter 10.

17. See the report in de Vaux, "Fouilles au Khirbet Qumrân: Rapport préliminaire sur la deuxième campagne," *Revue biblique* 61 (1954) 206–36.

18. "Fouilles," 210.

19. "Fouilles," 210–11.

20. "Fouilles," 212 (translation by J. VanderKam). See also de Vaux, *Archaeology and the Dead Sea Scrolls* (The Schweich Lectures 1959; rev. ed.; London: Oxford University Press, 1973) 29–33, which contains a related but longer account, one in which de Vaux reacts to criticisms later leveled against his interpretation of the tables.

21. "Fouilles," 228.

22. "Fouilles," 229 (translation by J. VanderKam).

23. "Fouilles," 231 (translation by J. VanderKam).

24. "Fouilles," 232.

25. "Fouilles," 233 (translation by J. VanderKam).

26. "Fouilles," 234.

27. "Fouilles de Khirbet Qumrân: Rapport préliminaire sur les 3e, 4e et 5e campagnes," *Revue biblique* 63 (1956) 533–77.

28. "Fouilles de Khirbet Qumrân," 535.

29. "Fouilles de Khirbet Qumrân," 538 (translation by J. VanderKam). See also his *Archaeology and the Dead Sea Scrolls,* 5.

30. "Fouilles de Khirbet Qumrân," 539.

31. "Fouilles de Khirbet Qumrân," 549–50.

32. "Fouilles de Khirbet Qumrân," 565–69.

33. "Fouilles de Khirbet Qumrân," 569–72.

34. "Fouilles de Feshkha. Rapport préliminaire," *Revue Biblique* 66 (1959) 225–55.

35. "Foreword" to de Vaux, *Archaeology and the Dead Sea Scrolls,* vi.

36. See his review of Allegro's book, *The Treasure of the Copper Scroll,* in *Revue Biblique* 68 (1961) 147.

37. See *Revue Biblique* 75 (1968) 205.

38. See *Revue Biblique* 73 (1966) 585.

39. Steckoll, "Preliminary Excavation Report in the Qumran Cemetery," *Revue de Qumrân* 6 (1968) 323–36.

40. See N. Haas and H. Nathan, "Anthropological Survey on Human Skeletal Remains from Qumran," *Revue de Qumrân* 6 (1968) 345–52.

41. Steckoll, "Marginal Notes on the Qumran Excavations," *Revue de Qumrân* 7 (1969) 33–34.

42. *Qumrân: L'établissement essénien des bords de la Mer Morte: Histoire et archéologie du site* (Paris: Picard, 1976).

43. Patrich wrote: "Our approach was first to identify the caves marked on de Vaux's map, learn what was done by his team, explore the caves's relation to Khirbet Qumran, and determine which caves could be still further explored by means of archaeological excavations. The excavations, carried out by a large crew, marked the second stage of our exploration." See "Khirbet Qumran in Light of New Archaeological Explorations in the Qumran Caves," in *Methods of Investigation of the Dead Sea Scrolls and the Khirbet Qumran Site,* ed. M. Wise, N. Golb, J. Collins, and D. Pardee (Annals of the New York Academy of Sciences 722; New York: New York Academy of Sciences, 1994) 74.

44. "Khirbet Qumran in Light of New Archaeological Explorations," 75.

45. "Khirbet Qumran in Light of New Archaeological Explorations," 75–76.

46. "Khirbet Qumran in Light of New Archaeological Explorations," 93–94.

47. "The Archeology of Qumran—A Reconsideration," in *The Dead Sea Scrolls: Forty Years of Research,* ed. D. Dimant and U. Rappaport (Studies in the Texts of the Desert of Judah 10; Leiden: Brill; Jerusalem: Magnes and Yad Izhak Ben-Zvi, 1992) 103–15.

48. "The Archeology of Qumran—A Reconsideration," 106.

49. "The Archeology of Qumran—A Reconsideration," 111.

50. "The Archeology of Qumran—A Reconsideration," 105.

51. "The Archaeology of Khirbet Qumran," in Wise et al., eds., *Methods of Investigation of the Dead Sea Scrolls and the Khirbet Qumran Site,* 1–38.

52. "The Architectural Context of Qumran," in *The Dead Sea Scrolls: Fifty Years After Their Discovery 1947–1997.* ed. L. Schiffman, E. Tov, and J. VanderKam (Jerusalem: Israel Exploration Society with the Shrine of the Book, Israel Museum, 2000) 673–83. The quotation is from p. 683.

53. Broshi and Eshel, "Residential Caves at Qumran," *Dead Sea Discoveries* 6 (1999) 328–48.

54. "L'espace sacré à Qumrân: Propositions pour l'archéologie," *Revue Biblique* 101–2 (1994) 161–214.

55. "A Villa at Khirbet Qumran?" *Revue de Qumrân* 63 (1994) 397–419.

56. "A Villa at Khirbet Qumran?" 419.
57. "Qumran Archaeology: Past Perspectives and Future Prospects," in *The Dead Sea Scrolls After Fifty Years: A Comprehensive Assessment,* ed. P. W. Flint and J. C. VanderKam (2 vols., Leiden: Brill, 1998–99) 1:47–77, esp. 65.
58. "The Chronology of the Settlement at Qumran in the Herodian Period," *Dead Sea Discoveries* 2 (1995) 58–65, esp. 64–65.
59. Meshorer, "Numismatics," *Encyclopedia of the Dead Sea Scrolls,* 620.
60. *Archaeology and the Dead Sea Scrolls,* 86.
61. *Archaeology and the Dead Sea Scrolls,* 46–47.
62. *Qoumrân,* 99–109.
63. "The Archeology of Qumran—a Reconsideration," 114.
64. "Did Extra-Mural Dwelling Quarters Exist at Qumran?" in Schiffman et al., eds., *The Dead Sea Scrolls: Fifty Years After Their Discovery,* 720.
65. "L'espace sacré à Qumrân," 175–77.
66. *Archaeology and the Dead Sea Scrolls,* 48.
67. "The Cemeteries of Qumran and Celibacy: Confusion Laid to Rest?" *Dead Sea Discoveries* 7 (2000) 220–53.
68. "The Cemeteries of Qumran and Celibacy," 237.
69. "The Cemeteries of Qumran and Celibacy," 242
70. "Another Settlement of the Judean Desert Sect at ʿen el-Ghuweir on the Shores of the Dead Sea," *Bulletin of the American Schools of Oriental Research* 227 (1977) 1–25.
71. *Archaeology and the Dead Sea Scrolls,* 89–90.
72. "The Archeology of Qumran—a Reconsideration," 115.
73. "'Qumran Type' Graves in Jerusalem: Archaeological Evidence of an Essene Community?" *Dead Sea Discoveries* 5 (1998) 158–71.

Chapter 4

1. See Donald W. Parry, David V. Arnold, David G. Long, and Scott R. Woodward, "New Technological Advances: DNA, Electronic Databases, Imaging Radar," in P. W. Flint and J. C. VanderKam, eds., *The Dead Sea Scrolls After Fifty Years: A Comprehensive Assessment* (2 vols., Leiden: Brill, 1998–99) 1:496–515.
2. W. Ryder, "Remains Derived from Skin," in *Microscopic Studies of Ancient Skins* (Oxford: Oxford University Press, 1965).
3. Michael Wise, Martin Abegg, Jr., and Edward Cook, *The Dead Sea Scrolls: A New Translation* (San Francisco: HarperSanFrancisco, 1996) 478.
4. Parry, Arnold, Long, and Woodward, "New Technological Advances," 505.
5. See Annette Steudel, "Assembling and Reconstructing Manuscripts," in Flint and VanderKam, eds., *The Dead Sea Scrolls After Fifty Years,* 1:516–34.
6. D. Barthélemy and J. T. Milik, *Qumran Cave I* (DJD 1; Oxford: Clarendon Press, 1955) 91–97, 118.
7. "Methods for the Reconstruction of Scrolls from Scattered Fragments," in L. Schiffman, ed., *Archaeology and History in the Dead Sea Scrolls: The New York University Conference in Memory of Yigael Yadin* (JSP-Sup 8, JSOT/ASOR monographs 2; Sheffield: JSOT Press, 1990) 189–220.
8. A. Steudel, *Der Midrasch zur Eschatologie aus der Qumrangemeinde [4QMidrEschat^a, ^b]. Materielle Rekonstruktion, Textbestand, Gattung und tradionsgeschichtliche Einordnung des durch 4Q174 ('Florilegium') und 4Q177 ('Catena A') repräsentierten Werkes aus den Qumranfunden* (Studies on the Texts of the Desert of Judah 13; Leiden: Brill, 1994).
9. "Assembling and Reconstructing Manuscripts," 529–30.
10. E. Schuller, "Prayer, Hymnic, and Liturgical texts from Qumran," in E. Ulrich and J. VanderKam, eds., *The Community of the Renewed Covenant: The Notre Dame Symposium on the Dead Sea Scrolls* (CJA 10; Notre Dame IN: University of Notre Dame Press, 1994) 153–71, esp. 168.
11. See Esther Boyd-Alkalay and Elena Libman, "Preserving the Dead Sea Scrolls and Qumran Artifacts," in Flint and VanderKam, eds., *The Dead Sea Scrolls After Fifty Years,* 1:535–44.
12. F. Frank, Unpublished letter to R. de Vaux (1962).
13. H. Plenderleith, "Unpublished notes and reports" (1962).
14. V. H. Foulkes, "Unpublished notes and reports" (1963).
15. See Gregory Bearman, Stephen J. Pfann, and Sheila I. Spiro; "Imaging the Scrolls: Photographic and Direct Digital Acquisition," in Flint and Vanderkam, eds., *The Dead Sea Scrolls After Fifty Years,* 472–95, esp. 472–87.
16. See Y. Yadin, *The Temple Scroll* (3 vols., Jerusalem: Israel Exploration Society, 1983) 1:5–8; and his *The Temple Scroll: The Hidden Law of the Dead Sea Sect* (Jerusalem: Steimatzky, 1985) 46–54.
17. R. H. Eisenman and J. M. Robinson, *A Facsimile Edition of the Dead Sea Scrolls* (Washington, DC: Biblical Archaelogy Society, 1991). According to Stephen Pfann, a set of Robert Schlosser's negatives was the actual source used to produce the prints in the *Facsimile Edition* (Bearman, Pfann, and Spiro, "Imaging the Scrolls," 483 n. 23).
18. See Bearman, Pfann, and Spiro: "Imaging the Scrolls," 487–94.
19. Bearman, Pfann, and Spiro, "Imaging the Scrolls," 493.

Chapter 5

1. Stuttgart: Deutsche Bibelstiftung (1967–77).
2. Stuttgart: Würtembergische Bibelanstalt (3d ed., 1937; 16th ed., 1971).
3. *Torah, Nebi'im, Uketuvim* (Tel Aviv: ADI Publishers and Tel Aviv University, 1973) [Hebrew].

4. *Biblia Hebraica Leningradensia* (Peabody, MA: Hendrickson, 2001).

5. M. H. Goshen-Gottstein, ed., *The Hebrew University Bible. The Book of Isaiah* (Jerusalem: The Hebrew University, 1995); S. Talmon, ed., *The Hebrew University Bible. The Book of Jeremiah* (Jerusalem: The Hebrew University, 1997).

6. W. Gesenius, *De pentateuchi samaritani origine, indole et auctoritate commentatio philologico-critica* (Halle: 1815).

7. *Letter of Aristeas,* trans. R. H. Charles (Oxford: Clarendon Press, 1913), ll. 301–7.

8. A. Rahlfs, *Septuaginta. Id est Vetus Testamentum Graece iuxta LXX interpretes* (Stuttgart: Deutsche Bibelgesellschaft, 1935).

9. For example, *The Septuagint Version: Greek and English* (Regency Reference Library; Grand Rapids, MI: Zondervan, 1986). The 1851 edition was published in London by Samuel Bagster.

10. *The Holy Bible, Containing the Old and New Covenant, Commonly Called the Old and New Testament; translated from the Greek {the Old Testament from the Septuagint]* (4. vols., Philadelphia: J. Aitken, 1808).

11. For several listings, see H. B. Swete, *An Introduction to the Old Testament in Greek* (New York, 1902; reprint, Peabody, MA: Hendrickson) 201–10.

Chapter 6

1. For an introduction and English translation based on the scrolls, see M. G. Abegg, Jr., P. W. Flint, and E. Ulrich, *The Dead Sea Scrolls Bible* (San Francisco: HarperSanFrancisco, 1999) 3–22. Hereafter AFU.

2. 1QGen, 2QGen, 6QGen, 8QGen.

3. 4QGen-Exod[a], 4QGen[b] 4QGen[c], 4QGen[d], 4QGen[e], 4QGen[f], 4QGen[g], 4QGen[h1], 4QGen[h2], 4QGen[h-title], 4QGen[j], 4QGen[k], 4QpaleoGen-Exod[l], 4QpaleoGen[m], 4QGen[n], and pap4QGen.

4. MasGen, Mur 1, MurGen (origin questionable), and Sdeir 1.

5. Introduction and English translation: AFU, 23–76.

6. 1QExod, 2QExod[a], 2QExod[b], 2QExod[c], pap7QLXX-Exod.

7. 4QGen-Exod[a], 4QExod[b], 4QExod[c], 4QExod[d], 4QExod[e], 4QExod-Lev[f], 4QExod[g], 4QExod[h], 4QExod[j], 4QExod[k], 4QpaleoGen-Exod[l], and 4QpaleoExod[m].

8. Introduction and English translation: AFU, 77–107.

9. 1QpaleoLev, 2QpaleoLev, and 6QpaleoLev.

10. 4QExod-Lev[f], 4QLev-Num[a], 4QLev[b], 4QLev[c], 4QLev[d], 4QLev[e], 4QLev[g], 4QLXXLev[a], pap4QLXXLev[b] (plus the Targum of Leviticus [4QtgLev]).

11. 11QpaleoLev[a], 11QLev[b].

12. MasLev[a] and MasLev[b].

13. Introduction and English translation: AFU, 108–44.

14. 1QpaleoLev,   2QNum[a],   2QNum[b],   2QNum[c], 2QNum[d](?), 4QLev-Num[a], 4QNum[b], and 4QLXXNum.

15. 5/6Hev/SeNum[a], XHev/SeNum[b], and Mur 1.

16. Introduction and English translation: AFU, 145–95.

17. 1QDeut[a], 1QDeut[b], 2QDeut[a], 2QDeut[b], and 2QDeut[c].

18. 4QDeut[a], 4QDeut[b], 4QDeut[c], 4QDeut[d], 4QDeut[e], 4QDeut[f], 4QDeut[g], 4QDeut[h], 4QDeut[i], 4QDeut[j], 4QDeut[k1], 4QDeut[k2], 4QDeut[k3], 4QDeut[l], 4QDeut[m], 4QDeut[n], 4QDeut[o], 4QDeut[p], 4QDeut[q], 4QpaleoDeut[r], 4QpaleoDeut[s], and 4QLXXDeut.

19. 5QDeut, pap6QDeut?, and 11QDeut.

20. Introduction and English translation: AFU, 201–7.

21. 4QJosh[a] and 4QJosh[b].

22. AFU, 202.

23. Introduction and English translation: AFU, 208–12.

24. 1QJudg, 4QJudg[a], and 4QJudg[b].

25. Introduction and English translation: AFU, 607–10.

26. 2QRuth[a], 2QRuth[b], 4QRuth[a], and 4QRuth[b].

27. Introduction and English translation: AFU, 213–59.

28. 1QSam, 4QSam[a], 4QSam[b], and 4QSam[c].

29. Introduction and English translation: AFU, 260–66.

30. 4QKings, 5QKings, and pap6QKings.

31. Introduction and English translation: AFU, 632–33.

32. Introduction and English translation: AFU, 634–35.

33. For comments on Esther, see AFU, 630–31.

34. Introduction and English translation: AFU, 590–93.

35. 2QJob, 4QJob[a], 4QJob[b], and 4QpaleoJob[c].

36. From Michael Wise, Martin Abegg, Jr., and Edward Cook, *The Dead Sea Scrolls: A New Translation* (San Francisco: HarperSanFrancisco, 1996); hereafter WAC. In WAC, translations are enumerated by scroll, fragment, column, and line.

37. Introduction and English translation: AFU, 505–89.

38. 1QPs[a], 1QPs[b], and 1QPs[c].

39. 2QPs, 3QPs, 5QPs, pap6QPs, and 8QPs.

40. 4QPs[a], 4QPs[b], 4QPs[c], 4QPs[d], 4QPs[e], 4QPs[f], 4QPs[g], 4QPs[h], 4QPs[j], 4QPs[k], 4QPs[l], 4QPs[m], 4QPs[n], 4QPs[o], 4QPs[p], 4QPs[q], 4QPs[r], 4QPs[s], 4QPs[t], 4QPs[u], 4QPs[v], 4QPs[w], 4Q522 *(Prophecy on Joshua,* including Ps. 122).

41. 11QPs[a], 11QPs[b], 11QPs[c], 11QPs[d], 11QPs[e], and 11QapocrPs.

42. MasPs[a], MasPs[b], and 5/6HevPs.

43. Pss. 151A, 151B, 154, 155, David's Last Words (= 2 Sam. 23:1–7), and Sir. 51:13–30.

44. It is possible that the *Eschatological Hymn* and *Apostrophe to Judah* are part of the same psalm (see below).

45. For a translation with comments, see AFU, 576–77.

46. For a translation with comments, see AFU, 573.

47. For a translation with comments, see AFU, 539–24, and WAC, 453–54.

48. Introduction and English translation: AFU, 594–96.

49. 4QProv[a] and 4QProv[b].

50. Introduction and English translation: AFU, 619–21.

51. 4QQoh[a] and 4QQoh[b].

52. Introduction and English translation: AFU, 609–18.

53. 4Cant[a], 4Cant[b], and 4Cant[c], and 6QCant.

54. Introduction and English translation based on the Scrolls: AFU, 265–381.

55. 1QIsa[a] (the *St. Mark's Isaiah Scroll*) and 1QIsa[b] (the *Hebrew University Isaiah Scroll*).

56. 4QIsa[a], 4QIsa[b], 4QIsa[c], 4QIsa[d], 4QIsa[e], 4QIsa[f], 4QIsa[g], 4QIsa[h], 4QIsa[i], 4QIsa[j], 4QIsa[k], 4QIsa[l], 4QIsa[m], 4QIsa[n], 4QIsa[o], pap4QIsa[p], 4QIsa[q], and 4QIsa[r].

57. Introduction and English translation: AFU, 382–406.

58. 2QJer, 4QJer[a], 4QJer[b], 4QJer[c], 4QJer[d], and 4QJer[e].

59. Introduction and English translation: AFU, 622–27.

60. 3QLam, 4QLam, 5QLam[a], and 5QLam[b].

61. Introduction and English translation: AFU, 407–16.

62. 1QEzek, 3QEzek, 4QEzek[a], 4QEzek[b], and 4QEzek[c], and 11QEzek.

63. Introduction and English translation: AFU, 482–501.

64. 1QDan[a], 1QDan[b], 4QDan[a], 4QDan[b], 4QDan[c], 4QDan[d], 4QDan[e], and pap6QDan (written on papyrus).

65. WAC: *The Last Days: A Commentary on Selected Verses.*

66. Introduction and English translation: AFU, 417–79.

67. 4QXII[a], 4QXII[b], 4QXII[c], 4QXII[d], 4QXII[e], 4QXII[f], 4QXII[g], and 5QAmos.

68. MurXII and 8ḤevXII gr.

69. M. Cross, *The Ancient Library of Qumran* (3rd ed., Sheffield: Sheffield Academic Press, 1995).

70. S. Talmon, "The Textual Study of the Bible—A New Outlook," in F. M. Cross and S. Talmon, eds., *Qumran and the History of the Biblical Text* (Cambridge, MA: Harvard University Press, 1975) 321–400, esp. 380–81.

71. "The Biblical Texts from the Judean Desert—An Overview and Analysis of all the Published Texts," in *The Bible as Book: The Hebrew Bible and the Judaean Desert Discoveries. Proceedings of the Conference Held at Hampton Court, Herefordshire, 18–21 June 2000,* ed. E. D. Herbert and E. Tov (London: The British Library, 2002), 139–66.

72. Tov's order is: "Qumran Practice," Proto-Masoretic, Pre-Samaritan, Pre-Septuagint, and Non-Aligned.

73. Tov, "The Biblical Texts from the Judean Desert," 153.

74. E. Ulrich, *The Dead Sea Scrolls and the Origins of the Bible* (Studies in the Dead Sea Scrolls and Related Literature; Grand Rapids, MI: Eerdmans; Leiden: Brill, 1999) 17–120.

75. For some of these items, see Tov, "Biblical Texts from the Judean Desert," 140. Tov's final count of the biblical scrolls is 200–201 from Qumran and 23 from other sites in the Judean Desert.

76. "Biblical Texts from the Judean Desert," 142.

77. See Tov, "Biblical Texts from the Judean Desert," 151.

78. See E. Tov, "Excerpted and Abbreviated Biblical Texts from Qumran," *Revue de Qumrân* 16 (1995) 581–600.

79. For further details, see M. Bar-Ilan, "Writing Materials," in Schiffman and VanderKam, eds., *Encyclopedia of the Dead Sea Scrolls,* 2:996–97.

Chapter 7

1. Compare the similar definition by Sid Leiman: "A canonical book is a book accepted by Jews as authoritative for religious practice and/or doctrine, and whose authority is binding upon the Jewish people for all generations" (ed., *The Canon and Masorah of the Hebrew Bible. An Introductory Reader* [New York: KTAV, 1974] 14).

2. From the Greek *biblia,* plural of *biblion,* the diminutive of *biblos,* "papyrus" or "book." *Biblos* is a loanword from the Egyptian, first denoting the papyrus reed, later the inscribed paper or scroll, and finally the writing as a book, letter, record, or statute. It is also used for individual books (e.g., Psalms in Acts 1:20) or groups of books (e.g., the whole Law in Mark 12:26).

3. For a survey of terms used for Scripture, see R. T. Beckwith, "Formation of the Hebrew Bible," in *Mikra: Text, Translation, Reading and Interpretation of the Hebrew Bible in Ancient Judaism and Early Christianity* (CRINT 2.1; Assen and Maastricht: Van Gorcum; Philadelphia: Fortress, 1988) 39–86, esp. 39–40.

4. WAC: Michael Wise, Martin Abegg, Jr., and Edward Cook, *The Dead Sea Scrolls: A New Translation* (San Francisco: HarperSanFrancisco, 1996).

5. J. N. Lightstone, "The Rabbis' Bible: The Canon of the Hebrew Bible and the Early Rabbinic Guild," in L. M. McDonald and J. A. Sanders, eds. *The Canon Debate: The Origins and Formation of the Bible* (Peabody, MA: Hendrickson, 2002), 163–84, esp. 171.

6. There is some fluidity in Hebrew tradition as regards the order of books in the Kethubim. For example, in the oldest complete manuscript of the Hebrew Bible, the Leningrad (or St. Petersburg) Codex, the order is: Chronicles, Psalms, Job, Proverbs, Ruth, Song of Songs, Ecclesiastes, Lamentations, Esther, Daniel, and Ezra-Nehemiah.

7. Julio Trebolle, "Origins of a Tripartite Old Testament Canon," in McDonald and Sanders, eds., *The Canon Debate,* 129–45, esp. 129.

8. P. Skehan and A. Di Lella, *The Wisdom of Ben Sira* (The Anchor Bible 39; New York: Doubleday, 1987) 452.

9. See J. VanderKam, *The Dead Sea Scrolls Today* (Grand Rapids, MI: Eerdmans; London: SPCK, 1994) 142–43.

10. Sir. 49:9, but the text is problematic.

11. Beckwith, "Formation of the Hebrew Bible," 52.

12. Compare J. A. Goldstein, *II Maccabees* (The Anchor Bible 41A; New York: Doubleday, 1983) 187.

13. See the notes to the *HarperCollins Study Bible: New Revised Standard Version, with the Apocryphal/Deuterocanonical Books* (New York: HarperCollins, 1993) 1807.

14. *On the Contemplative Life,* trans. F. H. Colson, in *Philo,* vol. IX (Loeb Classical Library 363; London: Heinemann; Cambridge, MA: Harvard University Press, 1960) 127.

15. See Siegert Folker, "Early Jewish Interpretation in a Hellenistic Style," in *Hebrew Bible/Old Testament: The History of Its Interpretation*, ed. Magne Saebo (vol. I/1; Göttingen: Vandenhoeck & Ruprecht, 1996) 130–98, esp. 176; Beckwith, "Formation of the Hebrew Bible," 54.

16. *Against Apion or On the Antiquity of the Jews*, trans. H. St. John Thackeray, in *Josephus*, vol. 1 (Loeb Classical Library 186; London: Heinemann; Cambridge, MA: Harvard University Press, 1926) 179, 181.

17. *Against Apion*, trans. St. John Thackeray, 179, note b; R. Beckwith, *The Old Testament Canon of the New Testament Church and Its Background in Early Judaism* (London: Clowes, 1985) 119; VanderKam, *Dead Sea Scrolls Today*, 148.

18. *Jewish Antiquities*, vol. 10, trans. Ralph Marcus, in *Josephus*, vol. 6 (Loeb Classical Library 326; London: Heinemann; Cambridge, MA: Harvard University Press, 1958) 177. See also Beckwith, *Old Testament Canon*, 99–100.

19. Beckwith (*Old Testament Canon*, 119) is somewhat vague in adding that Lamentations could replace either Ecclesiastes or Song of Songs in this list.

20. S. Mason, "Josephus on Canon and Scriptures," in Saebo, ed., *Hebrew Bible/Old Testament*, 215–35, esp. 234.

21. See J. Barton, *Oracles of God: Perceptions of Ancient Prophecy in Israel after the Exile* (London: Longman and Todd, 1986) 49; and Trebolle, "Origins of a Tripartite Old Testament Canon."

22. See van der Kooij, ("The Canonization of Ancient Books Kept in the Temple of Jerusalem," in *Canonization and Decanonization*, ed. A. van der Kooij and K. van der Toorn (Leiden: Brill, 1998) 17–40, esp. 22.

23. *The Jewish War*, trans. H. St. John Thackeray, in *Josephus*, vol. 3 (Loeb Classical Library 210; London: Heinemann; Cambridge, MA: Harvard University Press, 1961) 99, 101; see also O. Eissfeldt, *The Old Testament: An Introduction* (Oxford: Blackwell, 1966) 568; Trebolle, "Origins of a Tripartite Old Testament Canon."

24. See the survey of the nonbiblical scrolls in Chapter 9. For a translation, see WAC, 358–64.

25. P. Flint's translation of the Hebrew ‏[ואף כתבונ]ו אליכה‏ ‏שתבין בספר מושה [ובסספר]י הנביאים ובדוי[ד]‏. The preposition *bet (in)* before *Davi[d]* is important since it separates David from the Prophets.

26. The Hebrew for *in the book[s of* is preserved on the isolated fragment 17, while *[the Pr]ophets and in Davi[d]* is on fragment 15, which does not join directly with fragment 17. See E. Qimron and J. Strugnell, *Qumran Cave 4.V: Miqṣat Maʿaśe ha-Torah* (DJD 10; Oxford: Clarendon Press) 58 and plate VI.

27. Qimron and Strugnell, DJD 10.59.

28. "Origins of a Tripartite Old Testament Canon."

29. DJD 10.59.

30. WAC, 363; F. García Martínez, *The Dead Sea Scrolls Translated: The Qumran Texts in English* (Leiden: Brill; Grand Rapids, MI: Eerdmans, 1994) 79; G. Vermes, *The Complete Dead Sea Scrolls in English* (London: Penguin, 1997) 227.

31. Thus E. Ulrich, "Canon," *Encyclopedia of the Dead Sea Scrolls*, ed. L. Schiffman and J. VanderKam (2 vols., New York and Oxford: Oxford University Press, 2000) 1:117–20, esp. 119.

32. See Chapter 6, "The Scrolls and the Prophets"; and E. Tov, *The Minor Prophets Scroll from Naḥal Ḥever (8ḤevXIIgr)* (DJD 8; Oxford: Clarendon Press, 1990) 8.

33. For both readings, see J. C. VanderKam and J. T. Milik, "4Q228. Text with a Citation of Jubilees," DJD 13.177–85 + plate XII.

34. Translation by J. Sanders, *The Dead Sea Psalms Scroll* (Ithaca, NY: Cornell University Press, 1967) 87.

35. Hebrew ‏בנבואה‏.

36. J. VanderKam, "The Jubilees Fragments from Qumran Cave 4," in *The Madrid Qumran Congress, Proceedings of the International Congress on the Dead Sea Scrolls, Madrid. 18–21 March 1991*, ed. J. Trebolle Barrera and L. Vegas Montaner (2 vols., Studies on the Texts of the Desert of Judah 11; Leiden: Brill; Madrid: Universidad Complutense, 1992) 2:635–48, esp. 648.

37. J. T. Milik, *The Books of Enoch: Aramaic Fragments of Qumrân Cave 4* (Oxford: Clarendon Press, 1976) 256.

38. *The Hymns of Qumran: Translation and Commentary* (Society of Biblical Literature Dissertation Series 50; Chico, CA: Scholars Press, 1981) 48–55.

39. See M. Fishbane, "Use, Authority and Interpretation of Mikra at Qumran," in M. J. Mulder, ed., *Mikra: Text, Translation, Reading and Interpretation of the Hebrew Bible in Ancient Judaism and Early Christianity* (CRINT 2.1; Assen and Maastricht: Van Gorcum; Philadelphia: Fortress, 1988) 339–77, esp. 347–48.

40. See John I. Kampen, "The Diverse Aspects of Wisdom in the Qumran Texts," in *The Dead Sea Scrolls After Fifty Years: A Comprehensive Assessment*, ed. P. W. Flint and J. C. VanderKam (2 vols.; Leiden: Brill, 1998–99) 1:211–43, esp. 223–25.

41. For the methodology used here, see VanderKam, *The Dead Sea Scrolls Today*, 150–51.

Chapter 8

1. See R. E. Brown and R. F. Collins, "Canonicity," *New Jerome Bible Commentary* 1035–36 (§66.9–10).

2. For dates, see the introductions to the various apocryphal books in W. Meeks et al, ed., *The HarperCollins Study Bible. New Revised Standard Version, with the Apocryphal/Deuterocanonical Books* (New York: Harper Collins, 1993).

3. *1 Enoch* and *Jubilees* are traditionally categorized as Pseudepigrapha, but at least one historic Christian confession (the Ethiopian Church) seems to regard them as Scripture. See R. W. Cowley's short but important study, "The Biblical Canon of the Ethiopian Orthodox Church Today," *Ostkirchliche Studien* 23 (1974) 318–23. Roger Beckwith, however, concludes that the Ethiopian canon most likely includes the book of *Jubilees,* but not *1 Enoch* (*The Old Testament Canon of the New Testament Church and Its Background in Early Judaism* [Grand Rapids: Eerdmans, 1985] 494–500, 504–5).

4. Although the Hebrew original of *2 Esdras* was completed only in ca. 100–120 CE, it is loosely classified as Second Temple literature in view of its focus on the Temple and its destruction. Scholars disagree on the precise date of *4 Maccabees.* For dates, see the introductions to the various books in Meeks et al., eds., *The HarperCollins Study Bible.*

5. For an introduction and English translation based on the scrolls, see M. Abegg, Jr., P. Flint, and E. Ulrich, *The Dead Sea Scrolls Bible* (San Francisco: HarperSanFrancisco, 1999) 636–46. Hereafter AFU.

6. 4QpapTobit^a ar, 4QTobit^b ar, 4QTobit^c ar, 4QTobit^d ar, and 4QTobit^e.

7. *Ten Years of Discovery in the Wilderness of Judaea* (Studies in Biblical Theology 26; London: SCM, 1959) 139–40.

8. That is, the fourth-century text of Codex Sinaiticus (abbreviated א or S), in the eleventh-century miniscule 319 (Vatopedi 513, dated 1021 CE), and in Old Latin (La) manuscripts. See J. VanderKam, consulting ed., *Qumran Cave 4.XIV: Parabiblical Texts, Part 2* (DJD 19; Oxford: Clarendon Press, 1995) 2–4.

9. Introduction and English translation: AFU, 576, 597–606.

10. The Qumran scrolls are 2QSir, copied in the second half of the first century BCE, and 11QPs^a, copied 30–50 CE. The Masada scroll is MasSir (Mas 1h), copied in the first third of the first century BCE.

11. *Pe* is the seventeenth letter in the Hebrew alphabet. Unlike several comparable examples in the scrolls, the canticle is not written "stichometrically" (i.e., with each new verse beginning on a new line) in 11QPs^a.

12. See J. A. Sanders, *The Psalms Scroll of Qumran Cave 11 (11QPs^a)* (DJDJ 4; Oxford: Clarendon Press, 1965) 113, 116–17.

13. Y. Yadin, *The Ben Sira Scroll from Masada, with Introduction, Emendations and Commentary* (Jerusalem: Israel Exploration Society and the Shrine of the Book, 1965) 1:5.

14. Introduction and English translation: AFU, 628–29.

15. M. J. Bernstein, "Pseudepigraphy in the Qumran Scrolls: Categories and Functions," in E. G. Chazon and M. Stone, eds., with the collaboration of A. Pinnick, *Pseudepigraphic Perspectives: The Apocrypha and Pseudepigrapha in Light of the Dead Sea Scrolls, Proceedings of the International Symposium of the Orion Center for the Study of the Dead Sea Scrolls and Associated Literature, 12–14 January, 1997* (Studies on the Texts of the Desert of Judah 36; Leiden: Brill, 1999) 1–26.

16. M. E. Stone, "Categorization and Classification of the Apocrypha and Pseudepigrapha," *Abr-Nahrain* 24 (1986) 167–77, esp. 168.

17. "The Dead Sea Scrolls and the Pseudepigrapha," *Dead Sea Discoveries* 3 (1996) 270–95, esp. 269 (also 271).

18. Introduction and English translation: AFU, 585–86.

19. See the comments in *The HarperCollins Study Bible,* 1749.

20. See also AFU, 585–86.

21. Introduction and English translation: AFU, 572–73, 579–80.

22. A Nestorian manuscript (Mosul/Baghdad, Library of the Chaldaean Patriarchate 1113). See Sanders, DJDJ 4:53.

23. Michael Wise, Martin Abegg, Jr., and Edward Cook, *The Dead Sea Scrolls: A New Translation* (San Francisco: HarperSanFrancisco, 1996) 399–400. Hereafter WAC.

24. Sanders, *Dead Sea Psalms Scroll,* 109.

25. For a description, see AFU, 480–81. The Aramaic text and English translation of the Qumran fragments appears in J. T. Milik, *The Books of Enoch: Aramaic Fragments of Qumrân Cave 4* (Oxford: Clarendon Press, 1976), and a translation from the Ethiopic in E. Isaac, "1 (Ethiopic Apocalypse of) Enoch," in J. H. Charlesworth, ed., *The Old Testament Pseudepigrapha* (2 vols.; Garden City, NY: Doubleday, 1983–85) 1:5–89.

26. See R. H. Charles, *The Book of Enoch or 1 Enoch* (Oxford: Clarendon Press, 1912) xxvii, xxix.

27. 4QEn$^{a–b}$ ar, 4QEn$^{c–f}$ ar, 4QEn^g ar, and 4QEnastr$^{a–d}$ ar.

28. 7Q4, 7Q8, 7Q11–14, which together form pap7QEn gr.

29. Milik, *The Books of Enoch,* 5, 183–84.

30. 4QEn$^{a–b}$ ar and 4QEn$^{c–e}$ ar.

31. 4QEnastr$^{a–d}$.

32. 4QEn$^{c–f}$ ar.

33. 4QEn^c ar and 4QEn^g ar.

34. 1QEnGiants^a ar, 1QEnGiants^b ar, 2QEnGiants ar, 4QEnGiants^a ar, 4QEn of Giants^b ar, 4QEn of Giants^c ar, 4QEn of Giants^d ar, 4QEnGiants^e ar, 4QEnoch^e ar, and 6QpapGiants. Since 4QEnGiants^a ar and 4QEn^c ar were written by the same scribe, it is very likely that they belong to the same manuscript.

35. Milik, *Books of Enoch,* 4, 54, 57, 76–79, 91–106, 109, 183–84, 227, 310.

36. Milik, *Books of Enoch,* 7.

37. G. Boccaccini, *Beyond the Essene Hypothesis: The Parting of the Ways Between Qumran and Enochic Judaism* (Grand Rapids, MI, and Cambridge: Eerdmans, 1998) 185–89; cf. 160–62.

38. For a description, see AFU, 196–98. The edition and an English translation of almost all the Cave 4 fragments

appears in J. VanderKam, consulting ed., *Qumran Cave 4.VIII: Parabiblical Texts, Part I* (DJD 13; Oxford: Clarendon Press, 1994) 1–185.

39. 1QJub[a], 1QJub[b], 2QJub[a], 2QJub[b].

40. 3QJub.

41. 4QTanḥ frags. 19–21 (4Q176), 4QJub[a], pap4QJub[b]?, 4QJub[c], 4QJub[d], 4QJub[e], 4QJub[f], 4QJub[g], pap4QJub[h].

42. 11QJub.

43. VanderKam and Milik, DJD 13:24. Moreover, in earlier DJD editions 3QJub was misconstrued as 3QapProph and 4Q176 was incorrectly identified as frags. 19–21 of 4QTanḥumim.

44. S. Talmon, "Hebrew Written Fragments from Masada," *DSD* 3 (1996) 168–77, esp. 172.

45. R. A. Kugler, "Testaments," in L. H. Schiffman and J. C. VanderKam, eds., *Encyclopedia of the Dead Sea Scrolls* (2 vols.; New York and Oxford: Oxford University Press) 933–36, esp. 933.

46. For English translations and editions of the Qumran fragments, see J. VanderKam, consulting ed., *Qumran Cave 4.XVII: Parabiblical Texts, Part 3* (DJD 22; Oxford: Clarendon Press, 1996) 1–82.

47. 1QLevi ar, 3QTJudah?, 4QLevi[a] ar, 4QLevi[b] ar, 4QLevi[c] ar, 4QLevi[d] ar, 4QLevi[e] ar, 4QLevi[f] ar, 4QTNaph, and pap4QTJudah?.

48. For example, some parts of *Aramaic Levi* correspond to sections of the Cairo Genizah text, some parts to the Greek *Testament of Levi*, and some have no equivalent in these later texts.

49. See DJD 22:2.

50. DJD 22:73–82. WAC (260–61) calls this *The Last Words of Naphtali*, but see our comments in Chapter 9.

51. WAC, 429–36; see also the comments in Chapter 9.

52. M. Bernstein, "Pseudepigraphy in the Qumran Scrolls," 1.

53. "Pseudepigraphy in the Qumran Scrolls," 3.

54. "Pseudepigraphy in the Qumran Scrolls," 10–24.

Chapter 9

1. "The Qumran Manuscripts: Contents and Significance," in *Time to Prepare the Way in the Wilderness*, ed. D. Dimant and L. H. Schiffman (Studies on the Texts of the Desert of Judah 16; Leiden: Brill, 1995) 32–33.

2. "The Qumran Manuscripts," 35.

3. The translation of Qumran texts used throughout is M. Wise, M. Abegg, Jr., and E. Cook, *The Dead Sea Scrolls: A New Translation* (San Francisco: HarperSanFrancisco, 1996), abbreviated WAC. The translators often give titles to texts that are not the standard ones; this will be noted where it occurs.

4. This seems a better name for the texts in the category than a title such as "halakhic" works, since the Qumran texts do not refer to their legal teachings as *halakhah*, a word familiar from rabbinic literature and apparently the term employed by the pharisaic opponents of the covenanters.

5. 4Q158, 4Q364–67. In WAC these are separate, with 4Q158 as *A Reworking of Genesis and Exodus* (pp. 199–204) and 4Q364–65 as *An Annotated Law of Moses* (pp. 325–28). 4Q366–67 is omitted.

6. 11Q19–20, 11Q21?, 4Q365a?, 4Q524 (WAC, 457–92).

7. See the survey of views by F. García Martínez, "The Temple Scroll," *Encyclopedia of the Dead Sea Scrolls*, ed. L. Schiffman and J. VanderKam (2 vols.; New York and Oxford: Oxford University Press, 2000) 927–33.

8. 4Q394–99; in WAC (358–64) this work is named *A Sectarian Manifesto*.

9. E. Qimron and J. Strugnell, eds., *Qumran Cave 4.V: Miqṣat Maʿase Ha-Torah* (DJD 10; Oxford: Clarendon Press, 1994).

10. WAC, 271–74 (as *A Commentary on the Law of Moses*).

11. J. Baumgarten, "264a. 4QHalakha B," in Baumgarten et al., eds., *Qumran Cave 4.XXV: Halakhic Texts* (DJD 35; Oxford: Clarendon Press, 1999) 54.

12. WAC, 278–80 (as *Portions of Sectarian Law*).

13. 4Q274–78; WAC (281–85) considers these to be four different texts.

14. 4Q159, 513, 514, though not all may represent the same text (see WAC, 204–7).

15. 4Q284; WAC (289–90) calls this *Laws for Purification*.

16. 4Q284a, or *Laws about Gleaning* (WAC, 290–91).

17. 4Q414, paralleled by 4Q512; see WAC, 390–91 (*A Baptismal Liturgy*) and 418–20 (*A Purification Ritual*).

18. The standard abbreviation for this work, CD, stands for *Cairo Damascus*. Damascus is mentioned several times as a place where a covenant was made. Schechter published the text as *Fragments of a Zadokite Work* (Documents of Jewish Sectaries 1; Cambridge: Cambridge University Press, 1910).

19. 4Q266–73, 5Q12, 6Q15 (WAC, 49–74).

20. 1QS, 4Q255–64; 5Q11; see WAC, 123–43 (*Charter of a Jewish Sectarian Association*). In this book we use the accepted title *Rule of the Community*.

21. See Sarianna Metso, *The Textual Development of the Qumran Community Rule* (Studies on the Texts of the Desert of Judah 21; Leiden: Brill, 1997); and M. Knibb, "Rule of the Community," in Schiffman and VanderKam, eds., *Encyclopedia of the Dead Sea Scrolls*, 793–97.

22. WAC, 14–47 (*Charter for the Last Days*).

23. See S. Pfann, in *Qumran Cave 4.XXVI: Cryptic Texts and Miscellanea, Part 1*, consulting eds. J. VanderKam and M. Brady (DJD 36; Oxford: Clarendon Press, 2000), 515–74.

24. WAC, 147–49 (*Priestly Blessings for the Last Days*).

25. 1QM, 4Q491–96; see WAC, 150–72 (*The War Scroll*).

26. 4Q285 and 11Q14; see WAC, 291–94 (*The War of the Messiah*).

27. 1QpHab; see WAC, 114–22 (*A Commentary on Habakkuk*).

28. 4Q175 (*Testimonia*) is sometimes called a thematic *pesher,* but it is really just a collection of four citations with virtually no commentary (WAC, 229–31: *A Collection of Messianic Proof Texts*).

29. WAC, 225–28 (*The Last Days: A Commentary on Selected Verses*).

30. WAC, 233–37 (*The Last Days: An Interpretation of Selected Verses*); the very fragmentary 4Q182 is called *Catena B.*

31. WAC, 455–57 (*The Coming of Melchizedek*).

32. WAC, 74–84 (*Tales of the Patriarchs*).

33. In WAC 4Q534 is combined with 4Q535–36 to form *The Birth of the Chosen One* (pp. 427–29).

34. WAC, 429–30 (*A Vision of Jacob*).

35. WAC, 430–31 (*An Apocryphon of Judah*).

36. WAC, 258–59 (as part of *The Words of Levi*).

37. Though WAC calls it *The Last Words of Naphtali* (260–61), the title is appropriate only for column 2, which has now been separated from the first column as a distinct work (4Q215a).

38. WAC, 331–35 (*Stories About the Tribes of Israel*).

39. WAC, 431 (*The Last Words of Joseph*).

40. WAC, 432–33 (*The Last Words of Kohath*).

41. WAC, 433–36 (*The Vision of Amram*).

42. On 4Q158 and 4Q364–67 see WAC, 199–204 (*A Reworking of Genesis and Exodus*) and 325–28 (*An Annotated law of Moses*); and the comments on *Reworked Pentateuch* earlier in this chapter.

43. WAC, 457–92.

44. WAC, 172–74 (*Words of Moses*).

45. In WAC, 1Q29 and 4Q376 are termed *Three Tongues of Fire* (pp. 178–79), but 4Q375 is considered a different text, which is entitled *The Test of a True Prophet* (pp. 336–37).

46. WAC, 337–38 (*A Moses Apocryphon*).

47. WAC, 335–36 (*Discourse on the Exodus and Conquest*).

48. WAC, 377 (*Prayer of Praise*).

49. WAC, 339–42 (*Psalms of Joshua*).

50. WAC, 422–23 (*A Tale of Joshua*).

51. WAC, 207–9 (*An Account of the Story of Samuel*).

52. Thus WAC, 331–35.

53. WAC, 342–47 (*A Collection of Royal Psalms*).

54. WAC, 453–54 (*Songs to Disperse Demons*).

55. WAC, 347–48 (*An Apocryphon of Elijah*).

56. In WAC (pp. 349–56), 4Q384–90 are together termed a *Prophetic Apocryphon.* In his "Texts from the Judean Desert" in the *SBL Handbook of Style* (ed. P. Alexander et al.), Emanuel Tov (176–233, esp. 201–2) breaks up 4Q384–90 into no fewer than fourteen texts: 4Q383 (apocrJer A), 4Q384 (papApocrJer B?), 4Q385 (psEzek^a), 4Q385a (apocrJer C^a), 4Q385b (psEzek^c), 4Q386 (psEzek^b), 4Q387 (apocrJer C^b), 4Q387a (apocrJer D), 4Q388 (psEzek^d), 4Q388a (apocrJer C^c), 4Q389 (apocrJer C^d), 4Q389a (apocrJer D), 4Q390 (apocrJer E), 4Q391 (papPsEzek^e).

57. WAC, 414–17 (*The Songs of the Sage for Protection Against Evil Spirits*).

58. WAC, 437–39 (*The Tale of Bagasraw*).

59. WAC, 265–66 (*The Healing of King Nabonidus*); Nabonidus ruled from 556 to 539 BCE.

60. 4Q243–45 are translated in WAC (pp. 266–68) as copies of a single document, *The Vision of Daniel.*

61. WAC, 268–70 (*A Vision of the Son of God*).

62. WAC, 439–41 (*The Vision of the Four Trees*).

63. A sundial or roundel has also been found at Qumran.

64. See WAC, 319–20.

65. See WAC, 301–3.

66. See WAC, 314–16.

67. See WAC, 317–18.

68. See WAC, 320–21.

69. See WAC, 307–9.

70. See WAC, 243–46.

71. WAC, 303–5.

72. WAC, 444–45.

73. WAC, 408–10.

74. WAC, 410–14 (*The Words of the Heavenly Lights*).

75. WAC, 184–88.

76. WAC, 377–78.

77. WAC, 286–89 (*A Liturgy of Blessing and Cursing*).

78. WAC, 84–114 (*Thanksgiving Psalms*).

79. WAC, 342–47 (*A Collection of Royal Psalms*).

80. WAC, 378–90 (*The Secret of the Way Things Are*); also included are 4Q410, 412–13, 419–21.

81. WAC, 174–77 (*The Book of Secrets*).

82. WAC, 242–43 (*In Praise of Wisdom*).

83. They are included in *The Secret of the Way Things Are* in WAC.

84. WAC, 393–94 (*A Collection of Proverbs*).

85. WAC, 294–95.

86. WAC, 423–26 (*The Blessing of the Wise*).

87. WAC, 414–17 (*The Songs of the Sage for Protection Against Evil Spirits*).

88. WAC, 180–84 (*A Vision of the New Jerusalem*).

89. WAC, 420–22 (*Redemption and Resurrection*).

90. WAC, 188–98 (*A List of Buried Treasure*).

91. See A. Yardeni, "Appendix: Documentary Texts Alleged to be From Qumran Cave 4," in H. Cotton and A. Yardeni, eds., *Aramaic, Hebrew and Greek Documentary Texts From Naḥal Ḥever and Other Sites* (DJD 27; Oxford: Clarendon Press, 1997) 283–87. Plate XXI has the two fragments juxtaposed.

Chapter 10

1. *The Dead Sea Scrolls of the Hebrew University* (Jerusalem: Magnes, 1955) 29. The statement is drawn from the first fascicle of his Hebrew publication *Hidden Scrolls* (Jerusalem: Bialik, 1948) 16.

2. Quoted from G. Vermes and M. D. Goodman, eds., *The Essenes According to the Classical Sources* (Oxford Centre Textbooks 1; Sheffield: JSOT Press, 1989) 33. Goodman was responsible for the translations.

3. The literal rendering is "below these," but the translator has supplied the word *Essenes* to make clear what Pliny means here.

4. "Pliny the Elder," *Encyclopedia of the Dead Sea Scrolls*, ed. L. Schiffman and J. VanderKam (New York and Oxford: Oxford, 2000) 678.

5. Goodman, *Essenes According to the Classical Sources*, 59.

6. Ralph Marcus, trans., *Josephus VII: Jewish Antiquities Books XII–XIV* (Loeb Classical Library 365; Cambridge, MA: Harvard; London: Heinemann, 1966), 311, 313.

7. L. H. Feldman, trans., *Josephus IX: Jewish Antiquities Books XVIII–XIX* (Loeb Classical Library 433; Cambridge, MA: Harvard; London: Heinemann, 1981), 15.

8. WAC: Michael Wise, Martin Abegg, Jr., and Edward Cook, *The Dead Sea Scrolls: A New Translation* (San Francisco: HarperSanFrancisco, 1996).

9. Goodman, *Essenes According to the Classical Sources*, 47.

10. Goodman, *Essenes According to the Classical Sources*, 73.

11. WAC, 349–56; *Prophetic Apocryphon*.

12. WAC, 420–22; *Redemption and Resurrection*. The quote is from p. 421.

13. WAC, 266–68.

14. Goodman, *Essenes According to the Classical Sources*, 39.

15. Goodman, *Essenes According to the Classical Sources*, 39.

16. F. H. Colson, trans., *Philo IX* (Loeb Classical Library 363; Cambridge, MA: Harvard; London: Heinemann, 1985), 59, 61.

17. Recall Josephus's term *mingle* in *War* 2.122 (quoted above).

18. Goodman, *Essenes According to the Classical Sources*, 43.

19. For a helpful summary of the relevant information, see A. Oppenheimer, "Ḥaverim," *Encyclopedia of the Dead Sea Scrolls*, 333–36.

20. Josephus's term for the general membership is the Greek equivalent of the Hebrew term used for the community in the scrolls.

21. Goodman, *Essenes According to the Classical Sources*, 45.

22. Goodman, *Essenes According to the Classical Sources*, 29.

23. "The Pharisaic-Sadducean Controversies About Purity and the Qumran Texts," *Journal of Jewish Studies* 31 (1980) 157–70.

24. H. Danby, *The Mishnah* (London: Oxford University Press, 1933) 784.

25. *Reclaiming the Dead Sea Scrolls* (Philadelphia and Jerusalem: Jewish Publication Society, 1994) 75.

26. *Reclaiming the Dead Sea Scrolls*, 273.

27. Whether these could be called the founders of the group is more problematic since the earliest recensions of the *Rule of the Community* do not assign them the same status they have in the Cave 1 copy.

28. *An Unknown Jewish Sect* (Moreshet Series 1; New York: The Jewish Theological Seminary of America, 1976) 127. Ginzberg himself published the German original, *Eine Unbekannte Jüdische Sekte*, in 1922.

29. "The Community of the Renewed Covenant: Between Judaism and Christianity," in *The Community of the Renewed Covenant: The Notre Dame Symposium on the Dead Sea Scrolls*, ed. E. Ulrich and J. VanderKam (Christianity and Judaism in Antiquity 10; Notre Dame, IN: University of Notre Dame Press, 1994) 6–7.

30. Rengstorf's book is entitled *Ḥirbet Qumrân und die Bibliothek vom Toten Meer* (Studia Delitzschiana 5; Stuttgart: Kohlhammer, 1960); it was translated into English as *Ḥirbet Qumrân and the Problem of the Library of the Dead Sea Caves* (Leiden: Brill, 1963). Golb's views are most easily accessible in his book *Who Wrote the Dead Sea Scrolls? The Search for the Secret of Qumran* (New York: Scribner, 1995).

31. See, for instance, *James the Brother of Jesus: The Key to Unlocking the Secrets of Early Christianity and the Dead Sea Scrolls* (London and New York: Penguin Books, 1997).

Chapter 11

1. WAC: Michael Wise, Martin Abegg, Jr., and Edward Cook, *The Dead Sea Scrolls: A New Translation* (San Francisco: HarperSanFrancisco, 1996).

2. J. VanderKam, *The Book of Jubilees* (2 vols., Corpus Scriptorum Christianorum Orientalium 510–11, Scriptores Aethiopici 87–88; Louvain: Peeters, 1989) 2:7–8.

3. The abbreviation 1/12 means the twelfth day of the first month.

4. Purim would also have fallen on a sabbath in the 364-day calendar (12/14; see Esth. 9:21), something that was avoided.

5. For overviews of the Qumran calendrical texts, see J. VanderKam, *Calendars in the Dead Sea Scrolls: Measuring Time* (The Literature of the Dead Sea Scrolls; London and New York: Routledge, 1998) 43–110; S. Talmon with J. Ben-Dov, "Calendrical Documents and Mishmarot," in Talmon, Ben-Dov, and U. Glessmer, eds., *Qumran Cave 4.XVI: Calendrical Texts* (DJD 21; Oxford: Clarendon Press, 2001) 1–166.

6. This passage reads: "Any man who is not ritually clean in respect to his genitals on the day of battle shall not go down with them into battle, for holy angels are present with their army" (WAC, 157). The presence of the angels with the community has been adduced as the background for Paul's curious statement in 1 Cor. 11:10: "For this reason a woman ought have a symbol of authority on her head, because of the angels."

7. The translator has mistakenly written *Branch* here.

8. The sentence about the prophet and messiahs does not occur in 4Q259, where the unit found in 1QS 8.15–9.11 fails to appear. Whether the shorter or longer text is original is debated.

9. Some think the Teacher of Righteousness was expected to return and carry out prophetic functions at the end. One text that has been read in this sense is CD 6.10–11.

10. The translation in parentheses is to be preferred.

11. The translator prefers to render with *nation*, although the word is usually taken as meaning *congregation*.

12. Another text that may speak about a priestly messiah is 4Q541, which WAC includes under the rubric *The Words of Levi* (see pp. 259–60).

13. San Francisco: HarperSanFrancisco, 1999. Wise's book is a combination of a popularly written text (reading at times like a novel) and a series of long and learned footnotes tucked at the end of the volume.

14. It is likely that the Teacher was considered a prophet, but this does not follow from use of the word *meliṣ* in the Teacher hymns, as Wise suggests.

15. The paleographical date for 1QS is 100–75 BCE; the one-sigma AMS dates are 164–144 BCE and 116 BCE–50 CE.

16. Berkeley: University of California Press, 2000. The Hebrew original was entitled *In the Footsteps of the Messiah* (Jerusalem: Schocken, 2000). The order of the presentation has been changed somewhat from the Hebrew to the English version. For example, in the English translation the account of a day in the life of the messiah is placed first, whereas it comes later in the Hebrew version.

17. 4Q431 and 4Q471b seem to be from the same manuscript.

18. Quoted from Exod. 15:11 where God makes this statement about himself. See also Ps. 89:6.

19. R. Marcus and A. Wikgren, trans., *Jewish Antiquities Books XV–XVII*, in *Josephus vol. VIII* (Loeb Classical Library 410; Cambridge: Harvard University Press, London: Heinemann, 1980) 183.

20. Knohl, following Flusser, says this is like the reference to the sword of God in the *War Scroll* 19.11; God's sword there kills the enemies of the sons of light in the final war.

21. Knohl may be right that the speaker in the Qumran hymns is a messianic figure, but, as we have seen, there are other possibilities. One appealing approach is to compare what is said in *Priestly Blessings for the Last Days* (1Q28b), where in some places a person who may be the high priest receives a blessing and in others the sons of Zadok do. Some of the language there resembles what we find in the so-called Self-Glorification Hymn. So, for example, in 1Q28b column 4 we read: "and to place you at the head of the Holy Ones" (l. 23) and "May you abide forever as an Angel of the Presence in the holy habitation, to the glory of the God of hosts.

May you serve in the temple of the kingdom of God, ordering destiny with the Angels of the Presence, a society of the *Yahad* [with the Holy Ones] forever, for all the ages of eternity" (ll. 24–26). Because the text is so fragmentary, there is a debate about whether the high priest or an ordinary priest is being addressed here, but one may not even have to appeal to the blessing of the high priest for such exalted language. Another attractive possibility is to see a collective "I" behind the Qumran hymn. For a review of the evidence and the interpretations, see M. Wise, מי כמוני באלים, A Study of 4Q491c, 4Q471b, 4Q427 7 and 1QHᵃ 25:35–26:10," *Dead Sea Discoveries* 7 (2000) 173–219. Wise adopts the collective view, although, as we have seen, he thinks the Teacher's disciples put these words on his lips.

Chapter 12

1. E. Cook, who translates the *Commentary on Nahum* in WAC (Michael Wise, Martin Abegg, Jr., and Edward Cook, *The Dead Sea Scrolls: A New Translation* [San Francisco: HarperSanFrancisco, 1996]), renders the phrase as *the Flattery-Seekers*. This highly interpretive rendering misses the point of the expression and thus is not used here.

2. "Jealousy" may not be the nuance the text is suggesting; perhaps "zeal" or "animosity" would be better.

3. The expression for the Lion of wrath is *kefir ha-ḥaron*, while the one for the last priest is *kohen ha-'aharon*.

4. Another possible translation is that the Teacher is actually doing the rebuking here.

5. The translation in WAC is strange. The word means "only, unique"; it has been suggested that it be emended slightly so that it yields *Yahad*.

6. See H. Eshel, "The History of the Qumran Community and Historical Details in the Dead Sea Scrolls," *Qadmoniot* 30 (1997) 91 (Hebrew).

7. It is conceivable that the Qumranites held a different view of the Hasmonean state when Sadducees were dominant during Jannaeus's reign.

8. E. Eshel, H. Eshel, and A. Yardeni, "4Q448. 4QApocryphal Psalm and Prayer," in J. VanderKam and M. Brady, consulting eds., *Qumran Cave 4.VI: Poetical and Liturgical Texts, Part 1* (DJD 11; Oxford: Clarendon Press, 1998) 421.

9. So J. Fitzmyer, "4Q332. 4QHistorical Text D," *Qumran Cave 4.XXVI: Cryptic Texts and Miscellanea, Part 1*, consulting eds., J. VanderKam and M. Brady (DJD 36; Oxford: Clarendon Press, 2000) 284–85.

Chapter 13

1. The context is clear, but translating משפט as "Scripture" is not accurate. It means "statute" or the like.

WAC: Michael Wise, Martin Abegg, Jr., and Edward Cook, *The Dead Sea Scrolls: A New Translation* (San Francisco: HarperSanFrancisco, 1996).

2. Among the titles assigned to the priestly messiah is the same one—Interpreter of the Law (see *The Last Days: A Commentary on Selected Verses* 3.10–12).

3. We should recall that the Teacher was associated with a law in *Commentary on Psalms^a* (4Q171) fragments 1–2 4.8–10.

4. See L. Schiffman, *Reclaiming the Dead Sea Scrolls* (Philadelphia and Jerusalem: Jewish Publication Society, 1994) 247–49.

5. For the principle involved, see the *Rule of the Community* 8.15; Rom. 4:15.

6. Schiffman, *Reclaiming the Dead Sea Scrolls,* 247–48.

7. *The Temple Scroll* (3 vols.; Jerusalem: Israel Exploration Society, the Institute of Archaeology of the Hebrew University of Jerusalem, and the Shrine of the Book, 1983) 1.74.

8. *The Temple Scroll,* 1.76, 360–61 (he also mentions 1 Sam. 8:15–17 as a possible basis for the king's tenth).

9. Translation from VanderKam, *The Book of Jubilees* (2 vols., Corpus Scriptorum Christianorum Orientalium 510–11; Scriptores Aethiopici 87–88; Leuven: Peeters, 1989) 2:17.

10. The Hebrew for "his brother" and "his brothers" looks the same; in this context with "his sister" the translation "his brother" is preferable.

11. See L. Ginzberg, *An Unknown Jewish Sect* (Moreshet Series 1; New York: Ktav, 1970) 55–57, for the references and a discussion.

12. The text does not, of course, use names for the days of the week. It refers to them with ordinal numbers, which the translator, M. Abegg, then expressed with the corresponding names.

13. That is, the 17th day of the second month to the 17th day of the seventh month.

14. *Studien zum Habakuk-Kommentar vom Toten Meer* (Beiträge zur historischen Theologie 15; Tübingen: Mohr Siebeck, 1953) 150 (translation by J. VanderKam). He considered the second part of the hermeneutical principle to be the decisive one for the commentary and maintained that the interpretation had a practical, pastoral purpose (153–54).

15. The Hebrew letters *reš* (ר) and *dalet* (ד) are virtually identical in appearance, and are thus easily mistaken one for the other. Hence the two words under discussion look almost indistinguishable.

16. William Brownlee considered such separation of words into two or more parts one of the thirteen hermeneutical principles that he uncovered at work in the *Commentary on Habakkuk* ("Biblical Interpretation Among the Sectaries of the Dead Sea Scrolls," *Biblical Archaeologist* 14 [1951] 60–62). This is the eleventh principle in his list.

Chapter 14

1. "¿Papiros neo–testamentarios en la cueva 7 de Qumrân?," *Biblica* 53 (1972) 91–100. English translation by W. L. Holladay: "New Testament Papyri in Qumrân Cave 7?," Supplement to the *Journal of Biblical Literature* 91 (1972) 1–14.

2. See M. Baillet et al., *Les 'petites grottes' de Qumrân,* (DJD 3, 3a; Oxford: Clarendon Press, 1962) 144–45.

3. Although O'Callaghan's transcription includes only portions of Mark 6:52–53, for each passage the full text of vv. 52–54 is provided for context.

4. In the Greek text given here, the extant letters do not line up accurately when compared to the photograph of 7Q5. This is because the text found at Qumran is inscribed in Greek majuscules (capital letters), whereas the transcription is in minuscules (small letters), which distorts the alignment.

5. S. Enste, *Kein Markustext in Qumran* (Novum Testamentum et Orbis Antiquus 45; Freiburg, Schweiz: Universitätsverlag; Göttingen: Vandenhoeck & Ruprecht, 2000).

6. C. P. Thiede, *Rekindling the Word: In Search of Gospel Truth* (Leominster, UK; Gracewing, Valley Forge, PA: Trinity, 1995) 189–97.

7. G. Stanton, *Gospel Truth? New Light on Jesus and the Gospels* (Valley Forge, PA: Trinity, 1995) 27.

8. See DJD 3:143. In the Septuagint, the Epistle of Jeremiah comprises chapter 6 of the book of Baruch.

9. See DJD 3:143–44.

10. E. Tov, "The Biblical Texts from the Judean Desert—An Overview and Analysis of all the Published Texts," in *The Bible as Book: The Hebrew Bible and the Judaean Desert Discoveries. Proceedings of the Conference Held at Hampton Court, Herefordshire, 18–21 June 2000,* ed. E. D. Herbert and E. Tov (London: The British Library, 2002): "probably all biblical," p. 150.

11. V. Spottorno, "Una nueva posible identificacion de 7Q5," *Sefarad* 52 (1992) 541–43.

12. For further comments, see Thiede, *Rekindling the Word,* 189–95.

13. G. W. Nebe, "7Q4—Möglichkeit und Grenze einer Identifikation," *Revue de Qumrân* 13 (1988) 629–33. Nebe points out that the association of 7Q8 with *1 Enoch* 103:7–8 is not assured since the fragment could also belong to Zech. 8:8; Isa. 1:29–30; Ps. 18:14–15; Dan. 2:43; Qoh. 6:3; or Num. 22:38. None of these six passages, however, is near a text that can serve as an identification for 7Q4.1 (Nebe, "7Q4," 632–33, n. 26).

14. É. Puech, "Notes sur les fragments grecs du manuscrit 7Q4 = 1 Hénoch 103 et 105," *Revue Biblique* 103 (1996) 592–600; and "Sept fragments de la Lettre d'Hénoch (1 Hén 100, 103 et 105) dans la grotte 7 de Qumrân (=7QHén gr)," *Revue de Qumrân* 18/70 (1997) 313–23.

15. See E. Isaac, "1 (Ethiopic Apocalypse of) Enoch," in J. H. Charlesworth, ed., *The Old Testament Pseudepigrapha* (2 vols.; Garden City, NY: Doubleday, 1983–85) 1:5–89, esp. 72–89.
16. George Nicklesburg, *1 Enoch 1: A Commentary on the Book of 1 Enoch, Chapters 1–36, 81–108* (Hermeneia; Minneapolis, MN: Fortress Press, 2001) 10–11.

Chapter 15

1. *The Scrolls from the Dead Sea* (New York: Oxford University Press, 1955); *The Dead Sea Scrolls: 1947–1969* (New York: Oxford University Press, 1969).
2. *The Lost Years of Jesus Revealed* (Greenwich, CT: Fawcett, 1958).
3. *The Dead Sea Scrolls: A Preliminary Survey* (Oxford: Blackwell, 1952) 99. Translated from the French edition (1950).
4. *The Dead Sea Scrolls: A Preliminary Survey,* 99–100.
5. *Amazing Dead Sea Scrolls* (Chicago: Moody Press, 1956). Republished as *The Dead Sea Scrolls and the Christian Faith* (Chicago: Moody Press, 1962); see esp. 166–68.
6. *Qumrân Cave 4.I (4Q158–4Q186)* (DJDJ 5; Oxford: Clarendon Press, 1968).
7. "Notes en marge du Volume V des 'Discoveries in the Judaean Desert of Jordan,'" *Revue de Qumrân* 7 (1970) 163–276.
8. M. Bernstein and G. Brooke with the assistance of J. Høgenhavn, in consultation with J. VanderKam and M. Brady, *Qumran Cave 4.I: 4Q158–186* (DJD 5A, rev. ed.; Oxford: Clarendon Press), forthcoming.
9. P. Davies, "Allegro, John Marco," in L. Schiffman and J. VanderKam, eds., *Encyclopedia of the Dead Sea Scrolls* (2 vols.; New York and Oxford: Oxford University Press, 2000) 1:18.
10. *The Dead Sea Scrolls: A Reappraisal* (Harmondsworth, UK: Penguin, 1956; 2d ed., 1964).
11. *The Dead Sea Scrolls: A Reappraisal,* 2d ed., 109, 175.
12. *Time,* February 6, 1956, as quoted by J. Fitzmyer, in *Responses to 101 Questions on the Dead Sea Scrolls* (New York: Paulist, 1992) 164.
13. See Neil Asher Silberman, *The Hidden Scrolls. Christianity, Judaism, and the War for the Dead Sea Scrolls* (New York: Putnam, 1994) 133–34.
14. Silberman, *The Hidden Scrolls,* 134.
15. London: Hodder and Stoughton; Garden City, NY: Doubleday, 1970.
16. Newton Abbot, UK: Redwood Burn; Amherst, NY: Prometheus Books, 1979.
17. *The Dead Sea Scrolls and the Christian Myth,* 190–91.
18. J. M. Allegro with A. A. Anderson, *Qumrân Cave 4.I (4Q158–4Q186)* (DJDJ 5; Oxford: Clarendon Press. 1968). For the abbreviation DJDJ (Discoveries in the Judean Desert of Jordan), see Chapter 18 and Appendix IV.
19. Randall Price, *Secrets of the Dead Sea Scrolls* (Eugene, OR: Harvest House, 1996) 360.
20. Michael Baigent and Richard Leigh, *The Dead Sea Scrolls Deception* (New York and London: Summit, 1991).
21. *Jesus and the Riddle of the Dead Sea Scrolls* (San Francisco: HarperSanFrancisco, 1992); esp. 285–331.
22. Woodstock, NY; Beekman Publishing, 1992.
23. Glenn D. Kitler, *Edgar Cayce on the Dead Sea Scrolls* (New York: Warner Books, 1970).
24. Huntsville, AR: Ozark Mountain Publishers, 1999.
25. Los Angeles: The Essene Mystery School of Life, 1995.
26. J. Taylor, *The Immerser: John the Baptist Within Second Temple Judaism* (Grand Rapids, MI: Eerdmans, 1997) 47. For bibliography on the subject and discussions of the problems, see pp. 20–48.
27. WAC (Michael Wise, Martin Abegg, Jr., and Edward Cook, *The Dead Sea Scrolls: A New Translation [San Francisco: HarperSanFrancisco, 1996]): Charter of a Jewish Sectarian Association* (p. 123).
28. WAC call this text *Charter of a Jewish Sectarian Organization.*
29. J. J. Collins, *The Scepter and the Star. The Messiahs of the Dead Sea Scrolls and Other Ancient Literature* (Anchor Bible Reference Library 10; New York: Doubleday, 1995) 117–22, 205–6.
30. Craig A, Evans, "Jesus and the Dead Sea Scrolls from Qumran Cave 4," in C. A. Evans and P. W. Flint, eds., *Eschatology, Messianism, and the Dead Sea Scrolls* (Studies in the Dead Sea Scrolls and Related Literature; Grand Rapids, MI, and Cambridge: Eerdmans, 1997) 91–100, esp. 97.
31. *The Scepter and the Star,* 169.
32. *The Scepter and the Star,* 155.
33. É. Puech, "4Q525 et les péricopes des Béatitudes en Ben Sira et Matthieu," *Revue biblique* 138 (1991) 80–106.
34. B. Witherington III, *Jesus the Sage: The Pilgrimage of Wisdom* (Minneapolis, MN: Fortress, 1994).
35. "Jesus and the Dead Sea Scrolls from Qumran Cave 4," 96.
36. For the passage being discussed, see WAC, 133.
37. See E. Eshel, "The Rebukes by the Overseer," *Journal of Jewish Studies* 45 (1994) 111–22.
38. See WAC, 291–94.
39. See G. Vermes, "The Oxford Forum for Qumran Research: Seminar on the Rule of War from Cave 4 (4Q285)," *Journal of Jewish Studies* 43 (1992) 85–94; H. Shanks, "The 'Pierced Messiah' Text—An Interpretation Evaporates," *Biblical Archaeology Review* 18/4 (1992) 80–82.
40. San Francisco: HarperSanFrancisco, 1999.
41. Berkeley: University of California Press, 2000.

Chapter 16

1. There was debate among ancient Jewish groups regarding precisely when the Festival of Weeks was to be celebrated because of a perceived ambiguity in Lev. 23:15, but all groups observed it in the third month.

2. See J. Fitzmyer, *The Gospel According to Luke X–XXIV* (Anchor Bible 28A; New York: Doubleday, 1985) 879. They are paired in the *Testament of Issachar* 5:2 and the *Testament of Dan* 5:3, but whether these are pre-Christian is not certain. The two commands may be reflected in Philo, *On the Special Laws* 2.15.

3. *War* 2.120 and *Antiquities* 18.21; cf. Philo, *Hypothetica* 11.14.

4. For further comments on celibacy at Qumran, see Chapter 10.

5. See, for example, J. Fitzmyer, "Paul and the Dead Sea Scrolls" in *The Dead Sea Scrolls after Fifty Years: A Comprehensive Assessment*, ed. P. Flint and J. VanderKam (2 vols.; Leiden: Brill, 1998, 1999) 2:599–621, esp. 613.

6. With the possible exception of 4Q174 (*The Last Days: A Commentary on Selected Verses*) 3.7, where many scholars read *todah* ("thanksgiving") rather than *torah* ("law").

7. Note that the British Bible Society's translation of the New Testament into modern Hebrew (*Hebrew New Testament* [Yanetz: Jerusalem, 1976]) uses *ma'aśe ha-torah* for all eight occurrences of *erga nomou*. However, a later revision (1991) replaced the examples in Galatians with *miṣwot ha-Torah* ("commandments of the law").

8. J. D. G. Dunn, "4QMMT and Galatians," *New Testament Studies* 43 (1997) 147–53, esp. 148–50.

9. N. T. Wright, "Paul and Qumran," *Bible Review* 14/5 (1998) 18–54, esp. 54.

10. "Paul and Qumran," 54

11. "4QMMT, Paul, and 'Works of the Law,'" in P. W. Flint, ed., *The Bible at Qumran: Text, Shape, and Interpretation* (Studies in the Dead Sea Scrolls and Related Literature; Grand Rapids, MI: Eerdmans, 2000) 203–16, esp. 213.

12. E. P. Sanders, *Paul and Palestinian Judaism* (Philadelphia: Fortress, 1977) 239–328, esp. 319–20.

13. Abegg, "4QMMT, Paul, and 'Works of the Law,'" 214.

14. J. D. G. Dunn, *The Epistle to the Galatians* (Peabody, MA: Hendrickson, 1993) 135.

15. See VanderKam, "Identity and History of the Community," in *The Dead Sea Scrolls After Fifty Years*, 2:487–533, esp. 490–97.

16. This is another place where Paul collects a series of biblical passages to make a point. For his sources, see Lev. 26:11–12; Ezek. 37:27; Isa. 52:11; Ezek. 20:34; 2 Sam. 7:14; and Isa. 43:6.

17. This is an alternate form of the name *Belial* found in Greek texts.

18. "Paul and the Dead Sea Scrolls," 610–11; he documents the parallels in the scrolls on pages 611–12.

19. Paul does not use the term *sons of darkness* for unbelievers.

20. In *The Last Days: A Commentary on Selected Verses* (= 4Q174) 3.6 there may be a command that the community build for God "a temple of man."

21. See the argument in P. Barnett, *The Second Epistle to the Corinthians* (*The New International Commentary on the New Testament;* Grand Rapids, MI: Eerdmans, 1997) 337–41, who takes it as "a specific call for separation from the temple cults of Corinth, in direct continuity with the holiness-separation theme of 1 Corinthians" (p. 341). But why would a name like *Beliar* be used for such a purpose?

22. Since the words in brackets are supplied, we do not know whether a negative was read here, as some have suggested.

23. Yadin, "Pesher Nahum (4QpNahum) Reconsidered," *Israel Exploration Journal* 21 (1971) 1–12.

24. See the discussion of the issues by Fitzmyer, "Paul and the Dead Sea Scrolls," 607–9. See also M. Wise, "Crucifixion," in the *Encyclopedia of the Dead Sea Scrolls*, ed. L. Schiffman and J. VanderKam (2 vols.; New York and Oxford: Oxford University Press, 2000) 158–59.

25. For an argument against this reading, see Barnett, *The Second Epistle to the Corinthians*, 125–26. See also Acts 6:2, 5; 15:12, 30.

Chapter 17

1. See David E. Aune, "Qumran and the Book of Revelation," in P. W. Flint and J. C. VanderKam, eds., *The Dead Se Scrolls After Fifty Years: A Comprehensive Assessment* (2 vols.; Leiden: Brill, 1998–99) 2:622–48.

2. For an early synthesis of parallels found between the scrolls and Revelation, see Herbert Braun, *Qumran und das Neue Testament* (2 vols.; Tübingen: Mohr Siebeck, 1966) 1:307–26.

3. One exception is the commentary by J. Massyngberde Ford (*Revelation* [Anchor Bible 38; Garden City, NY: Doubleday, 1975]), which contains about 200 references to various texts in the Dead Sea Scrolls.

4. See L. H. Schiffman, *The Eschatological Community of the Dead Sea Scrolls: A Study of the Rule of the Congregation* (Society of Biblical Literature Monograph Series 38; Atlanta: Scholars Press, 1989), which focuses on 1QSa; J. J. Collins, "Was the Dead Sea Sect an Apocalyptic Movement?," in L. H. Schiffman ed., *Archaeology and History in the Dead Sea Scrolls: The New York University Conference in Memory of Yigael Yadin* (Journal for the Study of the Pseudepigrapha, Supplement Series 8, JSOT/ASOR Monographs 2; JSOT Press, 1990) 28–51;

Collins, *Apocalypticism in the Dead Sea Scrolls* (London and New York: Routledge, 1997).

5. See D. Dimant, "Apocalyptic Texts at Qumran," in E. Ulrich and J. VanderKam, eds., *The Community of the Renewed Covenant* (Christianity and Judaism in Antiquity 10; Notre Dame: University of Notre Dame Press, 1994) 175–91; also her "The Qumran Manuscripts: Contents and Significance," in D. Dimant and L. H. Schiffman, eds., *Time to Prepare the Way in the Wilderness: Papers on the Qumran Scrolls by Fellows of the Institute for Advanced Studies of the Hebrew University, Jerusalem, 1989–1990* (Studies on the Texts of the Desert of Judah 16; Leiden: Brill, 1995) 23–58.

6. In WAC (378–90) this work is termed *The Secret of the Way Things Are*.

7. In WAC (268–70): *A Vision of the Son of God*.

8. In WAC (420–22): *Redemption and Resurrection*.

9. Dimant, "Apocalyptic Texts at Qumran," 23–58.

10. É. Puech, "4QApocalypse Messianique," in his *Qumrân Grotte 4:XVIII: Textes Hébreux (4Q521–4Q528, 4Q576–4Q579)* (DJD 25; Oxford: Clarendon Press, 1998) 1–38, plates I–III.

11. Aune, "Qumran and the Book of Revelation," 628–29.

12. Collins, *Apocalypticism in the Dead Sea Scrolls,* 10.

13. WAC, 150–72.

14. J. Duhaime, "War Scroll," in J. Charlesworth, ed., *Damascus Document, War Scroll, and Related Documents,* (Princeton Theological Seminary Dead Sea Scrolls Project 2; Louisville, KY: Westminster John Knox; Tübingen: Mohr Siebeck, 1995) 80–83; idem, "The War Scroll from Qumran and the Greco-Roman Tactical Treatises," *Revue de Qumrân* 13/49–52 (Carmignac Memorial, 1988) 133–51; Aune, "Qumran and the Book of Revelation," 641.

15. See A. Yarbro Collins, *The Combat Myth in the Book of Revelation* (Harvard Dissertations on Religion 9; Missoula, MT: Scholars Press, 1976).

16. R. Bauckham, "The Apocalypse as a Christian War Scroll," in his *The Climax of Prophecy: Studies on the Book of Revelation* (Edinburgh: T. & T. Clark, 1993) 210–37 (first published as "The Book of Revelation as a Christian War Scroll," *Neotestamentica* 22 [1988] 17–40).

17. For further details, see Aune, "Qumran and the Book of Revelation," 646–47.

18. WAC (180–84): *A Vision of the New Jerusalem*.

19. F. García Martínez, "New Jerusalem," in L. Schiffman and J. VanderKam, eds., *Encyclopedia of the Dead Sea Scrolls* (2 vols.; New York and Oxford: Oxford University Press, 2000) 2:606–10, esp. 609.

20. See F. García Martínez, "New Jerusalem," 609.

21. "Qumran and the Book of Revelation," 635.

22. Aune, "Qumran and the Book of Revelation," 638.

Chapter 18

1. "Scholarship," *JQR* 39 (1948–49) 337–63; "The Fiction," *JQR* 44 (1953–54) 85–115; "The Antiquity," *JQR* 45 (1054–55) 1–29.

2. *The Ancient Library of Qumran and Modern Biblical Studies* (rev. ed.; Grand Rapids, MI: Baker Book House, 1980) 35.

3. "The Original Team of Editors," in T. Lim, H. MacQueen, and C. Carmichael, eds., *On Scrolls, Artefacts and Intellectual Property* (Journal for the Study of the Pseudepigrapha, Supplement Series 38; Sheffield: Sheffield Academic Press, 2001) 181.

4. Copies of these volumes that were reissued much later by the Clarendon Press lack the words "of Jordan."

5. Both the Hebrew and English editions were published in Jerusalem by the Israel Exploration Society, the Institute of Archaeology of the Hebrew University of Jerusalem, and the Shrine of the Book.

6. "Notes en marge du volume V des 'Discoveries in the Judaean Desert of Jordan.'" *Revue de Qumran* 7 (1963) 163–76. The text of DJD 5, with the index of Hebrew words, runs to 111 pages.

7. Strugnell has written that during Benoit's fourteen years some seven volumes were published and another seven during his term ("The Original Team of Editors," 188 [and 189, note 3]). Whatever these numbers are based on, he is clearly not referring to DJD volumes.

8. The Biblical Archaeology Society issued the remaining three fascicles in 1992, 1995, and 1996.

9. A copy of the letter, signed by Amir Drori and Emanuel Tov, dated September 22, 1991, and containing the suggestion of possible legal action can be found in *A Facsimile Edition of the Dead Sea Scrolls,* ed. R. Eisenman and J. Robinson (Washington, DC: Biblical Archaeology Society, 1991) 1.xliii (Figure 20). Regarding these volumes, see below.

10. Shanks published a copy of Drori's letter as Figure 9 in the Foreword to *A Facsimile Edition* (1.xxxii).

11. Actually, scholars were aware of the text before this. Milik, for example, had cited some words and passages from it in DJDJ 3:223, 225.

12. Shanks, "Intellectual Property Law and the Scholar: Cases I Have Known," in Lim et al., eds., *On Scrolls, Artefacts and Intellectual Property,* 64.

13. New York: Summit Books. 1991.

14. Shaftesbury: Element, 1992.

15. *The Dead Sea Scrolls Uncovered,* 3–4.

16. *The Dead Sea Scrolls Uncovered,* 4.

17. Numbers 35 and 36, 180–200.

18. *The Dead Sea Scrolls Uncovered,* 9. See also p. 182, where they reiterate the point. It is only fair to add that, in using the photographs, Eisenman and Wise had the advantage of all the work represented on those plates.

In other words, they did not start their work from scratch, but from Strugnell's placement of fragments on the plates.

19. This is what Robert Eisenman later reported (see M. Wise, N. Golb, J. Collins, and D. Pardee, eds., *Methods of Investigation of the Dead Sea Scrolls and the Khirbet Qumran Site: Present Realities and Future Prospects* [Annals of the New York Academy of Sciences 722; New York: New York Academy of Sciences, 1994] 484). Wise confirmed it in a statement he made at the conference (p. 496).

20. *The Dead Sea Scrolls Uncovered,* 198–99.

21. *The Dead Sea Scrolls Uncovered,* 182.

22. The text of the session can be consulted in *Methods of Investigation,* 455–95.

23. *Methods of Investigation,* 478–82.

24. *Methods of Investigation,* 490. After Golb presented this argument in testimony in an Israeli court (on the trial, see below), the judge, Dalia Dorner, wrote in her Judgment: "This does not seem to me an adequate explanation. In any case, his explanation does not account for the fact that while this decipherment of Exhibit 19 *[The Dead Sea Scrolls Uncovered]* is essentially identical to the composite text, another part of the Scroll (the calendar), which the Plaintiff [that is, Qimron] had deciphered but did not published [*sic*], is completely different from the decipherment of Exhibit 19." (*On Scrolls, Artefacts and Intellectual Property,* 31–32).

25. The statements may be found in *Methods of Investigation,* 496.

26, Leiden: Brill, 1993.

27. Strugnell had thought of placing photographs of scrolls on microfiche, with one placed in an envelope in each DJD volume so that creation of expensive plates would not be needed. That plan was not approved by the advisory committee of the IAA and never was implemented (see Strugnell, "On the History of the Photographing of the Discoveries in the Judean Desert for the International Group of Editors," in the *Companion Volume to the Dead Sea Scrolls on Microfiche Edition,* 132–33). The lists of manuscripts and corresponding photographs were the latest stage in a history of compiling such information. Basing himself on earlier work (from 1956, 1967, and 1981), from 1989 to 1992 Stephen Reed compiled the information that was then issued in fourteen fascicles. Later this appeared in *The Dead Sea Scrolls Catalogue: Documents, Photographs and Museum Inventory Numbers,* compiled by S. Reed; revised and edited by M. Lundberg with the collaboration of M. Phelps (SBL Resources for Biblical Study 32; Atlanta: Scholars Press, 1994). All of this and more has gone into an electronic database developed by S. Pfann.

28. As of 2002 a corrections volume was in the planning stages, and it is possible that there will be other volumes that incorporate texts not fully covered in the existing DJD volumes, but published outside the series.

29. "The Judgment," 32. T. Lim's translation of the judge's decision in the trial can be read in "The Judgment," *On Scrolls, Artefacts and Intellectual Property,* 26–62. In a forthcoming article, Lim reports that the sum was actually NIS 367,500, not 472,500.

30. Shanks testified that the first edition involved 413 copies, of which 200–300 had been sold ("The Judgment," 56).

31. "Intellectual Property Law and the Scholar: Cases I Have Known," in Lim et al., eds., *On Scrolls, Artefacts and Intellectual Property,* 66.

32. "The Judgment," 34.

33. "The Judgment," 39.

34. "The Judgment," 27.

35. "The Judgment," 57–60.

36. "The Judgment," 61–62.

37. Qimron is the author of *The Hebrew of the Dead Sea Scrolls* (Harvard Semitic Studies 29; Atlanta: Scholars Press, 1986). This is the standard grammar of Qumran Hebrew and is a revised, translated form of the doctoral dissertation he wrote at the Hebrew University (1976).

38. Shanks refers to this testimony in "Cases I Have Known," 66.

39. C. A. Carson, "Raiders of the Lost Scrolls: The Right of Scholarly Access to the Content of Historic Documents," *Michigan Journal of International Law* 16 (1995) 298–348; D. Nimmer, "Copyright in the Dead Sea Scrolls," *Houston Law Review* 38 (2001) 1–236.

40. C. A. Carson, "The Application of American Copyright Law to the Dead Sea Scrolls Controversy," in Lim et al., eds., *On Scrolls, Artefacts and Intellectual Property,* 74–98.

41. D. Nimmer, "Assaying Qimron's Originality," in Lim et al., eds., *On Scrolls, Artefacts and Intellectual Property,* 76.

42. Lim et al., *On Scrolls, Artefacts and Intellectual Property,* 233–43.

43. The district court had apparently forgot about this part of Qimron's original request.

44. *The Dead Sea Scrolls in English* (revised and extended 4th ed.; London: Penguin Books, 1995) 181.

45. "Discoveries in the Judaean Desert: Textes legaux (I)," *Journal for the Study of Judaism* 32 (2001) 71–89.

46. "Discoveries in the Judaean Desert," 76 (translation by J. VanderKam). García Martínez documents both claims in detail.

Index